Matthias Stern
Taxes and Authority in the Late Antique Countryside

Archiv für Papyrusforschung
und verwandte Gebiete

Begründet von
Ulrich Wilcken

Beiheft 55

De Gruyter

Taxes and Authority in the Late Antique Countryside

The Reach of the State and the Pagarchs of Byzantine Egypt (284–642 CE)

by
Matthias Stern

De Gruyter

The open access publication and prepress of this book have been published with the support of the Swiss National Science Foundation.

Swiss National
Science Foundation

ISBN 978-3-11-143592-3
e-ISBN (PDF) 978-3-11-149318-3
ISSN 1868-9337
DOI https://doi.org/10.1515/9783111493183

Library of Congress Control Number: 2024918764

Bibliographic information published by the Deutsche Nationalbibliothek
The Deutsche Nationalbibliothek lists this publication in the Deutsche Nationalbibliografie; detailed bibliographic data are available on the Internet at https://dnb.dnb.de.

Printing and binding: CPI books GmbH, Leck

www.degruyter.com

Questions about General Product Safety Regulation:
productsafety@degruyterbrill.com

MIX
Papier | Fördert gute Waldnutzung
FSC® C083411

Preface

This book is the revised version of my doctoral dissertation in ancient history, defended on June 4, 2019 at the University of Basel, the unrevised version of which is accessible at the University Library. Early ideas for a study of this kind were conceived during my involvement in the National Research Network *Imperium and Officium: Comparative Studies in Ancient Bureaucracy and Officialdom* at the University of Vienna, funded by the Austrian Science Fund. The topic was then developed as part of my *wissenschaftliche Assistenz* at the University of Basel's Institute of Ancient History, where alongside my *Assistenz* I was also part of the project *Change and Continuities from a Christian to a Muslim Society—Egyptian Society and Economy in the 6th to 8th Centuries*, funded by the Swiss National Science Foundation. The study took its final form in Munich during my time as *Juniorprofessor* of Papyrology at the German Archaeological Institute's Commission for Ancient History and Epigraphy and the Ludwig-Maximilians-Universität (LMU). All three cities proved to be the ideal research environments for the work that would ultimately become this book.

After my defense, a combination of private, professional, and pandemic-related circumstances prevented me from getting back to this study as early as planned, and many of my readers will be familiar with both the excitement and the challenges of bringing recently published and important unpublished material into dialogue with a "finished" manuscript. Some parts of the dissertation have been cut or streamlined for the book publication, while many others were expanded. But most importantly, there are few discussions that did not profit from then-unpublished sources and studies that the wonderful papyrological family brought to my attention after I presented findings from my dissertation at the twenty-ninth and thirtieth editions of the International Congress of Papyrology in Lecce and Paris, as well as at other conferences, workshops, and presentations.

I have incurred many debts of gratitude for the attention and support this work has received. First and foremost, this applies to my *Doktoreltern*, Sabine Huebner and Bernhard Palme, who provided me with constant advice, encouragement, and inspiration. Equally profound thanks go to Sven Tost, who also read large parts of the growing manuscript of the original dissertation and critically discussed them with me; I have benefited from the gift of his honest advice ever since my early days in Vienna. All three have, in their individual ways, shaped my thinking and provided me with inestimable opportunities during my early career. I am also grateful to the Commission, especially Christof Schuler and Rudolf Haensch, and the LMU, especially Martin Zimmermann, for being so welcoming and for the advice and support they provided, both during the pandemic transition period and later on while I was finishing the book; to the editors of the *APF-Beihefte*, in particular Fabian Reiter and Lajos Berkes, for accepting the manuscript for publication and providing helpful suggestions; to Mirko Vonderstein,

https://doi.org/10.1515/9783111493183-201

Jessica Bartz, Florian Ruppenstein, and the rest of the team at De Gruyter for their invaluable work throughout the production process; and to the Swiss National Science Foundation for the most-generous financial support that gave me the opportunity to publish this book open access.

During my work on this project, numerous colleagues in addition to those already mentioned kindly gave me their time to discuss my research or their own with them; granted me access to then-unpublished works; helped me obtain information about, access to, or images of papyri; or provided me with inspiration at crucial crossroads. These include Yasmine Amory, Danae Baffa, Gisela Bélot, Amin Benaissa, Graham Claytor, Charles Crowther, Jitse Dijkstra, Jean-Luc Fournet, Eugenio Garosi, Nikolaos Gonis, Anne Grons, Aaltje Hiddink, Alexandra Jesenko, Anna-Maria Kaiser, Sophie Kovarik, Claudia Kreuzsaler, Francesca Maltomini, Joseph Manning, Isabelle Marthot-Santaniello, Fritz Mitthof, Federico Morelli, Isabelle Mossong, Matthias Müller, Irene Nicolino, David Ratzan, Markus Resel, Stefanie Schmidt, Loreleï Vanderheyden, and Guus van Loon. The University of Basel's Max Geldner Fund financially supported the proofreading of the text, which was undertaken by Andrew Godfrey-Collins, Kate Sotejeff-Wilson, Laura Massey, Henry Heitmann-Gordon, and Colleen Kron, while Raphael Schneider did much of the practical indexing work. Naturally, I bear sole responsibility for all remaining errors and inconsistencies. I am grateful to all those mentioned, as well as to Roger Bagnall for the opportunity to spend time at New York University's Institute for the Study of the Ancient World during the earliest stages of writing up my dissertation in 2016 and to the Freiwillige Akademische Gesellschaft Basel for the generous support that made it possible. The few months I got to work in that incredible research environment and live in that marvelous city proved to be an intense and immensely inspiring time, without which this book would have looked fundamentally different.

Finally, as this my first academic book, no preface can adequately express the profound gratitude I feel toward all the academic teachers and colleagues I met and worked with in Magdeburg, Halle, Vienna, Liège, New York, Basel, and Munich. I owe the deepest gratitude, however, to a number of wonderful people who are not named here, and I would prefer to thank them in person for their support, friendship, and love. This book is dedicated to some of them—my family.

Munich, May 2024
Matthias Stern

Alle volte mi basta uno scorcio che s'apre nel bel mezzo d'un paesaggio incongruo, un affiorare di luci nella nebbia, il dialogo di due passanti che s'incontrano nel viavai, per pensare che partendo di lì metterò assieme pezzo a pezzo la città perfetta, fatta di frammenti mescolati col resto, d'istanti separati da intervalli, di segnali che uno manda e non sa chi li raccoglie.

Italo Calvino
Le città invisibili

At times all I need is a glimpse that opens in the midst of an incongruous landscape, a glint of lights in the fog, the dialogue of two passersby meeting in the crowd, to think that, setting out from there, I will put together, piece by piece, the perfect city, made of fragments mixed with the rest, the instants separated by intervals, of signals someone sends out without knowing who receives them.

Italo Calvino
The Invisible Cities

Contents

Preliminary Notes and Aids for the Reader

Citations of ancient sources, modern scholarly works, instrumenta, and online resources follow abbreviations that are defined in the back matter. For the sake of readability, information on the origins and dates of individual papyri is often restricted to nome/region and year where a more detailed entry is not crucial to the argument; approximate dates of sources by century are given in Roman numerals. All Julian dates are CE unless otherwise indicated, though I still frequently use CE in order to highlight that a number marks a year.

Dates in the papyri follow the Egyptian calendar, which was divided into twelve months of thirty days each plus five (or, in leap years, six) intercalary days (*epagomenai*). The corresponding dates given below are for nonleap years.

Akhet (inundation)	Thoth 1	August 29
	Phaophi 1	September 28
	Hathyr 1	October 28
	Choiak 1	November 27
Peret (growth)	Tybi 1	December 27
	Mecheir 1	January 26
	Phamenoth 1	February 25
	Pharmouthi 1	March 27
Shemu (harvest/low water)	Pachon 1	April 26
	Payni 1	May 26
	Epeiph 1	June 25
	Mesore 1	July 25
Heriu-renpet (epagomenal days)	birth of Osiris	August 24
	birth of Horus	August 25
	birth of Seth	August 26
	birth of Isis	August 27
	birth of Nephthys	August 28

Traditionally, the Egyptian year began on Thoth 1, but in late antiquity the beginning of the year varied from region to region, and even within these regions there were often divergences, for instance between a chronological and a fiscal year. These specific issues are discussed in the chapters where they are relevant; for an in-depth discussion of chronological reckoning in late antique Egypt, the reader is directed to *CSBE*².

In late antiquity, many papyrological documents were dated according to a cycle of fifteen *indictional years*. Where a document is dated to a first indiction, actually the first year of the *indictional cycle,* this may refer to different years of the Julian calendar,

https://doi.org/10.1515/9783111493183-202

for instance, 522/523, 567/568, or 627/628. Some corresponding Julian years from the period that is of central interest in this study are given below as a guide for documents dated only by indiction; for convenience, only the first possible Julian year is noted, i.e., 522 rather than 522/523:

1	522 / 537 / 552 / 567 / 582 / 597 / 612 / 627
2	523 / 538 / 553 / 568 / 583 / 598 / 613 / 628
3	524 / 539 / 554 / 569 / 584 / 599 / 614 / 629
4	525 / 540 / 555 / 570 / 585 / 600 / 615 / 630
5	526 / 541 / 556 / 571 / 586 / 601 / 616 / 631
6	527 / 542 / 557 / 572 / 587 / 602 / 617 / 632
7	528 / 543 / 558 / 573 / 588 / 603 / 618 / 633
8	529 / 544 / 559 / 574 / 589 / 604 / 619 / 634
9	530 / 545 / 560 / 575 / 590 / 605 / 620 / 635
10	531 / 546 / 561 / 576 / 591 / 606 / 621 / 636
11	532 / 547 / 562 / 577 / 592 / 607 / 622 / 637
12	533 / 548 / 563 / 578 / 593 / 608 / 623 / 638
13	534 / 549 / 564 / 579 / 594 / 609 / 624 / 639
14	535 / 550 / 565 / 580 / 595 / 610 / 625 / 640
15	536 / 551 / 566 / 581 / 596 / 611 / 626 / 641

Personal names are generally transcribed in their Greek forms, unless individuals are commonly known by their Latin or Anglicized name, such as emperors or ancient authors. The pseudo *nomina gentilia* Aurelius and Flavius are given in Latin, since by our period these had become status designations rather than personal names. To distinguish some pagarchs from namesakes, I include additional titles or epithets as part of their names (Kollouthos Cancellarius, Kollouthos Exceptor, Menas Scriniarius, Menas Stratelates, Strategios Paneuphemos, and Strategios Stratelates); other homonymous pagarchs are distinguished by context (notably Ioannes, Ioulianos, and Theodoros). I should add that apart from "Strategios Paneuphemos" these combined names do not appear in other scholarly works. Despite being the only pagarch of that name, the Arsinoite pagarch Apion is referred to here as Apion Stratelates in order to avoid confusion with the Apiones of Oxyrhynchos, who also occur frequently in this study. It has become common to assign a numerical order to these Oxyrhynchite Apiones (Strategios I, Apion I, Strategios II, etc.)—a practice to which I shall adhere, since it is so widespread and has proven merit.

Technical terms, such as ancient Greek words for offices, epithets, honorifics, weights, and coins, are, for reasons of accessibility, generally transliterated in the main text and in continuous footnote text but are not converted to their Latin equivalents, because oftentimes this "equivalence" may be less unambiguous than one would like—due, for example, to different contextual uses in the various languages. Consequently, μεγαλοπρεπέστατος becomes *megaloprepestatos*, not *vir magnificentissimus*; τρακτευτής becomes *trakteutēs*, not *tractator*; and so forth. If a Greek term is, however, a quasi-transcription of a Latin one, then the latter is given priority: *praipositos pagou* becomes *praepositus pagi* (although in Chapter One, I use *praipositos pagou* on occasion when referring specifically to the Greek form of this title), *doux* becomes *dux*, etc. An exception to this rule (for reasons explained in Chapter Five, Section I) is the epithet/title of *illoustrios*. The guiding aim has been to make the given epithets clear, even if this leads to constructions such as *lamprotatos scriniarius*. Honorary titles are retained as technical terms when their use did not depend on the speaker's position, such as *patricius*. By contrast, honorifics that relate to a vague hierarchy but are effectively more like polite formulas habitually used by speakers of lower, or sometimes equal, rank, such as *kyrios* ("lord") and *despotēs* ("master"), are generally translated.

Toponyms of cities are generally used in conventional forms, as in, for instance, Oxyrhynchos. When different conventions exist, I tried to balance readability and distinctiveness: I prefer, for instance, Antinoopolis over Antinoe, but Arsinoe over Arsinoiton Polis. For names of villages and hamlets, I usually use the form given by *TM* Places, so as to make them easier for the nonspecialist to look up. The Upper Egyptian village that we know by the name Aphrodito in the Islamic period was in Byzantine times called Aphrodites Kome ("village of Aphrodite"), or Aphrodite for short, but to avoid confusion I also use "Aphrodite" in the context of the early Islamic period; see Fournet 1992.

Transcriptions of ancient papyrological texts and inscriptions in the footnotes are annotated based on the adapted Leiden conventions:

[ ]	contain lost text or the approximate number of lost letters (lacuna).
[– – –]	indicates that the number of lost letters in a lacuna has not been estimated.
( )	define abbreviated text or symbols (or provide short explanatory comments).
(...)	indicates passages in the original text that I have omitted in the quotation.
⟨ ⟩	contain letters that have been added or changed by the editor in order to standardize the text.
{ }	contain text deleted by the editor.
⟦ ⟧	contain text deleted by an ancient writer.
\ /	contain supralinear additions from an ancient writer (preferred over ` ´ for the sake of clarity).
|	marks a line break when a papyrus or an inscription is quoted within continuous text.

Dots under letters (e.g., α̣β̣) indicate that the reading is uncertain.
Dots below the line (e.g., . .) indicate the approximate number of illegible letters.

When quoting from editions, I chose not to harmonize details such as parentheses around supralinear final letters, e.g., -ο(υ), accentuation of Egyptian names and months, or the spelling of ἰνδ(ικτίωνος)/ἰνδ(ικτίονος), but took them as they are in the texts of the editions—or as they are in the database of the *PN* if abbreviations are not expanded in the edition. On the case of ἰνδικτίωνος versus ἰνδικτίονος, see Danielewicz 2022 and Stolk 2022.

Translations of ancient sources are my own or, if available, adapted from that of the editor or from the translations listed in the back matter, unless otherwise indicated. To aid the nonspecialist, I chose to quote ancient sources in translation in the main text, displaying the original in the notes. The original text of longer passages from papyri is provided only in exceptional cases, as these passages are easily accessible through the *PN* at *papyri.info*. Translated numbers are written out or given in numerals, depending on the original Greek. Within translated texts, I use the following conventions:

( ) contain either relevant ancient terminology in transliteration, additions that are not in the edited text verbatim (≈ scil.), or brief explanatory comments (such as "i.e., ...") that I have added for clarity. If the parentheses are empty, they mark an (untranslated) technical term in abbreviation when the correct expansion is uncertain.
[ ] contain lost text; only sparingly used in translations.
(...) indicates passages that I have omitted in the quotation.
[– – –] indicates that the original text is too damaged to be translated.

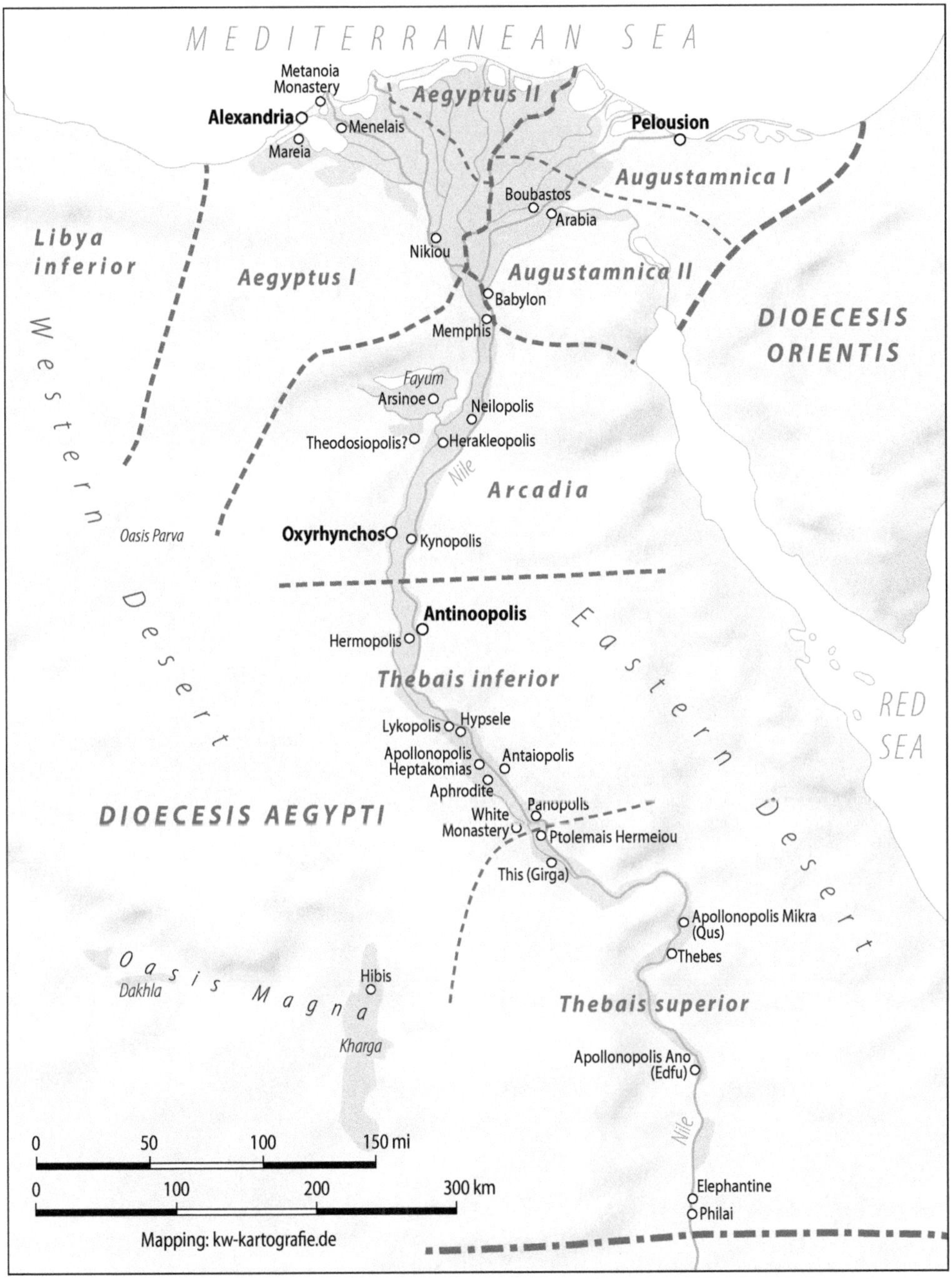

Figure 1: Egypt in late antiquity; administrative borders according to Hierocles's *Synecdemus* (c. 527–535 CE) and, for Aegyptus II, George of Cyprus's *Descriptio orbis Romani* (c. 603–606 CE).

Introduction

It is fashionable nowadays to ignore taxes altogether,
although they are one of the most crucial,
while tangible, instruments of Empire.[1]

I. Fiscal Authority in the Imperial Periphery

The Roman emperor Justinian, or Imperator Caesar Flavius Iustinianus Augustus,[2] would perhaps have endorsed the words quoted above when, in 539 CE, he issued a proclamation from the imperial capital of Constantinople. Its formal recipient was John the Cappadocian, Justinian's close confidant and praetorian prefect of the East, and thus supreme governor of one quarter of the empire.[3] In this document, which would become known to scholars as *Edict* 13, the emperor expressed deep concerns about the state of affairs in the Egyptian diocese, one of the subunits of the prefecture, and took great care to ensure the implementation of a major restructuring of Egypt's provincial administration.[4] In the *praefatio*, or preamble, to the edict, Justinian leaves no doubt as to why he deemed this necessary. Somewhere between the level of the taxpayers and that of the prefecture taxes were being lost, and the edict's accusations against the local administration are loud and clear. The culprits were the responsible authorities in the cities (*politeuomenoi*) and in the countryside (the pagarchs), their collecting staff on the ground (*praktores*), and the governors within the diocese, including the Augustalian prefect in Alexandria:

> To John, the *endoxotatos praefectus praetorio per Orientem*: Given that we regard even the smallest matters as deserving our consideration, much more shall we not ignore the most important ones that sustain our commonwealth (*politeia*), or let them go unconsidered or bereft of the proper condition of order, especially as we have the support of your excellency,

1 Van Minnen 2006, 165.

2 Cf. Iust. *inst.*, *prooemium*: *Imperator Caesar Flavius Iustinianus Alamannicus Gothicus Francicus Germanicus Anticus Alanicus Vandalicus Africanus pius felix inclitus victor ac triumphator semper Augustus*, "Imperator Caesar Flavius Iustinianus; conqueror of the Alamanni, the Goths, the Franks, the Germans, the Antes, the Alans, the Vandals, the Africans; pious, auspicious, and renowned, victorious and triumphant; forever Augustus." On Justinian's imperial titulature in the epigraphic sources, see *CIIP* I 785 and Di Segni 2011, 352–354 with further references. The consular diptychs from 521 CE, that is, before Justinian's accession in 527, give his name as Flavius Petrus Sabbatius Iustinianus; see *PLRE* II, s.v. Iustinianus 7, referring to *CIL* V 8210.3 (which should be 8120.3) and *CIL* XIII 10032.7.

3 *PLRE* III, s.v. Ioannes 11.

4 On *Edict* 13, see Palme 2013a, 103–105 with further references.

https://doi.org/10.1515/9783111493183-001

> whose responsibility it is to serve us unremittingly, to increase the tax revenue, and to care for our subjects. Accordingly, despite our view that other aspects of the tax collection had otherwise been quite well organized in times past, we have had in mind that in the Egyptian diocese it has reached such a confused state that there is no knowledge here even of what is going on out there (or: what is going on in the countryside). We have been surprised at the disorder over it hitherto; but God has granted that this, too, has been kept for our times and your excellency's ministrations. They (i.e., the officials) have been, as it were, tossing the grain over to us from there, and, that done, not deigning to bring in anything else; but, while the taxpayers were insisting that they were definitely having the whole assessment demanded of them in full, the pagarchs, the curials (*politeuomenoi*), the collectors (*praktores*) of the taxes, and in particular the governors (*archontes*) at the time have hitherto arranged the business in such a way that no one can find out anything about it, and that only they can profit from it. Should we, therefore, leave the business under a single administration, we would never be able to clear it up and organize it properly; so we have decided to reduce the responsibilities of the authority in charge of Egyptian affairs—of the *Augustales*, that is—for a single person's mind could hardly cope with so many burdens and administer the business in such a way as to give us a clear insight into it.[5]

By that point, Justinian had been ruling the Eastern Roman, or Byzantine, Empire for more than a decade. Extensive warfare—against the Persians in the east, as well as the invasion of the Vandal kingdom in northern Africa—was putting a continued strain on imperial finances.[6] With these and other large-scale military campaigns ongoing or recently concluded, Justinian's reign was a period of extraordinary financial distress, and one story behind *Edict* 13 concerns the efficiency of revenue extraction. It is a truism that fiscal interests are central to states, but that is even more strongly the case for premodern states such as the Roman Empire, which are thought to have generated and exercised public authority within their borders primarily in order to maintain stability and a constant stream of revenue: "This was the business of empire."[7]

---

5 Iust. *ed.* 13, *praefatio*. Here and elsewhere, translations of *Edict* 13 are adapted from Miller and Sarris's translation; the adaptations mostly provide a more technical rendering of various institutional terms. The passage concerning the officials reads οἱ παγάρχαι δὲ καὶ οἱ πολιτευόμενοι καὶ οἱ πράκτορες τῶν δημοσίων καὶ διαφερόντως ⟨οἱ⟩ κατὰ καιρὸν ἄρχοντες. For the period leading to *Edict* 13, discussed here in the *praefatio*, Justinian is referring to the governors (*archontes*) of the individual provinces at that time: *Augustalis* (Aegyptus), *corrector* (Augustamnica I), three *praesides* (Augustamnica II, Arcadia, Thebais Inferior), and *dux* (Thebais Superior). In Chapter 1, however, as part of the new regulations, the *archōn* is subordinate to the *dux et Augustalis* and must therefore be the *praeses*; see also Chapter 25. Miller and Sarris consistently translate *archōn* as "governor." For a list of the various governors of the individual provinces before and after *Edict* 13, see Palme 2007c, 246. The structure of the Egyptian provinces under Justinian is discussed in more detail in Chapter One, Section IV (see especially p. 54).

6 This is reflected in Procopius's rendering of John's warning to his emperor about the expected costs of such an adventure (Proc. *bell.* III 10.7–20). On the historical context of Justinian's situation at that point, see Haldon 2005, 53–55 and Bell 2013, 87–88 with further references. For recent guides to the scholarly discussions of the Justinianic age and their sources, see Haarer 2022 and Maas 2005.

7 Quote: Bang 2015, 541. Political scientist James Scott (1998, 2) refers to "the classic state functions

The present study seeks to advance our understanding of how the late Roman Empire ensured and protected its stream of revenue by maintaining public authority in its periphery. The majority of imperial subjects lived in the countryside.[8] It was here, at the ground level, that most tax revenue originated and that the Roman state and its representatives came face-to-face with most of its subjects. How and by whom was fiscal authority generated and enforced in these areas? How deep did the "reach of the state" go?[9] And how did its subjects in the country villages, hamlets, and estates perceive this authority? To find answers, I turn to the evidence on the pagarchs of Byzantine Egypt, who supervised tax collection in rural communities. The pagarchs suggest themselves for such a discussion for two chief reasons, both of which will be discussed in the course of this introduction: they operated at the intersection between provincial administration, cities, and rural areas, and they are attested in the papyrological evidence, which allows us to reconstruct their activities across multiple strata of society in significant detail.

This study seeks to investigate the functioning of the late Roman state's administrative network from a specific angle. Its aim is to accurately locate an essential fiscal institution within the "small politics" of the countryside and the "big politics" of the empire.[10] Alongside the army and the law, fiscal administration was the most visible manifestation of the empire in the countryside,[11] and the pagarchy, the institution of the office of the pagarch, played a major role in it.

---

of taxation, conscription, and prevention of rebellion." See also Roger Bagnall's (1989, 204) description of the Roman Empire (in the imperial period) as "a state with a highly concentrated central power and weak ties to local communities. Most villages in Roman Egypt had no permanent resident representatives of central authority, for the village officials were locals serving limited terms [...] and Roman military posts were sporadic at best. The state's interest in the village was largely one of collecting taxes, extracting labor, and preventing disturbance." In n. 12, Bagnall gives a comparable description of the Ottoman Empire's interests: "defense, public order, and taxes. Other things which we might regard as duties of government were either left to local authorities or ignored entirely." On the historiography of the "ambitions" of ancient governments, see Ando 2017b, 115–118. Some scholars even see the capacity to impose and collect stable tax revenue as the main condition for being able to talk of a *state*, using a broad definition of *tax* (see Valk 2021, 3–11 for a recent discussion and references, including "external taxes," or tribute, as well as "material resources and labor"), and hold that "[f]or the ordinary citizen, the power to tax is the most familiar manifestation of the government's ability to coerce" (Bonney 1999, 5; cf. Valk 2021, 7 and Haldon 2005, 34–35 and 42–44).

8 Ando 2017b, 115 estimates the percentage of the population dwelling in the countryside to be 85 percent, though that is for the imperial period and covers the empire as a whole. For Egypt, the figure is generally considered to be lower, but still equal to about two-thirds of the population; see Sarris 2006, 10–11 with references.

9 On this concept, see Manning 2003, 129 (who borrows the concept from the title of Shue 1988) and Ando 2017a, 1.

10 On the "small" politics of the late antique countryside, cf. Grey 2011; on the "big" politics of the Eastern Empire and especially the relationship between rulers and the state elite, see Begass 2018.

11 Of course, perceptions of this authority usually involved the intermediate layer of the cities:

II. Late Antique Egypt and the Pagarchs in Perspective

Chronologically, this study covers virtually the entire period of what scholars habitually call *late Roman Egypt, late antique Egypt*, or *Byzantine Egypt*, spanning from the accession of Emperor Diocletian in 284 CE to the Arab conquest, which was essentially completed by 642.[12] There has been some discussion about whether these terms should be used in general or more restricted senses, but so far no system has found common acceptance in the field.[13] The earlier part of this period, up until the latter half of the fifth century, will be central only to the first chapter, whereas the remaining five will focus on the period from about 500 to 642, since it is the pagarchs' position during that time that best lends itself to a study of the webs of authority in the late antique countryside. Except in the first chapter, I shall use the term *pagarch* in relation to these roughly one and a half centuries of Roman-Egyptian history. Occasionally, however, I refer to "later" pagarchs in order to distinguish them from the "early" pagarchs of the fourth and fifth centuries, who—as we shall see—differed in significant respects.

Late antique Egypt forms the latter part of the period that scholars label *Graeco-Roman Egypt*, referring to the roughly one thousand years during which Greeks and Romans ruled the lands along the Nile after the armies of Alexander the Great entered Egypt in 332 BCE.[14] Following Alexander's death in 323 BCE, the Graeco-Macedonian

"C'est par les impôts et les liturgies fiscales que se manifeste institutionnellement la domination de la campagne par la ville" (Gascou 1996, 343–344 = 2008, 410).

12 The year 284 CE is actually of minor importance for Egypt compared with 297/298, when Diocletian led an army into the country to quell the usurpation by Domitius Domitianus and Aurelius Achilleus. The inclusion of the year 284 in the title of this book is due to the historical context of late antiquity. Palme 2013a provides a thorough account of the historiography of Byzantine Egypt. A more recent overview can be found in various contributions to Bagnall 2021. Classic accounts of Egypt's administration in terms of imperial fiscal policy are Rouillard 1928 (first edition published in 1923) and Johnson & West 1949. The more recent study Bransbourg 2016 can be added to that list. On the period from Diocletian through the fourth century, see also Lallemand 1964; a shorter general survey can be found in Heinen 1991. Palme 1989 offers numerous illustrative accounts on the evolution of the taxation system from the High Empire to late antiquity and early Islamic Egypt, while Zuckerman 2004a provides an in-depth study of the fiscal process in a single locality, the village of Aphrodite in the Thebaid. Karayannopoulos 1958 and Jones 1964 remain authoritative works on late Roman (or early Byzantine) taxation in an imperial context, including references to—though not primarily focusing on—papyri.

13 See Palme 2013a, 96, which refers to Giardina 1989 and Bagnall 2003. Lajos Berkes (2017a, 4) makes a compelling case for a late antiquity covering the entire period from Diocletian to the Abbasids (284 to 750 CE), although one might question the descriptive value of a notion of "late antiquity" spanning such a long period. There is probably not going to be a consensus about this anytime soon and in order to avoid ambiguity, I adhere to the synonymous use of all three terms. The "Roman" character of the early "Byzantine" Empire in contemporary thought was recently explored in Kaldellis 2015.

14 Some scholars use *Graeco-Roman Egypt* to only refer to a shorter period, for instance, from the Ptolemies to 284 or 395 CE.

dynasty of the Ptolemies controlled the country for about three centuries until 30 BCE, when Octavian, the later Emperor Augustus, made Egypt a province of the Roman people. From that point on, with two intermezzos in the late third and early seventh centuries CE, Egypt was continuously part of the Roman Empire until the Arabs established control between 639 and 642. While modern historiography has somewhat distanced itself from the idea that Egyptian, Greek, and Roman (and other) cultures mingled into one *Mischkultur* during the millennium from Alexander to Emperor Heraclius, these groups' mutual influences are evident—especially, perhaps, in the use of Greek as the main language of written administrative and legal documentation during the entire period of Graeco-Roman Egypt.

In the Ptolemaic period and during the Principate, Egypt was subdivided into "nomes" (*nomoi*), the fifty or so districts that had constituted its administrative framework since Pharaonic times.[15] The nomes contained administrative centers, an estimated 2,000 to 2,500 villages, and an uncountable number of smaller hamlets.[16] But these settlements were not distributed evenly throughout the region. While the Roman province of Egypt looks extensive on political maps, most of it consisted of infertile deserts. Egypt's arable lands were concentrated on a narrow band along the Nile banks and in the wider region of its delta to the north that were among the most densely populated areas of the entire ancient Mediterranean. A notable exception was the Fayum depression, a large oasis some forty miles south of Giza that had been made arable under the pharaohs. This region was maintained through a sophisticated canal system and formed the Arsinoite nome, which extended over a larger area than other nomes.

Most people stayed close to the Nile because, as Herodotus famously noted, Egypt was the "gift of the river."[17] During the fall season, the water level would rise dramatically before receding again, leaving the plains with fertile silt deposits and thus resulting, during most seasons, in significant grain surpluses that were Egypt's most valuable asset for the Roman Empire. Extracted as tax from the province, Egyptian grain fed the armies and the larger cities, notably Rome and, later, Constantinople. *Edict* 13 from 539 CE gives an amount of 8 million artabas, some 310 million liters or about 82 million US gallons, in annual exports.[18] The start of the imperial fiscal year in Egypt was actu-

15 The traditional and religiously heeded number of nomes was forty-two, but over time, some nomes were merged and new ones established for administrative reasons. By the middle of the second century CE, there were probably fifty-two nomes in Egypt; see Eller 2022, 15.

16 On this estimate of the number of villages, see Bagnall 1993, 110, although Bagnall admits (n. 1) that the margin of error may be high given the small number of texts on which the calculation is based.

17 Hdt. II 5.

18 Iust. *ed.* 13.8. Mayerson 2007 has argued that the unnamed unit of measurement for the amount of "eight million" is not the artaba, but the modius. See, however, Bransbourg 2016, 335 n. 116, who refers to earlier arguments for the traditional view that Mayerson does not consider. On the measurement units and currencies used in this study, see Bagnall 2009c.

ally moved to harmonize with the Nile flood, so that tax collection in the nomes could be organized accordingly.[19]

The advent of Diocletian and the tetrarchic emperors sets the traditional starting date for the Byzantine period of Egyptian history at 284 CE, that is, even before Byzantium was turned into a "new Rome" in 330 CE and—under the name Constantinopolis, City of Constantine—became the new imperial center. There are various reasons why this periodization is commonly accepted. Aside from the increasing foothold that Christianity was gaining in Egypt, the first appearances of Coptic—the latest form of the Egyptian language—in written documents, and overall changes in documentary practice, the most obvious ones relate to politico-administrative changes. Beginning with Diocletian, the emperors restructured Egypt and other provinces, integrating them into a new empire-wide system of prefectures and dioceses with the corresponding official institutions. If Egypt had ever enjoyed any special administrative position, Diocletian and his successors effectively abolished it.[20] The country was divided into more and more provinces, up to four in 400 CE and seven in 539 (Figure 1).[21] At the local level, the nomes and their administrative centers, the *mētropoleis*, took the last steps toward being converted—from a legal perspective—into proper Roman cities (Lat. *civitates*; Gr. *poleis*) in the late third and early fourth centuries. Although the term *nomos* was still used as a geographical unit for centuries, and is used in this study too, a nome now formally referred to the hinterland (Lat. *territorium*; Gr. *enoria*) of its urban administrative center.

This hinterland of the cities was the pagarchs' area of responsibility. In the fourth and fifth centuries, the pagarchs were still minor civic officials with authority over only fractions of a nome, but their status was elevated at some point in the late fifth century, from which point onward there was only one pagarch (or one collegium) per *civitas*, and the officeholders were now veritable aristocrats from the ranks of a newly formed aristocracy of service. The fifth century had seen a dramatic shift in the distribution of power in the *civitates*—as will be explored in Chapter One—and it is this more or less established situation, extending from the later fifth century to the dawn of the Islamic age, that forms the background to the remaining five chapters of this study.[22] During this latter period, the pagarchs operated at the intersection between provincial

19 This issue is explored in relation to the pagarchs' tenures in Chapter Four, Section II.

20 Johnson & West 1949, 3. See Palme 2013b for an overview of Egypt's administration in late antiquity. Still, the question is to what extent Egypt was ever an exceptional case in the Roman Empire—it probably never differed much more from an "imperial ideal type" than any other province; see Keenan 2009; Jördens 2009, 53–58; Huebner 2019, 5–7 with additional literature; Bagnall 2020, 11 and 55–58; and Sarris 2022.

21 See p. xvii.

22 Cf. Bagnall 2003, 47, who argues for the distinctiveness of the period from around the mid-fifth century to the Islamic conquest, when the "great houses," the *oikoi*, dominated: "The councils lose out to the imperial administration and the church as the privileged locus of elite competition." Similar, already Oertel 1917, 404.

administration, cities, and rural areas. Residing in the urban centers, they were part of the local political elite, and some of them owed their standing to reputable posts in the provincial and imperial administrations. At the same time, many pagarchs are known to have owned landed estates in areas for which they were responsible by virtue of their office. They can therefore be of relevance to important ongoing debates in the field of late antique studies, concerning topics such as the links of the late antique cities to their rural territories, the power of the imperial center to impose its will in the periphery, the economics of the large estates, the role of the empire's aristocracy as power brokers, and the factor of bureaucracy in the "mechanics of empire."[23] Since the pagarchs were installed throughout Egypt, they may provide us with general insights into what the government attempted to achieve at the local level.

III. The Historiography of the Pagarchy

Given how central the pagarchy was to the late Roman tax regime, for all the reasons given above, it is surprising that, while it is often mentioned in passing, the institution has received little detailed attention in recent debates about the politics, economy, and society of late antique Egypt. The first scholar to contribute extensively to research on the Byzantine pagarchy was Matthias Gelzer in 1909, who took the view that the pagarchs' area of responsibility comprised only the rural hinterland of the cities, excluding the autopract villages, which handled fiscal matters largely on their own.[24] Gelzer argued that the central administrative authority in the urban center was still in the hands of the curials. In his view, the creation of the pagarchy was a telling reaction to the wretched state of Byzantine administration, which had caused the decline of the curial class over the course of the fifth century. In 1923, Germaine Rouillard argued that the pagarchs' area of responsibility was in general equivalent to the old nome.[25] She considered them the central authorities in the *civitates* and their *territoria*, who were responsible for collecting taxes in non-autopract regions but occasionally intervened in autopract villages as well. Given the important role that Justinian's *Edict* 13 assigned to the pagarchs, Rouillard assumed their office represented an attempt by the imperial government to integrate local elites into a new and more centralized administration precisely in order to counteract centrifugal tendencies in local administration. In 1974, Wolf Liebeschuetz took up Rouillard's view that the pagarchs were the central authorities in the *civitates*; one year earlier, Liebeschuetz had already suggested that the pagarch was the direct successor of the *exactor civitatis* and that the office was created

23 The expression is borrowed from Parker 2001.
24 Gelzer 1909, especially 90–99. The institution of *autopragia* is discussed in Chapter One, Section I.
25 Rouillard 1928 (first edition 1923).

by Anastasius I (r. 491–518).[26] Like Gelzer, Liebeschuetz took the creation of the pagarchy as a consequence of administrative chaos in Byzantine Egypt, and argued that centralizing tax collection in this way was a response to the increasing ineptitude of the city councils to effectively administer their territories.

In 1972, little before Liebeschuetz published his articles on the topic, Jean Gascou advanced a radical new interpretation of the pagarchy.[27] Gascou saw the Byzantine pagarchy as a *munus patrimonii*, an obligation that large landowners had to bear in order to finance certain public services. Subsequent scholarship has, with slight variations, tended to follow either Liebeschuetz or Gascou, or implicitly attempted to reconcile their accounts. An instance of the latter is Roberta Mazza's ambitious study of the Byzantine pagarchs from 1995, in which she compiled the evidence and reviewed different scholarly opinions in a way that had not previously been achieved.[28]

Recent contributions on Byzantine Egypt are divided in their interpretation of the pagarchy: while some follow a rather pessimistic narrative of the pagarchs undermining local state control, others take the pagarchy as, in essence, an effective means of exercising public authority.[29] The pessimistic narrative appears to have gained more ground, however, in historical circles outside papyrology, in terms of both small and big politics. The "small" perspective sees the pagarchs as violently confronting taxpayers to the detriment of public resources, and the "big" perspective sees a thriving insubordinate elite in the late Roman periphery. An essential feature of research on late antiquity was, for a long time, the slightly paradoxical notion of an allegedly oppressive state (*Zwangsstaat*) that slowly lost control over its branches and local hierarchies by allowing certain aristocratic families to take over important government posts and to establish local quasi-regimes, setting the stage for medieval feudalism.[30] But over the last five decades, some scholars have argued that the growing aristocratic responsibilities in the documents are instead indicative of a "strong state" incorporating local private resources for its ends. One key example is Gascou's seminal 1985 study on the "large estates" of Byzantine Egypt, which continued a path blazed a decade earlier by Roger Rémondon. Gascou argued that these large estates were deeply integrated into public structures

26 Liebeschuetz 1973 and 1974.

27 Gascou 1972a. The original study was substantially revised and even renamed in Gascou 2008.

28 Mazza 1995, including, however, a number of texts that must be—and some more that are probably—from the early Islamic period. A short overview, leaning toward Gascou, is also given by Verbeeck 1991.

29 Compare, for instance, Banaji 2007 (first edition 2001) and Sarris 2006 ("pessimistic") with Mazza 1995 and Palme 2007c ("optimistic"). Notably, each of these four scholars has a different idea of what the pagarchy was. The institution has largely been sidelined in recent publications on the fiscal process or fiscal authority in the countryside of late antique Egypt. Ruffini 2018a at least provides the reader with a definition: on p. 11 for the pagarchy ("the larger fiscal jurisdiction of a pagarch, an official subordinate to the local governor"; on this point, see Section VII below) and on p. 20 for the pagarch ("an official in charge of regional tax collection").

30 On the history of scholarship on this issue, see Keenan 1993 and Palme 2013a.

and in fact supported, rather than undermined, the public administrative system; this notion is often referred to as the model of fiscal participation, the model of fiscal shares, or the Gascou model.[31] However, in the last two decades the picture of disintegrating social or state structures has—albeit differing from the traditional "feudal model"—been gaining ground again. This is notably due to the influence of Peter Sarris and Jairus Banaji, whose works—which I cannot do full justice here—have become major points of reference for historians due to their scope and ambition.[32]

Despite this back-and-forth, the image of the pagarchy as "disintegrative" has largely persisted in modern scholarship, when reality was of course more complex. At the beginning of this Introduction, we saw that in *Edict* 13 Justinian accused the pagarchs of obstructing the flow of taxes, which would very much seem to fit this narrative. Yet the pagarchs still appear in Egypt nearly two centuries later, and we find a comparable narrative put to work by modern scholars, for instance in the case of the pagarch Basileios and his dispute with the Arab governor nearly a century after the Islamic conquest.[33] Such narratives of continuous institutional failure seem suspicious: it would be peculiar for so calamitous an institution to have prevailed for at least two hundred years, and even after the transition to the reign of the Caliphs, despite the numerous administrative changes that were implemented throughout this period. There is certainly more to the story here.

IV. The Structure of This Study

The previous section's short review of the relevant historiography raises questions about how local fiscal authority was constructed and deployed in Byzantine Egypt. Several comprehensive studies have been published in recent years that focus on key aspects of the late antique countryside—village administration, the large estates and

31 Rémondon 1974a; Gascou 1985. The model has since received strong support from Hickey 2008 and 2012 (see also Amin Benaissa's introduction to new documents from the Apion estate in *P.Oxy.* LXXXIV, pp. 154–166) and will be discussed in more detail in Chapter One.

32 Sarris 2006 argues for a "bitter struggle between the imperial authorities and aristocratic interests over access to the wealth created by—and extractable from—the labouring population of the empire" (p. 7). Banaji (2007; first edition 2001) points to the more rigid social hierarchy driven among other things by increased and direct exploitation and by an "economic revival" of the late antique countryside (p. 3), which created conflicts of interest between the state and the provincial aristocracy, concluding that "with the decline of a strong central authority late Byzantine Egypt was being progressively abandoned to the unfettered domination of the local and provincial aristocracy more or less on the lines described by Gelzer" (p. 100, where the pagarchs play a key role). In darker terms, the findings of Zuckerman 2004a may be read as essentially supportive of the hypothesis of an oppressive aristocracy; see Palme 2007b.

33 Cf. Papaconstantinou 2015. Basileios is generally seen as a pagarch of the village of Aphrodite, with his title *dioikētēs* being synonymous with that of pagarch. Isabelle Marthot (2013, I 187–196) has challenged this notion and pointed to significant inconsistencies in the traditional view.

their economy, the curial administrators, the agency of local communities[34]—but there has not been a systematic investigation of the pagarchs in their administrative and sociohistorical context.[35] Such an investigation is the goal of the present study, which is divided into six chapters, each of which builds upon the others.

Chapter One recontextualizes the creation and evolution of the pagarchy from the fourth to the early sixth centuries in order to understand where this institution so central to the administration of late antique Egypt originated.

Chapter Two discusses the central actors and their activities before, during, and in the wake of the tax collection process, leading to a more nuanced picture of the fiscal landscape in the nomes, while also analyzing the pagarchs' relation to higher, parallel, and subordinate actors, and the ways in which the pagarchs' administrative networks pervaded the cities' rural hinterlands.

Chapter Three engages with the same question through a close examination of the texts in which the obscure expression *kōmē pagarchoumenē*, referring to "pagarched" villages, occurs. The results help to separate different lines of authority in the countryside of late antique Egypt and establish a clearer picture of the distribution of power between various actors in the cities.

Chapter Four investigates the formal features of the pagarchy: the mode of appointment, the length of tenure, practices of substitution and representation, and the practical implications of a collegial pagarchy.

Chapter Five analyzes different patterns that pagarchic careers followed, as far as we are able to track them. Particular attention is paid to the composition of the local elite in different parts of Egypt, and an integrative political model of the pagarchy is developed that accounts for these differences.

Chapter Six reviews some densely documented events that unfolded in the village of Aphrodite in Upper Egypt in the years around 550 CE and in the late 560s, which relate to conflicts between the pagarchs and (parts of) the village community. This chapter tests many of the structural conclusions developed in the previous chapters against specific cases in a larger context, all while examining the pagarchs' relationship to this village and the way that both villagers and imperial authorities reacted to alleged transgressions of authority.

The Catalog presents all known pagarchs from around 500 to 642 CE. Primarily discussing potential identifications of pagarchs with namesakes, it goes into a level of papyrological detail that I wanted to avoid in the main chapters. The Catalog is still an essential part of the study, because it informs virtually all the analyses developed in the rest of the book.[36]

---

34 Berkes 2017a (village administration), Hickey 2012 (large estates), Laniado 2002 (curial administrators), and Grey 2011 (local communities) are the most recent studies on these subjects.

35 Cf. Berkes 2017a, 212, who points to our insufficient understanding of the space between village administration and the management of the large estates, and that between village and pagarchy.

36 To keep cross-references to the Catalog to a minimum, I restrict them to cases where they seem

V. Sources

Egypt occupies a key role in historical research on the Graeco-Roman world because it provides us with an exceptional wealth of sources that enables us to explore many historical subjects in remarkable detail compared with the rest of the Greek Mediterranean or the Roman Empire. This wealth is due above all to the hundreds of thousands of papyri the country has yielded, most of which are still unpublished and stored in collections around the world. Papyrological texts also constitute most of the sources on the pagarchs, supplemented by additions, scant though they are, from literary, legal, and epigraphic sources. Papyrus, the paper of the ancient world, was used throughout the Mediterranean for all kinds of records, and large quantities of papyrus documents were produced each day throughout the Roman Empire.[37] Because papyrus is an organic material, the vast majority of those documents are lost today. Egypt, thanks to its favorably dry climate, is the only region where papyrological evidence has survived in significant quantity and with comparatively wide distribution.[38]

Papyri[39] provide historians with a window into parts of the ancient world that seem far away from great wars, court intrigues, and abstract religious discourse.[40] Some contain literary or "semi-literary" texts, but typically they were used for more transient, what papyrologists call *documentary*, purposes, generating a wide range of documents—including, to name just a few examples, tax receipts, business accounts, family letters, leases of land, fiscal registers, and court proceedings. We can find pagarchs in all these various types of documents (and more besides), which allows us to bear as close witness to their activities across various societal and administrative strata as one can possibly hope to do for individuals from the ancient world. Of course, our sources offer but a fragmentary picture of the vast quantity of documentation that was once produced, and a large part of what constituted people's lives was not written down at all. Still, there can be little doubt that fiscal issues were not only vital to the empire but also influenced the way individuals perceived their world and operated within it. More-

absolutely necessary. The reader may want to consult the Catalog more often than that, since many issues of detail concerning individual pagarchs and texts are discussed there.

37 This also applies to the related writing materials that are included in the concept of *papyrological evidence*, such as ostraca (potsherds) and wooden tablets.

38 It has been noted that climate cannot be the whole answer, and that different archival and disposal practices may also have played a role. Parts of the Near East and North Africa, for instance, would have benefited from similar climatic conditions, yet have yielded few or no papyri. On this issue and for an overview of notable findspots outside Egypt, see Bagnall 2020, 8–13 and Gascou 2009.

39 When I speak of *papyri* here and throughout this book, I refer to documentary papyrological material; see n. 37 above. Only between four and six published ostraca (*O.Dor.* 5; *O.BirShawish* 3 and 29, and perhaps 27; *O.Sabil* 31; perhaps *O.Sarga* 107, which is undated) relate to a Byzantine pagarch, however.

40 But see Palme 2015 on how the papyri also contribute to each of these subjects at a more global scale, with a focus on the late Roman, or early Byzantine, Empire.

over, the fiscal administration was the most prolific and reliable producer of written documents, first and foremost papyri; if there was anything like a state apparatus in the Roman Empire, Egypt is where we can expect to witness it at work, and not only in an elite environment but also at lower strata of society.[41]

In contrast to literary sources, the number of published papyrus documents has grown vastly since the early days of papyrology over a century ago, and new documents continue to emerge. Every new historical study based on papyri can therefore draw on a much wider foundation than preceding ones. But not only do the sources become more numerous over time; it is equally important that scholarly work increasingly refines our understanding of those texts that were already available—through new readings, new dates, or new conceptions of the ways these documents were used. Such refinements alter the grounds of discussion significantly, as I hope will become evident in this book.

Rich and diverse as they are, papyrological sources have their own serious limitations. One of these is that the evidence is not distributed evenly over time and space, but forms clusters from around a certain time, from a certain place, and focusing on a particular type of content, thus creating multiple microcosms of Byzantine Egypt. I refer to this phenomenon as *clusters of evidence* throughout this book. Some scholars refer in this context to the "accident of preservation," cautioning us to remember that the documents that have come down to us are but a random snapshot of the world we are seeking to understand. These scholars would agree, however, that this is a simplification of a more complex issue. While it is true that we have only a tiny percentage of what was once written in Graeco-Roman Egypt, there are still patterns that we can observe.[42] Awareness of these patterns can sharpen our sense of which questions we can and cannot expect our material to answer.

As for local distribution, there are virtually no finds from the Nile delta, a region that includes, most importantly, the city of Alexandria. This city was Egypt's capital from the early days of Graeco-Macedonian occupation and continued to be so for as long as the region remained a single province, until Diocletian's reforms, but even afterward it was still a city unlike any other in Egypt. We know from papyri and from literary sources how the outside world saw Alexandria, but these sources concentrate on the exceptional, and we have little idea of what was going on day to day in the streets and offices of Egypt's political and cultural center. The distribution of papyrological evidence in the rest of the country also follows a distinctive pattern. Whereas many of the finds from the first four centuries CE originate from villages, most of what has come down to us from the fifth and sixth centuries is from the cities, notably (from north to south) Arsinoe, Herakleopolis, Oxyrhynchos, Antinoopolis, and Hermopolis.[43]

---

41 Cf. Palme 2015, 226–228.

42 Berkes 2016, 391, with reference to Bagnall 2011, 27–53.

43 Bagnall 2020, 25; Palme 2013a, 98. The notable exception is the large quantity of papyri from the "village" of Aphrodite in the Antaiopolite nome, but that settlement should not be considered a typical village; see Chapter Six, Section I.

If we look at the chronological distribution of papyri from the fourth century up until the Islamic conquest in 642 CE, it is notable that there are markedly fewer documents dating from the fifth century, a fact that has thus far eluded any commonly accepted explanation but may in essence be due to the lack of large archives from this century.[44] *Archive* is the papyrological term for a group of texts that share a common background or content and often relate to the same individuals. Archives allow for additional, contextual insights that isolated and often fragmentary papyri generally fail to provide. Some scholars distinguish between groups of texts that were deliberately kept together even in antiquity (archives in the strict sense) and groups of texts that may stem from different sources but still share a connection because they concern the same people, surroundings, or subjects, and thus were grouped together by modern scholars (dossiers).[45] Because the exact definitions of these terms are debated and since they are not used consistently in scholarly literature, I use the term *archive* in the general sense throughout this study.[46]

The most obvious criterion for identifying specimens relevant to this study among the tens of thousands of papyri from late antique Egypt is the occurrence of the title of pagarch or related words, but many other texts provide necessary comparative evidence or illuminate the wider context of the pagarchs' areas of activity. With some exceptions, the distribution of evidence for the pagarchy by and large follows the general pattern of distribution for late antique papyri. In the fourth and fifth centuries, papyri about the pagarchs—who at that time can be identified with the well-documented *praepositi pagorum*, discussed in Chapter One—come almost exclusively from Oxyrhynchos. After the generally poorly documented fifth century, the papyri again become more numerous due to the emergence of two of the largest papyrus archives of Graeco-Roman Egypt: the Apiones archive and the Dioskoros archive. These archives dominate the Egyptian evidence for the sixth and early seventh centuries, and have provided some of our most valuable sources on the pagarchy.

The Apiones were a magnate family or "house," apparently from Herakleopolis in Middle Egypt, who rose to the highest imperial honors during the late fifth and early sixth centuries. This family has left us an archive that spans from the mid-fifth century to the early seventh and features around four hundred Greek papyri dealing with the operation of the family's "large estate" in Oxyrhynchos in Middle Egypt: business let-

44 Palme 2013a, 98, with reference to Rémondon 1966 and Bagnall & Worp 1980; see also Habermann 1998.

45 In this sense, a dossier may contain one or multiple archives, and likewise an archive may contain multiple dossiers, depending on how finely one draws the line between them. On this issue, see Martin 1994, Jördens 2001, and Vandorpe 2009.

46 I occasionally use *dossier*, however, in order to refer vaguely to groups of texts, depending on context, such as the dossier of the pagarchs Ioannes and Serenos, which is part of the Dioskoros archive. For critical remarks on the narrow use of the terms *archive* and *dossier*, see Bagnall 2020, 48 n. 13.

ters, estate accounts, receipts of delivery, and much else.[47] The Apion estate has often served to exemplify the notion of late antique Egypt as a land dominated by incredibly wealthy landowning magnates, but there have long been doubts about whether this exceptionally well-documented estate is in fact representative even of Egypt, let alone of the Eastern Empire at large. Even though the Oxyrhynchite Apiones are not attested as pagarchs, Chapter Three draws extensively on their archive so that the pagarchs' responsibilities can be compared and contrasted with (other) responsibilities that large landowners were vested with in the late antique countryside.

By contrast, the Dioskoros archive contains some seven hundred papyri—evidence of the private and public dealings of the poet and notary Dioskoros and his family.[48] This archive is connected to the two smaller archives of Phoibammon (whose wife was Dioskoros's cousin) and Kollouthos, from which it is not always distinguished in modern scholarship.[49] Written in Greek and Coptic, the texts of these archives focus on Dioskoros's hometown, the "village of Aphrodite" in Upper Egypt, and its administrative district, the Antaiopolite nome, but also on the city of Antinoopolis, the provincial capital where Dioskoros was for some years active as a notary. He may have been born around 520 CE, and the earliest documents in his archive date back to the early part of the century, since Dioskoros kept some documents that were still of value and reused others that no longer served a purpose. We largely lose track of him in the course of the 570s, but his wife Sophia apparently continued to fill the family archive until at least 587/588. The texts of the archive do not deal solely with Dioskoros's family, friends, or business partners, however. Since he worked as a notary and thus put other people's affairs into writing, the range of individual activities documented by his papers is

47 *TM* Arch ID 15. See the highly readable discussion of the archive and its reconstruction in Azzarello 2015, as well as references to relevant literature on p. 353 n. 1; one should add Ruffini 2008a, 94–146 and, although controversial, Sarris 2006, *passim* to Azzarello's list. More recent additions include Bransbourg 2016, 346–399; McConnell 2017; Begass 2018, 317–351; and the discussion of new Apionic texts in *P.Oxy.* LXXXIII (focusing on their family history) and *P.Oxy.* LXXXIV (focusing on the administration of their Oxyrhynchite estate). On the early history of the Apiones, see Nikolaos Gonis's commentary on *P.Oxy.* LXXXII 5325 and Palme 2016. New insights will be provided by the various contributions in Azzarello forthcoming.

48 *TM* Arch ID 72. The authoritative works are the articles collected in Fournet 2008a; see also Fournet 1999, especially 317–336, MacCoull 1988 and Ruffini 2018a. The nature of the archive is discussed in Fournet 2008b and Ruffini 2018a, 5–10. Important forthcoming contributions include the re-editions of the petitions by Jean-Luc Fournet and the Greek letters by Yasmine Amory as well as the editions (including re-editions) of the Coptic letters by Loreleï Vanderheyden (forthcoming as *P.Aphrod.Let.Copt.* I, a revised and expanded version of her 2015 dissertation).

49 See Fournet 2016, 115–121 and 126–139; cf. Fournet 2008b, 18 n. 3. One could speak of "the Aphrodite papyri of the sixth and early seventh centuries," of which the Phoibammon archive (*TM* Arch ID 193), the Kollouthos archive (*TM* Arch ID 429; categorized as a "subarchive" of the Phoibammon archive, which is why the texts are not listed separately), and the Dioskoros archive in the strict sense (or, "Sophia archive"; see Fournet 2008b, 29) form interrelated parts.

greater than we could hope to find in other archives. Along with his father and other relatives, Dioskoros was also involved in the administration of his village as headman (*prōtokōmētēs*), which is why the archive also contains many documents of an official nature and reveals how Aphroditans interacted with higher authorities from the *civitas* or the province. Chapter Two, which reconstructs the mechanics of the pagarchy in the countryside, draws largely on evidence from this archive—as does Chapter Six, which discusses the pagarchs' activities in and around the village of Aphrodite.

Apart from these two archives, a large body of sources is formed by what could be called *the papyri of the Fayum elite*. These documents deal mainly with the business of various aristocrats and their associates in the Arsinoite nome from the late fifth century to the end of the seventh, and a considerable number of these aristocrats were pagarchs. But the Byzantine documents of this cluster only rarely reveal the pagarchs' official agenda. For the most part, they are concerned with the business of estate owners who *happened* to be pagarchs, although there are some exceptions. Still, this material has much to tell us about the prosopography and chronology of the pagarchs in the Fayum,[50] particularly for a period when there is virtually no evidence for the pagarchy from other nomes: namely, the early seventh century, including the decades of the Persian occupation of Egypt (619–629) and reestablished Roman rule (629–639).

The Catalog at the end of this book reveals that evidence for the pagarchs from other nomes is sparse in the Byzantine period. Barely a handful of relevant documents are known from Hermopolis, and only one uncertain instance may relate to Herakleopolis, which is striking since both are among the most prominent places of provenance for late antique papyri. I have no explanation for this discrepancy, except the aforementioned "accident of preservation" that has left us with the documents that we happen to have, and the fact that we lack large archives from these two places. It is perfectly possible that new publications may remedy this imbalance in the future.

Most of the documents referred to above were written in Greek, which was the dominant language for public purposes in Egypt from the time of the Ptolemies onward. In Egypt, Latin was usually the language of the higher echelons of the state apparatus or military. Coptic, the latest form of the Egyptian language, was used in private letters from the fourth century CE onward, but does not appear in administrative or legal documents until the sixth. It was only after the Islamic conquest that Coptic began to replace Greek at a somewhat faster pace, as increasing numbers of contracts, administrative letters, and tax receipts came to be written in the Egyptian language.[51] For this reason we would not expect large numbers of Coptic documentary texts to

50 Throughout this work, I shall for the sake of brevity speak of a "pagarch of Arsinoe" or a "pagarch of the Fayum," even though the proper title until at least 622 CE was in fact "pagarch of Arsinoe and Theodosiopolis." The city of Theodosiopolis in the Fayum was for much of the Byzantine period bound to her neighboring sister Arsinoe via a system of joint administration, discussed in Stern forthcoming (c).

51 Fournet 2009, 430–441; Clackson 2010; van der Vliet 2013; Fournet 2020a.

deal with Byzantine pagarchs, and indeed only three or four published specimens mention them.[52] Since the Coptic material is still largely unpublished, this may change in the near future.[53]

Nonpapyrological sources on the pagarchy are rare.[54] In the fourth and early fifth centuries, pagarchs figure in one passage from the *Codex Theodosianus*, in a municipal inscription from Asia Minor, and in two literary passages: one by Isidore of Pelusium, from Egypt, the other in the letters of Basil of Caesarea, from Asia Minor.[55] From the period after the pagarchs' rise to the city level, there are *Edict* 13, quoted at the beginning of this Introduction, and two Coptic literary texts: a *History of the Church* and the *Life of Aaron*.[56] The former relates to pagarchs during the reign of Emperor Marcian (r. 450–457), the latter to a pagarch in the late fourth century or early fifth. Both may, however, reflect the conception of the pagarchy at the time they were written, rather than at the time they are about, which is discussed in context in the relevant chapters.

VI. Methodologies

Anyone who uses papyrological evidence will sooner rather than later realize that attempting to work solely from the printed texts will prove unsatisfactory, and that the papyri themselves—their material side, their formal features, their appearance—will yield new insights, while also raising a host of new questions. I have therefore generally

52 *O.Sarga* 107 (the text is a private letter without a date, but may be assigned to the sixth or seventh century on palaeographical grounds; see Förster 2002, 600, s.v. πάγαρχος); *P.Sorb.Copt.* 30; MacCoull 1993, nos. 6 and 11. MacCoull's no. 6 is apparently lost, whereas no. 11 has been re-edited in Vanderheyden 2015 (soon to be published in revised form as *P.Aphrod.Let.Copt.* I) as no. 15. In addition, Vanderheyden presents two new texts that relate to pagarchs (nos. 11 and 13).

53 However, there will most likely not be scores of new texts mentioning pagarchs, given the preference for Greek for administrative purposes in the Byzantine period. It seems unlikely that there was a (yet undiscovered) genuine Coptic, i.e., Egyptian, official title for the pagarch, because Coptic texts generally render specific higher administrative titles as Greek loanwords throughout the Byzantine period; see also Berkes 2017a, 208–210.

54 Liebeschuetz 1974, 165 and 168 points to some "prefects" of cities in the work of John of Nikiou who may have been pagarchs (perhaps alongside other positions; the argument goes back to Jean Maspero; see Mazza 1995, 180 n. 32). But there are problems with this argument. John was writing much later, his sources are not well understood, and the text is only available in an early modern translation in Ge'ez of an Arabic translation of the (probably Coptic, perhaps Greek) original. In a later work, Liebeschuetz (2001, 270) is more careful on this point.

55 *C.Th.* VIII 15.1; *ICG* 182 (= *CIG* 3989); Isid.Pel. *epist.* 51; Basil. *epist.* III 2; all discussed in Chapter One.

56 On this *History of the Church* and the passage relating to pagarchs, see Johnson 1976 and López 2013, 145 n. 20. Although Tito Orlandi (2007, 11) has argued that the original title of the work was *The (Twelve) Histories of the Church*, the traditional title is used here, as it is prevalent in the scholarly discourse. On the *Life of Aaron* and the passage relating to pagarchs, see the new edition by Dijkstra & van der Vliet 2020 and Stern 2020, 41–43 with further references.

worked from the photos accessible to me through online databases or the generous help of colleagues,[57] and on that basis attempted to examine the texts. This work inevitably resulted in new readings that are relevant to my understanding of these documents, though they are certainly not without flaws. The benefits of this approach will hopefully become apparent throughout this book, and although most detailed papyrological discussions have been restricted to the footnotes or the Catalog, these discussions have fed into many arguments made in the main text or even become an essential new part of the study. This way of including and presenting papyrological detail is intended to encourage historians to engage more closely with the papyri.[58] Not the least due to the digital revolution, these sources have never been more accessible than they are today—and papyrologists and historians still have a lot to say to each other about the ancient world.[59]

But even though the papyri bring us closer to the lower strata of society, and to what empire looked like on the ground, than any other evidence we have on the ancient world, we must bear in mind that they are not representative depictions of the views or affairs of Roman-Egyptian society. As noted before, the vast majority of written documentation is lost, and the remainder is filtered by intention and custom. As regards intention, the term *documentary* does not imply objectivity, and there has been a lot of recent scholarly inquiry into the narrative content of documentary sources. One question concerns the degree to which certain types of documents, such as petitions, may also be deemed literary in nature.[60] Another factor concerns "the interplay of ability and need to read and write."[61] Most papyri relevant to the present study were written by professionals trained

57 Due to the ongoing repercussions of the cyber-attack on the British Library during the final revision of this book, I have not had the opportunity to recheck images from this collection.

58 Cf. Turner 1968, vi: "I have gone indeed some lengths to avoid making use of the words 'papyrologist' and 'papyrology.' They suggest a department of knowledge which is only too easily elevated into a 'mystique.' A [person] who wishes to work on Greek or Latin papyri needs no mystical powers."

59 See, for instance, Keenan 2009, adeptly articulated at 181 and 186–187, and, for a case in point, Chapter One, n. 23. This goes, *mutatis mutandis*, for all the many disciplines that work, or could work, with papyri—and naturally, the terms *papyrologist*, *historian*, *philologist*, *archaeologist*, *Egyptologist*, *Arabist*, etc., are not mutually exclusive. In this context, one may want to add to n. 58 above that most papyrologists today would agree that Greek and Latin texts, important though they are, no longer exclusively define "papyrology." Digital revolution and papyrology: Bagnall 2020, 97–103; digital tools such as the *Duke Databank of Dokumentary Papyri* (*DDbDP*, now integrated in the *PN*) and *Trismegistos* join invaluable "traditional" instrumenta such as the *Berichtigungsliste* (*BL*) and the *Sammelbuch* (*SB*).

60 See Davis 1987 for an insightful study on early modern letters of remission, a type of document that is comparable in many respects to the late antique petitions, for instance in the use of "documentary literacy" to gain a higher authority's grace. See also Brown 1991, 154 on the factor of storytelling. For a narratological interpretation of the petitions from the Dioskoros archive, see Kovelman 1991. On the "literacy" of late antique documentary sources, see also Fournet 2004 and Fournet 2015, 256–257.

61 Bagnall 2020, 22.

in handwriting, in legal or customary formulae, and in the use of "proper" language. What we see in written documents is therefore presumably different from the content, style, and register most people would have employed in their daily lives.[62] Documentary papyri were not created to tell modern scholars about that period in time, but served certain needs in the present.[63] It is therefore of paramount importance to place each document in relation to others that address comparable issues, but also in relation to other specimens of this formal type of document. Finally, we have to acknowledge the immense amount of documentation that has been lost, as well as the words, events, and practices that were never put into writing in the first place.

This study takes an administrative perspective and assumes that the public agenda played a considerable role in people's individual lives, an assumption that is somewhat biased by the available evidence. State business was a significant background factor for many surviving documents, which may create the impression that it was one of the primary concerns of the population of late antique Egypt.[64] This was certainly not the case. However, in a recent monograph on the Byzantine village of Aphrodite, it has been argued that "[a]t this level there is no state" and that "the state appears only at exceptional moments."[65] I believe that this goes too far in the other direction, as I hope to show in the course of this book. *State* should not, of course, be equated here with its modern incarnation, the nation state, let alone the capitalist nation state, but rather should be understood as an aggregate of institutionalized practices that are territorially centralized and backed by a monopoly on the use of coercive force.[66] *State power*, then, is the capacity that this entity has to impose its will on others.[67] The state thus conceived is only one of several overlapping networks that shape power relations between

62 In the context of the present study, this is perhaps most strikingly illustrated by *P.Oxy.* XVI 1831 (Oxyrhynchites; late V–early VI), a letter between two village headmen (*meizones*). The grammar and orthography in this text deviate so greatly from modern standard conventions of ancient Greek that it is hard to even grasp the author's main arguments; one sentence, discussed in Chapter One, Section III, has been regularized, and therefore interpreted, in five different ways by modern commentators. Although the author surely was in a position to have someone "more" literate write the letter, he did not bother to do so, presumably because he could expect that his addressee, the headman of a neighboring village, would have no problem following this text that modern scholars have struggled to make sense of.

63 Bagnall 2020, 12 (original emphasis): "Rather, the prime motivator for use was *need* for written documentation."

64 Bagnall 2020, 13: "This is the sense in which the social character of writing and its dependence on power act as another filter between our gaze and ancient society."

65 Ruffini 2018a, 213. Cf. also Ando 2017a, 5, referring to Millar 1981, an influential pessimistic voice on the presence—or, rather, visibility—of the state in the world of Apuleius's *Metamorphoses*.

66 This is in essence still the Weberian model. Among detailed recent discussions of the value of the concept of "state" in classical antiquity, see Scheidel 2013 for an optimistic position and Winterling 2014 for a pessimistic one.

67 On ancient state power in particular, see the comprehensive theoretical and historiographic survey in Ando 2017a.

groups and individuals, and an analysis of the infrastructural organization of each particular power network helps reveal how this power is generated. For this analysis, I draw on the sociology of Michael Mann, for whom the *autonomous power of the state* consists of two—complementary, rather than inversely related—kinds of power: *despotic power* on the one hand and *infrastructural power* on the other.[68] Despotic power refers to "the range of actions that the state elite is empowered to make without consultation of civil society groups," whereas infrastructural power denotes "the capacity of the state to actually penetrate civil society and implement its actions across territories."[69]

The analytical structure laid out in Section IV of this introduction thus aims at evaluating the pagarchs' contribution to the late Roman Empire's infrastructural power. I do not, however, draw on this concept as an all-encompassing explanation, but rather seek to deploy it as an analytical tool. I understand infrastructural power essentially as a network. This network is formed by a set of institutions, rules, resources, and people that enables the central government to impose its will at the regional and local levels. In the context of this study, that specifically means enabling the government to extract resources from taxpayers smoothly and efficiently. I postulate that the institutions and rules of this state network can either be legally prescribed or emerge out of customary practices. More importantly, these institutions and rules as well as the underlying resources can be *public/official* or *private* in character—as can the roles that individual actors play in this network—as long as they contribute to a more or less unobstructed flow of taxes to the top.[70] This allows us to grasp the different sources of power constituting empire in the countryside, and to differentiate between various actors and institutions that were part of the same administrative and political networks as the pagarchs.

---

68 See Mann 1986b, which builds on Mann's IEMP model; further nuance is added in Mann 2008. The IEMP model was articulated in Mann 1986a, the first volume of his monumental study *The Sources of Social Power*, of which three further volumes have since followed. Mann rejects the notion of one "unitary totality" of "society" (p. 2) and argues that social power is generated through ideological, economic, military, and political (IEMP) networks, which are separate but interrelated. Mann's political power is by definition the result of territorially centralized state activity. For a multifaceted discussion of Mann's social theory, see Hall & Schroeder 2006.

69 Mann 2008, 355; cf. Mann 1986b, 113–116. There is no space here to engage with the anachronistic nature of the concept of civil society as applied to the ancient world (cf. Ando 2017a, 9); for my purposes it will be sufficient to equate civil society with the "imperial subjects," however vague that notion may be.

70 This approach acknowledges that *official*, *public*, and *private* are not concepts that existed in the ancient world, but rather modern tools for making better sense of it. This approach also avoids the problem of having to characterize the use of private resources for official purposes as "semi-public" or similar, a problem that manifests most immediately in the role of the large estates described in Chapter Three. For a discussion of "public" and "private" spheres of activity in late antique Egypt and how they are perceived through a contemporary lens, see Tost 2012; for the Roman world, cf. the survey in Cooper 2007, 17–24.

The degree to which the administration of late antique Egypt featured *bureaucratic* elements will not be of primary interest in my discussion.[71] Although the number of officials grew in the late Roman Empire, it was still, by modern standards, severely under-administered.[72] One should not conceive of the late Roman state or any other premodern administration as a carefully laid-out structure in which each and every official had his own clearly delineated area of responsibility. Instead, administrative powers and competences were much more situational, and we must be careful when moving from particular to general and avoid the tendency to "totalize" when the evidence may be insufficient.[73] We have virtually no normative descriptions of the pagarchs' competences or areas of responsibility,[74] and a major challenge for this study is to make sense of a tangle of a relatively small number of direct sources. Most of these texts do not relate to the same events, and I am aware that, more than once, the interpretation of a single text weighs heavily.[75] Brian McGing once remarked of the office of the Ptolemaic *epimelētēs*:

> It is difficult to paint anything other than a rather disjointed picture of the epimeletes' job, as the papyrological evidence, while vitally informative, is also quite limiting. For the most part the texts allow us only to say that at a certain time in a certain place an epimeletes acted in a certain way, and that therefore, he had the power to act at that time and in that place (sometimes we can add that he was expected to act in this way).[76]

The same is true for the pagarchs, and for the overwhelming number of other regional and local functionaries in the ancient world. The interest that we have in episodes such as the conflict between the village of Aphrodite and the pagarchs of Antaiopolis is therefore multilayered. First, we can infer what the pagarchs were considered responsi-

71 See Eich 2015, especially 90–95 and 117–118 on the prospects and pitfalls of the (again, ultimately Weberian) concept of bureaucracy in a premodern context and 133–144 for a bureaucratic view of the organization of imperial administration in the late Roman period up to the fifth century. A highly intriguing inside perspective on the imperial bureaucratic apparatus is provided by John the Lydian (Lydus *mag.*), compellingly read in context by Kelly 2004. On the use of the terms *state, administration,* and *bureaucracy* as applied to the Roman Empire in general, see also Kruse 2002, 8–11.

72 There has been wide-ranging discussion about a growing late antique (proto)bureaucracy. The basic direction can be grasped through the account of Weisweiler 2017, notably regarding traditional ideas of a "privatization" of public authority. For numbers, see Kelly 2004, 110–111. With regard to the local level, Sven Tost (2012 and 2015) has highlighted aspects of late antique administrative practice that seem to mark a distinction from earlier periods, though it was still far from constituting a bureaucracy in the modern sense.

73 Keenan 1991, 162. Cf., however, Roger Bagnall's (2020, 110 n. 13) cautionary remarks about using this term that way.

74 Justinian's *Edict* 13 is, to a certain degree, an exception.

75 The most striking examples may be *P.Oxy.* XVI 1831 (Chapter One), *P.Cair.Masp.* I 67057 (Chapter Two), and *P.Oxy.* XVI 2040 (Chapter Three).

76 McGing 2002, 63.

ble for and what they were authorized or expected to do in order to meet this responsibility. Then, if the pagarchs transgressed their authority in a particular case, we can ask why they did so, how the upper and lower strata of society reacted, and whether this authority was the same as in other nomes. In light of what *Edict* 13 has to say about the pagarchs in its *praefatio*, which was quoted at the beginning of this introduction, we may safely infer that there were pagarchs throughout Egypt, but was their job the same in each of the nomes? What if in, say, Antaiopolis, the term *pagarchos* referred to something different than it did in Oxyrhynchos?[77] The sources show us many different activities that the pagarchs were involved in, but due to the clusters of evidence not all of these activities are documented to the same degree, in every region, or in every decade.

Let us take only the individual pagarchs: From the period of 500 to 642 CE, which this study takes into focus, we know approximately thirty individual pagarchs by name, yet only seven to nine appear explicitly as pagarch in three or more texts.[78] The majority of them instead figure in only one or two documents, and some pagarchs even remain anonymous. And even with our knowledge of these about thirty officeholders, considerable gaps remain. All sixty or so *civitates* of late antique Egypt—that is, the former nomes—presumably had at least one pagarch at a given moment, who was sometimes in office for a mere handful of years and at other times for considerably longer.[79] This means, at a *very* broad estimate, that there may have been at least twelve hundred pagarchs throughout Egypt from the beginning of the sixth century up until the Islamic conquest,[80] which gives us some sense of how much we are missing despite all the rich and diverse evidence we do have from Egypt.

---

77 Lajos Berkes (2017a, 46 and 210–211) has demonstrated that such regional differences also occur in late antiquity, which is often assumed to have been more standardized. One such instance is the term *prōtokōmētēs*, which in the Oxyrhynchite was not a term for a village headman like almost everywhere else, but rather an informal designation for a village notable.

78 Antaiopolis: Ioulianos, Menas Scriniarius, Ioannes, and Serenos. Antinoopolis: perhaps Kollouthos if Kollouthos Cancellarius and Kollouthos Exceptor are the same person. Arsinoe: Strategios Paneuphemos, Menas Stratelates, and Strategios Stratelates, although the count for the latter includes two unpublished documents. Theodorakios appears in one document from the Byzantine period but continues to be attested as pagarch in the early Islamic period. Of course, this count increases by means of prosopographical analysis, which underscores the relevance of the Catalog of prosopographical notes at the end of this book.

79 Sixty *civitates* is probably a conservative count. On the number of nomes, which by the fourth century had morphed into *civitates*, see n. 15 above. In the early sixth century, the "grammarian" Hierocles lists about seventy-two cities (*poleis*) for the Egyptian provinces (Hierocl. *Synecd.* 723.6–732.7; not counting the cities of Libya, which was also part of the Egyptian diocese); but there is reason to suspect that the surviving list contains some later additions and that some entries were lost in copying the text. Around 600 CE, George of Cyprus lists more than ninety localities (Georg.Cypr. 685–787), but for various reasons this compilation is more difficult to use for our question. On lengths of tenure and the phenomenon of joint pagarchs, see Chapter Four, Section II and IV.

80 Calculated on the basis of sixty *civitates*, one pagarch per nome, and a probably overestimated

One aim of this study is therefore to unify this seemingly disjointed picture. To begin with, in view of the small number of documents that directly attest the Byzantine pagarchy, it is remarkable that their distribution by and large follows the same pattern as late antique papyri in general. But more important are the cases in which there is indeed parallel evidence, such as when a deed of surety addressed to a pagarch, a type of document that is numerous in Arsinoe, surfaces in the Antaiopolite nome.[81] On other occasions, *mutatis mutandis*, different sets of evidence from two nomes complement each other. Such is the case when some Hermopolite tax receipts show us the exact procedure that an Antaiopolite contract only hints at.[82] A challenge here is that the clusters of evidence tend to document different hierarchical levels, and potential links between them may not be always immediately apparent. The Dioskoros archive from the village of Aphrodite in the Antaiopolite nome shows what fiscal activity looked like on the ground in that nome and related regions and how it impacted and challenged local communities. By contrast, the papyri of the Fayum elite and the Apiones archive provide us with a perspective that is presumably closer to how the pagarchs themselves and their aristocratic peers saw their world: here we can see how the pagarchs had their own holdings managed (Arsinoe) or how large estates administered their fiscal responsibility in parallel to that of the pagarchy (Oxyrhynchos). Other, scattered evidence adds to this picture.

Finally, a note on the early Islamic period. At least around two hundred Greek and Coptic texts from the postconquest era mention the title of pagarch, the pagarchy, or related terms,[83] significantly more than is the case in texts from the Byzantine period. But while the early Islamic evidence will for obvious reasons not be the focus of this book, which is interested in the late Roman Empire, the postconquest evidence may be valuable for testing the model or for forming new hypotheses. Provided that analogies are handled with care, this approach may occasionally help us identify *potential* indicators of practices or institutional arrangements that are obscure in relation to the Byzantine pagarchy. Generally speaking the value of the Islamic material for this study lies not in providing us with answers but in handing us a new set of questions. For instance, the Senouthios archive from the earliest years after the Islamic conquest has left us over a hundred documents from the desk of a subordinate official who sat in

---

average tenure of seven years. The margins of error for this estimate are high; the result can therefore only serve to illustrate the order of magnitude, but is likely to be on the low end.

81 *P.Cair.Masp.* I 67094 (Antaiopolites) and, e.g., *CPR* XXIV 24 (Arsinoites).

82 *BGU* XII 2196 and *P.Lond.* V 1753 (both Hermopolites) show us the aggregation and accounting of the taxes collected by the *boēthoi* at the level of the pagarchy and its *trakteutēs*, which is the exact procedure that *P.Lond.* V 1660 (Antaiopolites) refers to in a contract between two tax collectors, probably village *boēthoi*.

83 This count results from a search in the *PN* and therefore does not even include all published Coptic, let alone Arabic, documents, the numbers of which have risen sharply in the last few decades. The larger amount of evidence that has been found compared with the Byzantine period demands an explanation, and a tentative one is proposed at the end of Chapter Three.

the midst of a pagarch's administration, showing us the workings of the early Islamic pagarchy in intricate detail.[84] Other notable archives of pagarchs from the early Islamic era are those of Papas (Apollonopolis Ano), Nājid b. Muslim (Herakleopolis and Arsinoe), and perhaps of Basileios (Aphrodite/Antaiopolis) from the second half of the seventh century and the first half of the eighth.[85] The Byzantine period has left no comparable official archives of the pagarchs' administration.[86]

VII. Semantics

There were two ways to refer to a pagarch in Greek: *pagarchēs* and *pagarchos*.[87] The office as such is mentioned as early as the early fourth century,[88] yet the noun proper for the officeholder first figures in bilingual court proceedings from Oxyrhynchos from 353 CE.[89] This document also marks the earliest instance of the form *pagarchēs*, whereas the synonym *pagarchos* is first attested about five decades later.[90] Notably, the former instance occurs in fragmentary bilingual court proceedings that additionally may feature the unique term *pagarcha* in the Latin part of the document, although that reading is not entirely certain.[91] In legal documents and some other contexts, the title is given in extended form, in which case it includes the pagarch's administrative allocation. From at least the sixth century onward that was the *civitas*,[92] as in "pagarch of Antaiopolis," while around the end of the 630s, the prevalent expression was "pagarch

84 *TM* Arch ID 418. The main publications are *CPR* XXX and *CPR* XXXVI, edited by Federico Morelli.

85 Papas: *TM* Arch ID 170. Basileios: *TM* Arch ID 124 (but see n. 33 above). Nājid b. Muslim: no *TM* Arch ID; the main publication is Sijpesteijn 2013. Other relevant, albeit smaller, archives concerning pagarchs are that of the Herakleopolite pagarchs Appa Kyros, Christophoros, and Theodorakios from the Herakleopolite nome (640s CE; *TM* Arch ID 572) and that of the Arsinoite pagarch and later *dux Arcadiae* Atias/ʿAṭiyya (around 700 CE; *TM* Arch ID 27).

86 On these archives and the different pattern of survival of these documents compared to the Byzantine period, see Morelli 2013, esp. 172–173 and 183–184.

87 On παγάρχης versus πάγαρχος, see the full discussion in Stern 2024.

88 On παγαρχία and παγαρχέω, see below. There is a curious mention of οἱ πάγων ἄρχοντες as rendition of *magistri pagorum* in Magie 1905, 55, who refers to Dion.Hal. *ant.* II 76.1 and IV 15.2–3, dealing with the Roman regal period. But the context assures us that this is not supposed to be a technical term.

89 *Ch.L.A.* V 292.4 (Oxyrhynchos; 353 CE; new ed. Pedone 2020, 7–20).

90 *O.BirShawish* 29.1 (Oasis Parva; 398/399 or 413/414), although the reading is not entirely certain.

91 *Ch.L.A.* V 292.7 (Oxyrhynchos; 353 CE; new ed. Pedone 2020, 7–20): [± 10]*ịnari debebit pagarch*⟦ ⟧*a*. Pedone chose not to include the original editor's suggestion that the erased letter was perhaps *i*; based on the photo I think it is indeed likely that it was. The Latin term *pagarcha* follows the common derivation from Greek masculine nouns ending in -ης, and perhaps reoccurs in l. 10: [± 12] ̣ *praes*[*en*]*ṭe eodem super constituendo pa*[*garcha*].

92 In the fourth and fifth centuries, the *praepositus pagi* (i.e., the "early" pagarch) and the *pagarchia* are attested with the extension of the number or name of the *pagus*.

of this (!) (city of such-and-such)."[93] *Pagarchos* and *pagarchēs* continued to be used in parallel until well after the Islamic conquest of Egypt in 642 CE, and were apparently synonymous. There is no convincing pattern of preference for either form in specific contexts, and the use of one form rather than the other probably depended on personal custom, as the example of the Dioskoros archive illustrates. Here, in the middle of the sixth century, the only writers to use *pagarchēs* are Dioskoros himself and the notary Pilatos, while all other documents from this archive instead have *pagarchos*.[94] Similarly, the Arsinoite notary Panouphios, from the end of the sixth century, is distinguished by his use of *pagarchēs*.[95] Other instances of *pagarchēs* are scarce, but the form is found throughout the early Islamic period.[96] The Coptic parallels, where *pagarchos* is the only form documented, appear to support the general trend. Consequently, one should consider *pagarchēs* when resolving abbreviations of the title in documents from the hands of Dioskoros, Pilatos, Panouphios, or their associates, but based on the evidence available today *pagarchos* is the safer choice in all other cases.

The related term *pagarchia* (literally, "governance of a *pagus*") relates to the institution of the pagarchy, that is, the office of the pagarch and its authority as well as, in a later development, the district in which the pagarchs exercised this authority. The ambiguity is, however, largely a modern one, and an auxiliary conception of *pagarchia*

93 It is tempting to suppose that the change to the formula πάγαρχος/παγάρχης ταύτης τῆς πόλεως illustrates a reorganization of the pagarchy in the Persian or the post-Persian period, but ταύτης τῆς also occurs earlier in statements of origin (e.g., *BGU* XII 2202.4, perhaps from May 1, 565) or of locality (*P.Lond.* V 1714.19 from March 14, 570; see also *P.Mich.* XI 607.7–8 from March 1, 569: ἡγεμονικῆς τάξεως ταύτης τῆς Ἀντινοέων | [π]όλεως, which refers to the location of the bureau, not to the administrative circumscription, which in this case is the province). Thus, the use of ταύτης τῆς in these cases reflects that the city (or province) mentioned is the one that the authors of the document happen to find themselves in. This use of ταύτης τῆς πόλεως is ubiquitous in the Byzantine period (e.g., in *CPR* XIV 47.1, *P.Cair.Masp.* II 67158.17, and especially *P.Oxy.* XVI 1885.13) and apparently simply became fashionable for official titles during the 620s or the 630s. In Stern 2020, 34 n. 5 I therefore suggested restoring *CPR* XXIV 33.4 (653 CE) as δουκὶ ταύτης τῆς Ἀρκάδω]ṿ ἐπαρχίας rather than simply δουκὶ τῆς Ἀρκάδω]ṿ ἐπαρχίας, having missed that Sophie Kovarik (2014, 110 n. 189) had already had the same idea in her unpublished dissertation. This has consequences for the name of that pagarch; see the Catalog, n. 105.

94 That is, of course, in those instances where the word is not abbreviated. In *P.Lond.* V 1674.81, παγ̣ά̣ρχο̣[υ]ς̣ should be read as παγ̣ά̣ρχα̣ς̣; see Stern 2024, 288 and n. 30. Dioskoros is not consistent, however; see Stern 2024, 288–290.

95 *SB* XVIII 13952.6 (Arsinoe; 591/592) and *CPR* XIX 14 + P.Vindob. G 21029 + 25638 (Arsinoe; 590; edition forthcoming by Sophie Kovarik); cf. Stern 2024, 287 and n. 25.

96 Byzantine period: *Ch.L.A.* V 292.4 (Oxyrhynchos; 353 CE; new ed. Pedone 2020, 7–20); *P.Oxy.* LXIII 4371.9 (Oxyrhynchos; mid to late IV); *P.Oxy.* LXXXVII 5592.8 (Oxyrhynchos; early V). Islamic period: *SB* VIII 9755.1 (Herakleopolis; July 19, 642), *PSI* I 52.4 (Oxyrhynchos; September 18, 647; on the date, see Chapter Three, Section VI), *CPR* XXII 5.1 (Herakleopolis; mid-VII), *P.Lond.* III 1075.10 (unknown; VII; the newly uploaded online image was not accessible at the time of revision due to ongoing repercussions of the cyber-attack on the British Library), and *SB* I 5582 A.3 (Thebes; August 22, 724; no online image available).

might be "all matters pagarchs are considered responsible for," which may be seen as almost naturally manifesting into a territorial sense. Even the earliest occurrences of *pagarchia* in the fourth and fifth centuries appear to attest both meanings at least implicitly.[97] The pagarchy of the sixth and early seventh centuries, however, never related to the entire *civitas*,[98] and only began to do so in the early years of Islamic rule in Egypt, when it became the official term for the entire nome.[99] I present a hypothesis in Chapter Three as to what caused this change, but at this point it is sufficient to note that when I use the term *pagarchy*, I refer to its abstract institutional connotation.

Another derivative from the pagarch's title is the adjective *pagarchikos*, the only two Byzantine attestations of which occur in the Dioskoros archive.[100] Both cases refer to a pagarch's official authority (*pagarchikē exousia*), and are probably simply alternative renderings of the "institutional" *pagarchia*.[101] The verb *pagarcheō* and its participle, meanwhile, occur in a handful of cases in the active voice with the meaning "to act as pagarch," with two of those instances actually predating the first known occurrence of the noun proper.[102] The word also appears as a passive participle in sixteen papyri from the Oxyrhynchite and Kynopolite nomes that refer to *kōmai pagarchoumenai*, villages that were being "pagarched," an expression discussed in detail in Chapter Three. Finally, the last cognate, the noun *pagarchitēs*, appears twice in the edition of an internal administrative letter from the early Islamic period. This document supposedly deals with

---

97 In *P.Oxy.* XVII 2110.5 (October 6, 370) the institutional meaning is obviously intended, while *P.Oxy.* XLVI 3307.1 (early IV) mentions a *census* "of the pagarchy of Teis," which reveals an at least implicit territorial sense, as this list is ordered by localities.

98 See Chapter Two, Section I.

99 On the territorialization of the term, see Banaji 2007, 154–155. The earliest evidence cannot be precisely dated, but documents dated by indiction from the Papas archive of Apollonopolis Ano in Upper Egypt offer a conveniently close time frame, e.g., *P.Apoll.* 9 (660/661 or 675/676 CE) or *P.Apoll.* 13 (April 17, 661 or 676). The phenomenon occurs in Upper and Middle Egypt as far north as Memphis, at the southernmost tip of Lower Egypt; see the list in Banaji 2007, 154–155 n. 126. This distribution indicates that this was an Egypt-wide phenomenon, as we have to take into account the general lack of sources for Lower Egypt.

100 *P.Ant.* II 97.3 (Antinoopolis; VII) is another instance, but possibly from the Islamic period: ϗαὶ κτημάτων διακειμένων παγαρχικῷ[ν – – –]. See also *P.Heid.* XI 488.11 (Oxyrhynchites; mid to late VII): [Β]ίκτωρ σὺν Θ(εῷ) . . αρχικό(ς). The editor Lajos Berkes deems the reading παγαρχικό(ς) possible, but uncertain, and cautions that *pagarchikos* is not attested as a title.

101 In *P.Cair.Masp.* I 67019 verso 2–5 (Antinoopolis; 548–549), a petition to the emperor, the petitioners claim that they have never been brought ὑπ[ὸ π]αγαρχικὴν ἐξουσίαν ("under pagarchic authority") and therefore never paid their taxes to the pagarch, but rather directly to the provincial *officium*. Another attestation is the fragmentary petition *P.Cair.Masp.* III 67354 *descr.*, where πα]γαρχικῆς ἐξουσία[ς stands isolated in the first line of frg. 2 and therefore cannot be linked to what remains of the following line.

102 *ICG* 182 and *C.Th.* VIII 15.1 from the early fourth century; Iust. *ed.* 13.25; and the *Life of Aaron*, a Coptic hagiography, on which see n. 56 above.

procedures and guidelines for a pagarch in regard to the inheritance of late *pagarchitai*, but both instances are very uncertain.[103]

103 *P.Ross.Georg.* IV 15 frg. 1.7–9 (Aphrodite; 710): ἐὰν δὲ τελευτήσῃ τ[ις τῶν παγαρχιτῶν γράψον ἡμῖν περὶ αὐτ(οῦ)] | σαφηνίζων ἐν τοῖς αὐτοῖς γράμμασιν [τά τε γήδια αὐτοῦ καὶ τὸ πόσον] | ὃ ἐχείρησεν (l. ἐχείρισεν) καὶ τοὺς κληρονόμ[ους] τ[ῆς οὐσίας αὐτοῦ; frg. 2.3–4: τοῦ τοιούτου] | πα[γ]αρχ[ί]του τοῦτον διαδεχόμεθ[α. Only the uppermost part of πα[γ]αρχ[ί]του has been preserved and in a modern papyrological edition the word would be printed as π̣α̣[γ]α̣ρ̣χ̣[ί]τ̣ου; note especially how little space is available for the supposed χ[ί] and that there is no descender of a rho visible on the extant part of the fragment, contrary to what we would expect.

Chapter One
From Curials to Noblemen

The creation of the pagarchy must be understood in the light of numerous administrative developments that occurred between the third and fifth centuries. The first section focuses on three points that must be established at the outset in order to render comprehensible the context from which the pagarchy originated: the character of civic administration during this period, the institutional role of the emerging large estates and *oikoi*, and finally the dubious privilege of domanial tax collection. The second section identifies the very first mentions of pagarchs and pagarchies in the fourth century, and the third section follows them through the "dark" fifth century. Against this backdrop, the fourth section establishes a new explanation for the evolution of the pagarchy during that period, especially regarding the pagarchs' transformation from curial Aurelii into the high-ranking aristocrats of the sixth and seventh centuries.

Currently, there are two prevailing theories about the origins of the pagarchy as we see it in the sixth century: first, that the pagarchy was created to comprise all the territories left over after the widespread granting of *autopragia*, as argued by Matthias Gelzer, and second, that the pagarch was a creation of Emperor Anastasius intended to replace the *exactor civitatis*, as suggested by Wolf Liebeschuetz. The latter hypothesis is accepted by the overwhelming majority of scholars; an analysis of the early evidence, however, makes it all but certain that Gelzer was closer to the mark, although the development was more complex than he could have assumed based on the material he had at hand over a century ago.

I. A Late Antique Tax Regime: City, Village, and Estate

A particular feature of Egypt's internal administrative organization at the beginning of late antiquity was the process often referred to as the "municipalization" of Egypt, which entered its final stage around 300 CE. Formally civic institutions increasingly replaced the administration of the fifty or so "nomes," the traditional districts of Egypt, and the new city councils (Lat. *curiae*; Gr. *boulai*) were entrusted with significant responsibilities, notably concerning tax collection.[1] The old nome capital (*mētropolis*), which legally had once been nothing but a village (*kōmē*), turned into a Roman city (Lat. *civitas*; Gr. *polis*) and accordingly the old nome area became the hinterland (Lat. *territorium*; Gr. *enoria*) of its city. The term *nomos*, however, for centuries continued

1 Palme 2013a, 117–118, with further references. For an illustrative insight into the functioning of civic administration just after the tetrarchy, see Bowman 2008 with more literature on civic development in later Roman Egypt on p. 32 n. 3.

https://doi.org/10.1515/9783111493183-002

to be used to refer to what was now legally the district of a Roman *civitas*.[2] The fiscal authority of the former chief official of the nome, the *stratēgos*, was transferred to the *exactor civitatis*, who was answerable to the city council and was chosen from among the ranks of the curial class.[3] The countryside, formerly subdivided into several toparchies, was restructured into the slightly more numerous *pagi*, each of which was headed by a *praepositus pagi* and contained a small handful of villages, each in turn administered by a number of village officials.[4] The majority of municipal officials were now liturgists, individuals chosen by the city council to perform compulsory public services. Many of these liturgies entailed considerable financial risk for those nominated, and therefore candidates frequently either challenged their nomination or otherwise sought to escape these increasingly burdensome duties.[5]

The new organization of fiscal administration went along with a reorganization of the tax assessment,[6] as Diocletian introduced a system of mixed capitation and land tax commonly referred to as *capitatio-iugatio*. This system taxed individuals, or rather, their working capacity, in addition to the land, which was assessed on the basis of a handful of land categories, again as in the rest of the empire. Every year, a general tax announcement (*diatypōsis* or *indictio*) was sent out to the empire's four prefectures. The yearly indictions as a chronological device began under Diocletian in 297 CE and prevailed until well into the early Islamic age. After 312 CE, they were counted in fifteen-year cycles, which, however vaguely, provides a way to date documents.[7] Upon

2 Maresch 2007; Bagnall 1993, 54–62.

3 The late antique meaning of *bouleutēs* in comparison to its suspected equivalent *politeuomenos* has been much discussed for our period, and there seems to be no firm common ground. For the basic arguments, see the references in Sheridan Moss 2009, 51–52; but cf. Bogaert 1997, 107 and references. I shall maintain the distinction between the two and translate *bouleutēs* as "councilor," but *politeuomenos* as "curial" (as a noun). With the latter term, I refer to a member of the curial class (*ordo curialis*) who was subject to the pertaining liturgies but not necessarily part of the city council; here, I lean on Nikolaos Gonis's take on the problem in *P.Worp.*, pp. 195–201.

4 The term *toparchia*, however, is still employed after the introduction of the *pagus* system in several Hermopolite documents (see *P.Herm.Landl.*, pp. 9–10). This use is generally seen as an archaism, but Roger Bagnall and Giovanni Ruffini (*O.Trim.* I, p. 45) pose the question whether such differentiated terminology may be significant.

5 Service could be avoided by an alternative career in the provincial administration, the military, or the church; other nominees handed over their property (*cessio bonorum*) upon nomination in order to fall below the threshold of eligibility; yet others simply left their cities to avoid performing a liturgy. The standard work on liturgies in Roman Egypt remains Lewis 1997.

6 Palme 1989, 69–71 provides an instructive account of the new tax regime, particularly in relation to Egypt; Bransbourg 2015, 265–269 covers more-recent research and addresses the consequences for our perception of the imperial economy. See also Berkes 2017a, 220–222 for a discussion of how the process of redistributing the demands from above looked at the village level.

7 Originally, *indictio* was the designation for the entire five-year, then fifteen-year, cycle and one would refer to individual years as "the nth year of the present indiction," but soon the term referred also in legal documents to the particular year itself as "the nth indiction (of the current cycle)." In the present study, I use "indiction" to refer to the individual year, whereas the entire

reception of the imperial tax assessment, the *praefectus praetorio* of each of the prefectures partitioned the amount among the dioceses under him. For the diocese of Egypt, this entailed that the *praefectus Aegypti* and, after 382 CE, the *praefectus Augustalis* subdivided the demands among the governors (*correctores*, *praesides*, and *duces*) of the provinces (*eparchiai*). The governor repartitioned the due amount among the *civitates* in his eparchy, where they were distributed by the *exactor civitatis* to the city and its *pagi*. Finally, the *praepositus pagi* partitioned the demand received to the villages, and village authorities, for instance *kōmarchai*, in each village then calculated the sum due to each taxpayer.

A new factor in this system that became important especially in the fifth century, and is central to the history and historiography of late antique Egypt, is the late antique *oikos* (Lat. *domus*; literally, "household"), primarily rendered by scholars as either "Great House" or "large estate."[8] In Byzantine Egypt, this institution manifests in three forms: as an imperial (*theios* or *theiotatos*: "divine" or "most divine"), ecclesiastical (*euagēs*: "holy"), or, as often called, private or senatorial *oikos*. It is mainly the last of these, the "private" *oikos*, that is of interest here. While it figures most prominently as the *endoxos oikos* of the family of the Apiones in the Oxyrhynchite nome, there are examples, notably the oldest ones, of *peribleptoi oikoi*, that is, with a lower-ranking epithet, and therefore the status of an *oikos* was likely linked to that of its master.[9] A precise definition of *oikos* in this context has not yet been achieved: there apparently also existed large estates owned by wealthy magnates that were not styled as such,[10] but whether

cycle of fifteen years will be rendered as "indiction cycle." The fifteen-year indiction cycle was not introduced in Egypt until 314 CE, but was nonetheless counted later as if it had started in 312; see *CSBE*², 7–11.

8 Since Jean Gascou (1985) explicitly elaborated the concept of the *oikoi* that engage in public administration, there has been no comprehensive study. The comparatively recent contributions of Mazza 2011, especially pp. 265–266 and 268–269, and Tuck 2011 offer, with slightly different emphases, concise overviews of the material, the state of the art at the time, and questions still ahead. Important recent monographs on the economic mechanisms of the *oikoi* include Hickey 2012, Banaji 2007, Sarris 2006, and Mazza 2001; other seminal contributions include *P.Oxy.* LXXXIV, pp. 154–166 (Amin Benaissa), Bransbourg 2016, Hickey 2008, and Palme 1997a. Although McConnell 2017 is a commendable addition to our understanding of various details about the Apion estate, I do not think that the conception of the Apiones as tax farmers is supported by the sources; see Chapter Three, n. 256.

9 See Tuck 2011, 289 for instances and sources. I discuss the hierarchy of the rank epithets and their use in late antique papyri in Chapter Five, Section I. Gonis 2015a, 349 argues that the term *endoxos oikos* for the Apion estate is only used by its members or those associated with it, not by third parties.

10 Liebeschuetz 2001, 190–191. Count Ammonios, the most distinguished magnate in early sixth-century Aphrodite, directs an *ousia*, not an *oikos*; see *P.Hamb.* I 68.20–21, but cf. *SB* III 6704.4–5: τῷ ἐνδόξῳ οἴκῳ | τῆς αὐτῆς κώμης Ἀφροδίτης, which Zuckerman (2004a, 221) has identified with the *oikos* of Ioulianos, the former *eparchos* (see pp. 236–237 below). This man is, however, only known as owning an *ousia* (*P.Cair.Masp.* I 67060).

and how far those estates and the estates led by "heirs of N.N." differed from *oikoi* has hitherto not been answered conclusively.[11]

Yet there must be more to an *oikos* than landed property. Some *oikoi* and their owners can be seen handling a host of administrative responsibilities that one would expect to be part of the public—or state—agenda: they collected taxes, employed security forces, and even maintained prisons on the land in question. Furthermore, the *oikoi* assumed responsibility for certain tasks and staffed civic offices based on elaborately calculated shares, which resulted in documents such as a list in which four *oikoi* share the responsibility for filling the position of *riparius*, the chief police official of the city, for over a century.[12] Scholarly opinions vary widely regarding the extent to which the *oikoi* governed civic administration through the assumption of such shares,[13] as well as what this phenomenon reveals about the relationship between the state and its landed aristocracy.[14] The traditional interpretation takes the *oikoi* to be entirely property of aristocratic families who gradually gained hold of vast amounts of land. The *oikoi* seized administrative and executive powers at the expense of the state, and the land was in consequence effectively cut off from the reach of public authority and legislation. In this scenario, the farmers on these lands became a "servile" labor force at the disposal of "protofeudal" magnates that began to undermine state structures due to their socioeconomic dominance, contributing, or leading to, the eventual disintegration of Roman authority in the provinces.[15] The resulting model is basically one of late antique feudalism, based on developments that turned the Western Empire into an early medieval society and rooted in the view of late antiquity as a period of decline.[16]

The second line of argument, by contrast, roughly runs as follows: The *oikoi* cannot entirely be understood as owned property, because they took a pronounced role in public administration, which the head of an *oikos* assumed as an obligation toward the state. The organization of tax collection by these estates therefore does not imply

11 The formula "heirs of N.N." probably indicates a certain legal status, since it is so frequent and apparently institutionalized in documents such as *P.Oxy.* XVI 2020, 2039, and 2040: it would seem odd to assume that all those owners died just recently. The urge to avoid the division of inherited property (Banaji 1999, 205) cannot have been the main reason for the emergence of institutionalized *oikoi*, however, as most of them are attributed to individual holders. Tuck 2011, 287–289 renders *oikos* as "group of estates administered by a single 'household'" and assumes that the wealth of their owners was distinctive of *oikoi*; indications that this explanation may come close are established in Chapter Three, Section V. Mazza 2011, 276 speculates whether the title *geouchos* (!) marks the head of an *oikos*, which seems intriguing in the light of the *geouchōn* (!) address, discussed in Chapter Three, Section III.

12 *P.Oxy.* XVI 2039 with the new edition of Azzarello 2006.

13 See, e.g., Liebeschuetz 1996 for a pronounced minimalist position.

14 For the historiography of the large estates, see Hickey 2012, 5–7; Sarris 2006, 131–148 (cf. Sarris 2004, 60–62); and Keenan 1993.

15 The "servile" is from the title of Bell 1917, an influential contribution in this context.

16 Though, naturally, this account is simplified. Even Edward Hardy acknowledged an obvious administrative aspect to his "large estates"; see Hardy 1931, 47–48.

an occupation of state power by insubordinate magnates, but rather constitutes the public service of a landed aristocracy. This hypothesis emerged in the decades that witnessed the reevaluation of late antiquity and was in its outline explicitly articulated by Roger Rémondon, who pointed to certain "contradictions" between the evidence and the traditional narrative.[17] Essentially following Rémondon, Jean Gascou substantially underpinned and extended that hypothesis by a meticulous scrutiny of the evidence.[18] This second view is therefore often referred to as the Gascou model, or, after one of its fundamental assumptions, as the model of fiscal shares, emphasizing the idea that the large landowners shared the responsibility for public duties in the *civitas*.[19] The Gascou model has since received generally favorable reception from papyrologists,[20] although the feudal model is still present in some historiographical surveys of Byzantine Egypt. Recently, a revisionist stance to the Gascou position has received substantial scholarly credit in the work of Peter Sarris, who evaluated the economic aspirations of the late antique aristocracy. Sarris came to see the late antique large estates as "proto-capitalist" enterprises, and the imperial government and its elites as opponents in a bitter struggle for power.[21] Papyrologists had, however, considerable objections to Sarris's handling of the evidence from the Apion estate, which forms a central part of his book.[22] Most recently, Todd Hickey, in a survey of the exploitation of vineyards on the Oxyrhynchite large estate of the Apiones, forcefully undercut key economic assumptions of Sarris's model, concluding that "the central tenet of the Gascou model—that *oikoi* participated in the fiscal administration of the Oxyrhynchite on a system of shares—must stand."[23]

17 Rémondon 1974a. See also Rémondon 1974b, 372: "Le domaine est une entreprise économique. Mais il est aussi une institution."

18 Gascou 1985. Perhaps the best comprehensive summaries of Gascou's original ideas are his own short reviews of their scholarly reception in the preface to the revised edition of the article (Gascou 2008, 125) and in Gascou 2004, 97–98 (= 2008, 444–446); cf. the critical review of the topic by Carrié 1999, 351–352.

19 "Model of fiscal shares" in Hickey 2012, 6. Alternatives: "Gascou thesis" in Keenan 1993, 142 and Sarris 2006, 141 or "model of fiscal participation" in Banaji 2007, 93 and McConnell 2017, 6. Gascou himself has his reservations about the use of the term "model"; see Gascou 2004, 97 (= 2008, 445) and 2008, 125.

20 On the impact of Gascou's work, see Palme 2013a, 130–133.

21 Sarris 2006, which has gained much prominence, not least due to its accessibility and literary verve. "Proto-capitalist" is taken from Hickey 2012, vii, who puts the term within scare quotes and argues against this conception. Sarris himself speaks of his model as a *"tertium quid"* (p. 147; roughly, "third way") beyond both feudalist and cooperative interpretations of the relationship between the imperial government and the provincial aristocracies.

22 See, for instance, the reviews Ruffini 2009 and Mazza 2008.

23 Hickey 2012, 159; see also, with independent evidence, Hickey 2008 (discussing the *descriptum P.Oxy.* XVIII 2196 verso, now published as *P.Oxy.* LXXXIV 5464), and Amin Benaissa in *P.Oxy.* LXXXIV, pp. 154–166. Sarris's understanding of the Apion estate managed to establish itself as a dominant voice in the nonpapyrological scholarly discourse on the late Roman and early medieval periods. That the substantial objections from Hickey and other scholars (see the previous note) have gone largely unnoticed in that context—whereas Sarris himself has repeatedly

The origins of the institutionalized large estates are not quite clear. The imperial *oikos* surfaces in the 420s CE and the first "private" *oikoi* appear shortly afterward in the 430s, while the system of fiscal shares, if the aforementioned account for the staffing of the *riparia* through Oxyrhynchite *oikoi* is any indication, dates back at least to 460/461.[24] Traditional scholarship has connected the rise of the large estate with the *patrocinium*, the supposedly widespread phenomenon that saw independent farmers transfer their land to larger landholders who acquired these lands in exchange for legal and fiscal protection.[25] Modern opinions vary about the extent to which this development contributed to the rise of the *oikoi*, or was at all prevalent in Egypt. Some paragraphs of the *Codex Theodosianus* address it in an explicitly Egyptian context,[26] but the papyri tell a more nuanced story. On the ground, there is hardly any conclusive evidence for a fundamental change in the agricultural landscape in the fourth century, whether for the concentration of land in the hands of few magnates or for a decline of the peasantry into a class of serfs.[27] Furthermore, few signs of protocapitalist accumulation can be observed.[28] There remain political strategies, such as imperial patronage, marriage, and inheritance, which do seem plausible alternatives, but hard evidence for a downright drive to expansion is scant.[29]

---

defended his model against the counterarguments—may demonstrate the long way that papyrology still has to go to contribute to the general historical discourse on an equal footing. Yet, it is hardly possible to overstate the importance of approaches such as Sarris's, which brings the papyrological evidence from Egypt into dialogue with the rest of the late Roman Empire and the eastern Mediterranean, and thus promotes the use of papyri by more disciplines. The essential point here may be less about Sarris's view of the eastern Mediterranean than about the potential exceptionality of the Apion estate at Oxyrhynchos (in its administrative organization and economic aspirations), which is a point that Hickey has repeatedly made himself.

24 *P.Oxy.* XVI 2039, in which the fourteenth indiction of 460/461 is the first year listed; see Azzarello 2006, 210.

25 See Palme 2015, 230 with a nuanced picture and references.

26 *C.Th.* XI 24.1, 3, and 6 (on patronage of villages) explicitly deal with Egypt. But even in these passages, some scholars see reason to believe that landownership in these cases precisely did not change; see Grey 2011, 207–208 with references.

27 Bagnall 1993, 115 and 148–153; Palme 1997a, 118–119; van Minnen 2006, especially 165; Rathbone 2008; Venticinque 2014, 477–479; Berkes 2017a, 214–216. Telling may be a comment by Jairus Banaji (2007, 120–121, quote at 121 n. 69), who when discussing this lack of papyrological evidence has "no doubt, however, that papyri will turn up to illustrate the important social changes of this period (390–415)." For the world beyond Egypt, see also the nuanced evaluation by Grey 2011, 6–7 and 206–212, with further references.

28 Especially Hickey 2012 (partially in response to Sarris 2006) and Bransbourg 2016, 347–399 have established convincing common ground in rejecting this view regarding the mechanics of the Apion estate at Oxyrhynchos, a central witness to this hypothesis.

29 See Hickey 2012, 154–155 and Bransbourg 2016, 362 and 402. On expansion through marriage, see also Azzarello 2006, 210 n. 8 and Palme 2016, 341, particularly in connection with the rise of the Apiones. Cf. Ruffini 2008a, 4–5 for the suggestion that the expansion of the Apion estate at Oxyrhynchos "did not proceed through rurally based social ties." See Azzarello 2019, 343 and

Although the mechanics of the *oikoi* cannot be imagined without the substantial private resources that sustained them, it seems nonetheless plausible that public concerns contributed to the expanding importance of the large estates. Some obscure *oikoi* "of the city" figure in the papyri as early as the second and third centuries, and might have been institutionalized in order to administer ownerless land.[30] It is indeed conceivable that such ad hoc arrangements lay behind the institution of the first "private" *oikoi* that we know of—the *oikoi* of Theon and Timagenes, both of whom were dead by the time their *oikoi* first find mention.[31] But rather than being the physical foundations of the "private" *oikoi*, it seems conceivable that institutions like the *oikoi* "of the city" could have served as a model to organize the changing city landscape of the fifth century. The first *oikoi* that belong to living aristocrats appear not long after the first mentions of Theon's and Timagenes's *oikoi*, and the development from an auxiliary construction to an acknowledged part of the public administrative landscape must have followed soon.[32]

A much cited, if rarely discussed, problem in this context is the phenomenon called *autopragia* (literally, "self-handling"). This institution is regularly found in scholarly accounts as the right of the *oikoi* to collect taxes on their estates.[33] However, the term and its cognates are only rarely attested in a late antique fiscal context, and notable occurrences suggest that the privilege here is not the collection itself, although it is a part of it, but the mode of payment: the right to *pay* one's own taxes independently—that is, without intervention of the municipal officials—to the provincial treasury, thus dodging any attempt from intermediate instances to skim off surcharges.[34] It is true

---

n. 6 for a case of expansion because of unpaid loans, but this is hardly an instance of strategic accumulation.

30 Tuck 2011, 290–291. One prominent direction where to look for such land may be former temple land. Notably, the cases Tuck cites predate even the establishment of city councils in Egypt. On the handling of ownerless land, see Chapter Two, Section II 2.

31 See the prosopographical notes by Gonis 2009, 91–92 and his more recent discussion of the early development of the *oikoi* and the *merides*, i.e., "shares" or "(sub)districts," in both Oxyrhynchos and Hermopolis in *P.Oxy.* LXXXII, p. 169. It seems possible that, like Strategios I of the Apion family, at least Theon had been an imperial functionary, which would foster the link between the *oikoi* and the new service aristocracy. Cf. *P.Oxy.* XVI 2016, where their *oikoi* and that of a certain Eudaimon occur without an indication that the owners were dead at that time; unfortunately, this text is undated, although it likely is from the sixth century. In contrast to Theon's and Timagenes's *oikoi*, their "shares" already occur when they are alive in 437 (see *P.Oxy.* LXXXII, p. 173) and 432 CE (Gonis 2009, 91), respectively.

32 Apion I, for instance, was very much alive when an *oikos* of his was first mentioned in *SB* VI 9152 (Herakleopolis; 492). Note that the first text to feature a *kōmē pagarchoumenē* appears in 493 CE in the Oxyrhynchite; see Chapter Three, Section III. For the appearance of the Apion *oikos* at Oxyrhynchos before that date, see Azzarello 2006, 210–211, but also Gonis 2015a, 349–350, noting that *endoxoi oikoi* are attested throughout Egypt from the 530s onward.

33 Tedesco 2013 provides the most recent comprehensive discussion of "autopragia demaniale," by which he means domanial tax collection.

34 This was noted early by Wilcken 1913, 283–284 and Gelzer 1913a. The term *autopraktos* and its cog-

that large landowners increasingly became responsible for—or, according to the feudal model, arrogated the right of—collecting taxes from lands directly worked by them, and later also for land leased out to tenants.[35] Yet nowhere in the papyri do we see *oikoi* actually sideline civic authorities. Quite the contrary, as Jean Gascou has already noted: the fiscal business of the *oikoi* did not imply skipping the *civitas* level, but instead the *oikoi* were deeply integrated into the mechanics of civic administration.[36] Therefore, the concept of *autopragia* should probably be restricted to the payment of taxes directly to the province.[37] Its only certain manifestation in Egypt is, consequently, the Upper Egyptian village of Aphrodite, which legally enjoyed *autopragia* as an imperial privilege.[38]

The model for the participation of the *oikoi* in civic administration is necessarily largely an Oxyrhynchite one due to the distribution of the evidence, and for the same reason this city has yielded the majority of the early testimonies related to the pagarchy.[39]

---

nates are, in relation to the *autopragia* of the village of Aphrodite, attested in several sixth-century documents: *P.Cair.Masp.* I 67002 col. III 8; 67019 verso 3; 67024–25 (new ed. Fournet 2018) A 34, A' 58–59; and 67032.94. The *autopragia* of Aphrodite and what it entailed is also described in *P.Hamb.* III 230.6–11. The Latin form *autopractorium* is attested in *C.Th.* XI 22.4 (409 CE), which notes that this is a privilege granted by the emperor. The law is precisely about the unauthorized use of this concept by *possessores* who illegally tried to circumvent the local tax collectors, and Theodosius demands that *curiales vel apparitio provincialis* bring about the collections from these *possessores*, as usual. Although it is not made explicit, the autopract mode of payment appears to be also behind *C.Th.* XI 1.34 (429 CE). This law grants four months, counted from the promulgation of the tax assessment, to the *possessores* of Africa to pay their taxes to the province; otherwise, provincial officials would collect the taxes from them, too. We have no way of knowing whether legislation aimed at Africa was in a similar way adopted for Egypt (cf. Bagnall 2020, 55–56) and it may in fact refer to special and temporary privileges that were neither intended to be implemented universally nor in Egypt in particular. Africa had a lower density of *civitates* than Egypt, and *autopragia* may therefore have been a more practical matter there to bring in the taxes from the countryside.

35 Notable milestones were *C.Th.* XI 1.14 (371 CE) and *C.Th.* XI 24.6 (415 CE). The latter made the estate owners responsible for the personal dues, the liturgies, imposed on farmers and tenants of their estate; see Palme 1989, 96–97. The first "private" *oikoi* surface just some decades after these regulations.

36 Gascou 1985, 38–39 (= 2008, 160–161); a similar view about domanial tax collection is argued by Tedesco 2013, 15–17, who captures this, however, under the term *autopragia*. The public economies of the *oikoi* are discussed in more detail in Chapter Three.

37 With this specification, the question of whether domanial tax collection was legal, illegal, or illegal but tolerated (cf. Tedesco 2013, 16–17), would become obsolete.

38 Aphrodite's *autopragia* is discussed in Chapter Six.

39 The relevance of the Gascou model beyond the Oxyrhynchite is discussed in Chapter Three, Section VII.

II. Enter the Pagarchs: The Fourth Century

Explicit references to "pagarchs" or the "pagarchy" occur as early as the fourth century in Egypt (five to eight texts)[40] and the rest of the Eastern Empire (three texts).[41] Although these numbers are not very impressive, we may infer from these documents that the cognates *pagarchos/pagarchēs*, *pagarchia*, and *pagarcheō* were originally representations of the office of the *praepositus pagi*. Consequently, I refer to this as the "early" pagarchy, in contrast to the "later" pagarchy of the sixth and early seventh centuries. A liturgist chosen from the curial class, the *praepositus pagi* was the head of one of several districts called *pagi* in the countryside of the *civitas* and subordinate to the *exactor civitatis* and to the *logistēs* (*curator civitatis*). He was responsible for the allocation and collection of taxes, the maintenance of public security, nominations of minor liturgists in his district, "and, indeed, almost anything else."[42] Apart from rare exceptions, the *praepositi pagorum* always bore the name predicate Aurelius, instead of Flavius, which marked military or higher civil ranks.[43]

The identification of the fourth-century pagarch with the *praepositus pagi* is suggestive in a papyrus containing court proceedings.[44] Due to the document's fragmentary

---

40 *P.Oxy.* XLVI 3307 (Oxyrhynchos; early IV); *Ch.L.A.* V 292 (Oxyrhynchos; 353 CE; new ed. Pedone 2020, 7–20); *O.Sabil* 31 (Oasis Magna; third quarter of IV); *P.Oxy.* XVII 2110 (Oxyrhynchos; 370); *P.Oxy.* LXIII 4371 (Oxyrhynchos; latter half of IV). The ostraca *O.BirShawish* 3, 27, and 29 have been dated to around 400 CE and are discussed in the following section.

41 *C.Th.* VIII 15.1 (316/317?); *ICG* 182 (Lycaonia; early IV?); Basil. *epist.* III 2 (Pontus/Cappadocia; c. 360).

42 On the *praepositus pagi*, see Schmidt-Hofner 2008, 124–125 (though not differentiating between "early" and "later" pagarchs); Mitthof 2001, 146–147 with further references; Mazza 1995, 173 n. 9 with further references; Bagnall 1993, 61–62 (quote); Oertel 1917, 301–302; and Gelzer 1909, 57–60. An exemplary study of the *pagus* system in the Hermopolite nome can be found in *P.Col.* IX, pp. 106–134, especially 119–123, which also contains numerous remarks on the *pagus* system in general; see also Mitthof 1999b. Derda 2006, 263–266 provides a recent overview on the introduction of the system in Egypt. On the involvement of the *praepositus pagi* in issues of public security, see *P.Cair.Isid.* 126; Lewis 1948, especially 54 and n. 10; and Torallas Tovar 2000, 118. Some papyrus archives provide occasions to see these officials at work, for instance the archives of the *praepositi pagorum* Aurelius Heras (*TM* Arch ID 33) and that of Aurelius Asklepiades (no *TM* Arch ID; see *CPR* XVIIA and add *CPR* XXIII 30 and 31). One especially important archive is that of Papnouthis and Dorotheos, *boēthoi* of *praepositi pagorum* (*TM* Arch ID 172); see *P.Oxy.* XLVIII, pp. 74–76; Bagnall 1993, 158–159; and McConnell 2017, 58–62. The traditional date of the introduction of the office in Egypt is 307/308, but cf. the discussion (also of the connection to the *logistēs*) in *O.Trim.* I, pp. 45–46, which may point to 303 CE as a *terminus ante quem*.

43 Only two Flavii are attested as *praepositi pagorum*: the first figures in *P.Oxy.* IX 1190.2–3 (Oxyrhynchos; 347): Φλαουίῳ Π[..... καὶ] Αὐρηλίῳ Θέωνι | πραιπ(οσίτοις) ε πά[γου ἀδελ]φοῖς χαίρειν, where ἀδελφός means "colleague," while the second one is addressed in *P.Oslo* III 113.3 (Hermopolites; 346): [Φ]λ̣αυίῳ Ὀλ̣υμπιοδ[ώρ]ῳ τῷ καὶ Ἀ̣συνκ̣ριτ[ί]ῳ πραιπ(οσίτῳ) α π̣ά̣γ̣ο̣υ̣. Keenan 1974, 293–294 argued that these men must have been entitled to the Flaviate because of other magistracies unknown to us. On these "names" as status designations, see Keenan 1973, 1974, and 1983.

44 *P.Oxy.* LXIII 4371 (Oxyrhynchos; latter half of IV). The proceedings were held in Pelousion,

state the content remains vague; the main point seems to be that a certain Diogenes was assigned a—lost—office in connection to a *pagus*, but was for some reason incapable of performing it on his own.[45] The office in question was subject to the *exactor civitatis*, was a curial liturgy, and the later remark "we all have been pagarchs" is obviously used as an argument in relation to Diogenes's case.[46] Finally, the office was apparently entitled to make use of *boēthoi*, and on the whole there is strong evidence that we are dealing with the office of the *praepositus pagi* here and that *pagarchēs* is used as a synonym.[47]

A record of proceedings before the city council of Oxyrhynchos from 370 CE further illustrates the conditions for nomination to the early pagarchy and its municipal context.[48] Chosen as the party responsible for the military woolen garment, the city councilor Theon contests the validity of his nomination.[49] He claims that the *praefectus Aegypti* had appointed him to be one of the twenty-four men responsible "for the pagarchies and *conductoriae*," which implies several pagarchies in the Oxyrhynchite nome at that time.[50] His fellow councilors eventually release Theon from the additional nomination on the ground that he bears "more burdensome liturgies" as he is "one of the 24."[51] Obviously the pagarchy at that time was a civic office staffed with council-

probably before the *praeses Augustamnicae*, as the editor argues. Thus, at the time the papyrus was written, Oxyrhynchos was still part of that province, before the creation of Arcadia.

45 Office related to the *pagus*: καὶ νῦν ἐστιν αὐτὸς μὲν το[ῦ] πρώτου πάγου ̣ (l. 3), after which there is a lacuna. The traces immediately before the lacuna exclude pi, but rather look like iota or the lower part of epsilon or sigma and maybe ἐ̣[πικείμενος must be supplied. It is also possible that Diogenes was assigned a second liturgy in addition to the one related to the *pagus*.

46 Subject to the *exactor*: πρ]ο̣ν̣ο̣ίᾳ τοῦ ἐξάκτορος (l. 5). Curial liturgy: see ll. 2 and 3. Pagarchs used as an argument: πάντες παγάρχαι γεγόνα{σ}μεν (l. 9). The editor thought that the argument being made here might be that being pagarch does not exempt from being assigned to another liturgy. Cf., however, *P.Oxy.* XVII 2110, in which the opposite claim is made (see below).

47 See the introduction to *P.Oxy.* LXIII 4371. In l. 11, Diogenes is asked why he did not request a *boēthos*. The editor suggested that the document may have some connection to the archive of Papnouthis and Dorotheos; see n. 42 above.

48 *P.Oxy.* XVII 2110 (Oxyrhynchos). On this text, see Bowman 1971, 106–108 and 169.

49 The name is common in the Oxyrhynchite nome at this time but the status as *bouleutēs* make it possible to speculate that this Theon may be an ancestor of the *politeuomenos* Theon who is behind one of the first *oikoi* at Oxyrhynchos (see Section I above) and whose *floruit* dates to the 430s and 440s.

50 *P.Oxy.* XVII 2110.4–5: ἐ̣π̣ὶ̣ τῆς μελλόσης (read μελλούσης) κήρας εἰμὶ καὶ ἐν τοῖς εἰκοσιτεσσαρες (read εἰκοσιτέσσαρσιν) εἰμὶ τοῖς διατυπωθεῖσιν ὑπὸ τοῦ κυρίου τοῦ λαμ(προτάτου) Τατιανοῦ εἰς τὰς παγαρχίας καὶ κονδου|κτ̣ο̣ρίας. Wolf Liebeschuetz (1973, 39) argued on the basis of this text that there were twenty-four pagarchies in Oxyrhynchos; if this were so, there would be a difference to the number of Oxyrhynchite *pagi*, of which there were ten. It is not clear, however, whether "twenty-four" includes all pagarchs and *conductores* for one term, and even if this were the case, we cannot say whether each of these men was to be made "pagarch and *conductor*" or whether some of them were pagarchs and some others *conductores*, which seems more likely. On the *conductores*, see Lewis 1997, 21.

51 *P.Oxy.* XVII 2110, e.g., ll. 9 and 14.

ors through appointment by the prefect and so onerous a charge that being nominated for it would exempt one from being appointed for (certain?) other liturgies.

The fragmentary bilingual court proceedings *Ch.L.A.* V 292, dated 353 CE, fit into this picture, as they—in their recent re-edition—probably show us another testimony of the curial authority over the nomination of the "early" pagarchs. In this case it appears that one party of the dispute over a nomination asked that a decision made by the *praeses Augustamnicae* be executed by the city council of Oxyrhynchos. Particularly notable is the otherwise unattested Latin form *pagarcha*, although this reading is not certain.[52]

Further suggesting multiple pagarchies per nome in the fourth century is an "individual list of an assessment of the pagarchy of Teis," as translated by the editor.[53] Under this heading, the document lists various villages (*kōmai*) and hamlets (*epoikia*) along with the number of "men" in each of these localities who were liable for a certain tax.[54] With Teis being only one of several villages in that list, the editor was certainly right to suggest that the expression "pagarchy of Teis," was an alternative way of referring to the eighth *pagus* of Oxyrhynchos.[55] Similarly, *pagi* were sometimes named after a sort of chef-lieu, instead of being numbered as they usually were.[56] This does not mean that *pagarchia* manifests as a territory here: these villages were conceived to be under, and

52 *Ch.L.A.* V 292.7 (Oxyrhynchos; 353 CE; new ed. Pedone 2020, 7–20): [± 10]*ịnari debebit pagarch*⟦ ⟧*a*, on which see the Introduction, n. 91. The term perhaps reoccurs in l. 10: [± 12] ̣ *praes*[*en*]*ṭe eodem super constituendo pa*[*garcha.*] Cf. l. 4: [± 4 κατα]σ̣τ̣ῆναι παγάρχην, which from the photo I would correct to [± 4 κατα]σ̣τ̣ῆναι̣ π̣αγάρ̣[χ]ην̣, at least. Several letters raise doubts, as neither sigma nor iota are drawn the same way as in the remainder of the document, and the final nu has a small superfluous arch also not seen in the rest of the document.

53 *P.Oxy.* XLVI 3307.1 (Oxyrhynchos; early IV): κατ' ἄνδρα κήνσου παγιαρχίας (read παγαρχίας) Τήεως. According to Carrié 1981, 339–341, the "men" (ἄνδρες) in this document are not actual people, but abstract fiscal units.

54 The contributions from *epoikia* were apparently effectuated by the magnates who owned them; see *P.Oxy.* LXX 4787.9–10 and the commentary.

55 See *P.Oxy.* XLVI 3307.1 and the commentary. The list of villages resurfaces in the roughly contemporary *P.Oxy.* XII 1448 (after 324 CE), while in *P.Oxy.* LV 3788.1 (309 CE), the *praepositus* of the eighth *pagus* is responsible for the villagers of Teis. On the connection of these two texts to *P.Oxy.* XLVI 3307, see also Nielsen 1997, 756–764.

56 Identification by **village name only:** *P.Aktenbuch* fol. 28.9 and 16 (Hermopolis; 359) and *P. Kell.* I 27.3 (Oasis Magna; IV), but cf. *O.Trim.* I, p. 45. Identification by **number *and* village name:** *P.Ant.* III 200.1 (Hermopolites/Antinoites; first half of IV), *P.Charite* 14.1 (Hermopolites; 326/327?), and *P.Charite* 15.1 (Hermopolites; 329). A *pagus* named after **a "share" (*meris*)** is probably attested in *P.Lond.* III 1293.1 (Hermopolites; 346?): πάγ(ου) μερίδ( ) Δωροθέου καὶ Ἑρμαίωνος. By contrast, in *P.Oxy.* LXVII 4611 col. II 12 and *P.Oxy.* LXVII 4612 col. II 6 (both: Oxyrhynchos; 363) the references in the form *pagus* + village name are most likely to the particular village that makes the payment, not a name for this *pagus*. The *eirēnarchēs* of a *pagus* in *P.Sakaon* 45 (Arsinoites; 334) may be explained by a close association of a village with its *pagus* (instead of forming a new level of hierarchy of the *eirēnarchai* that Sänger 2005, 182 assumes), because *eirēnarchai* are usually attested for villages (or, earlier, for nomes), though there is insufficient evidence to say that with certainty. Apparently, the allocation of a village to a certain *pagus*

not necessarily within, a pagarchy.[57] A recently published list of names from the third quarter of the fourth century and excavated in the Great Oasis—that is, from outside the Oxyrhynchite or that nome's neighboring Small Oasis—refers to a *pagar(ch-)* and it is uncertain whether the *pagarchia* or the pagarch is meant here.[58]

The non-Egyptian record suggests that the term *pagarchos/pagarchēs* was used throughout the Eastern Empire in the fourth century as an alternative to *praipositos pagou* in Greek.[59] An allusion to their synonymy is extant as early as in a legal decision by Emperor Constantine, which has come down to us as part of the *Codex Theodosianus.*[60] Two women, Codia and Agrippina, had bought some undefined property from the brother of an unnamed official. In the document, Constantine makes the case that officials are not entitled to such purchases during their tenure and that any property so acquired falls to the fisc. Agrippina's argument is either that the man was not in office at the time the women purchased the property from his brother or that the brother himself was not an official. The document alternates between Greek (Agrippina) and Latin (Constantine), and while Agrippina's Greek statement "he was not pagarch to that *topos*" deploys the verb *pagarcheō*, Constantine's Latin response refers to the official's *pagus.*[61] The Greek word *topos* (literally, "place") can refer to many kinds of place or settlement below the level of a *civitas*, rendering Agrippina's argument equivalent to her insisting that "he was not *praipositos* of that *topos*."[62]

---

was subject to change; cf. *CPR* XVIIA 7.4–5 (Hermopolis; 317) and *P.Charite* 18.6–7 (Hermopolites; 320–350), where the village Sinarchebis changes its *pagus*.

57 Cf. the prevalent use of παγαρχία from the sixth century onward, which is defined by its *civitas* in the form "pagarchy of such-and-such city," also without being territorial. See the Introduction, Section VII.

58 *O.Sabil* 31.2–3 (Oasis Magna): Χ̣άρης Λωιτο(ς) ἐκ | τιμ̣[ῆ]ς̣ ε̣ἰ̣ς̣ παγαρ(χ-). The editors argue that the early date makes one tend to prefer παγαρ(χίαν), but in the light of the sources collected in the present section, πάγαρχ(ον) and παγάρχ(ην) do not seem inconceivable.

59 Cf. the conclusions in Palme 1989, 19 on the presence of *apaitētai* throughout the entire Eastern Empire.

60 *C.Th.* VIII 15.1. Constantine's death in 337 CE provides a *terminus ante quem*; Corcoran 1996, 259–260 (cf. Schmidt-Hofner 2008, 124 n. 22) dates the episode to 316/317 CE. On this text, though not in context of the pagarch, see Bianchini 1984.

61 *C.Th.* VIII 15.1: τῷ τόπῳ ἐκείνῳ οὐκ ἐ⟨π⟩αγάρχει (Agrippina) and *in suo pago* (Constantine). Gothofredus suggested the emendation ἐ⟨π⟩αγάρχει. The manuscript, a codex in the Bibliothèque Nationale, Lat. 9643, 118 recto, l. 1, has ουκετιαγαρχει, which is an easy copying mistake; for a photo, see https://gallica.bnf.fr/ark:/12148/btv1b10303686s/f247.zoom.

62 *C.Th.* VIII 15.1: τοῦ τόπου ἐκείνου πραιπόσιτος οὐκ ἦν. An unspecific use of *topos* is evident, e.g., in *P.Oxy.* VIII 1101.9–10 (Oxyrhynchos; 367–370: τοῖς κατὰ τόπον πραι|[ποσίτοις], implying not clearly defined nearby localities (the *praepositus* here is a military *praepositus*, not a civil *praepositus pagi*). In *P.Oxy.* LXXII 4867.2 (Oxyrhynchites; 122/123), the address is to σι(τολόγοις) Ὤφεως τόπ(ων), Ophis being a village; these *topoi* apparently could be understood to form a sort of district. Iust. *ed.* 13.24 lists a descending hierarchy of eparchies, cities, and *topoi* being under the fiscal authority of the *dux et Augustalis*; see also Chapter Two, Section I.

Asia Minor furnishes the remaining two instances of pagarchs in the fourth century. One is an inscription from Lycaonia for a late curial from his brothers that lists the pagarchy among his civic offices.[63] Finally, in a letter from the time of his Pontian retreat around 360 CE, Basil of Caesarea reports that an inhabitant of Anisa and several accomplices broke into his home, robbed the whole place, and assaulted the women who were present. Basil now addresses the governor Candidianus, with whom he was acquainted, and notes that "as far as I am concerned, the culprit's punishment would be sufficient only if he were arrested by the pagarch and locked up in jail for a short time."[64] The pagarch is obviously summoned within the context of a private dispute, and his capacity is that of a guarantor of public order.[65] This is in line with the areas of authority of *praepositi pagorum* typically displayed in the Egyptian papyri.

The fourth-century evidence, to conclude, shows that the pagarchy was then a municipal office under the *exactor civitatis*; its authority was of fiscal and coercive nature and extended over a small number of villages.[66] The *praepositus pagi* was not the predecessor of the pagarch—he *was* the pagarch.[67] It is not difficult to envision how *pagarchos* and *pagarchēs* might have originated as colloquial Hellenizing alternatives to the quasi-transcribed form *praipositos pagou* that were preferable to Greek speakers because they sounded more natural, or because they were unlikely to be confused with

---

63 *ICG* 182.4–14 (early IV?): Αἰλ⟨ί⟩ῳ | Καλπ(ουρνί)ῳ Ἀφθονί(ῳ) | Ἀντωνίου βου(λευτῇ) | τῆς Λα'(οδικέων) πόλε'(ως) | ὁ τὰ πάντα πε|πολειτευσά|μενος, δὶς ἄρ|ξας, ἐξακ⟨τ⟩ορ|εύσας, παγαρχή(σας), | πάντα ἀνεν|δεῶς ἐκτελέσας. The instance of παγαρχη( ) was not identified as such in the *editio princeps* (*CIG* 3989). The text was corrected by Ramsay 1888, 238–239, no. 11, restoring παγαρχή(σας), and even later in Ramsay 1918, 175–178, no. 16, where the author adds παγάρχη(ς) as yet another possibility. The latter seems unlikely since the formal coherence requires a participial construction. Ramsay dates the inscription to the early fourth century, at which time *pagarcheō* is attested; see *C.Th.* VIII 15.1. On the inscription, see also Breytenbach & Zimmermann 2018, 246–247.

64 Basil. *epist.* III 2 (trans. Deferrari; I have, however, supplied "pagarch" for "district magistrate"): γένοιτο δ' ἂν ἡμῖν ἀρκοῦσα δίκη, εἰ διὰ τοῦ παγάρχου συλληφθεὶς ἐν τῷ δεσμωτηρίῳ βραχὺν κατακλεισθείη χρόνον. Yves Courtonne renders the pagarch here as "chef du village." On the date, see Jeffrey Henderson's commentary on the passage (p. 29 n. 1). On the controversy whether Anisa (or Annisoi) was a Pontian or Cappadocian town, see Métivier 2005, 159 n. 195.

65 Métivier 2005, 287 n. 251, referring to Mitchell 1993, II 72 and Mitchell 1988, 113 n. 22, suggests that both this pagarch and the one from *ICG* 182 may have been overseers of imperial domains. For an interpretation of this passage in terms of criminal justice, see Krause 1996, 89 and 113. For more literature, in various contexts, see Cassia 2009, especially 77 n. 125, 78 n. 127, and 81 n. 130; the author's interpretation of the pagarch in this passage fails to convince.

66 Especially *P.Oxy.* LXIII 4371, *P.Oxy.* XLVI 3307, and *C.Th.* VIII 15.1 all but exclude the possibility that pagarchs of any sort existed alongside the *praepositi pagorum*.

67 Which strikes me as a different nuance compared to Mazza 1995, 180, where, following Liebeschuetz 1973, the "semantic" connection is given primacy: "Le connessioni con la carica di *praepositus pagi* sarebbero invece per così dire di tipo semantico." Mazza does not believe that the pagarch of the sixth century is the successor of the *praepositus pagi*.

the military (or yet other) *praepositi*.[68] It may be illustrative of their initially colloquial nature that *pagarchos* and *pagarchēs* were used interchangeably. However, in 353 CE, we find *pagarchēs* and, probably, the Latin form *pagarcha* employed in a legal protocol,[69] so the forms appear to have become part of the official jargon rather soon. Evidence for the term *praepositus pagi* disappears around 370 CE.[70] Henceforth, only *pagarchos* and *pagarchēs* are used, yet we do encounter *pagi* still in the fifth century, as we see in the next section.

III. The Fifth Century: A Changing Fiscal Landscape

Six to nine instances of the pagarchy or pagarchs can be assigned to the fifth century, but these documents are somewhat more obscure than their fourth-century counterparts.[71] The Greek rendering of the Latin term *praepositus pagi* no longer occurs; *pagi*, however, are still documented in the early fifth century.[72]

---

68 Gelzer 1909, 96 n. 1 assumed that Isidore's use of πάγαρχος/παγάρχης instead of πραιπόσιτος πάγου in Isid.Pel. *epist.* 51 (on which see Section III below) was a literary Hellenizing expression. For a possibly similar development, cf. the terms σύνδικος and ἔκδικος as Greek renderings of the *defensor civitatis*. On πάγαρχος and παγάρχης, see the Introduction, Section VII.

69 *Ch.L.A.* V 292.4, 7, and [10] (Oxyrhynchos; 353 CE; new ed. Pedone 2020, 7–20); cf. the Introduction, n. 91.

70 The latest evidence for a *praepositus pagi* is either *C.Th.* XII 6.8 from 365 CE (Lewis 1997, 42) or the "tavola di Trinitapoli" (if indeed the same office is meant in l. 6: *a{d} praepositis pagorum*), a fragmentary constitution from Apulia and probably dating from 368–375 (*AE* 2003, no. 359; see Pedone 2020, 16 n. 27 and Schmidt-Hofner 2008, 64–71). The Oxyrhynchite *P.Harr.* II 219.1 from August 5, 362 provides its latest occurrence in Egypt. The Greek transliteration of the office (πραιποσιτούρα) occurs only once in the papyri, in *P.Lips.* I 111.16 (unknown origin; IV?), a reference I owe to Guus van Loon.

71 *O.Dor.* 5 (Oasis Parva; 407/408 or 422/423); Isid.Pel. *epist.* 51 = Migne LXXVIII 536 (420–435/440? CE); *P.Oxy.* LXXXVII 5592 (Oxyrhynchos; early V); *Ch.L.A.* XLIII 1259 (unknown origin; V?); *P.Oxy.* LVI 3865 (Oxyrhynchos; V–early VI); *P.Oxy.* XVI 1831 (Oxyrhynchos; late V–early VI). *O.BirShawish* 3, 27, and 29 from the Small Oasis have been dated to around 400 CE and are discussed here for reasons of content. *P.Cair.Masp.* III 67295 col. I 10 is not taken into account here: for the restoration of "pagarchies," the editor leaned on *P.Cair.Masp.* I 67057 col. II 25 (mid-VI), but this seems dubious. Two Coptic literary texts contain references to pagarchs in the fifth century, but probably reflect later conditions; see the Introduction, n. 56.

72 *P.Oxy.* LV 3803.4 (Oxyrhynchos; August 16, 411); *SPP* XX 117.1, 2 (Herakleopolites; December 9, 411); *P.Select.* 13.3 (Herakleopolis; June 25, 421). The first two are contracts and the third is an official declaration, which one would expect to employ official terminology. Derda 2006, 266 n. 12 calls for a reexamination regarding the occurrence of *pagi* in the fifth century, but the dates can hardly be put into doubt. Even later instances are somewhat puzzling: *SB* XX 14505.17 (unknown origin; VI?) may palaeographically also be from the fifth century, as Lajos Berkes argues (personal communication), but there is no online image of *SPP* X 270.8 (Arsinoites; VII–VIII?). Assuming the reading and dating are correct, there may be some archaism at work that used the term *pagus* as a regional marker or approximation. The fact that both *SB* XX 14505 and *SPP* X 270

The probably earliest sources in the present section are three recently published ostraca from the Small Oasis, which date to the end of the fourth century or the beginning of the fifth. Nothing in these texts suggests that the character of the pagarchy and the pagarch had changed since the 370s CE.[73] The first ostracon contains a receipt to a liturgist that was issued in the name of—and perhaps signed by—an unnamed pagarch to confirm that the public service has been performed.[74] The second is a receipt, issued probably by a pagarch, for a tax payment in the form of chickens and eggs.[75] The third is a receipt of unknown content, again signed by a pagarch.[76] In another fragmentary ostracon that is said to be also from the Small Oasis, a pagarch appears in what is probably a tax receipt.[77] The pagarch Isak who appears in these ostraca at least once may be the *geouchos* (landlord) Isak who repeatedly appears in ostraca from the same context.[78]

---

concern a "7th *pagus*" leads me to speculate that this may be a fossilized designation that became the name of a place. This hypothesis of ζ πάγου (perhaps with a "frozen" genitive) being a locality of some sort would conveniently eliminate the problem (discussed by Derda 2006, 269–270) that the villages listed in ll. 1–7 of the fragmentary *SPP* X 270 are never situated in the sixth *pagus* (where they would be expected if the occurrence of ζ πάγου in l. 8 were the start of a new list); the figures in front of the lines in this part of the list are obscure in either interpretation (there is no online image to analyze the layout).

73 It is unclear whether these ostraca were meant to be stored together: while they were found in the same complex of three rooms, two of these rooms over time merged into one, and according to the editor, the field documentation is inconsistent; see *O.BirShawish*, pp. 23–27.

74 *O.BirShawish* 3.1 (388 or 403 CE): π(αρὰ) τοῦ παγάρχου, addressed to a *leitourgos* (l. 3). The editor points to *P.Lond.* V 1661.12: [λ]ειτουργῶν \ἤτοι φυλ̣[άκ]ω̣ν/—a text from sixth-century Aphrodite and addressed to pagarchs—and the possibility of linking the liturgy mentioned in *O.BirShawish* 3 to guard duties (pp. 32–33), more specifically, to an *agrophylakia* repeatedly attested in the Bir Shawish ostraca (pp. 164–165).

75 *O.BirShawish* 27.1 (398 or 413 CE): Ἰ̣σ̣ὰ̣κ π̣ά̣γ̣α̣ρ̣(χος). The editor, in addition to dotting the letters, explicitly highlights the uncertainty of the reading. On the chickens-and-eggs payments as a tax, see *O.BirShawish*, pp. 158–160.

76 *O.BirShawish* 29.1 (398/399? or 413/414?): Ἰσὰκ πάγαρχο̣ς̣ . . . The numeral for a fifth indiction (l. 4) is uncertainly read and the subsequent reference to a twelfth year (l. 5) may link this piece to *O.BirShawish* 27, which is a receipt from a twelfth indiction to the same recipient issued by perhaps the same pagarch; see the preceding note.

77 *O.Dor.* 5.1 (407/408 or 422/423): [– – –]κ πάγαρχος ς ἰνδικ(τίονος); for the mention of the indiction year as part of an official's titulature, cf. a number of ostraca (IV–early V) from the Great Oasis, e.g., *O.Douch* 220 and 257. The editor of *O.Dor.* 5 suggested the pagarch's name to be Isak (*exempli gratia*). Accepting this would make the pagarch Isak from *O.BirShawish* 29 (cf. the preceding note on the potential mention of a fifth indiction in that text) and, if the restoration is correct, *O.BirShawish* 27 a tempting match. A renewed yearly tenure for the same pagarch (= *praepositus pagi*) need not cause surprise, as we might be dealing with a limited pool of eligible candidates for that post in a comparatively peripheral region. But this identification is by no means certain, and even the oasis findspot of *O.Dor.* 5 is not beyond doubt; see *O.BirShawish*, p. 74.

78 Isak pagarch: *O.BirShawish* 27(?), 29; *O.Dor.* 5(?). Isak *geouchos*: *O.BirShawish* 7, 15, 18; *O.Sarm.* 1, 2, 3, 4(?), 6(?), 11, 12(?), 13(?).

This profile is completely in line with the *praepositi pagorum* as we see them during the fourth century.[79]

Two further testimonies are rather short notes in their present condition, and yield no valuable information for the question of the pagarchs' status. A bilingual Latin-Greek document contains, in the Greek section, a reference to a *pagarchia*, but the papyrus is poorly preserved and the word is completely isolated.[80] Finally, the Egyptian ascetic and theologian Isidore of Pelusium speculates about the etymology of the Areopagus (Gr. *Areios pagos*) in one of his letters; in order to explain the term *pagos*, Isidore states that "pagarchs are called, by some, those who govern (*archontes*) the villages and *topoi*,"[81] which is too general to be of much value, yet links the pagarchs to the countryside.

The remaining three instances provide more to work with, and taken together, they may be interpreted to indicate, in a subtle way, changes in the institutional character of the "early" pagarchy. The first is a fifth-century loan of money from Oxyrhynchos, recently published as *P.Oxy.* LXXXVII 5592.[82] One Flavius Horion and the priest Anouthis undertook the loan, about eight *nomismata*, from a certain Apion.[83] Apion credited the amount "on account of the expense for the bath, for the name (*onoma*, i.e., the fiscal registration) of our pagarch Theodoulos."[84] The reference to "our pagarch" without any rank epithet or polite reference such as "lord" or "master" would be unusual for the "later" pagarchs of the sixth century.[85] The lacking reference to "our

79 The master of the well-known *boēthoi* Papnouthis and Dorotheos (see n. 42 above) is at times referred to as *praepositus pagi*, at others as *geouchos*; see Berkes 2017a, 160–161. A comparable instance is the *boēthos* of the *praepositus pagi* Ision (*P.Sakaon* 46–48), who refers to his master as his *geouchos* (*P.Abinn.* 28.3 and 22). See also *P.Oxy.* LXVII 4599, where one Eutrygios pays in his official capacity as *praepositus pagi* for the *kōmētai* of the tenth *pagus* (ll. 8–9 and 15–16), but on the same occasions he also contributes as one of the *politai* (ll. 5–6 and 13), and the basis of these contributions must certainly be found in landed estates in the area of that same *pagus*. I owe the reference to this text to Nikolaos Gonis.

80 *Ch.L.A.* XLIII 1259.8 (unknown origin; V?).

81 Isid.Pel. *epist.* 51 = Migne LXXVIII 536 (420–435/440? CE): πάγαρχοι καλοῦνται παρά τισιν οἱ τῶν κωμῶν ἢ τόπων τινῶν ἄρχοντες; see Mazza 1995, 173–174.

82 I thank the editor Nikolaos Gonis for making me aware of this text ahead of its publication.

83 This man has no apparent connection to the famous family that scholars know as the Apiones, referred to later in this section.

84 *P.Oxy.* LXXXVII 5592.6–8: εἰς λόγον τοῦ ἀναλώματος | τοῦ βαλανί[ου (read βαλανείου) ὑ]π̣ὲ̣ρ ὀνόματος | τοῦ παγάρχη (read παγάρχου) [ἡ]μ̣ῶν Θεοδούλου.

85 In references to superior officeholders, ἡμῶν is generally linked to polite references such as κύριος or δεσπότης; see *P.Cair.Masp.* I 67068.10 (Aphrodite; VI): τοὺς λαμπρ̣[οτάτου]ς ἡμῶν δεσ[πό]τας παγάρχους or, earlier, *P.Abinn.* 45 (Arsinoites; June 23, 343): τοῦ κυρ̣ίου ἡμῶν δουκός. In rare cases, it is indeed linked to the office of such authorities; see *P.Oxy.* LIX 3987.5–6 (Oxyrhynchos; March 21, 457/502/532): τοῦ τὰ πάντα μεγαλοπρεπεστάτου καὶ σοφοτάτου (read σοφωτάτου) κοινοῦ | ἡμῶν ἄρχοντος and probably *PSI* XV 1569.11 (Antinoopolis?; VI): τῷ μεγαλοπρε̣π̣ε̣σ̣τ̣ά̣τ̣ῳ̣ κοι̣[νῷ] ἡμῶν ἄρχοντι, whereas *P.Oxy.* XVI 1885.15–16 (Oxyrhynchos; November 29, 509): τῷ τὰ πάντα μεγαλοπρ(επεστάτῳ̣) καὶ σοφωτά(τῳ̣) | [κοινῷ̣] ([κυρίῳ̣] *ed. pr.*) ἡμῶν ἄρχοντι is based on the

common lord/master"[86] in the reference to the pagarch, moreover, may suggest that Apion was not one of that pagarch's fiscal subjects, and that Theodoulos therefore was still one of multiple pagarchs of separate territorial authority within the Oxyrhynchite countryside, instead of a "pagarch of Oxyrhynchos."[87]

The circumstances of the loan are a little obscure. The facts that the public context of the loan is so meticulously stated, that Apion credits the sum on an account for public contributions, and that he does so in both public and private gold standards probably only make sense if we assume that the nature of the loan was not entirely private; rather, all three men involved are likely to have borne some responsibility for the contributions in question, and Apion may have been some minor fiscal administrator or someone's assistant.[88] This context invites comparison with a papyrus from sixth-century Aphrodite, in which two tax collectors acknowledge a loan given to them formally by two collegial pagarchs, but in practice perhaps rather by the two village headmen representing the pagarchs.[89] In this constellation, the loan was de facto a deferral of the retrieval of the collected taxes, which the village headmen framed as a loan for their security. A similar situation may be behind *P.Oxy.* LXXXVII 5592: Potentially Anouthis and Horion, as representatives of their village community, were to pay the bath contributions to Apion. This Apion perhaps was Theodoulos's assistant in the city or a minor administrator at

(likely) suggestion in *BL* XIII 154. ἡμῶν is also attested referencing a *geouchos* in *P.Oxy.* XLVIII 3398.17–18 (Oxyrhynchos; mid to late IV): ἄπελθε πρὸς τὸν γεοῦχον | ἡμῶν Διογένην. This man is perhaps to be identified with the superior *praepositus pagi* of the writer (a *boēthos*), since the writer in a different letter calls another man "my master (and) landlord" (*P.Oxy.* XLVIII 3400.25: τὸν δεσπότη μ̣ο̣υ̣ γεουχω Εὐλόγιων; read τὸν δεσπότην μου γεοῦχον Εὐλόγιον). The possessive is more naturally used by superiors referring to their subordinate managerial or official agents, such as *boēthoi* or *pronoētai*; e.g., in *P.Cair.Isid.* 94.5–6 and 21 (Arsinoites; May 4, 312).

86 Cf. *P.Lond.* V 1661.5–6 (Aphrodite; July 24, 553): τῶν μ]ε[γ]α̣λ̣οπρ̣επεσ̣τάτων κοινῶν | δεσποτῶν παγάρχων. It is conceivable, however, that *koinos* ("common") was not consistently used in such contexts.

87 The editor Nikolaos Gonis plausibly suggests in the commentary that the pagarch Theodoulos may be identical with the *riparius* Theodoulos from *P.Select.* 3.8 (421 CE). This match would fit well the curial background of the "early" pagarchs, and would entail a narrower dating rather to the early fifth century.

88 We have seen that Apion was unlikely to have been located in the same area as Horion and Anouthis, and perhaps was even a resident of Oxyrhynchos, where the papyrus was found; yet he is still sufficiently well-known to remain without a title, rank epithet, or origin in the address—an omission that we usually would consider a documentary *faux pas* at the beginning of a contract. The date of the loan underscores the de facto public background of the transaction: Repayment was due "on the fourteenth of the current month of Pachon" (*P.Oxy.* LXXXVII 5592.13–14), that is, within the first two weeks of the new fiscal indiction. Although the contribution itself is not linked to a specific year, this date thus suggests an annual public contribution instead of a one-time demand (notwithstanding the possibility that the obligation to pay may have rotated within a pool of potential contributors).

89 *P.Lond.* V 1661 (Aphrodite; July 24, 553).

the level of the *civitas*,[90] who accepted the payment as a quasi-debt because the money would be paid in the subsequent days.[91]

The division of the contribution into two payments of four *nomismata* each—one in the public, the other in the private standard—is curious.[92] This "double standard" may reflect Theodoulos's double capacity as an "early" pagarch with authority over villages and as landlord (*geouchos*) in the countryside.[93] However, the division of exactly 50 percent raises the suspicion that we may not be dealing with actual collections from two different areas of Theodoulos's activity. Furthermore, the formula *hyper onomatos* in a fiscal context usually implies private responsibilities, thus, that the entire sum of eight *nomismata* relates to Theodoulos's responsibilities as a *geouchos* rather than that of his office.[94] Either we need to assume an unusually generous use of *hyper onomatos*, or the contributions in public and private gold standards mentioned in this loan both result from Theodoulos's capacity as *geouchos*—a synthesis may be within reach later.

The next papyrus, *P.Oxy.* LVI 3865, refers to a "pagarch of the village."[95] The very irregular hand is not older than the fifth century; the early sixth century also seems possible.[96] Again, the pagarch is occupied with fiscal matters, as he sends an *apaitētēs*

---

90 Apion's position described above would suit well a *boēthos*, an "assistant," of the *praepositus pagi*, residing in the city but responsible for individual villages. This would put Apion on a still close-enough level in the official and social hierarchy that villagers such as Anouthis and Horion could address him as "my lord brother," the common reference for colleagues or hierarchically close individuals (the singular possessive need not cause surprise here). See the archive of Papnouthis and Dorotheos, *boēthoi* of a *praepositus pagi*, who were city residents (Bagnall 1993, 158), and, on similar administrative levels, e.g., the Florentine papyrus PL III/721.1 (Harrauer & Pintaudi 2012): τῷ κυρ(ίῳ) τῷ ἀδελφῷ Δωροθέῳ βοηθ(ῷ) σ̣ε̣[ι]τ̣(ολόγων) (read σιτολόγων) and *P.Oxy.* XVI 1948.2: τῷ κυρ(ίῳ) μου ἀδελφ(ῷ) Ἀφ[οῦ]ς (read Ἀφοῦτι) προ(νοητῇ) Πέλα (the relationship between the *boēthoi* and the *pronoētai* will be discussed in Chapter Three). It is not entirely inconceivable that Apion was a municipal officer processing such contributions, but he might then have been too high-ranking to be addressed with *adelphos*, and would probably not be so close to the villagers as to use his (rather common) personal name without a title.

91 For the time frame, see n. 88 above.

92 *P.Oxy.* LXXXVII 5592.10–11: (γίνονται) νο(μισμάτια) η, οὕτως· δ̣ημοσίῳ σταθμῷ | νο(μισμάτια) δ, ἰδιωτικῷ σταθ(μῷ) νο(μισμάτια) δ.

93 Or, in the language of the fourth century, as a "city dweller" (*politēs*) with landed estates in the hinterland of the *civitas*. For this double capacity in local accounts, see the *praepositus pagi* Eutrygios in *P.Oxy.* LXVII 4599, discussed in n. 79 above.

94 The expression ὑπὲρ ὀνόματος regularly refers to the fiscal duties of individual taxpayers, large landowners and their *oikoi*, and other private institutions such as communities of joint heirs. Its use in relation to the aggregated tax responsibility of a public official is, as far as I see, not attested. Officials might of course be named as an *onoma* but in this case the account still concerns the official in their private capacity, such as the *riparius* in *SB* XIV 11378 (cf. Tost 2012, 775).

95 *P.Oxy.* LVI 3865.63–64 (Oxyrhynchites): πάγαρ̣|χ̣ο̣ς τῆς κώμης, certainly relating to Orthoniou, although the text does not explicitly say so. If "the pagarch of the village" were to refer to Pakerke, this place would be too distant to plausibly explain why this pagarch would be sent to Orthoniou (cf. the "relative locality" sections for the mentioned places in Benaissa 2021, s.vv.).

96 The handwriting is prevalent throughout the fifth or the early sixth century, but the form of the

into the settlement Orthoniou to collect taxes on a mill.[97] The attribution "of the village" however, need not necessarily entail that this pagarch was responsible for this particular village only, since we have seen that *pagi*—and "early" pagarchies—could be named after a central village or, on occasion, the relevant place in a given context,[98] here: Orthoniou.[99] Three other villages occur in this document, all of which are scattered widely throughout the Oxyrhynchite nome: Senokomis, Akoutou, and Pakerke. In this context, a specific regional marker such as "of this-and-that village," instead of simply saying "the pagarch," suggests the necessity for clear identification and indicates that, at that time, several pagarchs were active in several different administrative circumscriptions throughout the nome. Accordingly, it seems likely that we are still dealing with an "early" pagarch here, a *praepositus pagi*.

The letter *P.Oxy.* XVI 1831, finally, from the late fifth century or the beginning of the sixth, documents a quibble between two neighboring villages.[100] The village headman (*meizōn*) of Tholthis complains to the village headman of Takona that field guards from Takona started a fight against men from Tholthis and stole their cattle. The head-

---

staurogram at the beginning of l. 2 probably points to the late fifth or early sixth century, as Nikolaos Gonis informs me. The editor suggested a date in the late fifth century by assuming that the pagarchy was created in this period at the earliest.

97 The *apaitētai* are attested at the city level as well as in villages; see Palme 1989, 129–133.

98 Another possible instance is *P.Oxy.* XLVIII 3425.7–8: π(αρὰ) Εὐλογίου πραι(ποσίτου) | κώμης Τερύθεως (see the editor's commentary). For pagarchies and *pagi* named after villages, see the discussion of *P.Oxy.* XLVI 3307 in the previous section. For an analogy, Tomasz Derda (2006, 154–158) has shown that the attribution of a place to the title of *kōmogrammateus* (who was at times responsible for multiple villages) in the Roman period can sometimes be explained by the fact that this was the relevant place in the given context, not the entire circumscription of this official. In our case, this interpretation may be all the more likely since this text is a private letter, which would not adhere to precise administrative attributions but only intends to make clear that the pagarch *who is responsible for that particular village* has intervened. This interpretation would imply that the mentioned pagarch is not the pagarch with whom the author and his addressee would normally interact with, and therefore his title required specification. A similar interpretation for *hypodektai* "of the village" by the editor of *P.NYU* I (p. 10), however, fails to convince in that particular context; see Chapter Two, n. 131.

99 The structure of the text suggests that Orthoniou is a village here (l. 64; likewise: Benaissa 2021, s.v.), but this runs into the fact that no other known text refers to Orthoniou as a *kōmē*. Instead, it is referenced as a *ktēma*, an *epoikion*, or (in *SPP* X 198.3, ignoring the dubious *SB* I 1945.19) a *chōrion*, although all these mentions are probably younger than our text. The latter is interesting, however, because *SPP* X 198 was dated to the Arab period, when *chōrion* usually refers to village-like fiscal units. If Orthoniou is *not* a *kōmē* in *P.Oxy.* LVI 3865, then by using the expression "pagarch of the village" the writer is most probably referring to the village that Orthoniou administratively belonged to. This, however, would entail that "pagarch of the village so-and-so" was indeed the proper title of this pagarch, which might indicate a change in the character of the pagarchy at that time. It seems risky to extrapolate such a conclusion from *P.Oxy.* LVI 3865 alone, though this explanation fits the development I propose toward the end of the present section.

100 The editor assigned the text to the late fifth century based on the occurrence of the pagarchy, but the handwriting could well belong to the early sixth century, as Nikolaos Gonis informs me.

man of Tholthis now demands that his colleague summon the men involved, and adds a warning:

> For we must not start skirmishes between each other, nor do we litigate with the protection of our/your pagarch/pagarchs, so that you summon those who are in discord with us, young and old, (and?) lest we start a fight against each other [– – –] nor our *boēthos* [– – –] the pagarch (nominative). Therefore, see to it that they (i.e., the cattle) be returned, lest his (i.e., the pagarch's?) watered field (*mēchanē*) remain unsown.[101]

The text is rather difficult to make sense of at times due to its fragmentary preservation and the fact that its grammar is hard to follow. The passage "nor do we litigate with the protection of our/your pagarch/pagarchs" is particularly problematic, since the Greek text makes little sense (to us) as written in the document[102] and the writer frequently confuses the spelling of the possessives "our" and "your" on account of their phonetic similarity. But even if there were only one pagarch mentioned here, this would not discount the possibility of an "early" pagarch, a *praepositus pagi*.[103] The sender apparently uses the potential involvement of the pagarch(s) as a threat to his colleague.[104] From this obscure sentence, it is not possible to decide whether we are dealing with the *praepositus pagi* or with a pagarch at the *civitas* level, as the characteristics—possibly several officeholders within a single nome; superiority to village headmen; coercive authority—are compatible with both options.[105]

---

101 *P.Oxy.* XVI 1831.8–13 (Oxyrhynchites; late V–early VI); cf. O'Callaghan 1963, no. 24.

102 *P.Oxy.* XVI 1831.8–9: οὐδὲ γὰρ ἔχο|μεν πρᾶγμα μετὰ τῆς ἀδ̣ι̣α̣ς (*sic*) τῶν ὑμῶν π̣α̣γαρχον (*sic*). Contra the commentary in the *editio princeps*, I read ἀδ⟨ε⟩ί̣α̣ς̣ instead of ἀ⟨η⟩δ̣ί̣α̣ς̣ since the text shows a pattern of phonetic spelling. The phonetic argument would furthermore point to τῶν (…) π̣α̣γάρχ⟨ω⟩ν, the interchange of ο/ω being common in Coptic. See also *P.Lond.* IV 1540.20 (Aphrodite; 709–714), where των is written for τὸν (ἐνδ(οξότατον) πάγαρχον). Cf., however, the spelling τον for τοῦ in *P.Oxy.* LIX 4008.2 (Oxyrhynchos; VI–VII). A search in the Text Irregularities section of *Trismegistos* lists ninety-four instances of ων instead of ου; see www.trismegistos.org/texirr/124. Other scholars read this passage differently; see Stern 2015, 143–144.

103 The close links between the two mentioned villages are evident in the sixth century, when we find a single *prostasia* (management district) of the Apion estate named "Takona and Tholthis"; the *prostasiai* generally bore the name of only one settlement. The *prostasia* system is discussed in Chapter Three. The two villages were, however, probably part of different *pagi* (see Benaissa 2021, s.vv.). This would entail that the pagarchy in our text already transcends the *pagi*. While this seems a far-fetched conclusion to draw from this text alone, it fits a development I propose in the next section.

104 The background of out-of-court dispute resolution and the use of official intervention as a threat have been laid out by Harries 2001. Cf. *P.Neph.* 19 (Herakleopolites; IV) for an illustration of how fearful people were of official involvement in private disputes, and Bagnall 1993, 170–171.

105 What is striking here is the pagarch's involvement in dispute resolution, of which there is little evidence for the "later" pagarchs until the Islamic conquest. Maybe the pagarchs handled minor civil cases in the countryside while formal litigation at the *civitas* level was, since the early fourth century, in the hands of the *defensor civitatis* (Gr. *ekdikos* or *syndikos*), on whom see Palme

Toward the end of the letter the writer refers to "the pagarch" in the singular, and the addressee is apparently urged to return the stolen cattle by the prospect of letting this pagarch's fields go unsown.[106] The close ties that the headman as representative of his village appears to have to this pagarch—with the village community assuming responsibility for this man's fields—is reminiscent of the close relationship that several villages in the Oxyrhynchite nome later maintained with the aristocratic family of the Apiones and their large estate, the *endoxos oikos*. Several papyri from the Apion estate discuss issues related to *mēchanai*, and some of them refer to villages that are called *kōmai pagarchoumenai*, villages being "pagarched" by the Apion *oikos*.[107] In 550 CE, this formula is also attested for Takona, the other village appearing in *P.Oxy.* XVI 1831.[108] In fact, of the six settlements mentioned in *P.Oxy.* LVI 3865 and *P.Oxy.* XVI 1831, five are attested later in connection to the *endoxos oikos* of the Apiones.[109] Members of this aristocratic family of imperial ranking, however, probably would not have been referred to by the simple title of pagarch, but rather with at least one of their senatorial epithets or honorary titles. Although it is not a given that a village headman would always employ such titles when referring to an aristocrat in the third person in a nonlegal document, it is a strong indication that these texts are older than the Apionic presence in these villages.[110] Consequently, the pagarch in *P.Oxy.* XVI 1831 was probably an elusive local landowner who was important enough that the well-being of the village community of Tholthis was linked to that of his property, but in neighboring Takona he was apparently not perceived primarily through his socioeconomic dominance, which is why the headman of Tholthis refers to him with his title of pagarch, rather than by a reference such as "our common master (*despotēs*)." That is, this pagarch is likely to have owned some, but not the lion's share of, land in Tholthis and was distant enough from the village headman of Takona to be referred to by his official title only.

2008a, 63 with references in n. 27. Palme suspects the *riparius* to have handled minor civil cases at the village level.

106 *P.Oxy.* XVI 1831.12–13:]ṭε ọ̔ π̣ά̣γαρχος. θ̣ε̣λ̣ή̣σ̣α̣τ̣[ε . .] ν̣ῦ̣ν̣ ṭαῦτα | ἀπολῆσαι εἵνα μὴ ἄσπορος μίνῃ (read ἀπολῦσαι ἵνα μὴ ἄσπορος μείνῃ) ἡ τούτου μηχανή.

107 These villages are discussed in detail in Chapter Three, Sections III and IV.

108 *P.Oxy.* I 133.

109 This concerns Takona and Tholthis in *P.Oxy.* XVI 1831 and Senokomis, Pakerke, and Orthoniou in *P.Oxy.* LVI 3865. No immediate Apionic presence is attested so far for Akoutou. Gonis 2015b suggested we read Ἀκ[ούτ]ου̣ in the undated *P.Oxy.* XVI 1856.2 (VI–VII), but this reading, which would yield the first testimony of an Apionic connection to that settlement, is not certain, at least from the online image; for an alternative plausible reading of the following words, influencing what we can expect to read in Ἀκ[. . .] . . . ., see Benaissa 2021, 152.

110 The growth of the Apion estate in the late fifth century is hard to follow. In *SB* XXVIII 17150 (489–497 CE?), the money payments, presumably, by Strategios II among a number of Oxyrhynchite contributors for an unknown purpose amount to 22 percent of the total; see Gonis 2002a, 88–93. Compared to the "usual" Apion share of 25 to 30 percent over a large part of the sixth century (see Chapter Three, Section V), this may illustrate a development and point to their extending fiscal responsibility.

An attractive interpretation of these relations seems to me that by the time of *P.Oxy.* XVI 1831, the "early" pagarchy had evolved, at least de facto, into a responsibility of local *geouchoi* for extended periods of time. This would probably have at first concerned only some of the *geouchoi*, perhaps resulting from frequent reappointment of the same men from an ever smaller pool of suitable candidates.[111] This hypothesis does not only fit the context I suggested for *P.Oxy.* XVI 1831; it would also explain several features of the fifth-century documents assembled here: (1) the expression "our pagarch(s)" in *P.Oxy.* LXXXVII 5592 and *P.Oxy.* XVI 1831, which appears around that time and is extremely uncommon for superior officeholders in this form; (2) the expression "the pagarch of the village" in *P.Oxy.* LVI 3865; and finally (3) the curious use of the term *onoma* in connection with the combined responsibilities of being pagarch and *geouchos* in *P.Oxy.* LXXXVII 5592. This proposed development fits well into the administrative context of the late fifth century by providing one step toward the administration of the nome through fiscal "shares" that we see more clearly in the later part of the century.[112] The list of shares for the Oxyrhynchite *riparia* mentioned in Section I implies that this liturgy was shared among the *oikoi* from the 460s CE at the latest,[113] with *P.Oxy.* LVI 3865 and *P.Oxy.* XVI 1831 probably being written not much later than that.

IV. The Elevation of the Pagarchy

Some scholars have pointed to the synonymy of the pagarch with the *praepositus pagi* in the fourth century, but this has occasionally led to descriptions in which the "later" pagarchs of the sixth and early seventh centuries still figure as mere *pagus* officials.[114] To others it was obvious that the pagarchs of exalted aristocratic standing, like Ioulianos the ex-*eparchos* or Strategios the *paneuphēmos patricius*, had little in common with

111 Cf. *P.Oxy.* LXIII 4371.9, in which a councilor comments that πάντες παγάρχαι γεγόνα{σ}μεν, referring to the burdens shared by his colleages of the *boulē*. In the context of the document the implication is that no one got around it as early as the second half of the fourth century. See also the pagarch Isak from the Small Oasis, who appears to have held multiple tenures around 400 CE, although the readings are not beyond doubt; see nn. 76–78 above.

112 See Chapter Three. In the sixth-century list *P.Oxy.* XVI 2040, contributions for probably another bath are (still?) shared by the large landowners of Oxyrhynchus through participation via their "fiscal shares." The amount of twenty-seven *nomismata* does not concern (all) "expenses" as our eight *nomismata*, but explicitly only the fuel. Yet it is unclear whether the twenty-seven *nomismata* were intended for a specific indiction or for a longer period. A specific indiction in that text is explicitly linked only to a separate contribution for the village of Takona, made by the *endoxos oikos*, that is, the Apion *oikos*.

113 *P.Oxy.* XVI 2039. Public responsibilities assumed by *oikoi* are attested earlier still (e.g., *P.Oxy.* L 3583 from 444 CE).

114 So, apparently, in Wilcken 1892, 298–299 and especially 299 n. 5; Schmidt-Hofner 2008, 124 n. 22; and Mazza 2018, equating the Egyptian *pagi* "roughly with the nomes."

Theon who once before the city council contested his nomination to a *pagarchia*.[115] It remains obscure exactly when the small curial subordinate of the *exactor civitatis* of the fourth century, with responsibility over only a handful of villages at most, became the dominant civil authority in the city territory of exalted aristocratic standing that we see in the sixth century.

The most widespread theory on the origin of the pagarchy as we see it in the sixth century was established by Wolf Liebeschuetz, who noted that the pagarch assumed the main tasks of the *exactor civitatis* and that sixth-century testimonies possibly attesting the *exactor* are few in number and, in his view, disputable.[116] The *exactor* is last attested in 504/505 CE,[117] which led Liebeschuetz to conclude that this office had been reformed and renamed into that of the pagarch under Anastasius I (r. 491–518). But after 504/505, there is still evidence for the "exactorical office" (*exaktorikē taxis*), the running of which was still a civic liturgy that no longer fell on the curials, but on the *oikoi*.[118] Apparently, the office of the *exactor*—or rather, its responsibilities—continued to exist into the sixth century, but at least in Egypt its power was significantly diminished.[119] Liebeschuetz's hypothesis that the "later" pagarchy was created under Anastasius, ultimately, builds on plausible reasoning: he argues that this move would have fit well with the creation of the *vindex*, an official who was handed the main oversight of tax collection from the curials in certain cities of the Eastern Empire, including Alexandria.[120] According to John the Lydian, the *vindex* was appointed by the praetorian prefect and the relevant passages suggest that local administration was to be kept out of the appointment procedure; apparently the state tried to rationalize tax collection by filling central positions at the local level with men who owed their standing to the

115 This disparity was highlighted early by Bell 1908, 103–104 (albeit mingling the Byzantine pagarchs with their successors from the early Islamic period) and Wilcken 1912, 83. Drecoll 1997, e.g., 30 and 155, separates pagarchs and *praepositi pagorum* entirely and finds them at different levels in the same hierarchy (comparably, Cassia 2009, 75–98). A moderating view is articulated by Johnson & West 1949, 324–325; they see the continuities but acknowledge considerable changes over time.

116 See Liebeschuetz 1973, who acknowledges earlier evidence for pagarchs as *praepositi pagorum*, but argues that the connection between the two is no more than nominal. On the *exactor civitatis*, see Palme 1989, 70–71 and n. 290 with further references.

117 *P.Stras.* V 486 (Hermopolites).

118 Gascou 1985, 41–44 (= 2008, 163–167); Mazza 2011, 270–271; Tuck 2011, 298. Because of the connection to the *oikoi*, the *exaktorikē taxis* was taken as a private bureau by Liebeschuetz 1973, 40 and Thomas 1959, 136–138.

119 The pagarchs' relationship to the "bureau of the *exactor*" is discussed in Chapter Two, Section II 2. Iust. *nov.* 128.5 (545 CE) mentions *exactores* as tax collectors in the eastern provinces (cf. § 16 of the same text and see Chapter Two, n. 70 for § 8). In the Aphrodite Cadaster, *SB* XX 14669.203 (Aphrodite; 524 CE): τόπ(ου) τοῦ ἐξάκτορ(ος) is perhaps a fossilized name of this particular *topos*, given that it is ὑπ(ὸ) Μ[ουσ]ῆν Ψιμανωβέτ. Or may this be a plot that was administered by the *exactor* for the city? See Chapter Two, Section II 2 on possible similar cases.

120 On the *vindices*, see Laniado 2002, 29–36.

central authority and had no local connections.[121] But there is no evidence whatsoever that the "later" pagarch and the *vindex* were part of the same administrative measures and it is perfectly plausible that one predated the other. The characteristics of both offices are also hardly comparable: the *vindices*, as far as we can see, were responsible for civic finances and were outsiders to their cities, while the pagarchs were still in general responsible for the countryside, and most of them are known to have owned land in the areas under their authority.[122] To conclude, the evidence does not support the hypothesis that the office of *exactor* was renamed to *pagarchos/pagarchēs* under Anastasius.

More than a century ago, Matthias Gelzer suggested that an increasing number and extent of autopract estates (and autopract villages) in the countryside was what made the small-scaled *pagus* system obsolete.[123] Gelzer's hypothesis has been virtually ignored since Liebeschuetz's article[124] but the evidence of the fourth and fifth centuries, most of which had not yet been published by Gelzer's time, suggests that he was nearer the mark. An important nuance is added if we introduce Jean Gascou's model of fiscal participation into this discussion: I suggest that it was not the disintegrative powers of insubordinate landowning magnates that made the *pagi* obsolete as subdistricts, but the extension of administrative responsibilities vested to the *oikoi* by the state, notably tax collection. This becomes especially plausible when one recalls that these estates were mostly not contiguous areas but were scattered throughout the countryside, and thus the same estate could be part of multiple *pagi*.[125] While with the law of 415 CE, landowners had in general been made responsible for the taxes and other liabilities of their tenants,[126] a cornerstone of the model of fiscal participation is the contention that some landowners collected taxes also on land *beyond* what was owned by them,[127] and Chapter Three will show that the administrative framework for this was the institution of the *kōmē pagarchoumenē*, which described a village as being "pagarched" by a *geouchōn*. Consequently, for one, the estates that collected taxes on their own holdings practically dropped out of the *pagus* system. But so did the villages that began to be administered by some of these *oikoi* when some of these "early" pagarchies assumed by

121 Lydus *mag.* III 49; Liebeschuetz 1973, 42.

122 Liebeschuetz 1973, 41 admits that the cities in which *vindices* are attested cannot be convincingly put into a common frame. The pagarch's (territorial) area of responsibility will be discussed in Chapter Two, Section I.

123 Gelzer 1909, 89; cf. his view on the meaning of *autopragia* in n. 34 above. Gelzer placed the creation of the office of the pagarch at the beginning of the sixth century (p. 96), but this interpretation of *P.Cair.Masp.* I 67002 col. II 18 is unlikely in view of what we now know about the tenures of the pagarch of Antaiopolis; see Chapter Two, Section II.

124 It has, however, found continuous support from Bernhard Palme (1989, 98 and 2013a, 107).

125 See, for instance, *P.Charite* 12 (Hermopolites; early to mid-IV), with its interpretation by Palme 1989, 145, for an early illustration of this phenomenon. See also Palme 1997a, 118–119.

126 On *C.Th.* XI 24.6, see n. 35 above.

127 See n. 18 above.

geouchountes turned into *kōmai pagarchoumenai*. The remaining, scattered, territories were united into one single pagarchy.

The earliest papyrus to attest a "pagarched" village, published only recently, supports this reconstruction. It contains an Oxyrhynchite lease dating to 493 CE, in which the leased land is part of one such *kōmē pagarchoumenē* in the responsibility of the young Strategios II, a member of the Apion family.[128] In this text, as in others from around that time, Strategios is represented by a certain Theodoros *hypokatastatos*; the precise meaning of this term is not clear but it certainly relates to someone acting as a substitute, probably because Strategios was still a minor.[129] The same Theodoros *hypokatastatos*, however, assumes the additional function of *diadochos*, or liturgical substitute, in a document that addresses Strategios as *riparius*.[130] The fact that Theodoros is not *diadochos* in the lease from the "pagarched" village can therefore only mean that whatever is behind the *pagarchoumenē* formula, it is not a liturgy or an office borne by Strategios. A formal and administrative analysis of the formula concerning the *kōmai pagarchoumenai* reveals that this expression does not relate to the pagarchy of Oxyrhynchos either, but rather to villages in which large landowners also collected taxes on land other than their own.[131] I believe the only logical explanation for all this is that by 493 CE, at the latest, some *oikoi* had been entrusted with tax collection for village land, including land they did not own, on a long-term basis and no longer by virtue of the "early" pagarchy.[132] These areas of authority were no longer contiguous districts as the *pagi* were, but lands adjacent to estate parcels, such as villages in which the magnate would have already owned some, probably a considerable amount of, land. The areas subject to the fiscal authority of the "early" pagarchs not attached to one of the *oikoi* would then have been scattered throughout the nome, and presumably have varied widely from *pagus* to *pagus*. Consequently, these lands were united into a single pagarchy at the level of the *civitas*.

If one follows my argument that the several "early" pagarchies in a city's *territorium* were first, de facto, entrusted to the *geouchoi*—a sort of predecessor to the *kōmai pagarchoumenai*—before there was one unified pagarchy for the *civitas*, the key question is no longer when and why the aristocratic magnates start to be entrusted with a new

128 *P.Oxy.* LXXXII 5337.

129 For a discussion of the meaning of *hypokatastatos*, or *hypokatastatēs*, see *P.Oxy.* LXVII, pp. 233–234.

130 *P.Oxy.* LXVII 4614 (late V).

131 See Chapter Three, Sections III and IV.

132 In Berkes 2017a, 14–15, *SB* XXII 15318.13 (Hermopolis; 442–447): μερ(ίδος) Ταυρ(ίνου) Φο[ιβάμμ](ων) Χλωτίωνος ἀπὸ Πτεμ[ενκύρκεως] is taken to show that a village, (P)Temenkyrkis, was at that time under the fiscal purview of an *oikos*—that of Taurinos, who is responsible for a "share" (*meris*). I do not believe that this is a necessary conclusion to draw from that passage. The text only states that Phoibammon, son of Chlotinos, who paid for the *meris* of Taurinos, was from Temenkyrkis; it would not be unheard of that he worked for, or in some place within the "share" of, Taurinos (for instance, as a lessee) without being registered there.

and more powerful pagarchy, but when and why those pagarchies that in practice were not already borne by *oikoi* on a long-term basis were turned into one single pagarchy. By assuming two steps in the evolution of the office—first the de facto long-term assignment of the charge to the *geouchoi,* then a unification and extended administrative purview—the transition becomes more gradual, unlike the abrupt change in organizational and hierarchical aspects that other explanations had to assume so far.

This line of argument probably places the "creation" of the "later" pagarchy before 493 CE, at least for Oxyrhynchos, and an Arsinoite papyrus might attest this system in place six years earlier.[133] For other regions, evidence for the "later" pagarchy is virtually nonexistent before Justinian's *Edict* 13 of 539 CE.[134] This proclamation fundamentally changed the provincial organization of the Egyptian diocese, but in its introduction presupposes pagarchs throughout Egypt who were independent from the city councils.[135] A *terminus post quem* is more elusive. In 548/549 CE, the villagers of Aphrodite

133 *SPP* XX 128 (May 23, 487), a deed of surety for the tax collection duties of a *sitometrēs* for a Theodosiopolite village. The document is addressed to a "Flavius Eustochios, *megaloprepestatos* and *endoxotatos comes domesticorum* and *prōteuōn* (= *principalis*) of Arsinoe." Gelzer 1909, 91 took this text to mean that there were villages directly administered by the city council. This man, however, is probably the same Eustochios whose heirs were responsible for fiscal shares in the Fayum around 620 CE (*SPP* X 249, discussed in Chapter Three, Section VII), and his title of *prōteuōn* mirrors the situation of Strategios II's titulature when he exercised authority over a *kōmē pagarchoumenē* as *geouchōn*; see Chapter Three, Section III. I therefore believe that an intriguing, although by no means certain, explanation for the *prōteuōn*'s being addressed in this particular case is the assumption that the village was part of Eustiochios's fiscal share, with *prōteuōn* supplanting the address as *geouchōn* just as in Strategios's case. The fact that the village is not described as *pagarchoumenē* need not speak against this, as this term is only attested when either the person under surety or the guarantor hails from such a village, which is not the case here. In addition, the parallel formula for *epoikia*, using the participle *diapherōn* ("belonging"), is notably less consistently used in the Fayum than it is in Oxyrhynchos, so the use of *pagarchoumenē* may also have been inconsistent. See also *P.Flor.* III 325 (Oxyrhynchite; 489), a contract involving Strategios II in which a *ktēma* is not described as *diapheron*, so even in Oxyrhynchos this designation was not used consistently.

134 On *Edict* 13, see the Introduction, Section I. On its consequences before the backdrop of the fourth- and fifth-century developments, see Palme 2007c, 245–249.

135 In 567 CE, the villagers of Aphrodite in the Thebaid note that there had been eight pagarchs of Antaiopolis so far under whom they had never been in arrears with their imperial taxes (see *P.Cair.Masp.* I 67002 col. II 18–19), but this must refer to the time after they had lost their autopract status and were put under the fiscal authority of the pagarchy (see Chapter Six, Section III). In the two decades before 567 CE, five or six individual pagarchs are known, with plenty of "documentary fog" in these years (on the chronology of the pagarchs of Antaiopolis, see Chapter Four, Section II and note that Patrikia must be placed somewhere in the 550s, while Makarios cannot be dated with certainty). If one still sees the comment of the Aphroditans as referring to the inception of the Antaiopolite pagarchy as an institution, one may wish to assume the minimum count, that is, four pagarchs in twenty years (assuming for now that Menas was only a stand-in for Patrikia during these years), thus taking, hypothetically, another two decades to reach eight pagarchs, which results in 527 CE as hypothetical "inception date," and thus rath-

argue that they received their privilege of *autopragia* from Emperor Leo I (r. 457–474) and they note on the same occasion that they had not been placed under pagarchic authority "since the time of their fathers and forefathers."[136] The town is attested in the status of a village (*kōmē*) possibly as early as the third century CE[137]—and in the fourth century, the villages were allocated to the *pagi*, which entails that Aphrodite should then formally have been subject to a "pagarchy," namely that of the *pagi*.[138] But the rhetoric of the Aphroditans may simply mean that since then—that is, since Leo's providing the privilege—they had *no longer* been subject to pagarchic authority. It may not be a coincidence that the Aphroditans were awarded *autopragia* around the same time that I suspect the pagarchy was transferred on the *oikoi* at least in Oxyrhynchos.[139] In any case, since the last securely dated *pagus* appears in 421 CE,[140] this can be taken as the minimum *terminus post quem* for the establishment of the "later" pagarchy. If my arguments about the "early" pagarchy's relation to the *oikoi* are accepted, we may put this establishment into a range from about the 460s, when the participation of the *oikoi* in civic liturgies becomes apparent, to 493 (or 487), when the first "pagarched" village

---

er late in comparison to Oxyrhynchos, which seems less likely to me. Instead, it is possible the Antaiopolite pagarchs of the early sixth century were less likely to work in collegia than their colleagues from the middle of that century, as discussed in Chapter Four, Section IV.

136 *P.Cair.Masp.* I 67019 verso 4–6: μηδέποτε κ̣λη[ρω]θ̣ε̣ῖ̣[σ]α̣ ὑπ[ὸ π]α̣γα̣ρχικὴν ἐξουσίαν ἀπὸ γονέων | α̣ὐ̣τῶ̣ν καὶ προγόνων, ἐχόντω̣[ν] τὸ προνόμιο̣ν̣ αὐτ̣[ῶ]ν ἀπὸ θείο̣[υ] τύπου | τοῦ τῆς θείας λήξεως Λέ̣[ον]τ̣ο̣ς. As Ruffini 2008a, 118 notes, the reading of Leo's name is not certain. The term κληρόω ("allot," "assign") is extremely rare in this period, but the traces, although uncertain, fit well. This passage has been adduced to argue that there must have been ("later") pagarchs in place by 474 CE (cf. Rouillard 1928, 53 with references), but this is not supported by the text (see also Liebeschuetz 1973, 39 n. 11), although it may have been so.

137 *O.Ont.Mus.* II 223 (Aphrodite; III?); *P.Col.* VIII 235 (Antaiopolis; 229/312?); *P.Kell.* I 30 (Oasis Magna; 363); *P.Kell.* I 42 (Oasis Magna; 364). Cf. the discussion on Aphrodite's potential *polis* status in Chapter Six, n. 11.

138 Was the village subject to a *praepositus pagi* or did it already enjoy a privilege similar to that *pronomion* described in *P.Cair.Masp.* I 67019 verso? The various rudimentary forms of civic administration in the "village" would point to the latter alternative and Leo may just have formally renewed this privilege in light of the newly empowered pagarchs, in which case the elevation of the pagarchy to the *civitas* level would have to be assumed as roughly contemporary to Leo's granting of the privilege, but this is speculative.

139 A curious passage in the Coptic *History of the Church* attributes to Emperor Marcian (r. 450–457) a decision to prohibit *boēthoi* from entering a village to collect taxes. Instead, the pagarchs are supposed to collect the taxes themselves and hand them over to the ⲉⲡⲓⲧⲣⲟⲡⲟⲥ ⲕⲁⲧⲁ ⲉⲡⲁⲣⲭⲓⲁ (fol. II recto col. a). This depiction is confused: both the "early" and the "later" pagarchs had *boēthoi* at their disposal, and certainly did not collect the taxes themselves in each village. While the "early" pagarchs would seem to be more suitable candidates to enter their villages on a regular basis, they would not hand over the taxes to the provincial office, but to the *exactor civitatis*. Perhaps this account, coming from a later perspective, blurs different stages in the evolution of the pagarchy but still contains the vague idea of reform in or around Marcian's reign. Cf. Chapter Two, n. 182.

140 See n. 72 above.

occurs and the (hypothesized) de facto "village pagarchies" had been transformed into administrative extensions of the large estates.[141]

By 539, at the time of *Edict* 13, the pagarchy at the *civitas* level had become an established part of the administration throughout Egypt. There were now seven provinces, or eparchies, in Egypt proper: Aegyptus I and II, Augustamnica I and II, Arcadia, and Thebais Superior and Inferior. The "double provinces" of Aegyptus, Augustamnica, and the Thebaid each received superior civilian and military authority in the form of the *dux et Augustalis*, to which a civilian officer, the *praeses*, was subordinated.[142] These *duces et Augustales* were directly subordinate to the praetorian prefect of the East, so there was no longer one superior authority for the Egyptian diocese. Arcadia, whose treatment is missing in the edict because of its fragmentary state, never had its own *dux* until some years before the Arab conquest; there are indications that this province, however, was at least temporarily subject to the *dux* of the Thebaid in the latter half of the sixth century.[143]

The edict's *praefatio* alludes to pagarchs being crucial fiscal actors throughout Egypt,[144] but only the relevant passages for Aegyptus and the Thebaid survive. The papyrological documentation furnishes abundant evidence for Byzantine pagarchs in Arcadia and the Thebaid. By contrast, Augustamnica remains a bit of a blind spot, as the only securely attested references to pagarchs in that province are references to "early" pagarchs in some Oxyrhynchite papyri from the fourth century, when Oxyrhynchos was still part of Augustamnica, not of Arcadia as later.[145] Yet, a Coptic name list of unknown origin mentions a "lord Theode, pagarch of Arabia and Jioubastin, and his whole household," no doubt referring to the two Augustamnican nomes of Arabia and Boubastos in the southeastern Nile delta.[146] The text is dated to the seventh century on

141 For the alternative 487 CE, see n. 135 above.

142 See Palme 2007c, 246 for a table showing the development of the Egyptian provinces and their governors. I shall therefore speak of Aegyptus, Augustamnica, and the Thebaid simply as "provinces," in contrast to the "eparchies" of Aegyptus I, Aegyptus II, and so forth. Yet, *Edict* 13 appears to speak of *praesides* for the Thebaid in the plural, which begs the question of whether that means that each eparchy had its own *praeses*; see also Zuckerman 2004a, 53. On the power of the *dux et Augustalis* in Egypt, see Kaiser forthcoming and cf. Legendre 2016.

143 See Palme 2013c with further references, and Derda 2006, 44–56 (cf. the table on p. 57). The potential subordination of Arcadia under the authority of the *dux et Augustalis* of the Thebaid is based on an analysis of Dioskoros's poems to the *dux* Athanasios (Morelli 2008a). But in this case, it would seem unusual that this authority was not covered by his regular titulature. Ultimately, it is possible that the authority over Arcadia to which Dioskoros alludes was grounded in some other of Athanasios's capacities that yet escapes us.

144 See the Introduction, n. 5.

145 *P.Oxy.* XLVI 3307 (early IV); *Ch.L.A.* V 292 (Oxyrhynchos; 353 CE; new ed. Pedone 2020, 7–20); *P.Oxy.* XVII 2110 (October 6, 370 CE); *P.Oxy.* LXIII 4371 (mid to late IV). Named after Emperor Arcadius, Arcadia must have been founded between 386 and 398 CE; see Palme 2013c.

146 See P.Mich. inv. 1525, edited in Heisler 1984, with references in the commentary, although the *chōrion* Bouba( ) in *SB* I 5339.31 cited in the article certainly refers to the well-known Fayum

palaeographical grounds and the fact that one pagarch is apparently responsible for two cities may indicate a date from the early Islamic period.[147] However, in combination with the fourth-century evidence and the *praefatio* of *Edict* 13, the papyrus practically assures us that there were Byzantine pagarchs throughout Augustamnica, too.

While *Edict* 13 subordinated the pagarchs to the recently installed *duces et Augustales*,[148] this did presumably little to change the pagarch's day-to-day business: before and after 539 CE, they would probably deal mainly with the bureaus of the eparchies in issues of accounting.[149] The intention of *Edict* 13 seems to have been rather about giving the *duces* a more immediate hold of the pagarchs and entitle them to intervene in critical cases.[150] Although the curials still had their part to say in issues of tax collection, the regulations of the pagarchs' replacement leave no doubt about the pagarchs' importance: the *dux* was not entitled to dismiss them on his own but had to notify the praetorian prefect of the East, who would then seek imperial approval for any further way of proceeding.

We cannot say whether the transformation of the pagarchy took a similar path outside Egypt. Evidence for its sister phenomenon, the model of fiscal participation, has not surfaced anywhere else in the form we find in Egypt.[151] A curious passage from *Edict* 13 raises some speculation in this regard. Here, Justinian orders that the districts of the Mareotes and the Menelaites, both in the eparchy of Aegyptus I, henceforth be under the authority of the *dux* of Libya. Yet nowhere is there any mention of what should happen to the pagarchs (or other local administrators) of these places, suggesting, if only vaguely, that the local administration of Libyan *civitates* level essentially resembled that in Aegyptus.[152] A second indirect indication that pagarchs were known

---

village of that name. It may be added that the nomes of Arabia and Boubastos are listed next to each other as early as in *P.Rev.* col. 31.9–10 (259–258 BCE). Also the nomes' appearances in *P.Flor.* II 278 col. II 3 and 20 (Memphis or Babylon; after September 24, 203 CE) indicate proximity.

147 On "double pagarchies," cf. the Catalog, s.v. Anonymous pagarch (Apollonopolis Heptakomias or Antaiopolis).

148 Strictly speaking, this regulation is extant only for Aegyptus and the Thebaid, but the edict is incompletely preserved.

149 See *P.Mich.* XI 624 (Arcadia; mid-V–early VI), where two collegial pagarchs are said to have rendered a fiscal report (*anaphora*, on the meaning of which see the Catalog, s.v. Antiochos & Theon) to the praesidial bureau of Arcadia, and Iust. *ed.* 13.25. The *exactores* had taken their orders from the *praesides*; see Thomas 1959, 125.

150 Palme 2013b.

151 See Durliat 1990 for an ambitious attempt at reconstructing in the world of the Western Empire and its successors phenomena that seem closely comparable to Gascou's ideas of elite fiscal participation. This attempt has met with criticism for its handling of the evidence, and indeed the argument, while remaining essentially possible, fails to convince based on the evidence available to date. Moreover, the structure and the character of private landholding seems to have been different in the West; on this latter point, see Begass 2018, 440–449.

152 Iust. *ed.* 13.18–22. The edict holds that Libya would not be able to cover its expenses without the taxes from these two newly incorporated places. The text contains no regulations concerning the authority of the Libyan *dux* over pagarchs as are extant for Aegyptus and the Thebaid. But

outside Egypt in the sixth century may be drawn from the drafts of an imperial rescript that the Egyptian village leader Dioskoros wrote and redacted around 551 and which he brought to Constantinople to have it redacted again by a local expert before submitting it.[153] In the three different versions of the draft that have come down to us, Jean-Luc Fournet notes at least two instances of a particular usage of technical terms in the latest draft of the rescript that we have. He argues convincingly that this usage was intended to deliberately avoid provincial jargon that might have even led to misunderstandings in the imperial administration.[154] In light of this it may be significant that the title "pagarch of Antaiopolis" is used in this text without explanation, which can only mean that this title was generally known in wider circles of the imperial administration in the mid-sixth century.[155] If this was because the pagarchs were considered particularly important for the administration of one of the empire's wealthiest provinces, or because pagarchs were a phenomenon throughout the East also after the fifth century, we cannot say.

No other text allows for a comparable reasoning.[156] Did other provinces resort to different solutions in the fifth century when transforming the office of the *praepositus pagi*? New evidence may illuminate these local conditions of the late Roman eastern

in these latter two instances the edict aimed at defining the authority of the *newly* implemented posts of the *duces et Augustales* in Aegyptus and the Thebaid. Since Libya was already governed by a *dux* before the edict was issued, such regulations would perhaps not be expected here.

153 *P.Cair.Masp.* I 67024–25 (new ed. Fournet 2018). It is likely that neither of these manuscripts was the final draft that would have been presented to the imperial chancery in Constantinople: A and A' were written by Dioskoros and B is a version redacted by an expert from the capital; Fournet provides an in-depth analysis of these different versions and their relationship to one another.

154 Fournet 2018, 621, who put the motivation of the redactor of this rescript as "le débarrasser des expressions qui sentent trop le terroir." See also Fournet 2024, 148–149.

155 We might have hypothesized this already from the prominent references to pagarchs in the rescript *SB* VI 9102 (548 or 551 CE), authored by a leading member of the imperial administration in Constantinople, and Justinian's *Edict* 13, but these texts are addressed *to* the province of Egypt and thus would have been finally redacted by someone with local expert knowledge. Thus I think *P.Cair.Masp.* I 67024–25 is a more intriguing lead in this question, because it may be assumed to have gone through quite some hands, or ears, in the capital and therefore must have been comprehensible to a wider part of the imperial administration. Note also how the abovementioned Menelaites, i.e., in the form of the word that marks the old district (*nomos*), is called a "city" (*polis*) in Iust. *ed.* 13.1 (cf. 13.17: τὸν Μαρεώτην).

156 Two inscriptions from columns in the hippodrome of Tyre that describe "places" of the circus factions (V–VI) read τόπο(ς) παγ( ) | Βενετῶν and τόπο(ς) παγα( ) | ⟦– – –⟧, respectively (Rey-Coquais 2002, 331–332; *AE* 2002, nos. 1535 and 1536). The editor proposes the readings παγ(άρχου) and παγά(ρχου), respectively, and, after considering some less likely hypotheses, ultimately argues that the word "désignerait simplement le chef d'une faction." Provided this is supposed to mean that a high-ranking title from the public administration was used here to designate a position of authority within the faction (which the editor does not state expressly), then this does not seem impossible, but should on current evidence still be regarded as far from certain. See also the nuanced discussion in Feissel 2003, who instead opts for παγ(ανῶν)/παγα(νῶν).

provinces, but tenable results are more likely to emerge from another direction, namely the former Roman provinces of the early Islamic Empire outside Egypt. The administrative language of the early Islamic Empire drew in considerable measure upon local traditions, and the documentary evidence from the Syrian and Palestine regions of the early Islamic period has only begun to be exploited in this regard.[157] So far, we must resort to speculation.

V. Summary

In 307/308 CE, in the final stage of Egypt's long process of municipalization, the office of the *praepositus pagi* was created and a new administrative division into *pagi* imposed on the rural parts of the *civitas* territory. The abandonment of Egypt's particular form of administration reflects an empire-wide effort and consequently, the Latin title of the *praepositus pagi* was also employed, in Greek quasi-transliteration, for the official's title in the Eastern Empire. Yet from the beginning, the office was rendered as *pagarchia*, and the act of discharging that office found a convenient expression in the verb *pagarcheō*. The official's title of *praipositos pagou* found a Hellenized alternative in two synonymous terms: *pagarchos* and *pagarchēs*, which both may initially have been colloquial expressions before they entered official jargon in the 350s. There is no sign that this terminological change entailed any administrative adjustments; the "early" pagarchs, the *praepositi pagorum*, were in control of conglomerates of several villages, while estates and hamlets permeated their *pagi*. Although there is no unambiguous evidence that *pagarchia* acquired a territorial meaning, it could well be called after a central village, from which point the expression found in one text, "pagarch of the village," becomes understandable. The "early" pagarchs were curials and subordinate to the *exactor civitatis*, acting on their own or collegially.

In the course of the fifth century the pagarchy was, like other civic liturgies, entrusted to the *oikoi*, which had only recently been institutionalized. This possibly resulted from a gradual process that perpetuated the authority of some of the "early" pagarchs, the *praepositi pagorum*, for particular territories around their landed estates. As the large estates had begun to be vested with the duty to collect taxes on their territories, the official authority of the pagarchies at that time extended no longer over contiguous areas but rather over those fractions of the territories that the scattered *oikos* plots of the large landowners had left. From this situation it was only a small, and logical, step to render fiscal authority over villages to those magnates who already had interests and an elaborate administration present in these areas, and some of the de facto "village pagarchies" were thus turned into *kōmai pagarchoumenai*, villages over which a large landowner exercised fiscal authority. The remaining villages fell under one unified pag-

157 The majority of the Arabic material has yet to be published. For Egypt, see Sijpesteijn 2013, 66–71. For the early Islamic Empire as a whole, see Garosi 2022, 263–322.

archy; this stage had probably been reached in Oxyrhynchos at the latest by 493 CE.[158] The exact status of the *kōmai pagarchoumenai*, their administration, and their share of the countryside in relation to the pagarchy are explored in Chapter Three, which will further support the development outlined here. The discussion there also provides further indications that the development proposed here was, *mutatis mutandis*, structurally comparable to what must have happened in other nomes to different degrees.

By the end of the fifth century, pagarchs were significantly higher in rank than the old *praepositi pagorum*. They appear to have gained independence from the civic authorities and perhaps became subject to the governors of the eparchies, while the pagarchs' superiors of old, the *exactores civitatum*, apparently lost much of their former areas of authority with the exception of recordkeeping business,[159] and their charge was also transferred to the *oikoi*. Following *Edict* 13 and the reform of Egypt's provincial administration in 539 CE, the pagarchs were more immediately bound to the central authorities: their appointment ultimately depended on imperial approval and they were formally subordinate to the newly installed *duces et Augustales*, while in practice they perhaps still worked closely with the *praesides* at the level of the eparchies. Apart from rather subtle allusions, evidence is lacking for what happened to the *praepositi pagorum* in other provinces in the fifth century.

158 Or even earlier in the Fayum, if one accepts my interpretation of *SPP* XX 128, dated 487 CE; see n. 133 above.

159 Perhaps the *exactor* still had some authority over tax collection in the urban parts of the *civitas*. The relationship between the pagarchy and civic institutions in the sixth century is discussed in the next chapter.

Chapter Two
The Mechanics of Extraction

Operating at the intersection between the provincial bureaus and the local level of the countryside, the pagarchs played a distinctive role in the fiscal process. This chapter evaluates that role.[1] The pagarchs' networks pervaded the fiscal landscape of the cities and by studying those networks, we can retrace both the flow of taxes and the exercise of public authority at the local level. Specifically, this chapter interrogates the widespread idea that the pagarch was the head of the nome. The reality, as we might expect, was more complex, especially in diachronic perspective. Wolf Liebeschuetz noted not too long ago:

> We lack the evidence to decide whether, or to what extent, the administration of civic and imperial expenditure was kept separate in the cities of Egypt. Was the pagarch involved in municipal finance as well as the collection of taxes? Was the *dēmosion logistērion* concerned with municipal accounts as well as the updating of the imperial tax register? Did cities like Oxyrhynchus have significant income from civic estates or urban properties? What precisely were the remaining functions of the decurions?[2]

A closer look at the mechanisms of the pagarchy cannot answer all these questions, but does nonetheless contribute greatly to clarifying some of the underlying mechanisms.

Reconstructing the pagarchs' network is not easy, however. The doings and dealings of the various fiscal officials at the provincial, city, and village levels, their interactions, and the administrative procedures are difficult to pin down exactly and uniformly. We do not encounter the strict bureaucratic administration of modern times, with its abstract and clearly defined areas of responsibility, in the classical and late antique world. In what follows, my aim is not to provide a handbook of late antique Egypt's fiscal administration but rather to illustrate how the fiscal authority of the pagarchs was accepted (or tolerated) and how it was expected that it would be exercised. Due to the available evidence, this perspective is largely an Antaiopolite one. Notably, about eighty tax receipts that were issued in the name of pagarchs have survived. Some sixty of these were collected as part of at least three codices from the Dioskoros archive in the strict sense.[3] A smaller, yet substantial, amount of about two dozen receipts has come down to us as individual papyri, mostly from the archive of Dioskoros's cousin-in-law

1 The title of this chapter is borrowed from the title of a 2016 conference, now the subtitle of Valk & Soto Marín 2021.

2 Liebeschuetz 2001, 197 n. 177.

3 (1) *P.Cair.Masp.* III 67325, (2) (*P.Aphrod.Reg.* +) *P.Flor.* III 298 + *P.Stras.* VII 699, and (3) a largely unpublished one from the Strasbourg collection; for a description of the latter, see Fournet 2008d, 297–298. I am currently preparing the tax receipts from this third codex for publication.

https://doi.org/10.1515/9783111493183-003

Phoibammon, but also from other nomes.[4] But although evidence from other nomes is scant beyond the tax receipts, we will see that where such evidence does exist it points in the same direction or, at least, does nothing to refute the hypothesis that essential cornerstones of the Antaiopolite pattern fit other nomes, too.

I. The Fiscal Landscape of Late Antique Egypt and the Territorial Pagarchy

From Diocletian onward, the administrative organization of the empire from the imperial level down to the provinces, with prefectures and dioceses as intermediary levels, largely balanced both military and fiscal considerations.[5] Local administrative organization equally had to provide stability and conform to the necessities of tax collection, so as to secure a smooth flow of contributions from the lowest taxable entities upward.[6] The hub of this organization was the *civitas*, which in a legal sense was much more than just the urban center, which in Egypt was the former *mētropolis* of the nome. The *civitates* had become identical to what used to be the nome, comprising both the urban center and the country villages and hamlets. In his classic account of the later Roman Empire, Arnold H. M. Jones put it as follows:

> The Roman empire was an agglomeration of cities (*civitates*, πόλεις), self-governing communities responsible for the administration of the areas which they occupied, their territories. In each *civitas* there was a town which was its administrative capital and in varying degrees its economic and social centre, but there was no legal distinction between the urban and rural members of the community. Constitutionally and administratively, then, the cities were the cells of which the empire was composed.[7]

Despite the legal unison of the urban and rural parts of the *civitas*, in practice there were fiscal subdivisions, which can be glimpsed in Justinian's *Edict* 13. The wording of the edict lists the "provinces (*eparchiai*), cities (*poleis*), and rural places (*topoi*) under him (i.e., the *dux et Augustalis*)," thus effectively distinguishing *provincia*, *civitas*, and

---

4 **From the Antaiopolite:** *P.Cair.Masp.* I 67045; 67046; 67047; II 67228; *P.Gen.* IV 193; *P.Lond.* V 1665; 1666; *P.Vat.Aphrod.* 16A; *SB* XVI 12370; XX 14121; 15013.1–3 and 4–7; 15015.1–5 and 6–9; XXIV 15975; P.Mich. inv. 3272 (ed. Keenan 2012). Add the two related rent receipts *SB* XX 15014 and 15016. **From the Hermopolite:** *BGU* XII 2196; *P.Lond.* V 1753 (perhaps from the early Islamic period) and 1865 *descr.* (ed. Gascou & Gonis 2022, no. 5); perhaps *P.Münch.* III 152 (origin uncertain). **From the Antinoopolite:** *P.Leid.Inst.* 72. Some of these may originally have been part of a codex. I discuss both the "individual" and the "codex receipts"—and their writers—in Stern forthcoming (a) and (b).

5 For an overview of the imperial fiscal and military administration under Justinian, including structural charts, see Haldon 2005, 41–48.

6 Roger Bagnall (1993, 137 and 316), for instance, has argued that the village organization essentially came into being only when confronted with the public fiscal regime.

7 Jones 1964, 712.

territorium.[8] A later chapter specifies the governor's duty to "dispatch to Alexandria the amount (i.e., of the tax grain) that the rural regions (*chōrai*) and cities (*poleis*) under him ⟨contribute⟩."[9]

This may merely represent a descending administrative hierarchy, but there seems to be more to it than that. The explicit distinction between city and hinterland correlates with the evolution of the pagarchy presented in Chapter One, as will become clearer when we examine the pagarchy's spatial dimension. Evidence from the sixth century suggests that, at that time, *pagarchia* was mostly used in an abstract sense that referred to the institution.[10] As we have seen, *Edict* 13, which certainly conveys official terminology, apparently does not conceive of a pagarchy as a territorial entity but instead distinguishes *poleis* from *topoi*.[11] We have also seen in Chapter One that these *topoi* served to designate different kinds of settlements in the countryside, among them the hamlets (*epoikia*).[12] The pagarchy would thus not comprise a clearly defined or necessarily contiguous territory, but rather a list of particular places or localities.[13] At the same time, the pagarchy was occasionally understood as a geographic area.[14] In one

8 Iust. *ed.* 13.24: ταῖς αὐτοῦ ἐπαρχίαις τε καὶ πόλεσι καὶ τόποις. Here the virtual subordination of the τε καὶ (...) καί clause under ἐπαρχίαις might be taken as an illustrative indication of the urban center and the city territory as distinct entities under the head of a province.

9 Iust. *ed.* 13.26: ὥστε ἐκπέμπειν αὐτὸν (...) κατὰ τὴν Ἀλεξανδρέων κατ' ὅσον ⟨αἱ⟩ ὑπ' αὐτὸν τεταγμέναι χῶραί τε καὶ πόλεις ⟨εἰσφέρουσι⟩; both emendations go back to Zachariae and suggest themselves by the context of the passage.

10 See the Introduction, Section VII.

11 The edict refers only twice to a παγαρχία, the context being the dismissal and replacement of fraudulent pagarchs in Aegyptus (Chapter 12) and the Thebaid (Chapter 25); e.g., Chapter 25: τῶν δὲ ἐπιλεγέντων ἐν τῇ χώρᾳ τούτων (...) ἀντικαθισταμένων καὶ εἰς τὰς ἐκείνων παγαρχίας τε καὶ οὐσίας ἐμβαινόντων, "and those selected will be appointed in their stead (...) and they will take over their (i.e., the former incumbents') pagarchies and properties (*ousiai*)."

12 See especially Chapter One, Section III on *C.Th.* VIII 15.1 and Isid.Pel. *epist.* 51.

13 The situation in the fourth century appears to be similar: most instances of *pagarchia* refer to the office or institution, though occasionally a territorial connotation seems plausible, referring to a *pagus* that comprised certain villages and hamlets. See the discussion of *P.Oxy.* XLVI 3307 in Chapter One, Section II.

14 Apart from the papyri discussed in this section, there are some fragmentary and dubious instances, starting with *P.Mich.* XV 742.14–15 (unknown origin; VI), most likely referring to costs raised by (or for) the office, not the territory; see n. 117 below. Then there are two fragmented and dubious attestations from *SB* I, neither of which is securely dated or available as a digital image: *SB* I 4812.11 (Arsinoe; 591–602? or 610–640?) and *SB* I 4848.10 (Arsinoe?; Byzantine?). Another papyrus from that era, *SB* I 4707 (Arsinoites; Byzantine) was revised by Jördens 1992, 286, but her revision is only partially rendered in *BL* X 179–180. Although Jördens reads another line before the beginning of the text in the *editio princeps*, she sticks to the line count of the *editio princeps*. The text has [‒ ‒ ‒]ημένην παγαρχίαν in l. 6 and [‒ ‒ ‒ ημ]ένης π̣αγαρχί̣α̣ς̣ in l. 11. Given the relative rarity of the ending and in view of the comparable expression ἐ]κ τῆς αὐτῆς παγαρχίας in *P.Rain.Cent.* 81.5 (on which see below), the two lines can possibly be restored as τὴν εἰρ]ημένην παγαρχίαν and τῆς εἰρημ]ένης π̣αγαρχί̣α̣ς̣, respectively. It is tempting to connect the latter phrase to ἐν τῷ πραιτωρίῳ in the preceding line, but this restoration does not appear to fill all the lost

petition, the inhabitants of the village of Aphrodite complain about the misconduct of the pagarch Menas Scriniarius:

> He (i.e., Menas) did not stop his mad behavior to tear apart and turn upside down, as they say, the pagarchy, which he plundered, and whose goods he transferred into the (monastery of) Apa Senouthios.[15]

The Greek verbs for "to tear apart" and "to turn upside down" are attested only in transitive uses and therefore most likely imply the pagarchy as their direct object.[16] Later in the sentence, it is, then, clearly the pagarchy that is plundered and whose goods are removed by Menas. There is therefore a territorial aspect of the pagarchy in this instance, though that might also be read metaphorically, relating to the office, an ambiguity probably intended by the petition's author.[17]

What does it entail, then, when a pagarch or a pagarchy is assigned to a certain *civitas*, as in "pagarch(y) of Antaiopolis"?[18] Basically, there are two positions. The first holds that this expression entails that a territorial pagarchy was congruent with the entire nome, that is, the *civitas*. This position was most influentially articulated by Harold Idris Bell.[19] By contrast, Matthias Gelzer, coeval with Bell, argued that the pagarchs were responsible for the villages in the *territoria* of the *civitates* only, excluding localities that were specifically exempt from their authority such as autopract villages.[20] Germaine Rouillard tried to strike a balance between the two: pointing to the pagarch's (supposed) intrusion into the issues of the autopract village of Aphrodite, she concluded that he was the central civil authority in the *civitas* and, while being deprived of the responsibility for the tax collection in autopract villages, still had his

---

text in the left half of the papyrus. Some enjambments make it obvious that there must be more than eight lost letters; see, e.g., ll. 3–4, 5–6, and 12–13. Probably some apposition to πραιτωρίῳ has been lost at the beginning of l. 11 and the sense of ll. 3–6 could approximately be "that N.N. (-odoron) hands over sureties [and comes/goes/returns into the] aforementioned pagarchy," but this is speculative.

15 *P.Cair.Masp.* I 67002 col. III 20: οὐκ' ἐπαύσατο μανιῶν διόλο(υ) διαρπάξαι καὶ ἀθετῆσαί φησιν τὴν παγαρχίαν, ἣν ἐξεπόρθησεν ἀποτεθεικὼς τὰ τα(ύ)της χρήματα εἰς τὰ Ἄπα Σενουθί[ο(υ)].

16 The word for "to tear apart," διαρπάζω, can also mean "to spoil" or "to corrupt" (see *LSJ*, s.v.). The basic meaning of "to turn upside down," ἀθετέω, is "to negate" (i.e., a clause or a contract; see *WB*, s.v.).

17 I had the pleasure of discussing this idea with Jean-Luc Fournet, who came to the same conclusion during his work on his forthcoming new edition of the petitions of Dioskoros of Aphrodite. In another instance in *P.Cair.Masp.* I 67002, the petitioners note that Menas had "taken over" the Antaiopolite pagarchy: ἀντελάβετο τῆς παγαρχίας | Ἀνταίο(υ) (col. I 10–11), again an ambiguous use of *pagarchia*.

18 There is no difference in meaning between τῆς Ἀνταίου or τῆς Ἀνταιοπολιτῶν here; see, e.g., *P. Cair.Masp.* I 67002 col. I 6 and 10–11 and col. II 18–19.

19 Bell 1908; see Mazza 1995, 186 n. 55 on this and other early literature on this issue.

20 Gelzer 1909, 94 and 95; cf. the critical review of Maspero 1911, 182–183 on this point.

say in the event of irregularities.[21] The current *communis opinio* is in essence Rouillard's formulation of Bell's argument, but scholarly references mostly go back to the Bell's work. His arguments, however, drew on the early Islamic evidence, with no immediate intention to describe the pagarchy's extension within the nome.[22] Rather, he sought to illustrate the more general claim that the pagarchies of the early Islamic period had their roots in the structure of the old nome/*civitas*. Making Bell the authority for the relation "pagarchy = entire nome" *in the Byzantine period* is therefore problematic. Bell's view regarding the Byzantine period in fact tended more toward Gelzer's, as becomes clear in Bell's later assertion that the pagarch of this era "had no authority over the municipality, which after the creation of his office ceased to be responsible for the finances of the rural territory."[23]

Although the evidence is patchy, it seems likely that at least in the sixth century the pagarchs' authority did indeed not extend to the entire *civitas*, probably due to its emergence out of the much more fragmented authority over the various *pagi*. The most uncontroversial claim about the pagarchs' fiscal authority is that it extended over the villages (*kōmai*) in the countryside. This authority is also the pagarchs' most immediate link to their earlier incarnation, the *praepositi pagorum*. The fact that the pagarchs' title incorporated the name of a city does not necessarily mean that their authority extended into the urban center, even though they surely had their residence there.[24] As we have just seen, Justinian's *Edict* 13 distinguishes between the cities and the rural areas. Its *praefatio*, quoted in the Introduction above, complains about the disorder in Egyptian tax collection and draws a telling distinction between the pagarchs and other fiscal authorities:

> The pagarchs, the curials, the collectors of the taxes, and in particular the governors at the time have hitherto arranged the business in such a way that no one can find out anything about it, and that only they can profit from it.[25]

---

21 Rouillard 1928, 61.

22 This was noted early on by Gelzer 1909, 90.

23 Bell 1948, 121; cf. 120 (my emphasis): "The whole *rural area* now forms a single district, financially administered by an official called a pagarch." See also Bell 1917, 99, which takes a position close to Gelzer's on the development of the pagarchy out of the *pagi*.

24 The exclusion of the urban center from the scope of the pagarchy's power is a point in Gelzer's and Bell's original arguments that is frequently passed over. Gelzer did not elaborate on this point but appears to have simply taken it as self-evident, given the origin of the pagarchy from the *pagi*. On official titles including city names, see Oertel 1917, 302, distinguishing "Spezialorgane der städtischen […] Verwaltung im engeren Sinne" from "Organen staatlicher Zweckbestimmung für den Sprengel 'Stadt.'"

25 Iust. *ed.* 13, *praefatio*: οἱ παγάρχαι δὲ καὶ οἱ πολιτευόμενοι καὶ οἱ πράκτορες τῶν δημοσίων καὶ διαφερόντως ⟨οἱ⟩ κατὰ καιρὸν ἄρχοντες, κτλ. On the meaning of *archontes* here, see the Introduction, n. 5.

The pagarchs are distinguished from the curials in the same way in a later passage, which first describes the pagarchs' standing vis-à-vis the *dux et Augustalis* of the two Aegypti before proceeding to describe the curials' relationship to him.[26] This distinction is also obvious in the parallel passage concerning the subordinates of the *dux et Augustalis* of the Thebaid:

> As we said earlier, the local *praesides* shall, of course, be subject to him, with responsibility for the said provinces (*eparchiai*), as also shall the members of their *officia* and the entire provincial (*politikē*) or civic (*dēmosia*) auxiliary staff, including the pagarchs and the curials, and in general everyone present (*ontes*) or resident (*oikountes*) in these provinces, or acting as pagarchs (*pagarchountes*) or working in any way on public business (*dēmosia*).[27]

Again, the pagarchs are mentioned next to the curials and somewhat apart from anyone else involved in the fiscal process. All of this suggests that the pagarch's authority was distinct from that of the civic authorities.

Another probable instance is an administrative letter from the sixth or early seventh century that concerns a controversy between the bureau of the *defensor civitatis* of Hermopolis on the one hand and a *megaloprepeia*, presumably the *praeses*, on the other.[28] The reason for this controversy was apparently an order by the *megaloprepeia*, which involved "the summoning of those from the said pagarchy who have been subject to accusations."[29] Roberta Mazza has suggested that this text may indicate that the

---

26 Iust. *ed.* 13.12.

27 Iust. *ed.* 13.25. On this meaning of *politikos*, see P.Sorb. inv. 2743 recto l. 1 (Hermopolis/Antinoopolis; early V) with discussion in Gascou 2014, and, e.g., *P.Cair.Masp.* I 67019 verso 2–3: ὑπὸ τὴν ἐ[πι]χώριον σεμνὴν | π̣ο̣λ̣ι̣[τι]κὴν τάξιν; see also Chapter Six, n. 148 and Appl 2012, 52. The participle *oikōn* designates someone who temporarily dwells in a certain place, in contrast to an individual's *origo*; see *CPR* XXIV, p. 196.

28 *P.Rain.Cent.* 81 (Hermopolis; VI–VII). The editor uses palaeographical observations for the rough date and further argues from the occurrence of a *taxis* (Lat. *officium*) of the *defensor* that the text must be from later than than 535 (based on Iust. *nov.* 15, but the law does not actually say that the *taxis* is new). One may infer from the term *dēfēnsoria taxis* (l. 2) that the text predates the Islamic conquest. Although the *ekdikos* is still attested well into the eighth century (cf. Fournet 2020a, 110 n. 88, where by "allusions to the *defensor*" he means the occurrence of the word *ekdikos*, not that of the Graeco-Latin form *dēfēnsōr*), it seems unlikely that his bureau would be rendered with the transliterated Latin title as *dēfēnsoria taxis* under Arab administration if the Greek form of the official title had been widely used; indeed, all papyri that attest the Greek transliteration of the Latin *defensor* come from the fourth and fifth centuries. Moreover, the ἐκλήμπτωρ (ll. 2 and 6) has not so far appeared in any early Islamic evidence.

29 *P.Rain.Cent.* 81.4–5: τὴν παραγωγὴν τῶν ὑπὸ αἰτίασιν | γινομε̣[νων ἐ]κ τῆς αὐτῆς παγαρχίας. There appear to be only two parallels for the connection of παράγω with ἐκ in the *PN*, and they date all the way back to the Ptolemaic period: *P.Lond.* VII 1979.4–5 (Alexandria; c. 253 BCE) and *P.Köln* XI 453.6–7 (Herakleopolites; January 24, 159 BCE). It is, theoretically, conceivable that the accused individuals were received "from the pagarchy," as in, from the hands (or through the assistance) of the pagarch and his subordinates; see Mazza 1995, 185 n. 52 (who considers this to be unlikely, however) and cf. *WB*, s.v. παράγω § 5. However, I am not aware of any instances in the

pagarchy was "a territorial entity related to the city but distinct from it, consequently moving it to a meaning close to '*pagus*.'"[30] The papyrus is damaged, so it remains unclear what sort of pagarchy or pagarch had previously been mentioned in the text. Still, it seems plausible that this pagarchy was that of Hermopolis, since the *defensor civitatis* was responsible for one *civitas* and would normally not extend his authority to other nomes. The term, then, appears to relate to the countryside of Hermopolis in its entirety, which would define any territorial boundaries of the pagarchy roughly along the lines assumed by Gelzer.

Such developments are illustrative of the "more and more formal supreme authority" that the curials wielded over the rural territory, which now basically consisted of three parts: territories gathered under the *oikoi*, autopract villages, and the villages under the authority of the pagarch.[31] Furthermore, as we have seen, Justinian's *Edict* 13 handed the supervision of the pagarchs' fiscal authority over to the new provincial governors, the high-ranking *duces et Augustales*. The edict thus aimed at strengthening the governor's position vis-à-vis a concentrated mélange of local elites, and at providing the central authorities with more immediate access to local administrative procedures.[32] According to the edict's *praefatio*, the opacity of the local networks created by pagarchs, curials, local collectors, and (at that time lower-ranking) provincial governors was the main reason for this reorganization, which underscores that these developments were largely a response to, and continuation of, wider socioeconomic trends around the transformation of the city landscape since the third and especially during the fifth century.[33]

All these actors at the city level—*oikoi*, autopract villages, the pagarchy, and civic administration—did not form enclosed areas of authority under the provincial bureau. Rather, they were interlinked at various points. The *oikoi* are discussed in Chapter Three and the autopract villages in Chapter Six; the remainder of the present chapter

---

papyri in which an office such as the *pagarchia* is styled as an actor on its own; one would instead expect a personal reference to a pagarch or his subordinates in such cases.

30 Mazza 1995, 185: "un'entità territoriale correlata alla città, ma da essa distinta, risalendo quindi a un significato prossimo a *pagus*."

31 See Palme 1989, 98 (parentheses in the original): "So hat man unter der mehr und mehr formellen Oberhoheit der Bule (*curia*) ab dem 5. Jh. n. Chr. auf dem Territorium einer *civitas* drei Arten von Verwaltungseinheiten: 1. die οἶκοι der autoprakten Grundherren (private und kirchliche), 2. die autoprakten Dörfer, 3. die Pagarchen." We should not understand these three entities as clearly delineated and contiguous territories, however. Instead, this was probably a matter of registration. The degree to which autopract villages were present in late antique Egypt is debated; see the discussion in Chapter Six, Section 1.

32 See the Introduction, Section I.

33 See Laniado 2002 for a detailed analysis of this transformation and Liebeschuetz 2001 as well as the articles collected in Krause & Witschel 2006 for other influential perspectives. The discussion about Egypt's curial dignitaries and their careers during the period of this transformation is placed within a modern historiographical context by Palme 2013a, 119–120. The implications of this transformation for the fiscal landscapes of late antique Egypt are discussed in Chapter One.

will instead explore the pagarchs' links to the civic administration and the mechanics of tax collection in the villages under the pagarchy.

II. Fiscal Operations at the City Level

The preceding section established a conceptual difference between the urban center of the *civitas*/nome and the countryside from an administrative point of view. Building on this, this section examines the pagarchs' relation to civic institutions in matters of tax collection, which includes their relationships to the *dēmosion logistērion* and to civic business in the countryside, as well as their own administrative infrastructure at the city level.

*1. The Public Accounting Office (*Dēmosion Logistērion*)*

One central node of fiscal operations at the city level was the *dēmosion logistērion*, the "public accounting office" or "central treasury," which was a genuinely civic institution.[34] Since the pagarch is sometimes described as the "director" of taxation in the late Roman-Egyptian *civitas*, it would seem only natural to assume that he directed the operations of the *logistērion*.[35] Some scholars have explicitly or implicitly done so, usually drawing on the idea that the pagarchy's territorial purview was congruent with the entire nome/*civitas*.[36] Allan Chester Johnson and Louis West made the case for identifying the *dēmosion logistērion* as the bureau of the pagarchy;[37] later, Ewa Wipszycka put forward the same hypothesis and described the *dēmosion logistērion* as the "accounting office of the pagarchies."[38] Following Wipszycka, Bernhard Palme pointed to the communication between the *apaitētai* and officials from the *logistērion*, such as the *boēthos tou logistēriou* and the *diastoleus*; he took those officials as an intermediate level between the pagarch and the villages, and assumed the pagarch's bureau and the *logistērion* to be one and the same.[39]

---

34 On the *dēmosion logistērion*, see the literature in *CPR* XXIV, p. 43 n. 23. The working of this institution is vividly described, with specific reference to Hermopolis, by Wipszycka 1971 and Gonis 2007a and illustrated by the extensive *P.Sorb.* II 69. See also Gascou & Gonis 2022. On imprisonments in the *logistērion*, see Krause 1996, 104, 140, 160, 162, 166–167, and 194. Court proceedings also appear to have been held there; see *P.Panop.* 30 (Panopolis; 332), where the *exactor* presides over one of these cases. On the *logistērion* in the first three centuries CE, cf. Kruse 2002, 799–800.

35 "Director" of taxation: Liebeschuetz 2001, 188.

36 See the preceding section.

37 Johnson & West 1949, e.g., 174–175.

38 Wipszycka 1971, *passim*, especially 109: "bureau des comptes des pagarchies."

39 Palme 1989, e.g., 105, 108, and 172; cf. the reservations on this point expressed by Gascou 1992, 354.

Although their connection must have been close, the *dēmosion logistērion* and the pagarchy appear to have operated separately. In equating the (Byzantine) *logistērion* with the pagarchs' bureau, Wipszycka drew on Roger Rémondon's observation that the *logistērion* was "the accounting office of the city and, very likely, of the pagarchy."[40] In 622 CE, Rémondon goes on to argue, the *dēmosios logos* (!)—which is represented by the *boēthos tou logistēriou*—possessed only limited autonomy vis-à-vis the central government represented by the pagarch.[41] In another, albeit fragmentary, text from the early Islamic period to which both Rémondon and Wipszycka refer, the sender apparently requests that the pagarch issue an order to the *boēthos tou logistēriou*.[42] It is notable, however, that the sender still perceives the *boēthos* as an administrative entity and does not, for instance, demand directly that the pagarch comply with the request. This highlights that the *boēthos logistēriou* was not merely the pagarch's clerk, but an official acting on his own authority,[43] and that consequently equating the *dēmosion logistērion* with the pagarch's bureau runs the risk of conflating distinct administrative entities.[44] Yet, a receipt from sixth- or early seventh-century Hermopolis signed by the pagarch was "written in a hand suggestive of the *dēmosion logistērion*" of that city, which may indicate that pagarch's office was part of the operations of the *logistērion* or that their staff were recruited from the same professional pool.[45]

Other evidence from the Byzantine period may further suggest a nuanced relationship between these two institutions. Recently, some tax receipts from the Dioskoros and Phoibammon archives, that is, from the Antaiopolite nome, have been taken to illustrate that the *dēmosion logistērion* was the pagarch's bureau; *boēthoi* signed these receipts in the name of the pagarchs and thus are taken to be *boēthoi tou logistēriou*.[46]

---

40 *P.Apoll.*, p. 118: "bureau des comptes de la cité, et très probablement de la pagarchie," cited by Wipszycka 1971, 109, where "*P.Apoll.* 47" must be read for Wipszycka's "*P.Edfou* 47."

41 *P.Apoll.*, p. 118: "A cette époque [that is, the date of *P.Würzb.* 19] le δημόσιος λόγος ne doit jouir que d'une autonomie restreinte vis-à-vis du gouvernement central répresenté par le pagarque."

42 *P.Apoll.* 47.3: παρακαλῶ ψηφίσασθαι μηκέτι τὸν βοηθ[ὸν τοῦ λογιστηρ(ίου) – – –]; for the restoration, cf. l. 8. The text is from the archive of the pagarch Papas (i.e., from the second half of the seventh century) and probably addressed to him.

43 See also *P.Apoll.* 47.4 and 8, mentioning ἰδικὰ προστάγματα, apparently in relation to the *boēthos tou logistēriou*. Furthermore, if the latter were merely the pagarch's subordinate, it would be difficult to comprehend why the Aphroditans so frequently had dealings with him in the Dioskoros papyri, given (as Dioskoros claims) the villagers' fierce resistance to the pagarch's involvement.

44 Lajos Berkes notes in *P.Heid.* XI, p. 120 that it is not currently possible to establish how tasks and duties were divided among the staff even within the *dēmosion logistērion*.

45 *P.Lond.* V 1865 *descr.* (new ed. Gascou & Gonis 2022, no. 5). The writers and secretaries at the administrative level of the *civitas* were no doubt trained in the same circles, and may therefore in similar contexts have adopted similar handwriting. On this type of hand, see *P.Sorb.* II 69, pp. 13–15. Cf. Chapter Three, Section VII for a discussion of this text in the context of the Hermopolite *merides*.

46 Berkes 2017a, 164 n. 282: "An keiner dieser Stellen werden die βοηθοί als Dorf-βοηθοί definiert, und da sie im Namen des in Antaiopolis residierenden Pagarchen quittieren, handelt es sich wohl um βοηθοί des λογιστήριον von Antaiopolis." This statement is used to reject the idea that the

This would entail that the officials signing these receipts (or certificates) on behalf of the pagarchs were attached to and placed in the *dēmosion logistērion* of Antaiopolis rather than in or around the village of Aphrodite—and that they were issuing confirmations long after the payments had actually been made. Analyses of the tax receipts from the Dioskoros and Phoibammon archives cast doubts on this assumption, as the handwriting and subscription patterns suggest that the signatories were closely linked to the payments themselves.[47]

The documents concerning the *dēmosion logistērion* provide evidence to support this point. The *boēthos (tou) logistēriou*, for instance, rather than signing tax receipts as someone else's intermediary, appears regularly as an authority in his own right in these documents. Instead of writing receipts in the name of the pagarchs, he had the authority to use intermediaries himself.[48] One transfer of tax responsibilities (*epistalma tou sōmatismou*) illustrates that the *boēthos tou logistēriou* was not simply part of the *logistērion*, he *was* the *logistērion*.[49] In the Antaiopolite receipts, *hypodektai* and *boēthoi* fulfill comparable roles for different taxes, whereas receipts or certificates from the *logistērion* of Hermopolis suggest that the *boēthos tou logistēriou* managed certain accounts for the *hypodektai* and was thus not on the same administrative level.[50] The formal separation of the *boēthos tou logistēriou* from the business of the pagarchy is, finally, illustrated by an account of civic expenses from Antaiopolis: in this document, the remuneration of the *boēthos tou logistēriou* and expenses for the pagarchy are listed under separate headings.[51]

---

boēthoi in these receipts were village *boēthoi*—which I think they were. These texts and the role of the *boēthoi* in this context are discussed in Section III 2 below.

47 Stern forthcoming (a) and (b).

48 This can be seen in certain documents from the large body of evidence that the Hermopolite *logistērion* has left us: *BGU* XVII 2720 (588/589?), *CPR* VII 29, *P.Berl.Cohen* 20, and *P.Herm.* 85 (all VII). The amounts in these receipts are strikingly low, only in *BGU* XVII 2720 reaching six *keratia* (which is, *cum grano salis*, the most common amount in the Antaiopolite receipts, too). Are these amounts payments to balance or finalize accounts? Moreover, in *P.Aphrod.Reg.* (Aphrodite; 526/527) the *boēthos tou logistēriou* appears (ll. 75 and 162) as an authority in his own right—here for the collection of the *embolē*—and draws remuneration from the village's *dēmosia* (l. 176).

49 *P.Würzb.* 19.3, 15, and 16 (Hermopolis; March 3, 622); Mitthof 1999a, 136; Gascou 1986, 100–101 (= 2008, 226–227). This text comes from the time of the Persian occupation (note the missing regnal formula), but I do not think that this is significant for the question under discussion here.

50 See *CPR* XXIV, pp. 45–46 (mostly concerning Hermopolis) and especially the explanation of *P.Princ.* II 89 (concerning Antaiopolis). A comparable case is *SPP* III^2 43 from Hermopolis, where the *diastoleus* of the *logistērion* issues a receipt for a payment that was effectuated not by the contributor Daniel, but by a certain Georgios, who is probably to be identified with a Georgios who is a βοηθὸς κωμοκατοίκων, i.e., a *boēthos* with responsibility for a particular tax; see the discussion by the editor.

51 *P.Cair.Masp.* I 67057 col. II 10 (Antaiopolis; c. 551/552?): [συν]ή̣θ(ειαι?) βοηθ(οῦ) [λο]γιστηρ(ίου) {λογιστη̣ρ̣(ίου)} ν(ομίσματα) ι̣β̣ (with haplography, according to *BL* I 106). Also in *P.Aphrod.Reg.*

2. *Civic Business in the Countryside*

Even though the pagarchs' main area of authority was the countryside it is evident that they maintained close ties to the civic administration. Not only were they responsible for tax collection from plots taxed as *astika* (literally, "pertaining to the city")[52] but they probably also had their hands on civic land in the countryside. *SB* XX 15016, a receipt in which a *boēthos* confirms a rent payment (*phoros*) to the pagarchs, may illustrate this point:

> From the *endoxotatoi* pagarchs through me, Matoi, *boēthos*, to Menas, the tenant. I have received in full from you the rent (*phoros*) of my third share, which is under you(r care), of the plot that is of the "barren" (*aporos*) (category), called Karkarou, for the tax assessment (*kanōn*) of the eighth indiction, in accordance with the legal force of the assigned? registration (*sōmatismos*), and for your legal security I have made this receipt as it is here. The *endoxotatoi* pagarchs through me, Matoi, *boēthos*, who agrees with this receipt as it is here. The Holy Trinity.[53]

It is generally agreed that in late antique Egypt the line between rents and taxes had blurred due to a mingling of the private and public spheres,[54] and here too the *phoros* payment is linked to the tax assessment of the present indiction. But there is more to it. The land is explicitly in the pagarchs' possession—despite the confusion of the singular and plural number, which is common.[55] It therefore seems unlikely that this document is a record of an ordinary tax payment. Are the pagarchs, consequently, joint

---

176, the *boēthos tou logistēriou*, at a time when Aphrodite was not yet subject to the pagarchy (526/527 CE), receives a salary out of the *dēmosia* of the village of Aphrodite.

52 *P.Cair.Masp.* I 67045; 67046; *SB* XX 14121. All these are tax receipts signed by *hypodektai*.

53 *SB* XX 15016 (Antaiopolite; 559/560). The end of l. 1 should read: βοηθ(οῦ) Μ̣η̣ν̣ᾶ̣ μ̣ι̣σ[θ(ωτῇ); cf. *SB* XX 15017.2 and Marthot 2013, II 114. In ll. 3–4, one must probably restore ἐκ πλ[ή]ρ̣[ο]υ̣[ς] κ[α]τ̣[ὰ] τ̣ὴν τήναμιν (read δύναμιν) τοῦ | προσπε\τ(ω)κ̣ό̣τ̣ο̣ς̣?/ (read προσπεπτωκότος) σωμα(τισμοῦ). There is no room for κ[αὶ πρὸς τ]ὴν, and σώμα(τος) makes little sense in this context; see further Stern forthcoming (a), s.v. Matoi. The name of the *topos* is given in other documents either as "Pkarkarou" or, as here, without the Coptic definite article, as "Karkarou."

54 On Gascou's "rent-tax," see Chapter Three, Section IV and n. 113, where a more nuanced picture is proposed.

55 *SB* XX 15016.1–2: ἐ]δεξάμεν (read ἐδεξάμην) καὶ ἐπλη|ρώθην παρ̣ὰ̣ [σοῦ] τ̣ὸ[ν] φόρο[ν] τοῦ ὑπὸ σ̣ἑ̣ [μο]υ τρίτον (read τρίτου) μέρους τ̣ο̣[ῦ] κτήματος. The phenomenon of singular stylization of such receipts even for plural senders is widespread; see, e.g., P.Mich. inv. 3272.8–9 (ed. Keenan 2012), where the same writer, Matoi, even more blatantly confused the grammatical and logical order; for a different but parallel context, see *SPP* III² 68.1, 3, and 4 (Herakleopolites; late VI–early VII). Ruffini 2011, s.v. Matoi 1 (a) wonders whether [μο]υ may instead be referring to Matoi, but parallels such as *P.Cair.Masp.* III 67327.37–49 show that the nominal issuing party (here, the landowner) is still the subject of the sentence in such cases and referred to by μου (l. 39): the intermediary is a "slave" (*pais*, probably used as a relational term, a humble self-reference) and overseer (*pronoētēs*) and therefore certainly not the owner of the field in question. On the ὑπὸ τὸν δεῖνα formula, see Gascou 1987, 111–113 (= 2008, 256–257).

owners of the land and collecting the rent in their private capacity? That does not seem to be the case either: the pagarchs are not addressed by their personal names but anonymously as a collective—unlike, for instance, to the Arsinoite pagarchs Christophoros and Strategios Stratelates when these appear in documents linked to their estate.[56] In addition, during this eighth indiction of 559/560 CE, no fewer than three pagarchs were in office, including Ioulianos, who is known to have controlled an estate of his own.[57] Finally, the signing *boēthos*, Matoi, is well known and his public role is evident from other documents.[58]

The reference to a registration (*sōmatismos*), which apparently defined the terms of payment, raises another point. *Sōmatismos* (literally, "embodiment," that is, of a legal arrangement) is mostly a technical term for the transfer of tax liabilities. The new owners had to enter their name in the public register through a "commission of registration" (*epistalma tou sōmatismou*), while the former owners had to formally request through a "commission of remission" (*epistalma tou kouphismou*) that their name be removed from the register.[59] In Hermopolis, this register was kept by the *dēmosion logistērion*,[60] and in Oxyrhynchos, by the "bureau of the *exactor*" (*exaktorikē taxis*),[61] whose responsibilities included maintaining land registers.[62] Moreover, the *dēmosios*

---

56 Christophoros and Strategios Stratelates repeatedly appear in private contexts (e.g., *CPR* XIV 11, but also in two unpublished texts, of which Sophie Kovarik makes me aware) and they bear the same patronymic, that is, they were siblings. If we furthermore assume that *SB* XX 15016 is about private rents, then the pagarchs' appearance in the plural would imply that they were joint owners of an *oikos* and therefore had assumed the pagarchy together, something for which there is not yet any evidence from the Thebaid. That officials signing on behalf of their superiors sometimes omit the personal names of these superiors is not the standard pattern, but there are examples dating back as far as the second century (cf. *P.Lond.* II 309.14–19; Kruse 2002, 793). Moreover, the anonymous reference to the office makes little sense in the context of personal ownership.

57 *SB* XVI 12370; *P.Cair.Masp.* I 67060.

58 The role of the *boēthoi* in general and Matoi in particular is discussed in Section III 2.

59 *P.Oxy.* LXXXII, p. 170. *P.Würzb.* 18 (Arsinoites; latter half of IV) is an example of the former, *P.Würzb.* 19 (Hermopolis; March 3, 622) of the latter. This register may be identical to the *dēmosios codex* that appears in five papyri from Aphrodite (*P.Cair.Masp.* I 67097.41; *P.Gascou* 30.11–12; *P.Michael* 40.24–25; 41.23; 42a.19), one of unknown origin (*P.Herm.* 32.10), and two from Petra in the province of Palaestina Salutaris (*P.Petra* III 19.4; V 61.56), all from the sixth century. On the term δημόσιος κώδιξ, see also *P.Petra* V, p. 187 and *P.Gascou*, p. 161.

60 *Epistalma tou sōmatismou*: *P.Laur.* III 77. *Epistalma tou kouphismou*: *P.Würzb.* 19.

61 *Epistalmata tou sōmatismou*: *P.Oxy.* I 126; *P.Oxy.* XVI 1887; *P.Warr.* 3; cf. *P.Oxy.* L 3583 (see l. 4). *Epistalmata tou kouphismou*: *P.Oxy.* LXXXII 5339–5341. Note that *P.Oxy.* L 3583 (444 CE) is *not* addressed to the *exaktorikē taxis* but to the *meris* of the *oikos* of Timagenes through (*dia*) two *boēthoi exaktorias* of the city. These documents' stated purpose is "the security of the *dēmosios logos*," though *P.Warr.* 3 and *P.Oxy.* L 3583 use *dēmosion* only here (the relevant passage is lost in *P.Oxy.* LXXXII 5339 and 5341).

62 Liebeschuetz 2001, 187–188. One may want to add the *caveat* that after 500 CE the *exaktorikē taxis* appears only in the Oxyrhynchite nome; the *exactoria*, however, occurs in the Petra papyri from the sixth century. With the evidence we have, it seems impossible to establish under what

logos—the more abstract fiscal interest of the *civitas*[63]—at times functions as a legal entity for leases of public land, in which cases it is represented by civic or provincial authorities.[64] In the autopract village of Aphrodite, publicly owned land, as well as the registration of tax liabilities, fell under the authority of its own *dēmosios logos*,[65] which was represented by the village *boēthos* or the village headmen (*prōtokōmētai*).[66] But the *dēmosios logos* is not synonymous with the *dēmosion logistērion*: the former is the abstract fiscal interest[67] that may in certain contexts manifest as an authority, while the latter is a concrete institution.[68]

---

exact conditions the bureau of the *exactor* and the *dēmosion logistērion* might have coexisted. Cf. *P.Oxy.* LXXXII 5341.3–4 (Oxyrhynchos; June 16, 575), addressed τῇ ἐξακτορικῇ τάξει τη τε (*sic*) βοηθοῖς | λογιστηρίου. A document from a similar context from Nessana in the province of Palaestina Salutaris, *P.Ness.* III 24 (569 CE), is instead addressed to the *logographos* of the *civitas*, on whom see Section II 3 below.

63 The *dēmosios logos* should not be confused with the formula εἰς λόγον δημοσίων: the latter is simply an alternative to ὑπὲρ δημοσίων in the context of tax payments and, at least in the Antaiopolite tax receipts, depends on the writer's personal style. The form εἰς λόγον δημοσίον (*SB* XX 15013 and 15015) instead of εἰς λόγον δημοσίων, however, is the spelling preferred by the *boēthos* Pninnos, not a reference to the *dēmosios logos*.

64 *P.Cair.Masp.* I 67105 (September 28–October 27, 532) concerns the village territory of Phthla. In *P.Cair.Masp.* I 67103 (September 16, 526), the village is lost. See also *P.Oxy.* LXXXII, p. 144 on land under the *exaktorikē taxis* and the civic management of lands associated with the city council. On the revenues of cities from publicly owned land, see Liebeschuetz 1996, 389, 390 n. 6, and 391. On publicly owned land in villages, cf. Berkes 2017a, 23–24.

65 No *dēmosios logos* of any other village is known, so this is clearly yet another reminder of Aphrodite's pseudo-city administration. Vanderheyden 2015, 152–153 and Keenan 2008a, 291 both equate the status of Aphrodite's *boēthos* with that of a *boēthos logistēriou*, while Zuckerman 2004a, 129–130 does not. No *boēthos logistēriou* from the village is known, however; the instances of a *boēthos logistēriou* in accounts from Aphrodite are all from contexts relating to Antaiopolite officials. In practice, Aphrodite's *boēthos* was certainly comparable to a *boēthos logistēriou*, most notably because, unlike other village *boēthoi*, he was not employed by the pagarch: he figures, for instance, among the signatories of a petition against the pagarch Ioulianos (*P.Cair.Masp.* III 67283 col. II 24).

66 Lease of public land: *P.Cair.Masp.* I 67106 (October 10, 539); the land here is "barren" (l. 11: *aporos*), which is significant. The *boēthos* is the *boēthos* of the village, the title being specified in *P.Cair.Masp.* I 67118.9. Requests for the transfer of tax liabilities (*epistalmata tou sōmatismou*): *P.Cair.Masp.* I 67119 (511/512?); *P.Cair.Masp.* I 67117 (June 25–July 24, 524); *P.Cair.Masp.* I 67118 (September 29–October 28, 547). The proceedings of *P.Cair.Masp.* III 67329, however, refer to a transfer of parcels from an Antaiopolite village to the autopract village of Aphrodite and thus are negotiated before Antaiopolite officials, among them the *boēthos tou logistēriou*.

67 E.g., in *P.Cair.Masp.* I 67001.20; 67002 col. III 14. Cf. the probably synonymous or closely related *dēmosia agora* in *P.Stras.* I 46.6, which takes the same role (and is represented by the same man) as the *dēmosios logos* in the parallels *P.Stras.* I 47.32 and *P.Stras.* I 48.4.

68 The *dēmosios logos* in Hermopolis is at times represented by the *boēthos tou logistēriou* (*BGU* XIX 2788; *P.Würzb.* 19), but at Aphrodite we witness other institutions (*P.Cair.Masp.* I 67103; 67105; *P.Lond.* V 1687; *P.Stras.* I 47–49 and 51), and *P.Würzb.* 19 appears to imply that in Hermopolis, too, *dēmosios logos* and *dēmosion logistērion* were not synonymous, for in ll. 15 and 16 the *logistēri-*

Does the pagarchs' formal possession of land in *SB* XX 15016 relate to public land of this kind? That does indeed seem to be the case, for the plot is described as "of the barren (*tou aporou*)"—a land category whose administration by public authorities is well documented.[69] *Novel* 128 from 545 CE shows more clearly how Justinian's government looked to distribute among local authorities land that was abandoned or whose owners were unable to pay the taxes:

> On any occasion when the owner of any holding whatsoever either does not appear, in the event, or is incapable of meeting the tax payment, that being what has caused the necessity for the impost (…) we command that records are to be made before the *praeses* of the province showing the quality and condition of the said holding and everything found on it, so that the curials, that is to say, collectors, or *vindices* or *officiales* may take it over.[70]

In *SB* XX 15016 the tax liability appears to have been assigned to the pagarchs as the "owners."[71] The plot is administered in the name of the pagarchs by Matoi as village

---

on is named on its own as an institution representing someone. The Basileios archive from the early eighth century yields examples of, perhaps, a pagarch representing the *dēmosios logos*, but always with the *symboulos*, the Arab governor of Egypt, as (formal) intermediary, as, for instance, in *P.Lond.* IV 1494 frg. 2.6–8 (Aphrodite; April 8, 709); but cf. the discussion about Basileios's pagarchy in the Introduction, n. 33. See Berkes 2014, 78–81 for a passage of *P.Köln* XIII 548 (Oxyrhynchites?), although largely restored, in which a pagarch directly represents the *dēmosios logos*; the style and content seem to point to the mid or later seventh century in this case.

69 On the *aporos* category and the management of these parcels by the city and village authorities, see *P.Sorb.* II 69, pp. 28–29 and Johnson & West 1949, 21–22 and 95–96. Cf. *SB* XVI 12370, a tax receipt for "ownerless" (*adespotos*) land, issued by three (!) pagarchs, which is a singular instance. On the *adespotos* category, see Johnson & West 1949, 21 and 97. Cf. *BGU* XIX 2788.8 (Hermopolis; 607/608), addressed to the *dēmosios logos* and certainly referring to some matter of land registration. At the end of the document, the officiating *boēthos tou logistēriou* is said to have chosen a new farmer for a certain plot of land. The fragmentary text mentions that taxes had been overdue and that the former lessee (or owner; the text is not clear) of the plot had died, but it is unknown whether either of these facts was the reason for reassigning the land.

70 Iust. *nov.* 128.8 (translation adapted from Miller and Sarris; cf. Ruffini 2008a, 146): εἴ ποτε δὲ συμβαίη δεσπότην οἱασδήποτε κτήσεως ἢ μὴ φαίνεσθαι ἢ πρὸς τὴν τῶν δημοσίων καταβολὴν μὴ ἀρκεῖν (…) κελεύομεν ὑπομνήματα γενέσθαι παρὰ τῷ τῆς ἐπαρχίας ἄρχοντι δηλοῦντα τὴν ποιότητα καὶ κατάστασιν τῆς αυτῆς κτήσεως καὶ πάντα τὰ ἐν αὐτῇ ἑυρισκόμενα, ἵνα οὕτως αὐτὴν οἱ πολιτευόμενοι ἤγουν ἐξάκτωρες ἢ βίνδικες ἢ ταξεῶται παραλαμβάνουσιν. In this context, *exactor* is a more general term and is not referring specifically to the *exactor civitatis*; cf. Mitthof 2001, 128. The full text of the law demands that the land is "to be made over to owners of estate and village properties" before being handed over to the curial administration, but in *SB* XX 15016 the pagarchs, as argued above, probably do not receive the land in their private capacity.

71 There are—earlier—instances in which *sōmatismos* refers to the tax liabilities of the tenant rather than the owner (see *WB*, s.v. σωματισμός § 2; *P.Fay.* 33), but given that after 371 CE the landowners were responsible for the taxes of their tenants (Liebeschuetz 2001, 184), this seems an unlikely scenario in our case. The use of the word *phoros* may even support the above reconstruction: the *phoros* paid to the pagarchs is technically still rent but substitutes for the taxes the owners have to

boēthos,[72] who was probably employed by the pagarchs to do so.[73] This reconstruction seems to be supported by two land registers from the early Islamic period, in which Karkarou is classified as *astika* land.[74] Karkarou is mentioned in yet another document from the sixth century, featuring a pagarch along with his accountants (*trakteutai*) and, again, a *boēthos*.[75] Although the text is fragmentary, it appears that this group was to oversee, again, *aporos* land and that a land registration of the Karkarou plot was at stake here.

The de facto public character of the "rent" payment from *SB* XX 15016 may also be implied by another rent receipt signed by a certain *pronoētēs* Psates in the name of "the *endoxotatoi* pagarchs," that is, once again on behalf of an anonymous collegium.[76] If this were a private estate, and individual ownership were the essential information, it would seem odd to refer anonymously to the pagarchs, given that the pagarchy was not a lifetime attribute. It is therefore more plausible that these two receipts show us the pagarchs as formal "owners," or rather administrators, of public land they had rented out in this capacity.[77] In this case, the pagarchs rely on a *pronoētēs* ("supervisor"), a private employee that we find so frequently as a "*pronoētēs*, or *hypodektēs*," managing, among other things, taxes for the large estate of the Apiones at Oxyrhynchos.[78]

Another interesting text in this regard is an Antaiopolite lease in which the pagarch Ioulianos leases out a plot "for as long as [I shall be in charge] of the pagarchy of the same city (i.e., Antaiopolis),"[79] which may imply that the land will change ownership

---

pay in lieu of their tenant. The word "assigned" in the text is based on an uncertain new reading (see n. 53 above), but the formal documentary context of the receipt makes the fact as such clear.

72 Dioskoros's complaints that the *boēthos* of Phthla has seized his land, leaving him the tax payments (*P.Cair.Masp.* I 67002 col. I 14–15; *P.Lond.* V 1677.13–16), appear to reflect such a responsibility.

73 Section III 2 below shows that Matoi was most likely a *boēthos* at the village level. Village *boēthoi* were not genuine village officials, but employed by higher authorities for certain localities.

74 *P.Lond.* IV 1419.826 (Aphrodite; 716/717): (ὑπὲρ) κτήμ(α)τ(ος) Καρκάρο(υ) (ὑπὲρ) ἀστικο (read ἀστικῶν) Ἀνταίο(υ); restored in l. 1362. *SB* XX 15099.275 (Aphrodite; 716/717): (ὑπὲρ) κτήμ(α)τ(ος) Καρκάρ[ου under the heading [ἀστικ(ῶν)] Ἀνταίου (l. 273). The link between these texts and *SB* XX 15016 has already been pointed out by Marthot 2013, I 232. She later (II 114) links the *topos* Karkarou tentatively to the village of Phthla, i.e., outside Aphrodite's potentially special area.

75 *SB* XX 14241 (Aphrodite; c. 553?). I am indebted to Yasmine Amory for sharing some insights from her forthcoming new edition of this and other texts. The pagarchs' *trakteutai* are discussed in Section II 3 below.

76 *SB* XX 15014 (Antaiopolite; VI), in which l. 2 should read: παρ̣ὰ̣ σοῦ̣ ἀπ̣ὸ̣ τ̣ῶ̣ν̣ ἐ̣κφ̣ο̣ρ(ίων) ἕκτης ἰνδ(ικτίωνος); cf., e.g., *BGU* XII 2184.1 (Hermopolis; VI).

77 Cf. the *ekphorion* receipt *P.Lond.* III 1072 (Hermopolis; VI), addressed to the Holy Church through the intermediary of the "*pronoētēs* of the share (*meris*) of Hermopolis," and the interpretation by Gascou 1985, 40–41 (= 2008, 162–163).

78 This institution is discussed in Chapter Three, Section IV.

79 Following Lemaire 2010, 398, *PSI* IV 283.9–10 reads: ἐ]φ̣' ὅσον χρόνον . . [± 7] | τ̣ὴν παγαρ̣χείαν τ̣ῆς α̣[ὐτῆ]ς̣ πόλεως, which she translates as "for as long as [we shall be in charge] of the pagarchy of the same city"—without, however, restoring the essential verb. Her reading seems fine to me, though the traces before the lacuna look like *αι* or *αν*. Also possible is delta with a pro-

as a matter of course at the end of Ioulianos's pagarchy.[80] The contract expressly notes that the plots to be leased previously belonged to a now deceased curial, which prompts the intriguing question of whether this is noted here because the plots fell (back?) to the city after the curial's death.[81]

Even though the sample is small, it seems plausible to infer from all these observations that the Antaiopolite pagarchs at some point took over the administration of (some) public land from the civic officials who acted on behalf of the *dēmosios logos*. It is possible, of course, that some allocations or divisions of responsibilities among these institutions simply elude us.[82]

In any event, these documents suggest that the pagarchs sometimes assumed the role of guardians of civic interests in the countryside. With Egypt's municipalization,

---

longed downward stroke; the same appearance of delta can be noted in l. 5: ἐνδοξό̣τ̣[(ατος), l. 13: δια[κειμένας], and l. 16: ἰδίων, although in the latter case the letter's "belly" is fully closed at the top. The restoration δ̣[ιακατέχω], meaning "to hold an office," therefore has its attraction, although it remains hypothetical; cf. *WB*, s.v. κατέχω and *P.Giss.* I 40 col. II 3 (Apollonopolites Heptakomias; ca. 215 CE): ε̣[ἰς τὸ δια]κατέχειν ἢ λα[μβ]ά̣νειν τὰς πολ[ιτι]κ̣ὰ̣ς [τ]ι̣μ̣άς; perhaps *P.Tebt.* I 88.16 as well (Arsinoites; 115–114 BCE). The construction "for as long as I ..." is attested in similar contexts in *P.Grenf.* I 59.5–6 (Antaiopolites or Apollonopolites Heptakomias; V–VI): ἐφ' ὅσον χρόνον γεωγροῦμεν τὸ κτῆμα τῆς σῆς | λαμπρότητος and *P.Horak* 9.16 (Hermopolites; VI): ἐφ' [ὅσο]ν̣ χρόνον γεωργῶ τῶν (αὐτῶν) σου ἀρουρῶ̣ν̣ (see the commentary on the genitive). In *P.Eirene* II 12.13–14 (Herakleopolis; 492): εἰς πάντα τὸν χ̣ρ̣ό̣ν̣ο̣ν̣ τῆς λογιστίας (read λογιστείας) τοῦ προειρη|μένου οἴκου looks quite comparable (the same formula is extant in *CPR* V 17.9–10); note the contrast to *SB* XII 11079.15–16, where the duration is fixed, probably because the duration of the *logisteia* was fixed beforehand (ll. 7–8).

80 The rent is measured τῷ̣ φορικ]ῷ̣ μέτρῳ̣ (l. 24), i.e., probably according to Ioulianos's "private" standard; see Keenan 1985b, 144.

81 On the identification of this man, see Ruffini 2011, s.v. Kuros 16 (which presents a new reading of Kyros's name in *PSI* IV 283 by Florence Lemaire). This Kyros was a *megaloprepestatos politeuomenos* and had ties to Dioskoros's family, which may provide the link to the lessee Phoibammon; see Ruffini's entries (b), (d), and (f). One may point to the *geouchos* Flavius Kyros (Ruffini's Kuros 22) who receives aggregated tax payments from an Aphroditan *boēthos* in *P.Cair.Masp.* I 67049 (535/536?; see n. 170 below), whom I deem to be a likely match, which might support the reconstruction given above. Ruffini speculates that Ioulianos might have been an heir of Kyros's land in *PSI* IV 283. But his entries in my opinion suggest otherwise, as Kyros seems to have long-held ties to Antaiopolis, whereas Ioulianos bears the nickname "the Arsinoite" in *P.Cair.Masp.* I 67024–25 (new ed. Fournet 2018) A' 55 and B 29. Moreover, the fact that *PSI* IV 283.12–13 explicitly states the origin of this plot of land makes it to my mind unlikely that the document concerns the transfer of a regular inheritance. Cf. the case discussed in Fikhman 1974.

82 The recto of *SPP* III 264 (Arsinoites or Herakleopolites; VI), which is very fragmentary, reads as follows: ἐπλήρωσ(ε) ὁ κύρ[ιος – – –] | παγαρχ( ) τὸ ἐνοίκ[ιον – – –] | τῶ(ν) ἀπὸ Φαρμ(οῦ)θ(ι) α [ἕως – – –]. The wording pattern for this type of document makes it quite likely that a pagarch "fully paid" the rent for some place here; cf. *BGU* I 47 and 173 (both Arsinoites; VII–VIII). The lacuna in l. 1 leaves enough space for the personal name and an epithet if one adds the name of the relevant plot in l. 2. The alternative interpretation, namely that the renter is a subordinate "of the pagarchy," is without precedent in such a context; in *P.Cair.Masp.* I 67057 col. II, where this specification occurs, it is required to draw a contrast to other institutions in the same document.

the responsibility for tax collection fell to the cities and their councils. Curial liturgical officials such as the *hypodektai*, *epimelētai*, and *apaitētai* discharged their liturgies under the supervision of the *exactor civitatis*, and at least some of these officials reoccur later under the authority of the pagarch. The evidence for the *exactoria* after 500 CE, though scant, suggests that this institution continued to fulfill a central function in the fiscal process even after the nome-level pagarchy was introduced.[83] This rudimentary *exactoria* was probably confined to the urban center, however,[84] and thus became a sort of anachronistic concession to the councils that acknowledged their former privileges. The *dēmosion logistērion* was still in place; councils and civic administration had not disappeared but were mostly marginalized to a point that literary sources can hold they no longer existed.[85] Social power in the *civitates* was now concentrated in the regime of notables, comprising the bishops, the *possessores*, and the *honorati*. An Oxyrhynchite papyrus from the latter half of the sixth century is illustrative in this regard:[86] in a list of contributions for a bathing house from "the whole city," the pagarchy, shared by two *endoxotatoi*, is only one contributor among many parties, including individual aristocrats, *oikoi*, heirs of aristocrats, and a single village. While the document refers to institutions rather than to geographical entities, it still shows that the pagarchy was only part of the fiscal landscape of the *civitas*, not congruent with it. This may be conceived as part of a continuous process during which the pagarchs took their fiscal and executive authority from the level of the *pagi* to the level of the *civitates*.[87] Certain responsibilities were apparently still granted to the city councils, particularly in regard to tax collection in the urban center, but there is, to my mind, little question that pagarchs like Strategios Paneuphemos and Ioulianos had their say in all fiscal matters, and likely more than that, in their *civitates*, but how these powers were negotiated among the new elites of the cities remains hidden from our view. It is significant in this context that the civic expenses for the pagarchy in mid-sixth-century Antaiopolis were paid out of taxes earmarked for "external" purposes, highlighting the pagarchy's position as related to, but distinct from, civic administration, as the next subsection explains.

3. The Pagarch's "Bureau" in Antaiopolis

There is no direct evidence of an official bureau of the pagarch, if we mean by that an actual building. We are on firmer ground, however, if we take the term *officium* to refer

83 See Chapter One, Section IV on the supposed "ousting" of the *exactor civitatis* by the pagarch.

84 Cf. Liebeschuetz 1996, 394 for a comparable reconstruction—assuming that the "bureau of the *exactor*" is not an Oxyrhynchos-exclusive anachronism.

85 See Tuck 2011, 287 for the sources.

86 *P.Oxy.* XVI 2040 (Oxyrhynchos; 566/567?). This text is discussed in Chapter Three, Section II.

87 Cf., by contrast, the marginalization of civic offices such as that of the *defensor civitatis*, whose tenure lasted five years (*C.J.* I 55.4) until 535 CE but was then reduced to two years (Iust. *nov.* 15; Tuck 2011, 301).

to the entirety of an official's staff.[88] The pagarchs, though often personally engaged in their duties, did not get very involved in day-to-day fiscal operations but instead had various officials and employees carry out the work of keeping accounts and checking individual payments.[89] As with many minor administrative staff in late antique Egypt, little synthetic work has been done on these subordinate officials and employees.[90] Some of the following observations are therefore rather tentative, but may nonetheless illuminate the fiscal network that formed around the pagarchs. An extensive "tax account" (*logos dēmosiōn*) of the city of Antaiopolis dating from the mid-sixth century provides a starting point, although some critical passages are damaged.[91] The document lists the city's expenses, divided into four categories: *annona* (the grain tax, here including some adaerated extraordinary expenses for military expeditions), "*kanonika* and others" (various imperial taxes), *synētheiai* (official salaries, apparently for provincial officials), and, finally, expenses "for the pagarchy." It appears that this document was supposed to be a comprehensive account of taxes due from the city after civic expenses had been settled, and probably covers an entire year.[92] The separate accounting for the pagarchy in this document highlights that the office was both part of the *civitas* and formally separate from the civic administration. The section for the pagarchy is structured as follows:[93]

88 Palme 1999, 100 n. 78 and *nFWB*, s.v. τάξις § 5.

89 *P.Cair.Masp.* III 67295 col. I 9–10: τῶν ἐξ[υ]π̣[ηρ]ετουμένων | [ταῖς παγαρχίαις contains an *exempli gratia* restoration and is therefore not considered here; see Chapter One, n. 71.

90 Cf. Bagnall 2020, 79: "In a papyrologist's dream world, every office would have a recent monograph devoted to it."

91 *P.Cair.Masp.* I 67057. I will focus on the account of the pagarchy; for discussions of various aspects of this text, see Bransbourg 2016, 310–311; Zuckerman 2004a, 54–56; and Johnson & West 1949, 275–285 and 294. We probably owe the survival of this document to Dioskoros who may have brought it home as writing paper from his time working for the provincial administration in Antinoopolis (Gelzer 1913b, 347), but it is unclear whether the list was drawn up in Antinoopolis or had been sent there from Antaiopolis.

92 Gelzer 1913b, 348.

93 *P.Cair.Masp.* I 67057 col. II 24–31:
εἰς λ(όγον) τοῦ ἐπ[...]λογ( ) ν(ομίσματα) μγ
εἰς λ(όγον) τῶν ὑ̣π̣[ο(υ)]ρ̣γ(ῶν) τῆς̣ δ̣ι̣ο̣ι̣κ̣(ήσεως) [τῆς παγα]ρ̣χ(ίας) ν(ομίσματα) ρκ̣[δ κ(εράτια)] ς ∠
τοῖς τρακτ(ευταῖς) [τ]ῆς παγαρχ(ίας) ν(ομίσματα) ν
τῷ ὑποδέκτ(ῃ) τῆς (αὐτῆς) ν(ομίσματα) λς
τῷ λογωγράφῳ̣ (read λογογράφῳ̣) τῆς (αὐτῆς) ...... ν(ομίσματα) ιβ
τοῖς πολιτ(ευομένοις) [(ὑπὲρ)] διδομέ̣ν̣ω̣ν̣ ... προσ̣ώπ[ων]
ν(ομίσματα) λς κ̣(εράτια) [ις]
(γίνεται) ν(ομίσματα) τ[α κ(εράτια)] κβ ∠
Johnson & West 1949, 294 n. 8 compare the total of 301 *nomismata* 22 ½ *keratia* with the 300 *nomismata* that are excluded from a tax reduction in *P.Oxy.* XVI 1907.9–10 (Oxyrhynchos; 574–582) and conclude that that passage refers to the expenses for the Oxyrhynchite pagarchy, but there is nothing to support this claim and the suspiciously rounded sum of 300 *nomismata* (whose purpose, it should be added, is unspecified) seems instead to indicate that this was some kind of guaranteed amount.

On the account of the (singular) *ep*[– – –]*log*( ) 43 *nomismata*.
On the account of the servants of the administration of the pagarchy 124 *nomismata*, 6 ½ *keratia*.
To the *trakteutai* of the pagarchy 50 *nomismata*.
To the *hypodektēs* of the same (pagarchy) 36 *nomismata*.
To the *logographos* of the same (pagarchy) [– – –] 12 *nomismata*.
To the curials for the [– – –] people nominated[94] 36 *nomismata*, 16 *keratia*.
Total 301 *nomismata*, 22 ½ *keratia*.

The order of these entries does not appear to reflect the amounts involved. The amount of thirty-three *nomismata* for a single *hypodektēs* stands out, however, especially in comparison with the fifty *nomismata* for two or more *trakteutai* (Lat. *tractatores*) or with the twelve *nomismata* for a single *logographos*, and may therefore indicate a rough hierarchy.

The first entry remains a mystery. It contains the largest individual amount, and since all other entries refer to people, the fragmentary line was probably referring to an official rather than an institution—but which one? The palaeography is not conclusive.[95]

The second entry is likewise prefixed with "on the account of," and the "servants of the administration of the pagarchy" are probably staff appointed by the pagarch personally.[96] This interpretation is supported by the fact that the *trakteutai*, the *hy-*

94 On the use of δίδωμι for nominating people to liturgical offices, see *WB*, s.v. and Lewis 1997, 59. The archive of Basileios from the early eighth century preserves lexically close parallels of πρόσωπα for inhabitants assigned to a διοίκησις, e.g., in *P.Berl.Frisk* 6.18–19 and *P.Lond.* IV 1345.5–6; cf. *P.Lond.* IV 1343.3 and *P.Ross.Georg.* IV 6.10.

95 One might be tempted to see the *epimelētēs* ("caretaker") of the *dēmosion logistērion* here; cf. *P.Oxy.* I 125.3 (560 CE) and *P.Got.* 9.3–5 (564 CE), which are both from Oxyrhynchos and concern the same man; see also *P.Oxy.* I 126 (572 CE), in which the same man is instead addressed as *epimelētēs* of the city of Oxyrhynchos and then as the *epimelētēs* of the *oikos* of Theon, suggesting that the "house of Theon"—or, rather, the *oikoi* now responsible for its share—staffed the *epimeleia* of the *dēmosion logistērion*. But note that in *P.Cair.Masp.* I 67057 col. II 10 (with *BL* I 106), the *boēthos logistēriou* appears under the heading of *synētheiai*, not under that of the pagarchy. Alternatively, an *epikeimenos* may be conceivable. However, while επ seems certain, the lacuna probably does not exceed two letters, and one can in fact spot traces on the photo. The writer started the lambda with a connecting stroke from a preceding letter that is lost in the "lacuna," which appears to rule out an abbreviation beforehand. I doubt that an official called ὁ ἐπί is hidden here.

96 *P.Cair.Masp.* I 67057 col. II 25: τῶν ὑ̣π̣[ο(υ)]ρ̣γ(ῶν) τῆς δ̣ι̣ο̣ι̣κ̣(ήσεως) [τῆς παγα]ρ̣χ(ίας), although the reading looks doubtful; cf. the same editor's *exempli gratia* restoration of the pagarchy in *P.Cair.Masp.* III 67295 col. I 10 (see Chapter One, n. 71). Consulting the online image, I doubt that there is enough space in the last lacuna for τῆς; one can spot, however, traces of π̣α̣γ̣α̣. Furthermore, while the first τη (*sic*) seems clear and δ̣ι̣ο̣ι̣κ̣ possible, I have difficulties spotting traces of ς in between. However, the fact that officials are to hire their own staff is attested in, e.g., *P.Oxy.* VI 904.3–4 (Oxyrhynchos; V), according to which a liturgist for the *riparia*, responsible for maintaining public security, promised to provide his substitute with servants, messengers, and

podektēs, the *logographos*, and the unidentified official of the first entry are each listed with their own entry and are thus apparently tied to the office rather than to the actual incumbent.[97] These servants were presumably mainly officials or assistants working at lower levels, such as local clerks or *boēthoi* (literally, "assistants"). It was common for personal staff such as the *boēthoi* to be partially remunerated by the local population.[98] But there also must have been a number of clerks and secretaries in the pagarch's bureau hidden behind this entry. In the Senouthios archive from the first years after the Arab conquest, Federico Morelli has identified at least twenty-four different hands in documents from the office of the pagarch Athanasios,[99] and although not all of these writers were working at the same time, this does illustrate that the pagarchs' clerical staff must have been far more numerous than their mentions in the documents appear to suggest.

Trakteutai were accountants at various administrative levels[100] and our list shows that there were at least two *trakteutai* "of the pagarchy."[101] Their role appears to have been essentially that of tax clerks rather than collectors, as apparent in one agreement where a subcontractor assures his superior, certainly a village *boēthos*:[102]

> (I assure you I will) draw up a full calculation (*logopoiia*) and (effectuate) the formal fulfillment (*apoplērōsis*) of the aforesaid *dēmosia* and other payments in the presence of the aforementioned pagarchs and their *trakteutai*.[103]

---

guards for the work on the ground, the difference being that in our case these men are (partially?) remunerated from civic funds.

97 The signature patterns in the tax receipts issued in the name of pagarchs conform to this hypothesis; see Section III 3 below.

98 See generally Berkes 2017a, 146–147 and Zuckerman 2004a, 140. *SPP* III^2 furnishes numerous instances of this phenomenon, e.g., no. 22 + 84. For the *boēthoi* in particular, see Berkes 2017a, 161–162 and Section III 2 below.

99 See *CPR* XXXVI, pp. 23–35.

100 *P.Sijp.*, pp. 236–237; Zuckerman 2004a, 124–127.

101 *P.Cair.Masp.* I 67058 col. III (Aphrodite; 549/550?) is part of a collection of accounts similar to *P.Cair.Masp.* I 67057, but for the autopract village. It has separate entries for payments to two *trakteutai* (col. III 3 and 8); the first payment is specified as (ὑπὲρ) συνηθειῶ[ν], the latter is not; both *trakteutai* receive the same amount of five *nomismata*. The recipients are, according to Zuckerman 2004a, 40–42, members of the unit of the Numides. Bell (*P.Lond.* V, p. 212), however, took the one in l. 3 to be the *trakteutēs* of the pagarch.

102 The editor already suspected that the superior was a *boēthos*, which finds support in the contexts in which village *boēthoi* appear (see Section III 2 below). Cf. also *P.Oxy.* I 125.7–8, which concerns a man in need of a surety in order to become *diadochos* ("deputy") to a village *boēthos* for one year.

103 *P.Lond.* V 1660.20–23 (Antaiopolites; c. 553?): ὡς πᾶσαν λογοποιείαν (read λογοποιίαν) θέσθαι καὶ ἀποπλήρωσιν τῶν | εἰρη[μένων] δ̣η̣μ̣ο̣σ̣ίων κα[ὶ] ἑτέρων δομάτων ἐγγὺς τῶν προλεχθέντων | παγάρχων καὶ τρακτευτῶν αὐτῶν.

In these lines, the subcontractor lays out the procedure that would usually apply to his superior, the (actual) *boēthos*: the collected amounts were delivered to the pagarchs and their auditing *trakteutai*, who held the *boēthos* accountable. A Hermopolite tax receipt, though possibly from the early Islamic period, illustrates the procedure by showing its result: a pagarch, represented by his *trakteutēs*, issues a tax receipt to a village *boēthos* who has turned in the *eumeneia* (official salaries) he collected from his village.[104] Note that the *eumeneia* is also part of the agreement made in the aforementioned contract.[105] Another Hermopolite tax receipt signed by a *trakteutēs* in the name of a pagarch is for the *embolē*.[106] The receipt is issued to someone's heirs, and we might be dealing with a later confirmation of payment to a taxpayer in this case. Yet since this document relates to the same administrative level as the other Hermopolite *trakteutēs* receipts just mentioned, these heirs might also have been the representatives of an *ousia* that had its *embolē* contributions handled through the pagarch's office.

The second-largest individual payment is given to the *hypodektēs* of the pagarchy, who is listed by himself. The *hypodektai* were "receivers" of taxes and are therefore discussed in the following section of this chapter.

Logographoi, who dealt with with financial matters, served the staff of various officials from the time of Diocletian onward.[107] In our Antaiopolite account for the pagarchy, the *logographos* is granted the lowest individual contribution but was obviously important enough to receive an individual entry. It is puzzling that we do not find the pagarchs' *logographos* in any other document from the Byzantine period, perhaps due to terminological inconsistency: in one receipt from the early Islamic period, the same Ieremias who is identified in the beginning as a *logographos* and intermediary for the pagarch signs at the bottom of the document as "Ieremias, *notarius*."[108] The term *notarius* might thus be a marker of profession rather than an official position. In a "list of vouchers from a Byzantine provincial office," a *notarius* receives the substantial amount of more than twenty-seven *nomismata*, whereas the *logographos* in the same document has to content himself with about three *nomismata*.[109] Another text from the early Islamic period suggests that a *logographos* (in this case, of the *dēmosion lo-*

---

104 *P.Lond.* V 1753; for a discussion of the date, see the Catalog, s.v. Ioannes (Hermopolis).

105 *P.Lond.* V 1660.9.

106 *P.Lond.* V 1865 *descr.* (VI–VII), for the text of which see Gascou & Gonis 2022, no. 5. The document is certainly from Hermopolis, as is suggested by the name of the *trakteutēs*, Pkylis, and made certain by the occurrence of the formulae ἐπὶ ṭ[όπου ἐμβολῆς] in l. 3 and μέτρ(ῳ) Ἀθην(αίῳ) in l. 5. On this text, see also Section II 1.

107 Wipszycka 1971, 112–113; *P.Sijp.*, pp. 233–234.

108 *SB* VI 9144.1–2 (Hermopolites; after 641): Φλ(αύιος) Ἰωάννης σὺν θ(εῷ) πάγαρχ(ος) δι' ἐμοῦ Ἰερεμία | λογογρ(άφου) and l. 6: Ἰερεμία(ς) νοτάριο(ς).

109 Traianos Gagos and James Keenan suggested based on *P.Sijp.* 35 that the term *logographos* could have been used to designate the same types of writers as, e.g., *exceptores* or *tachygraphoi*, given that these do not show up in this text (*P.Sijp.*, pp. 233–234). The authors refer to the equation *logographos* = *notarius* in *SB* VI 9144 (see the previous note) but do not comment on the fact that the two positions are mentioned separately in *P.Sijp.* 35.

gistērion) was not entitled to sign tax receipts—or in this case, rather, certificates of payment or copies of the receipts—on his own,[110] but in another one, a *logographos* of unknown affiliation does exactly this, though for extraordinary surcharges (*proskairoi*) and issued to his own *geouchos*, so this may have been a documentary exception.[111] This illustrates that there were a variety of *logographoi* in different institutions, and therefore the *logographos tou logistēriou* and the *logographos* of the pagarchy were probably not one and the same post.[112]

Finally, the Antaiopolite curials (*politeuomenoi*) apparently nominated (and appointed?) peers for several lower liturgical posts connected to the pagarchy, who were collectively paid significantly less than the pagarchy's "servants" in the second entry.[113] Like the "servants," these curial officials will presumably have acted, however, as a local arm of the pagarch and as clerks in his office. The available evidence does not allow for a clearer distinction.

In short, we may envision the pagarchs' bureau being staffed by the *hypodektēs*, who collected certain taxes and appears to have been more or less frequently present in the villages as well, several *trakteutai*, who kept track of the sums coming in from the various local collections, notably via the *boēthoi*, and the *logographos*, who drafted documents and generally organized correspondence, though his precise role is less clear. Two receipts from the bureau of the pagarch of Hermopolis show us village *boēthoi* delivering the amount collected from the villages to the pagarchy.[114] In one of these papyri, possibly from the early Islamic period, a *trakteutēs* serves as intermediary for the pagarch for the issuing of the receipt to the *boēthos*,[115] but the second one, certainly Byzantine, appears to be personally signed by the pagarch.[116] A fragmentary list of expenses

110 *P.Herm.* 85 (unknown origin; VII) has a *logographos* representing the *boēthos logistēriou* in a receipt/certificate for the *annona* (l. 2: ἀννώνῃ).

111 *BGU* III 799 (unknown; VII–VIII), addressed to a landowner (*geouchos*).

112 Some variety among the *logographoi* is also suggested by *CPR* XIX 39 (September 28–October 27, 542 or 557?), in which the *logographos* is an Aurelius, not a Flavius. Cf. the *logographos* of a *civitas* who is addressed directly (i.e., not as an intermediary) in *P.Ness.* III 24 (Palaestina Salutaris; 569) and in a function (he receives an *epistalma tou kouphismou*) that may make him equal to the homonymous *logistērion* official in Egypt.

113 Jean-Luc Fournet (1999, 567) quotes this line in connection with an interpretation by Roger Rémondon according to which *prosōpa* may refer to the arrival of the imperial images of Justin II in Antaiopolis. See Chapter Six, Section III on *P.Aphrod.Lit.* IV 17, which refers to the arrival of Justin's images in Antinoopolis.

114 It is also conceivable that the money was not actually processed by the pagarchs' staff but simply credited to the accounts of the various subordinate officials. Both receipts, discussed below, are for payments of multiple *nomismata*, representing a considerably higher amount than the Antaiopolite receipts issued to individual taxpayers. Consequently, the amounts in both receipts probably represent aggregated tax payments from multiple payers.

115 *P.Lond.* V 1753 (VII); see n. 104 above.

116 *BGU* XII 2196.3 (VI): Δωρόθεος στοιχεῖ μοι, κτλ. The different hand cannot be attributed to a change of style by the same writer. Note how the δεκα has been left out in ll. 4 *and* 5 but is correct in l. 3: apparently, the signatory believed that the paid amount comprised only seven *keratia*,

probably mentions papyrus rolls in connection to the pagarchy and thus probably relates to their supply.[117] We therefore may have to assume an actual bureau in which tax revenues were accounted for and allocated to the various beneficiaries at the village, city, provincial, and higher levels. In this bureau, the pagarchs also had their fiscal reports (*anaphorai*) drawn up for the provincial officials.[118] Justinian's *Edict* 13 proclaims that pagarchs may be removed from office if they are "fraudulent in regard to the auspicious grain shipment (*sitopompia*) or in regard to what has been paid for the freight charges and for local expenditures," which we can assume delineated the pagarch's responsibility beyond the city level.[119] The evidence does not provide more detail, and the reality was certainly more complex—but acknowledging that ancient administration was far from being rigidly compartmentalized, this reconstruction is probably not too far from the truth.

---

which he writes twice, instead of seventeen as stated in the upper part of the receipt. A pagarch, Menas Scriniarius, also certainly signed on the verso of *P.Cair.Masp.* I 67060, an internal administrative letter.

117 *P.Mich.* XV 742.14–15 (unknown; VI): (ὑπὲρ) χάρτ(ου) εἰς τ̣ὰ̣ς̣ π̣ρα[. .]ιοτ .ηρ . . . . | παγαρχ( ) . [.]η. . [.]τιπ . . . . ( ) νο(μισμάτια) [– – –]; cf. (ὑπὲρ) χαρτί(ων) in *P.Cair.Masp.* I 67058 col. I 5. The indent at the beginning of l. 15 signals that the two lines belong together. It is possible but far from certain that the *endoxotatos stratēlatēs* in l. 3 is the pagarch whose pagarchy is probably referred to in l. 15. In that case, the text very likely comes from the Arsinoite nome, since it must be from the Byzantine period—see the use of the term χωρίον in connection with a *pragmateutēs* in l. 1, that is, as "vineyard," not as the later fiscal unit—and since the Byzantine pagarchs of the Fayum before 623 CE whom we know were all *endoxotatoi stratēlatai*; on the latter argument, see Chapter Five, Section V 4. On the discussion about the translation of χάρτης as "papyrus roll," see the references in Rendsburg 2017, 151–152. For the alternative reading (ὑπὲρ) χαρτ(ουλαρίου) in l. 14, see *P.Louvre* III, p. 284.

118 *P.Mich.* XI 624.9, cf. 16 and 28 (mid-V–early VI), on which see the Catalog, s.v. Antiochos & Theon (Arcadia); this document comes from the Arcadian provincial administration. The pagarchs in *P.Cair.Masp.* I 67068 might have been present in Antinoopolis, the provincial capital of the Thebaid, to deliver (and defend) such a report; see the Catalog, s.v. Anonymous pagarchs (Thebaid). The *typoi* ("records") of a pagarchy that figure in *P.Oxy.* XVI 1829 are perhaps comparable to these *anaphorai*; see the Catalog, s.v. Anonymous pagarch (Arcadia). See also *SPP* VIII 1028, which appears to relate to a pagarch dealing with an *advocatus fisci* connected to the provincial level (cf. *P.Cair.Masp.* I 67057 col. II 23); see the Catalog, s.v. Ammonios (Hermopolis?). See Haensch 2013, 344–345 on the imperial context of the monthly reports that local officers had to submit to the governors, and the reports that the governors in turn had to submit to the praetorian prefects.

119 Iust. *ed.* 13.25, speaking of the Thebaid. The parallel in Chapter 12 for the two Aegypti reveals a similar construction: "the grain (*siton*) or the freight charges (*naula*) or the other taxes (*dēmosia*) pertaining to the causes stated, or for local expenditures."

III. Tax Collection on the Ground

This section elaborates on how the business of the pagarchy was carried out at the lowest level, in the maybe 2,000 to 2,500 villages and uncountable hamlets of late antique Egypt. This task is complicated by the fact that each tax payment—and the processing of each payment—involved multiple interconnected variables, and any conclusion drawn here may be valid only for specific contexts:[120] Who paid? For whose account (*onoma*)? How much did they pay? Which tax was it for? Who was the recipient? At what administrative level? In what region? At what time of the year? In what period? Changing any of these variables potentially entails others changing, too. And many of these connections are opaque, not least because we only have access to a small fraction of the documentation that was once produced in late antique Egypt.

As for the pagarchy, much of the evidence in this section comes from the Antaiopolite nome. In the archives of Dioskoros and Phoibammon we find a large number of tax receipts, many of which were formally issued by the pagarchs through various representatives. This representation is visible in the final confirmation clauses and signatures, which take the form "the pagarch(s) N.N. through me (*di' emou*), N.N.," followed by a verb of confirmation or approval. Unlike the two Hermopolite receipts issued by pagarchs to village *boēthoi* that were mentioned at the end of the previous section, the extant Antaiopolite receipts from pagarchs were issued to individual taxpayers. The pagarchs did not personally oversee the handover of such receipts to individuals; rather, these documents were routinely drafted in local bureaus or on the spot.[121] The intermediary signatories of these receipts, and thus the "actual issuers," are varied in nature. The most frequent are *boēthoi*, followed by *hypodektai* and *notarii*. Numerous signatories sign with only their name and do not mention their official capacity. A *singularis*, a *pronoētēs*, and a *presbyteros* and *dioikētēs* occur only once each. Based on the pattern of dates and signatures in the Antaiopolite tax receipts, most of these signatories must have been agents who were locally active in the villages.[122] Starting from these observations, the pagarchy's rank and file can be outlined in some detail. The resulting picture will, of necessity, be rooted in a very specific Antaiopolite context—namely, that documented in the family papers of Dioskoros of Aphrodite—but this material is complemented by evidence from other nomes.[123]

---

120 See the Introduction, Section VI.

121 Such "local bureaus" might in practice have consisted of a desk the tax collector or a secretary would set up temporarily when in town.

122 See the overview in Table 1 in Section III 3 below.

123 Because of Aphrodite's unique—or at least unusual—administrative status, observations about the evidence from the Dioskoros archive often raise the question of whether we are dealing with a special case. The receipts from pagarchs do not, however, solely concern the village of Aphrodite. Indeed, while the connection to the neighboring village of Phthla is made explicit in several receipts, only one makes specific reference to Aphrodite (this is explained further in Section III 1 below). Non-Antaiopolite sources are discussed in Section III 4.

1. *The* Hypodektai

The account of civic expenses quoted earlier shows the pagarchy's *hypodektēs* (literally, "receiver") being remunerated by the city of Antaiopolis.[124] Is this "*hypodektēs* of the pagarchy" the same official as the city *hypodektēs* who frequently appears in the papyri?[125] The city *hypodektai* were liturgical officials, probably appointed for one year, and were the major receivers of tax payments at the level of the *civitates*.[126] In general, they are seen distributing and transferring the taxes collected at lower levels, for instance, by *sitologoi, apaitētai, boēthoi, kōmarchai*, and *prōtokōmētai*, to higher branches of the fiscal network.

So, again, are the *hypodektēs* of the pagarchy and the city *hypodektēs* in fact one and the same position? The small amounts the *hypodektai* sign for in the name of the pagarchs would seem to suggest otherwise: four of the seven extant receipts list amounts from 10 ½ to as low as 2 ½ ⅓ *keratia* and consequently certainly refer to individual payments from a single taxpayer.[127] What seems clear is that some *hypodektai* were at least occasionally active at the local level in villages.[128] It has been disputed whether there were *hypodektai* "of" villages; much of the evidence comes from the village of Aphrodite, which is known to have possessed rudimentary city institutions despite its nominal village status.[129] But even discounting the Aphrodite evidence, we find explicit

124 *P.Cair.Masp.* I 67057 col. II 24–31; see Section II 3 above.

125 This identification is proposed by the editor of *CPR* XXIV (p. 41). But a terminological fuzziness between different hierarchical levels is ubiquitous in Byzantine administration, as will also be evident in the case of the *boēthoi* in the next subsection.

126 On the *hypodektai*, see Mitthof 2001, 108–119 and *CPR* XXIV, p. 41 with earlier literature. See also n. 129 below on Aphrodite's *hypodektēs*. On the length of tenure, see *CPR* XXIV, p. 41 and cf. *P.Petra* III 25.2 (Palaestina Salutaris; 559): ὑποδέκτῃ τῆς παρούσης ἑβδόμης ἰνδ(ικτίωνος). Some liturgists were partially remunerated; see n. 228 below.

127 See *P.Cair.Masp.* I 67045 (10 ½ *keratia*); *P.Cair.Masp.* I 67047 (7 *keratia*); *SB* XX 14121 (2 ½ ⅓ *keratia*); *SB* XXIV 15975 (8 + 3 ½ *keratia*). By contrast, *P.Cair.Masp.* I 67046 (2 *nomismata*, 10 *keratia*) looks like an aggregated payment. *P.Cair.Masp.* II 67228 appears to comprise a larger payment as well, based on new readings that require more discussion than can be provided here. *P.Vat.Aphrod.* 16A is too damaged to determine the amount. The various *hypodektai* are consistent in noting the installments *(katabolai)* that the payments were made for during the indiction, so these do not seem to be summary certificates for entire tax years.

128 *CPR* XXIV, pp. 42–43.

129 Tost 2012 demonstrated this using the example of the *riparii*, the security officials of the *civitas*. See Zuckerman 2004a, 180–182 on Aphrodite's *(chryso)hypodektēs*, who in *P.Hamb.* III 230 (Antinoopolis; mid-VI) is referred to as the Aphroditans' "own" *hypodektēs* (l. 8: ἰδίου ὑποδέκτου), an expression that marks a contrast with the city of Antaiopolis in that same line, at a time when the village was not subject to the pagarchy. Consequently, Aphrodite's *hypodektēs*, who paid directly to the provincial treasury, should be conceived of essentially as a city, not a village, *hypodektēs*, as Zuckerman 2004a, 181 also seems to suggest. Cf. *P.Petra* III 19.1 (Palaestina Salutaris; 539/540): χρ[υ]συποδέκταις τῆσδε τῆς μητροπόλεως.

instances of *hypodektai* "of" villages in numerous Fayum papyri.[130] It has been suggested that these are "elliptical locution[s]" and that the *hypodektai* mentioned there were still city officials, but the argument for this conclusion rests on fairly flimsy grounds.[131]

Still, a conclusive link between the *hypodektai* mentioned in the pagarchs' receipts and the city *hypodektēs* can be found in a receipt, or certificate, that is without parallel in this form:

> Apollos, son of Dioskoros, has given through Phoibammon for the *diagraphon* of the 2nd indiction three and a half *keratia* in gold, that is, 3 ½ *keratia* and nothing more than that, and I am willing to hand you the receipt of the *hypodektēs* of the city and to take back mine. I, Petros, *diastoleus*, agree.[132]

---

130 E.g., in *SB* XXVI 16718 (late VI–early VII), *SPP* VIII 953, 954, and *SPP* III² 23 (all VI). In *SPP* VIII 1040.1 (VI) two (considerations of space seem to exclude more than that) *hypodektai* of the village of Magais and of (the Arsinoite village) Hermopolis occur (see the correction by Palme 1989, 248 n. 202), but it is unclear whether both *hypodektai* were responsible for both villages or whether one was responsible for Magais and the other for Hermopolis. Note that in *P.Prag.* I 68.3 (VII–VIII), however, this phrase must be corrected to Μαγαίδος καγκ(έλλῳ) (*SPP* III² pt. V, p. 193). See also *SPP* III² 7 (VII), in which a *hypodektēs* receives the remuneration for a *symmachos* from a village scribe; and *SPP* III² 23 verso (VI?) for a *hypodektēs* of Kaminoi, a village known to have been under the pagarchy.

131 The editor of *CPR* XXIV discards evidence for a village *hypodektēs* of (Roman) Karanis on p. 42 and in n. 20 by referring to arguments made in *P.NYU* I, pp. 10–11, from where the above quote is taken. But the sources cited by the editor of *P.NYU* I do not support his argument. He cites *P.Cair.Isid.* 11.56 (312) as an analogy for his hypothesis, translating ἀποδέκταις Καρανίδος (usually, "*apodektai* of Karanis") as "*apodektai* for Karanis," i.e., for Karanis among others, but the text does not seem to support his case for the "elliptic" nome *apodektai*. Quite the contrary, it features one *apodektēs* of another village (l. 57), and even two *apodektai* "of the city" (l. 59). Moreover, the "*apodektai* of the harbor" (referred to in *P.NYU* I, p. 10) were clearly not nome *apodektai*, as shown by *P.Cair.Isid.* 47.1, 15, and 38–39, in which two collegia for different harbors occur within the same nome. For the *hypodektai*, *P.NYU* I, p. 10 n. 1 refers to *P.Hamb.* I, p. 198 n. 2 to make the case that *P.Hamb.* I 56 col. VI 28 (Aphrodite; late VI–early VII) shows that the *hypodektēs* who drew up that list "collected from more than one village." But that does not seem plausible. The relevant passage refers to a contribution π(αρὰ) τῶν λειτουρ(γῶν) κώμ(ης) Θμο̣νε̣χθη (a new reading I shall explain with more context elsewhere) and states only that some *leitourgoi*—possibly guards; cf. *P.Lond.* V 1661.12: λ]ειτουργῶν \ἤτοι φυλ̣[άκ]ω̣ν/—of Thmonachte (in the *TM* spelling), Aphrodite's neighboring village, paid their professional contributions (cf. Rémondon 1965, 418–419) to the village account of Aphrodite; the passage does not show that the *hypodektēs* who drew up that list was also responsible for Thmonachte as a village, which is also obvious from the fact that no other contributions besides the one from the *leitourgoi* appear. We cannot say whether *P.Hamb.* I 56 dates from the time of Aphrodite's *autopragia*—in which case the *hypodektēs* would be Aphrodite's own *hypodektēs* as a result of its pseudo-city administrative regime (cf. *P.Hamb.* III 230)—or from a later period when Aphrodite was subject to the pagarchy (see Chapter Six, Section III), but in any case *P.Hamb.* I 56 should not be used to make a point about the existence of "regular" village *hypodektai*.

132 *P.Princ.* II 89 (553/554 CE?); see especially *BL* III 150 on l. 1 and *BL* VI 118 on l. 4. The writer wrote the usual symbol for (ὑπέρ) in l. 1, although the document template requires δ(ιά).

In her seminal study of the *dēmosion logistērion*, Ewa Wipszycka reconstructs the context of this document in accordance with the extant legal instructions.[133] Before this certificate was written, Phoibammon would have paid the *diagraphon* in the name of Apollos, for which he obtained a receipt from the collecting *hypodektēs*.[134] Subsequently, Phoibammon brought this first receipt, certainly along with others, to Antaiopolis in order to have his payment properly registered in the accounts of the *dēmosion logistērion*. As he, for some reason, needed proof of payment, the *diastoleus* of the *logistērion* issued him an official confirmation, which is the above certificate, or (second) receipt. The *diastoleus* declares that he would be willing to hand over the first, original receipt if needed, implying that the original receipt had been properly registered in the *logistērion* and, consequently, that Phoibammon had paid the tax; "mine" in the above translation is thus referring to the very document it appears in.[135] One can hardly avoid the conclusion that the "*hypodektēs* of the city" who is mentioned here is the same type of official as, for instance, the *hypodektēs* Phoibammon to whom the taxpayer Phoibammon paid for the *diagraphon* in Apollos's name in one of the tax receipts:

> Apollos, son of Dioskoros, has given through Phoibammon for the *dēmosia* of the third installment (*katabolē*) of the third indiction eight *keratia*, that is, 8 *keratia*. The *endoxotatoi* pagarchs through me, Phoibammon, *hypodektēs*: I have issued this receipt as it is above. For the *diagraphon* three and a half *keratia* in the full standard, that is, 3 ½ *keratia*.[136]

Although this particular specimen might have been a copy issued on the spot, this receipt was the kind of document that the taxpayer Phoibammon would have brought to the *logistērion* and whose delivery the *diastoleus* Petros confirmed in the receipt/certificate quoted earlier.

Yet another point links the "receipt *hypodektai*" to the city level.[137] The tax titles of the receipts reveal the striking pattern that whenever the *dēmosia* are specified, *hypodektai* issue receipts for *astika* payments,[138] whereas receipts for *kōmētika* payments

---

133 Wipszycka 1971, 115–116. On the payment and certification procedures that *P.Princ.* II 89 illustrates, see also Palme in *CPR* XXIV, pp. 38–53; Mazza 1995, 214–215; and Gascou 1986, 100 n. 26 (= 2008, 227 n. 26).

134 On the *diagraphon* or *diagraphē*, see Zuckerman 2004a, 44 and *P.Gascou*, p. 69. It will also be discussed by Loreleï Vanderheyden in the forthcoming *P.Aphrod.Let.Copt.* I.

135 The procedure described in the document is certainly a hypothetical one, and the *diastoleus* was in practice never forced to produce the original receipt, though in theory he was supposed to.

136 *SB* XXIV 15975 (554/555 CE).

137 All *hypodektai* sign with elaborate paraphs and frequently use technical shorthand. This is consistent with the view that they were well-educated men from the administrative center of Antaiopolis, presumably members of the curial class. Compare the clumsy writing and nonstandard spellings by Matoi, the *boēthos* discussed in the next subsection.

138 *P.Cair.Masp.* I 67045; *P.Cair.Masp.* I 67046; *SB* XX 14121. The *dēmosia* are not specified in the *hypodektēs* receipts *P.Cair.Masp.* I 67047 and *SB* XXIV 15975. In *P.Cair.Masp.* II 67228 and *P.Vat.Aphrod.* 16A, the relevant part of the texts did not survive. The village territory at issue is

are issued by *boēthoi*.[139] The *astika*—literally, "(things) pertaining to the city"—were originally taxes on land held by inhabitants of the city, while the *kōmētika*, "(things) pertaining to the village," were taxes on land held by villagers; but these categories soon became ossified: "once *astika*, always *astika*," even if there was a change of ownership.[140] The specification of the city in the tax title—as "*dēmosia astika* of Antaiopolis," for instance—is certainly why the *hypodektai* in these receipts do not bear a specification. The *hypodektēs* receipts do not indicate to which village circumscription the *astika* land that was paid for belonged; it would, however, be an enormous coincidence if the *hypodektēs* receipts were all from Aphrodite, given that between eight and ten out of eleven "noncodex receipts" issued by *boēthoi* concern the neighboring village of Phthla.[141] Even though the sample is small, the reason for so clear a pattern cannot be the "accident of preservation" of the papyri. The responsibility of a *hypodektēs* for the *dēmosia* on *astika* lands in the village was therefore certainly not unique to Aphrodite. Why, then, were the two similar entries for the grain tax (*embolē*) in the codex receipts—written by the *hypodektēs* Zacharias—not signed by him in the name of the pagarchs?[142] There are three possible explanations. First, these receipts may show that Aphrodite still had its own *hypodektēs*, who assumed this role that was usually held by the village scribes in other villages. Second, it may have been irrelevant whether the signatories signed in their own name or explicitly, using *dia*, as an intermediary.[143] Third, it may be significant that these receipts do not acknowledge the payment, but rather the shipping of the grain tax; the other Antaiopolite receipts of this kind, all signed by

never mentioned because the tax title always refers to the *civitas* Antaiopolis. For the link to the *astika*, see also *P.Lond.* V 1672 (Aphrodite?; VI), an account of expenses with an entry (ὑπὲρ) τοῦ ὑποδέκτ(ου) (ὑπὲρ) συνηθιῶν (read συνηθειῶν) | τῷν ἀστ̣ι̣κ(ῶν) νο(μισμάτια) δ (ll. 7–8), though it is not clear what exactly this is supposed to mean. The editor suggested that this amount was paid for "extras" linked to the collection of the *astika*.

139 *P.Gen.* IV 193; *P.Lond.* V 1665; *P.Lond.* V 1666; *SB* XVI 12370; *SB* XX 15013.1–3 and 4–7; *SB* XX 15015.1–5 and 6–9.

140 On the character of the *astika* and *kōmētika*, see Gascou 1987, 113–114 (= 2008, 257–258, also pointing to evidence from outside the Antaiopolite) and Bagnall 1992, 136–137 (quote). From among the Antaiopolite tax receipts, passages such as *P.Gen.* IV 193.1–2: εἰς λόγον ἐμβολῆς | πεντεκαιδεκάτης ἰνδ(ικτίονος) (ὑπὲρ) κωμ(η)τ(ικῶν) κώμ(ης) Φθλᾶ suggest that *astika* and *kōmētika* are not the actual taxes themselves, but rather land tax categories.

141 From Phthla: *P.Gen.* IV 193; *P.Lond.* V 1665; *P.Lond.* V 1666; *SB* XX 15013.1–3 and 4–7; *SB* XX 15015.1–5 and 6–9; *SB* XX 15016 (for the location, cf. Marthot 2013, II 114). Not stated, but both issued by Matoi, *boēthos* of Phthla: P.Mich. inv. 3272 (ed. Keenan 2012); *SB* XX 15017. From Aphrodite: *SB* XVI 12370. On the "codex" and "noncodex" receipts, see nn. 3 and 4 above.

142 *P.Cair.Masp.* III 67325 fol. III verso 1–3 and 4. In both its occurrences in Zacharias's receipt, the word ὑ̣π̣ο̣δ̣έ̣κ̣(της) is written with a rather extravagant flourish, and it appears that it served as a paraph in its own right, marking a point of similarity between Zacharias and the *hypodektai* who sign for the pagarchs.

143 This is suggested by Thomas Kruse in a study on Roman administrative assistants (Kruse 2016, 1764). Cf. *P.Ant.* II 90 (Antinoopolis; VI), a receipt for a payment εἰς λόγ(ον) δημ(οσίων) πόλ(εως) Ἀντι(νόου), signed by a *hypodektēs* in his own name.

village scribes, likewise do not refer to the pagarchs. This last option gains plausibility if considered in connection with the business of the *boēthoi*, as discussed in the next subsection.

In conclusion, the role of the *hypodektai* seems to be more extensive and more engaged at the local level than previously acknowledged, although we cannot entirely exclude the possibility that the *hypodektēs* of the city and the *hypodektēs* of the pagarchy were two distinct positions.

2. *The* Boēthoi

The *boēthoi* furnish the most instances of intermediary signatories in the Antaiopolite tax receipts. There are many types of these "assistants," and the texts are often unclear about which institutions they actually belong to. Any institution of some significance, whether public or private, can plausibly be assumed to have had *boēthoi*.[144] Section II of this chapter established a negative definition, arguing that the *boēthoi* who signed the tax receipts for the pagarch are unlikely to be the *logistērion* officials some scholars have taken them to be.[145] Building on this, the present subsection develops a positive defini-

144 *Boēthoi* explicitly linked to a *geouchōn* or an *oikos*: e.g., *P.Oxy.* XVI 2049.3 (Oxyrhynchos; VI) and *SB* VI 9153.11, 31, and 37 (Herakleopolis; 596). See also *P.Bad.* VI 173.2 for a *hypoboēthos* of the imperial *oikos*. It seems, however, only natural that the village *boēthos* also dealt frequently with the local *geouchōn*; see *SB* XVI 12485 (Oxyrhynchos; VI) or, without the village attribution, *P.Harr.* I 159 (unknown; V–VI). Many "official" *boēthoi* may have also conducted technically "private" business for their superiors. In *P.Oxy.* XIX 2244.27, 47, and 75, for instance, *boēthoi* preside over districts of an *oikos* and may well be village *boēthoi*. In short, I wonder whether some, if not all, of these *boēthoi* "of" *oikoi* may be, in fact, village *boēthoi* (meaning that rather than one person holding two positions, there is in fact just a single position with different names in different contexts). The model established by Tost 2012 would seem to fit here: *riparii* "of the city" maintained and paid by local magnates were sometimes addressed as *riparii* "of the *oikos* of N.N.," though notably, this happens exclusively in the context of private business. This may perfectly explain the situation of the village *boēthoi*, who were hired by the responsible officials and also by large landowners in the case of "pagarched" villages: The *boēthos* who provides surety to Flavia Anastasia in *P.Oxy.* XLIV 3204.6–7 (Oxyrhynchos; January 2, 588) refers to himself as her *boēthos*, but may also have been hired by Anastasia to be responsible for the *kōmē pagarchoumenē* (discussed in Chapter Three) that is the residence of the person under surety (the sureties in such documents are often in some way responsible for the place where the person under surety is from; see, e.g., village headmen acting as sureties in *P.Cair.Masp.* I 67094). Note that Papnouthis and Dorotheos appear both as *boēthoi* of certain villages and as *boēthoi* of a certain *geouchos* (see Berkes 2017a, 160–161). Similarly, the *boēthos* of the *praepositus pagi* Ision (*P.Sakaon* 46–48) refers to him as his *geouchos* (*P.Abinn.* 28.3 and 22). Cf. also some village *grammateis* who on other occasions identify as *grammateis* of a particular shipper (*CPR* XXIII, pp. 215–216 n. 11).

145 It is unclear who the *boēthoi* of *P.Cair.Masp.* I 67070 are (cf. Berkes 2017a, 161 n. 255 and 164 n. 282). They refuse to issue a receipt for eighteen *keratia* on the grounds that they did not receive the full amount (*symplērōsis*), since the gold coins (*holokottina*) they received were found to be too light in weight (cf. *P.Cair.Masp.* II 67198 *descr.*, which appears to concern a similar issue);

tion. No case is as illuminating as that of the *boēthos* Matoi, who is now known to have issued at least six receipts in total, five of them in the name of pagarchs:[146]

- *P.Cair.Masp.* III 67325 fol. VIII verso 1–6, a receipt for two cash payments from the eighth indiction, effectuated through Dioskoros in the name of his father Apollos. One of these payments is for the *diagraphon*, the other for the (adaerated) *embolē*. The receipt lacks a reference to the issuing party or a signature but can still be attributed to Matoi by virtue of his characteristic hand; it was presumably written on the same occasion as the following receipt, with the signature on the latter intended to be valid for both receipts.

---

the writer of the letter consequently demands that the addressee send seven *keratia* "for the sake of God and for the sake of the *embolē* of your village" (l. 4). The addressee may be one Apollos (see the verso for the reading Ἀ̣π̣ο̣λ̣λ̣ῶ̣[τος?] but there is no online image to verify this reading), so perhaps this is Dioskoros's father and *prōtokōmētēs* or Dioskoros's colleague as *prōtokōmētēs* (or someone else entirely). Since the writer is not prone to phonetic spelling elsewhere, it does not seem convincing to understand l. 4: τῆς κώμης ὑμῶν ("your village") as τῆς κώμης ἡμῶν ("our village"); therefore, there is some distance between the writer and the addressee. For "your village" in a similar context, cf. *P.Cair.Masp.* I 67060.1. The term *holokottinon* usually refers to a *nomisma/solidus*, but even if it were being used here more generally to mean "gold" or "gold coins" (as in *P.Rain.Cent.* 161.22–23), the word choice all but confirms that the transferred amount exceeded eighteen *keratia* (cf. the editor's commentary), as there were no gold coins below a *solidus*, a half-*solidus* (*semissis*), or a third-*solidus* (*tremissis*). The combination of an amount of probably multiple *nomismata,* the writer's distancing himself from the village, and the urgency in tone would fit a tax collector who was transferring an aggregated amount to the higher level, either to Antinoopolis (assuming this payment is linked to the *autopragia*; and if these *boēthoi* are low-ranking secretaries in the provincial office, and thus very far away from "your village," it might explain why the sender does not use their names) or to Antaiopolis. In the latter case, the *boēthoi* would perhaps be those of the *logistērion*, but we may recall that the village *boēthoi* Papnouthis and Dorotheos were also city residents (see Chapter One, n. 90) and their Antaiopolite counterparts, as employees of the pagarch, would have probably found it unproblematic to refer to their own administrative circumscription (here, Phthla or post-autopract Aphrodite) as "your village." In addition, as noted in Section II 1 above, the *boēthos tou logistēriou* never signs in the name of someone else but is usually himself the superior authority. Other possibilities are that the letter was written from Aphrodite or Phthla to Dioskoros while he was living in Antinoopolis, or that the letter was sent only a short distance within the immediate surroundings of Aphrodite because the matter was urgent, perhaps due to the limited amount of time the *boēthoi* were around. There seem to be collegia attested for the village *boēthoi* in *SPP* III 399.1 (Herakleopolites; VI; see Berkes 2017a, 161 n. 255) and also for *boēthoi* of the *logistērion* in *P.Oxy.* LXXXII 5341.3–4 (Oxyrhynchos; June 16, 575): τῇ ἐξακτορικῇ τάξει τη τε (*sic*) βοηθοὶς | λογιστηρίου. An instance of the latter can perhaps also be found in Hermopolis; see Gonis 2007a, 128. By contrast, Wipszycka 1971, 113–114 argues for one central *boēthos tou logistēriou*.

146 See Stern forthcoming (a), s.v. on Matoi's dossier and on palaeographic and formulaic aspects of this identification, which confirm that the two receipts in *P.Cair.Masp.* III 67325 fol. VIII verso 1–6 and 7–13 were both written by him. Coming from a different direction, Loreleï Vanderheyden came to the same conclusion about Matoi's authorship of *P.Cair.Masp.* III 67325 fol. VIII 7–13 in her doctoral dissertation; see Vanderheyden 2015, 77–78, soon to be published as *P.Aphrod.Let.Copt.* I.

- *P.Cair.Masp.* III 67325 fol. VIII verso 7–13, a receipt for a *dēmosia* payment in money, again by Dioskoros in the name of his father, from the eighth indiction, issued by Matoi in the name of the pagarchs.
- *P.Lond.* V 1666, a receipt for a single monetary payment from the eighth indiction in the name of the same Apollos for both the *dēmosia kōmētika* of the village of Phthla and the monks of a monastery, issued by Matoi in the name of the pagarchs.[147] No intermediary payer is given.
- *SB* XX 15016, a receipt for "rent" (*phoros*) for the third part of a barren (*aporos*) land lot from the eighth indiction, issued by Matoi in the name of the pagarchs. The receipt is issued to a tenant called Menas and the third part of the lot is declared to be "under" that tenant but, in terms of actual ownership, "mine." No amount or currency is specified; it is only stated that the *phoros* has been paid in full.[148]
- *SB* XX 15017, a receipt for another payment by (probably the same) Menas, son of Phoibammon, for the crops (*hyper genēmatos*) of a lot[149] belonging to the "holy catholic church of the village of Euphrosynon," for the sixth, seventh, and eighth indictions. The payment is made in kind, but it is not clear whether in advance or for arrears. The receipt is issued by Matoi in the name of the church.
- P.Mich. inv. 3272 (ed. Keenan 2012), a receipt for an *embolē* payment in kind by the heirs of Psimanobet, son of Kyros, in Psimanobet's name from the eleventh indiction, issued by Matoi in the name of the pagarchs.

The diverse content of these receipts helps sort some things out. First, we see Matoi handling various taxes, paid both in cash and in kind: (unspecified) *dēmosia*, the *dēmosia kōmētika* of the village of Phthla, adaerated *embolē*, unadaerated *embolē*—a picture that fits the hypothesis that Matoi was a village *boēthos*.[150] But then, Matoi also confirms the receipt of crops in the name of a church.[151] The church of Euphrosynon

147 The name of the monastery is heavily damaged and the reading Ạ[γ]ị[ο]ụ poses a challenge. If we accept it, the monks probably appear here because Apollos had leased land from them (Wipszycka 1972, 90 n. 1).

148 On this text, see Section II 2 above, especially n. 53.

149 On the expression ἀπ̣ὸ τοῦ | λόγου (ll. 2–3), cf. *P.Sorb.* II 69, p. 34.

150 On the village *boēthos* (βοηθὸς τῆς κώμης), see Berkes 2017a, 157–167. The author argues, however, that the texts I collected here concern *boēthoi* of the *logistērion* (p. 163 n. 282); on this point, see the discussion in Section II 1 above. The "model" village *boēthoi*, Papnouthis and Dorotheos, also handle taxes both in cash and in kind (*P.Oxy.* XLVIII, p. 75). Their documents play a large part in Berkes's meticulous account, which will be discussed in context below; on their archive, see Chapter One, n. 42.

151 One may suspect that Matoi, besides being village *boēthos*, was employed by the church of Euphrosynon; cf. Berkes 2017a, 160 and *P.Sorb.* II 69, p. 61 n. 32 on *boēthoi* in service of monasteries. In *P.Lond.* V 1666, however, one payment is designated for the *kōmētika* and, at the same time, for a monastery; this payment is confirmed in a single receipt and may therefore relate to the same capacity and to Matoi's job as village *boēthos*, in which role he acted on behalf of anyone who had fiscal interests in the village.

is, however, known as a landowner in the village of Aphrodite,[152] so it could plausibly have owned land in the neighboring village of Phthla.[153] Matoi is therefore probably the village *boēthos* of Phthla and also handled various payments for absentee local authorities as part of either that role or an additional, or previous, job.[154] Village *boēthoi* having multiple assignments would not be unheard of, since they were not village officials, but personal agents employed by higher authorities for various localities.[155] Collecting rent (*phoros*) for apparently public lands administered by the pagarchs was another of Matoi's duties.[156]

The receipts signed by *boēthoi* in the name of pagarchs attest their responsibility for village land taxes.[157] While the *hypodektai* collected the taxes from *astika* lands, the *boēthoi* collected what was due from *kōmētika* lands.[158] It is certainly no coincidence that a *boēthos* wrote what is known as the Aphrodite Register, which exclusively con-

152 Zuckerman 2004a, 33–34; Keenan 1985b, 160.

153 Alternatively, Matoi was responsible for Aphrodite as well, though this seems less likely. But note that Λυκᾶ, the relevant plot in *SB* XX 15017, was apparently an Aphroditan land lot in the eighth century (*P.Lond.* IV 1442 G 68). Phthla must have been immediately adjacent to Aphrodite's eastern outskirts; see Marthot 2013, I 10 and n. 15, who compellingly rejects the hypothesis that Phthla should be identified with modern el-Wa'adlah, more than five miles north of Aphrodite (for this identification, see Ruffini 2018a, 18; Fournet 1999, 545; and *TM* Geo ID 3022).

154 The pattern suggests that the eighth indiction from *SB* XX 15017 is the same as the eighth indiction from *SB* XX 15016, *P.Lond.* V 1666, and *P.Cair.Masp.* III 67325 fol. VIII verso 1–13, which entails that the payments made in *SB* XX 15017 (for the sixth, seventh, and eighth indictions) are for arrears. Perhaps Matoi, as village *boēthos*, stepped in because there were some irregularities that threatened the use of the crops for tax payments? Cf. the *boēthos* Makarios, who signs one receipt for *dēmosia* not in the name of the pagarchs as he does on other occasions, but *per procuram* of the landowners' *koinon* (*P.Cair.Masp.* III 67325 fol. VII verso 20–22); in that instance, however, he does not include his being *boēthos* in his signature. But *SB* XX 15017 might also be an advance payment issued in the sixth indiction; for an example of advance payments of this kind from the Dioskoros archive, see, e.g., *P.Cair.Masp.* I 67097 verso A.

155 Papnouthis and Dorotheos were, for instance, responsible for several villages at once. Moreover, they are styled both as *boēthoi* of villages and as *boēthoi* of the *praepositus pagi*, though not in the same document. See Berkes 2017a, 160–161 and Zuckerman 2004a, 130. See also *P.Lond.* V 1677.51, where Dioskoros might be noting that he asked the pagarch to issue an order to the *boēthos* concerning taxes: ἐ̣κ τ[ού]ṭο(υ) ἤτησα τὸν π̣ά̣γαρχον ἀ̣λλότριον τὸν βοηθὸν | [– – – χρυσι?]-κ̣ὰ̣ δ̣[η]μ̣ό̣σ̣ια (assuming ἀ̣λλότριον refers to the pagarch). The context is not very clear, as the passage is surrounded by lacunae.

156 On this interpretation of *SB* XX 15016, see Section II 2 above.

157 Cf. *P.Oxy.* XLVIII 3392 (Oxyrhynchos; June 14, 360), a receipt issued by a *praepositus pagi* through the (village) *boēthos* Dorotheos; the structure of this receipt is completely parallel to the tax receipts from the pagarchs, and also impersonally styled.

158 These are usually *dēmosia* in the sense of money taxes, but cf. *P.Gen.* IV 193.1–2: εἰς λόγον ἐμβολῆς | πεντεκαιδεκάτης ἰνδ(ικτίονος) (ὑπὲρ) κωμ(η)τ(ικῶν) κώμ(ης) Φθλᾶ. On this fiscal category, cf. *P.Cair.Masp.* II 67139 fol. IV recto 5: εἰς τὴν ἐμβολ(ὴν) τῶν κτημ(άτων) ἀστικ(ῶν) τε καὶ κωμητικ(ῶν). This formula probably means that in the Geneva text we are dealing with the *embolē* from land that is in the *kōmētika* category, and underscores that *astika* and *kōmētika* are not themselves taxes whose revenues go to the city or the village. Cf. n. 140 above.

cerns *kōmētika*.[159] Analogous to the *hypodektai*, the specification of the village in the tax title—as in "*dēmosia kōmētika* of the village of Phthla," for instance—plausibly explains the missing specification of the *boēthoi* in the signature. The business of the *boēthoi* concerning the grain tax (*embolē*) seems less clear-cut, at least on the first look: how does Matoi's receipt for an *embolē* payment in kind relate to several other extant Antaiopolite receipts for the *embolē*, signed by the village scribes Pilatos and Timotheos, but also by the *hypodektēs* Zacharias? These latter receipts confirm the loading of Aphrodite's grain onto the ships that the monastery of Metanoia provided as a service to the state.[160] By contrast, Matoi's aforementioned receipt confirms the *payment* of the *embolē*.[161] This difference likely reflects two distinct procedures, as is suggested by a receipt confirming an *embolē* payment for the *kōmētika* of Phthla, signed in the name of the pagarch. To this receipt, the *boēthos* Pninnos adds a note stating that it was issued according to a shipment receipt (*prosgraphon*) from Timotheos, Aphrodite's village scribe.[162] Pninnos obviously felt the need to be clear that he had not witnessed the actual payment being made himself—apparently an unconventional procedure in such cases. Payment and shipping were probably handled separately because (a portion of) the grain would be sent directly to the provincial capital Antinoopolis and Alexandria without going through the nome capital Antaiopolis.[163] These Aphroditan "loading

159 Zuckerman 2004a, 27–28 and 128–133. This official bears the title βοηθὸς τῶν δημοσίων κώμη[ς Ἀ]φροδίτης in *P.Cair.Masp.* III 67283 col. II 24; on the institutional character of Aphrodite's *boēthos*, see n. 65 above. Cf. MacCoull 1993, no. 11 (new ed. Vanderheyden 2015, no. 15), where a *boēthos* is concerned with both the *kōmētika* and the *astika*, but that man is Ioannes, the *boēthos tou logistēriou* (see Vanderheyden's restored text) of Antaiopolis(?), and the text explicitly concerns the payment of arrears (or payments that the village shepherds had collected but not transferred), which is probably why the *boēthos tou logistēriou* got involved.

160 **Pilatos:** *P.Cair.Masp.* III 67325 fol. II recto 6–10; *P.Flor.* III 298.53–56 and 74–76 (new ed. of both documents as no. 8 in Fournet 2020b). **Timotheos:** *P.Cair.Masp.* III 67286.1–10 and 12–22 (new ed. of both documents as no. 6 in Fournet 2020b); *P.Cair.Masp.* III 67347 col. I recto 1–7 and 9–12 (new ed. of both documents as no. 5 in Fournet 2020b). **Zacharias:** *P.Cair.Masp.* III 67325 fol. III verso 1–3 and 4. On the role of Metanoia, see Fournet & Gascou 2002.

161 P.Mich. inv. 3272 (ed. Keenan 2012). The *embolē* payment in cash that is attested in *P.Cair.Masp.* III 67325 fol. VIII verso 1–6 represents an adaerated contribution.

162 *P.Gen.* IV 193.2–3: δι(ὰ) προσγράφ(ου) Τιμοθέου γραμ̣(ματέως) | κ̣ώμ̣(ης) Ἀφροτίτ(ης) (read Ἀφροδίτης). See *P.Sorb.* II 69, p. 33 for a similar use of this type of διά in a fiscal account from early seventh-century Hermopolis. On the *prosgraphon* (literally, "supplementary document") as loading receipt, see *P.Gen.* IV, p. 231 and *P.Hamb.* III 230.9 including the commentary. See also *CPR* XXIII, p. 216 (and additional literature in n. 14). The editor of *CPR* XXIII finds the interpretation as two distinct administrative procedures attractive, but ultimately discounts it because some of these "loading receipts" do not refer to themselves as *prosgraphon* but rather as *entagion* (e.g., *CPR* XXIV 23). To my mind, that line of argument assumes a rigid use of largely formulaic terminology at the most local administrative level that we hardly see elsewhere, even at higher levels of late antique administration or in notarial contracts.

163 See Morelli 2008b (cf. Hoogendijk 1998) for an analysis of *SB* XXIV 16222, in which tensions arise over the use of the (state) fleet to transport this *embolē*; involved was the *paneuphēmos patricius* Athanasios, *dux et Augustalis* of the Thebaid and *curator domus divinae*. These services were

receipts" do not usually refer to the pagarch, but one of them does in fact attest some involvement of the pagarch(s or the pagarchy) in the procedure; however, the papyrus is unfortunately too fragmentary to grasp what exactly is going on there.[164] A Coptic letter from the Hermopolite might allude to a pagarch intervening at the village level in what seems to be a problem concerning the registration or acknowledgment of *dēmosia* and *embolē* payments.[165] In the latter case, a *prosgraphon* has already been issued to the letter writer, apparently by village authorities.[166] This would fit the procedure we see in the Antaiopolite evidence, so the constellation in these documents does not seem to be a result of Aphrodite's status as an autopract village.[167]

Two receipts from Hermopolis shed some light on the job of the *boēthoi* at a higher level.[168] They are the addressees rather than the signatories of these documents, this time clearly identified as *boēthoi* of particular villages:[169] the pagarchs confirm that the *boēthoi* have paid the taxes from their villages.[170] This is clearly an upper level of ad-

---

often outsourced to larger institutions such as the Apion *oikos* in Oxyrhynchos, or that of the *patricia* Sophia in the Fayum, or the monastery of Metanoia for the Antaiopolite nome, to name some prominent instances. This is Rémondon's (1974a, 20) "super-autopragie"; on the use of the term *autopragia* in this context, see Chapter One, Section I.

164 See Fournet 2020b, no. 1.7 (p. 115), which refers, after a lacuna and immediately before the signature of the *grammateus*, to παγαρχ( ) τῆς αὐτῆς γιν̣. . . .[– – –].

165 *P.Sorb.Copt.* 30.9–10 (Hermopolites; VI–early VII): "[– – – and when] the Lord Theodore, the pagarch, comes, visit him (?), say, concerning them, that [– – –]," [– – – ⲉⲣϣ]ⲁ̣ⲛⲡⲕⲩⲣⲓ̈ⲥ ⲑⲉⲟⲇⲱⲣⲉ ⲡⲁⲅⲁⲣⲭⲟⲥ (read ⲡⲡⲁⲅⲁⲣⲭⲟⲥ) ⲉⲓ ϭⲁⲧϥ̄ ϫⲟⲟϥ ⲉⲣⲟⲟⲩ ϫⲉ̣ | [– – –]. I am indebted to Anne Grons for contacting me about this papyrus ahead of publication.

166 *P.Sorb.Copt.* 30.7: "[– – –] also the *embolē*, until I send the *prosgraphon* to you [– – –]," [– – –] ̣ⲣⲱ̣ⲛⲉ ⲉⲧⲕⲉⲙ̄ⲃⲟⲗⲏ ϣⲁⲛϯϫⲟⲟⲩ ⲡⲉⲡⲣⲟⲥⲅⲣⲁⲫⲟⲛ ⲛ̣ⲁ̣ⲕ̣ ̣ⲉ̣ ̣ ̣[– – –]. Later, in l. 10, the writer mentions that he will receive an *entagion* once he has paid (?) the *dēmosia* for an eleventh indiction. Due to the fragmentary state of the papyrus it is, however, not clear whether the pagarch's involvement might extend to only one of the two, the *dēmosia* or the *embolē*.

167 It remains uncertain whether the "lord Kolthe, *boēthos*" (*P.Sorb.Copt.* 30.1: ⲡⲕⲩⲣⲓ̈ⲥ̄ ⲕⲟⲗⲑⲉ ⲡⲃⲟⲏⲑⲟⲥ) mentioned at the beginning of the letter refers to a *boēthos* of the village in question or perhaps to the *boēthos* of the *logistērion* who became involved due to irregularities.

168 The two texts are compared in Mazza 1995, 214.

169 *BGU* XII 2196 (VI) and *P.Lond.* V 1753 (VII); cf. *P.Herm.* 83 and *P.Lond.* III 1035 (both Hermopolites; VI), parallels addressed to a *magister*, in which the amounts are, however, measured ζυγ(ῷ) ἰ(διωτικῷ), which might point to the model of fiscal shares (see Chapter Three). The date of *P.Lond.* V 1753 was established on palaeographical grounds, and the papyrus may date from the early Islamic period; see the Catalog, s.v. Ioannes (Hermopolis).

170 Cf. *P.Cair.Masp.* I 67049 (550/551?), where a certain Flavius Kyros (Ruffini 2011, s.v. Kuros 22) receives some remainders of the *dēmosia* from Aphrodite's *boēthos*; Kyros is referred to as *geouchos* and is represented by his *meizoteros*. How does this man relate to the pagarch Ioulianos? Cf. the parallel *P.Cair.Masp.* I 67044, where the sender can be identified as *trakteutēs* (Ruffini 2011, s.v. Origenes 1). We might suspect that Flavius Kyros was the *megaloprepestatos politeuomenos* of Antaiopolis (Ruffini 2011, s.v. Kuros 16 and cf. Section II 2 above on *PSI* IV 283) who dealt with some of Aphrodite's "local" taxes. That man, however, was dead by 539 CE, so *P.Cair.Masp.* I 67049 might instead date to 535/536.

ministration, as is obvious from the signatures: one receipt is signed by a *trakteutēs*, certainly one of the aforementioned *trakteutai* of the pagarchy, the other probably by the pagarch himself.[171] The tax titles and amounts paid can also be compared with the Antaiopolite evidence, which would suggest that these receipts concern aggregated payments: one comprises five *nomismata* and six *keratia* for the *eumeneia*;[172] the other, thirty-three *nomismata* and seventeen *keratia* for unspecified *dēmosia*. Despite the comparatively large amounts, both appear to have been partial payments: they are said to be "of" (*apo*) the taxes and are effectuated on Epeiph 4 and Hathyr 4, respectively, that is, two and six months into the indictions that the payments are made for.

The three taxes mentioned thus far in connection with the *boēthos*—the *dēmosia kōmētika*, the *embolē*, and the *eumeneia*—are basically the same titles (*dēmosia*, *aisia embolē*, *eumeneia*) that appear in an agreement between two unknown individuals about tax collection from the village of Phthla.[173] The beginning of the document is lost, but both contracting parties appear to be part of a tax-collecting collegium, with one party subcontracting their share of the responsibility to the other.[174] Both parties explicitly note their accountability to "the aforementioned pagarchs and their *trakteutai*,"[175] meaning that we have here not only the same taxes but also the same tasks and hierarchy as in the receipts issued by or to *boēthoi*—the superior contracting party was therefore no doubt a *boēthos* of the village of Phthla.[176] The contract underscores that the *boēthoi* were more akin to entrepreneurs than village officials,[177] not unlike the *pronoētai* of the *oikos* of the Apiones in Oxyrhynchos. Matoi's example also suggests that the *boēthoi* could hold multiple jobs or at least have dealings with with other local authorities—in Matoi's case with the church of Euphrosynon. Similar to Matoi, the *boethos* Makarios generally signs as *boēthos* for the pagarchs but in one instance "as authorized representative (*ex epitropēs*, i.e., *per procuram*) of the *koinon* of landowners (*ktētores*)."[178]

171 See Section II 3 above on the pagarch's "bureau."

172 In the main text of the receipt, *P.Lond.* V 1753, the tax title is ἀπὸ̣ τῆς εὐμε(νείας) τῆς (αὐτῆς) κώμ(ης), whereas the summary on the verso identifies the document as an ἐντάγι(ον) εὐμε(νείας) το(ῦ) β̣ο̣η(θοῦ).

173 *P.Lond.* V 1660.8–10 (c. 553?): εἴτε περὶ τῶν εἰρημένων δημοσίων καὶ τῆς αἰσίας ἐμβολῆς | κα[ὶ] τ̣ῆ̣ς ε[ὐ]μ̣ε̣νείᾳ[ς] εἴδε (read εἴτε) πάλιν καὶ περὶ τῆ̣ς ἀ̣ναλ̣ι̣σ̣κομένης ῥώγας (read ῥόγας) καὶ | ἑτέρας ζημίας προφάσει τῆ̣ς εἰρη[μ]έ̣ν̣[ης] κ̣[ώ]μ̣η̣ς [Φ]θ̣λ̣ᾶ̣. The separation by εἴτε may indicate that the "*roga* and other payments (i.e., fines?)" are to be understood as extraordinary payments of some kind, in addition to regular taxes.

174 See l. 19: συμμετέχειν and the editor's commentary.

175 *P.Lond.* V 1660.21–22.

176 This hypothesis was already put forward by the editor.

177 The *boēthoi* were no regular members of the village *koinon* and ranked above village officials (Berkes 2017a, 158–159).

178 *P.Cair.Masp.* III 67325 fol. VII verso 20–22: δι' ἐμοῦ̣ Μ̣ακαρίου | ἐξ ἐπιτροπῆς τῶν κο̣ι̣νῶν (read τοῦ κοινοῦ?) τῶν κτητ(όρων) | σεσημ(είωμαι). See Chapter Six, n. 20 for a discussion of the expression τῶν κοινῶν τῶν κτητόρων.

The *boēthoi* collected taxes from individual taxpayers (or amounts already aggregated by some village officials) and in the case of cash payments exchanged comparatively small change into amounts of gold as required by the state. This role provided them with ample opportunity for profit,[179] but also involved considerable risk: some *boēthoi* ran into debt in order to guarantee the required tax volume, or even to pay it up front.[180] Obviously, the combination of financial peril and the prospect of personal gain might not exactly have encouraged the sort of conduct that would have been met with affection or gratitude by the local population. Figures with a reputation as explicitly bad as that of Kyros, the *boēthos* of Phthla, are rare,[181] but in the eyes of the locals he was by no means an isolated case in the Egyptian countryside. The Coptic *History of the Church* claims that Emperor Marcian attempted to gain popularity in Egypt by prohibiting the *boēthoi* from entering the villages to collect taxes, and instead directed the pagarchs to gather what was due.[182] Whatever the historical core of this episode, the literary argument assumes people's general distrust of, if not outright disdain for, the *boēthoi*. In one of his poems, Dioskoros asks the governor to "reject these *boēthoi*," comparing them to raging barbarians.[183] Some *boēthoi* were locals but others were not,[184] which makes it hard to determine whether they generally shared a common background. One can imagine that their job required local connections and

179 *P.Oxy.* XLVIII, pp. 75–76; Berkes 2017a, 158–159. Opportunities for profit must have been great enough to attract subcontractors; see the aforementioned *P.Lond.* V 1660.

180 As *P.Oxy.* XLVIII 3393 (Oxyrhynchos; 365) suggests, Papnouthis and Dorotheos were expected to pay taxes in advance before actually collecting them. An instance from the second half of the sixth century is *SB* XII 10810 (origin unknown; possibly from the Fayum or the Hermopolite nome), in which a village *boēthos* takes a loan from a banker: the document was issued on Epeiph 7 of the eighth indiction, but repayment was due in Phaophi (i.e., after the harvest), shortly after the beginning of the *tenth* indiction, suggesting that the *boēthos* expected the collection of the due amount to take a long time. *SB* VIII 9750 (Herakleopolis; 642/657?), from the early years after the Islamic conquest, shows that a pagarch had lent to the *boēthos* and a village headman an amount equal to the taxes due from their village; they are supposed to pay it back five days later, presumably after having been able to collect arrears (Berkes 2017a, 76).

181 Ruffini 2011, s.v. Kuros 26. Another malevolent village *boēthos*, who "tore down the whole village," appears in *P.Cair.Masp.* I 67005.19–22 (Antinoopolis; c. 568). See also, e.g., the complaint against a *boēthos* in *PSI* XIII 1342 (Hermopolites/Antinoopolites; latter half of V?).

182 See Johnson 1976, 10–11. Cf. López 2013, 145 n. 20, arguing that Marcian sought to secure the support of the urban elites by curbing the right of *autopragia*. This seems unlikely to me for the simple reason that the *boēthoi* were direct subordinates of the pagarchs. The passage may be confusing different stages of the development of the pagarchy during the fifth century. Cf. Chapter One, n. 139.

183 *P.Aphrod.Lit.* IV 11.82; Ruffini 2018a, 169–170.

184 The *boēthoi* Papnouthis and Dorotheos were residents of the city; see Chapter One, n. 90. However, a number must have come from "their" villages, as illustrated by the village *boēthos* known to have been *prōtokōmētēs* in the same village; see Berkes 2017a, 159. Note also *P.Lond.* V 1660.10: τῆ̣ς̣ εἰρη[μ]έ̣ν̣[ης] (!) κ̣[ώ]μ̣η̣ς̣ [Φ]θ̣λ̣ᾶ̣, which means that Phthla must have been mentioned before in the (lost) beginning of the text; this suggests that at least one, if not both, contracting parties (very likely to be *boēthoi*) hail from that village.

knowledge, but the apparently widespread antipathy toward the *boēthoi* suggests a lack of integration into the communities of "their" villages. The *boēthos* of Aphrodite who signed a petition against the pagarch Ioulianos seems to be a notable counterexample, but at that time the village was autopract and its *boēthos* was therefore not an employee of the pagarch.[185]

Other texts highlight that there was, however, also a certain degree of separation between the pagarchs and their *boēthoi*. Kyros, the *boēthos* of Phthla, was on good terms with the pagarch Menas but took the job before Menas assumed the pagarchy,[186] so it is not a given that Kyros had been part of Menas's personal network. In another document, Dioskoros states that he paid taxes directly to the pagarch rather than the *boēthos* and that the latter went back to Dioskoros's tenants in order to "wear them out."[187] Although it is unclear what exactly happened here, the way this incident is described appears to suggest a certain distance between the pagarch and the *boēthos* Kyros. Finally, the Coptic *History of the Church*, in the passage referred to before, draws an explicit contrast between the (benevolent) pagarchs and the (malevolent) *boēthoi*, implying that the latter were not perceived as simply part of the pagarchs' business.[188]

3. Personal or Office Assistants?

Before moving on to the signatories who appear less frequently than the *hypodektai* and the *boēthoi*, one peculiar phenomenon should be considered. In the Antaiopolite receipts, the writers and/or signatories often refer to the responsible pagarchs anonymously as "the *endoxotatoi* pagarchs" (*hoi endoxotatoi pagarchoi*), while on other occasions they give individual names. This happens under different tenures and so is not just a momentary phenomenon. Economics of space also cannot account for the anonymous formula, since one document refers to an anonymous pagarch in the singular (*ho endoxotatos pagarchos*).[189] The attributions of these formulae (singular or plural, anonymous or named) to the individual writers are captured in Table 1.[190]

185 Given Aphrodite's pseudo-city status in many regards, Aphrodite's *boēthos* probably shared characteristics of both a village *boēthos* and a *boēthos logistēriou*; see n. 65 above.

186 Good terms with Menas: *P.Cair.Masp.* I 67002 col. I 17–18. In office before Menas: MacCoull 1993, no. 11 (new ed. Vanderheyden 2015, no. 15).

187 *P.Lond.* V 1677.48–52, showing, again, that profits from this business were apparently worth pushing for. But when Dioskoros says that he paid directly to the pagarch, he certainly would not have been handing the taxes over to him in person, but still relying on intermediaries. What does this reveal about the way that people perceived some minor officials as the pagarchs' agents, but not others?

188 See Chapter One, n. 139

189 *P.Cair.Masp.* II 67228: ὁ ἐνδοξ(ότατος) πάγαρχος δ̣(ιὰ) ἐοῦ (read ἐμοῦ) Κολλούθο̣υ̣ ὑποδέκτ(ου).

190 For a catalog of the writers, discussing their palaeography, style, and identifications, see Stern forthcoming (a). When writers are attested using the particular formula of that column multiple times, their names are given in bold; writers using more than one type of formula, and therefore

Table 1: Anonymous and named references to pagarchs in the signatures of the Antaiopolite receipts and the official or professional titles of the writers who used these references.

	ho endox. pag. **(anon.)**	**Ioulianos**	**Ioannes (⅔)**	**Serenos (⅓)**	***hoi endox. pag.*** **(anon.)**	***hoi endox. pag.*** **+ names**
hypodektai	Kollouthos	Petros			**Menas**; Phoibammon; Anon. *hyp.* 1	Anon. *hyp.* 2 (= Petros?)
boēthoi		**Pninnos**		***Makarios 1**	Biktor; *Makarios 1; **Matoi**	Makarios 2
notarii **and** ***grammateis***			***Christodoros 1**; **Damianos**	**Mousaios**	***Christodoros 1**	
other posts			Iosephis *presbyteros* & *dioikētēs*		Menas *singularis*; Psates *pronoētēs*	
post lost (Anon. 1) or not mentioned			***Gennadios**; Anon. 1	**Christodoros 2**; **Daniel**; *(Gennadios)[191]	**Hermias**; **Komasios**	

The table shows that some signatories only ever use one type of reference when signing in the name of a pagarch, such as the *boēthos* Pninnos, who always signs for Ioulianos. Others, such as Makarios *boēthos* 1 and Christodoros 1, switch from using the anonymous plural to the named singular for their respective pagarchs.[192] With the exception of the *hypodektai*, to which I shall return, the use of a particular type of formula did not depend on the writer's official position: *boēthoi* as well as *notarii* and *grammateis*—and Christodoros 2—are attested using singular as well as plural, and anonymous as well as named references. But it is noteworthy that writers never switch between the pagarchs Ioannes and Serenos, who held the office jointly. Two observations suggest that this is not accidental, but follows a pattern. First, in the single instance in which Gennadios did indeed sign a receipt for the pagarch Serenos rather

appearing twice in the table, are preceded by an asterisk. For instance, the *hypodektēs* Kollouthos is attested only in one receipt, where he signs in the name of one anonymous pagarch (*ho endoxotatos pagarchos*); the *boēthos* Makarios 1, however, issues multiple receipts in the name of the pagarch Serenos, but in one additional case signs in the name of unnamed pagarchs (*hoi endoxotatoi pagarchoi*). The one receipt signed by Liberis (*P.Cair.Masp.* III 67325 fol. III recto 5–7), in which the payment is made "for security of the third share of (the pagarch) Serenos, *illoustrios*," is not included here, since it is not formally issued in the name of the pagarchs "through" Liberis.

191 Gennadios signs once for Serenos, but in this case is careful to expressly state that he was acting on Serenos's order; see below.

192 Makarios changes his habit at some point during the sixth or seventh indiction, Christodoros in the course of the fourth indiction.

than the pagarch Ioannes, he added an explicit comment that this payment was due to an *epistalma* ("commission," "order") by Serenos,[193] probably because he deemed an apparently unusual procedure worthy of note. Second, the *notarii* Damianos and Mousaios actually split their signatures at the bottom of the same receipts: Damianos, on two occasions, wrote the receipts and afterward signed in the name of Ioannes, whereas Mousaios, on the same two occasions, added his signature to the receipts in the name of Serenos.[194] Consequently, it seems that (some of) the writers were attached to one pagarch but were free to sign in the name of either that particular pagarch or the entire collegium as they pleased, without affecting the value of the document. In other words, when writing the receipt, the *notarius* Damianos, for instance, could have signed in the name of Ioannes alone or in the name of "the pagarchs," as he preferred;[195] the one thing he would not do was sign in the name of Serenos.[196]

It follows from these signature patterns that at least those men who signed for individual pagarchs were local agents of individual pagarchs and not of the collegium as a whole.[197] This hypothesis makes sense for *notarii* and other lower administrative staff.[198] But while it is also plausible that *boēthoi* were employed by individual pagarchs and not by the collegium as a whole, this contention seems incompatible with the administrative position of the *hypodektai* at the city level. We have no *hypodektēs* receipts from the joint tenure of Ioannes and Serenos that would allow us to see whether the final clauses written by *hypodektai* switched between pagarchs. Only two receipts were signed by a *hypodektēs* in the name of an individual pagarch: one by Kollouthos (for an

193 *P.Flor.* III 298.12–16; the additional note in l. 13 reads: ἐξ ἐπιστάλμ(ατος) τοῦ ἐνδοξ(οτάτου) ἰλλ(ουστρίου), referring to the pagarch Serenos. The following [παγ(άρχου) (l. 14) should be deleted; see Stern forthcoming (a), s.v. Gennadios.

194 *P.Cair.Masp.* III 67325 fol. III verso 5–9 and 10–12.

195 Or possibly even without referring to any of the pagarchs; cf. the hypothesis that the reference to a formal issuing party was not strictly relevant to the legal value of such receipts (Kruse 2016, 1768).

196 Or if he did, he would have made it explicit, as Gennadios did in the only receipt he signed for Serenos; see n. 193 above.

197 See the specification of Christodoros 1, a *notarius* and *grammateus*, in *P.Cair.Masp.* III 67325 fol. VII recto 6 as: Χρ̣ι̣σ̣τ̣ο̣δώρο(υ) γρ̣(αμματέως) . . (διμοίρου) μέρ(ους). The reading of the title is uncertain and the traces in front of (διμοίρου) are unclear. In any case, the "two-thirds share" seems to be part of Christodoros's official title. The case of Gennadios signing once for Serenos suggests, however, that such boundaries, while formally respected, may in practice have been rather blurry and would often be handled according to the needs of the situation, though it is notable that deviations from usual administrative practice apparently had to be justified; cf. the discussion of *P.Gen.* IV 193 in Section III 2.

198 The position might have been omitted in some cases because these men were well known locally and easy to identify, but this explanation is unsatisfactory for an official document. Christodoros, Hermias, and Komasios (who do not sign with an official title) do not have particularly unusual personal names; by contrast, "Pninnos" certainly qualifies as a rare personal name, yet he always states his position.

anonymous pagarch), the other by Petros (for Ioulianos).[199] Only Petros's receipt gives an amount in *nomismata*, and it therefore certainly concerns an aggregated payment of some sort. Looking at the *fasti* of the Antaiopolite pagarchs, it is quite likely that Ioulianos was indeed the sole pagarch before Patrikia joined him to form a collegium.[200] If Anonymous *hypodektēs* 2 can be identified with Petros, which is plausible but not certain,[201] this would suggest that Petros switched from writing the named singular to writing the named plural once Patrikia joined Ioulianos in office. Kollouthos's receipt, by contrast, gives the anonymous singular, which implies that there was only one incumbent pagarch at that time. The *hypodektai*, therefore, cannot be linked to individual pagarchs—unless only one was in office—but were probably assigned to the collegium in its entirety. What this entails for the distribution of authority between joint pagarchs is discussed in Chapter Four. The next subsection instead addresses the issue of how the remaining, mostly lower-ranking, signatories conform to this conception.

4. The Other Signatories of the Tax Receipts

Besides the *hypodektai* and the *boēthoi*, a number of other agents signed tax receipts in the name of the pagarchs. Of those, the *notarii* Damianos and Mousaios were certainly attached to individual pagarchs, as was Christodoros 1, who signs as *notarius* and as *grammateus* on different occasions. Comparative evidence shows that *notarii* could be an official's personal assistants. Despite the etymology, the late antique *notarius* was not a notary but rather a scribe or secretary, and his job does not appear to have been strictly defined.[202] In many cases, both *notarius* and *grammateus* probably designate professions rather than official positions. A well-known parallel from the earliest years of the Islamic occupation would be Senouthios, *notarius* and *anystēs* to the pagarch Athanasios for a subdistrict of the Hermopolite nome.[203]

All signatories who sign in the name of the pagarchs without stating their position conform to the hypothesis established in the previous subsection and may thus ten-

199 *P.Cair.Masp.* II 67228 (Kollouthos); *P.Cair.Masp.* I 67046 (Petros).

200 See Table 4 (pp. 165–167). That Ioulianos was sole pagarch through 552/553 CE is suggested by *P.Cair.Masp.* I 67094, a deed of surety issued to Ioulianos, and by *SB* VI 9102, an imperial rescript dating from the time of the "Ioulianos affair" (discussed in Chapter Six), which refers only anonymously to "the pagarch."

201 *P.Vat.Aphrod.* 16A. See the discussion in Stern forthcoming (a), s.vv.

202 On the status of *notarii*, see Schmelz 2002, 250 and Kovarik 2014, 273. Cf. Teitler 1985, especially 52 and 75, and Diethart & Worp 1986, 9 and 13, including on the unclear distinction, if there was any at all, between *grammateis* and *notarii*. See also *P.Sijp.*, pp. 232–233. *Grammateus kōmēs*, by contrast, is a technical term that refers to the village scribe.

203 For the early Islamic period, see also *CPR* XIV 1 (Arsinoites; July 8, 651/666); *CPR* XXIV 33 (Arsinoe; 653), possibly addressed to the same man (see the Catalog, n. 105); *P.Mert.* II 100 (Arsinoites; October 20, 669); and *SB* VI 9144 (Hermopolites; after 641), on which see *BL* XII 194 and n. 108 above.

tatively be identified as personal assistants of individual pagarchs, although Hermias and Komasios, who use the anonymous plural to refer to the pagarchs, might have been serving the collegium as a whole. The role of the *pronoētēs* Psates for the collegial pagarchs was discussed in Section II 2: he was apparently employed for a public lot that was administered by the pagarchy.

Another possible exception from the "personal assistants" model is Menas, the *singularis*.[204] Since he is the only writer in these receipts to use the Antinoopolite measure, he is no doubt one of the provincial *singulares* who spread over the countryside and regularly appear as local collectors in the papyri.[205] In light of this, we may take his mistake of writing "Promantinoos" instead of "Philantinoos" as a telling slip of the pen due to unfamiliarity with the locals: he may have simply misheard or misread the name.[206] A certain Georgios who appears under obscure circumstances in a receipt signed by Christodoros 2 can possibly also be identified with a homonymous *singularis*.[207] Liberis, the only (explicit) Flavius among the signatories, was probably a provincial official too, or a collecting soldier.[208] Notably, Liberis does not sign in the name of any pagarch, but instead notes that he received the payment "for the security (*asphaleia*) of the one-third share of Serenos, *illoustrios*."[209] This might be a formality to account for the fact that Liberis was not a "proper" local tax collector or was not a part of Serenos's local apparatus.[210]

---

204 On the *singulares*, see Palme 1999, 105; *P.Sorb.* II 69, p. 61; and *P.Horak* 9.15–16 including the commentary.

205 *P.Cair.Masp.* III 67284 (Aphrodite; 538/539?); *P.Flor.* III 291 (Aphrodite; 538/539?); *P.Cair. Masp.* II 67210 (Aphrodite; c. 548?); *P.Horak* 9 (Hermopolites; VI). These officials also appear as intermediaries for Aphrodite's fiscal administration (*dēmosios logos*) during the period when Aphrodite enjoyed autopract status, e.g., in *P.Cair.Masp.* I 67103 (September 16, 526). Note that the *singulares* in *P.Cair.Masp.* III 67284.5–6 have the additional function of *apaitētai*, viz., tax collectors (cf. *P.Cair.Masp.* I 67105.7–8).

206 *P.Cair.Masp.* III 67325 fol. VIII recto 5: δέδωκ(ε) Κορνήλιος Προμ[αντ]ινό(ου). The Coptic expression ⲡⲣⲟⲙ ⲁⲛⲧⲓⲛⲟⲟⲩ translates to "the man from Antinoopolis," which is a common construction to identify an individual and thus might have come easily to the writer's mind.

207 *P.Flor.* III 298.24–25 (574/575 CE): τὰ καὶ δοθ(έντα) τῷ κρ( ) Γεωργίῳ ἀπὸ τῶν β | [. . . . .], followed by the signature. Based on the digital image, κρ( ) can be corrected to κυρ(ίῳ); cf. *BL* X 73: κυρ(ῷ). Georgios may be identical with the homonymous *singularis* in *P.Cair.Masp.* I 67056 col. II 4 (around May 25, 551?), if we compare the *singularis* Menas in a similar position in *P.Cair.Masp.* III 67325 fol. III recto 1–6. The name is not rare, however, and the two Georgioi are separated by about two decades; on the new dates that I propose for the receipts in *P.Flor.* III 298, see Table 4 (pp. 165–167).

208 Liberis is the only signatory who certainly had someone write the receipt for him, as his clumsy signature reveals; see *P.Cair.Masp.* III 67325 fol. III recto 5–7.

209 *P.Cair.Masp.* III 67325 fol. III recto 6–7: τὰ δοθ(έντα) Λιβερίο(υ) (ὑπὲρ) ἀσφαλ(είας) τοῦ τρίτου | μ̣έρ[ο]υς Σιρινο̣ς (*sic*) ἰλλουστρίο̣υ̣.

210 Though perhaps this hypothesis is trying too hard to look for formal explanations in a highly flexible administrative system.

Finally, Iosephis, the *presbyteros* and *dioikētēs*, was also doubtless a local actor, as is suggested by parallel evidence that attests *dioikētai* of church property.[211] In one papyrus, a *presbyteros* and *dioikētēs* acts as intermediary for a monastery with regard to a lease that includes the payment of taxes (*synteleia*) "in grain and in gold, the freight charges (*naula*), and any kind of supply levy (*annōniakoi titloi*)."[212] Perhaps Iosephis had a similar job and processed the tax payments for Apollos's *onoma* because of an older lease arrangement. But Iosephis's *dioikēsis* may also refer to a public, presumably local, responsibility: a *presbyteros* who was *dioikētēs* of a village acts as intermediary in a (very fragmentary) petition from the province of Palaestina Salutaris concerning taxes.[213] Perhaps Iosephis signed for the pagarch Ioannes, instead of the collegium, because he was in contact with him.[214]

5. Evidence from Outside the Antaiopolite Tax Receipts

While the accounts so meticulously kept by Dioskoros's family provide us with a fairly clear picture for the Antaiopolite nome, there is little evidence for the lower-level operations of the pagarchy in other nomes.[215] Still, the available material fits the Antaiopolite model. Two tax receipts from Hermopolis show the *boēthoi* delivering the aggregated taxes from their villages to the pagarch,[216] and a sixth-century tax receipt from the Antinoopolite nome also corresponds to the situation in the Antaiopolite receipts: the *boēthos* signs a receipt for *dēmosia* "of the village" in the name of the pagarch of Antinoopolis.[217] A Coptic letter from the Hermopolite aligns with the twofold pro-

211 Wipszycka 1972, 141–142.

212 *P.Mich.* XIII 667 (mid-VI). The title of *presbyteros* and *dioikētēs* (l. 8 and 37) is abbreviated and partially restored and therefore disputed by Fournet & Gascou 2002, 31 n. 25, who instead suggest a *diakonētēs*, which would then probably further link the pagarchs to the shipment of grain by the monastery of Metanoia (cf. earlier Mazza 1995, 217–218 for a similar hypothesis), on which see Section III 2 above. In Iosephis's case (*P.Cair.Masp.* III 67325 fol. VIII recto 22), the palaeography does not fit the (conceivable) alternative διακ( ). Cf. *P.Cair.Masp.* I 67060.1, which explains that a *diakonētēs* has reported to the pagarch Menas Scriniarius that Aphrodite has not sent its taxes (*astika* and *kōmētika*), and *P.Cair.Masp.* I 67002 col. III 19: a *grammateus* and *diakonētēs* tells Menas not to persecute the villagers. In any event, the manager in *P.Mich.* XIII 667, whatever his title, was the intermediary for a monastery whose tax payments were handled by its lessee.

213 *P.Ness.* III 54.2 (Palaestina Salutaris; late VI or early VII): ἐ]λεεινοῦ πρεσβ(υτέρου) καὶ διοικητοῦ Χαφρεα[των κώ]μης. On the restoration, see the commentary on l. 2.

214 Territorial divisions of the pagarchy are unlikely to be at play here; see Chapter Four, Section IV.

215 An explanation for this situation is offered by the "clusters of evidence," as discussed in the Introduction.

216 *BGU* XII 2196 (VI) and *P.Lond.* V 1753 (VII, possibly from the Islamic period); see Section III 2 above.

217 *P.Leid.Inst.* 72.

cedure for processing the payment and shipment of the grain tax.[218] In Oxyrhynchos, a *boēthos* "of" the landowner Anastasia stands surety for one inhabitant of a *kōmē pagarchoumenē*, and we regularly find *boēthoi* in other "pagarched" villages.[219] The only non-Antaiopolite text attesting a *hypodektēs* in connection with a pagarch is extant in a small fragment of an Arsinoite papyrus: the *hypodektēs* here is involved in the business of tax collection in a village.[220] However, in their professional titles the managers of the Apion estate active in villages call themselves "*pronoētēs*, or *hypodektēs*," certainly referring to their "semi-public" capacity to collect taxes for the Apionic holdings within these "pagarched" villages.[221] Some papyri from the Arsinoite nome are similar in that administrators of large estates are referred to as *hypodektai*.[222]

One prominent tax collection officer, the *apaitētēs*, is completely absent from the tax receipts issued by the pagarchs.[223] In fourth-century Oxyrhynchos, still under the *praepositus pagi*, the *apaitētai* aggregated the various taxes sent in by the local *boēthoi*.[224] In a fifth-century text from the same nome, however, the pagarch (= *praepositus pagi*?) sends an *apaitētēs* to a village to collect directly from a taxpayer and hand over the proper receipt.[225] In a sixth-century contract from the Antaiopolite nome, two "*apai-*

218 *P.Sorb.Copt.* 30; see Section III 2 above.

219 The *kōmai pagarchoumenai* and their relationship to the pagarchy are discussed in Chapter Three, Sections III and IV.

220 *SB* I 4781 (Arsinoites; c. 600) with the new reading by Bernhard Palme in the commentary on *P.Messeri* 44, who also discusses the parallels to this type of document. On the verso, *SB* I 4781 identifies as a ὁμο(λογία) παρακλήσ(εως) ὑποδοχ(ῆς) κώμ(ης) Ἀρσινόης ὑπὸ Αὐρ(ηλίου) | Εὐλογίου ὑποδέκτ(ου) μετ' ἐγ(γυητοῦ) τούτου [– – –]. Palme argues that we are dealing here with an estate *hypodektēs* of Strategios (*P.Messeri*, p. 264). On the one hand, the *hypodektēs* of the *ousia* of the (late) pagarch Menas in *SPP* III^2 153.1–2 (Arsinoites; 629 or 644) might be a parallel instance and it is true that the managers of the Apion estate in the Oxyrhynchite (on whom see the following note), who were responsible for the rents and taxes from estate property, refer to themselves as "*pronoētēs*, or *hypodektēs*," in contracts. On the other, in cases where only one title is used, these men are always referred to as *pronoētai*, and these managers' authority did only relate to estate parcels within the village, not to the village in its entirety (as I discuss in Chapter Three, Section IV). I therefore believe that it is still possible that Strategios's relation to a city *hypodektēs* is at issue in *SB* I 4781. As to the nature of the business dealt with in the contract, plausibly analyzed by Palme, *SB* I 4781 is perhaps functionally comparable to *P.Lond.* V 1661, an Antaiopolite contract between the pagarchs and two "*apaitētai* of the liturgists," possibly including a precollection credit, which is discussed below. *SB* I 4815 = 4792 and *P.Messeri* 44 are parallels to *SB* I 4781, also addressed to Strategios Paneuphemos and also concerning a *hypodochē*, but the part in which the *hypodektēs* occurs in *SB* I 4781 is missing in both parallel texts.

221 A *hypodochē* of a *pronoētēs* occurs, for instance, in *P.Oxy.* XVI 1915.10. The Apionic *pronoētai* and their collections are discussed in Chapter Three, Sections IV and V.

222 See Chapter Three, Section VII.

223 On the *apaitētai*, see Palme 1989.

224 See the example of the *boēthoi* Papnouthis and Dorotheos in *P.Oxy.* XLVIII 3393.12 (June 8, 365) and *P.Oxy.* XLVIII 3397.6 (IV); cf. Berkes 2017a, 2 n. 7.

225 *P.Oxy.* LVI 3865.63–70 (Oxyrhynchos; V); see Chapter One, Section III.

tētai of the liturgists of the village of Aphrodite" appear.[226] The *apaitētai* acknowledge to the pagarchs a debt of twelve *nomismata* for "the said liturgists—namely, guards (*phylakes*)—of the said village of Aphrodite for the present second indiction."[227] The contract provisions—for instance, repayment in accordance with the three official tax installments (*katabolai*)—leave no doubt that this debt is connected to the tax collection duties of the *apaitētai*, maybe as a remuneration for the liturgical guards.[228] Because the contract is dated Epeiph 30, two months into the same indiction for which the taxes were due and in the harvest season, the editor proposed that it might be a "disguised" tax collection contract—or a job description, as it were—in the form of a debt contract through which the *apaitētai* guaranteed their share to the pagarchs up front.[229] In any case, these *apaitētai* collected a specific tax in the countryside.[230] It was the job of the pagarchs, and their *trakteutai*, to collect such amounts at the higher level and pass them on.

Other officials not present in the tax receipts but whose dealings with the pagarchs are otherwise frequently attested are the village headmen (*prōtokōmētai*).[231] We only have evidence for Aphrodite, where in the mid-sixth century the *prōtokōmētai* were appointed by the provincial office on the recommendation of Ammonios, an *endoxotatos comes sacri consistorii*.[232] When Aphrodite later lost its autopract status (or had it suspended or limited), appointing the village headmen apparently became the duty of the pagarch. At least in one case a villager deems the pagarch Menas capable of installing a *prōtokōmētēs*,[233] and this fits the situation described in a recently edited papyrus from

226 *P.Lond.* V 1661.9–10 (Aphrodite; July 24, 553): ἀπαιτητῶν τῶν λειτουργῶ̣[ν] | τῆς αὐτῆς κώμης Ἀφροδίτης. This title is not attested anywhere else.

227 *P.Lond.* V 1661.11–13: ὑπὲρ | τῶν αὐτῶν [λ]ειτουργῶν \ἤτοι φυλ̣[άκ]ω̣ν/ τῆς αὐτ̣ῆς κώ[μ]ης Ἀφροδ̣ί̣τ̣ης ὑπὲρ τῆς παρούσης | δε[υ]τέρας ἰν[δ(ικτίονος)]. *Leitourgoi* as a specific term for guards (cf. l. 4: μάχην) may also occur in *PSI* I 71.6 and 10 (Oxyrhynchos; VI) and, as assumed by Gascou 1983, 101 (= 2008, 103), in *P.Hamb.* I 56.25 and 28, on which see n. 131 above.

228 The editor discounts this possibility (*P.Lond.* V, p. 25), but remunerated liturgists are nothing unusual, e.g., *eirēnarchai* in *P.Neph.* 20 (Herakleopolites; IV) and in *SB* XXVIII 16872 (Arsinoites; VI–VII). In the latter, it is the village *grammateus* who remunerates the *eirēnarchai* out of the current indiction's crops (see also Sänger 2005, 193 n. 149). See also Maurer & Tost 2016, 1840 with additional evidence in n. 38.

229 Cf. n. 180 above for a similar procedure that was followed by the *boēthoi* Papnouthis and Dorotheos.

230 The official titulature of *apaitētai* frequently includes a specific tax title.

231 On the *prōtokōmētēs*, see Berkes 2017a, 25–53. In the Oxyrhynchite, this term refers more generally to a village notable, while the term for the village headman is *meizōn* (see, e.g., *P.Oxy.* I 133); on the *meizones*, see Berkes 2017a, 53–82.

232 *P.Cair.Masp.* III 67323 (Antinoopolis; c. January–July 540); Zuckerman 2004a, 123. On Ammonios, see Chapter Six, Section I. The signature of one *prōtokōmētēs* in Dioskoros's petition *P.Cair. Masp.* III 67283 col. II 21 against the pagarch Ioulianos also dates from this period. It is perhaps revealing that only one *prōtokōmētēs* signed this petition; did the other *prōtokōmētai* refrain from taking a stand against the pagarch?

233 *P.Lond.* V 1677.23–26 (Antinoopolis; c. 568–570).

immediately after the Islamic conquest, in which *prōtokōmētai* appear to have been replaced by agents of the pagarch.[234] The *prōtokōmētai* acted as mediators on behalf of their village community vis-à-vis the higher administrative levels but, conversely, were also the pagarchs' link to the village community. They are documented as intermediaries for the pagarchs in a deed of surety, probably for a criminal suspect,[235] as well as in the aforementioned formally private acknowledgment of debt by two *apaitētai* of Aphrodite to the pagarchs that was connected to tax collection in the village.[236]

Absent from the documentation of the pagarchs after 500 CE are the *sitologoi*, who regularly appear in connection with the *praepositus pagi* in the early to mid-fourth century. This may, however, be explained by Lajos Berkes's observation that after 400 CE these officials are no longer attested anywhere but in the Hermopolite nome,[237] from which we do not have abundant papyri concerning the pagarchs.

IV. Summary

Despite somewhat limited evidence, it is possible to draw a reasonably detailed picture of the pagarchs' place in the process of tax collection in the countryside. In the sixth century the pagarchs' territorial purview was not equivalent to the entire *civitas*, the ancient nome, and although their job entailed a fair amount of interaction with the civic administration, the Byzantine pagarchs were formally not the heads of the cities. Instead, fiscal operations at the city level were channeled around the *dēmosion logistērion* and the pagarchs' apparatus was, from a bureaucratic viewpoint, part of these operations. The pagarchs even acted as representatives of civic interests, for instance, in the administration of civic land in the countryside, and the city in turn paid for some of the pagarchy's subordinate functionaries.

In Antaiopolis, the pagarchs' apparatus at the city level consisted of several accountants (*trakteutai* and a *logographos*) and a *hypodektēs*, or "receiver." This official continued a tradition in collecting *dēmosia* from land plots classified as *astika*, that is, from those parcels in the countryside that had once belonged to city dwellers, but apparently had nothing to do with the collection of *dēmosia* coming from *kōmētika* plots. This was the job of the *boēthoi*, who collected these taxes from villages and delivered them

234 *CPR* XXXVI 2 (Hermopolites; c. 643–644), with the interpretation of the editor Federico Morelli.

235 *P.Cair.Masp.* I 67094 (Aphrodite; April 1–25, 552 or March 27–31, 553). It is hard to tell what the *anagnōstēs* Enoch is accused of, but the context points to a criminal offense rather than, e.g., *anachōrēsis*; cf., along similar lines, Palme forthcoming, 20–21. A surety for a liturgical task may be less likely because the document contains a conventional penalty instead of a demand for compensation that we might expect in the event of nonperformance of a liturgy. Enoch's six (!) guarantors guarantee for the considerable sum of six *nomismata*.

236 *P.Lond.* V 1661 (Aphrodite; July 24, 553).

237 Berkes 2017a, 205.

directly, without the mediation of the *hypodektēs*, to the pagarchs and their accountants. Unlike the *hypodektai*, the *boēthoi* were private entrepreneurs, some with multiple jobs. A number of minor administrative staff, such as *notarii*, also appear as issuers of receipts and must have been present in the villages at least on certain occasions. The pattern of their signatures for individual or collegial pagarchs suggests that these minor ranks were assigned to individual pagarchs rather than the entire collegium, but there are a number of officials who do not state their position, so this picture remains tentative. There were probably other collecting officials whose connection to the pagarchs eludes us due to the nature of our evidence. Glimpses of such links can be caught in a number of collectors whose titles occur only once in connection with pagarchs, such as the *singularis,* further attesting the provincial administration's local reach, and a church or village *dioikētēs*.

During the sixth century, the pagarchy was both part of and separate from the city's fiscal operations. Rather than being integrated into the civic apparatus, it had its own staff, who were paid from the city's budget for "external" expenses; from a civic point of view, expenses for the pagarchy had a similar character to those for imperial and provincial needs. The pagarchy was interlinked with the city administration, but distinct from it, and at least since *Edict* 13 (539 CE) it was directly subordinate to the provincial governor. This development is, to my mind, a far cry from the picture of the pagarchs as usurpers of local power at the expense of the state. Instead, it suggests that the rise of the pagarchy under various emperors was a continuous response to the inefficiency, and often opacity, of local government. The countryside and its resources were effectively cut off from civic authorities and put in the hands of dignitaries who were closer to the reach of the central government.[238] It was potentially this double role as a representative of central government who was at the same time still "of the city" that brought pagarchs like Ioulianos and Menas Scriniarius into conflict with the (initially) autopract village of Aphrodite.[239] All this fits the evolution outlined in Chapter One: instead of being conceived as civic officers, the "later" pagarchs of the sixth century consolidated their own administrative apparatus from the local level of the *pagi* to that of the "pagarchy" as part of the fiscal organization at the *civitas* level, but with responsibility outside the urban center. Little evidence is available that allows us to compare these results with the situation in *civitates* other than Antaiopolis. Evidence for the pagarchs' apparatus in the city or in the villages is almost completely absent from the records of the Fayum, which concern other layers of society. The Oxyrhynchite papyri shed light on the country villages from the perspective of the Apion estate, which is equally important for this question but requires a different analytical approach; that analysis is undertaken in Chapter Three.

238 Over the longer term, the replacement of pagarchs from the Christian Byzantine elite by pagarchs of Arab origin around the end of the seventh century and the beginning of the eighth was, therefore, a continuation of this trend rather than a fundamental break with tradition.

239 See Chapter Six.

The question remains of how this formally somewhat limited administrative role within the *civitates* in the sixth century made the Byzantine pagarchs into such powerful players, who in the early Islamic period at the latest became the formal heads of the cities; one can hardly imagine that a man like Strategios Paneuphemos had much reason to fear civic rebukes for any of his actions. This topic is addressed in Chapter Five. Soon after the Islamic conquest (639–642 CE), the Roman-Egyptian *civitates* began to identify their administrative circumscriptions as "pagarchies," but it remains unclear whether this was an abrupt administrative rearrangement or simply a change of terminology acknowledging the pagarchs' predominance among the leading authorities in the cities. The Senouthios archive from the 640s shows the pagarch Athanasios's strong sway over the entirety of the Hermopolite nome: the pagarchy had, effectively, become synonymous with the *civitas*. It may be that this had happened even earlier, and that related evidence from the time of the Persian occupation (619–629) or the reestablished Byzantine control (629–639) simply has not turned up so far. This question is relevant to the discussion of the late antique *oikoi* that is the focus of the next chapter.

Chapter Three
The State, Estates, and Elite Participation in a Rural World

Earlier, I argued that the evolution of the pagarchy to the level seen in the sixth century should be seen in terms of a continuous rearrangement of public responsibilities between the large estates and officials proper.[1] How, then, did the pagarchs' authority relate to the role the large landowners and their "houses" (*oikoi*) played in tax collection, which some scholars have understood as a privilege and others as an obligation? The model of fiscal shares was developed mainly from the evidence of the Oxyrhynchite nome, where the documentary situation for the pagarchy is peculiar: most sixth- to early seventh-century papyri from this nome that appear to pertain to the pagarchy do not attest pagarchs or a pagarchy of Oxyrhynchos but refer to *kōmai pagarchoumenai*, villages "pagarched" by a large landowner.

The present chapter expands upon this observation. Based on an analysis of the *kōmai pagarchoumenai* and their occurrence in the documents (mainly) from the Apion estate, it will establish a conception of fiscal authority in the Oxyrhynchite that not only supports basic assumptions of the Gascou model from an administrative perspective, but also refines it in significant aspects. I argue that the expression *kōmē pagarchoumenē* does not relate to the pagarchy of Oxyrhynchos but rather to a separate institution that most likely should be seen as a manifestation of the model of fiscal shares. These "pagarched" villages appear to have been under the quasi-permanent administration of the *oikoi* not only in fiscal terms, but for virtually everything one might expect officials to deal with in villages. This institution appears to have grown alongside the responsibilities of the *oikoi* for civic duties and was apparently abolished or significantly limited and downgraded at some point between 626 and 647 CE. There are indications that a system akin to the Oxyrhynchite one was in place but simply not as prominent in other nomes.

I. Large Estates and Fiscal Shares

Traditionally, domanial tax collection has been seen as a major limit to the pagarchs' authority in the countryside of late antique Egypt, particularly since these large estates were not contiguous landholdings in a coherent area, but rather consisted of many parcels scattered throughout the hinterland of the *civitates*.[2] These regions featured a host of landowners of different magnitude and, naturally, all of them paid taxes for the land they owned. With time, these landowners also became responsible for the taxes

1 See Chapter One.
2 Hickey 2007, 295; see also Chapter One, n. 125.

https://doi.org/10.1515/9783111493183-004

and personal liabilities of workers and tenants on their estates and collected these dues via their own administrative apparatus. Some of these landowners—at least in the Oxyrhynchite nome—were even in the position to collect and pay taxes for land they did *not* own, as the model of fiscal shares by Jean Gascou has established.[3] Gascou's ideas profoundly changed the scholarly perception of the large landowners' involvement in public administration.[4] Yet it remains unknown why some estates assumed such a pronounced "public" role when others did not; presumably, this status required a degree of administrative sophistication and a certain territorial extension of the estate.

Curiously enough, Gascou never explicitly addressed the question of how the fiscal shares maintained by these public-private institutions, the *oikoi*, related to the institution of the pagarchy and its fiscal authority. So far as I am aware, only Jairus Banaji has been explicit on this issue, arguing that the pagarchy was synonymous with the extended fiscal responsibilities that the *oikoi* assumed.[5] There is evidence for the opposite, however:

(1) In an Oxyrhynchite list of contributions for a public bath, the contributions that were due to a landowner or their heirs are kept separate from that individual's share of the pagarchy. The text also shows that there was only one Oxyrhynchite pagarchy and that the term *oikos* is used independently from it.[6]

---

3 On the large estates and the Gascou model, see Chapter One, Section I. The validity of the Gascou model beyond the Oxyrhynchite is discussed in Section VII below.

4 Hickey 2007, 289; Hickey 2012, 5–6.

5 Banaji 2007, 97–98 and 148–149, pointing to Gascou's silence on the pagarchs in Gascou 1985. Banaji deems it "only logical" (p. 149) to link Gascou's terminology of fiscal shares to the pagarchy because he sees the latter as "an institution which delegated fiscal authority to local landowners." Hickey appears to deem Banaji's view plausible (Hickey 2007, 298), but is cautious as to a potential technical meaning of the verb *pagarcheō*; see Hickey 2008, 89 n. 11 and Hickey 2012, 49, the latter questioning whether Sarris was correct to implicitly equate the pagarchy with the Apiones' fiscal shares. For a more explicit criticism of Sarris's view, see Ruffini 2009, 631–632. Yet my findings in this chapter suggest that also Ruffini's own conception—in which fiscal shares, village pagarchies (p. 631 and n. 4), and a *civitas* pagarchy (p. 632) could seemingly coexist—needs to be modified. Another prominent instance of an implicit distinction of the pagarchy and the landowners' fiscal responsibilities is Liebeschuetz 2001, 187–188.

6 *P.Oxy.* XVI 2040, discussed in the next section. While the *endoxos oikos* appears in l. 5, the entries for the pagarchy occur in ll. 10 and 13–14. Quotations of this passage (Gascou 1972a, 65 = 2008, 46; Mazza 1995, 190; Ruffini 2008a, 103) lack an important word. For the entries for the pagarchy are not twice "for the half share of the pagarchy," possibly relating to a "pagarchy" that would have amounted to about 50 percent of each aristocrat's personal fortune, as Mazza infers. Rather, the second entry reads "for the other (!) half share of the pagarchy," ll. 13–14: (ὑπὲρ) τοῦ ἄλλου (ἡμίσους) μέρ(ους) τῆς παγαρχ(ίας), which demonstrates that these two amounts are for the (only) pagarchy of Oxyrhynchos; cf. Ioannes and Serenos, pagarchs of the "two-thirds" and "one-third" part, respectively. Note that the shares of Ptolemaios and Ioustos without the pagarchy remain nearly exactly the same between *P.Oxy.* XVI 2040 and *P.Oxy.* XVI 2020, as discussed in Section II below.

(2) In the Fayum, pagarchs bore the title of "pagarch of Arsinoe and Theodosiopolis" at least from 556 to 622 CE. This reflects a system in which Theodosiopolite administration was generally taken care of by Arsinoite authorities, notably in the dealings of officials at the city level. The "double pagarchy" for two cities thus cannot be referring to magnates acting individually on "their" parts of the *civitas* territory, but must indicate sole pagarchs or a fixed number of responsible pagarchs that were organized in a collegium and jointly responsible for one *civitas* territory.[7] The Arsinoite yields indicators for the presence of the system of fiscal shares as well as one papyrus that may be indirectly attesting the distinction between the responsibility for fiscal shares and responsibility for the pagarchy.[8]

(3) In the Antaiopolite nome, the distinction is not as evident, as we do not clearly see the fiscal shares in that nome in relation to the pagarchy.[9] What seems clear is that there was only one "pagarchy of Antaiopolis,"[10] and that at certain times there was only one sole "pagarch of Antaiopolis."[11] And while it is possible that this man would have controlled the only *oikos* in the nome,[12] he did not exercise a (hypothetical) "fiscal-shares pagarchy" via that *oikos*: we can see that the value of the Antaiopolite pagarchy was, at least occasionally, divided in three "parts" (*merē*), shared by two or three pagarchs, which cannot be explained by inheritance of one single *oikos*, as these pagarchs originate from different families or regions.[13]

7 On Theodosiopolis and the system of joint administration, see the Introduction, n. 50. This argument is in line with the observation that from 556 to 622 CE no pagarch bore only one of the two city names (Arsinoe or Theodosiopolis) in his official titulature.

8 These documents are discussed in Section VII on the evidence outside the Oxyrhynchite nome.

9 See Section VII on the evidence outside Oxyrhynchite nome.

10 *P.Cair.Masp.* I 67002 col. I 10–11 and *P.Cair.Masp.* III 67283 col. I 2 (ἑλκ[έσ]θαι εἰς π̣α̣γαρχίαν τῆ[ς Ἀνταιο(υ)]π̣ο̣λ̣ιτῶν ἧς κεκράτηκ̣εν) speak of someone "entering into" and "getting hold of" the pagarchy—i.e., in the singular—of Antaiopolis. The Antaiopolite pagarchy has its own (single) entry in an account of civic expenses (*P.Cair.Masp.* I 67057 col. II 24–31, discussed in Chapter Two, Section II 3). And Ioulianos's "own" (*oikeios*) pagarchy is equated with the pagarchy of Antaiopolis; cf. *P.Cair.Masp.* I 67024–25 (new ed. Fournet 2018) A 32, A' 57, and B 31: ὑπὸ τὴν οἰκείαν παγαρχίαν ποιήσασθαι and A 31, A' 56, and B 29–30: παγάρχην τῆς Ἀνταιοπολιτῶν; see also *P.Cair.Masp.* III 67283 col. I 2.

11 In *P.Cair.Masp.* I 67003, a petition from a community of monks vexed by a man who is contesting their land, the provincial governor is asked "to order the pagarch of Antaiopolis and the *topotērētēs* of the same (city) to keep him away from us" (ll. 25–26: προστάξαι τῷ παγάρχῃ τῆς Ἀνταίο(υ) καὶ τῷ τοποτηρητῇ ταυτῆς ἀφ' ἡμῶν αὐτὸν ἀποτρέψαι). The tax receipt *P.Cair.Masp.* II 67228 is signed by a *hypodektēs* of Antaiopolis—that is, an official at the city level (see Chapter Two, Section III 1)—in the name of "the *endoxotatos* pagarch," whose name is not given. See also Chapter Four, Section IV.

12 See Chapter Six, Section I on the question of whether the pagarch Ioulianos controlled Aphrodite's *endoxos oikos*.

13 These are the pagarchs Ioulianos, Patrikia, and Menas in the early 550s CE (and possibly Ioulianos and Menas as a duo in 553); Ioulianos, Kometes, and Euthymios in 560; and Ioannes (pagarch of the "two-thirds part") and Serenos (pagarch of the "one-third part") around 570 CE; see Chap-

Consequently, as explained in the remainder of this chapter, the pagarchy existed alongside the fiscal authority exercised by the large landowners—now as *geouchountes*, in the participle form, rather than *geouchoi*. It is, however, not easy to grasp this relationship, owing to the profusion of various settlement types in the countryside of late antique Egypt. Besides villages (*kōmai*), several types of settlements were scattered throughout a city's hinterland; at this point, a short survey of them seems advisable.[14] Probably the smallest was the *epoikion*, which scholars often render as "hamlet" or "farmstead"; *epoikia* were maintained by sometimes only a handful of workers and were owned by individual magnates but also by village institutions.[15] On a comparable scale, a *ktēma* (literally, "property") can refer to a particular land parcel but also, more generally, to property in an abstract or comprehensive sense.[16] On a larger scale, *ousia* ("fortune," "estate") refers to an assembly of landed property that consisted of the aforementioned smaller units: an *ousia* was a concrete unit to which administrators were assigned,[17] *epoikia* were a part thereof,[18] and property within the urban center of the *civitas* could also be part of the *ousia*.[19] Somewhat comparable to an *ousia* is a *ktēsis* ("property") in that it was private property, was burdened with *munera*, and had managers allocated to it.[20] It was a fiscal *onoma* (a taxpaying account) and paid its taxes to a higher administrative level, which in the early Islamic age were clearly villages, but this is not obvious for the Byzantine period.[21] All in

---

ter Four, Section II on the chronology of the pagarchs and the Catalog on their possible backgrounds.

14 A *mēchanē*—technically an irrigation machine using a waterwheel—can refer to a farm of irrigated land, but seems not to have been a settlement in the legal sense; on this term, see *P.Oxy.* LXXXIII, p. 119 and Bransbourg 2016, 374 n. 218. For instance, no party in a legal document ever hails from a *mēchanē*.

15 Hickey 2007, 295–296; Berkes 2017a, 221.

16 See *P.Gen.* IV 198 (December 27, 633–January 5, 634), in which an *epoikion* (l. 6) is also referred to as a *ktēma* (l. 8).

17 *BGU* I 3 (*enoikiologos*); *P.Genova* II 72 and *SPP* X 251 B.6 (*phrontistēs*); *SPP* VIII 1061 and *SPP* III^2 44 (*pronoētēs*); *SPP* III^2 153 (*hypodektēs*); *SPP* XX 209.7 (*epikeimenos*).

18 *BGU* II 364 (September 11, 553).

19 *CPR* VII 51 (644 CE, from the early Islamic period); *SB* I 4492 (VI).

20 On *ktēseis* and *munera*, see *P.Cair.Masp.* II 67169.27; *BGU* XIX, pp. 82–83; and *SPP* III^2 pt. V, p. 148. For managers of *ktēseis* (all *pronoētai*), see *BGU* XIX 2791, *P.Oxy.* XVI 1902, and *SPP* VIII 1026; on the latter text, see Benaissa 2010.

21 On *ktēseis* as fiscal *onomata*, see *P.Sorb.* II 69, pp. 38–43. On *ktēseis* and villages in the early Islamic period, see *SPP* III^2 pt. V, p. xxvi. For the Byzantine period, this subordination is less clear. See, for instance, the editor's commentary on *P.Köln* XI 460, but this text lacks a village and the editor's reference to Kreuzsaler's discussion in *SPP* III^2 pt. V therefore risks comparing administrative apples and oranges. *BGU* XVII 2724A is a list of payments by (1) villages, (2) *ktēseis*, and (3) the harbor, all of which apparently are distinct entities and placed side by side at the same administrative level. *Ktēseis* pay to the account of the *civitas* in *P.Bad.* IV 95.447 (see *BGU* XIX, pp. 82–83) and in *P.Eirene* II 21. The document *Ch.L.A.* XLI 1194 = *P.Cair.Masp.* III 67329.6–7 reads: [κ]ạị ἐπειδ̣ὴ τ̣ὴν ὑπόλοιπ[ό]ν μο(υ) πᾶσαν ἐλαχίστην κ̣τ̣[ῆ]σιν ọ[ὖ]σ̣αν καὶ τελοῦσαν ὑπὸ τὴν εἰρημ(ένην) μοι | [κώμης Ἀφροδίτης, and also in *P.Cair.Masp.* III 67313.19 and 23–24, a *hypoloipos ktēsis* is part of a *ktēma* that in turn pays taxes to the village. But these latter two cases are possibly

all, *ktēsis* appears to denote landed property in a more general way than does *ousia*, perhaps comparable in this regard to the term *ktēma* at a lower level.[22]

What formally distinguished an *ousia* from an *oikos* can only be speculated upon so far, but an *oikos* was clearly more than an *ousia*. In one text, a certain late *endoxotatos* Olybrios owned "the three *ousiai* and the *ktēma* Thmoun Pamoun," which form (part of?) an *endoxos oikos*, managed by two *endoxotatoi dioikētai*; it appears that *apaitētai* and soldiers (*stratiōtai*) were responsible for collecting taxes from this estate.[23] In another text, Apion III's estates are not referred to as *endoxos oikos*, as they usually are, but as his *ousia*, and there are parallel examples for both Apion II and (for the Arsinoite *oikos* of) Strategios Paneuphemos.[24] I suspect that this terminological difference is significant and reflects different institutional roles of *ousiai* and *oikoi*. It is important to be aware that the pagarchy is nowhere linked to an *oikos*.[25] Quite the contrary: *Edict* 13 mentions that the pagarch's *ousiai* are in jeopardy in case of misconduct.

Which landowners were subject to the pagarchy, and which were not? It seems that as early as the fourth century the "early" pagarchs, the *praepositi pagorum*, had their say over *epoikia* whose contributions were paid through the magnates who owned them.[26] These magnates presumably owned *ousiai*. In the sixth century, the *ousia* of the *endoxotatos* Ioulianos in the Antaiopolite nome paid at least some of its dues to the pagarchy.[27]

---

invalid points of comparison due to the, in many aspects, *civitas*-like administration of the "village" Aphrodite.

22 Cf. *SB* XX 14669, the Aphrodite Cadaster, in which the terms *idiotikē/basilikē/nēsiotikē ktēsis* figure next to *basilikē/nēsiotikē patremounialia* in ll. 295–299. But cf. *BGU* XIX, p. 82 for a possible correlation of *ktēma* and *ktēsis* in the Hermopolite nome.

23 *P.Flor.* III 377.5, 9, 12–13, and 19–20 (Ptolemais Hermeiou; VI); Palme 1989, 146.

24 Apion III: *P.Oxy.* XVI 1917.127 (616/617? CE); Apion II: *P.Oxy.* LI 3641.9 (February 7, 544); Strategios Paneuphemos: *SPP* XX 209.7 (Arsinoe; February 27, 610). Nikolaos Gonis holds that *ousia* was not used for the Apion estate at the time *P.Oxy.* LXXXIII 5375 was written (June 18, 557) and that the *endoxotatos* Apion in l. 6 bears an unusual titulature (*P.Oxy.* LXXXIII, p. 130). He concludes that the *ousia* of this man was probably not the *endoxos oikos* of Apion II, to whom this text is addressed, but the *ousia* of a different Apion. The date of *P.Oxy.* XVI 1917 is not entirely certain and there is an outside chance that the papyrus is older than the *endoxos oikos* documents (see the discussion in *P.Oxy.* LVIII, pp. 114–115), but the text that mentions the *ousia* of Strategios Paneuphemos is younger than the text in which his *endoxos oikos* appears (*CPR* XXIV 26.4 from 602/603; on the provenance from Arsinoe, which is probable but not certain, see the editor's introduction. This suggests that *ousia* and *oikos* of the same magnate could coexist without being synonymous.

25 For the "pagarched" villages, which are indeed connected to the *oikoi*, see Sections III and IV below.

26 See *P.Oxy.* XLVI 3307.

27 It is hard to interpret *P.Cair.Masp.* I 67060 (mid-VI) other than to mean that the *ousia* of the *endoxotatos* ex-*eparchos* Ioulianos, who is not described as pagarch here, paid (part of) its taxes under the pagarchic regime. This might mean that in the Antaiopolite, the fiscal shares were (partially?) organized by the pagarchs, or that even a man of Ioulianos's standing was not involved in the local fiscal share system, possibly suggesting its more limited role in the Antaiopolite and the

In the earliest years of the Islamic period, one text from the Senouthios archive may reflect the pagarch's authority over ecclesiastical *ousiai*,[28] and indeed the entire archive gives the impression of the pagarch being the node for complaints or requests by the landowners within the nome.[29] In addition, this period yields numerous examples of *ousiai* paying (at least some of) their taxes into a village account,[30] a model that would provide a plausible context for Ioulianos's *ousia*. It is thus conceivable that *ousiai* occurred in the context of landowners' renting and fiscal obligations, whereas there must have been more to an aristocratic *oikos*—perhaps the administration of fiscal shares.

II. The Fiscal Shares of Oxyrhynchos

The quintessential site to study the relation of the pagarchy to the fiscal shares must be the city of Oxyrhynchos, which holds the most relevant evidence. In this section, two accounts are explored to establish a broad idea of the balance between various fiscal actors in this nome; these are *P.Oxy.* XVI 2040, probably dating from 566/567 CE, and *P.Oxy.* XVI 2020, which must be dated later for prosopographical reasons, but is most likely earlier than 588 CE.[31] The account *P.Oxy.* XVI 2040 provides an overview of contributions from various individuals and institutions, mainly for the fuel for a public bath,[32] but also for something unspecified at the village of Takona. The document has been described as an illustration of "the principal units of fiscal allocations" at Oxyrhynchos or "a snapshot of the Oxyrhynchite elite."[33] The complete list reads as follows:

> Estimate (*synopsis*)[34] of (contributions for) the fuel of the public northern new bath of 27 *nomismata*, and for the 15th (indiction for) Takona 1 *nomisma*, 19 ¼ *keratia*, in total 28 *nomismata*, 19 ¼ *keratia*, of the whole city, as follows:

Thebaid. Cf. *SPP* VIII 1061 (VI?) and the discussion in the Catalog, s.v. Neilammon (Arsinoites?), but we cannot say whether this is a tax payment, and the date is uncertain.

28 *CPR* XXX 25 (Hermopolis; c. 643/644), if indeed issued by the pagarch Athanasios.

29 *CPR* XXX, p. 11.

30 *SPP* III² pt. V, p. xxvi.

31 See Gonis 2002a, 95–96 and Gascou 1985, 48 n. 277 (= 2008, 170–171 n. 275) (*BL* XIII 156).

32 *P.Oxy.* XVI 2040.1–2: † σύνοψις τῶν ἐγκαυμά(των) τοῦ δημοσ(ίου) βορρινοῦ | νέου λουτρ(οῦ) (…) καὶ (ὑπὲρ) ιε Τακόνα. The interpretation of ἐγκαύματα proposed by Gascou (1972a, 64–65 = 2008, 46) should probably be modified, since only three other attestations of that term occur in the papyri; these are either unclear (*SB* XXIV 16192.5, although the term is joined with "pitch" in this fragmentary attestation), clearly relate to fuel (*P.Oxy.* XVIII 2206.9–10), or can only with difficulties be interpreted as anything other than fuel (*P.Hels.* I 12.12 and 21, as ἐνκαύματα and ἐ̣νκαύμασιν, respectively).

33 Gascou 1972a, 65 (= 2008, 46): "des principales unités d'assignation fiscale de cette cité." "Snapshot": Ruffini 2008a, 105. With these exceptions (add Mazza 1995, 189–190), *P.Oxy.* XVI 2040 is curiously absent from discussions of the Oxyrhynchite pagarchy.

34 For the technical rendering of σύνοψις as *taxatio*, see Gascou 1985, 46 (= 2008, 168).

Through the *endoxos oikos* 8 *nomismata*, 15 *keratia*, of which for the 15th (indiction for) Takona 1 *nomisma*, 19 ¼ *keratia*, remainder 6 *nomismata*, 19 ½ ¼ *keratia*.
Through the Holy Church 3 *nomismata*, 6 ¼ *keratia*.
Through the *oikos* of the *endoxotatos* Kometes 4 *nomismata*, 8 *keratia*.
Through the heirs of the *endoxotatos* Ptolemaios 2 *nomismata*, 19 ¼ *keratia*.
Through the same (man) for the half-share of the pagarchy 1 *nomisma*, 10 ½ *keratia*.
Through the *endoxotatos* Ioustos and his brothers 2 *nomismata*, 16 *keratia*.
Through the same (man) for the other half-share of the pagarchy 1 *nomisma*, 10 ½ *keratia*.
Through the heirs of the *comes* Oualerios 21 ¼ *keratia*.
Through the *megaloprepestatē* Euphemia 1 *nomisma*, 16 ½ *keratia*.
Through the heirs of the *peribleptos* Theodoulos 1 *nomisma*, 14 ¼ *keratia*.
Through those from Ieme 1 ½ ¼ *keratia*.

Note that the contributors are not very numerous, yet are still characterized as representative of "the whole city."[35] And while the payments for the northern bath differ for each of the contributors and presumably were allocated based on some sort of quota system, the amount given for Takona is paid for entirely by the *endoxos oikos* of the Apiones. This amount is likely to be connected to a bath at Takona,[36] and the reference to a payment for a specific indiction[37] suggests that this is also a contribution for a public service.[38]

35 *P.Oxy.* XVI 2040.3: πάσης πόλεως. Only two *oikoi* are explicitly mentioned while the other aristocrats' entries are personal ones. The presence of several heirs (*klēronomoi*) in lines 9, 15, and 17, however, suggests that inherited estates were behind them.

36 The editor proposed that this payment represents a contribution to the "postal" stables at Takona (*P.Oxy.* XVI 2040, commentary; on Takona as a stage point of the *cursus publicus*, see *P.Oxy.* LXXXIV, p. 213). Contributions of the Apion estate to the stables of Takona would have an obvious parallel in *P.Oxy.* XVI 2028 (Oxyrhynchos; VI); cf. ll. 1–2: † γνῶσ(ις?) χρυσίου δοθ(έντος) τῷ τραπεζ(ίτῃ) ὑπὲρ τῶν στάβλ(ων) | Τακόνα θ καὶ ι τῶν ἰνδ(ικτιόνων) δ(ιὰ) τῶν ἑξῆς προσώπ(ων); see Gonis 2000a, 182. But why would contributions to the stables at Takona figure in an account for an entirely different building apparently someplace else, if they were not even related by subject? Alston 2002, 314 suggested that the payment for Takona in *P.Oxy.* XVI 2040 implies a bath in this village.

37 The amount for Takona is significantly smaller than the amount for the "public northern new bath." Although it poses little problem to assume that a village bath might have been considerably smaller than one in the city of Oxyrhynchos, size alone probably cannot account for the much lower sum. The relevant year is twice made explicit for Takona but is not mentioned for the main payment, suggesting two interpretations: (1) The payment for the fifteenth indiction is for arrears (which might partially explain the smaller amount) from a past indiction, but in that case one would expect an explicit reference to this prior indiction. Also, it seems unlikely that wealthy magnates such as the Apiones were unable to pay this comparatively small amount in time. (2) Perhaps, since the "northern bath" is said to be "new," the indiction year next to Takona implies running costs for that indiction while the payments for the "new" bath represented a kind of starting investment for a longer period, which would partly explain the much higher amount.

38 A bath at Takona is known from an Apionic context, and this bath is called *geouchikos*, so would have been a bath of the Apion estate; see *P.Oxy.* XVI 1921.12 (561 or 621 CE): τοῦ γεουχι(κοῦ) λουτρ(οῦ) τῆς κόμ(ης) (read κώμης) Τακόνα and, for baths on the Apion estate, Benaissa 2012, 196.

It is certainly significant in this context that Takona is referred to as a *kōmē pagarchoumenē*, a village "pagarched" by the Apiones, about a decade earlier.[39] I shall discuss these villages in detail later; for now it suffices to point out that the Apiones apparently did not hold the Oxyrhynchite pagarchy by the time of *P.Oxy.* XVI 2040, which instead was shared equally by Ioustos[40] and (the heirs of) Ptolemaios.[41] The Apiones, however, were entirely responsible for the contributions for a bath at Takona. As multiple pagarchies per nome are hardly likely,[42] the reason for this contrast can, I believe, only be that the Apiones' responsibility for this village was grounded in a position comparable to, but distinct from, the pagarchy of Oxyrhynchos.

The aforementioned interpretation of *P.Oxy.* XVI 2040 assumes that this text is a representative illustration of Oxyrhynchite elite composition—an assumption that is supported by a list compiled in the second and third columns of the later *P.Oxy.* XVI 2020.[43] This list is structurally comparable to *P.Oxy.* XVI 2040, but concerns grain payments: Twenty-eight "joint contributors" (*syntelestai*) pay 15,688 artabas in total.[44] Six of these contributors clearly played in a different league than the rest: the imperial *oikos* (*theios oikos*, "Divine House"), the Holy Church, the *oikos* of Kometes, the heirs of Ptolemaios, the heirs of Ioustos, and the heirs of Euphemia. These contributors bore comparatively excessive amounts from c. 1,498 to 3,490 artabas each, altogether 75 percent of the total, while the next closest entry, for the heirs of Theodoulos, lists "only" c. 708

In order to explain how payments for a part of the Apion estate became part of a list for contributions πάσης πόλεως in *P.Oxy.* XVI 2040, we would need to assume that this list was drawn up by the Apionic estate administration for their internal records, which does not seem too much of a stretch. But even so, the way the Takona contribution is processed in *P.Oxy.* XVI 2040 (fuel "paid" in money) would strike me as unusual if this was internal estate business. In any case, *P.Oxy.* XVI 1921 may be much later than *P.Oxy.* XVI 2040 (see *BL* IX 191 and *BL* X 145 for a 621 date against *BL* VIII 251, arguing for 561). In the list, two entries refer to the delivery of fifty *specula* for an "estate bath" at Takona and eighty *specula* for a (non-"estate") bath at the village of Ophis. *Speculum* must refer to window panes here (Krüger 1989, 117) and the sheer number indicates significant construction works. Cf. also *SB* VI 9368 (577/578?) about the delivery of lead for a "public bath" (*dēmosion loutron*), in which a *dioikētēs* of Flavia Anastasia is involved; see Gascou 1972a, 70–71 n. 3 (= 2008, 49–50 n. 33). On Anastasia and her archive, see the Catalog, s.v. The Apiones and Anastasia (Oxyrhynchos).

39 *P.Oxy.* I 133 (October 19, 550).

40 Or rather, by his *oikos* if αὐτοῦ refers to the collective of Ioustos and his brothers.

41 The wording of ll. 10 and 13–14 (payments ὑπέρ, i.e., "for" the pagarchy) does not imply payments "to," but rather "on behalf of," the pagarchy; cf. *P.Herm.Landl.*, p. 22.

42 See Section I above and Chapter Four, Section IV. Moreover, the pagarchy of Ptolemaios and Ioustos is explicitly mentioned in *P.Oxy.* XVI 2040; if the Apiones, or other grandees, held "their own" pagarchy or pagarchies, one would expect to find them on the same list.

43 For a profound approach to this text in comparison to *P.Oxy.* XVI 2040, see Ruffini 2008a, 102–105. On the aristocrats showing up in both accounts, see also Gad 2016. The first column of *P.Oxy.* XVI 2020 is ignored at this point for reasons that will become clear later in this section.

44 When Hickey's corrections of ll. 24 and 25 are taken into account (see nn. 48 and 50 below), the missing contribution in l. 28 amounts to 111 ½ 1/24 artabas.

artabas.[45] It is probably not coincidental that the six leading contributors are not individuals but institutions, and also the only ones who pay "for various *onomata*."[46] With the exception of the imperial *oikos*, these leading contributors and the heirs of Theodoulos from *P.Oxy.* XVI 2020 are also listed in the earlier *P.Oxy.* XVI 2040, which attests to the longevity of the economic system they helped to sustain. While *P.Oxy.* XVI 2040 deals with cash payments, the list in *P.Oxy.* XVI 2020 comprises payments in grain. Still, a comparison of the shares given in the two documents is possible through the percentages allocated to those contributors that appear in both lists (and, for comparison, to some other significant contributors that do not appear in both lists), as captured in Table 2.[47]

Table 2: Percentages from contributors who appear both in *P.Oxy.* XVI 2040 and in columns II–III of *P.Oxy.* XVI 2020, plus the pagarchy and the imperial *oikos* for comparison.

	***P.Oxy.* XVI 2040 (c. 566/567)**	***P.Oxy.* XVI 2020 (c. 580–588)**		***P.Oxy.* XVI 2040 (c. 566/567)**	***P.Oxy.* XVI 2020 (c. 580–588)**
endoxos oikos	25%	0.5%	**heirs of Ptolemaios**	10%	11%
theios oikos	–	22%	**(heirs of) Ioustos**	10%	10%
***oikos* of Kometes**	16%	13%[48]	**(heirs of) Euphemia**[49]	6%	10%[50]

45 It was not status alone that provided this extraordinary position. In *P.Oxy.* XVI 2020 we find *endoxotatoi* whose contributions pale before those of the heirs to the lower-ranking *peribleptos* Theodoulos. The new *P.Oxy.* LXXXVII 5592 attests a pagarch Theodoulos at some point in the fifth century and it is possible that this is the same person; see the editor's comments on potential identifications. At the time of that text Theodoulos may have occupied a pagarchy somewhat in between the "early" and the "later" pagarchy, possibly comparable to a *praepositus pagi* with fiscal jurisdiction for other places adjacent to his holdings, later turning into his fiscal share (see Chapter One on this hypothesis about the development of the pagarchy).

46 The entry for the imperial *oikos* lacks this note, but the *oikos* figures in a separate entry in l. 14 as payer for a smaller *ktēma*.

47 Some clarifications for Table 2: Ioustos and Euphemia were apparently alive at the time of *P.Oxy.* XVI 2040, but had passed by the time of *P.Oxy.* XVI 2020, when their heirs are listed instead. All entries over 1 percent are rounded up or down to the next full percent. The figures include only the contributions for the "public northern new bath," not those for (the bath at?) Takona. For the percentages of *P.Oxy.* XVI 2040, cf. Alston 2002, 315; the chart and figures for this text in Hickey 2007, 297, by contrast, include the amount for Takona. Naturally, since my table includes only selected contributors, the percentages do not add up to 100 percent.

48 See Hickey 1998, 163 for the reading Αϡξε δʹ ηʹ (1,965 ¼ ⅛) instead of Αρξε δʹ ηʹ (1,165 ¼ ⅛), which I find convincing from the photo (contra Gascou 1985, 48 n. 278 = 2008, 171 n. 276).

49 The papyrus is abraded at the end of the name in *P.Oxy.* XVI 2020, but this suggestion (instead of Euphemios) by Gad 2016, 1793 cannot seriously be doubted. That Euphemia is referred to as *megaloprepestatē* in the earlier text but as *endoxotatē* in the later one does not necessarily imply a promotion; see Chapter Five, Section I on the use of the epithet *megaloprepestatos*.

50 See Hickey 1998, 163 for the reading Αυϙζ ∠ δʹ ηʹ (1,497 ½ ¼ ⅛) instead of Αϡξε δʹ ηʹ (1,965 ¼ ⅛), which I find convincing from the photo.

Holy Church	12%	10%	**heirs of Theodoulos**	6%	5%
pagarchy, total	10%	–[51]			

First, the shares differ.[52] To explain the smaller share of Kometes in the later list, we find some documents that may indeed illustrate his family's increasing economic difficulties.[53] Such an evolutionary explanation is plausible, but at the moment unavailable for the significantly higher share of Euphemia; in her case, the change from personal contributions (in *P.Oxy.* XVI 2040) to those of an institution that included her heirs (in *P.Oxy.* XVI 2020) may partially be responsible for the increase. Since we are dealing with different sorts of contributions, shares are expected to vary somewhat and therefore any arguments need to be based on the orders of magnitude.[54] With this in mind, the relative stability of the shares of Ptolemaios, Ioustos, Theodoulos, and the church is striking. The absence of the imperial *oikos* in the earlier list, however, defies convincing explanation.[55]

The value of these lists as a representative illustration of the distribution of fiscal shares in the Oxyrhynchite has been questioned, not least as the *endoxos oikos,* which pays 25 percent of the total in *P.Oxy.* XVI 2040, is all but absent from *P.Oxy.* XVI 2020, which, after all, is a list for *arkarika*, taxes designated for the prefecture.[56] Scholars have noted that the Apiones paid only a comparably insignificant sum because they paid only for one particular *onoma*:[57] "Through the *endoxos oikos* the aforementioned 76 ½

51 If, as Gascou 1972a, 70–71 n. 3 (= 2008, 49–50 n. 33) argues, Anastasia and Maria, who each paid 479 ⅛ artabas, paid on behalf of the pagarchy (which the text does not say), then that aggregated amount would comprise 6 percent of the total, much lower than the pagarchy's dues in *P.Oxy.* XVI 2040. Moreover, if we accept Gascou's suggestion, it is puzzling that Anastasia's and Maria's *own* shares do not figure here in *P.Oxy.* XVI 2020, while the shares of Ioustos and Ptolemaios in *P.Oxy.* XVI 2040 are each explicitly divided. For these reasons, I am more convinced by the hypothesis that Anastasia and Maria were sisters and simply inherited an identical share, as suggested by van Haelst 1966, 588.

52 The change of other contributors between *P.Oxy.* XVI 2040 and 2020, however, may simply be owed to the natural cycle. Even so, the list of contributors in *P.Oxy.* XVI 2020 is considerably longer than that of *P.Oxy.* XVI 2040.

53 See Ruffini 2008a, 75–80 and Amin Benaissa in *P.Oxy.* LXXXIV, p. 239.

54 The new papyrus presented by Gad 2016 advises us to remain cautious of too strict a comparison. There, the context of the contributions is elusive, but the heirs of Ioannes pay more than the heirs of Ptolemaios, while it is the other way around in *P.Oxy.* XVI 2040 and *P.Oxy.* XVI 2020. By orders of magnitude, however, the amounts in these texts are comparably high.

55 See Johnson & West 1949, 302 (pointing to *C.Th.* I 1.11) for the suggestion that the imperial estate's income went *entirely* to the department of the *arkarika* and that it is therefore absent from *P.Oxy.* XVI 2020, which I do not find particularly convincing, though I do not have a better alternative. Is the *theios oikos* absent from *P.Oxy.* XVI 2040 because the latter concerns a "municipal" expenditure?

56 On the *arkarika*, see Hickey 2012, 110, with further references in n. 89.

57 Gascou 1985, 48 (= 2008, 171). Cf. other landowners in this text who are paying "for various *onomata*," thereby illustrating one assumption of the model of fiscal shares.

artabas for Phoibammon, son of Kephalas."[58] In the papyrus, however, this list, comprising the second and third columns, is preceded by a column that is very fragmentary and therefore not easy to comprehend, although it appears to concern adaerated grain payments, that is, grain contributions commuted into cash.[59] But this column notably features one in-kind amount amid various cash payments for the *arkarika*:[60]

58 *P.Oxy.* XVI 2020.15: δ(ιὰ) τοῦ ἐνδόξ(ου) οἴκ(ου) τὰ\ς/ προκειμένας ὑπ(ὲρ) Φοιβάμμωνος Κεφαλᾶ (ἀρτάβας) ος ∠. The account *P.Oxy.* XVI 1919.13 notes a payment τῷ λαμπρο(τάτῳ) Ἀγαπητῷ (ὑπὲρ) τιμ(ῆς) κριθῶν (ἀρταβῶν) ος ∠ ὀν[όματος] Φοιβάμμωνος κεφαλ(αιωτοῦ) Ἀλεξ(ανδρείας) νο(μίσματα) ε. We therefore see the exact same amount of 76 ½ artabas of barley in both texts (although commuted into five *nomismata* in the latter)—certainly not a coincidence. In l. 9 of *P.Oxy.* XVI 1919, however, we read: ὀνό]μ(ατος) [Φ]οιβάμμωνος κεφαλ(αιωτοῦ), so the abbreviated κεφαλ( ) from l. 13 is unlikely to be a slip of the pen; it is impossible to read Κεφαλᾶ on the papyrus, as the abbreviation is clearly marked by the use of ʃ. Certainly, the same reading was intended in both *P.Oxy.* XVI 1919 and 2020, and one of these two writers must have confused something. The first possibility is that "Phoibammon, son of Kephalas" is the presumed reading in both cases. If this is true, we need to explain the fact that Kephalas usually figures as an *onoma* of his own in other papyri (on which see Hickey 2012, 60 n. 111 and Bransbourg 2016, 363 n. 185). Thus we need to assume that both *P.Oxy.* XVI 1919 and 2020 are from around 580 CE or later, i.e., later than the other attestations of that *onoma* or the *dikaion*, and that at that time the registration of these (quite extensive) holdings had changed from Kephalas to that of his son. This would seem a little odd, as "Kephalas" as the name of a *dikaion* seems to be a fossilized nomenclature in other documents. Alternatively, the writer of *P.Oxy.* XVI 1919, copying from another document, may have simply been unaware of the meaning of Κεφαλᾶ and "corrected" or misread it to a more familiar term, namely as an abbreviated reference to a *kephalaiōtes*. The second possibility is that the reading in both *P.Oxy.* XVI 1919 and 2020 should be "Phoibammon, *kephalaiōtēs*." If so, then the interpretation of Gascou 1972b, 250–252 may be closer to the truth than he later admits (Gascou 1985, 48 n. 280 = 2008, 171 n. 278). However, this hypothesis is challenged by the problem that if a "Phoibammon, son of Kephalas" did not exist and we adapt the principle of *lectio difficilior*, it would not be the most natural assumption that a writer mistakenly "corrected" the common κεφαλ(αιωτοῦ) to Κεφαλᾶ in *P.Oxy.* XVI 2020. I therefore argue for the first possibility: the figures in *P.Oxy.* XVI 1919.9 and 13 are both for the *onoma* of Phoibammon, son of Kephalas, and the writer made a mistake by misreading Κεφαλᾶ (from another document) to mean κεφαλα(ιωτοῦ), which he then shortened more regularly to κεφαλ(αιωτοῦ). I think the form of the abbreviation (ʃ) makes it unlikely that the writer intended it to stand for Κεφαλ(ᾶ), as Fikhman 1976, 176 n. 359 suggests.

59 On the monetization of the countryside and the trend toward cash payments to the state in late antiquity, see Banaji 2007, 51–88 and 169–170 and Bransbourg 2016, 317–321, 358, and *passim*.

60 *P.Oxy.* XVI 2020 col. 1:
[λόγος – – –] πολιτευομέ(νου)
[– – – οὗ]τ(ως)·
[ὑπὲρ – – – ἐξαρ]γυρι[σ]μ( ) ὄβρυζ(α) νο(μίσματα) Αωνβ κ(εράτια) κγ ∠ καὶ
[– – – ὡ̣ς̣] τ̣(ῶν) ξ νό(μισμα) α̣ νο(μίσματα) τξθ κ(εράτια) ις ∠, γί(νονται) νο(μίσματα) Βσκβ κ(εράτια) ιε ∠ (read ις).
[– – – ὑ]πὲρ παντοίων ἐξαργυρισμ(ῶν) νο(μίσματα) μγ κ(εράτια) γ δʹ,
[– – –] . νο(μίσματα) γ κ(εράτια) η,
[– – –] νο(μίσματα) β κ(εράτια) ιβ,
[– – – ἄ]λ̣λα ἐν εἴδεσιν κριθ(ῆς) καν(κέλλῳ) (ἀρτάβαι) ος ∠,
[(γίνονται) ὁ(μοῦ) ὑπὲρ παν]τοίων ἀρκαρικ(ῶν) ὄβρ(υζα) νο(μίσματα) Βσοα κ(εράτια) ιδ ∠ δʹ.

> [Account[?] – – –] *politeuome*( )
> [– – –] as follows[?]:
> [for[?] – – –] *adaeratio*, in "pure" value, 1,852 *nomismata*, 23 ½ *keratia* and
> [– – – as[?]] of 60 per 1[?] *nomisma*, 369 *nomismata*, 16 ½ *keratia*,[61] in total 2,222 *nomismata*, 15 ½ *keratia*.[62]
> [– – –] for *adaerationes* of all sorts 43 *nomismata*, 3 ¼ *keratia*
> [– – –] 3 *nomismata*, 8 *keratia*
> [– – –] 2 *nomismata*, 12 *keratia*
> [– – –] but in kind, barley, 76 ½ artabas by the *cancellus* (measure).
> [Grand total for] *arkarika* of all sorts, in "pure" value, 2,271 *nomismata*, 14 ½ ¼ *keratia*.

Strikingly, it has not yet been noted that the isolated amount of barley is identical to the one that the *endoxos oikos* pays for the aforementioned isolated *onoma* in the second column. Though much about the first column remains obscure due to its fragmentary state, I find it inevitable to conclude that (at least a part of) that column relates to the Apiones' share for the *arkarika* and that the Apiones paid for this share in adaerated grain, that is, by commuting payments in kind into gold.[63] Yet, the Apiones also registered a single smaller payment in kind for another *onoma*, and this payment in kind was then included both in the list of adaerated payments in the first column (in order to fully account for the Apiones' due share) *and* again in the second column, where all in-kind payments are listed.[64] This neatly explains why the first entry is introduced with "but in kind," marking the contrast of the in-kind and cash payments, and it also explains why the second entry refers back to the first one via "the aforementioned (artabas)," which had so far found no explanation.[65]

61 The line has in fact νο(μίσματα) ψνθ ϖ η′ = 759 ⅔ ⅛ *nomismata* (henceforth "original figure"), but τξθ κ(εράτια) ις ∠ is written above the line. The original figure is neither crossed out nor erased, which suggests that it is not a copying mistake, yet only the superscribed amount yields the correct result. Although various number games result in intruiging accordances with "share" figures calculated from other texts, all of these calculations require crucial assumptions about what we see in this first column that might or might not be true for this fragmentary text, and I therefore refrain from too much speculation here.

62 According to what can be read, the subtotal at this point should be 2,222 *nomismata*, 16 *keratia*, but the calculation continues with the apparently wrong amount.

63 On the topic of the Apion *oikos* and adaeration, see Bransbourg 2016, 366–373.

64 An amount for the *onoma* of Kephalas is also added separately in *P.Oxy.* XVIII 2195.144; see McConnell 2017, 52 n. 48.

65 Cf. Ruffini 2008a, 102 for other speculation upon the meaning of τὰς προκειμένας here.

Since large parts of the left half of the first column are missing, we cannot infer what defined these payments.[66] A conversion rate appears to have been given,[67] and assuming a rate of ten artabas per *nomisma* for the purpose of taxation and for a nome-wide operation,[68] the value contained in the first column exceeds that of the following list of grain payments from columns II and III (15,688 artabas, or 1,568.8 *nomismata*).[69] A conceivable hypothesis would be that the grain amounts of columns II and III are, in adaerated form, part of column I and that therefore in the latter sixth century the Apiones, being in a better position to exchange grain into much-needed gold,[70] were involved in commuting the grain contributions from *all other contributors*. Admitted-

66 Perhaps *P.Oxy.* XVI 2020 col. I 1: [λόγος – – –] πολιτευομέ( ) can be restored according to *P.Oxy.* XVI 2039.1: † λόγ(ος) ῥιπ[α]ρ(ίων) οἴκ(ου) Θέωνος σὺν θεῷ ια ἰνδ(ικτίονος). Thus, [† λόγ(ος) ἀρκαρικ(ῶν) οἴκ(ου) Θέωνος] πολιτευομέ(νου) may be conceivable. We know that Theon was a *politeuomenos* (Gonis 2009, 91–92) and if, which is not certain, the 1,852 *nomismata*, 23 ½ *keratia* of l. 3 are the basic contribution of the *endoxos oikos* without surcharges, then this may have amounted to about 48 percent of the total of all three columns (c. 3,840 *nomismata*, with the amounts of the columns II and III adaerated by a ratio of one *nomisma* per ten artabas; on the conversion, see below). In *P.Oxy.* XVI 2039, by way of comparison, the Apiones cover 47 percent of the share of Theon's *oikos* (based on the new readings by Azzarello 2006). But although these figures match intriguingly well, I do not think that linking *P.Oxy.* XVI 2020 to ancient responsibilities of Theon's *oikos* might be the best way to explain the document. By way of comparison, in *P.Oxy.* XVI 1909, the money taxes paid by Oxyrhynchos and Kynopolis together amount to 24,500 *nomismata*. Judging from the height of columns II and III of *P.Oxy.* XVI 2020, col. I 1 of the edited text might have been preceded by a line that is now lost.

67 I wonder whether it might even be possible to read [– – – τῶν (ἀρταβῶν) *n*] Ἀλ[ε]ξ(ανδρείας) νό(μισμα) α̣ instead of [– – – ῳ̣ς̣] τ̣(ῶν) ξ νό(μισμα) α̣ in l. 4. This expression is attested, e.g., in *P.Oxy.* LXXXIV 5470 col. I 3 and *passim*. A comparable connection of αλ that is close to a ligature is seen repeatedly in Apion accounts (e.g., in *P.Oxy.* I 132.6, 9, and 12) and the trace below the end of the first lacuna may even be the rest of an iota, yielding the conversion rate of ten artabas per *nomisma* I point to below. The online image is not very good; the faint traces before ξ may actually be ink, but there appears to be no abbreviation stroke through ξ (cf. l. 3: ἐξαρ]γυρι[σ]μ( )). The surface appears to be damaged in both spots, however.

68 *P.Oxy.* XVI 1909 (late VI); Bransbourg 2016, 367. The text shares the context of tax payments but it is unclear what sort of grain is at issue here. For other attested conversion rates, see Bransbourg 2016, 327 n. 72 and cf. *P.Oxy.* LXXXIV 5470, commentary on col. I 3, mentioned in the previous note. See also Bransbourg 2016, 373, suggesting that conversion rates for barley differed from those for wheat. Thus, for an alternative, we might want to read in our text the conversion rate of sixty artabas of barley per *nomisma* that Bransbourg cites (on p. 373) from *P.Lond.* V 1674, a text from the Antaiopolite nome. *P.Oxy.* XVI 2020 col. I 4 might then read: [– – – τῶν ἀρ]τ̣(αβῶν) ξ νό(μισμα) α̣. However, the context of *P.Lond.* V 1674 suggests that this rate was exceptional—the petition is complaining about it—as would the abbreviation, given that in thirty other instances in *P.Oxy.* XVI 2020, the artaba symbol is used.

69 A rate of, for instance, twelve artabas per *nomisma* (a recurring one in Apion accounts; see the references in the previous note) results in an even higher value of the gold amount in column I (when it is converted into artabas) compared to the grain amounts in columns II and III.

70 On the Apiones' capacities to generate cash in comparison to others, see Bransbourg 2016, 372–373.

ly, this would seem excessive if it were true for all taxes and can, for instance, be all but excluded for the *embolē*.[71] Still, the observation that the Apiones were involved in adaeration operations of this magnitude in this particular case—whether for their own *oikos* or also for others'—is itself a good indicator that we are close to Emperor Maurice's "full adaeration regime,"[72] which supports Gascou's prosopographical case for dating the text to the 580s CE.[73]

Whatever the exact distribution of these amounts between the Apiones and other aristocrats, bringing the *endoxos oikos* back into *P.Oxy.* XVI 2020 assures us that both *P.Oxy.* XVI 2040 and *P.Oxy.* XVI 2020 are, by and large, reliable indicators for the distribution of public shares among the main players in the Oxyrhynchite. In this light, the observation made at the outset of this section—that the Oxyrhynchite pagarchy in *P.Oxy.* XVI 2040 is separate from the Apiones' responsibility for the village of Takona—becomes significant for the main question of this chapter about how aristocrats' fiscal shares relate to the pagarchy.[74] As noted, in one document Takona is referred to as a *kōmē pagarchoumenē*, a village "pagarched" by the Apiones, which seems paradoxical at first sight given that in *P.Oxy.* XVI 2040, the Apiones' responsibilities for that village are separate from the pagarchy. Therefore, the following sections discuss the *kōmai pagarchoumenai* and their relationship to the Apion estate, starting with the "documentary habit" that governed when and how this formula was used.

III. The *Kōmai Pagarchoumenai*: A Notary's Tale?

Given that scores of late antique papyri come from Oxyrhynchos, it is remarkable that after the fifth century pagarchs are, with two exceptions, absent in documents from that nome.[75] These two instances are greatly outnumbered by texts that concern

---

71 On potential adaeration rates for the Apiones' *embolē*, see Bransbourg 2016, 366–368.

72 On this topic, see Gascou 1985, 11 (= 2008, 132–133) and Bransbourg 2016, 313, 358 n. 168, 393–395, and 403–404.

73 See n. 31 above.

74 My finding that the gold and grain payments in *P.Oxy.* XVI 2020 must be related also makes it possible that the Oxyrhynchite pagarchy was part of the calculations in the first column, since the business of the pagarchs and their *boēthoi* also involved dealing with taxpayers' grain and commuting it into tax gold; see Chapter Two, Section III 2.

75 *P.Oxy.* XVI 1858 and, implicitly, also in *P.Oxy.* XVI 2040, discussed in the previous section, although in the latter, the suspects Ptolemaios (or his heirs) and Ioustos are not titled "pagarch," but are listed as contributors ὑπὲρ τῆς παγαρχίας. The list in Gascou 1972a, 70–71 n. 3 (= 2008, 49–50 n. 33) contains—apart from the men mentioned in *PSI* I 52 and *P.Oxy.* XVI 1858—no instance of anyone actually being referred to as pagarch; see the introduction to the Catalog for a discussion. The restoration of a pagarch in *PSI* VIII 955 + *SB* XX 15181 is far from certain; see the Catalog, s.v. Anonymous pagarch (Oxyrhynchos). As shown in Section VI below, *PSI* I 52 should be dated to the early Islamic period. Cf. also *P.Oxy.* XVI 1829 and *P.Mich.* XI 624, discussed in the Catalog, s.vv. Anonymous pagarch (Arcadia) and Antiochos & Theon (Arcadia), respective-

kōmai pagarchoumenai, which are known virtually exclusively from the Oxyrhynchite nome.[76] The expression *kōmē pagarchoumenē* literally translates to "pagarched village" but is often rendered as "village under pagarchic authority."[77] All documents concerning a *kōmē pagarchoumenē* are contracts that refer to their addressee not as pagarch but as *geouchōn* ("landowner," but in the participle form),[78] and then add the *pagarchoumenē* formula only later in the main body of the text when a specific village is mentioned.[79] The expression is used exclusively with villages; in connection with hamlets (*epoikia*), the analogues "of N.N.'s property (*ktēma*)" or "belonging (*diapheron*) to N.N." appear in similar contexts.[80] This is not surprising, for the hamlets were integrated into the structure of their respective estate, paying their taxes and meeting their obligations via their landlord. Yet, the *kōmai pagarchoumenai* also occur in contexts obviously linked to landowners' business: in two papyri that involve men from *kōmai pagarchoumenai*, the issues at stake are explicitly labeled as "pertaining to the landowner" (*geouchikos*) while in a third, the land to be leased "belongs" (*hyparcheō*) to a *geouchōn*.[81] Nothing beyond the power of an ordinary landowner is at stake here, and

ly; these documents may refer to Byzantine pagarchs of Oxyrhynchos after 500 CE, but this is just one of many options.

76 On some of the following points, see Nikolaos Gonis in *P.Oxy.* LXX 4787.9–10, commentary. The (seeming) exception from outside Oxyrhynchos is *P.Lond.* III 776 from the Kynopolite nome (but from the context of the Apion *oikos*), discussed in Section VII below.

77 Of course, "pagarched" is an ugly word, but it is meant to illustrate the construction of the expression *kōmē pagarchoumenē* without imposing up-front assumptions about its meaning. The word is regularly translated as "under pagarchic authority/control/administration" (vel sim.), for instance, in Sarris 2006, Banaji 2007, Hickey 2012, and *P.Oxy.* LXXXIV, which is a translation I would go along with. Whether this translation is meant to invoke the authority of the actual pagarch or something different, varies from author to author.

78 I think that this terminology may be significant and that its use in the headings of these contractual documents might be intended to differentiate these fiscally responsible landowners from simple *geouchoi*.

79 Until January 2, 588 (*P.Oxy.* XLIV 3204) writers use παγαρχουμένης ὑπό, whereas from October 21 of that same year onward all documents have παγαρχουμένης παρά (*P.Oxy.* LXXXIII 5390). Consequently, *P.Oxy.* LXX 4787.9–10 (March 12, 564) should be restored as παγαρχουμ(ένης) | [ὑπὸ τῆς ὑμ]ετέρα⟨ς⟩ ὑπερφυείας. There is no apparent change in meaning between ὑπό and παρά in this usage. Both prepositions do appear in connection with an *oikos* rather than a person (ὑπό: *P.Oxy.* I 133.8; παρά: *P.Oxy.* XVI 1981.16 and *P.Oxy.* XXIV 2420.12–13), so this cannot be a factor in choosing one rather than the other. Cf. *P.Cair.Masp.* I 67024–25 (new ed. Fournet 2018) A 32, A' 57, B 31 (Aphrodite; c. 551), and the expression ὑπὸ (τὴν) παγαρχίαν ποιήσασθαι: "to bring (the villagers) under the pagarchy." *P.Oxy.* LXXXII 5337 from 493 CE is the earliest attestation of the passive participle; the verb *pagarcheō*, however, is attested as early as the fourth century in the nonpapyrological evidence from outside Egypt; see pp. 38–39 above.

80 In Greek: κτήματος τῆς or διαφέροντος τῇ, respectively, generally followed by an abstract reference to the landowner (e.g., "your Highness" vel sim.), never to the *oikos*; but cf. *P.Oxy.* XVI 1900 and *SB* XVIII 14006, referring to the church. Cf. the parallel construction in *BGU* XII 2184.1–2 (Hermopolis; VI): τοῦ γεωργίου τοῦ ὑπό σου γ̣ε̣ωρ̣γ[ο]υ|μένου.

81 *P.Lond.* III 776.8 and *P.Oxy.* LXX 4785.13 (*geouchikos*); *P.Oxy.* LXXXII 5337 (*hyparcheō*).

whatever lies behind the *pagarchoumenē* formula is not the reason for the landowner's involvement in these cases.[82] It appears therefore that the *pagarchoumenē* formula marked a general (legal) status of a village that was mentioned in legal documents regardless of whether an official or a private issue was at stake.[83] It was used to mark a village in any case where someone from that village was involved as a contracting party or as the person under surety in deeds of surety. Similarly, the expressions "of N.N.'s property (*ktēma*)" or "belonging (*diapheron*) to N.N." were used to describe an *epoikion* in cases where someone from that place was involved. These formulae therefore seem to define the landowner's relationship to the individual in question.[84]

Given that all these texts are contracts or receipts—legally enforceable documents in which meticulous attention to unambiguous terminology would be expected—it seems reasonable to assume that the written designation of the villages as *kōmai pagarchoumenai* served a purpose. There have been two main ways of interpreting this expression. On the one hand, Nikolaos Gonis has argued that it might indicate that the villages "were normally under the control of the pagarch, but it appears that their fiscal administration could be exercised by great landowners, whose authority was similar to that of a pagarch."[85] On the other, some scholars have taken this expression to mean that the addressees of the respective document were responsible for that village

---

82 The occurrence of the *pagarchoumenē* formula is therefore no indicator of a public character of the matter at issue, so it remains elusive whether, say, *P.Oxy.* XXIV 2420 (614 CE), where no immediate public background is apparent, relates to private interests between Apion and the two goldsmiths (for instance, because they worked for him or had fled from an estate parcel in the village) or to public interest (for instance, because they were awaiting trial or had fled from a non-estate parcel in the village), but again these interests are not easy to disentangle. On the public interest in securing the presence of goldsmiths, see Bagnall & Worp 1985.

83 Cf. Hickey 2012, 82, who argues that deeds of surety for *enapographoi geōrgoi* in *kōmai pagarchoumenai* were essentially private in nature and that these people resided in parts of the village belonging to the landlord (see also Nikolaos Gonis in *P.Oxy.* LXIX 4757.1, commentary; on the *enapographoi geōrgoi* and their status, see Benaissa 2020, who also summarizes previous discussions). Hickey's interpretation entails that the *pagarchoumenē* formula is not necessary for the business dealt with in the document, and I agree; see also Hickey 2012, 89 n. 11, carefully differentiating between the landlord's relationship to the village on the one hand and the reason for the document's drafting on the other.

84 In the work contracts for *pronoētai* to the Apiones *P.Bagnall* 33 (496 CE), *P.Oxy.* I 136 (583 CE), and *P.Oxy.* LVIII 3952 (610 CE), villages that are known from elsewhere as *pagarchoumenē* are mentioned without the term, apparently because no one from that village was involved (the *pronoētai* in each case hail from Oxyrhynchos); see also *P.Oxy.* LXIII 4397.23. The rare cases where people from those villages *are* involved and the villages are still not labeled as *pagarchoumenē* are discussed later.

85 *P.Oxy.* LXX 4787.9–10, commentary; cf. the same author in *P.Oxy.* LXIX 4757.1 (original parentheses): "Yet the presence of ἐναπόγραφοι in κῶμαι need not cause surprise, if we bear in mind the fiscal character of the *adscriptio*, and that these κῶμαι were in the administrative or fiscal control (παγαρχούμεναι) of those great landlords who also controlled ἐποίκια." See Fikhman 1978 (followed by Mazza 1995, 195–196) for a comparable view, although Fikhman seems less inclined than Gonis to conceive of this as an administrative arrangement.

as pagarchs—that is, by virtue of their office.[86] The latter hypothesis implies that we are dealing with an alternative Oxyrhynchite notarial custom for referring to pagarchs.

As will become clear in the remainder of this section (and this chapter), it is highly unlikely that the *kōmai pagarchoumenai* form part of a "notary's tale" and represent an alternative notarial way of referring to a pagarch. Not only would it seem odd to suppress the pagarchy from an aristocrat's formal address, only to add it much later in the text, but a rigid pattern in the usage of the title of *geouchōn* in the address suggests the opposite, namely that if aristocrats are addressed as *geouchōn* in a legal document, they did not hold the pagarchy or another nome-level office in that nome. In order to reveal this pattern, one needs to systematically look at the addresses in these contracts. Above, I noted that all landowners with authority over *kōmai pagarchoumenai* are addressed as *geouchountes*. An exception is provided by a papyrus dating to 530 CE, in which Strategios II appears not as *geouchōn* but as *prōteuōn* (Lat. *principalis*).[87] This phenomenon is consistent in three other papyri from the period 530–535 CE, and perhaps longer than that.[88] All four texts, however, concern the maintenance of estate infrastructure (waterwheels and a mill), which in each case is explicitly labeled as "pertaining to the landowner" (*geouchikos*).[89] There can therefore hardly be any doubt that Strategios was still considered *geouchōn* and that *prōteuōn* replaced the more general title in addresses.[90] Pushing this observation further, one notes that no one bearing the title of *geouchōn* in the address of a contract holds any public office in the area covered by this expression (usually a nome/*civitas*).[91] The inverse is also true: no one addressed in a legal document with their public office in a nome/*civitas* is given the *geouchōn* title in that same address. It appears that mentioning an office in a *civitas* entailed the sup-

86 See Banaji 2007, 150, although he refers to "the pagarch's function" and later argues that the pagarchy is synonymous with the responsibility for fiscal shares; cf. Mazza 1995, 195–196. Giovanni Ruffini's conception of this phenomenon as a "village pagarchy" (Ruffini 2009, 631 and n. 4; cf. 633) does not seem so far from the truth, as we shall see below, but in his view this phenomenon could apparently exist alongside the *civitas* pagarchy *and* the fiscal shares (cf. n. 5 above). Cf. Gascou 1985, 67 n. 378 (= 2008, 190 n. 376): "une sorte de pagarchie permanente sur certains villages de la région"; cf. p. 25 n. 143 (= 2008, 147 n. 143) and p. 78 (= 2008, 202).

87 *P.Oxy.* LXX 4785 (October 19, 530). On the *prōteuontes*, see Laniado 2002, 201–211 and more recently Fabian Reiter in *P.Köln* XI, pp. 238–244, who also points to this change in Strategios II's titulature, as does Nikolaos Gonis in the commentary to *P.Oxy.* LXX 4784.4.

88 The other documents are *P.Oxy.* LXX 4784 (September 23, 530), *P.Oxy.* XXXVI 2779 (December 30, 530), and *P.Oxy.* XVI 1983 (July 28, 535); cf. *P.Oxy.* LXX 4783 (528/533/534 CE?) and *P.Oxy.* LXX, p. 89. Strategios is explicitly called *geouchōn* (but not *prōteuōn*) until at least December 31, 526 (*P.Oxy.* LXXXIII 5365) and then again on February 18, 542 (*P.Oxy.* LXIII 4396).

89 A fifth text, *P.Oxy.* LXX 4783 (see the preceding note), in which *prōteuōn* is restored, is too fragmentary to determine its content.

90 Cf. the lease *SB* XVI 12948 (Hermopolites; 448): the document is addressed to an *aidēsimos prōteuōn* of Antinoopolis (ll. 3–4), while in l. 12 the same individual appears as *geouchōn*. Fabian Reiter (*P.Köln* XI, p. 242) has suggested that a *prōteuōn* may be a more elevated *geouchōn*.

91 This means actual functions, not honorary titles such as *comes* or *patricius*. These titles are discussed in Chapter Five, Section I.

pression of a potential address as *geouchōn*, provided that both distinctions were held in the same place.[92]

Evidence from other nomes may be enlightening, as it takes us outside the Apion bubble.[93] Private leases from the Arsinoite, for instance, underscore the pattern: the *geouchōn* address occurs frequently in leases of estate property but is absent when the lessor is an official.[94] The trend is also evident in deeds of surety—documents in which one person swears to an authority that a third person will continue to reside in a certain place.[95] Such documents were drafted mostly in order to guarantee that individuals fulfilled their legal dues, such as liturgies or taxes; in some cases, the person under surety has already committed an offense, be it a crime or escaping their dues, and is released from prison, as it were, on probation (*Enthaftungsbürgschaft*).[96] Officials were the natural addressees of such documents, but a host of sureties for people dwelling on estate property (in *epoikia, ktēmata*, or as part of villages and cities) are also addressed to *geouchountes*, of which the Apiones easily furnish the most examples. The large landowners of course had an interest in their workers and tenants abiding by the rules, staying where they were, and paying their rents and taxes. Most revealing for us are, however, the examples in which estate property and the responsibilities of the *geouchōn* are at issue—that is, where it would strictly speaking be irrelevant to the deed whether or not the addressee held any public office. These documents may be addressed to officials or to *geouchountes*, but, again, even if their responsibilities as *geouchountes* are the reason for the deed, officials are never addressed as *geouchountes*.[97] In other words, officials in

92 In the same vein, a local office usually makes the formula of origin (ἀπό + place) superfluous as long as both pertain to the same location. Conversely, the presence of this ἀπό in the description of contract parties usually implies that this individual did not hold office in the same location.

93 The main point can also be illustrated with non-Apionic Oxyrhynchite evidence, such as the deed of surety *P.Oxy.* IV 306 (December 16, 413), in which the addressee is *nauarchos* of Oxyrhynchos, but the relevant duties are γεουχικὰ ἔργα in an *epoikion*.

94 Addressed to *geouchountes*: *BGU* II 364; *P.Lond.* I 113.5A; *P.Ross.Georg.* III 32; *SB* XVIII 14001. Addressed to officials (all pagarchs): e.g., *BGU* I 305; *CPR* XIV 10; *CPR* XIV 11; *SB* I 5256. For other types of document from a private context addressed to officials (here, pagarchs) without the *geouchōn* formula, see for instance *CPR* XIX 32 (a receipt for a delivery of reed to be used on estate grounds), *CPR* XXIV 28 (a contract with an estate employee), or *SPP* III 392 (a receipt for rent).

95 On the deeds of surety, see the references in Stern 2016, 1847 n. 9.

96 A term that has found no equivalent outside German.

97 In order to highlight my main point, the following instances are restricted to deeds of surety for people from *epoikia*, since there are no *geouchountes* to be found in deeds of surety for villagers outside Oxyrhynchos; this may, however, be due to the lower number of surviving examples of deeds of surety from the Arsinoite. **Addressed to pagarchs:** *CPR* XIX 14 + P.Vindob. G 21029 + 25638 (Arsinoe; 590, edition forthcoming by Sophie Kovarik), *SB* XVIII 13952 (Arsinoe; 591/592), *P.Lond.* I 113.5C (Arsinoe; 600), and *CPR* XXIV 27 (Arsinoe; 610). **Addressed to officials other than pagarchs:** *BGU* II 401 (Arsinoe; 618) and *CPR* XIV 17 (Arsinoites?; 652?), both addressed to *ekdikoi* who apparently did not own the *epoikia*. **Addressed to *geouchountes*:** *P.Vind.Sijp.* 7 (Herakleopolites; 463), *SPP* X 127 (Herakleopolites; 463), and *CPR* X 127 (Arsi-

such deeds were undoubtedly still *geouchountes*, but they are not addressed as such, as an office bears higher prestige.[98] This pattern of suppressing the *geouchōn* title once a public office is involved seems rather straightforward and suggests that individuals addressed as *geouchōn* do not hold public office; ergo, the addressees in our documents concerning *kōmai pagarchoumenai* are not pagarchs of Oxyrhynchos.

It may be objected that these landowners might have simply been the responsible authorities for a, or the, pagarchy despite not actually performing the liturgy (as in the case of women or absentee landlords)—"formal" pagarchs, as it were—and were therefore not directly addressed as pagarchs. Strategios II would be a natural candidate here since he held the offices of *praefectus Augustalis* in Alexandria by 524 CE and *comes sacrarum largitionum* in Constantinople shortly after 532, probably residing in the imperial capital until the end of his life.[99] The only non-Apion to deal with *kōmai pagarchoumenai*, Flavia Anastasia, would also fit here, being a woman.[100] But this hypothesis is unlikely for two main reasons. First, while Strategios was still a minor, he was usually represented by a certain Theodoros *hypokatastatos*.[101] This Theodoros *additionally* assumed the function of a *diadochos*, a liturgical stand-in, when representing Strategios in a civic liturgy as *riparius*.[102] Theodoros does not, however, bear the title of

noe; 584). The latter is in fact addressed to four women who are referred to as *prōteuousai* (see Laniado 2002, 204–206 on the hereditary character of this title), which, as we have seen, supplants the *geouchōn* title. Interestingly, the document is the only one outside Oxyrhynchos using the *diapheron* formula to describe the hamlet in question. There are more examples of these texts addressed to (apparent) non-officials without the *geouchōn* address, so it seems that neither formula was a necessary element. But my point here is mainly that *when* the *geouchōn* address is used, the addressee is *not* an official in the area covered by the expression.

98 It is therefore often unclear whether these documents refer to an official background to the case in question or are linked to the official's capacity as owner of the particular *epoikion*. It could be argued, for instance, that in *P.Oxy.* XLVIII 3400 (Oxyrhynchos; c. 359–365), a village *boēthos* (Papnouthis) addresses his master Eulogios as *geouchos* despite the high probability that Eulogios's involvement was based on his being *praepositus pagi*. But this text is an internal communication, not a legal document, and the change of formula in this case contrasts with, and therefore highlights the rigidity of, the pattern found in contracts.

99 By 530, Strategios had become *patricius*. On the chronology of Strategios's titles, see Hickey 2012, 12–13. The *oiketēs* formula, which may hint at the absence of the Apiones in question (see Chapter Five, n. 111), is attested with Strategios II in 493 CE (*P.Oxy.* LXXXII 5337.5–6, but it is absent in multiple attestations of Strategios around that date) and then again after 523 (*P.Oxy.* LXXXII, p. 165). On the date of Strategios's death, see *P.Oxy.* LXIII, p. 146.

100 On her archive, see the Catalog, s.v. The Apiones and Anastasia (Oxyrhynchos).

101 *P.Flor.* III 325 (Oxyrhynchos; May 20, 489). On the term *hypokatastatos* or *hypokatastatēs*, see Chapter One, n. 129.

102 *P.Oxy.* LXVII 4614 (Oxyrhynchos; late V). Strategios's father, Apion I, was apparently still alive on October 1, 497 (*P.Oxy.* XVI 1982), but it appears that Strategios II nonetheless had formal authority over an estate as *geouchōn* (Nikolaos Gonis in *P.Oxy.* LXVII, pp. 233–234 and *P.Oxy.* LXXXII, p. 165). On *diadochoi* as liturgical substitutes, see Laniado 2002, 221–222. See also the discussion of this text on p. 51 above. The modalities of liturgical representation are discussed in Chapter Four, Section III.

diadochos in a roughly contemporary land lease that refers to a village as *pagarchoumenē* by Strategios,[103] which can only mean that the *pagarchoumenē* formula does not relate to an office or liturgy to which a person was appointed. And second, the *pagarchoumenē* formula cannot be explained in Anastasia's case simply by her being a woman, since in the Antaiopolite a woman named Patrikia *is* addressed as pagarch.[104] The use of the formula is therefore not triggered by absence or by some other sort of incapacity on the part of the landlord.

Consequently, if one is not to assume that the Oxyrhynchite developed a most unusual—and illogical—notarial practice in which important offices were suppressed from an aristocrat's titulature against all notarial custom,[105] the only remaining plausible explanation is that the *kōmai pagarchoumenai* were an institution that was distinct from the Oxyrhynchite pagarchy. This is finally illustrated by the example of the notary Ioannes, who signed three of the six documents concerning *kōmai pagarchoumenai* on which the notarial signature has been preserved.[106] In another document, though presumably a later one, this same Ioannes does explicitly refer to an Oxyrhynchite pagarch (not from the Apion family), which strongly discourages the idea that Ioannes used the *pagarchoumenē* formula to refer to the pagarchy of Oxyrhynchos in the other cases.[107]

"When you have eliminated the impossible, whatever remains, however improbable, must be the truth."[108] While the present section has analyzed the documentary practice around the use of the formula *kōmē pagarchoumenē*, the following sections, beginning with an analysis of the *kōmai pagarchoumenai* in the context of the Apiones' management of villages, present additional positive evidence that these villages were very likely distinct from the pagarchy of Oxyrhynchos, even though this seemingly complicates the picture and thus appears to contradict Ockham's razor.

---

103 *P.Oxy.* LXXXII 5337 (Oxyrhynchos; June 10, 493).

104 *P.Vat.Aphrod.* 16A.2: [– – – ο]ἱ ἐνδοξότατοι πάγαρχοι Πατρ[ικία καί – – –]; on this reading, see the Catalog, n. 251. No equivalent of the *oiketēs* formula (see n. 99 above) is known for Anastasia, and from a simple representation (διά) by her *dioikētēs* it is difficult to make her an absentee landlord of the same level as the Apiones.

105 On this custom in aristocrats' addresses, see Chapter Five, Section II.

106 Ioannes issued *P.Oxy.* XVI 1981, *P.Oxy.* I 139, and *P.Oxy.* LXVI 4536 within a span of only three days in 612 CE, but Diethart & Worp 1986, 82 opt against reading his name in *P.Oxy.* XXIV 2420 (February 25–March 26, 614). We can rule out the possibility that he was responsible for the remaining two documents: the signature of *P.Oxy.* LXX 4802 (early VII) is badly damaged, but the traces that remain do not fit Ioannes's name (see also Gonis 2002b, commentary on *SB* XXVIII 17002.26, who argues that this is a different hand) and the signature of *P.Oxy.* I 133 (October 19, 550) reveals a different notary at work.

107 *PSI* I 52, on which see Section VI below.

108 Sherlock Holmes in Arthur Conan Doyle's *The Sign of the Four*.

IV. The Apiones and Their Villages

We know sixteen instances of *kōmai pagarchoumenai*, comprising twelve different villages and two instances in which the village name is lost. All twelve known villages appear frequently in economic and administrative accounts from the Apion estate, and consequently must have been integrated into the network woven by the Apiones' highly complex estate management.[109] It is, however, only in contracts involving one of their inhabitants that these villages figure as *kōmai pagarchoumenai*. The villages are listed in Table 3.[110]

Table 3: Attested Apionic *kōmai pagarchoumenai* in chronological order; Tampeti, the only village to occur multiple times, is highlighted in bold type.

Date	Village	Evidence
June 10, 493	Spania	*P.Oxy.* LXXXII 5337
October 19, 530	**Tampeti**	*P.Oxy.* LXX 4785
October 19, 550	Takona	*P.Oxy.* I 133
September 7, 551	Sephtha	*P.Oxy.* LXXXIII 5371
August 24, 552	Sepho	*P.Oxy.* LXXXIII 5373
September 13, 552	Keuothis	*P.Lond.* III 776
March 12, 564	Paneuei	*P.Oxy.* LXX 4787
565/566 or 580/581	probably **Tampeti**	*P.Oxy.* LXXXIII 5377
571–578	**Tampeti**	*P.Oxy.* LXXXIII 5378
October 21, 588	name lost, c. 5 letters	*P.Oxy.* LXXXIII 5390
October 25, 612	Ophis	*P.Oxy.* XVI 1981
October 26, 612	Adaiou	*P.Oxy.* I 139
October 27, 612	Pleein	*P.Oxy.* LXVI 4536
February 25–March 26, 614	Seryphis	*P.Oxy.* XXIV 2420
early VII	Episemou	*P.Oxy.* LXX 4802

The regular inclusion of these villages in estate accounts and especially the fact that at least four of them—Sephtha, Spania, Takona, and Tampeti—were the centers of Apionic *prostasiai*[111] can only mean a more or less permanent allocation of those villages to the Apion estate management and its *prostasia* system, further undermining the

109 Although in the meantime many sources have further illuminated the Apion estate and its management, the most comprehensive account to date remains Mazza 2001, 76–156; for a more recent introduction to the basic structure of the estate and the issues at stake in the Apion dossier, see Hickey 2012, 18–27 and Amin Benaissa's discussion of new Apion accounts in *P.Oxy.* LXXXIV, pp. 154–166; for more literature, see the Introduction, n. 47.

110 The only non-Apionic instance is *P.Oxy.* XLIV 3204 (January 2, 588), addressed to Flavia Anastasia, in which the village name is lost.

111 *P.Oxy.* LXXXIV 5457 (536 CE); *P.Oxy.* XVI 2032 (540/541 CE); *P.Oxy.* LXXXIV 5458 (mid-VI);

hypothesis that the *kōmai pagarchoumenai* fell under the authority of the pagarchy of Oxyrhynchos.[112]

The Apion estate was organized and managed via a system of management districts (*prostasiai*), each placed under a *pronoētēs* who collected rents and taxes—hence Jean Gascou's concept of "rent-tax"[113]—for land owned by the Apiones (and some other land, as discussed later).[114] At one point in the later sixth century, thirty-three of these *prostasiai* were in place at the same time; recently published evidence suggests that this number remained relatively stable throughout the sixth century.[115] The *kōmai pagarchoumenai* were clearly allocated to such *prostasiai*, given their appearance in the relevant documents, mostly accounts and lists,[116] and *pronoētai* are attested in connec-

P.Oxy. LXXXIV 5460 (569 CE); *P.Oxy.* LXXXIV 5466 (latter half of VI); *P.Oxy.* XVIII 2207 (VI–VII; new ed. in Benaissa 2015).

112 Their integration into the Apion estate administration is underscored by other evidence; see Benaissa 2021, s.vv.

113 See Gascou 1985, especially 12–19 (= 2008, 134–141) on these interactions between rent and tax collection on the Apion estate; see also McConnell 2017, 44–45. One has to bear in mind, however, that this does not mean that rent and tax became the same—for instance because the Apiones were tax farmers, as it is sometimes understood—but that the *geouchoi* handled taxes *from their tenants* in the same way they handled the rents they received from these tenants. Rent and tax from estate grounds were thus handled in an analogous way, leading to frequent (involuntary, one assumes) interchange between the terms. See my explanation of *P.Oxy.* LXXXIV 5464 in Section V for the argument that the situation for non-estate grounds is different.

114 For concise accounts of the *prostasia* system, see McConnell 2017, 41–47; Hickey 2012, 26–27; Benaissa 2007, especially 75 n. 2; and Ruffini 2008a, 106–119. Todd Hickey (2012, 26 and n. 31), has established that the appropriate term for the district is *prostasia* and that *pronoēsia,* which is sometimes thought to be a synonym, "refers to the office [...]; it is not an equivalent [for *prostasia*]." The earliest evidence for this use of *prostasia* is provided by *P.Oxy.* VIII 1134 (March 3, 421), here concerning the *domus divina*.

115 For the number of *prostasiai*, see Amin Benaissa's account in *P.Oxy.* LXXXIV, pp. 158–166 and Benaissa 2015. This undermines the hypothesis brought forward by McConnell 2017, 62–66 and McConnell 2016 according to which the number of *prostasiai* would have increased from the second quarter to the latter half of the sixth century, but McConnell had no access to these new accounts at the time those studies were written.

116 **Lists and accounts (selected):** *P.Oxy.* XVIII 2207 (Tampeti and "Takona and Tholthis"; new ed. Benaissa 2015); *P.Oxy.* XVIII 2204 (Spania); *P.Oxy.* VII 1053 verso and *P.Oxy.* XVIII 2206 (Sepho, Spania, Takona, and Tampeti; note that the amounts allocated to the villages in these two documents are identical); *P.Oxy.* XXVII 2480 (Sephtha and Takona); *P.Oxy.* XIX 2243B (Takona and Episemou); *P.Oxy.* XVI 1921 (Takona and Ophis); *P.Oxy.* XVI 2028 (Pleein, Sepho, and Takona); *P.Oxy.* XVIII 2196 (Adaiou and Episemou); *P.Oxy.* LVIII 3960 (Adaiou and Episemou); *P.Oxy.* XVI 2044 (Adaiou; cf. Hickey 2012, 166); *P.Oxy.* XVI 2025 (Pleein, Paneuei—here as an *epoikion*; maybe the small village, as an *epoikion,* became part of the Apion estate—Ophis, and Episemou); *P.Oxy.* XVI 2032 (Adaiou, Ophis, and Takona); *P.Oxy.* XVI 2034 (Sepho, Spania, and Tampeti); *P.Oxy.* I 127 with the corrections by Hickey 1998, 161 (Adaiou, Episemou, Pleein, Seryphis, Sepho, and Ophis). **Working contracts:** *P.Bagnall* 33 (Sephtha) and *P.Oxy.* I 136 (Episemou and Adaiou). **Letters:** *P.Oxy.* XVI 1856 (Keuothis) and *P.Oxy* XVI 1859 (Seryphis; cf. Hickey 2012, 180), both of which are part of the Biktor archive, which belongs to the realm

tion with most of them.[117] But the Apiones never owned entire villages,[118] only parts of them.[119] It therefore seems only natural that the titles of the *pronoētai*, as attested in their "job descriptions," do not relate to villages but to the lands owned by the *geouchōn* within these villages.[120] One of these contracts is even explicit about the fact that the

---

of the Apiones, from the second decade of the seventh century; see Gonis 2015b. **Contracts/settlements:** *P.Oxy.* LXIII 4397.23 (Ophis). These villages are also ubiquitous in the new Apion documents of *P.Oxy.* LXXXIV.

117 See Benaissa 2021, s.vv. (updating Mazza 2001, Appendix 6).

118 For the curious claim that "great estates do own entire villages," see Ruffini 2018a, 211.

119 See for instance *P.Oxy.* XVI 2025 (VI–VII), a list of contributions in grain and money from hamlets and villages, in which the amounts from the former match or exceed those from the latter. Such estate property in villages could then apparently be termed "*ousiakon* of the village" (*P.Oxy.* LXXXIII 5377.2 and commentary). Note also the large number of *possessores* in the village of Spania as recorded by *P.Oxy.* XVI 2058. This village is, notably, the only village in our period to which *geouchountes* are attributed in addresses of legal documents (instead of the usual general "*geouchōn* in Oxyrhynchos," vel sim.), as attested in *P.Wash.Univ.* I 17 (see Gonis 2007b, 271) and *P.Bad.* VI 172, where, in addition, a location within the village is described as "in the village, in the precinct/district (*amphodon*) of the *megalē oikeia*" (ll. 14–15). The only other instance of a village being part of the *geouchōn* address that I am aware of can be found in *P.Gen.* II[2] 10 (Herakleopolites; 316).

120 *P.Oxy.* XVIII 2196.4–6: προ(νοητοῦ) Ματρεῦ καὶ | ἐν κώμ(ῃ) Ἐπισήμου καὶ ἐν κώμ(ῃ) Ἀδαίου καὶ ἄλλ(ων) ἐξωτικ(ῶν) | τόπων, "*pronoētēs* of Matreou and in the village Episemou and in the village Adaiou and of other *exōtikoi topoi*." The *pronoētēs* is the *diakonos* Serenos, whose work contract from three years earlier is preserved in *P.Oxy.* I 136, with the same area of activity described in ll. 14–17: ἐπὶ τῷ με τὴν | χώραν τοῦ προνοητοῦ ἤτοι ὑποδέκτου ἀποπληρῶσαι παρ' αὐτῇ ἐμ (read ἐν) προστασίᾳ κτήματος Ματρέου | καὶ τῶν ἐν ταῖς κώμης (read κώμαις) Ἐπισήμου καὶ Ἀδαίου καὶ τῶν ἐξωτικῶν αὐτῶν τόπων τῶν διαφερόντων | τῇ ὑμῶν ὑπερφυείᾳ, "under the condition that I fill the post of *pronoētēs*, or *hypodektēs*, for/under you in the *prostasia* of the hamlet Matreou and those (places) in the villages Episemou and Adaiou and their *exōtikoi topoi* that belong to your *hyperphyeia*." Both Episemou and Adaiou are known as *pagarchoumenē*. On the meaning of *exōtikoi topoi*, see Benaissa 2007, 80–86. Although damaged, *P.Oxy.* LVIII 3952.17–20 may have contained a comparable specification. The probably but not definitely Apionic *P.Bagnall* 33.7–8 (496 CE) contains a lacuna, but I take [– – – Β]ακιν καὶ Σαραλαου καὶ Σεσφθα καὶ Θμοιναχη τῶν ὑμῶν τόπων to mean that this refers again to "your *topoi*" within the villages (Sephtha and Thmoinache) or the hamlets (Bakin and Saralaou in their entirety), but the lacuna at the beginning cannot have contained much text. One restoration that suggests itself is ἤτοι ὑποδέκτου ἐν, which would, however, not leave much space for a specification. On the working contracts, see the evidence and literature assembled by Nikolaos Gonis in *P.Oxy.* LXXXIV, p. 245. Cf. the earlier *SB* VI 9527.7–8 (Arsinoe; 385–412): προνοητῶν κώμης Βου[β]άστου τῶν [γεουχι]|κῶν πραγμάτων for another indication that the basic responsibility of the *pronoētai* in the villages lay on the estate property of their *geouchountes*, and which may be taken to suggest that the abovementioned phrase τῶν ὑμῶν τόπων refers to "your *topoi*" *within* the villages. Notably, *P.Oxy.* I 136 explicitly refers in ll. 14–17 (see above) to *those* territories within the villages that belong to the Apion household, whereas ll. 18–19 refer to the "villagers who are liable." These two passages together illustrate that references to "village(r)s" in such contexts (cf., for instance, "village farmers" in the new *P.Oxy.* LXXXIV 5474.22 and 27) should probably not be taken to encompass the *entire* village. See Berkes 2017a, 172 n. 3 and Ruffini 2008a, 112, with comparable views on this

pronoētēs received as salary for his service in the villages only half the amount he received for the hamlets,[121] which again strongly suggests that his services did not extend to the entirety of these villages, but only to his master's parcels within them. Such a position was naturally on the borderline between what we would today call the private and the public realms, and it is certainly telling that these managers were contracted to "fill the post of *pronoētēs*, or *hypodektēs*,"[122] alluding to "private" and "public" sides to this position.[123] Given that these villages were, as mentioned above, eponymic centers of management districts called *prostasiai,* the *pronoētai* of the Apion estate are best understood not as *pronoētai* "of (the village of) Tampeti," etc., but as *pronoētai* "of (the *prostasia* of) Tampeti," etc.

Even though *kōmai pagarchoumenai* were not owned as a whole by the Apiones, it seems that considerable parts of their administration proceeded under Apionic authority. This did not simply mean having their taxes handled by Apion estate employees but apparently also included directing village institutions. For instance, the Apiones assumed responsibility for guards, *phylakes,* in order to maintain public security in *kōmai pagarchoumenai* and their own adjacent holdings. In two cease-and-desist letters addressed to Apion III, some *prōtophylakes* from *kōmai pagarchoumenai* agree not to steal nor to provide shelter to those who do.[124] The administrative routine that

---

important detail. Is this distinction between village land that was and was not owned by a large estate the source of the phenomenon that some *kōmai* and *ousiai* of the same name appear side by side? See, for instance, Theaxenidos Kome and Theaxenidos Ousia in Berkes & Haug 2016, no. 1.7–8; see also n. 229 below on Dikaiou. Cf. the discussion by Banaji 2007, 171–180 about "estate villages" and his statement that "[i]t is as if villages (*kōmai*) were simply immune to ownership" (p. 173).

121 *P.Bagnall* 33.14–15. The villages are Sephtha and Thmoinache, of which the former is known as *pagarchoumenē.* The latter is, curiously, known to have been part of the Herakleopolite nome in the fifth century (*SPP* X 233.8). It was likely situated in the southern part of that nome, fairly close to Sephtha, the northernmost known locality of the Oxyrhynchite nome. The missing καί in the formula γεουχοῦντι ἐνταῦθα τῇ λαμπρᾷ καὶ λαμπροτάτῃ Ὀξυρυγχιτῶν πόλ(ει) in *P.Bagnall* 33.2 may indicate that Thmoinache had changed its affiliation to the Oxyrhynchite nome, but the editors concede that the use of καί in this context might have been inconsistent.

122 The two roles, linked by ἤτοι, would thus be two sides of the same coin, not two distinct functions. The *hypodektēs* here needs to be understood not as the "city *hypodektēs,*" on whom see Chapter Two, Section III 1, but in the general sense of a "receiver" of taxes on what I call the "pronoetic territory," i.e., lands that *belonged* to the Apiones; cf. Section V below. Cf. *P.Ross. Georg.* III 45 (Aphrodite; VI) and the reference to a *pronoētēs* (l. 6) as *phorologos* (l. 2), highlighting the "private" side of the position.

123 See also *SB* XX 15014 from the Antaiopolite, in which a *pronoētēs* issues a rent receipt for land owned collectively by a pagarchic collegium, probably linked to their officeholding (see Chapter Two, Section II 2). Note also that the *pronoētēs* of *P.Oxy.* I 136 and *P.Oxy.* XVIII 2196 is a *diakonos* and that the Antaiopolite pagarch Menas Scriniarius receives his information about Aphrodite's overdue tax payments in *P.Cair.Masp.* I 67060 from a *diakonētēs*; on clerics involved in tax collection, see Schmelz 2002, 295–318, especially 316–317.

124 *P.Oxy.* I 139 (October 26, 612) and *P.Oxy.* LXVI 4536 (October 27, 612). An obvious parallel,

is evident from these documents and the context in which they were written suggest that similar agreements were routinely demanded from such guards, and that the Apiones acted as their superiors.[125] The *phylakes* also serve as a link to the pagarchs, who are in other contexts evidenced as a superior authority to *phylakes*, or to *eirēnarchai* and *phylakes*,[126] illustrating the parallel authority of the pagarchs on the one hand and the landowners that exercised authority over *kōmai pagarchoumenai* on the other. The Apiones, moreover, maintained a prison where they detained people from *epoikia* and *ktēmata* as well as from *kōmai pagarchoumenai*.[127]

The superior position of the Apiones over village institutions in *kōmai pagarchoumenai* is also apparent in a contract between Apion II and the collective of village notables of Takona, represented by the *meizōn* (the village headman) and, nominally, all *kōmarchai* (senior village officials).[128] It is obvious that Apion in this case was not concluding a contract with the farmers of his estate parcels but with the village as an administrative entity—and yet he appears in his capacity as *geouchōn*. The villagers borrow seed corn from the harvest of the present year, credited against the next harvest from Apion, who was of course only nominally involved.[129] They pledge to pay it back "together with our *phorikos phoros*" from the crops of the next harvest, in the month of Payni—that is, *during* the next harvest.[130] The character of this transaction is formal-

P.Oxy. XVI 1981 (October 25, 612), does not mention the professions of the contracting party, but was apparently issued on behalf of the entire village community; see Stern 2015, 126.

125 See Stern 2015, 125–126. The upkeep of local military detachments, the *bucellarii*, on such estates seems to be a different matter, but they certainly do not represent warlord-style "private armies"; see Gonis 2016 and Begass 2018, 449–456 on the current state of the debate and its implications.

126 *P.Oxy.* LXX 4802 (Oxyrhynchos; early VII) and *P.Bodl.* I 53 (Arsinoe; 605); cf. *P.Lond.* V 1786 (Arsinoites; c. 592–596), in which Kyrillos (see the Catalog, s.v.) is not addressed as pagarch, but the letter is not a legal document and Kyrillos may still have received it in his capacity as pagarch. The security personnel the pagarchs had at their disposal are discussed in more detail in Chapter Six, Section IV.

127 On estate prisons, see Stern 2016, 1857–1862 and 1866–1867. It appears that the Apiones were still using a city prison by August 24, 552 and, most probably, by June 18, 557 (see *P.Oxy.* LXXXIII 5373 and 5375, respectively, with the editor's commentary). The earliest document to mention their estate prison is either *P.Oxy.* LXXXIII 5377 (565/566 or 580/581 CE), *P.Oxy.* LXXXIII 5378 (571–578), or *PSI* VIII 953 (probably 567/568). On prisons in late antiquity, see recently Syrkou 2021, 31–36.

128 *P.Oxy.* I 133 (October 19, 550). As far as we know, the term *prōtokōmētēs* generally refers to a village headman throughout the Greek-speaking eastern Mediterranean, including most of Egypt; in Oxyrhynchos, however, it appears to have been a rather unspecific term for leading villagers, while the term for a village headman was *meizōn*; see Berkes 2017a, 207 and Chapter Two, Section III 5.

129 The document was drafted in the month of Phaophi, which is about two months after the end of the harvest season.

130 *P.Oxy.* I 133.17–20: ἐπάναγκες | ἀποδώσομεν τῇ ὑμῶν ἐνδοξ(ότητι) μετὰ καὶ τοῦ φορικοῦ ἡμῶν φόρου ἐν τῷ Παῦνι μηνὶ | τοῦ ἐνεστῶτος ἔτους σκζ ρϙς τῆς αὐτῆς παρούσης τεσσαρεσκαιδεκάτης ἰνδ(ικτίονος) | ἐκ νέων καρπῶν τῆς σὺν θεῷ πεντεκαιδεκάτης ἐπινεμ(ήσεως). While prima facie the term *phorikos phoros* suggests rent payments of those holdings belonging to the Apion estate, this

ly private,[131] and there are other examples of village communities acting as collectives vis-à-vis large landowners in business transactions.[132] It is notable, however, that the corn the villagers borrowed from Apion had been taken "from the harvest of the present fourteenth indiction."[133] This specification suggests that Apion regularly received "the" harvest of the village; presumably the contract does not relate to actual (physical) redistributions but was merely a matter of accounting. At the same time, the seed corn was to be used not for Apionic holdings in the village (*geouchikai arourai* vel sim.) but for the villagers' land ("our arouras").[134] This shows that parts of the land from which Apion regularly received the harvest were in the villagers' possession, again indicating Apion's fiscal responsibility, which is no doubt linked to the status of the village as *pagarchoumenē*. The entire procedure thus takes a public or at least "semi-public" character.

Other documents underscore the impression that the Apion estate regularly assumed responsibility for essential administrative tasks in certain villages. It was, for instance, an Apionic *chartoularios* who received a report from Takona concerning the rise of the Nile flood,[135] while other papyri show the Apiones managing the water supply for fields they did not own[136] or organizing the upkeep of public dikes.[137] Also striking in this regard is a list of expenses from the estate: all entries in which village officials receive considerable amounts (probably salaries) concern villages known as *kōmai pagarchoumenai*.[138] Because, as shown in the previous section, the connection between a *geouchōn* and a *kōmē pagarchoumenē* cannot be explained by the assumption that the particular *geouchōn* held the pagarchy of Oxyrhynchos, it follows again that the Apion

need not exclusively be the case here (though it is evidently so in the parallel *P.Oxy.* LXIII 4398, on which see the next note), since *phoros* in the estate accounts is frequently associated with tax payments; see *P.Oxy.* LXIII, p. 169 on the use of the adjective *phorikos* in regard to tax payments. This led Jean Gascou to develop the concept of "rente-impôt"; see n. 113 above.

131 Cf. *P.Oxy.* LXIII 4398 (Oxyrhynchos; 553), which attests an advance of seed corn from a *geouchōn* in almost exactly the same words, but concerns a (non-Apionic) *epoikion*, i.e., a settlement in possession of the landlord. This document is, moreover, the only other attestation for the expression *phorikos phoros*.

132 See for instance *P.Oxy.* LVIII 3954 (which, however, does not address the *geouchōn* but rather his *dioikētēs*).

133 *P.Oxy.* I 133.12–13: ἀπὸ γενήματος τῆς παρούσης | τεσσαρεσκαιδεκάτης ἰνδ(ικτίονος).

134 *P.Oxy.* I 133.13: εἰς σπερμοβολίαν τῶν ἡμῶν ἀρουρῶν καρπῶν. That "our arouras" refers to ownership is suggested by the contrasting formula in *P.Oxy.* LXIII 4398.20–21: εἰς σπερμοβολίαν τῶν ὑπ' ἐμὲ | γεουχικῶν (!) ἀρουρῶν καρπῶν, where the plot is only under tenancy. On the late antique village community as a collective landowner, see Berkes 2017a, 16–19.

135 *P.Oxy.* XVI 1830 (VI), sent by *pragmateutai*.

136 Hickey 2012, 50–51.

137 *P.Oxy.* LXXXIV, p. 240.

138 *P.Oxy.* VIII 1147, concerning *meizones*, *boēthoi*, and a *stablitēs*. The *riparius* (who acts at the city level) is not a village official, neither are the *pronoētai* (estate employees only assigned to a village). On this text, see also Berkes 2017a, 70.

estate was burdened with an institutional arrangement that was distinct from the pagarchy.

What has been said so far in this section suggests that the *kōmai pagarchoumenai* and their public institutions were under *oikos* administration regularly and on a long-term basis. Yet, these villages retained their proper administrative infrastructures.[139] Scholars dealing with the working contracts for the men called "*pronoētēs*, or *hypodektēs*," have assumed that the *pronoētai* also dealt with the tax payments of these villages beyond what was owned by the *geouchōn*,[140] but it must be cautioned that such an activity was apparently not covered in their "job description."[141] What is more, *kōmai pagarchoumenai* still had their own *boēthoi*, who would be natural candidates for handling at least some taxes in a village, but we may here simply be dealing with different layers of management and issues of accounting.[142] This separated responsibility may also have extended over arrangements unrelated to tax collection.[143] By way of comparison, *hypodektai* are well known from the Antaiopolite tax receipts, where we have already seen them acting as collectors (and receivers) of taxes from *astika* lands, whereas *kōmētika* taxes were collected and administered by the *boēthoi*. The terminology for the "rendering of accounts" that we find in one Antaiopolite de facto working contract for *boēthoi* is clearly parallel to that found in the Oxyrhynchite contracts for *pronoētai*,[144] which begs the question of whether the Oxyrhynchite "*pronoētai*, or *hypodektai*" fulfilled comparable functions in *kōmai pagarchoumenai* as the Antaiopolite *hypodektai* did in villages under the pagarchy.

Such an arrangement would seem natural, given that the city *hypodektai* were not assigned to individual pagarchs, but to the collegium as a whole. The landowners

139 Many types of village officials are attested in *kōmai pagarchoumenai*, e.g., *prōtophylakes* (see above), *kōmarchai* (*P.Oxy.* I 133: Takona), *meizones* (*P.Oxy.* I 133: Takona; *P.Oxy.* VIII 1147: Tampeti), village *grammateis* (*P.Oxy.* XVI 1997: Spania; the *katholikos* is certainly an estate employee and not the landowner as the editors believed), and, although not actually "village" officials, village *boēthoi* (*P.Oxy.* VIII 1147: Spania, Sepho, and Takona; *P.Oxy.* XVI 2032: Takona). This list is far from exhaustive; for more officials in *kōmai pagarchoumenai*, see Benaissa 2021, s.vv.

140 For instance, Hickey 2008, 89, discussed below.

141 Cf. n. 120 above.

142 Cf. *P.Oxy.* XVI 2032, where Takona has a *boēthos* (l. 4) but also a *pronoētēs*. The *boēthoi* may still have been involved in managing the tax payments from the non-Apion owned parts of the village before these were transferred to the estate management for tax accounting purposes. It is not surprising to find the *boēthoi* Papnouthis and Dorotheos also in the position of *pronoētai* under a large landowner, for these two positions were indeed comparable (Bagnall 1993, 158–160). On the *boēthoi*, see Chapter Two, Section III 2. Some documents among those identified by Mazza 2001, Appendix 8 as *pronoētēs* accounts mention villages, but none of them suggests responsibility for the entire village.

143 Cf. *SPP* VIII 989 (Hermopolis; V–VI), in which a *lamprotatos* Kallinikos orders a village *boēthos* to remunerate guards (*phrouroi*), and *BGU* XIX 2792 (Hermopolis; VI), where a *lamprotatos* Zacharias writes exactly the same, but to a *pronoētēs*.

144 *P.Lond.* V 1660.20 (Antaiopolis; c. 553): λογοποιείαν (read λογοποιίαν) θέσθαι versus, e.g., *P.Oxy.* LVIII 3958.31: τῶν λογοθεσιῶν. The comparability of the terms was noted by Gagos 2008, 66.

would not have access to these officials, and thus had their *pronoētai* fill this role for individual villages. On the other hand, there was no problem in handing a landowner the responsibility for *boēthoi* in individual villages under their own fiscal authority because the *boēthoi* were allocated to particular villages anyway (also under the pagarchy), and not to the city level like the *hypodektai*.[145] This could represent another interplay of "public" and "private" models of administration, but that must remain speculative.

The role of other village institutions in relation to the Apiones and other large landlords has recently been discussed in detail by Lajos Berkes in his survey of late antique village administration,[146] in which he also argued for a reconsideration of the traditional view that the late antique village community was irrelevant as a legal entity.[147]

Were *kōmai pagarchoumenai* a special group among villages under a fiscal share, or were all villages whose taxes were managed by the Apion estate *kōmai pagarchoumenai*? This is difficult to answer conclusively, but I see strong arguments for the latter option. In one instance, the village of Ophis, which is known as a *kōmē pagarchoumenē*, does not bear the formula even though we would expect it to,[148] suggesting that the formula could be omitted without affecting the legal value of the document, though it rarely was.[149] This interpretation seems to be supported by the parallel *diapheron/ktēma* formula that is used for hamlets (*epoikia*) and that is also absent in some cases where one would expect it.[150] Apparently, even without the designation it was still clear that

145 This scenario would perfectly fit *P.Oxy.* XLIV 3204 (January 2, 588), in which a *boēthos* of Flavia Anastasia's stands surety for a villager from a *kōmē pagarchoumenē*. This *boēthos* is probably a village *boēthos* whom Anastasia employed for this village under her fiscal authority.

146 Berkes 2017a, 66–75, where *pronoētai* are involved at several stages.

147 Berkes 2017a, 19.

148 *P.Oxy.* LXXXIII 5395 (592–602 CE), a deed of surety for villagers from Ophis, which is *pagarchoumenē* in *P.Oxy.* XVI 1981 (October 25, 612). The continuous presence of that village in earlier Apion accounts makes it somewhat unlikely that it became *pagarchoumenē* only after the date of *P.Oxy.* LXXXIII 5395.

149 Cf. the cases of P.Col. inv. 523 (May 16, 571; ed. Papathomas & Vergados 2021) and *P.Oxy.* LXIX 4756 (March 10, 590), both addressed to Flavia Anastasia; both documents are deeds of surety for villagers in which the villages are not described as *pagarchoumenē*. Another Apionic instance in which an expected *pagarchoumenē* is absent is *P.Oxy.* LVIII 3959 (January 12, 620; the contract lacks a regnal formula and is therefore certainly from the time of the Persian occupation), a deed of surety for a villager from Seryphis (which is *pagarchoumenē* in *P.Oxy.* XXIV 2420 from 614). That document is formally addressed to the *endoxos oikos* of the late Apion III, possibly accounting for the missing formula, which in its construction requires some kind of reference to a natural, living person—either "you" or "your *oikos*," vel sim. Formulaic considerations may also account for the missing *pagarchoumenē* formula in *P.Oxy.* LVIII 3954 (February 12, 611), in which a Kynopolite village is not *pagarchoumenē* despite the fact that the Apiones were probably responsible for the taxes of the entire nome (on this assumption, see the next section), for the document is addressed only to a subordinate of Apion III, not to the *geouchōn* himself.

150 For instance, *PSI* III 179 (December 25, 601 or 602 CE), addressed to Apion III. The *diapheron/ktēma* formula occurs only once outside the Oxyrhynchite, namely in *CPR* X 127 (Arsinoe; 584), but deeds of surety for individuals from hamlets are generally rare, e.g., *P.Vind.Sijp.* 7 (Herakleo-

such a village was *pagarchoumenē*. The Apion accounts further support this view, since they do not distinguish between different categories of villages.[151] It has been suggested, however, based on a different interpretation on a minor point, that they do draw such a distinction. In one account from the Apiones archive, the editor Todd Hickey pointed to one passage that looks as follows:

> Grand total (for receipts of the *pronoētai*): 108,816 ½ artabas, 4 *choinikes* of grain;
> and for the receipts of the villages: 53,4__ artabas.
> Grand total of receipts: 162,313 ½ artabas, 4 *choinikes* of grain by the *cancellus* measure.[152]

At the time, Hickey noted the distinction made between grain received from the estate's *pronoētai* and the villages. This distinction, he argued, suggests that

> since villages might be included in the territory of a *pronoetes,* the *komai* in *P.Oxy.* 18.2196.v must have been segregated because they were beyond easy incorporation into the estate's management structure. The best explanation for this is that the Apiones owned no (or limited) property in (or near) them, that the estate's *primary* relationship with these settlements was fiscal.[153]

In an accompanying footnote, Hickey implicitly identified these latter villages as the *kōmai pagarchoumenai*, but we have just seen that the Apiones' authority over these settlements included much more than merely collecting their taxes. It would also seem a confusing choice to refer simply to "villages" if contributions from villages were also included in the entry for the *pronoētai*.[154] The idea that some villages were included

---

polites; 463). Deeds of surety for villagers in other nomes than the Oxyrhynchite or Kynopolite are always addressed to officials (mostly pagarchs). Note that the earlier *P.Oxy.* XVI 1899.7–8 (Oxyrhynchos; May 8, 476), by contrast, still uses the most natural way of expressing possession of an *epoikion*: ἐποικίου | Πιάα̣ τοῦ αὐτοῦ ἐνδοξοτάτου ἀνδρός. This text may therefore provide a *terminus post quem* for the introduction of the *kōmai pagarchoumenai* (and hence the elevation of the pagarchy to the level of the *civitas*), but this is a risky argument because, as just stated, the formula could also have simply been "hidden" in even earlier documents.

151 Cf. the list *P.Oxy.* LXXXIV 5454 and the editor's introduction to the text, although he does not explicitly make the above claim.

152 *P.Oxy.* LXXXIV 5464 col. I 4–6 (c. 587 CE; cf. the identically structured passage with explicit reference to the *pronoētai* in *P.Oxy.* LXXXIV 5461 col. I from 569 CE). The passage was first discussed in Hickey 2008, 89–91. The document is the former *descriptum P.Oxy.* XVIII 2196 verso, discussed in its entirety in Hickey 2008. For the edition as *P.Oxy.* LXXXIV 5464, Hickey refers back to his 2008 article in lieu of a general introduction. The last two digits of the village figure are damaged; the grand total suggests 53,497 artabas. This assumes that the amounts of the *pronoētai* and the villages are measured in *cancellus* artabas, as is the grand total; see *P.Oxy.* LXXXIV 5464, commentary on col. I 4–6.

153 Hickey 2008, 89; see also Hickey 2012, 50 and *P.Oxy.* LXXXIV 5464, commentary on col. I 5.

154 Bransbourg 2016, 314–315 identifies these "villages" as the "other villages" from *P.Oxy.* XVI 1918 verso 12, implying that the latter provides an explicit reference to Hickey's distinction between these two categories of villages. Bransbourg's view appears to be a result of the author's wording

in the *pronoētai* contributions was based on the assumption that the *pronoētai* were responsible for *entire* villages, but the examples explicitly cited by Hickey actually deal with specific parcels *within* these villages (*en kōmais*).[155] The *pronoētai* did still handle taxes from land the Apiones did not own, but in a different context; the laws say that landlords could, but were not obliged to, effectuate tax payments for land owned by their farmers *outside* the estate proper.[156] This must be what is meant by the entries "for (his/her) private land" to which Hickey refers, and it is probably telling that so few of these explicit instances occur.[157] Additionally, some smaller independent landholders, who otherwise largely escape our notice due to the Apiones' "gravitational pull,"[158] may have relied on the *endoxos oikos* to pay their taxes in a "mutually profitable sym-

---

in Hickey 2008, 92, but I do not think that Hickey intended to attribute such significance to the formula "other villages." In *P.Oxy.* XVI 1918 verso, the amount for the "other villages" follows an entry for Σεφῶ̣, clearly a village, in l. 11 and two obscure entries for Παρ̣ο . . . . [and Πα̣κ̣έ̣ρ̣[κη in l. 10. As Hickey 2008, 92 n. 25 notes, these are not villages, but the papyrus is helplessly abraded in these spots. The sum (all my following figures ignore *keratia* for the sake of readability) in l. 9 is 13,950 *nomismata*; after the obscure entries in l. 10 it is 13,964, and after the entry for Sepho *and* the conversion to the Alexandrian standard it amounts to 14,061 in l. 11 and, after another addition, to 14,325 in l. 12, to which the amount of 5,685 *nomismata* for the "other villages" is then added, which results in the final 20,010 *nomismata*; for the restitution of these lines, see Maresch 1994, 102–103. The "other" is therefore used in contrast to one or more previously mentioned villages, but we have seen that there were many more villages administered by the Apiones than just these one or two (see above the several villages that form the centers of *prostasiai*). Therefore, these are not distinct categories of villages under the Apion administration, but rather Sepho (and, potentially, the two obscure places mentioned before) were calculated separately here for reasons that escape us due to the fragmentary state of these lines. If we, consequently, add the entry of l. 11 (plus, potentially, that of the obscure l. 10) to the amount of the "other villages" in order to arrive at an amount for all villages, this results in 5,818 (5,832 when l. 10 is included) *nomismata*, which still fits neatly within the range provided by the money receipts in *P.Oxy.* LXXXIV 5464 col. I 9–13 (= *P.Oxy.* XVIII 2196 verso; see also Hickey 2008, 92)—namely (the document is fragmentary here) between around 5,629 (resulting from the rho = 100 in l. 13 of the new edition) and 6,526 *nomismata*—and entails only a minor change to Bransbourg's calculation (Bransbourg 2016, 354) for the villages' nonpronoetic territory (from 40,882 to 41,835 arouras). I wonder whether the resulting decrease of 4.6 percent of the villages' nonpronoetic territory from 540–542 to 586/587 CE (cf. Bransbourg 2016, 361, where it is 2.4 percent) is already significant and calls for comment. Does this illustrate an expansion of the pronoetic lands at the cost of village land in *kōmai pagarchoumenai*, i.e., an expansion of the Apiones' possessions *within* the villages?

155 Cf. Hickey 2008, 89 n. 10, referring to *P.Oxy.* I 136.15–17 and *P.Oxy.* LXXXIV 5464 (= XVIII 2196 verso) col. I 4–5 (the commentary of that edition refers back to the 2008 article); see n. 120 above. See also, for instance, the *pronoētēs* account *P.Oxy.* XVI 1912 where in col. VI a heading ἐν κώμ(ῃ) Πέτνῃ follows after several headings "ἐποικ(ίου) so-and-so." Recently, Hickey acknowledged that ἐν ("in," "within") in such contexts suggests that pronoetic responsibilities did not extend over the entire village; see *P.Christodote*, p. 60 n. 54.

156 Iust. *nov.* 128.14; McConnell 2017, 91 and 109; Hardy 1931, 53.

157 Hickey 2008, 89 n. 9, frequently cited by Bransbourg 2016, e.g., 377, where n. 233 lists such entries.

158 "Gravitational pull": Ruffini 2009, 634. On a "much more nuanced social and economic land-

biotic relationship."[159] Bransbourg estimates the total share of the pronoetic lands *not* owned by the Apiones to be about 10 percent, but the margin of error is considerable and it seems more likely to be an over- rather than an underestimate.[160]

This reconstruction does, of course, not take anything away from Hickey's main and most important point—that the Apiones collected taxes from land they did not own. In fact, it supports that point, because now that we have removed a rather complicated conception of villages connected to the Apion estate, the aforementioned grain account looks much more natural: it refers to (1) grain from pronoetic lands—that is, estate property[161] outside and inside villages, plus some land that Apionic farmers owned *outside* the Apion estate but for which the Apiones paid the taxes, plus potentially some smaller independent landholders—and (2) grain from village land that was not part of the estate. The distinction between revenues from villages and those from *pronoētai* have since appeared in three other Apion documents.[162] Therefore, in the absence of any evidence of a distinction between different types of villages that the estate dealt with fiscally, it would seem the natural conclusion to take the phenomenon of *kōmai pagarchoumenai* as a manifestation or consequence of the model of fiscal shares.

---

scape in the Oxyrhynchite," noting the presence of smaller and medium-sized landholdings, see Hickey 2007, 297–298.

159 Bransbourg 2016, 373 and 403. "Mutually profitable" because the estate experienced an increasing need for gold to meet its tax requirements while the smaller landholders would have been spared from this business, which entailed quite some risk for them.

160 Bransbourg 2016, 374–379. My "pronoetic" is Bransbourg's "under direct fiscal management." On margins of error, cf. in particular the impact of a probably even lower rent than that assumed by Bransbourg (five artabas per aroura), as discussed on p. 375, on the percentages in Table 18 on p. 377.

161 On the question whether the *pronoētai* figure includes *autourgia* lands—land worked directly by the Apiones using wage labor, see Bransbourg 2016, 375–376 and Hickey 2008, 97 n. 45.

162 *P.Oxy.* LXXXIV 5458.3–4; 5460.36; 5461.4–5. The payment "from the *pronoētēs* of Tampeti," a village known as *pagarchoumenē*, in the *pronoētai* column is thus not a payment for the village, but for the *prostasia* named after the village (cf. p. 130 above). This *prostasia* then comprised Apion land within Tampeti as well as smaller hamlets completely in the Apiones' possession. This would be equally true for the other village names listed under the *pronoētai* heading. See n. 120 above for support for this hypothesis and see also the threefold association of the Apiones with Tarouthinou, noted by Amin Benaissa in *P.Oxy.* LXXXIV, p. 196. Provided that Benaissa's hypothesis that this place, usually known as an *epoikion*, had become a village is correct—and I see no obstacle—I would suggest that "*pronoētēs* of Tarouthinou" (*P.Oxy.* LXXXIV 5468.7) means that this man was responsible for the *prostasia* named after the village and that for some reason in this case, a different "*pronoētēs* of those in (οἱ ἐν) Tarouthinou" (*P.Oxy.* LXXXIV 5460.20) was responsible for the estate parcels within the village itself. On the quasi-technical usage of ἐν here, see nn. 120 and 155 above. Finally, Georgios, who held the "*boētheia* of Tarouthinou" (*P.Oxy.* LXXXIV 5466.32) would then be the link to everything pertaining to non-estate village land, and individuals from these parcels would be called "those from (οἱ ἀπό) Tarouthinou," who indeed appear in *P.Oxy.* LXXXIV 5468.8 (cf. again the *pronoētēs* of Tarouthinou in l. 7) and elsewhere.

Some parts of these villages were owned by a *geouchōn*; for the remainder, the *geouchōn* acted, in practice, like a pagarch, as captured in Figure 2.[163]

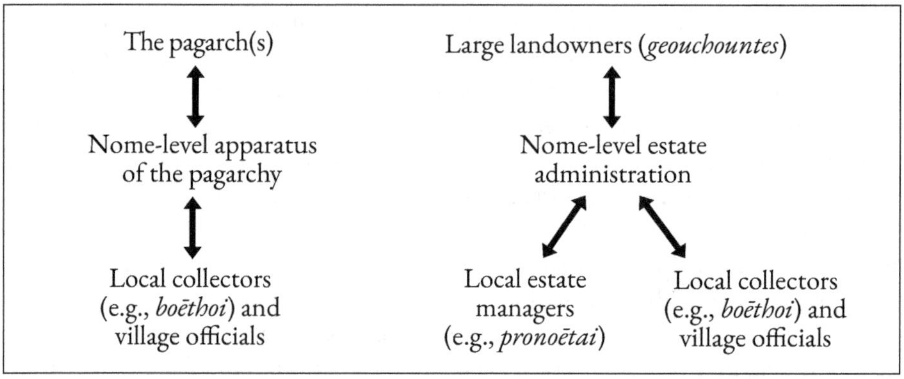

Figure 2: Administrative layers under pagarchs and large landowners responsible for fiscal shares in the sixth and early seventh centuries (simplified).

V. Landownership, Fiscal Shares, and the Pagarchy

With the *kōmai pagarchoumenai* established as a phenomenon distinct from the pagarchy of Oxyrhynchos, and having further analyzed their particular place within the administrative network of the Apion estate, it seems natural to look at this institution's relative fiscal share in the nome. First, the Apion estate proper. The contributions that the *endoxos oikos* in the Oxyrhynchite *and* Kynopolite made in unison for the grain tax in a late sixth-century account amount to 140,618.5 artabas,[164] which is about 40 percent of the 350,000 artabas given for the combined contributions from Oxyrhynchos and Kynopolis by another account dating to 582–602 CE.[165] The actual area *owned* by the estate was first estimated by Arnold H. M. Jones, who simply applied the only artabas-per-aroura ratio at his disposal, albeit one from the Antaiopolite, to convert the aforementioned 140,618.5 artabas to about 112,000 arouras (roughly 31,000 hectares or 77,000 acres) for the territorial basis of the Apion contributions in the Oxyrhynchite and Kynopolite nomes.[166] Todd Hickey, arguing that in light of the Gascou model this figure refers instead to the extent of the Apiones' fiscal share, arrived at a much small-

163 For the nome-level apparatus of the pagarchy, see Chapter Two, Section II 3. For the pagarch's local collectors, see Chapter Two, Section III.

164 *P.Oxy.* I 127 gives 87,818 ½ artabas for the Oxyrhynchite (ll. 1–2) plus around 52,8__ (the last two digits of the figure are damaged, so that the actual figure is slightly higher than the one given above) for the Kynopolite (l. 8); cf. Hickey 2008, 90.

165 *P.Oxy.* XVI 1909; Hickey 2012, 23.

166 Jones 1964, 784. *P.Cair.Masp.* I 67057 (Antaiopolis; mid-VI) provides the ratio for this exercise: 1.25 artabas per aroura, a figure that Hickey 2008, 97 n. 43 deems to be "on the low side."

er area of 29,500 arouras for the estate proper. Hickey took the figure of 825 arouras he calculated for the Apiones' lands used for viticulture and combined it with a second-century petition in which vineyards make up 2.8 precent of the entire agricultural land of one apparently rather moderate estate.[167] He acknowledged that the margin of error in this calculation is considerable but argued that this figure, rather than Jones's, must be the order of magnitude we are talking about.

To account for potential adjustments to individual variables, Hickey posited a "ceiling figure" of 1,250 arouras for the area the Apiones used for viticulture.[168] If we, for the sake of determining the size of the Apion holdings, substitute the 825 arouras mentioned above with 1,250, the calculation comes to 44,643 arouras. However, essential to Hickey's estimate of the area of the Apiones' vineyards (825 arouras) is the number of Apionic *prostasiai* (management districts) attested at one particular moment—a figure that has since slightly more than doubled due to the recent publication of further estate accounts.[169] If we acknowledge this by taking two steps back and calculating the extent of the Apiones' vineyards on the basis of thirty-three *prostasiai* instead of sixteen,[170] again leaving all other variables unchanged, the calculation yields 1,540 arouras.[171] This

167 Hickey 2012, 150–155; cf. Hickey 2008, 96–100. At the other end of the spectrum is Sarris 2006, 85, who argues that the Apion estate was even larger than Jones had estimated; cf. Chapter One, n. 23.

168 See Hickey 2012, 153.

169 Hickey (2012, 153 n. 50) acknowledged a general increase shortly before his book went to press, but defended his "ceiling figure" as a maximum.

170 For the number of *prostasiai*, see n. 115 above. We have to recall that the number of thirty-three—in contrast to the number of sixteen, which was a minimum gathered from incomplete documentation—represents a total for the entire estate at a certain point in the late sixth century.

171 The relevant mathematical operations are outlined in Hickey 2012, 152–153; all my following calculations are made with intermediate results rounded to the nearest whole number. The area of 825 arouras mentioned above consists of 175 arouras of vineyards under leases in kind and 650 arouras of vineyards under cash leases (p. 153). It is the latter figure that depends on the number of *prostasiai* and that, with thirty-three *prostasiai*, amounts to 1,365 arouras. To obtain this result, we first have to recalculate Hickey's "apotactic *solidi*" (p. 152; *solidi* = *nomismata*) using thirty-three *prostasiai* instead of sixteen, which results in 1,287 *nomismata*. This amount is then substituted in the calculation of p. 153 n. 47, yielding the result of 0.42, or 42 percent (see p. 153; Hickey's calculation based on sixteen *prostasiai* leads to 20 percent). This share is then, in form of a multiplier of .42, inserted into the calculation on p. 153 n. 49 (instead of .2), which yields 1,365 arouras. I have to leave open here whether the resulting contrast of 175 (vineyards under leases in kind) and 1,365 (vineyards under cash leases) arouras suggests that the first figure is unrealistically low, and thus the logic of the calculation requires modification, or whether it reflects "a thoroughly monetized countryside" (Banaji 2007, 169 in a general context; on the topic, cf. n. 59 above). The 175 arouras depend on a probably rather high yield estimate of 33.5 hectoliters per hectare (see Hickey 2012, 74–75 and 152), and we may push it up to 239 (calculated with a yield of 25 hectoliters per hectare) or perhaps even 593 arouras (10 hectoliters per hectare); see Clarysse & Vandorpe 1997, 70 for these alternative yield ratios for ancient vineyards. In these cases, the entire calculation for the extent of the Apion estate comes to 57,286 or 69,929 arouras, respectively. The latter figure is very close to, and even slightly larger than, Bransbourg's result (see below), which

results in an estate of 55,000 arouras, which can be characterized as the updated total of Hickey's calculation. It shows that even with the total number of *prostasiai* known for the entire estate, the result remains way below Jones's estimate.[172]

Other complex calculations of the size of the Apion estate and its fiscal responsibilities have been presented by Gilles Bransbourg in an article that among many other things demonstrates the validity of Hickey's approach and the order of magnitude presented above.[173] Bransbourg follows Hickey in segregating areas under the Apiones' "direct fiscal management" from "[t]he independent villages under the indirect tax umbrella of the Apiones," that is, he assumes that *entire* villages fell in the latter category, which is not the case, as we have seen.[174] However, this does not invalidate his figures, which, according to my hypothesis, only need to be relabeled.[175] For the 586–587 CE Oxyrhynchite and Kynopolite combined, Bransbourg's analysis yields the area of what I termed the Apiones' pronoetic lands as 64,972 arouras and the area of what I call the non-estate village territories under administration of the Apion estate as 39,893 arouras.[176] This equates to a total of 104,865 arouras under Apion management in both

is derived from independent analyses. None of these figures is going to be the Holy Grail, but the point is that all of them are significantly below Jones's (and, by extension, Sarris's) estimate. To reconcile the 55,000 arouras with the calculations in Hickey 2008, 90–91 (derived from yet another context), we probably need to assume a more "conservative" (i.e., lower) percentage of the land that was exploited directly by the Apiones than that assumed by Hickey in the 2008 article.

172 Although it still depends on a single extant vineyard-estate relation, namely from *P.Amh.* II 79, which is about four hundred years older. However, this share of vineyards (2.8 percent) may be confirmed as plausible by the percentage that emerges for the estate of Count Ammonios from the "Cadastre" of the village of Aphrodite, which amounts to 10 percent for vineyards and gardens; on this percentage, see Hickey 2007, 300. Note that using a higher vineyard percentage than Hickey does would make the Apion estate even smaller.

173 An inspiring aspect of Bransbourg's contribution is how he is able to integrate data from different regions to arrive at a largely coherent picture for Egypt as a whole. However, these calculations often depend on more complex ones made much earlier in Bransbourg's article; the following references are therefore to pages where Bransbourg makes an essential point in more summarized form. Bransbourg is himself reasonably cautious about his own figures, as some of these calculations depend on assumptions that are impossible to verify. But again, we are dealing with orders of magnitude here. Although some accounts from the later published *P.Oxy.* LXXXIV modify the numbers and some of the underlying assumptions of Bransbourg's article, I retain Bransbourg's figures to make the argument more easily retraceable, as my focus here is on the general differentiation of the land under Apion management and administration. On my relabeling of Bransbourg's categories as "pronoetic lands" and "non-estate village lands," see Section IV above.

174 See nn. 120 and 155 above.

175 For the basic considerations behind this relabeling, see the previous section. Bransbourg's areas under "direct fiscal management" (2016, 356 and 361, Table 15) become "pronoetic lands" in my model; Bransbourg's taxable area from "independent" villages (pp. 314; 352; and 361, Table 15) become my "non-estate village territories," that is, village land that was *not* part of the Apion estate.

176 Bransbourg 2016, 352–363. Around 10 percent, but probably less, of these pronoetic lands were

nomes,[177] or 40 percent of those nomes' combined taxable area, which Bransbourg calculates to be 260,996 arouras: 221,623 arouras for the Oxyrhynchite and 39,373 arouras for the Kynopolite.[178] Since, as Bransbourg convincingly argues, the Apiones fiscally managed the *entire* Kynopolite by the end of the sixth century,[179] their fiscal responsibility in Oxyrhynchos alone can be established at 30 percent,[180] which is strikingly close to the Apiones' share in the aforementioned *P.Oxy.* XVI 2040, which was about 25 percent—or about 30 percent if Takona is included in the calculation.[181] Again, it is hard to believe that this is a coincidence. Jean Gascou has previously pointed to other texts where the Apiones' share of public contributions amounts to around one-third of the total,[182] but again it is the order of magnitude that is relevant here. What these figures cannot tell us, however, is how much of the land within a particular village was actually owned by the Apiones.

Still, these numbers are impressive. If other Oxyrhynchite *oikoi* participated in similar arrangements for other villages, there would not have been many villages left subject

---

not part of the estate, but still had their taxes managed by the Apionic *pronoētai*; see the previous section and especially n. 159.

177 This is the area that Jones had calculated as 112,000 arouras; see n. 166 above.

178 Bransbourg 2016, 355. On the difference from the fourth-century figures for the *entire* nome territory from Bagnall 1993, 334–335, see Bransbourg 2016, 312 and 346. Compare this 40 percent to the virtually identical figure taken from *P.Oxy.* I 127 and *P.Oxy.* XVI 1909 mentioned at the beginning of this section.

179 Bransbourg 2016, 346–348. Bransbourg's suggestion is supported by considerations of administrative structures, for it seems that the Apiones essentially controlled the nome administration of Kynopolis; see Section VII below.

180 Bransbourg 2016, 359. A more traditional calculation, relying solely on *P.Oxy.* I 127 and *P.Oxy.* XVI 1909, yields roughly the same result. In this case, one needs to subtract the entire Apionic Kynopolite share in *P.Oxy.* I 127 (since the Apiones managed the entire tax volume of Kynopolis) from the total of *P.Oxy.* XVI 1909 (Oxyrhynchos + Kynopolis as a whole) and then compare the result against the Apionic Oxyrhynchite share from *P.Oxy.* I 127, which results in: 87,818.5 / (350,000 – 52,800) = 0.295 = 29.5 percent.

181 See Section II above. Note that *P.Oxy.* XVI 2040 is entirely unrelated to Bransbourg's calculation. Since the text probably dates from the 560s, the difference between the 25 percent figure and Bransbourg's 30 percent may be due to the roughly 30 percent increase in the Apiones' pronoetic lands that Bransbourg notes between the early 540s and the late 580s; cf. Bransbourg 2016, 361, Table 15 (a more detailed discussion of the expansion of the Apion estate can be found on pp. 395–399).

182 Gascou 1985, 45–46 (= 2008, 168–169). Gascou points out, however, that all these texts deal with different sorts of contributions and cannot be dated with certainty. The new readings of *P.Oxy.* XVI 2039 (Azzarello 2006), in which some *oikoi* share the responsibility of the (defunct) *oikos* of Theon for maintaining the office of the *riparius*, do not make this text an exception, as Bransbourg 2016, 364 n. 187 seems to argue. The 47 percent (or rather, 45/96) refers only to the share that the *endoxos oikos* bore in relation to the *oikos* of Theon, and since Theon's *oikos* in this list bears 63 percent of the Oxyrhynchite *riparia*, the Apiones' share of the total would be, again, 30 percent.

to the pagarchy of Oxyrhynchos.[183] The village of Tampeti is—in two of the three instances where it is described as *pagarchoumenē*—said to be "*pagarchoumenē* also (*kai*) by/under" the Apion addressed,[184] which suggests that there were multiple landlords with fiscal authority over "pagarched" villages active at the same time in Oxyrhynchos. There is, however, only one such text that explicitly links a "pagarched" village to a non-Apion: a deed of surety issued to Flavia Anastasia, in which the village name is lost.[185] However, since the thus-established dimensions of the Apion estate match so closely the percentage of their fiscal share of the nome in *P.Oxy.* XVI 2040, we may assume that some of the landowners listed there also had authority over villages.[186] Why

183 The arguments of Ruffini 2008a, 119 and 145 regarding autopract villages in the Oxyrhynchite should now be modified by the model established in the present chapter. Berkes 2017a, 13 has suggested that the villages cited by Ruffini may have been subject to the pagarchy of Oxyrhynchos, and my hypothesis on the separate authority of the pagarchy and landowners with fiscal shares would imply that they were. Cf., however, the village Ieme, which contributed outside the aristocrats' fiscal shares or the pagarchy in *P.Oxy.* XVI 2040, before occurring in some connection to Flavia Anastasia (*P.Oxy.* LXIX 4757), perhaps as a pagarched village, unless Anastasia is simply a landowner within this village and in that text is dealing with her farmers in this capacity alone; see also n. 185 below.

184 *P.Oxy.* LXX 4785.11–12 (530 CE): παγαρχουμένης | καὶ ὑπὸ τῆς ὑμετέρας ὑπερφυείας, addressed to Strategios II; see also *P.Oxy.* LXXXIII 5377 (565/566 or 580/581) and *P.Oxy.* LXXXIII 5378 (571–578), addressed to Apion II, although καί is restored in both texts. The restoration seems probable in the case of *P.Oxy.* LXXXIII 5377 due to the dimensions of the lacuna. I do not think, however, that there is enough space to restore καί at the beginning of l. 5 of *P.Oxy.* LXXXIII 5378. If the traces of ink between the two lacunae really are ọị, then this fragment should be placed slightly further left than in the online image, as is also suggested by l. 12: π̣άσης [τ]ῆς αὐ̣τ̣ῶν. Given the letter sizes in the other lines of the left fragment and especially the large forms of kappa at the beginning of ll. 10 and 12, there is room for thirteen characters, at most, in the lacuna at the beginning of l. 6. The writer does not use abbreviations but places the upsilon of ου above the omicron; this would fill the lacuna perfectly without καί.

185 *P.Oxy.* XLIV 3204.11–13 (588 CE): ὁρμωμενος (read ὁρμώμενον) ἀπὸ | [– – – πα]γαρχουμένης ὑπὸ τῆς ὑμῶν ἐνδοξότητος τοῦ Ὀξυρυγχίτου | [νομοῦ. A village known to have been linked to Flavia Anastasia is Ieme (Benaissa 2012, 110–111) and ἀπὸ | [κώμης Ειεμη would fit the lacuna well. This spelling (instead of Ιεμη) is attested in the only contemporary parallels for this village: *P.Oxy.* XVI 2040.18 and *P.Oxy.* LXIX 4757.14, the latter of which is also probably part of Flavia Anastasia's archive: since the Makarios under surety in *P.Oxy.* LXIX 4757 is an *enapographos geōrgos* (see l. 1 and cf. *P.Oxy.* XLIV 3204.16) from a village (the village of Ieme), this village may have been *pagarchoumenē* by Anastasia (the relevant section of the text is lost). But note that in *P.Oxy.* XVI 2040, Ieme contributes to public expenses independently of any magnate (or the pagarchy, for that matter).

186 See Section II; see in that section also the discussion about *P.Oxy.* XVI 2020 and the observation that the landowners who paid the largest shares are all listed as paying "for various *onomata*." A landowner with authority for a *kōmē pagarchoumenē* other than the Apiones or Anastasia may also figure in *P.Hamb.* III 228 (VI?). This text reports that an entire village (l. 2: πάντες οἱ γ̣ε̣ω̣ργοὶ τῆς κώμης) refused to pay taxes until the *geouchos* sends the *monopolarius* to purchase some commodities (Banaji 2007, 87), which may illustrate how local communities struggled with generating cash—contrary to Banaji's (2007, 169) picture of a "thoroughly monetized countryside"; cf.

did landlords exercise this authority over some villages but not others? And why were certain landowners entrusted with this authority while others were not? As with the question of why some magnates had control over *oikoi* and others did not, we can only retreat to arguments of plausibility here. Presumably, a landowning magnate had a dominant position in a village that was handed to him as *pagarchoumenē*, and presumably this magnate's estate administration had to be sufficiently complex to guarantee the proper performance of those additional tasks. We cannot say whether other landlords were responsible for the maintenance of public security in "their" *kōmai pagarchoumenai* the way the Apiones were, but this seems likely. Beyond the Apiones, evidence for the maintenance of estate prisons is sparse, however.[187] The church appears to have controlled prisons in the Oxyrhynchite,[188] but Flavia Anastasia, at a time when the Apiones had started to use an estate prison, still used a city prison of Oxyrhynchos.[189]

With multiple landlords holding pagarchy-like authority over Oxyrhynchite villages, the 10 percent share that the pagarchy contributes for a public bath in *P.Oxy.* XVI 2040 may reflect the relatively minor significance of the pagarchy of Oxyrhynchos compared with the large landowners' obligations in the region during this period.[190]

---

n. 59 above. The papyrus is from the Oxyrhynchite village of Senyris, which in the fifth century is attested in connection to Strategios I as a manager of imperial land (*P.Oxy.* L 3586), but the *geouchos* in *P.Hamb.* III 228 is unlikely to be the head of the Apion family (though this cannot be ruled out): First, referring to a *geouchos* without any epithets or titles would seem to be inappropriate if a member of the Apiones was meant, but this may be accounted for by the villagers' somewhat indignant tone. Second, the villagers demand that the *presbyteros* actually meet the *geouchos* in person in order to present the villagers' message to him (l. 6), which means that this man must have been around in the Oxyrhynchite, which the heads of the Apion family—for most parts of the sixth century—were not.

187 On the Apiones' use of city and estate prisons, see n. 127 above. No clear evidence for estate prisons other than the Apiones' or the church's has yet been identified, though there is some ambiguous evidence (see, for instance, the document republished in Berkes 2015: the prison itself bears no specification and the addressed *pronoētēs* may have made use of a public prison for his ends). *P.Cair.Masp.* I 67002 col. II 4 is often cited as an instance of a private jail but was more likely a public village prison, although the petitioners of this text are certainly trying to insinuate illegality in their accusations against the pagarch Menas; see Stern 2016, 1855 and 1868. Some individuals are sent εἰ(ς) τ(ὴν) φυλακ(ὴν) | τοῦ οἴκ(ου) Ἀνιανοῦ in *P.Oxy.* XVI 2056.1–2 (Oxyrhynchites; VII); this *oikos* is not known from anywhere else. Since a *mēchanē* called "farm (*gēdion*) of Anianos" is under Apion management in *P.Oxy.* I 137 (Oxyrhynchos; 584), is it possible that this land or parcel became "independent" after the decline of the Apion *oikos* (see Section VI below)?

188 See *P.Oxy.* XIX 2238 (Oxyrhynchos; August 7, 551) and *SB* XVIII 14006 (Oxyrhynchos; January 22–September 1, 635).

189 *P.Oxy.* XLIV 3204 (January 2, 588) and *P.Oxy.* LXIX 4756 (March 10, 590), in both of which the detainee hails from a village, in the first case noted to be a *kōmē pagarchoumenē*.

190 Cf. Ruffini 2008a, 248: "On surviving evidence, the Apions probably did not have a major fiscal role in more than a quarter of the forty-eight or more villages attested in the Byzantine Oxyrhynchite. The great estates as a whole may not have been able to shoulder the fiscal burden for all of these places either." Perhaps this was not what Ruffini had in mind but I think the missing institution covering the remaining villages is precisely the small share that was left to

The hypothesis that the *kōmai pagarchoumenai* were part of a fiscal institution distinct from the pagarchy of Oxyrhynchos may thus account for the seeming paradox that despite the enormous amount of late antique papyri this city has yielded, only two texts attest pagarchs in this nome between the disappearance of the "early" pagarchs (the *praepositi pagorum*) and the Islamic conquest.[191]

VI. The *Kōmai Pagarchoumenai* and the Rise and Fall of the Apiones

The institution of the *kōmai pagarchoumenai* was certainly not older than the system of institutionalized *oikoi* and their shared public responsibilities, which was in place as early as 460/461 CE.[192] Some light may be shed by the village of Tampeti, which in at least two of the three instances in which it occurs as *kōmē pagarchoumenē* is said to be "*pagarchoumenē* also (*kai*) by/under" the Apiones.[193] This *kai* has been taken as an indication that two or more *geouchountes* occasionally shared fiscal responsibility for a village,[194] and in this particular case Todd Hickey has suggested this may be due to the presence of the church as a large landowner in the area.[195] This may indicate that when villages were assigned to *oikoi*, the institution of the *kōmai pagarchoumenai* acknowledged certain property rights that were already manifest in a given area.[196] The magnates who had prominent landholdings in a particular village would have been the

---

the pagarchy of Oxyrhynchos, which could well have been assumed by the Apiones from time to time; see *P.Oxy.* XVI 1829, which some scholars assign to the dossier of the Apiones, but the prosopographical connections in this text are unclear; see the Catalog, s.v. Anonymous pagarch (Arcadia).

191 See n. 75 above.

192 See Azzarello 2006, 210, with the fourteenth indiction of 460/461 CE as the first year listed in *P.Oxy.* XVI 2039; but see also Chapter One, n. 113.

193 See n. 184 above.

194 The same phenomenon appears in the clause identifying someone as a *geouchōn* "also here in (the *civitas* of such-and-such)," usually taken to mean that they owned property in other nomes as well. However, in *SB* VI 9527 (Arsinoe; 385–412), the Alexandrian church is *geouchousa* "in Arsinoe," i.e., without *kai*, which in this strict interpretation would entail that the Alexandrian church did not hold land in any other nome, which is quite implausible. Possibly the *kai* in *P.Oxy.* LXX 4785 is instead supposed to mean "*also* a village pagarched by you," i.e., like other villages. In the case of the landholdings, this interpretation would entail that the addressee is *geouchōn* in the nome among other *geouchountes* (which would, however, probably seem too banal to write at all). See also *P.Bagnall*, p. 145, where Todd Hickey and James Keenan acknowledge the possibility that this *kai* was used inconsistently, which is probably the easier explanation; see also, along similar lines, Hickey 2012, 9 n. 40. Cf. *P.Oxy.* LXIII 4398.15–16 (Oxyrhynchos; 553) where an *epoikion* is styled κτήματος κ[α]ὶ τῆς ὑμῶν | παιδεύσεως.

195 Hickey 2012, 181, referring to *P.Oxy.* XIX 2244.81–85 (mid-VI).

196 For instance, Spania, the earliest attested *kōmē pagarchoumenē* (in *P.Oxy.* LXXXII 5337 from 493 CE) was probably located close to the border of the Herakleopolite nome (see Benaissa 2021, s.v.), where the young Strategios II was also active.

natural choice to assume administrative responsibilities in lieu of civic authorities and to oversee local village institutions. The consistent use of *pagarchoumenē* in case of the village of Tampeti suggests, moreover, that this status was long-term or permanent and was given to individual villages. This comes close to what was said about "village pagarchies" in Chapter One and may conveniently be explained by the genesis of the *kōmai pagarchoumenai* from the "early" pagarchy in the several *pagi* of a nome. This new system probably included only those *geouchountes* whose estates were able to provide the necessary infrastructure to guarantee effective tax collection from adjacent territories, as the *prostasia* system on the Apion estate certainly did. The remaining villages, then, would have been united under a single pagarchy sometime before 493 CE, when the formula is attested for the first time.[197] Hence also the lexical link of the *kōmai pagarchoumenai* to the pagarchy, which can be plausibly explained by their being remnants of the old *pagus* organization.

Even though the verb *pagarcheō* is clearly used to mean "act as pagarch" in official documents,[198] the passive participle *pagarchoumenos* appears to have been understood as a technical term, hence its careful, and most likely deliberate, attribution to the village instead of the person responsible. Consequently, one may think of this institution as a "quasi-pagarchy" formally restricted to individual villages, which certainly accounts for its attribution to villages instead of being part of the landowners' titulature.[199] The main difference in exercising this authority was apparently that the pagarchs' power rested on official staff from the *civitas* level downward, while the landlords with extended fiscal shares relied, at the upper tier, on their estate administration, with supporting village liturgists plus hired employees at the lower tier.

At the other end of the timeline, the disappearance of the *komai pagarchoumenai* can also be narrowed down with some probability, mainly owing to *PSI* I 52, a deed of surety issued to an Oxyrhynchite pagarch. The beginning of the document reads as follows:

> In the name of the lord and master Jesus Christ, our God and savior, Thoth 20, 6th indiction. To Flavius Ioulianos, *megaloprepestatos* pagarch of this city of Oxyrhynchos, (from) the Aurelii M[– – –]s, son of Apa Or and Eudoxia, and Kephalon, son of [– – –], hailing from the

---

197 *P.Oxy.* LXXXII 5337.

198 *C.Th.* VIII 15.1, *ICG* 182, and Iust. *ed.* 13.25. Hence, I refrain from describing the *geouchountes* with extended fiscal shares and responsibility for "pagarched" villages as "pagarching" landowners or similar.

199 I believe it is significant that the *geouchountes* are precisely not described as *pagarchountes* or the like, but that the "status" is only visible in the description of a village. In an Antaiopolite rescript draft, the "pagarch of Antaiopolis" (*passim*) Ioulianos is accused of trying to bring the village of Aphrodite "under his own pagarchy"; see *P.Cair.Masp.* I 67024–25 (new ed. Fournet 2018) A 31–32, A' 56–57, and B 30–31: τὴν κατ' αὐτοὺς κώμην ὑπὸ τὴν οἰκείαν παγαρχίαν ποιήσασθαι. In *P.Cair.Masp.* I 67283 col. I 2, however, the villagers state that Ioulianos was trying "to drag us into the pagarchy of Antaiopolis" (ἡμᾶς ἑλκ[έσ]θαι εἰς π̣α̣γαρχίαν τῇ̣[ς Ἀνταιο(υ)]π̣ο̣λ̣ιτῶν), which leaves no doubt that Ioulianos's "own" pagarchy was the *civitas* pagarchy.

> *ktēma* Leonidou in the vicinity of Tampeti in the Oxyrhynchite nome. We voluntarily agree, swearing the holy and august oath, to provide surety for, and receive from your *megalopre-peia*, Aurelia Theonoe, daughter of Georgios and Tap[– – –] from the same *ktēma* (...).[200]

The dating of this papyrus is disputed. The editor assigned it to the sixth century for palaeographical reasons, but Johannes Diethart and Klaas Worp then put the date to 602 or 617 due to a small dossier of texts signed by the same notary, Ioannes—the same man mentioned toward the end of Section III and who is attested in the years 611, 612, and 613.[201] Later, Worp pointed to the missing imperial dating formula in this document and argued, on the basis of a suggestive pattern, that its absence may indicate that Oxyrhynchos was not under Byzantine control at the time the papyrus was written, which would put the document to 647 CE.[202] The coincidence of the notary Ioannes's activity being documented in such a concentrated manner as above and then surfacing again some three decades years later does not seem negligible, but the pattern concerning the absence of the imperial dating formula has since found further support and seems strong.[203]

The case in favor of a 647 date for *PSI* I 52 can be strengthened by reference to the *kōmai pagarchoumenai*. The woman under surety hails from the *ktēma* Leonidou, which is a well-known part of the Apion estate.[204] Leonidou is then said to be in the vicinity of Tampeti, a village that was *pagarchoumenē* in 530 and in the later sixth century,[205] and under Apion administration both the *ktēma* and the village were centers

---

200 The text of the edition reads μεγάλ(ῳ) in l. 4 but the parallels leave μεγαλ(οπρεπεστάτῳ) beyond doubt; see Berkes 2014, 78.

201 *P.Oxy.* LXX 4800 (November 19, 611?); *P.Oxy.* XVI 1981 (October 25, 612); *P.Oxy.* I 139 (October 26, 612); *P.Oxy.* LXVI 4536 (October 27, 612); *PSI* I 62 (September 27, 613); Diethart & Worp 1986, 82. I follow Diethart and Worp in excluding *P.Oxy.* XXIV 2420 (February 25–March 26, 614) from that list. Previously, the editor of *P.Oxy.* XVI 1979 opted for "probably 617" (p. 229) as the date for *PSI* I 52.

202 Worp 2005, 155–158, though Worp is careful not to make this suggestion too definite.

203 *CSBE*², 105–108. This makes *PSI* I 52 an outlier when it comes to attestations of the notary Ioannes, but some notaries indeed appear to have enjoyed extraordinarily long spans of activity; see Kovarik 2023a, 197–198. As a side note, this date would also make the papyrus one of the few early Islamic texts from Oxyrhynchos; cf. Berkes 2017b. The rudimentary form of the imperial oath used in *PSI* I 52.11–12: ἐπọμνύμενοι τὸν θεῖον καὶ σεβάσμιον ọ̔ρκον is not a decisive argument here, since it is still attested, now probably understood in a less specific sense as a "divine and august oath" in *SB* VI 8988.106, which probably dates to the 640s, that is, to the early Islamic period; the document is part of the small archive of Philemon and Thekla (*TM* Arch ID 190). Finally, while the invocation used in *PSI* I 52 figures most abundantly under Emperor Heraclius and during the Persian occupation, there are instances from Middle Egypt datable to after the Arab conquest, one (*T.Varie* 8 from March 22, 669) even from the Oxyrhynchite nome; see *CSBE*², pp. 104 and 108.

204 See Benaissa 2012, 165–166 and Hickey 2012, 172. See also *P.Oxy.* LXXXIV 5470 col. II 8: δ(ιὰ) τοῦ πρ(ονοητοῦ) Λεωνίδου περὶ Ταμπετι, where the exact same phrase is used.

205 *P.Oxy.* LXX 4785 (October 19, 530); *P.Oxy.* LXXXIII 5377 (565/566 or 580/581); *P.Oxy.* LXXXIII 5378 (571–578).

of their own *prostasiai*. But in *PSI* I 52 the woman under surety, from Leonidou, is under the authority of the pagarch Flavius Ioulianos, which—if one accepts my characterization of the *kōmai pagarchoumenai*—strongly suggests that the Apion *oikos* had been disbanded or at least reduced as an administrative entity by the time this text was written. The death of Apion III, the last known head of the family, became known on the estate sometime between July 5, 619, and January 12, 620, but we know that his *oikos* survived the transition to Persian rule and was still functioning as late as August 29, 626.[206] *PSI* I 52, which is therefore likely from 647 CE, shows us a post-Apionic Oxyrhynchite where much of what once constituted the *endoxos oikos* had been put under the purview of the pagarchy, including the *kōmai pagarchoumenai*.[207] When exactly this happened, whether still during the Persian occupation, as part of Byzantine rearrangements, or under the new Arab government, is unknown,[208] though evidence from outside Oxyrhynchos may provide us with some possible leads.

VII. Beyond the Oxyrhynchite

If Oxyrhynchite magnates other than the Apiones also administered *kōmai pagarchoumenai*, one might suppose that this phenomenon was also prevalent in other *civitates*. The phenomenon was indeed not strictly limited to Oxyrhynchos, as one papyrus from the Kynopolite nome shows,[209] although this text still belongs to the Apiones archive and the close ties between the Apiones' estates in the Kynopolite and the Oxyrhynchite nomes are evident. Several documents show that these two *civitates* were considered two distinct tax units[210] but were so closely linked that their fiscal contributions, in

206 See Hickey 2012, 17–18 and the references given there. For an assessment of the economic potential of the *endoxos oikos* under the Persian occupation, see Bransbourg 2016, 397–398.

207 In *P.Oxy.* LVIII 3959 (January 12, 620), the village Seryphis, known as *kōmē pagarchoumenē* from *P.Oxy.* XXIV 2420 (February 25–March 26, 614), appears in a deed of surety and is *not* referred to as *pagarchoumenē*. Since the *oikos* apparently still held authority over the village, the reason for the missing reference is probably that it is formally not a person but the *oikos* (of the deceased Apion III) that is being addressed in the document; see n. 149 above.

208 Cf. Booth 2022, 244–246, suggesting that the *endoxotatos scholastikos* Marinos of *P.Oxy.* XVI 1863 (July 25, 624?) and 1864 (623/624?) might have been a pagarch. Marinos handles substantial sums for (part of?) the taxes of both Oxyrhynchos and Kynopolis to the Persian authorities, and a post-Apionic pagarch for both Oxyrhynchos and Kynopolis may fit the reconstruction above. *Scholastikos* is a fitting title for a pagarch (see the Byzantine pagarch Serenos in the Antaiopolite nome or the *ellogimōtatos scholastikos* Gennadios, father of the pagarch Theodorakios; see *CPR* VII 51 from 629 or 644) and in these letters we do not necessarily expect Marinos's full titulature including the title of pagarch to appear, even if he was one. But the link to the pagarchy is uncertain and multiple explanations are possible, particularly because the amount that is handed over by Marinos does not appear to constitute the full tax payments.

209 *P.Lond.* III 776 (September 13, 552).

210 E.g., *P.Oxy.* LI 3636 (V); *P.Oxy.* I 127 (late VI); *P.Oxy.* XVI 1843 (November 6, 623).

practice, were handled as one.[211] In the sixth century, Kynopolis was certainly not administered under a system of joint administration like Theodosiopolis in the Fayum, since the city nominally had its own officials.[212] The estate management of the Apiones in the Oxyrhynchite and Kynopolite nomes, controlling much of the fiscal business in the area, accordingly formed two distinct branches but was in practice administered centrally from Oxyrhynchos.[213] This structure remained in place even during the Persian occupation after the death of the estate's last head, Apion III,[214] and may be reminiscent of the joint administration of both nomes by Oxyrhynchite magistrates at some time during the Roman period.[215] This arrangement was therefore possibly the reason for—rather than the result of—the Apion estate's beginning to assume administrative responsibility in the Kynopolite nome.

The Apiones also exerted considerable influence on the administration in Kynopolis. In one text, an *ekdikos* of Kynopolis is compelled to approach an employee of the Apionic *antigeouchos* because he wants to receive his remuneration via a different channel; this probably reflects a *munus patrimonii* of financing the *ekdikia* that the Apiones bore.[216] The Apiones' influence is more immediately apparent in another text where several actors—among them the village of Pleein and *zygostatai* of Kynopolis—pay contributions to an Apionic *trapezitēs* for the stables at Takona.[217] Both Pleein and Takona are known, from other texts, as *kōmai pagarchoumenai* in the Oxyrhynchite nome, suggesting that the management of the two Apion estates in Oxyrhynchos and

211 See for instance *P.Oxy.* XVI 1909 (Oxyrhynchos; 582–602) and *P.Oxy.* LV 3797 (April 26–May 25, 624). Note also that *P.Lond.* III 776, though dealing with a village in the Kynopolite nome, addresses Apion as *geouchōn* "here in renowned Oxyrhynchos"; see also *P.Oxy.* XIX 2243A.87 and 93. For other close links, see for instance *P.Oxy.* XVI 1854 (early VII). An uncertain instance is *P.Wash.Univ.* I 8 (on which see Hagedorn 2005, 130–132): although the connection to the Apiones is suggestive because of the joint listing of Herakleopolis, Oxyrhynchos, and Kynopolis—*civitates* where the Apiones held estates—the document seems more likely to be internal communication from the level of the provincial administration of Arcadia.

212 *Ekdikoi: P.Oxy.* XVI 1860.17 (VI–VII); *P.Oxy.* VI 902.1 (465 CE); *zygostatai: P.Oxy.* XVI 2028.5, 7, and 10 (VI); *chartoularioi: P.Oxy.* XIX 2243A.93 (October 28–November 26, 590). Kynopolis also had *politeuomenoi* of its own; see *P.Oxy.* L 3599 (December 9, 460). On the system of joint administration in the Theodosiopolite nome, see the Introduction, n. 50.

213 See Hickey 2012, 19 n. 124 and *P.Oxy.* I 127 (Oxyrhynchos; late VI). The links between the Oxyrhynchite and Kynopolite estates of the Apiones were pointed out early, for instance, by Hardy 1931, 81–85.

214 *P.Oxy.* XVI 1843 (November 6, 623) and *P.Oxy.* LV 3797 (April 26–May 25, 624).

215 Cf. their joint administration in the Early Empire (Kruse 2002, 26–29) and also Kynopolis's status as one of the "towns between villages and cities," as presented by van Minnen 2007, 207 n. 2, where the village of Aphrodite (see Chapter Six) and Theodosiopolis in the Fayum would also be well placed.

216 *P.Oxy.* XVI 1860; see n. 116 above on the connection of the Biktor archive to the Apiones archive. Another striking point in this text is that the magistrate refers to the *antigeouchos* as "our common master."

217 *P.Oxy.* XVI 2028 (VI); see n. 36 above.

Kynopolis in some way bridged the administrative division between the two cities.[218] Therefore, the Kynopolite contributions, under the Apiones' supervision, for the stables at Takona (a *kōmē pagarchoumenē* in the Oxyrhynchite nome) again illustrate that the phenomenon of the *kōmai pagarchoumenai* was grounded in the large landowners' administrative responsibilities within the framework of their *oikoi*, rather than in their assuming the Oxyrhynchite pagarchy.

It is difficult to tell whether there were *kōmai pagarchoumenai* outside the Oxyrhynchite and Kynopolite, since no village is explicitly attested as such in other nomes. Based on the evidence so far available, it seems possible to attribute this absence to a difference in documentary practice.[219] A more compelling explanation may be found in the ratio between the fiscal shares assumed by the *oikoi* and that of the pagarchy of Oxyrhynchos. We have seen above that other nomes, particularly the Arsinoite and the Antaiopolite, yield numerous instances of pagarchs, but no explicit mentions of *kōmai pagarchoumenai*, whereas the Oxyrhynchite evidence includes few instances of pagarchs but a considerable number of *kōmai pagarchoumenai*. This stark contrast may suggest a lower prevalence of this institution outside Oxyrhynchos, and thus a larger share for the pagarchy in these nomes. A proxy to test this hypothesis may be the question of whether or not the prevalence of large estates and the extent of their participation in civic administration and tax collection were comparable to other nomes, based on my argument—presented above—that being in possession of an estate of a certain size, accompagnied by a correspondingly complex estate management, was a prerequisite for being vested with the authority over *kōmai pagarchoumenai*.

In his seminal articles on the large estates of Byzantine Egypt and their fiscal shares, Jean Gascou found essential parts of this system at work well beyond the Oxyrhynchite, namely in Herakleopolis, Arsinoe, Antinoopolis, Hermopolis, and Antaiopolis,[220] though he appears more cautious in his introduction to the revised version of "Les grands domaines," where he points to Constantin Zuckerman's analysis of the Aphrodite Register as a "confirmation" of his views with regard to the Antaiopolite.[221]

218 See *P.Oxy.* LV 3797 (Oxyrhynchos; 624), from the time of the Persian occupation, in which the two nomes' fiscal obligations are processed jointly (though they are still accounted for separately). See also Hickey 2012, 19 n. 124, who refers to *P.Oxy.* XVI 2025.13 as illustrative of the joint administration of the Oxyrhynchite and Kynopolite estates.

219 For the observation that the *pagarchoumenē* formula could be omitted, see Section IV, especially n. 149 above. The counterpart for *epoikia*, the *diapheron/ktēma* formula, does occur twice outside Oxyrhynchos, which suggests that this formulaic system was indeed known but simply not as prevalent in other nomes; see *CPR* X 127.7 (Arsinoe; August 28, 584) and *P.Michael.* 41.7–8 (Aphrodite; 539/554?).

220 Gascou 1985, especially 38–44 (= 2008, 160–167) and Gascou 2004 (= 2008, 441–451).

221 Gascou 2008, 125, referring to Zuckerman 2004a, 221–222. Zuckerman elaborated on the relation of the Aphrodite Register to *P.Ross.Georg.* V 62 (misidentified as *P.Ross.Georg.* III 62), which records a substantial payment for the ex-*eparchos* Ioulianos. Ironically, however, Zuckerman argued that this text relates to the extent of Ioulianos's *ousia*, and precisely did not consider fiscal shares to be at work here. The precise context of this document is indeed not easy to de-

Giovanni Ruffini and Roger Bagnall have suggested that the dominant position of the estate of the ex-*eparchos* Ioulianos in the village of Aphrodite, as argued by Zuckerman, may reflect fiscal shares.[222] At the same time, Ruffini is careful about accepting the importance of the large estate outside the Oxyrhynchite, but appears to lean toward a positive view as well when he argues that the impression of an Oxyrhynchite exceptionality may be due to the uneven documentary strata represented by the sources.[223] On the other hand, Todd Hickey—despite being arguably, after Gascou, the most prolific advocate of the model of fiscal shares *in the Oxyrhynchite*—admits that "I find myself skeptical."[224]

Jairus Banaji and Nikolaos Gonis introduced *SPP* X 249 into the discussion about fiscal shares. This papyrus contains a list of grain contributions from some Fayum villages and from certain well-known large landowners from that region. The end of the document, in the second column, reads as follows:

> The lord Theodosios, the *stratēlatēs*: 4,000 artabas.
> The lord *patricius*: 1,388 artabas.
> The lord Kyrillos: 925 artabas.
> The heirs of Eustochios: 1,850 artabas.
> That is, in total, 8,163.
> That is, in total, altogether 20,963, remainder 1,237 artabas, which also have to be carried over by those from Neilopolis.[225]

Banaji has shown how the amounts shared by the four aristocrats relate to one another, and argued that we see here a system of fiscal shares at work outside the Oxyrhynchite—

termine. *P.Cair.Masp.* I 67060 provides a possible context for Ioulianos's role: the writer of this letter understands the expression μεγάλοι κτήτορες (l. 2) to include Ioulianos's *ousia* paying (for) the *astika* and *kōmētika*, which brings to mind the *syntelestai* of *P.Oxy.* XVI 2020, discussed in Section II above.

222 Ruffini 2008a, 246 and Bagnall 2008, 188. The latter speaks a little more ambiguously of Ioulianos's role as "fiscal agent," implying that an office may also have been behind these payments.

223 Ruffini 2008a, 244–251. For an overview of the discussion of whether the Oxyrhynchite was the exception rather than the rule, see the still valuable survey by Keenan 1993, 142–143. Cf. Mazza 2011, 277: "In Oxyrhynchus, *oikoi* were apparently perceived as 'entities,' or better, enterprises and fiscal subjects much more than elsewhere in Egypt."

224 Hickey 2012, 160. See also p. 6 there: "the core of Gascou's thesis—the 'fiscal participation'—is certainly valid for the Byzantine Oxyrhynchite," the wording of which implies Hickey's caution in regard to the validity of his results for Egypt as a whole.

225 I provide here only the Greek of *SPP* X 249 col. II 13–14 as I understand it from Wessely's handwritten transcription, as it may not be intuitive: /ὁ(μοῦ) τ(ὸ) π(ᾶν) γί(νεται) β̣϶ξγ λοιπ(αὶ) (ἀρτάβαι) Ασλζ αἱ (καὶ) ὀφειλ(όμεναι) μ(ε)τ(α)κομ(ισθῆναι) | δ(ιὰ) ṭ(ῶν) ạπ̣ọ̣ Νειλουπ(ό)λ(εως).

indeed a compelling interpretation of these figures.[226] The papyrus is fragmentary,[227] but a list of administrators from before the section quoted above survived. Each of them is allocated an amount of grain followed by the names of two to four settlements, mostly villages, such as in the following example:

> Apa Or, *dioikētēs*, 500 artabas:
> Tristomon,
> Kerkeuris,
> Eleusis.[228]

The fragmentary state of the papyrus does not, however, allow us to determine whether these entries are collections from a single large estate, as has been suggested,[229] and so are a breakdown of the shares of one of the four magnates, or whether these entries are part of the 12,800 artabas implied by the calculation at the end of the document *before* the addition of the four magnates' shares (8,163 artabas). The contributions visible on the extant part of the papyrus only amount to 3,700 artabas, which means that in any case a considerable part of the document must be lost.[230]

226 Banaji 2007, 155–166. See also Gonis 2008, 207–208 (who accepts Banaji's argument) for an analysis of the aristocrats involved. Against Banaji, however, one might argue that it is not intuitive (and Banaji does not elaborate on the matter) why Strategios, Kyrillos, and the heirs of Eustochios would in his reconstruction be subject to a "4 per cent surcharge on a total payment of 4,000 artabas," while Theodosios, who pays exactly 4,000 artabas, would not. I instead suspect that the surcharge was 300 artabas of Theodosios's share, since with 3,700 he would have to be responsible for exactly ⅙ of the grand total (Strategios: 1/16; Kyrillos: 1/24; Eustochios's heirs: 1/12). In *SPP* VIII 1111, Theodosios also appears in relation to his fiscal share, which at that time (no date is given) amounted to ¼ 1/96; see Gonis 2008, 205.

227 See the editor's description of a *kollēsis* very close to the left margin of the papyrus. Wessely's transcription immediately begins with village names, not with a heading or an administrator. I suggest that in col. I 1 the village name Πτανψαει should be read; on this well-known settlement, see *SPP* III² 497.2 and the commentary. Moreover, col. I 8: τῶν γαστρησιν must certainly be something like γαστρησί(ω)ν or γαστρησι(α)ν(ῶν) (read καστρησίων or καστρησιανῶν); see *SPP* VIII 1149.2 (Arsinoites?; undated).

228 *SPP* X 249 col. I 13–16. There is no online image, but l. 15: Κερκευ̣φις of the *editio princeps* is probably Κερκευρις (cf. *P.Hamb.* I 32.2 from January 17, 120 CE; the reading is certain), which would place this latter village in the *meris* of Polemon.

229 See Banaji 2007, 155 and especially Palme 1997a, 109–119 on the comparable list *SPP* X 138, probably for the *oikos* of Strategios Paneuphemos. Note, however, that some localities might appear in both *SPP* X 138 and *SPP* X 249; this concerns Δικαίου (*SPP* X 138 col. II 17) or οὐσί(α) Δικαίου (*SPP* X 249 col. II 2) and Οὐῶ β(oρρίνη) (*SPP* X 138 col. II 16) or Οὐώ (*SPP* X 249 col. II 5). They occur in relative proximity, so it might be plausible that we are dealing with the same two settlements here. This estate would have had possessions in these villages from which it would collect these contributions. In that case, the listed names are probably the names of the corresponding *prostasiai* (or however these units would have been termed in the Arsinoite), whose managers would report to the central estate administration.

230 The amounts listed in *SPP* X 249 at the beginnings of ll. 1, 5, and 11 are 500, 500, and 1,500 artabas

But regardless of whether the amounts represent part of an individual aristocrat's share or not: in comparison with *P.Oxy.* XVI 2040 it is remarkable that the contributions of four of the most dominant Fayum aristocrats of that period make up only about 37 percent of the grand total (22,200 artabas). Although there are many unknowns as to the nature and content of this papyrus, a possible explanation for this may be that the 12,800 artabas were handled by the pagarchy. The document does not bear a date, but only two Arsinoite pagarchs are known from around the time the text must have been written, in the early seventh century:[231] Strategios Paneuphemos and Menas Stratelates. Both are attractive possibilities: Menas because he is absent from the list even though he must have been one of the leading aristocrats in the Fayum at that time; Strategios because he is the only one of the four listed men to appear only with his title (*patricius*), which indicates that he had been mentioned earlier.[232] Again, much is unclear about these amounts, but the remainder at the end implies that what we have here is a balance and, therefore, that these are actual payments.[233] The grand total is far too low to represent the grain taxes of the entire Fayum.[234] But since the majority of the known localities in this list are located in the ancient Polemon district, the lower figure might be explained by the hypothesis that this was an account for the Theodosiopolite nome, which had been carved out of the Arsinoite nome in the fifth century.[235] While this is, admittedly, very speculative because of the fragmentary condition of this docu-

---

and no doubt belong to a preceding column that is mostly lost (Wessely's transcription of l. 18 is unclear in this regard), so that col. I of Wessely's text should actually be col. II. The amounts still visible in this preceding column are noteably higher than those in the other two extant columns, I and II (actually II and III), which range from 50 to 500 artabas.

231 On the dating, see Gonis 2008, 207–208.

232 Gonis 2008, 207 notes Menas's absence, but neither Banaji nor Gonis explain the absence of the pagarchy, which in Banaji's is probably due to his assumption that the fiscal shares are identical with the pagarchy (see n. 5 above).

233 Banaji 2007, 146. Gonis 2008, 207 states that these contributions were "apparently for tax purposes." Cf. Palme 1997a, 116, who argues instead that the rounded sums in the similar list *SPP* X 138 refer to surpluses from these villages.

234 By way of comparison, in *P.Oxy.* XVI 1909 (582–602 CE?) Oxyrhynchos (plus Kynopolis) and Herakleopolis pay 350,000 artabas each. The figure for Arsinoe is lost, but since the Arsinoite was, even after the third and fourth centuries, the largest Egyptian nome, we may assume that it contributed on a comparable scale; the 22,200 artabas of *SPP* X 249 only amount to c. 6 percent of this figure. A problem with this hypothesis is that the contribution from Neilopolis, the only other city mentioned in the fragmentary *P.Oxy.* XVI 1909, appears to amount to only 10,000 artabas (l. 8), though that passage is heavily damaged.

235 In *P.Oxy.* LI 3636 (V), the ratio between the Arsinoite and the Theodosiopolite "for the account of flat-bottomed boats" is 163 to 13 ½ *nomismata*. The Theodosiopolite contribution thus amounts to c. 8 percent of the Arsinoite one, which is in about the same ballpark as the 6 percent drawn from the previous note. However, the ratios of the contribution from Oxyrhynchos (+ Kynopolis), Herakleopolis, and Neilopolis in *P.Oxy.* XVI 1909 (582–602 CE) do not match those in *P.Oxy.* LI 3636. Does this difference reflect a chronological development in the cities' economic strength?

ment, Theodosios's share of c. ⅙ in our text may be compared with the ¼ 1/96 share for which he is responsible in another papyrus.[236] This share might have been inherited from his mother Sophia, who is attested as responsible for a share of ¼ 1/24 in Theodosiopolis.[237] Theodosios reappears after the end of the Persian occupation as *eukleestatos stratēlatēs, dux et Augustalis* of Arcadia.[238]

The hypothesis that these four aristocrats' contributions reflect fiscal shares separate from the pagarchy may underscore the distinction of the pagarchy from the fiscal shares that has been discussed with regard to the Oxyrhynchite throughout this chapter. Although this would not prove that *kōmai pagarchoumenai* were involved in any of the four magnates' shares, this seems likely, if only due to the size of their share of the total. If this admittedly tentative hypothesis hits the mark, then the pagarchy's share in this document was significantly larger than the 10 percent in *P.Oxy.* XVI 2040 from Oxyrhynchos, which would suggest that the "public-private" responsibilities of the *oikoi* were considerably more widespread in Oxyrhynchos than they were in the Fayum and, presumably, elsewhere.[239] Why the problem of administrating fiscal responsibility in the countryside was dealt with so differently—if we accept this interpretation—is an intriguing question. Perhaps the large estates of the Fayum were simply not as large as in the Oxyrhynchite, and their administrative infrastructure was not fit to guarantee effective administrative coverage of most of the fiscal landscape.[240] This point will become relevant again in Chapter Five, where the social composition of the aristocratic elites of Oxyrhynchos, the Fayum, and the Thebaid is analyzed.

As for the later development outside Oxyrhynchos and potential parallels to the decline of the Apion estate, the large estates did not entirely vanish as administrative or economic entities immediately after the Persian conquest.[241] Oxyrhynchite evidence is scant for the turbulent period from the Persian conquest through the middle of the seventh century, but the survival of three Arsinoite estates may illustrate this point. A *hypodektēs* of an *ousia* of Menas Stratelates is attested when Menas was apparently still alive in 629 or 644 CE, while a *bucellarius* of this *ousia* is attested in a document that has

236 Share of ⅙: see n. 226 above. Share of ¼ 1/96: *SPP* VIII 1111 (January 3, 633?).

237 *SPP* VIII 1091. On these texts and their dates, see Gonis 2008, 204–205.

238 *P.Prag.* I 64 (Arsinoe; May 28, 636).

239 See the discussion of *P.Cair.Masp.* I 67060 in n. 27 above.

240 Hickey 2007, 299 suggests that the large estates of the Fayum may generally have been smaller than those of Oxyrhynchos; see also Palme 1997a, 116–117.

241 Beyond that, the untechnical use of *oikos* remains in use without relating to remnants of the late antique large estate. For instance, a register of unknown origin from the late eighth century may list *oikoi* in some obscure subordinate position under a *dioikētēs*; see *SPP* XX 249 recto. For the date and new readings, especially of l. 1 of the recto: διοκ(η)δ(ής) (read διοικητής), see Gonis 2019b, 202–203, also for the line numbering. This *dioikētēs* may have been active at the nome level, as is frequently attested in this period as well as in the Byzantine era. Note also the contribution from a *chōrion* (which in the early Islamic period designates village units), if the interpretation of the abbreviation χ(ωρίου) holds, in col. II 2 of the verso.

Menas as deceased in 643 or 658.[242] A papyrus from 653 CE that shows the *oikos* of the late (!) Strategios Paneuphemos may illustrate that these estates had become less important. The *antigeouchos* (the chief manager of an *oikos* within a nome) in that text is of lower status (*lamprotatos*) than even this estate's *dioikētai* and *meizoteroi* (the estate managers one level below the *antigeouchos*) had been during Strategios's lifetime.[243] Notably, in this text, the *antigeouchos* of Strategios's former estate acts as a representative for the pagarch. Since the papyrus is a receipt concerning the price for an item connected to a mill—that is, estate business—it probably shows a former *oikos* now being administered by the pagarch, which conforms to my interpretation of the "post-Apionic" *PSI* I 52 above. The estate of the *endoxotatos stratēlatēs* and later *eukleestatos dux Arcadiae* Theodosios also occurs after his death, under the Arab regime, as a fiscal-administrative unit.[244] The fact that those three estates are still named after these men even when they are deceased and no heirs are mentioned suggests that these were no longer "living" estates.[245] The reason might be that the social dynamic behind the system was bro-

242 *SPP* III^2 153 (April 11, 629 or 644) and *SPP* III 344 (October 8/7, 643/658). On these dates, see the Catalog, s.v. Menas Stratelates (Arsinoe). Cf., before the conquest, the *lamprotatos dioikētēs* and *chrys(o)hypodektēs* in *SPP* VIII 1111 (603 or 618 CE). This man certainly belongs to the administration of Theodosios's *ousia* or *oikos* (on the discussion about Theodosios's fiscal shares, see above). Bearing the personal name Tzittas, he is probably identical with the homonymous *megaloprepestatos comes* who later appears as estate administrator of Strategios Paneuphemos; for a discussion, see the Catalog, s.v. Neilammon (unknown province).

243 *CPR* XXIV 33.4–6 (May 29/June 8/June 18, 653): [Φλ(αουίῳ) – – – τῷ εὐκλεεστάτῳ δουκὶ ταύτης τῆς Ἀρκάδω]ν̣ ἐπαρχίας καὶ παγάρχ(ῳ) ταύτη[ς τῆς | Ἀρσινοϊτῶν πόλεως διὰ – – – τοῦ λαμ]π̣ροτάτου ν̣ο̣ταρ̣ίο[υ] καὶ ἀντιγε̣[ούχου | τοῦ ἐνδόξου οἴκου ? τοῦ τῆς πανευφ(ήμου) μνήμης Στρατ?]ηγίου γενομένου παγάρχ(ου); on the restorations in the first lacuna of l. 4, see the Introduction, n. 93. *Endoxoi oikoi* are not attested after the Islamic conquest and the editor explicitly provided this term in l. 6 *exempli gratia*. A more likely supplement seems to be a reference to Strategios's *ousia* or *oikos* (both are attested after his death) in connection with a written-out epithet, for instance, for his memory: τῆς οὐσίας (or τοῦ οἴκου) τοῦ τῆς πανευφήμου μνήμης Στρατ]ηγίου. The alternative τῆς οὐσίας (or τοῦ οἴκου) ἐν ἁγίοις Στρατ]ηγίου (see *SPP* X 1.1–2 and cf. *SPP* III 344.1) seems too short. On the structure of Strategios's estate, the personnel, and their standing, see Palme 1997a, 112–115. On the hierarchy of rank epithets, see Chapter Five, Section I.

244 *BGU* I 323.4–5 (before June 14, 651). In the context of the search for tax fugitives, a *dux* is addressed by a *meizōn* via an *endoxotatos illoustrios* and a *dioikētēs* of "the *ousia* of Theodosios of *endoxos* memory" (ll. 4–5). It is notable that this document is not addressed to a pagarch, because the pagarch's responsibility for tax refugees is frequently attested in the early Arab period. The *illoustrios* has a second title that is largely lost in a lacuna; see ll. 3–4: τοῦ ἐνδοξοτάτου ἰλλουστρίου καὶ κ̣τ̣ ̣[. . . . .] | τῆς Ἀρσινοιτῶν πόλεως. However, it is not possible to restore the title of pagarch in that lacuna unless one assumes dittography: καὶ {κ̣α̣ὶ̣} π̣[αγάρχ(ου) ταύτης] | τῆς Ἀρσινοιτῶν πόλεως, which is not convincing and brings to mind the *lex Youtie*. It seems that this specific constellation finds its explanation in the identity of the addressee, who was probably a *dux* of the Thebaid, even though we are in Arcadia; for more context, see Bernhard Palme's comments in *CPR* XXIV, p. 204 n. 12.

245 Cf. recently Booth 2022, 248, who, although pointing to a potential "shrinkage" of estates, puts emphasis on the continuity.

ken, so these sort of fossilized institutional landholdings were still in place at least for a while as a sort of administrative subdivision, but apparently were no longer "private" estates.[246] As surviving administrative units, these estates must have been prime candidates for subsumption under the pagarch's authority in the early Islamic period at the latest,[247] perhaps under modalities comparable to the pagarchs' responsibility for civic land in the countryside described earlier.[248]

There are no other documents that would allow for comparable hypotheses about the balance between fiscal shares and the pagarchy outside the Oxyrhynchite nome. We do, however, have a number of papyri that attest *merides* ("parts") that are generally interpreted as shares through which the notables of a *civitas* divided certain responsibilities among themselves.[249] In Hermopolis, for instance, these *merides* were always named after a person, sometimes deceased, and constituted abstract divisions used by the central accounting office, the *dēmosion logistērion*.[250] Whether the responsibility of the local pagarch would comprise one or more of such shares, perhaps in turn, is hard to determine, but one recently republished tax receipt for *embolē* that appears to originate from the *dēmosion logistērion* of Hermopolis is notably issued by the pagarch through a *trakteutēs*, whereas the documents from this context are usually issued by officials of the *dēmosion logistērion*.[251] The editors point to a potential parallel, also for the grain tax, from Antinoopolis, signed by the pagarch Kollouthos Exceptor through a *boēthos*.[252]

In a list from the neighboring city of Antinoopolis from the sixth century, a money amount is shared among a number of aristocrats:

246 At the same time, I do not think that we can assume that these are confiscated properties; see Stern 2020, 37–38. Similar institutional estate structures perhaps formed the foundations of "estate villages" we encounter in the early Islamic period, as remnants of the possessions of large estates in villages; on this hypothesis, see n. 120 above.

247 Cf. the discussion of the Oxyrhynchite *PSI* I 52 in Section VI above. In contrast to estate territory, the villages that had been administered by the (now-dissolved) *oikos* administration were probably put directly under the pagarch's watch sometime after the Persian conquest.

248 See Chapter Two, Section II 2, especially the discussions of *SB* XX 15016 and *PSI* IV 283.

249 For overviews and further references, notably to the works of Jean Gascou and to the Hermopolite and Antinoopolite sources mentioned below, see Fournet 2020b, 112–113; Lajos Berkes in *P.Gascou*, pp. 66–67; and Mazza 2011, 271–272.

250 See, for instance, the sources collected in Gascou 1985, 44–45 n. 261 (= 2008, 167–168 n. 259). On the *dēmosion logistērion*, see Chapter Two, Section III 1.

251 *P.Lond.* V 1865 (new ed. Gascou & Gonis 2022, no. 5). Cf. the "*trakteutēs* of the pagarchy," discussed in Chapter Two, Section II 3. The papyrus has been assigned to the late sixth or early seventh century and is "written in a hand suggestive of the *dēmosion logistērion* of Hermopolis." The editors point out that "[t]he pagarch is an unusual signatory" for this type of receipts, which are mostly seen as certificates of payment made from a central register. Cf. Chapter Two, Section II 1.

252 *P.Leid.Inst.* 72 (VI).

Apportionment (*merismos*) of 24 gold *nomismata* according to the 8 shares (*merides*), as follows:
Share of the heirs of Erythrios of *endoxos* memory: 6 ¼ *nomismata*.
Share of the heirs of Palladios of *hyperphyēs* memory: 4 ½ *nomismata*.
Share of the *hyperphyestatos patricius* Ioannes: 3 ½ *nomismata*.
Share of the *endoxotatos* Dioskoros and the (*endoxotatoi*) heirs of Theodoros: 2 ½ *nomismata*.
Share, formerly[?], of the late Phosphoria: 2 *nomismata*.
Share, formerly[?], of the late Phosporos: 2 *nomismata*.
(Here the papyrus breaks off.)[253]

Was a small contribution of the pagarchy hidden in the lost part of the list?[254] Or was the share of the pagarchy just not identified as such? Or was this particular *merismos* about a business that did not involve the pagarchy at all, just like the imperial *oikos* is absent from *P.Oxy.* XVI 2040, although it features in the comparable *P.Oxy.* XVI 2020?[255] Or was the local pagarch the supervisor of a process like this? With these questions outstanding, we cannot establish a balance between the fiscal shares—assuming we touch upon the same phenomenon in Oxyrhynchos, Arsinoe, Antinoopolis, and Hermopolis—and the pagarchy in Antinoopolis and Hermopolis. But immediately after the Islamic conquest, as early as the 640s, the evidence from the Senouthios archive shows us the pagarch Athanasios and his staff having their hand in everything important in Hermopolis and its nome. While the Senouthios archive is a collection of sources that we do not have in this form from any Byzantine pagarch, Chapter Two and the present chapter provide indications that in the sixth century, the pagarch was formally only part of the equation—although this part was probably often dominant. A development akin to the one described here and in Section VI above may explain this transition that seems to be implied by the more central position that Athanasios and other early Islamic pagarchs occupied. If that is the case, the early date of the Senouthios archive makes it less likely, though not impossible, that these were implementations by the Arab conquerors. It is more probable that we are dealing with innovations that had their origin in Persian (619–629 CE) or "late Byzantine" (629–639 CE) administration. This point is supported by an analysis of the diverse social backgrounds of the pagarchs in the various nomes and provinces of Egypt, developed in Chapter Five.

253 *P.Ant.* II 110, for instance ll. 1–3: μερ(ισμὸς) χρυσ(οῦ) νομ(ισμάτων) κδ κατὰ τῶν η μερί(δων) | οὕτως | μερ(ὶς) τῶν κλ(ηρονόμων) τοῦ τ(ῆς) ἐνδόξου μν(ήμης) Ἐρυθρίο\υ/ νο(μίσματα) ς δ′. There is no online image but the editor explicitly deems the reading of the symbols in ll. 8–9 as "formerly" (πρότερον) uncertain and considers the alternative that these may be fractions.

254 The amounts are listed in descending order and there must be three and one-fourth *nomismata* hidden in the lost part, apparently portioned onto two other shares.

255 One might ask whether the share of the pagarchy in *P.Oxy.* XVI 2040 was perhaps only valid for this specific contribution, and not a general share. By comparison, however, the Apiones's share in *P.Oxy.* XVI 2040 and other documents is remarkably consistent, as discussed in Section II above.

VIII. Summary

This chapter set out to address the relationship between the fiscal shares of the aristocratic "houses"—as posited by Jean Gascou and others—and the pagarchy. I started from the apparent paradox that in one list of fiscal contributions from Oxyrhynchos, both half-shares of the pagarchy are listed separately from the main contributors of the nome, the Apiones and their *endoxos oikos*, whose dossier contains frequent allusions to *kōmai pagarchoumenai*. A formal analysis of the documentary practice exhibited in these texts has established that the Apiones did not hold the pagarchy of Oxyrhynchos at the moment these documents were drafted, but that their formal status was that of "simple" *geouchountes*. Separating the institution of the *kōmai pagarchoumenai* from the pagarchy serves as independent support that the Gascou model is valid, and this support is further strengthened by a refined look at the responsibilities of the Apiones' *pronoētai* in villages. Thus, it became clear that the *endoxos oikos* administered these villages as a whole despite the fact that the Apiones did not hold all the land in them. This distinction was respected by the Apion estate management, whose *prostasia* system extended only to those parts of villages that were owned by the Apiones. The *kōmai pagarchoumenai* retained their administrative institutions, yet their superior administrative authority was not the pagarchy and its official apparatus, but the sophisticated Apion estate management. Within the *prostasia* system, estate property in these villages was attached to the *pronoētai*, as were some individual parcels not owned by the Apiones. Land remaining in the hands of "independent" landowners in the villages was, however, still accounted for by village officials and as such was included separately in the estate accounts. This organization reveals an administratively relevant distinction between estate land and non-estate land that was respected by the *endoxos oikos* and that runs counter to notions of private estates "taking over" villages or an occupation of public infrastructure by the late antique magnates. Formal observations about the documentary habit suggest that all villages in the Apiones' fiscal responsibility had this status. From a terminological perspective, this reinforces the interpretation that the large estates acted as de facto administrative units—which in turn explains the survival of some of them under a "fossilized" name, without heirs or new owners mentioned, in the early Islamic period. Substantial wealth and infrastructure were prerequisites for assuming such an influential public position, though the source of this wealth has yet to be found.[256]

256 On private resources as the foundation of the "public economy" of the *oikoi*, see Bagnall 1993, 160 and n. 58. On the sources of the Apiones' wealth, see Hickey 2012, 154–155. More recently, McConnell 2017 argued that the Apiones' fiscal responsibilities may have been grounded in a contractual tax-farming arrangement. McConnell's hypothesis was favorably received by Bransbourg 2016 and Ruffini 2018b, but has been met with skepticism from Azzarello 2019 and van Minnen 2019, since there is little evidence; see also Chapter One, n. 8. On the "upper tier," the hypothesis relies on plausible reasoning. At the level of the *pronoētai*, McConnell's ideas regarding the potential for profit are more intriguing. In this context, he addresses the additional 15 percent

While Todd Hickey, focusing on the private economy of the Apion estate, has repeatedly found strong evidence in support of the model of fiscal shares, the results presented here strengthen the model from a revised administrative perspective. They remove a major uncertainty from the Gascou–Hickey model and further refine our understanding of the mechanics of the Byzantine fiscal apparatus in the countryside of late antique Egypt. They also have important implications for our conception of the pagarchy. With the *kōmai pagarchoumenai* removed from the evidence for the pagarchy, the latter acquires a significantly more "official" character; it has become more likely that the pagarchs' main link to villages under their control was through their official apparatus, presented in Chapter Two, although borderline situations would still arise where the pagarchs may have had significant economic self-interest in the administered areas.

Though explicit terminology such as the *kōmai pagarchoumenai* has not yet been found outside the Oxyrhynchite and Kynopolite nomes, this system is likely to have been prevalent in other nomes as well, since comparable kinds of fiscal shares are attested and we have identified the *kōmai pagarchoumenai* as a manifestation of these fiscal shares. The account *SPP* X 249 from the Fayum may even suggest the larger purview of the pagarchy in other nomes compared with Oxyrhynchos, which may partially account for our lack of documentation for *kōmai pagarchoumenai* elsewhere.[257] The administrative double structure of pagarchy and *kōmai pagarchoumenai* is also an attractive context for the evolution of the pagarchy as charted in Chapter One. It likely developed from a situation where large landowners obtained total fiscal responsibility for their lands and in the fifth century increasingly assumed civic responsibilities through the institution of their *oikoi*. It is probable that the *praepositi pagorum*, at that time already called pagarchs, were effectively turned into "(greater) village pagarchs," a role then filled by the heads of local *oikoi*. As a result of this development, the remaining lands—those that could not be easily managed by the complex administrative structures of an adjacent large estate—were around the same time united and placed under the authority of the pagarchy and its own administrative apparatus.[258]

The system even survived the Persian conquest and the demise of key actors—among them the Apiones—but ultimately fell victim to the decline of the *oikoi* shortly after. The pagarchs' status of central civil officials in the nome and their increased presence in the early Islamic documentation are probably in part attributable to the retreat of the *kōmai pagarchoumenai* and the resulting expansion of the pagarchy over

that the Apionic *pronoētai* agree to extract above their regular collections. But this percentage, central to the model, is more readily explained as representing freight charges (Bransbourg 2016, 349). Tax farming was, however, not entirely obsolete, particularly in regard to indirect taxes, as attested in the position of the *arabarchēs* who farmed, *inter alia*, customs duties; see Kramer 2011, 175–184.

257 Or the use of the term *kōmē pagarchoumenē* for these villages was an Oxyrhynchite particularity.

258 See Chapter One, Section IV.

the entire nome. I believe this development is encapsulated by the "territorialization" of the term *pagarchia*, which beginning in the early decades of the Arab occupation denoted the entire administrative circumscription of the old *civitas*/nome throughout Egypt.[259] This meaning had been virtually nonexistent in the Byzantine period, and its terminological implementation probably reflects the declining importance and status of the institutional large estates and the more elevated position the pagarchs came to occupy in the *civitates* in general.

259 See the Introduction, n. 99. See also the pagarch's position as representative of the *dēmosios logos* in *P.Köln* XIII 548 (Oxyrhynchites?; mid or late VII), although largely restored, which marks a difference from the situation in the sixth century; see Chapter Two, Section II 1 and especially n. 68.

Chapter Four
Becoming and Being Pagarch

Separating the *kōmai pagarchoumenai* from the administrative institution of the pagarchy removes the explicit link between the pagarchs and the institution of the *oikoi* and thus appears to create a challenge to Jean Gascou's interpretation of the pagarchy as a depersonalized *munus patrimonii*. The present chapter therefore examines the formal characteristics of the pagarchy (modes of appointment, length of tenure, modes of representation, and the implications of their shared authority) to better understand the organizational framework of the pagarchs' activity.

I. Appointment

We have no direct information concerning the appointment procedure of pagarchs. The single normative text that concerns the Byzantine pagarchy is Justinian's *Edict* 13 from 539 CE, which provides instructions to the praetorian prefect pertaining to the removal of a fraudulent pagarch, among other things. The edict orders that the new incumbents be chosen by the governor and confirmed by the emperor, although this procedure need not have been the regular way pagarchs were appointed.[1] Nominal imperial confirmation of officials was common in late antiquity, and notable officials responsible for civic business, such as the *defensor*, the *curator*, the *sitona*, or the *pater*, also fall into this category. The laws have these officials chosen by the collegium of notables consisting of the bishops, imperial dignitaries, and the principal landowners, yet they still received their position by virtue of an imperial appointment through the praetorian prefect—a point which has led Wolf Liebeschuetz, among others, to characterize these men as "semi-imperial officials," given that we cannot trace their origins back to the curial order with certainty.[2] When these officials appear in Egypt, they, like the pagarchs of the sixth century, no longer bear the common status predicate of Aurelius, but instead the more distinctive Flavius, which places them on a higher social and administrative level than the curial

1 Cf. Iust. *ed.* 13.12 (for Aegyptus) and 25 (for the Thebaid). The *dux et Augustalis* shall "look around for" (περισκοπέω) or "search" (ἀναζητέω) potential successors for the pagarchy who may be "suitable," "fit," or "able" (ἐπιτήδειος) for this "matter," "function," or "undertaking" (πρᾶγμα). The term ἐπιτήδειος especially recalls liturgical vocabulary; see Palme 1989, 113–114 and Wilcken 1912, 343–344 and 344 n. 1, citing *P.Amh.* II 82, in which someone contests his nomination for a liturgy on the grounds that he is ἀνεπιτήδειος. Still, this seems anything but decisive.

2 Liebeschuetz 2000, 219–221 (quote on p. 221) with the relevant sources. Cf. Palme 2007c, 263 arguing precisely for a curial background of these new elites. Cf. *P.Cair.Masp.* III 67281, where the village *koinon* of Aphrodite appoints a *riparius*, probably a reflection of the pseudo-city administration inherent to that village.

https://doi.org/10.1515/9783111493183-005

administrators of the fourth century.[3] The framework of these "semi-imperial" offices has been considered a model also for the pagarchy, about which the laws, with the exception of *Edict* 13, are silent. Candidates for the pagarchy would, in this conception, have been chosen from among the large landowners of the city. This nomination would be sent to the Augustalian prefect—or, after *Edict* 13, to the *dux et Augustalis*—who would forward this nomination to the praetorian prefect and the emperor.[4] When the edict demands that the *dux* is to look around for potential successors for a fraudulent pagarch, it does not mention any involvement of the city notables; however, a passage from 535 CE in Justinian's *Novels* may reveal the same situation in the event of the replacement of a *defensor civitatis*, who without a doubt was, under usual circumstances, nominated by this collegium.[5] The college of city notables, however elusive this institution still is to us, should therefore be the starting point until further evidence surfaces.[6] One episode from the "Menas affair" in the village of Aphrodite in the 560s suggests that the pagarch Menas Scriniarius knew about one month in advance that he would become pagarch.[7]

It has often been held that local landholding was a fundamental condition of eligibility for the pagarchy, since the pagarchs for whom we have more information tended to be landowners,[8] but this seems not very distinctive. Some scholars have rightly been hesitant to assume that the early Byzantine aristocracy consisted entirely of large

3 On these "names" as status designations, see Chapter One, n. 43.

4 See Liebeschuetz 1974, 164 (followed by Mazza 1995, 199–200), who speculated that still after *Edict* 13 these notables may have in practice had their say by appealing to the *dux et Augustalis* in the first place, before he reported the case to the prefect.

5 See n. 1 above for the pagarchy and Iust. *nov.* 15.1 for the *defensor*.

6 Liebeschuetz 1974, 164; Mazza 1995, 200. In 569 CE, Justinian's successor Justin II issued *Novel* 149, which proclaimed that provincial governors would henceforth be chosen (or at least a number of candidates preselected) by a provincial collegium of notables in order to be ratified later by the emperor. It is possible, however, that this had been the practice previously, since Justinian had ordered the same for the reconquered province of Italy in his *Pragmatic Sanction* (554 CE). This development has found two lines of interpretation: either that it marked the government's finally giving in to the overwhelming power of local networks, or that it was an ingenious move to have—instead of predatory external governors—men at the helm who were bound by expectations and social control from among their peers (and clients). On this discussion, see Pieler 1990 and Laniado 2002, 225–252. Either way, it is unknown what effect *Novel* 149 had on the procedure of appointing pagarchs, if any. In practice, they were probably chosen after consultations among the local elite both before and after *Novel* 149.

7 When Menas had some villagers arrested while they were travelling (*P.Cair.Masp.* I 67002 col. II), he apparently did so (possibly several weeks) ahead of his tenure. See pp. 251–253 below.

8 The main point is made cursorily, e.g., by Liebeschuetz 1974, 164; Gascou 1972a, 69–70 (= 2008, 49); and Banaji 2007, 140–141. **Ioulianos:** *P.Cair.Masp.* I 67060 (*ousia*); *PSI* IV 283. **Patrikia:** *P.Lond.* V 1660, via her having a *dioikētēs*. **Menas Scriniarius:** *P.Lond.* V 1714, via the connection to his son, who was a *geouchōn* in Antaiopolis. **Kyrillos:** most of his dossier concerns private business; *SB* XXX 17412 contains an explicit reference to a *dioikētēs*. **Strategios Paneuphemos:** possibly as many as three known *oikoi* in Arsinoe, Herakleopolis, and Oxyrhynchos. **Menas Stratelates:** e.g., *CPR* XIX 32 and *SPP* III 344 (*ousia*). **Serenos:** if identical with the Serenos of *P.Cair.Masp.* I 67002, who controlled *dioikētai*. **Kollouthos Cancellarius:** if identical with

landholders,[9] but landed property as an economic basis was certainly not only prevalent among pagarchs. *Edict* 13 places emphasis on the wealth of a potential replacement for a fraudulent pagarch, in which case the successors, by virtue of an imperial order and an edict by the praetorian prefect, were to "take over their (i.e., the former incumbents') pagarchies and properties (*ousiai*)."[10] Wealth was a natural prerequisite for state officials or liturgists involved in tax collection, notably to make up for shortcomings.[11] Apart from the landlords who exerted fiscal authority over "pagarched" villages, however, only Strategios Paneuphemos is known to have been in control of an *oikos* while other high-ranking pagarchs, such as Ioulianos and Menas Stratelates, explicitly controlled "only" *ousiai*, but the differences between such categories of institutionalized landholdings are not fully understood.[12] Ultimately, the quoted passage from the edict is interesting in that it makes the *ousiai* part of what is transferred from the dismissed

(some of) the homonymous bureaucrats active in the Antaiopolite nome. On all these men, see the Catalog, s.vv.

9 See Bjornlie 2007 (no internal numbering): "Despite the high profile of certain provincials at Constantinople [...], it is not a given that the bureaucratic elite at the capital were predominantly estate owners. Such a claim would require as a companion study a detailed prosopographical examination of actors visible in Constantinople, where the political polemic generated." It has indeed recently been highlighted that, for instance, officeholding could prove a means of generating wealth apart from landholding, although wealth seems to have habitually been invested in land as a source of more secure and stable income, given the relative, up- *and* downward, social mobility among aristocratic circles in late antiquity; see Begass 2018, 431–434, 447–449, and 481–485. As for the provincial level, Hickey 2012, undermining conceptions of protocapitalist drives for economic gains among the Egyptian landed elite, has highlighted that we still do not know much about where those families' wealth came from. See Bagnall 1993, 68–78, especially 73, for sources of wealth other than land. Some pagarchs are known to have also owned real property within the urban center of the *civitas* (e.g., *CPR* XIV 10), but was such fortune considered sufficiently reliable to be considered when it came to choosing a pagarch? Cf. Chapter Three, n. 256.

10 Iust. *ed.* 13.25: εἰς τὰς ἐκείνων παγαρχίας τε καὶ οὐσίας ἐμβαινόντων, relating to the Thebaid; the parallel in Chapter 12 for the two Aegypti speaks of a "transmission" (*paradosis*) that comprises "all the things appertaining to the pagarchies, and to their (i.e., the former pagarchs') properties (*ousiai*)."

11 Cf. the distinction between ταῖς πολιτικαῖς λειτουργίαις on the one hand and πρὸς μόνα̣ς̣ τ̣ὰ̣[ς] ο̣ὐ̣σ̣ί̣ας διαφέρουσι on the other in ll. 13–14 of *P.Flor.* III 382 (= *P.Flor.* I 57) from c. 223 CE; Wilcken 1912, 344 n. 4. A passage in an account of expenses of the city of Antaiopolis, however, shows that a pagarch was not, or only in part, charged with the remuneration for various, sometimes high-ranking, subordinate staff. These were instead (partially) paid by the *civitas* (*P.Cair.Masp.* I 67057 col. II 24–31; see Chapter Two, Section II 3) and otherwise would have presumably been major expenses of the officeholders.

12 See Chapter One, Section I, and Chapter Three, Section I, suggesting that *oikos* in this context relates to more than actually owned land and included territories for which this estate assumed administrative responsibilities, such as in *kōmai pagarchoumenai*. In *SPP* X 249 col. II 8–9, the *endoxotatos stratēlatēs* Theodosios is responsible for a fiscal share close to three times as large as that of Strategios Paneuphemos (ὁ κύριος πατρίκιος). This seems difficult to reconcile with the contention that Strategios held the pagarchy on his own for so long because he was the leading

pagarchs to their successors, suggesting that the pagarchy was bound to certain *ousiai.* Still, the next section will show that it is difficult to argue that a fixed number of *ousiai* continuously bore the pagarchy; there must have been some appointment to the position, even if in variable intervals. Chapter Five discusses some indications that pagarchs, contrary to current opinion, can sometimes be shown to have been recruited from outside the local elite, which would explain their peculiar position in *Edict* 13 and suggest that the city notables were occasionally sidelined in the appointment procedure, but this is so far merely an alternative explanation that has its own problems.

II. Tenure

The length of the pagarchs' tenures casts doubt on the notion of the pagarchy as a liturgy shared among the local landowning magnates. By way of comparison, the tenure of the *defensor civitatis* was restricted to two years, and performance of this charge explicitly rotated among a set number of eligible candidates.[13] The office of the *riparius*, the head of local security, was also a short-term liturgy distributed by rotation among the city's *oikoi* based on elaborately calculated shares.[14] The available chronologies for the pagarchy, however, do not reveal a clear pattern, and given that not many pagarchs are known at all, tenures spanning a decade or more appear not to have been uncommon. Such chronologies can so far only be established for Antaiopolis and Arsinoe, where sources for the pagarchy from the sixth and early seventh centuries emerge in sufficient numbers. The testimonies in the following tables are arranged conforming to indiction years, drawing on a petition stating that the pagarch Menas Scriniarius took up his post at the beginning of a fifteenth indiction.[15] This indeed seems reasonable for a fiscal office, as in the Thebaid the indiction started on Pachon 1 (April 26), which is linked to

economic power in the Fayum throughout this period. Chapter Five will develop a model that may explain this apparent paradox.

13 Iust. *nov.* 15.6 (535 CE).

14 *P.Oxy.* XVI 2039 with Azzarello 2006. Since *riparii* who were installed by an *oikos* could be named "*riparius* of the *oikos*" in private contexts (see Tost 2012), it seems unlikely that the same *riparius* would have served as a stand-in for several different *oikoi*, and thus would have served over longer parts of the chronological list contained in this papyrus.

15 *P.Cair.Masp.* I 67002 col. I 10–11: ἀπὸ προοιμίων τῆς ἔναγχος διαδραμο(ύ)σης πεντεκαιδεκάτης ἐπινεμήσεως, ἀφ' ἧς ἀντελάβετο τῆς παγαρχίας | Ἀνταίο(υ). Cf. *P.Lond.* V 1674.66–67: καίτοι ἀφ' ἧς | παρέλαβεν τὴν παγαρχίαν, which uses a different verb. See also Maspero's restoration of *P.Cair.Masp.* III 67283 col. I 2–3: Ἰουλιανὸς ὁ λαμπρ(ότατος) βούλεται παρὰ τὸ] ἔ̣θ̣ος ἡμᾶς ἑλκ[έσ]θαι εἰς π̣α̣γαρχίαν τῆ[ς Ἀνταιο(υ)]π̣ο̣λ̣ιτῶν ἧς κεκράτηκε̣ν [ἀπὸ προ|οιμίων τῆς – – – ἐπινεμήσεως. The first lacuna is restored *exempli gratia* and Ioulianos's titulature, in the "short form" of reference (see Chapter Five, Section II) should probably rather contain one of his honorary titles, the title of pagarch, or perhaps the epithets *endoxotatos* or *megaloprepestatos*. For the use of the term ἐπινέμησις for the indiction year, see *CSBE*², 11 n. 36.

the date of the *praedelegatio* of the imperial tax schedule.[16] Based on this assumption, the Antaiopolite papyri provide us with the following picture, as displayed in Table 4.[17]

Table 4: Known Antaiopolite pagarchs from the mid-sixth century.

Indiction	**Attested pagarchs**	**Evidence**
9 = 545/546	Makarios(?)	*P.Cair.Masp.* I 67055(?)[18]
10 = 546/547		
11 = 547/548	Ioulianos	*P.Cair.Masp.* III 67283[19]
12 = 548/549	"the pagarch" = **Ioulianos**	*SB* VI 9102; ***P.Cair.Masp.* I 67019 verso**[20]
13 = 549/550		

16 On Pachon 1 (April 26) as the beginning of the Thebaid indiction year and its relation to the *praedelegatio,* which was actually due on May 1, see *CSBE*², 30 and 34. On the specific use of ἐπινέμησις for relating to this "*praedelegatio* indiction," although in a discussion of the Oxyrhynchite, see *CSBE*², 31–32. On the phenomenon of equating Roman with Egyptian months (e.g., Pachon 1 = May 1), see *CSBE*², 21, 27, and 127–128.

17 Entries in bold from the tenures of Ioulianos and Menas refer to the texts that provide individual names where the other testimonies simply refer to "the pagarchs." The papyri from the tenures of Ioannes and Serenos are mostly collections of tax receipts, some of which mention the pagarchs' names. The tax receipts collected in P.Strasb. gr. inv. 1622 and 1658 are currently being prepared by me for publication. The tax receipt *P.Vat.Aphrod.* 16A mentions "pagarchs" and names Patrikia before breaking off (see n. 73 below); since the extant part of this papyrus does not contain an indiction and Patrikia does not appear in first position when named next to the pagarch Ioulianos in *P.Lond.* V 1660 (whose date is lost), I refrain from dating this text to a specific year. Since the latter text mentions Ioulianos and Menas as pagarchs alongside Patrikia, its date should be somewhat close to 553 (*P.Lond.* V 1661). This table notably diverts from the *communis opinio* in dating the tenure of the pagarchs Ioannes and Serenos. Fournet 2000 established a widely accepted chronology that places these pagarchs in the indiction cycle of 552 to 567 CE. In my dissertation I developed a chronology that assigns both pagarchs to a later indiction cycle (the one from 567 to 582 CE), which I explain in detail in Stern forthcoming (b). Just before this book went to press, I learned of Sofie Remijsen's redating of the receipts of *P.Cair.Masp.* III 67325, *P.Flor.* III 298, and *P.Stras.* VII 699 to yet another indiction cycle later (the one from 582 to 597 CE; Remijsen 2024, with arguments partially similar to mine). While I believe that her chronology is generally possible, the one presented in Table 4 is more likely for a mix of several reasons, which I present in the mentioned article.

18 Or 530/531 CE, but both dates are not very certain. Moreover, the fragmentary state of the papyrus does not allow to be sure that Makarios actually was a pagarch; see the Catalog, s.v.

19 This is the latest possible indiction for this document. Recently, Jean-Luc Fournet (2015, 256; cf. Azzarello 2012, 78 n. 231) has dated this text to 540–545 CE. This hypothesis cannot be assessed until his new edition of Dioskoros's petitions is published. See Palme 2021, 325 n. 27 for a collection of other contributions to this question.

20 Or 551 CE.

14 = 550/551	Ioulianos	*P.Cair.Masp.* I 67046; *PSI* IV 283; *SB* XX 15015
15 = 551/552	Ioulianos	*P.Gen.* IV 193; *P.Cair.Masp.* I 67024–25
1 = 552/553	Ioulianos	*P.Cair.Masp.* I 67094;[21] *SB* XX 15013
2 = 553/554	Ioulianos & Menas	*P.Lond.* V 1661
3 = 554/555	"the pagarchs"	*SB* XXIV 15975(?)
4 = 555/556		
5 = 556/557		
6 = 557/558	"the pagarchs"	*P.Lond.* V 1665(?)
7 = 558/559		
8 = 559/560	"the pagarchs" = **Ioulianos & Kometes & Euthymios, represented by Christodotos *procurator***	*P.Cair.Masp.* I 67045(?); *P.Cair.Masp.* III 67325; *P.Lond.* V 1666; ***SB* XVI 12370**;[22] *SB* XX 15016
9 = 560/561	"the pagarchs"	*SB* XX 14121(?)
10 = 561/562		
11 = 562/563	"the pagarchs"	P.Mich. inv. 3272[23]
12 = 563/564		
13 = 564/565		
14 = 565/566		
15 = 566/567	"the pagarchs"(??), i.a. **Menas (1st year)**	***P.Cair.Masp.* I 67002**; *P.Cair.Masp.* I 67047(??)[24]
1 = 567/568	Menas (2nd year)	*P.Cair.Masp.* I 67002
2 = 568/569		[25]
3 = 569/570	"the pagarchs"	*P.Cair.Masp.* III 67325
4 = 570/571	"the pagarchs" = Ioannes (⅔) & Serenos (⅓)	*P.Cair.Masp.* III 67325
5 = 571/572	Ioannes (⅔) & Serenos (⅓)	*P.Cair.Masp.* III 67325

21 Or, though less likely, 551/552 CE; see Reiter 2003, 232–235 and 239 and n. 78.

22 Or, though less likely, 544/545 CE.

23 Ed. Keenan 2012. An alternative, but less likely, year is 547/548 CE.

24 The year is far from certain, but if one is to pick one among the possible fifteenth indictions in the early and mid-sixth century, this should be preferred.

25 During this year, the pagarch Kollouthos Cancellarius is attested acting in the area of Aphrodite; see the Catalog, s.v.

6 = 572/573	"the pagarchs" = Ioannes (⅔) & Serenos (⅓)	*P.Cair.Masp.* III 67325; *P.Flor.* III 298; P.Strasb. gr. inv. 1622
7 = 573/574	Ioannes (⅔) & Serenos (⅓)	*P.Flor.* III 298; *P.Stras.* VII 699; P.Strasb. gr. inv. 1622; P.Strasb. gr. inv. 1658
8 = 574/575	Serenos	*P.Flor.* III 298; *P.Stras.* VII 699; P.Strasb. gr. inv. 1720[26]

It is important to note that the appearance of only one pagarch in a document does not necessarily mean that he was the sole incumbent local pagarch at that time, as is obvious from the dossier of Ioannes and Serenos. Instead, it depends on the context and above all the type of document whether the appearance of only one pagarch is significant for the question of collegiality. In fact, collegiality seems rather to have been the norm. Still, it appears that Ioulianos was sole pagarch—at least in 548/549, when the imperial chancery could refer to him in a rescript anonymously as "the pagarch," and in 550/551, when he appears as sole superior of a *hypodektēs*[27]—before he formed a collegium in 553/554 at the latest, with either Menas or Patrikia or both.[28] By 559/560, the composition of this collegium had changed, although Ioulianos was still part of it. It remains elusive whether Menas was then sole pagarch from 566/567 until 568/569, before Ioannes and Serenos are attested in a collegium of two. In combination with the uneven lengths of tenure, particularly in the case of Ioulianos, who held the pagarchy for probably over a decade, this alternation between sole and shared pagarchy seems difficult to reconcile with a liturgy regularly shared among a circle of city magnates according to precisely drawn shares.

Two documents may indeed suggest that the pagarchs' tenure was generally longer than that of other liturgies, but not clearly defined: When the Aphroditan villagers filed a petition in order to henceforth be safe from Menas's alleged pursuits, Menas was in the sophomore year of his pagarchy; still the villagers obviously did not expect him to step down anytime soon.[29] And when Ioulianos leased out a plot of land, he probably did so "for as long as [I shall be in charge?] of the pagarchy of the same city (i.e., Antaiopolis)."[30] The tenure of such contracts is usually made explicit for a number of years or is left indefinite for the time being; our text actually gives a defined time period whose duration cannot yet be envisaged, probably because the pagarchy was not bound to a fixed term.

26 Ed. Fournet 2008d, 302–303.

27 "The pagarch": *SB* VI 9102. *Hypodektēs*: *P.Cair.Masp.* I 67046; perhaps also in *P.Cair.Masp.* II 67228. The *hypodektai*, officials at the city level, never sign for individual pagarchs in a collegium, in contrast to lower ranking officials; see Chapter Two, Section III 3.

28 Depending on whether Menas was Patrikia's representative at that time and when exactly Patrikia's texts are to be dated. For a discussion, see Section III below.

29 See n. 15 above.

30 See Chapter Two, Section II 2, especially n. 79.

The Arsinoite timeline largely conforms to the picture established for Antaiopolis.[31] While the time span from which pagarchs are attested in the Fayum is much wider than in the case of the Antaiopolite, there are considerable gaps throughout. The table below again follows the pagarchy by years of the fiscal indiction, which in the Fayum is for two months one count higher than the local chronological indiction.[32] With that said, the Arsinoite timeline currently looks as presented in Table 5.[33]

---

31 The obvious differences in the aristocratic hierarchy are discussed in Chapter Five, especially in Section V.

32 In the Fayum, the indiction started on Epeiph 1 (June 25), although as anywhere in Egypt, in fiscal contexts the indiction started with the *praedelegatio* of the imperial tax schedule, on Pachon 1 (April 26; see *CSBE*², 33 and 34; the *praedelegatio* was actually due on May 1, but there was a tendency to equate this date with Pachon 1). Writers in the Arsinoite nome generally acknowledge this difference by rendering any date that falls between Pachon 1 (start of the new "*praedelegatio* indiction") and Epeiph 1 (start of the new Arsinoite indiction) as "at the end of the *n*th (i.e., Arsinoite) indiction"; see, e.g., *BGU* I 305.2: Παῦνι ιθ τέλ(ει) δ ἰν(δικτίωνος). This difference is acknowledged in the following table in the way that, for instance, "at the end of the fourth (Arsinoite) indiction" the pagarch's tenure had already advanced to the fifth (fiscal) indiction, which relates to 556/557 CE. In the table, I assume that the pagarchs of the Fayum, like their Antaiopolite counterparts, assumed their office with the start of the fiscal indiction on Pachon 1, which to me seems more consistent with the pagarchs' responsibilities; see n. 15 above. It would appear natural that the pagarchs as fiscal officials took up their posts immediately before the harvest was initiated, thus following the *praedelegatio* indiction, not the Arsinoite one, if only to have sufficient time to collect potential arrears. The general alignment of local fiscal business with the fiscal indiction is illustrated, for instance, by *P.Oxy.* XVI 1997 (Oxyrhynchos; VI), where a payment for the fourth indiction is effectuated on "Mesore 7 of the 3rd indiction at the beginning of the fourth (indiction)." The Oxyrhynchite chronological year would coincide with its era reckoning and start Thoth 1 (August 29); therefore, Mesore 7 (August 1) is at the end of the third Oxyrhynchite indiction but at the "beginning" of the fourth fiscal indiction, which the Oxyrhynchite, too, counted from the *praedelegatio* of the imperial tax schedule, i.e., Pachon 1, actually May 1; see *CSBE*², 30–33 and 128.

33 In *BGU* II 364, *SB* XXVIII 16873, and *SB* XXX 17412, individuals who are attested as pagarchs in other years are *not* mentioned as pagarchs. Since such contracts are expected to give peoples' proper titles in the description of the parties (see Chapter Five, Section II), we can infer that these men were not pagarchs at the time these documents were composed. The three texts are therefore added below. I left out papyri that have too wide a chronological range to be useful for the purpose of establishing a sequence of pagarchs. On *SPP* VIII 1228 and whether this text refers to the pagarchy, see the Catalog, s.v. Kyrillos. Notable texts left out because of their lacking an indiction include *SB* I 5256 (anonymous pagarch), *BGU* XXI 2893, *SB* I 4781, and *SB* I 5253 (all Strategios Paneuphemos), and *SB* XXIV 16287 (Menas Stratelates). Included even though they do not preserve an indiction: *CPR* XIV 10, *CPR* XXIV 24, and P.Vindob. G 24302; each of these papyri most likely attests a pagarch beyond the period known from the dated documents or an entirely new pagarch, however vaguely. For my correction of the date of *P.Lond.* V 1786 (c. 592–596), in which Kyrillos certainly acts as pagarch and which has been assigned to the early seventh century, see the Catalog, s.v. Kyrillos (Arsinoe). Sophie Kovarik is currently working on a project about the aristocratic elite of the Arsinoite nome in the sixth and seventh centuries, for which she is studying scores of unpublished papyri from various collections. I am greatly indebted to her for providing access to her unpublished dissertation on the late antique notaries

Table 5: Known Arsinoite pagarchs of the Byzantine period, including texts that are at least roughly dateable.

Indiction	Attested pagarchs	Evidence
2 = 553/554	not Apion Stratelates?[34]	*BGU* II 364
end of 4 → 5 = 556/557	Apion Stratelates	*BGU* I 305
? = 556/557–577/578	Apion Stratelates (as *paneuphēmos apo hypatōn*)	*CPR* XIV 10
12 = 578/579	Christophoros & Strategios Stratelates	*CPR* XIV 11
5? = 586/587	Christophoros & Strategios Stratelates (as *eukleestatoi hypatoi*)	Louvre E 6573[35]
6/7 = 588	Strategios Stratelates (as *eukleestatos hypatos*; *pagarchos* restored)	P.Berol. 3387[36]
8 = 589/590	an [*endoxotatos*] *stratēlatēs*	*SB* I 4721
9 = 590/591	*endoxotatoi* heirs of a former *stratēlatēs*	*CPR* XIX 14 + P.Vindob. G 21029 + P.Vindob. G 25638[37]
10 = 591/592	[*endoxotatoi*] heirs of a *hyperphyestatos* [*patricius*]	*SB* XVIII 13952[38]
? = after 591/592	Kyrillos	P.Vindob. G 24302[39]
11 = 592/593	not Strategios Paneuphemos(?)[40]	*SB* XXVIII 16873

(Kovarik 2014), in which some of these documents are mentioned. As these texts are currently being prepared for publication, I have not made use of them with the exception of Louvre E 6573, P.Berol. 3387, P.Vindob. G 24302, and *CPR* XIX 14 + P.Vindob. G 21029 + P.Vindob. G 25638—documents that have already been introduced in the scholarly discourse elsewhere.

34 If Apion Stratelates is the *stratēlatēs* in *BGU* II 364, then he was not pagarch at the time the text was written; see the Catalog, s.v.

35 This papyrus is currently being prepared by Sophie Kovarik for publication in Azzarello forthcoming; cf. n. 33 above.

36 This papyrus is currently being prepared by Sophie Kovarik for publication in Azzarello forthcoming; cf. n. 33 above.

37 The new fragments were kindly brought to my attention my Sophie Kovarik, who is preparing the newly restored document for publication. See https://data.onb.ac.at/rec/RZ00000254.

38 With the restorations in Gonis 2008, 203.

39 See *BGU* XXI, p. 92, including the date, which appears to assume that Kyrillos could not have been in office with the preceding pagarchs.

40 This assumes that this text is indeed from the Arsinoite nome, and that this *paneuphēmos* Flavius Strategios is Strategios Paneuphemos. The editor restored the address to τῷ πανευφήμ[ῳ καὶ ὑπερφυεστάτῳ ὑπάτῳ] in l. 4. As the following lines show, l. 4 probably was not long enough to contain also παγάρχῳ τῆς Ἀρσινοιτῶν καὶ Θεοδοσιουπολιτῶν—the two cities are never abbre-

14 = 595/596	an *endoxotatos stratēlatēs* [= Kyrillos]	*BGU* XXI 2892
15 = 596/597	not Kyrillos[41]	*SB* XXX 17412
? = 595–600	Strategios Paneuphemos	*CPR* XXIV 24 + P.Vindob. G 21202[42]
end of 3 → 4 = 600/601	Strategios Paneuphemos	*SB* XXIV 16288
4 = 600/601	Strategios Paneuphemos	*P.Lond.* I 113.5C
9 = 605/606	Strategios Paneuphemos	*P.Bodl.* I 53
11 = 607/608	Strategios Paneuphemos	*CPR* XIV 9
13 = 609/610	Strategios Paneuphemos	*CPR* XXIV 27
15 = 611/612	Strategios Paneuphemos	*CPR* XXIV 28; *CPR* X 131
3 = 614/615	Strategios Paneuphemos	*P.Eirene* IV 40[43]
4 = 615/616	Menas Stratelates	P.Vindob. G 26585[44]
6 = 617/618	Menas Stratelates	*SPP* III 303[45]
10 = 621/622	Menas Stratelates	*CPR* XXIV 30[46]
11 = 622/623	Menas Stratelates	*CPR* XIX 32

viated. For the precise date (November 27–December 26, 592), see Nikolaos Gonis in *P.Oxy.* LXXXIII, p. 192 n. 1.

41 The text features Kyrillos as one party in a contract without mentioning his being pagarch, and since one expects that type of document to give the parties' full titles, Kyrillos was most likely not pagarch on October 5, 596, and, thus, probably not during the entire fifteenth indiction

42 See *BGU* XXI, p. 92. Cf. *P.Eirene* IV, p. 206 n. 5 on the newfound fragment P.Vindob. G 21202 and the resulting new date of the entire papyrus, although I am skeptical that the pattern concerning the occurrence of either *hyperphyestatos* or *paneuphēmos* as sole epithet can be taken so far; see, e.g., *SB* I 5271 (December 10, 615), which refers to Strategios as *hyperphyestatos patricius*, although according to the editor of *P.Eirene* IV 40, *paneuphēmos patricius* should be expected at that time.

43 The date in the edition is October 5, 614–October 4, 615. If I am correct in assuming that the pagarchy generally started on Pachon 1 and if Strategios Paneuphemos and Menas Stratelates were not jointly in office, then the date of *P.Eirene* IV 40 can be narrowed down to October 5, 614–April 25 (or 30), 615; cf. nn. 15 and 16 above.

44 See van Loon 2017. Technically, P.Vindob. G 26585 mentions Strategios Paneuphemos in a third-person reference that uses the "short form" of address (see Chapter Five, Section II) and is thus no proof that he was no longer pagarch. Yet, the "clustering" of papyri suggests that he and Menas Stratelates were not in office collegially.

45 The alternative date 632/633 CE seems too far off the rest of Menas's attestations.

46 The lack of a regnal date suggests that the tenth indiction fell in a period when no Roman emperor ruled Egypt. Moreover, the alternatives seem too distant from Menas's other attestations and in 636/637, the title "pagarch of Arsinoe and Theodosiopolis" was no longer in use.

2 = 628/629	Theodoros(??)	*BGU* II 694(??)[47]
13 = 639/640	Theodorakios	*W.Chr.* 8

The table encapsulates the "aristocratic density" of the Fayum as well as the strong sway of Strategios Paneuphemos and Menas Stratelates over the Fayum pagarchy. The distribution of the documents suggests that both were sole pagarchs—Strategios at least in and after 605 CE[48]—and their long tenures of at least fifteen and eight years, respectively, appear to mirror that of Ioulianos in Antaiopolis. An important difference, however, is that the majority of documents concerning the Fayum pagarchs are texts that relate to their estate business, not to their official function, and would therefore not be expected to list all incumbent pagarchs.[49] More so than in the Antaiopolite cases, it is therefore not certain that a pagarch attested in one document was the only incumbent at that time, as often assumed. The attestations of Strategios Paneuphemos as pagarch at least, however, are so strictly chronologically separated from those of Menas Stratelates that one may assume Menas was Strategios's successor, although I would not be surprised if new evidence proved otherwise.[50] In the case of Kyrillos, too, the clustering of the dated texts seems to be rather straightforward and suggests that

47 The date is very uncertain and may be later; see the Catalog, s.v. Theodoros (Arsinoe).

48 *P.Bodl.* I 53, in which Strategios contracts with *eirēnarchai* and supporting *phylakes*, probably in his official capacity as pagarch. Therefore, the lack of colleagues may suggest he was indeed the only pagarch at that date.

49 The deeds of surety to Strategios Paneuphemos (*CPR* XXIV 24; 27; *P.Eirene* IV 40; *P.Lond.* I 113.5C) are probably for individuals linked to his estate, but *P.Bodl.* I 53, a contract with public guards, may indeed show Strategios as the sole pagarch on September 16, 605 (see n. 48 above). In *CPR* XXIV 24.6 one should probably restore [ἐποικ]ί̣ο̣υ instead of [χωρ]ί̣ο̣υ, since the latter is highly suspicious in this context (that is, in a sense approaching κώμη) before the Islamic conquest: admittedly, Phanou is attested as a *kōmē* around that date, but varying use of these terms (or change of status) is not unheard of in this period. Sophie Kovarik (2014, xxiii in Kapitel 3) has come independently to the same conclusion about this restoration.

50 Strategios's last attestation as pagarch falls between October 5, 614 and October 4, 615 (*P.Eirene* IV 40; cf. n. 43 above), while Menas is first attested as pagarch on February 20, 616 (P.Vindob. G 26585; van Loon 2017). Four papyri that appear to have Strategios alive (may) fall into the period after his last attestation as pagarch: *BGU* II 368 (June 25, 615), *SB* I 5271 (December 10, 615), P.Vindob. G 26585 (February 20, 616), P.Vindob. G 50349 (619 CE; see van Loon 2017, 129 n. 10). But these references all occur in contexts where writers generally use the "short form" of aristocratic titulature (on this concept, see Chapter Five, Section II) and are therefore expected to prefer, e.g., Strategios's more distinguished title of *patricius* over the less exclusive title of pagarch, particularly since the full title in the Fayum at that time was the longwinded πάγαρχος τῆς Ἀρσινοιτῶν καὶ Θεοδοσιουπολιτῶν. The fragmentary receipt *SPP* VIII 1228 shows Strategios in some fiscal responsibility together with "the heirs of Kyrillos" in 623/624 (for the date, see the Catalog, s.v. Kyrillos); yet it seems unlikely that this responsibility was the pagarchy, since pagarchs always appear personally (or with their official title) in such texts, so we would expect the heirs' names to be written out here. This text therefore certainly relates to the fiscal shares of these magnates.

Kyrillos was pagarch before 596/597, when Strategios Paneuphemos took over, which would extend Strategios's tenure to nearly two decades.[51]

Christophoros and Strategios Stratelates, both *endoxotatoi stratelatai* in the earlier documents, apparently received a promotion during their tenure and became *eukleestatoi hypatoi*, which makes both of them unlikely matches for the anonymous *endoxotatos stratēlatēs* attested for 589/590, since we would expect them to be referred to by their higher title.

The tight clusters in which the papyri attest Strategios Paneuphemos and Menas Stratelates in the Fayum and Ioulianos, Ioannes, and Serenos in Antaiopolis leave little doubt that these pagarchs, in all probability, were in office continuously.[52] Finally, the cases of Strategios Paneuphemos and Menas Scriniarius, who are attested alive after their tenures,[53] may suggest that tenure as pagarch was not for life, although it would seem natural that pagarchs occasionally died in office, given tenures of a decade or longer. These results support the impression that short-term rotas as attested for the *defensoria civitatis* and the *riparia* are unlikely to have been the basis for determining a pagarch. The rather short tenure of Menas Scriniarius—and that of Kollouthos Cancellarius, if he was pagarch of Antaiopolis—may then be explained by the hypothesis that both may have found themselves confronted with special circumstances, or that they were "performing" as pagarchs for higher grandees, as discussed in the next section.[54]

---

51 The tendency of some aristocrats to suppress certain honorary titles when higher ones are obtained (for the case of Strategios Paneuphemos, see the Catalog, s.v.) suggests that Strategios Paneuphemos, too, might have been a *stratēlatēs* before becoming *hypatos*, which leaves open the distant possibility that he was himself the *endoxotatos stratēlatēs* of *BGU* XXI 2892.

52 Strategios Paneuphemos: indictions 4, 9, 11, 13, 15, and then 3 again, plus several fragmentary documents in which the date is lost. Menas Stratelates: indictions 4, 6, 10, and 11. Ioulianos: indictions [11,] 12, 14, 15, 1, 2, and (the "outlier") 8. Ioannes & Serenos: indictions 4–8, although Ioannes is not yet attested in the eighth indiction.

53 For Strategios Paneuphemos, see n. 50 above. For Menas, see *P.Lond.* V 1714. A pagarch who apparently died in office is alluded to in *P.Oxy.* XVI 1829.2–3 (uncertain date): οἱ τύποι τῆς | π̣αγαρχίας τοῦ τῆς ἐνδόξου μνήμης ὑμῶν πατρός; cf. ll. 12–13: τῶν τύπων τοῦ τῆς ἐνδόξου | [μν]ήμης ὑμῶ[ν] πενθεροῦ. The papyrus contains two letters of more or less the same content but directed to different addressees; on its value for the study of the pagarchy, see the Catalog, s.v. Anonymous pagarch (Arcadia). Perhaps Ioulianos can be added here; see *P.Lond.* V 1674.36–38 ("c. 570") where he is mentioned next to a late *procurator*, although the lacuna in l. 37 may have contained a reference to his being deceased; see the Catalog, n. 222.

54 The case of Kyrillos may, however, provide us with a comparably short tenure from the Arsinoite, if Kyrillos is not to be identified with one of the *endoxotatoi stratelatai* who were pagarchs around 590 CE.

III. Agency, Substitution, and Female Pagarchs

The business of the pagarchy was often conducted by someone other than the office-holder, a situation marked by the use of the expression "the pagarch through (*dia*) N.N." In most cases, this expression was used by subordinates conducting their daily business at the local level in the name of the pagarchs. These subordinates may be seen to act by virtue of *implied actual authority* and were examined in Section III of Chapter Two. By contrast, the present section deals with representatives in a stricter sense, with deputies who held the pagarchy as stand-ins, by virtue of *express actual authority*, when the "formal" incumbent would be unwilling or unable to do so. There are two possible attestations of this practice, the first of which being *P.Lond.* V 1660. In this document, a subcontracting tax collector declares to his superior, probably a *boēthos*,[55] that he will shield him against claims by

> the *megaloprepestatoi* common masters (and) pagarchs Ioulianos, the *megaloprepestatos apo archontōn*, and the *endoxotatē* Patrikia, through the *lamprotatos* lord Menas, her *dioikētēs* and pagarch.[56]

It has been suggested that *dioikētēs* here refers to a "deputy," but this meaning does not seem to be attested in documents from the sixth century.[57] Instead, *dioikētai* frequently figure as estate managers of higher grandees, but also in what are apparently regular of-

55 Cf. *P.Oxy.* I 125, in which someone aims to become *diadochos* for a village *boēthos*.

56 *P.Lond.* V 1660.5–8 (Antaiopolites; 553): τῶν μ]ε[γ]ạḷοπρẹπεσ̣τάτων κοινῶν | δεσποτῶν παγάρχων Ἰουλιανο(ῦ) τοῦ μεγαλοπρεστάτου (read μεγαλοπρεπεστάτου) ἀπὸ ạṛχ[όν]ṭ[ων] | καὶ τῆς ἐνδοξοτάτης Πατρικίας δ(ιὰ) τοῦ λαμπρο(τάτου) κυρίου Μηνᾶ αὐτῆς διοικητοῦ καὶ | παγάρχ(ου).

57 Ruffini 2008a, 191 translates *dioikētēs* in *P.Lond.* V 1660.7 as "deputy," yet throughout his book *dioikētai* are connected to the realm of estate administration. See Kruse 2002, 43 for the meaning "deputy" in the Roman period. For the use of διαδέχομαι with an acting (!) *logistēs*, see *SPP* VIII 1010.3 (Hermopolites?; IV–V); *SPP* III 369.4–5 (Hermopolites; IV–V), probably the same man as in the former text (see Gonis 2000b); and *P.Mich.* XVIII 794.5–7 (Herakleopolis; early VI). The verb occurs frequently in the first to third centuries CE, mostly in connection with the offices of the *stratēgos* and the *kōmogrammateus*. Evidence becomes scarce in the fourth century and the potential instance from the fifth (*SPP* VIII 1010.1 and 3, where both terms are used in regard to the same person) suggests that διοικέω and διαδέχομαι were used synonymously to refer to temporary replacements of officials.

ficial positions.[58] The reference "her *dioikētēs*," then, suggests that Menas was Patrikia's estate manager.[59]

Aristocratic bureaucrats of the rank of *lamprotatos* or even *megaloprepestatos* and *endoxotatos* were regularly involved in the estate business of higher-ranking elites and were the obvious choice when it came to appointing a liturgical stand-in.[60] Indeed, Jean Gascou suggested that Menas was a liturgical substitute, a *diadochos* (literally, "successor"), which is a term frequently used for deputies, substitutes, and indeed any kind of legal successors.[61] In this interpretation, Patrikia would have been the originally liable liturgist, but as a woman she was unable to exercise a public function, which would be the reason why she had herself represented by Menas.[62] Patrikia's appearance in *P.Lond.* V 1660 may then be explained by her financial interest in, and responsibility for, what happened under Menas's tenure.[63] One basic characteristic of the liturgical system of Roman (including late antique) Egypt was the incumbents' liability for their conduct in office. Even in cases where a substitute was involved, the original holder of the liturgy remained ultimately liable—a connection the papyri acknowledge in certain contexts by referring to the "principal" liturgist, the first instance, as *prōtotypos*.[64]

58 Some *dioikētai* with public areas of responsibility are attested well before the Arab period, for instance in *P.Grenf.* I 63.3–5 (Apollonopolis Heptakomias; VI–VII; see Benaissa 2008, 184–187, but compare 186–187 with Palme 1997a, 106 n. 23): Φλ(αουίῳ) Μηνᾷ τῷ λαμπρο(τάτῳ) διοικητῇ τῆς Ἀπολλωνοπολ(ι)τ(ῶν) | καὶ τοῖς μετὰ σοῦ παραλημψομένοις τὴν | διοίκησιν καὶ φροντίδα Ἀπόλλωνος, which appears to be a regular official position. On this context, see the discussion in the Catalog, s.v. Anonymous pagarch (Apollonopolis Heptakomias or Antaiopolis). See also *P.Köln* V 240.5 (Antaiopolites?; VI) for a *dioikētēs* of Antaiopolis and *P.Cair.Masp.* I 67088.10 (Aphrodite; c. 548?) for a village *dioikētēs*; the latter function also occurs in *P.Ness.* III 54.2 (Palaestina Salutaris; mid-VI). On the village *dioikētēs*, see Berkes 2017a, 129–135.

59 The alternative "his *dioikētēs*" is also attested and occurs, like "her *dioikētēs*," regularly in cases when the landowner has been mentioned before. It is therefore synonymous with, not a contrast to, "*dioikētēs* of the *ousia*/*oikos* of N.N."

60 For *megaloprepestatoi dioikētai* see, for instance, *P.Erl.* 67.4–5 (Herakleopolis; 591). For *endoxotatoi dioikētai* see, for instance, *P.Haun.* III 60.5 (Oxyrhynchites?; 618). These epithets and their hierarchy are discussed in Chapter Five, Section I.

61 Gascou 1972a, 70 (= 2008, 49).

62 On the character of Patrikia's pagarchy, see n. 73 below.

63 Cf. the deeds of surety concerning the *logisteia*, e.g. *P.Eirene* II 12 (Herakleopolis; 492), mentioned in nn. 72 and 74 below. Although the intermediary Apollos bears the title of *logistēs* and although the deed was about responsibilities related to the *logisteia*, the document nonetheless addresses the *oikos* of Apion, on which the liturgy was ultimately due; see ll. 13–14: τῆς λογιστίας (read λογιστείας) τοῦ προειρη|μένου οἴκου.

64 On liability of the substitute, see Reiter 2013, 4118; Lewis 1997, 105; Drecoll 1997, 309–352, especially at 323 § 5; Oertel 1917, 357; Palme 1989, 138 and 152. One frequently finds πρωτότυπος translated as "the aforementioned" in the sense of "who has been mentioned first" (e.g., in *P.Bad.* VI 168.11 as well as in *WB*, s.v.). But the word clearly has a specific sense (see the appropriate translation in *P.Oxy.* I 136.11 or *P.Oxy.* VI 904.8) and refers to the original holder of a liability, e.g., an individual whom someone else stands surety for (in contrast to the guarantor), the one originally chosen for a liturgy (in contrast to the substitute), or the original owner of property (in contrast,

Both the principal and the substitute could in different circumstances be attributed with the official title: In one text from the late fifth century, Strategios II from the family of the Apiones is addressed as *riparius*, while his intermediary is a certain Theodoros who is *diadochos* and at the same time *hypokatastatos*.[65] In a text from 489 CE in which Strategios is not *riparius*, however, the same Theodoros is *hypokatastatos*, but not *diadochos*,[66] while in yet another text, from 503 or 518 CE, Strategios is again addressed as *riparius*, but Theodoros is completely absent.[67] These three texts have been taken to indicate that Strategios II was still a minor in the former two texts and had Theodoros as a guardian (*hypokatastatos*), but in the first text was additionally subject to a liturgy for which Theodoros acted as Strategios's substitute (*diadochos*).[68] In the third text, however, Strategios was no longer in need of either a guardian or a liturgical substitute.[69] Apparently, officeholders were given the official title, and a potential deputy was noted adequately. In other cases, however, the *riparii* who bore the title were obviously the substitutes,[70] which is also apparent in case of the *logisteia*: in three cases

---

e.g., to the heirs). This is especially obvious in instances where the translation "aforementioned" makes little sense or would seem oddly placed, e.g., in *P.Oxy.* VI 904.8; *P.Stras.* I 40.21, 28, and 39; *P.Cair.Masp.* II 67167.12; *P.Lond.* I 113.1.65; *P.Cair.Masp.* I 67096.8; and *P.Lond.* I 113.2.15.

65 *P.Oxy.* LXVII 4614 (Oxyrhynchos; late V). On this man, see also pp. 125–126. The exact meaning of the term *hypokatastatos* (or *hypokatastatēs*) is disputed but I deem the following reconstruction highly plausible.

66 *P.Flor.* III 325 (Oxyrhynchos; May 20, 489). The interpretation of the editor of *SPP* III² 10, who sees an official in the *hypokatastatos* (or *hypokatastatēs*) *P.Flor.* III 325.3, does not seem to be correct (though it may be for the *katastatēs* in *SPP* III² 10); see also *P.Lips.* I 55.9–10 (Hermopolites; 375–379): ἐπιμελητὴν ἤτοι ὑποκαταστά|την Ἀπολλωνίου Ἥρωνος.

67 P.Harr. inv. 550a, from Oxyrhynchos and still unpublished; see *P.Oxy.* LXVII, p. 232.

68 See the discussion in *P.Oxy.* LXVII, pp. 233–234 and *P.Oxy.* LXXXII 5337 with the commentary. Strategios may have been head of a small estate liable to curial duties in the Oxyrhynchite before the heyday of the famous *endoxos oikos* of the Apiones in that nome. That minors were liable for liturgies need not cause surprise; see Beaucamp 1990, 32.

69 Another document, *CPR* XIV 48 (Herakleopolis; 506), is a petition addressed ἀναδεδεγμένοις τὴν ῥιπ̣αρίαν τῆ[ς πόλεως (l. 3), among whom we find Strategios, which may suggest that in Herakleopolis he was merely responsible for the office via a *munus patrimonii* (Maurer & Tost, 1828–1829 n. 7). Indeed, ἀναδέχομαι refers to the acceptance of the overall responsibility and the liability for a *munus* in *P.Ryl.* II 77.38–39 (Hermopolis; 192) and *P.Oxy.* LV 3796 (Oxyrhynchos; 412). In the former, the term clearly relates to an office, while in the latter a *systatēs* (on this title, see Lewis 1992, 128) had appointed someone for a liturgy who, however, refused to perform it; the *systatēs* now acknowledges taking over (ἀναδέχομαι) the responsibility for this liturgy (ll. 7–8), and, possibly, that he has received compensation in order to hire someone else to perform the actual duties; see the discussion in *P.Oxy.* LV, p. 73. A similar meaning occurs in the deeds of surety, where ἀναδέχομαι refers to the main responsibility for the liabilities of the party under surety; see Palme forthcoming, 45 n. 142. But why would a petitioner want to address, as in *CPR* XIV 48, the "principal" *riparii*, instead of their *diadochoi*, i.e., the active officials? Possibly, Leon and Strategios were still in a state of being "designated" *riparii* (cf. the appointment procedure in *P.Flor.* III 304) or this was a mere formality.

70 E.g., in *P.Oxy.* LV 3805.11 and 116 (after 566 CE), *P.Oxy.* VIII 1147.10 (late VI), and *P.Oxy.* LVIII

from Oxyrhynchos, the principals of the *diadochoi* are termed *lachōn* (masc.) or *lachousa* (fem.), respectively, "who has been assigned (the charge of such-and-such)."[71] All three cases concern the same three offices (the *logisteia*, the *proedria*, and the *pateria civitatis*) and involve large landowners (*geouchountes*) who were supposed to bear these charges. Again, a *diadochos* came into play in order to provide the services in question, usually some capable estate manager who, in addition, could bear the proper title of the office he represented.[72]

These observations may be dismissed as minor points, but become significant in light of *P.Lond.* V 1660, quoted above, in which Ioulianos and Patrikia are styled as joint pagarchs, with Patrikia being represented by Menas, who is *also* given that title. The addition of Menas's pagarchy makes it clear that Patrikia, not Menas, is part of the expression "common pagarchs" and a new reading of a fragmentary Antaiopolite tax receipt eliminates all doubt as to whether Patrikia herself bore the title of pagarch.[73] There is no parallel, however, for both the "nominal" liturgist *and* the substitute be-

---

3949.6–7 (June 4, 610), all from Oxyrhynchos. See also *riparii* "of the *oikos*," convincingly explained by Tost 2012 as the substitutes nominated by the *oikos* to fill the post of *riparius* of Oxyrhynchos.

71 *SB* XX 14964.4–6 (517 CE); *P.Oxy.* XXXVI 2780.6–13 (553 CE); *SB* XII 11079.5–12 (571 CE); cf. *CPR* V 17.10 (late V) from Herakleopolis. In the first case, the *diadochos* does not bear any other title or epithet, the latter two both are *aidēsimos* (a nonaristocratic rank epithet). Note that *SB* XII 11079, while being formally addressed to Apion via his *diadochos*, employs a construction that aims at the *diadochos* (see l. 15), which is not the case in the other two instances.

72 E.g., *P.Eirene* II 12.3–4 (Herakleopolis; 492), addressed τῷ οἴκῳ Ἀπίωνος ṭοῦ ἐνδοξοτάṭου καὶ ὑπερφυεστάτου διὰ | Ἀπολλῷ (read Ἀπολλοῦ) λογιστοῦ (ll. 4–5); ll. 13–14 mention "the *logisteia* of the same *oikos*." See also *P.Oxy.* LVIII 3949 (Oxyrhynchos; 610), where a certain Enoch appears who is *riparius*, *logistēs*, and *boēthos* of the public bath. He is of the same rank (*aidēsimos*) as the *diadochoi* of *P.Oxy.* XXXVI 2780 and *SB* XII 11079.

73 *P.Vat.Aphrod.* 16A.2: [– – – ο]ἱ ἐνδοξότατοι πάγαρχοι Πατρ[ικία καί – – –]; see the Catalog, n. 251. By contrast, Beaucamp 1992, 12 sees an "hesitation à dénommer une femme pagarque" in *P.Lond.* V 1660. The second lacuna in *P.Vat.Aphrod.* 16A leaves open the possibility that the signature continued "Patrikia through Menas (i.e., the pagarch)" vel sim. but there is no precedent for this in the receipts from pagarchs; cf. *SB* XVI 12370, in which a *procurator* acts instead as representative for the entire collegium, and *P.Leid.Inst.* 72 (Antinoopolis; VI), where the pagarch Kollouthos Exceptor—who was probably a *lamprotatos* and, thus, of Menas's status—is the responsible signatory for the tax receipt. I am still hesitant, however, to argue that *P.Vat.Aphrod.* 16A.2 shows that Patrikia was actively performing the pagarchy. On women in relation to public duties and officeholding, see Grubbs 2002, 74–80; van Bremen 1996, 41–81 and 114–141; Mazza 1995, 194, especially n. 81; Beaucamp 1990, 29–35 and 1992, 5–21; and Lewis 1990. An intriguing observation by Joëlle Beaucamp (1990, 33–34) has made it at least conceivable that "personal" liturgies were distinguished from "physical" liturgies, and that women therefore could well be conceived to exercise functions that did not involve actual physical, but for instance intellectual or advisory, work. May this also have been the case for the pagarchy? Bagnall 1995, 71 points out that "financial responsibility had always been the main point of such functions [i.e., civic offices, including nonliturgical ones], and in any case it is only asserted, not actually proven, that in the sixth century the women mentioned did nothing except accept financial liability."

ing given the official title in the same document,[74] which would suggest that Menas, although Patrikia's estate manager, was still pagarch on his own and assumed the role of Patrikia's substitute in addition to that.[75] If this hypothesis is correct, the prominent and confident position Menas took during his first and second pagarchies would be much more understandable,[76] and fit the "tripartite" pagarchy that is documented not much later when three pagarchs are attested (in 559/560) and when Ioannes and Serenos later had their pagarchy split into three parts in the early 570s. *P.Lond.* V 1660 does not bear a date, but is certainly close to *P.Lond.* V 1661 from July 24, 553, in which Ioulianos and Menas both appear as pagarchs again, but this time without Patrikia.[77] This document is a debt acknowledgment from two *apaitētai* who have apparently borrowed from the pagarchs, in advance, the equivalent of the tax amount that they were to collect.[78] Patrikia's absence may therefore be conveniently explained by the assumption that this transaction was formally private and arranged by Ioulianos and Menas in their own name and out of their own funds—regardless of whether at that time Menas was pagarch for Patrikia, pagarch on his own without Patrikia, or pagarch on his own *and* for Patrikia.

Another potential instance of express actual authority occurs in an Antaiopolite tax receipt from 559/560 CE, but the situation is more complicated here:

> Apollos, son of Dioskoros, has given for ownerless land (*adespotos*) to the account of the taxes of the village of Aphrodite of the tax assessment (*kanōn*) of the eighth indiction thirteen and one-fourth *keratia* in the (public) standard, that is 13 ¼ *keratia* in the (public) standard. The *endoxotatoi* pagarchs Ioulianos, Kometes, and Euthymios through the *peribleptos comes* Christodotos, *procurator*, through me, Makarios, *boēthos*: I agree to this receipt of thirteen and one-fourth *keratia* in the (public) standard as it is above. (The amount has been) handed over by the fellow (*adelphos*) Dioskoros, his son.[79]

---

74 The Oxyrhynchite evidence in fact suggests that the *diadochoi* were only attributed the formal title in case their principal liturgist was not mentioned in the document; cf. n. 72 above on the formulae of *P.Eirene* II 12.3–4 (the document is addressed to the *oikos*; the substitute is referred to as *logistēs*) versus that of *SB* XX 14964.4–6, *P.Oxy.* XXXVI 2780.6–13, and *SB* XII 11079.5–12 (the document is addressed to the *geouchōn* or *geouchousa*; the substitute is referred to as *diadochos*).

75 *P.Lond.* V 1714 suggests that Menas himself had landholdings in the Antaiopolite nome.

76 Discussed in Chapter Six, Section III. In some cases (*P.Cair.Masp.* I 67060–67061; 67083; III 67322; *P.Lond.* V 1682–1684; *PSI* VIII 939; *SB* XX 14241) it is not certain whether these relate to Menas's first (in the 550s) or second (in the 560s) pagarchy. At least for *P.Cair.Masp.* I 67060, however, the mid-550s seem to be the best bet because Dioskoros is attested as *prōtokōmētēs* during these years and was no longer in his native village when Menas became pagarch again in 566. Apart from *P.Lond.* V 1660, the documents connect all of Menas's activities to him alone and Patrikia is never mentioned even formally.

77 *P.Lond.* V 1661.5–6 (July 24, 553): Φλ(αουίῳ) Ἰουλιανῷ τῷ μεγαλοπρεπεστάτῳ ἀπὸ ἀρχόν̣τ̣ων̣ καὶ Μηνᾷ λαμπροτάτῳ | σκρ̣ινιαρίῳ καὶ παγάρχαις τῆ̣ς Ἀνταιοπολιτῶ̣ν̣.

78 Palme 1989, 105.

79 *SB* XVI 12370.

The twofold representation of the pagarchs, first through a *procurator* and then through a *boēthos*, suggests that the *procurator* Christodotos was not an ad hoc intermediary like the *boēthos* Makarios, but an institutionalized representative of some sort. But which? There were generally two sorts of *procuratores* in late antique Egypt: managers of large estates and representatives of officials.[80] Given the increasing interference of public and private business of the *oikoi*, however, these categories may in fact be two different aspects of the same position: that of a personal agent managing all sorts of affairs. The same *procurator* Christodotos is referred to posthumously in a fragmentary petition from the "Menas affair," in which he is mentioned in connection with the pagarch Ioulianos.[81] Christodotos plays no role in the conflict some villagers of Aphrodite had with Ioulianos in the late 540s, and perhaps he arrived on the scene only later and for the reason that Ioulianos became an absentee pagarch around the mid-550s.[82] But in the case that Christodotos was only Ioulianos's estate manager or his stand-in for the pagarchy, it would seem notable that his representation in the tax receipt extended over the entire collegium, and not just Ioulianos.[83] More decisively, however, the fragmentary petition appears to say that Ioulianos decided to change the taxation rate "at the persuasion (*peismonē*) of Christodotos, the late *procurator*," though it was Ioulianos who had the final say.[84] This suggests that Christodotos had his own interests in matters concerning Aphrodite;[85] the fact that he is absent from the petitions against Ioulianos, on the other

80 Azzarello 1998, 25–27: "Guts- bzw. Vermögensverwalter" versus "Geschäftsführer von Amtspersonen." Cf. Laniado 2002, 114 n. 104: a Latin epitome of Iust. *nov.* 134 renders σκρινιάριοι as *procuratores*. For the equivalence of *procurator* and *dioikētēs* in the sense of "estate manager," see Mazza 2001, 137. But see also *CPR* VII 24 recto 5 (Oxyrhynchos; V–VI), where a *procurator* is a woman's representative in court, *pace* Azzarello 1998, 26.

81 *P.Lond.* V 1674.36–38 (c. 570?): κατὰ πεισμονὴν Χριστοδότọ[υ] | τοῦ ἀπογενομέ(νου) π̣ροκ̣[ουράτορος ± 14]ης Ἰουλιανο(ῦ) τοῦ [ἀπ]ὸ ἐπάρχων̣ | κ̣α̣ί̣ [– – –]. On this passage and the restorations of the lacunae here, cf. the Catalog, s.v. Ioulianos (Antaiopolis). The name Christodotos is extremely rare, and the link to Ioulianos makes the match therefore close to inevitable. Since the name is so rare and because Christodotos belongs to a rather mobile stratum of the Thebaid's bureaucratic realm, *SB* XIV 12116 (see the new edition in Keenan 2015) and *SPP* III 436 may show him at some other point of his career, but this is not certain.

82 This reconstruction would be tempting in case Ioulianos is identical with the *endoxotatos stratēlatēs* of that name, who in *P.Cair.Masp.* I 67008.3 (Antinoopolis?; 567/568?) represents the provincial governor of the Thebaid, viz. in Antinoopolis. This identification, which is of course uncertain, would also imply a promotion of Ioulianos after the incidents of the late 540s, fitting my reconstruction of this episode's result as discussed in Chapter Six, Section V.

83 The term *procurator* may have been used as an equivalent for *dioikētēs*, which is the term relating to the pagarch Menas in *P.Lond.* V 1660. But both terms are, on their own, rather general. On collective authority, see the next section.

84 *P.Lond.* V 1674.36–37; see n. 81 above. It is not ultimately certain from the damaged text whom Christodotos persuaded, but Ioulianos would seem the most likely option.

85 Christodotos may be the *procurator* who is mentioned in *P.Cair.Masp.* I 67074 (note the addendum on p. 206), a very fragmentary letter that, given the context of the find, may have been addressed to the *prōtokōmētai* of Aphrodite, and which in l. 3 reads [– – – ἀπ]ήλλαξαν τὸ πρᾶγμα

hand, makes it all but certain that he was not simply someone attached to Ioulianos, an observation that conforms to his intermediary role for the entire collegium in the tax receipt.

All this makes for intriguing speculation. Perhaps Christodotos was acting in a capacity that was somewhat comparable on a hierarchical level, but at the same time not part of the hierarchy under the pagarch. He may have been the *procurator* of imperial land at Aphrodite, or rather, in the Thebaid,[86] a hypothesis that is intriguing due to the fact that the village, or considerable parts of it, had been patronized by the imperial household.[87] Accepting this hypothesis would have interesting consequences, since no *procurator* in a comparable role is known either from the early years of Ioulianos's pagarchy around 550 CE or from the later dossier of the pagarchs Ioannes and Serenos from 570/571 and beyond.[88] Are we looking at a transitional period in which Aphrodite was formally subjected to the Antaiopolite pagarchy and during which an imperial *procurator* who was apparently on good terms with Ioulianos supervised the relevant transactions?[89] More generally, does this text, then, indicate that the pagarchs' authority extended over taxes from imperial lands? This cannot be answered with certainty—perhaps the special category of *adespotos* land plays a role here as well—but the reconstruction is intriguing because it would suggest that Aphrodite's struggle against the pagarchs was not a fight against aggressive potentates but rather a restructuring of the village's fiscal organization after persistent problems concerning due taxes.[90] A potential, though uncertain, identification may be tempting here. If the Theodosios *procurator* from an Aphroditan rent receipt is the same as the homonymous *megaloprepestatos* who (allegedly) embezzled Aphrodite's taxes at the end of the 540s after the death of Count Ammonios, who had been a *comes sacrii consistorii*, one might suggest

αὐτῶν, "they carried out their affair/matter/business/lawsuit." The context is obscure, but the *procurator* figures as someone who has his proper decisions effectuated: [– – – ἐπ]οίησεν ὁ προκουράτωρ, μὴ θέλων | [– – –] (l. 1–2).

86 Delmaire 1988, 130 takes Christodotos as a *procurator domus divinae*, a hypothesis dismissed by Azzarello 1998, 26–27 with the argument that *SB* XVI 12370 shows Christodotos as "agent" of the pagarchs' collegium, but this, as I argued above, is ambiguous. A *procurator*, perhaps the *procurator rei privatae*, figures in *P.Sijp.* 35 recto col. II 13 and verso col. II 8 (Oxyrhynchos?; VI–VII) in a list of vouchers from a provincial office, where he receives fifty-seven *nomismata*, the highest individual amount after the governor, the *comes* Ioannes, and a certain oil-seller named Stephanos. On this type of *procurator*, see *P.Sijp.*, p. 235.

87 *P.Cair.Masp.* III 67283; *P.Cair.Masp.* I 67002.

88 But cf. some earlier *procuratores*: *P.Aphrod.Reg.* 603 (525/526 CE), where his role is not evident, *pace* Zuckerman's commentary on p. 271; *P.Flor.* III 304 (V–VI), in which a *procurator* of Count Ammonios appears; and *P.Cair.Masp.* I 67104.3 and 5 (August 19, 530). The Menas in the latter is unlikely to be Menas Scriniarius (*pace* Banaji 2007, 163); see the Catalog, s.v. On the *procurator* Theodosios who appears in *P.Ross.Georg.* III 45, see below.

89 On this transition, see also *P.Lond.* V 1674, referring to the "yoke" (or, more prosaic, "measure") of the pagarchy (l. 16) that Aphrodite had fallen under.

90 This problem is discussed in Chapter Six.

that this Theodosios was Christodotos's predecessor and that he was responsible for the imperial patronage over Aphrodite.[91] This hypothesis would suggest that we are dealing with *implied*, rather than *express*, actual authority. In this scenario, the *procurator* Christodotos became involved by virtue of his position as he was the necessary intermediary within the usual hierarchy at that time, which may have seen this particular land (and the whole of Aphrodite?) under an imperial *procurator* but with ultimate authority of the pagarch. But this is, again, hypothetical.

IV. Individual and Collective Authority

The fourth century occasionally saw two "early" pagarchs/*praepositi* in charge of a single *pagus*, and I have already alluded to several instances from the sixth century in which two or three pagarchs shared the office. In this context, some questions emerge from the previous sections: Why did Ioulianos begin as sole pagarch but later come to share the office with one or two other grandees? And why did Arsinoe have collegial pagarchs, but after c. 590 CE apparently individual pagarchs only? Why was the pagarchy in the Arsinoite sometimes taken over by brothers and how does this relate to the pagarchic collegia in Antaiopolis? And finally, how did these colleagues operate in practice and what does this entail for the pagarchs' authority, liability, and shared responsibilities? In the first years after the Arab conquest, we encounter subdistricts called *skelē* (Sg. *skelos*) in some nomes.[92] These probably date back at least to the last years of the Byzantine administration in Egypt, and it may seem tempting to assume a continuity from the *pagi* as subdistricts of the nome to the *skelē* of early Islamic Egypt

91 *P.Ross.Georg.* III 45; see especially the sender in ll. 1–2, who is distinguished enough to have a *phorologos*, a rent manager (the only other late antique attestation is *P.Cair.Masp.* III 67327.22 from July 27, 539, in a clearly private context), as an intermediary: [– – – δ(ιὰ)? Θε]οδοσίου προκουράτορος δ(ιὰ) Πόννιτος | φορολόγο[υ]. The supplement χαίρ(ειν) in l. 2 should be deleted and the text might have, alternatively, started with παρά in l. 1, but the lacuna there seems too spacious to make Theodosios the sender. It fits comfortably a longer beginning, such as a reference to the *domus divina* or the pagarch Ioulianos (or another *geouchōn*) and the addition of δ(ιὰ) τοῦ μεγάλοπρ(επεστάτου) κόμετ(ος), further abbreviated if necessary, before Theodosios's name (cf. the arrangement of the titles in the potential parallel *SB* XVI 12370). In l. 4 instead of λόγῳ δ⟦.⟧ιτρọπ̣ικ̣(ου) the reading λόγῳ δ̣ι̣α̣τροφῇ[ς] would fit this type of document and, judging by the online image, seems to fit the traces, although the image is very blurry. See also *P.Flor.* III 304, in which Count Ammonios has a homonymous *procurator* dealing with official matters, in this case the appointment of a *riparius*. Fournet 1999, 318 also tentatively approached Theodosios to the management of the *domus divina*.

92 These *skelē* are prominently attested in the archive of Appa Kyros, Christophoros, and Theodorakios, pagarchs of the Herakleopolite nome (*TM* Arch ID 572), and in the Senouthios archive (*TM* Arch ID 418). See *CPR* XXXVI, p. 16 and 194; *CPR* XXX, pp. 15, 18, and 106–112; Sijpestein 2013, 72 and 139. Some papyri suggest that there were *skelē* in the Oxyrhynchite nome, too; see Azzarello 2013 and Berkes 2014, 79.

by assuming a territorially divided pagarchy. The evidence of the sixth century suggests otherwise, however.

The only known named pair of pagarchs in the Arsinoite timeline are Christophoros and Strategios Stratelates, who appear in two leases,[93] but the idea that we are faced with an exceptional case is difficult to reconcile with the frequent occurrence of collegial pagarchs in Antaiopolis and also more recently discovered fragmentary occurrences in the Fayum. Since the evidence for Arsinoite pagarchs almost always comes from the world of the private estates, we cannot expect that pagarchs mentioned in such texts were the only incumbents. In 590/591, the pagarchy in the Fayum was held by two *endoxotatoi* heirs (let us name them for the moment A + B) of an *endoxotatos stratēlatēs* (X), whereas during the next indiction, two *endoxotatoi* heirs (C + D) of a *hyperphyestatos patricius* (Y) are attested in this position.[94] It seems conceivable that we have encountered a transmission of the pagarchy from A + B to C + D, and both collegia only *happen* to consist of siblings. Another possibility is that their collegiality is linked to their status as heirs, and that we are confronted with a hidden multitude of pagarchs: These private documents do not aim to provide us with a complete list of incumbent pagarchs, but they address joint estate owners who happen to be pagarchs at that time. In this reconstruction, the *endoxotatos stratēlatēs* (X) and the *hyperphyestatos patricius* (Y) would have been the original "shareholders" of the pagarchy before each was succeeded by his heirs (X → A + B; Y → C + D) who were jointly responsible for their share, resulting in A + B + C + D being collective pagarchs.

But what, then, to make of the long tenure of Christophoros and Strategios Stratelates, who are attested in two testimonies spanning nine years? Should the two have been joint heirs this long before things were finally settled? Or was the pagarchy not imposed on the *ousia* but on their father's person, and afterward transferred onto his heirs personally? A list of contributions from the joint *syntelestai* of the city of Oxyrhynchos may point in the latter direction. The pagarchy is here shared in equal parts between the *endoxotatoi* Ptolemaios and Ioustos, but it is notable that their shares of the pagarchy are listed next to contributions by boards of shareholders whose members were apparently related by family:

> Through the heirs of the *endoxotatos* Ptolemaios 2 *nomismata*, 19 ¼ *keratia*
> Through the same (man) for one half-share of the pagarchy 1 *nomisma*, 10 ½ *keratia*.
> Through the *endoxotatos* Ioustos and his brothers 2 *nomismata*, 16 *keratia*.
> Through the same (man) for the other half-share of the pagarchy 1 *nomisma*, 10 ½ *keratia*.[95]

93 *CPR* XIV 11 (578 CE) and Louvre E 6573 (586/587). It cannot be excluded that Christophoros and Strategios leased out these properties in their official capacity (see Chapter Two, Section II 2), yet there is nothing in the text that would suggest this.

94 See Table 5 (pp. 169–171).

95 *P.Oxy.* XVI 2040.9–14. On this text, see Chapter Three, Section II.

Ptolemaios had obviously passed away by that time, as his heirs paid for his share, and in a similar way Ioustos and his brothers appear to form a sort of consortium, certainly as their father's heirs.[96] The payments from both consortia are not identical but are in the same order of magnitude compared to the remaining contributors in this text; this fits with the liturgical hypothesis in the light of the fact that both drew an equal share of the pagarchy, according to their estimated wealth. On the other hand, the list separates the personal shares from those that were due to the pagarchy; the pagarchy, in turn, was apparently linked to Ptolemaios and Ioustos as individuals, even though Ptolemaios was already dead.[97] This would again be an argument that the pagarchy was formally an individual appointment, not one that fell automatically on the owners of particular *ousiai*.

In the Antaiopolite, the picture looks a little different, at least there is no indication that any of the known pagarchs were from the same family.[98] In case Menas was not pagarch on his own in the 550s, but only through his substitution for Patrikia, then the transition of the pagarchy from Ioulianos and Patrikia to the trio of Ioulianos, Kometes, and Euthymios in 559/560 may be explained by Kometes and Euthymios being Patrikia's heirs.[99] In this scenario, Ioulianos would presumably have shouldered 50 percent of the pagarchy and Kometes and Euthymios 25 percent each, although we have no way of knowing whether Ioulianos and Patrikia had shared the pagarchy equally.[100] An alternative scenario may be that from some point in the 550s the Antaiopolite pagarchy was shared in three equal parts by Ioulianos, Patrikia, and Menas, followed by Ioulianos, Kometes, and Euthymios, and later these shares were distributed between Ioannes, "pagarch of the two-thirds share of Antaiopolis," and Serenos, "pagarch of the one-third share of Antaiopolis." But in 550/551, and possibly from as early as his first attestations as pagarch until 552/553, Ioulianos had probably been sole pagarch of Antaiopolis, which might entail either that Ioulianos got into some financial trouble during the late 540s and early 550s, that the division of the pagarchy responded to an

96 Cf. *P.Oxy.* XVI 2020.17 and 18, where Ptolemaios's and Ioustos's heirs pay "for various *onomata*," and therefore certainly constituted *oikoi*; on this interpretation of the term, see Chapter Three, Sections I and II.

97 That Ioustos apparently held the pagarchy may account for the fact that he and his brothers, in contrast to Ptolemaios's offspring, are not styled as heirs of their father.

98 We may, however, once again be suffering from documentary bias here: if the hypothesis that the pagarchy formally rested on the individual person is true, then there would be no need to refer to the incumbents as heirs in the Antaiopolite documents, since the latter generally relate to the pagarchs' official capacity.

99 Or heirs of whoever may hide as pagarch in the late 550s; see Table 4 (pp. 165–167).

100 Patrikia, strikingly, appears in the first position in a collective signature of *P.Vat.Aphrod.* 16A.2: [– – – ο]ἱ ἐνδοξότατοι πάγαρχοι Πατρ[ικία καί – – –]; see the Catalog, n. 251. No date is extant on the fragmentary papyrus, but the hand may be that of the *hypodektēs* Petros, who is the signatory of *P.Cair.Masp.* I 67046 (550/551).

order from above, or that the fiscal responsibilities of the pagarchy increased,[101] as indicated by the general rise in tax demands during this period.[102]

In this light, Menas's second pagarchy may be notable since it remains unclear whether he was acting for some higher aristocrat when he became pagarch in 566/567: an Aphroditan petition states that he assumed the pagarchy in that year, and does not allude to his former tenure.[103] No other pagarch is known from that period, although one tax receipt that refers anonymously to "the *endoxotatoi* pagarchs" may also be placed to 566/567.[104] By contrast, on at least two occasions Aphroditans refer to Menas as simply "the pagarch," which would appear to imply that he was sole pagarch at that time, or at least the only one to regularly engage with the village.[105] Menas may have been representing some high-ranking aristocrat during these years, or even acting as a representative for an entire collegium, but in these cases it would be hard to understand why the villagers would refer only to him only as "the pagarch," which implies that this reference was unambiguous.[106] Did the *lamprotatos* Menas acquire enough wealth on his own to be an eligible candidate for the pagarchy? The liturgical hypothesis seems to fall short of explaining how a *lamprotatos scriniarius* was able to hold the pagarchy on his own, while six years prior the same duty was borne by three *endoxotatoi*, one of them being the *endoxotatos illoustrios* Ioulianos who was one of the most important grandees in the region. The pagarch Kollouthos Cancellarius also appears to have acted on his own, despite being only *lamprotatos*.[107] Do Menas's and Kollouthos's links to the provincial administration in Antinoopolis play a role here, and were they installed

---

101 All these explanations can be linked, either as cause or result, to Ioulianos's confrontation with the autopract village of Aphrodite toward the end of the 540s, which is explored in Chapter Six, Section II. *P.Cair.Masp.* II 67228 may also illustrate Ioulianos as sole pagarch; it is a tax receipt signed by a *hypodektēs* (viz., an official from the city level) on behalf of a single "*endoxotatos* pagarch," with no name given. I am currently preparing this receipt for re-edition.

102 See Chapter Three, Section II and Chapter Six, Section V.

103 *P.Cair.Masp.* I 67002 col. I 10–11. In the same text, col. II 11–12 implies that Menas had himself the authority to issue tax receipts.

104 *P.Cair.Masp.* I 67047; this date is far from certain, however.

105 *P.Lond.* V 1677.51 and Vanderheyden 2015, no. 11, a private Coptic letter, where "the pagarch" is not further identified, neither by name nor epithet. Perhaps also *P.Cair.Masp.* I 67002 col. I 17 (however, with rank epithet) may count here. See also *SB* XX 14241.12–13: τοῖς λαμπρ(οτάτοις) τρακτευτ(αῖς) καὶ τῷ βοηθῷ καὶ τῷ κοινῷ δεσπό(τῃ) τῷ κυρίῳ | Μηνᾷ, where Menas appears alone in what may be an official hierarchy, but this text may also date to Menas's first pagarchy in the 550s.

106 It is also hard to see how Dioskoros or the Aphroditans would have been able to single out and accuse Ioulianos and Menas in such a direct and pronounced manner before the imperial chancery and the *dux et Augustalis* if both men had not been sole pagarchs at the time of their "conflicts" with Dioskoros's family.

107 This is apparent from Dioskoros's poems addressed to Kollouthos and from *P.Cair.Masp.* I 67003—if this is Kollouthos, but the singular pagarchy seems clear. What is not clear, however, is whether Kollouthos was pagarch *in Antaiopolis*. For a discussion, see the Catalog, s.v. Kollouthos Cancellarius (Thebaid IV: Unknown Nome).

due to situational considerations?[108] In any case, the contrast between sole pagarchs and collegia in both Antaiopolis and Arsinoe does not seem negligible.

The Antaiopolite tax receipts allow some insight into what a shared responsibility may have looked like in practice. What did it entail, for instance, when the pagarchs Ioannes and Serenos were at one point pagarchs of, respectively, the two-thirds and one-third shares of Antaiopolis? The initial scholarly consensus of a territorial division is incompatible with the fact that the collegial pagarchs Ioulianos and Menas act as authorities for the same area in two contracts.[109] The pattern of the signatures in the tax receipts further discourages this hypothesis; the *notarii* Damianos and Mousaios signed two receipts together, but each *notarius* signed for "his" pagarch.[110] Most receipts, however, bear only one signature, either in the name of an individual pagarch or of the collegium. This observation makes it quite hard to believe that there would have been plots registered on Ioannes's share, plots registered on Serenos's share, and yet other plots registered on both shares; signatures in the name of one or the other pagarch also are not exclusive to particular taxpayer accounts (*onomata*). It seems more likely to assume that references to the pagarchs' shares relate to the aggregated tax quota, and that it was irrelevant whether one pagarch or the entire collegium issued a particular receipt.[111] As seen in Section III 3 of Chapter Two, the pagarchs' local subordinates issued tax receipts in a pattern where signatories switched between signing in the name of one individual pagarch and signing for the collegium as a whole according to their preference.[112] But the same signatory never switched between individual pagarchs, which suggests that these men were assigned to one particular pagarch instead of being assigned interchangeably to both; still, their fiscal authority was obviously valid for the entire collegium. Each pagarch thus disposed of his own staff, apparently scribes, accountants, and collectors for local fiscal operations,[113] in addition to staff assigned to

108 This cannot be discussed here but is explored in Chapter Six.

109 These contracts are *P.Lond.* V 1660 and 1661 (the former including Patrikia) and have been interpreted as arguments against a territorial division by Rouillard 1928, 55–56. The discussion is outlined by Mazza 1995, 191–194, who also argues against the territorial division.

110 *P.Cair.Masp.* III 67325 fol. III verso 5–9 and 10–12; see Table 1 (p. 96).

111 This phenomenon is not uncommon in other offices and collegial institutions; see, e.g., Palme 1989, 120 and 152 on the *apaitētai*, on the latter occasion citing *O.Bodl.* II 782 (Thebes; 160), which was issued by a collegium even though the subscription names only two (ll. 4 and 5) or even only one of the partners (l. 7).

112 "Local" here means "below the level of the *civitas*," thus excluding the *hypodektai*. Jean Gascou (1972a, 66 = 2008, 46–47) thought instead that this "fractionnement de l'autorité pagarchique" entailed that contributors had to receive receipts from *both* pagarchs in order to have their contribution fully validated, which to me seems quite unlikely in view of the assembly of the Antaiopolite receipts.

113 See the occasional references to individual shares in the descriptions of the payments (*P.Cair. Masp.* III 67325 fol. III recto 6–7: Liberis) or in the titles of these officials (*P.Cair.Masp.* III 67325 fol. VII recto 6: Christodoros *notarius*, but the reading is not beyond doubt) or in their signatures (*P.Cair.Masp.* III 67325 fol. III verso 8 and 9: Damianos *notarius* and Mousaios *notarius*).

the “entire” pagarchy (that is, to all pagarchs) at a higher administrative level, such as the *hypodektai*, *logographoi*, and *trakteutai*. It was apparently also an individual writer’s habit, and not necessary for the legal value of the receipts, whether or not to include a reference to the two-thirds and one-third shares of Ioannes and Serenos in the subordinates’ signature.[114]

It is unclear whether there was a formal hierarchy within a collegium. In Antaiopolite documents, Ioulianos is always mentioned in first position, be it with Patrikia and Menas, with Menas only, or with Kometes and Euthymios. In one fragmentary receipt, however, Patrikia was in first position but the names of her colleagues are lost.[115] In the two receipts in which Ioannes and Serenos appear jointly, the *endoxotatos comes* Ioannes, pagarch of the two-thirds share, is mentioned before the *endoxotatos illoustrios* Serenos, pagarch of the one-third share.[116] Having a minor share did not, however, exclude one from actively performing the pagarchy, as Serenos in one case sent an *epistalma* (“order,” “commission”) in an official context.[117] Both Ioannes and Serenos issued tax receipts throughout the fiscal year; there is no apparent pattern that would show them acting only during specific months. The writer of one administrative letter, in a passage in which he refers to the pagarchs Antiochos and Theon, switches to the singular at one point,[118] indicating that the actual contact was only through one of the pagarchs, presumably Antiochos.

The hypothesis according to which these shares were not linked to subdistricts within a nome is not entirely satisfactory,[119] but on current evidence remains more convincing than the opposite.[120] A document from the realm of the Arcadian provincial administration from the early sixth century holds the pagarchs Antiochos and Theon

114 See the previous note. The explicit mention of the ratio (two-thirds versus one-third) in the case of Ioannes and Serenos may suggest that a 50 percent share may have been the regular one in other collegia. But cf. *P.Oxy.* XVI 2040, where a 50 percent share is explicitly noted as such.

115 *P.Vat.Aphrod.* 16A.2; see the Catalog, n. 251.

116 *P.Cair.Masp.* III 67325 fol. III verso 5–9 and 9–12. It was, however, Ioannes’s *notarius*, Damianos, who wrote these receipts before Serenos’s *notarius* Mousaios added his signature, which might also explain on its own why Ioannes was mentioned first.

117 *P.Flor.* III 298.12–16.

118 *P.Mich.* XI 624.14–15: ὑπομνήσας τοὺς αὐτούς, τουτέστιν Ἀντίοχον καὶ Θέωνα, | τὰ κτήνη αὐτῶν παρασχῖν (read παρασχεῖν) πρὸς μετ[α]φορὰν τούτων καθὼς καὶ ἐπηγγίλατο (read ἐπηγγείλατο). “Remind the same (men), that is, Antiochos and Theon, to supply their donkeys for the transfer of it (i.e., the hay) just as he announced.”

119 If there was no difference, then it is not easy to explain why the signatory Gennadios, who usually signs for the pagarch Ioannes, once signed for Serenos at all (*P.Flor.* III 298.12–16), and why he felt obliged to point to the apparently unusual circumstances of this procedure (l. 13), or why the signatory Flavius Liberis expressly notes that the received payment was “for the security of the third share of Serenos,” as in *P.Cair.Masp.* III 67325 fol. III recto 6–7: (ὑπὲρ) ἀσφαλ(είας) τοῦ τρίτου | μ̣έρ[ο]υς Σιρινο̣ς (read Σερήνου).

120 It should be highlighted here that the evidence for the Antaiopolite pagarchs is not limited to the potential “special case” of the village of Aphrodite.

collectively responsible for a report and for the disposition of donkeys for transportation purposes.[121] Whatever divisions of authority existed between two or more pagarchs may have been negotiated between the members of the collegium rather than dictated from above.

V. Summary

The pagarchy was borne either alone or in a collegium, and may have fallen to the heirs of a former holder of the charge. Although sufficient real property (*ousia*) was apparently a prerequisite, there are indications that the burden of officeholding was not imposed on landed estates, but that formally individuals were personally appointed. The college of city notables may or may not have had their say in the nomination of a pagarch, but the appointment was probably by virtue of an imperial confirmation, via the praetorian prefect and the provincial governor, at least in the mid-sixth century. In this, the pagarchy mirrors "semi-imperial" offices such as that of the *defensor civitatis*. Pagarchs started their tenure probably with the *praedelegatio* on Pachon 1, which marked the beginning of the indiction for fiscal purposes throughout Egypt. Although no case is attested for certain, it seems that pagarchs could have had themselves substituted, but still hold the main responsibility. Women could be part of pagarchic collegia, hold the proper title, and tax receipts could even be signed in their names; the limited evidence does not show that they were actively performing the charge, but it also does not prove that they were not. Authority within a collegium was probably based on the aggregated tax quota of the territories under the pagarchy, and if there were divisions of responsibility, these were most likely negotiated and fixed on the basis of private agreements among the members of the collegium.

All this seems in line with the liturgies as attested throughout Roman and late antique Egypt, even though the major arguments for the pagarchy being a *munus patrimonii* have been undermined by the distinction of the *kōmai pagarchoumenai* from the pagarchy proper, as discussed in Chapter Three. Other characteristics hardly fit the model of a traditional liturgy. Even though few pagarchs are attested in total, the known tenures vary between probably three or four years for Menas Scriniarius in the 560s and fifteen, possibly up to nineteen, years for Strategios Paneuphemos, with other pagarchs continuously attested over six (Ioulianos) or five years (Ioannes and Serenos). This is a remarkable difference from known liturgical offices and would suggest a rather unbalanced distribution of the charge among a local aristocracy. By way of comparison, the office of the *defensor civitatis* alternated biannually between the city notables.[122] It is also curious that a *lamprotatos scriniarius* was able to hold the pagarchy apparently

121 *P.Mich.* XI 624.8–10 and 13–15, respectively. See also the anonymous pagarchs in *P.Cair.Masp.* I 67068.

122 Iust. *nov.* 15.6 (535 CE).

on his own while six years prior the same charge was borne by three *endoxotatoi*, among them the *endoxotatos apo eparchōn* Ioulianos, one of the most-distinguished personae in the region. What precise political or economic considerations determined the choice of one or several pagarchs remains therefore to be studied, and this will be pursued in the following chapter by tracking down the pagarchs' career patterns.

The involvement of women appears to be the clearest indication of the liturgical nature, but it seems difficult to make a classical liturgy out of the pagarchy. One may, then retreat to the vague notion that the pagarchy was "a function that had liturgical elements as well as characteristics of a state office,"[123] though in this case, especially with the absentee Apiones removed from the list of pagarchs proper and the notable imbalance in the distribution of the charge on various aristocrats, I opt rather for a state office with liturgical elements.

123 Mazza 1995, 196: "una funzione che aveva elementi liturgici e caratteristiche proprie delle cariche statali."

Chapter Five
Careers of a Service Aristocracy

Modern historiography has long seen the late antique aristocracy in Egypt as a socioeconomically dominant class oppressing the local peasantry and undermining the authority of the imperial government. Recent decades have seen a forceful insurgency against this model, and in the wake of this change of paradigm, some scholars have come to see the pagarchy as a public obligation that large landowners assumed. Yet the pagarchs to this day enjoy mostly a notorious reputation as the principal representatives of an insubordinate elite that assumed local dominance at the expense of the state. Both sides largely agree, however, that the pagarchs were essentially local magnate administrators focusing primarily on their local standing. This chapter will challenge that idea, not to dispense with it completely, but to add important nuances to the picture, especially in view of the results of Chapter Three that highlighted the formal administrative distinction between fiscal shares and the pagarchy proper.

The aforementioned typification of the pagarchs as local magnates trying to detach their local sphere of influence from the reach of the central government became particularly influential in the discussion of the extent of change and continuity in the early Islamic period. Here, the pagarchs frequently serve to illustrate an alleged major administrative development during the latter seventh century that had local estate-owning administrators turned into delocalized or, as it were, "supralocal" career bureaucrats. In this argument, the new Arab government saw its authority in the province threatened by the persistent disloyalty of the pagarchs vis-à-vis the central government, which was grounded in the pagarchs' focus on their local interest.[1] Consequently, starting in the late seventh century the new rulers are said to have increasingly replaced the Byzantine-Christian and estate-owning magnate pagarchs with a more bureaucratic Muslim elite whose power and influence did not rely on local landholding and to whom their tenures as pagarchs would have been but one further step in their career.[2] This interpretation of these "new" pagarchs has been summarized in the statement that "their loyalty lay with their Arab Muslim colleagues, not with a local agricultural estate."[3] Well-known representatives of this type of pagarchs are ʿAṭiyya b. Juʿayd and Nājid b. Muslim. The former, also known as Flavius Atias, son of Goedos, held the pagarchy of Arsinoe from 694 to 697 CE before being promoted to *dux* of Arcadia (and, at times,

1 For a discussion of this reasoning, see Papaconstantinou 2015.

2 The underlying general argument of a more "efficient" administration set in place by the new rulers goes way back to the earliest day of papyrology but was perhaps most prominently formulated by Harold I. Bell in *P.Lond.* IV, pp. xxiii, xxxv–xxxvii, and Grohmann 1964, 132–134. See Sarris 2006 for a Byzantine perspective of this argument, emphasizing the importance of agricultural production to these large landowners' autonomy in the preconquest period.

3 Sijpesteijn 2013, 210.

https://doi.org/10.1515/9783111493183-006

also of the Thebaid) until 703 or 712. The latter was pagarch of Herakleopolis at least from 728 to 729 and afterwards was appointed pagarch of Arsinoe for some time between 729 and late 743.[4]

In the course of this chapter I argue that the reality of the Byzantine pagarchy may not have been as straightforward as the distinction between old "magnate pagarchs" and new "bureaucrat pagarchs," though ideal-typical, makes it seem. Especially in terms of their connections and mobility, the traditional picture of the pagarchs as a coherent group of landowning aristocrats who were focused on their local powerbase requires some qualification. The pagarchy served different ends for different types of elites and thus emerges as a flexible instrument. I begin, in the first two sections, with some general observations about aristocratic hierarchy and how to classify it. Then, I establish the pagarchs' career patterns first for the Thebaid, and then for Arcadia, before comparing the two regions. Additionally, the Apiones and Flavia Anastasia are featured because of their position as magnates of *kōmai pagarchoumenai*, which permits a more comprehensive look at the composition of the elites in the late antique countryside in terms of fiscal authority. The distinction between "upper-tier" and "lower-tier" aristocrats in the present chapter is not meant to evoke two social classes but rather facilitates the conceptual argument being advanced. As such, it separates aristocrats with the rank of *endoxotatos* or higher from those ranking beneath.[5]

I. Aristocrats and Hierarchy

There is no agreed-upon definition of the social and political elites of the late antique Roman Empire, although several criteria have been proposed.[6] The term *aristocracy* often implies, in historical perspective, a link between status and heredity that was not as prominent in the late antique Roman world as in other periods and regions, and in no way was it prerequisite.[7] Scholars still widely use *aristocracy*, stressing its meritocratic aspect, and there can be little doubt that elites up to senatorial ranks were a meritoc-

4 On ʿAṭiyya/Atias and Nājid, see the references in Stern 2020, 34 n. 5. For Atias, add Morelli 2024, 172. For Nājid, add the new findings by Garel & Vanthieghem 2022, especially 88–89.

5 For instance, some "lower-tier" pagarchs such as Ioannes in Hermopolis (if his tenure still dates to the Byzantine period) were in some way close to Ioulianos in Antaiopolis, but not quite *endoxotatos*.

6 See, e.g., Börm 2010, 164, referring to Wickham 2005, 154 (parentheses in the original): "distinction of ancestry; landed wealth; position in an official hierarchy; imperial or royal favour (what the Germans call *Königsnähe*); recognition by other political leaders; and lifestyle," or, with different accentuation, Rebenich 2008, 154: "Herkunft aus einer bedeutenden Familie," "Bekleidung hoher prestigeträchtiger Ämter," "hinreichende materielle Ressourcen," "moralische Integrität," and "Bildung"; membership in the senate was complementary.

7 For a theoretical overview and a review of trends in this topic, see Beck et al. 2008b and more recently Fisher & van Wees 2015.

racy. This is not to say that heritage did not help in attaining certain ranks, but it was no guarantee. Status was primarily purchased by office, and office was purchased by effort—or protection. With this in mind, I shall use the term *aristocrat* generally in an absolute sense in regard to anyone bearing at least the epithet *lamprotatos*, the Roman clarissimate, which originally marked eligibility for the Roman senate.[8] In addition, all these men—and women—whom I discuss in regard to the Byzantine pagarchy are Flavii/Flaviae, marking their elevated status as part of the civil or military state apparatus.[9] By contrast, the term *elite* will be employed in a relative sense for village elites, imperial elites, and so forth without being too strict in this regard.[10]

Status in late antique papyri notably manifests in the various forms of address or reference to individuals, typically including the following elements: (1) (rank) epithets, that is, adjectival words marking an individual's social rank; (2) honorary titles, that is, nouns that refer to concrete honors or dignities that are officially bestowed upon a person but are not offices;[11] and (3) official titles, that is, a reference to an office that this person held. Consequently, I begin this chapter with a brief survey of various categories of aristocratic status in the sixth and early seventh centuries. This survey does not aim for completeness or absolute validity but rather wants to provide a guideline of the approximate ranking of the titles that will occur most frequently throughout this chapter.[12]

---

8 One may also call them *senatorial epithets*, although in the sixth and seventh centuries their holders were no longer entitled to actually attend senate meetings, which became a more exclusive right; see Begass 2018, 55–57 and Haldon 2005, 39–40.

9 Mazza 1995, 203 notes that Menas Scriniarius is never referred to as a Flavius, and indeed, the abbreviation of the word in *P.Lond.* V 1661.5–6 (Aphrodite; July 24, 553): Φλ(αουίῳ) Ἰουλιανῷ τῷ μεγαλοπρεπεστάτῳ ἀπὸ ἀρχόντων καὶ Μηνᾷ λαμπροτάτῳ | σκρινιαρίῳ καὶ παγάρχαις τῆς Ἀνταιοπολιτῶν does not contain the additional lambda (Φλλ$) that usually appears in the extant attestations for Φλ(αουίοις); this is a description of parties in a notarial contract and, consequently, the only reference where we would expect Menas's Flaviate to be mentioned; by contrast, the contract *P.Lond.* V 1714 contains only a patronymic reference to Menas. However, there are instances in which only Φλ$ is used to mark the plural Φλ(αουίοις): e.g., *SB* XXVIII 17188.4 (unknown origin; April 17, 370) and *P.Mich.* XI 613.4 (Herakleopolis; August 19, 415). Interestingly, the few attestations for Αὐρηλ(ίοις), all from the third or fourth century, all seem to use only one lambda. Ruffini's entry for Menas in *P.Lond.* V 1661 grants him the Flaviate; see Ruffini 2011, s.v. Menas 13 (c).

10 A person such as Dioskoros of Aphrodite would thus count as "village elite," but, in my system, not as aristocrat, even though he was a Flavius. For an overview of research traditions and terminologies concerning late antique Roman elites, and aristocracies in particular, see Rebenich 2008.

11 In this definition, *comes* and *patricius*, for instance, are titles. Honorifics such as *kyrios* or *despotēs*, however, are not, as these are polite addresses rather than titles. See also n. 49 below.

12 There are scores of minor epithets and titles that could be categorized in a similar way, but I will discuss these only when they are part of an argument. This concerns epithets that primarily appear to be linked to certain professional domains, e.g., *logiōtatos*, *theophylaktos*, *thaumasiōtatos*, or *aidēsimos*, or titles such as *scholastikos*.

In Imperial Rome, *clarissimus* (Gr. *lamprotatos*) had been the most distinguished aristocratic epithet marking a particular status.[13] It is not until the time of Constantine that it was joined by two additional and more distinguished ranks: *spectabilis* (Gr. *peribleptos*) and, as the highest, *illustris* (Gr. *illoustrios*). This development explains a peculiar ambiguity in the later use of *lamprotatos*, which denotes members of the third and lowest aristocratic "class," but may also refer to members of the aristocratic circle in general.[14] Finally, the epithet *magnificentissimus* (Gr. *megaloprepestatos*) apparently arose as an alternative attribute for men and women from the highest aristocratic circle, the *illoustrioi*.[15] The threefold structure (*lamprotatos*, *peribleptos*, *illoustrios*) opened more and more over time, as lower administrative duties or honors than before made individuals eligible for the epithet *lamprotatos*. In the fifth century, the status of *lamprotatos* was increasingly attributed to groups such as retired officials, and therefore, higher provincial officers such as the *praeses* or the *dux* tended to be immediately promoted to the rank of *peribleptos* or *megaloprepestatos*.[16] Hence, these epithets generally "descended" and new ones had to be found for the top of the pyramid.

In the sixth century, the hierarchy of rank epithets had developed to the point where the place above *megaloprepestatos* was now occupied by *endoxotatos* (Lat. *gloriosissimus*), and at the uppermost end of the spectrum we find new and even more distinctive epithets such as *paneuphēmos* (Lat. *famosissimus*), *hyperphyestatos* (Lat. *excellentissimus*),[17] and *eukleestatos* (Lat. *celeberrimus*?).[18] These three epithets usually designate the highest imperial officials or dignitaries, such as *consulares* or *patricii*. The term *illoustrios* retreated from this hierarchy, as it were, and transformed into an honorary title, which is discussed below, although one may encounter echoes of its former

13 For all the epithets cited in this section, see Koch 1903 and Hornickel 1930, s.vv. A systematic modern study that includes the vast material published in the meantime remains a desideratum. A more recent overview of some general developments is given by Haldon 2004, especially 184–192, although his account differs from mine in details, as I am focusing on the use of these epitets and titles in the papyri.

14 Hornickel 1930, 26; Koch 1903, 12–13. An illustrative example may be the dating formulae that include the consulate of Basileios, who is habitually styled *lamprotatos* but especially in the Aphrodite papyri bears the epithet *paneuphēmos* (see MacCoull 1993, 26), which is probably the widest span conceivable in late antique aristocratic hierarchy. Admittedly, this is not really "ambiguous" if one takes *lamprotatos* to refer to "any notable," while the other attributes would serve as complementary further distinctions. Moreover, in the case of the consular dating, tradition seems to play a role as well, as the earlier senators and consuls had been *lamprotatoi*; see Begass 2018, 42.

15 Cf. Begass 2018, 42–44.

16 Koch 1903, 18, 21, 25, and 56. This development is behind the idea that the Byzantine period witnessed an "inflation" of such ranks. One must acknowledge, however, that this "inflation" appears not to have been as chaotic as often stated but is rather retraceable, as outlined in this paragraph.

17 See also Begass 2012, but note that "Fl. Marianos" is better known as the *dux et Augustalis* Athanasios, on whom see Ruffini 2011, s.v. Athanasios 4.

18 Occasionally, aristocrats entitled to these three epithets were addressed simply as *endoxotēs*; see, for instance, *P.Oxy.* LXVII 4616.2 and 8; *P.Oxy.* I 133.4 and 8; and *P.Oxy.* I 128.5 and 14.

use as an epithet.[19] The aforementioned ambiguity of *lamprotatos* remained common in later times[20] and we should not be surprised to find someone styled *endoxotatos* and *lamprotatos* on different occasions in one and the same document, although in the papyri this phenomenon is rare. Finally, *megaloprepestatos* does no longer appear to designate a rank in the strict sense, but instead seems to be used as a general term to refer to individuals of higher standing.[21] As such, it frequently occurs in connection with *lamprotatos, peribleptos,* and *endoxotatos* or even replaces these epithets. It is, however, not attested with any of the three highest-ranking epithets *paneuphēmos*, *hyperphyestatos*, and *eukleestatos*. This observation is especially relevant for prosopographical questions, as some currently accepted relative datings of documents are based on the argument of a hierarchical progression from *megaloprepestatos* to *endoxotatos*. If, for instance, an aristocrat appears in one text as *megaloprepestatos* and in another as *endoxotatos*, the latter must be younger than the former. A handful of cases urge caution here. There are a number of instances of men being referred to as *megaloprepestatos* during a period in which they are clearly also referred to as *endoxotatos*. Among the pagarchs, these are Ioannes[22] and Ioulianos[23] of Antaiopolis as well as Kyrillos[24] and Theodorakios[25] of Arsinoe.[26] So, changes in addressing a person as either *megaloprepestatos* or *endoxotatos*

---

19 For instance, in the somewhat unusual word order τῷ (…) ἰλλο(υ)στρίῳ μεγ[αλ]οπρε(πεστάτῳ) Σερήνῳ in *P.Cair.Masp.* I 67002 col. II 2. On the combinations "*illoustrios* pagarch" and "*illoustrios* and pagarch," cf. n. 46 below.

20 Koch 1903, 21–22, 26, and *passim*, with examples.

21 Gonis 2009, 92 n. 11 and *CPR* XXIV, p. 66.

22 Ioannes appears repeatedly in the tax receipts of (at least) three codices from the Dioskoros archive (see Chapter Two, n. 3) whose writers and signatories I discuss in Stern forthcoming (a), from which catalog the following identifications are taken. Most writers of these receipts consistently refer to Ioannes as *endoxotatos*, not counting here anonymous collective references to οἱ ἐνδοξότατοι πάγαρχοι. These writers are Christodoros 1 (fourth indiction), Damianos (fifth indiction), Iosephis (fifth indiction), and Gennadios (seventh and eighth indictions). But Gennadios refers to Ioannes as *megaloprepestatos* in the fifth indiction, that is, when other writers instead use *endoxotatos*. This is also attested in an unpublished receipt (P.Strasb. gr. inv. 1622.4–6) from the seventh indiction by a writer whose name is lost (Anonymous 1), if this man is not identical with Gennadios.

23 See the Catalog, nn. 207 and 210.

24 On the verso of *P.Lond.* V 1786, Kyrillos, an *endoxotatos stratēlatēs* (see the address on the recto, ll. 3–4) is rendered as *megaloprepestatos stratēlatēs*—or simply, *megaloprepestatos*, since *stratēlatēs* is entirely in a lacuna: το (read τῷ) μεγαλο̣πρε̣[π(εστάτῳ) στρατ(ηλάτῃ)] Κ̣υ̣ρ̣ί̣λ̣λ̣ῳ̣. An image of this papyrus was put online only recently—recently enough that due to the repercussions of the cyber incident at the British Library it was no longer accessible when I tried to recheck it in order to estimate the length of that line. But the restoration of the *stratēlasia* here raises doubt, as this title is never borne in connection with *megaloprepestatos* alone. Assuming the editor was correct in his estimate of the available space, we should consider the reading μεγαλο̣πρε̣[πεστάτῳ] Κ̣υ̣ρ̣ί̣λ̣λ̣ῳ̣ or, following the idea that titles are combined with specific epithets (see n. 28 below), μεγαλο̣πρε̣[π(εστάτῳ) παγάρχ(ῳ)] Κ̣υ̣ρ̣ί̣λ̣λ̣ῳ̣.

25 See the Catalog, s.v.

26 See also the case of Count Ammonios in the Antaiopolite nome (Ruffini 2011, s.v. Ammonios 1),

in different texts need not represent an actual change in rank of that person, although this may have been the case.

This detail of documentary practice concerning the epithet *megaloprepestatos* links to the general feature of this rank system that we frequently find epithets of different value combined in the same reference.[27] Both observations underscore that we are not dealing with enclosed classes that would bear the names *endoxotatos* or *megaloprepestatos*. Rather, the use of these and other rank epithets can be shown to be context-sensitive.[28] It seems that certain offices or honors would increasingly be accompanied by a specific epithet.

To the rank epithets must be added numerous honorary titles, of which I mention those most relevant to the pagarchs. The *comes* title was an honor of three grades that was relatively widespread among the late Roman-Egyptian aristocracy, and it is normally not made explicit which grade is meant. Most Egyptian *comites* of the sixth or early seventh century bear the epithets of *peribleptos, megaloprepestatos* and *endoxotatos*, in which case it probably refers to the titles of *comes sacri consistorii* and *comes domesticorum*.[29] Some *comites*, however, rank as low as *lamprotatos*.[30] The title *illoustrios* had once been the highest-ranking epithet but turned into an honorary title attested for *megaloprepestatoi* and *endoxotatoi*, and in this use it appears to have been linked to certain offices.[31] The title of *stratēlatēs* originally served to designate the office of

---

where the changing use of these epithets is equally visible and does not seem to follow a chronological development.

27 To list only a few instances, in ascending hierarchy: *P.Lond.* V 1714.12 (Antinoopolis; 570): *peribleptos* and *lamprotatos*; *P.Lond.* V 1786.2–3 (Arsinoites; c. 610): *megaloprepestatos* and *endoxotatos*; *P.Oxy.* XVI 1984.2 (Oxyrhynchos; 523): *endoxotatos* and *hyperphyestatos*.

28 The petition *P.Cair.Masp.* I 67002 (Antinoopolis; May–July 567 CE) provides a striking illustration of that point. Note how meticulously its author Dioskoros of Aphrodite assigns to each title the appropriate epithet, first in the case of the *dux* Athanasios: τῷ [ἐνδ]οξοτά(τῳ) στρατηλάτῃ [ἀπὸ] ὑπάτων καὶ ὑπ(ερ)φ[υε]στά(τῳ) πατρικίῳ (in the *praefatio*), but also when referring to a certain Serenos, who is probably identical with the Antaiopolite pagarch: τῷ περιβλέπτῳ κόμε(τι) καὶ ἰλλο(υ)στρίῳ μεγ[αλ]οπρε(πεστάτῳ) Σερήνῳ τῷ λωγιωτ(άτῳ) (read λογιωτάτῳ, a professional epithet primarily used for nonaristocratic bureaucrats) σ̣χ̣\ο/λ̣(αστικῷ) (col. II 2); το(ῦ) ἐνδοξ(οτάτου) ἰλλ(ουστρίου) Σερήνο(υ) (col. II 4).

29 As revealed by a search in the *PN*. See also *P.Oxy.* LXIX, p. 213 and, more generally for the imperial perspective, the still useful collection of material in Scharf 1994 and, for the period from 457 to 518 CE, Begass 2018, 53–54.

30 This cannot be accounted for by the connotation of *lamprotatos* including *all* aristocrats, as the example of *SB* XVI 12673 verso (Arsinoites; mid-VI) makes clear, which reads λαμπρο[τ(άτῳ)] καὶ εὐδοκ(ιμωτάτῳ) κόμιτι. See also *P.Sorb.* II 69, p. 62.

31 Koch 1903, 44–45; Hornickel 1930, 17; Haldon 2004, 222–223; *P.Oxy.* LXIX, p. 213 (on the supposed link between the title of *illoustrios* and the pagarchy, see, however, the introduction to the Catalog). The *illoustrioi* may have formed a reservoir of "retired" (*apo*) provincial or imperial servants. Note how, for instance, the title of *illoustrios* interchanges with *apo archontōn* (or *apo eparchōn*) in the pagarch Ioulianos's titulature in contracts; see the discussion of his titles in the Catalog, s.v. Ioulianos (Antaiopolis).

the *magister militum* but at some point also became a mere honor.[32] It is found with aristocrats who held the rank of *endoxotatos* or higher.[33] Certainly an imperial honor, *hypatos* denotes the honorary consulate, which could be held continuously for several years.[34] Along with its derivate *apo hypatōn*, it was borne only by aristocrats with the rank of *endoxotatos* or higher.[35] Possibly the most elevated title open to a person outside the imperial family was *patricius*, granted exclusively to the highest-ranking aristocrats from the level of *hyperphyestatos*, *paneuphēmos*, and *eukleestatos*, and marking direct relations with the imperial administration or even the imperial family.[36]

---

32 Noteworthy instances that would appear to suggest an office proper include: a στρατηλάτης τῆς χώρας in *P.Cair.Masp.* I 67032.57 (Constantinople; July 11, 551), perhaps an actual *magister militum*, and the three στρατηλάται ταύτης τῆς Ἀρσινοιτῶν πόλεως in *SPP* III 344.1–2 (October 8/7, 643/658), *P.Ross.Georg.* III 53.6–7 (674/675), and *SPP* III² 72bis.3–5 (latter half of VII). On the date of *SPP* III 344 and my correction of ll. 1–2, see the Catalog, s.v. Menas Stratelates (Arsinoe), especially n. 71. Jairus Banaji's (2007, 140) suggestion that being *stratēlatēs* entitled to control *bucellarii* may be interesting in this regard (earlier still: Rémondon 1974b, 369, followed by Liebeschuetz 2001, 194–195), or the *stratēlasia* became indeed a real office after the Persian conquest or in the early Islamic age (though admittedly, the title becomes rare in the Islamic period). As to the Byzantine period, three arguments support the idea that *stratēlatēs* was an honorary title: (1) The title is attested for a woman, the *endoxotatē* Theophania (*CPR* X 127.4 and most probably also *SPP* VIII 1091.1), who would not have assumed a military office; she was the wife of a certain *endoxotatos* Strategios (*CPR* X 127.4–5), who cannot be identical with the pagarch Strategios Stratelates; see the Catalog, s.v. Strategios Stratelates (Arsinoe). (2) The title occasionally appears alongside the titles *prōteuōn* (*P.Oxy.* XXXVI 2779.3) and *geouchōn* (*P.Oxy.* LXX 4781.3), both of which are expected to be suppressed from titulatures in case an office proper is involved (see Chapter Three, Section III). (3) The title is suppressed from the titulature of Arsinoite aristocrats from the moment they become *hypatos*. This phenomenon can be seen in the case of the pagarchs Apion Stratelates and, with even two men at the same time, Christophoros and Strategios Stratelates; see the Catalog, s.vv.—Banaji 2007, 139 n. 37 cites *BGU* I 3 (Arsinoe; 605) as an example of a, supposedly, *stratēlatēs* of Arsinoe from the Byzantine period; the whole passage, naming the sender, reads (ll. 7–10): Αὐρήλιος Μηνᾶς υἱὸς Ἡλία ἐ[ν]οι|κιολ[ό]γος οὐσίας Θεοδοσακίου τοῦ ἐνδοξο|τάτου στρατηλάτου ἀπὸ τῆς Ἀρσινοιτῶν πό|λεως ἀπὸ ἀμφόδου Κατωτέρου, in which Arsinoe is clearly referring to the origin of Menas, not to that of Theodosakios. Furthermore, a person of the rank of *endoxotatos stratēlatēs* is generally not referred to by origin.

33 *P.Lond.* V 1786.30, concerning the pagarch Kyrillos, seems to be an exception, but in the same text this man is also addressed as *endoxotatos* (see l. 3) and the restoration of the *stratēlatēs* title in the lacuna of l. 30 should probably be deleted; see n. 24 above.

34 As in the case of Strategios Paneuphemos; see below. Aristocrats who were *consules ordinarii*, by contrast, would refer to this extended form—such as Apion II, who was ordinary consul in 539 CE (see Nikolaos Gonis in *P.Oxy.* LXX p. 93). On the ordinary consulate, see Begass 2018, 47–49.

35 Our sources possibly fall short of capturing every case, since at least the honorary consulate appears to have been held also by *megaloprepestatoi* and *lamprotatoi*; in the early 490s, a Flavius Klementinos is *megaloprepestatos comes* and *apo hypatōn* (*P.Oxy.* LXIII 4394; *SB* XXII 15580). The consul Basileios, who frequently occurs as *lamprotatos* in the dating formula, is in fact (also) *paneuphēmos*; see n. 14 above.

36 For the imperial perspective, see Begass 2018, 45–46.

Generally, attribution of a certain honorary or official title entailed the eligibility for a certain epithet, and certain titles follow a clear pattern of which epithets can be attributed to them.[37] While in the sixth century, we find pagarchs referenced by a lower-ranking *lamprotatos* epithet, pagarchs in the seventh century were entitled to the epithet, or chosen from the rank of, *megaloprepestatos*. It is only when we find them with more-distinguished honorary titles or offices (*stratēlatēs, illoustrios*, etc.) that they rank beyond that, as *endoxotatos* or higher.[38]

All this leads to the hierarchy as presented in Table 6, intended as a working hypothesis to facilitate orientation regarding the pagarchs' careers:[39]

Table 6: Approximate hierarchy of aristocratic rank epithets and honorary titles from c. 500 CE up to the Islamic conquest, in descending order, with *megaloprepestatos* being subject to the qualifying comments about its use given above.

Rank epithet in Greek	Rank epithet in Latin	Honorary titles
paneuphēmos *hyperphyestatos* *eukleestatos*	*famosissimus* *excellentissimus* *celeberrimus?*	*patricius*
endoxotatos	*gloriosissimus*	↑ *hypatos* ↑ *stratēlatēs*
megaloprepestatos	*magnificentissimus*	↑ *illoustrios*
peribleptos	*spectabilis*	
lamprotatos	*clarissimus*	↑ *comes*

37 See nn. 24 and 28 above.

38 No rule without exceptions; see, e.g., the "*endoxotatos* pagarch" Zacharias, mentioned in *P.Ross. Georg.* III 52.6 (Arsinoe; October 3, 674), a receipt in contract form (and thus expected to use the "extended form" of titulature, on which see the next section).

39 This hierarchy is based on the pairing of epithets with the same person in the same reference, usually connected by καί, for which I searched the *PN*. For instance, *peribleptos* joins *lamprotatos* and *megaloprepestatos* in documents, but not *endoxotatos* or higher epithets; *endoxotatos* joins *eukleestatos* and *megaloprepestatos*, but not *peribleptos*, and so forth. In this respect, *paneuphēmos, hyperphyestatos*, and *eukleestatos* appear to be comparable insofar as they are all frequently found alongside each other (see *P.Oxy.* LXIII 4396, where the titulature of Strategios II displays all three of them) and with *endoxotatos*, but not with epithets ranking lower than that. An exception is that *lamprotatos* rather frequently joins *megaloprepestatos*, for which the particular genesis of these two epithets may account. The arrows indicate that the honorary title could also be borne by higher ranks than the one indicated, though it would have often been suppressed once the aristocrat obtained a higher-ranking honor.

Women were in general entitled to the epithets and honorary titles of their spouses.[40] Scions generally inherited at least a general affiliation to the nobility, the status of *lamprotatos*.[41] The superlative epithets also transferred to "private" *oikoi* in the reduced forms of *lampros*, *megaloprepēs*, and *endoxos*.[42]

II. How to Address the Elite

There is a difference between the titles that the elite held and the titles by which they were referred to, as not every document lists all titles of a given individual. This becomes obvious when we follow an individual through several papyri, where we can distinguish an *extended* and a *short form* of address or reference. The extended form is used most notably to introduce parties in legal documents such as contracts, whereas the short form may occur in any other case. The extended form of reference aims for a comprehensive rendering of an individual's status and contains all major components of titulature: the status predicate of Flavius,[43] epithets (either the highest or, occasionally, the one corresponding to the title or office that follows), honorary titles (at least the highest),[44] and current offices (all locally relevant).[45] In this extended form of reference, honorary titles are connected to offices either asyndetically or via *kai* ("and").[46] By con-

40 Koch 1903, 23.

41 Koch 1903, 23; Gonis 2002a, 94. This is due to the aforementioned "ambiguous" character of *lamprotatos*. Children of *endoxotatoi* or higher appear, however, to have been entitled to the epithet *endoxotatos* (see, for instance, *P.Cair.Masp.* I 67003.11–12), but for the lower levels the pattern is not so clear.

42 Koch 1903, 36. By contrast, ecclesiastical and imperial *oikoi* go with the epithets *hagios* and *theios*, respectively; see Chapter One, Section I.

43 On Aurelius and Flavius as status designations, see Chapter One, n. 43.

44 In rare cases, we can see that an honorary title was omitted, as appears to be the case in *P.Cair. Masp.* I 67094 (Aphrodite; March 27–31, 553). In this deed of surety, the pagarch Ioulianos is addressed "only" as *megaloprepestatos* pagarch without either *apo archontōn* or *illoustrios*, titles that usually accompany him. Ioulianos may have been granted the title of *apo archontōn* later, but the first certainly dated document to give him the title, *P.Lond.* V 1661, dates only to about four months after *P.Cair.Masp.* I 67094. On the other hand, Ioulianos held the dignity of *illoustrios* by 550 CE at the latest; see *PSI* IV 283.

45 In case the aristocrat holds no locally relevant office, the participles *geouchōn* and *prōteuōn* may appear in this position; see Chapter Three, Section III. In some documents from Oxyrhynchos, Strategios II is addressed as *prōteuōn* of both Herakleopolis and Oxyrhynchos; see, for instance, *P.Oxy.* LXX 4785 (530 CE), but here the "additional" title in another nome is the same title Strategios held in the local area, and thus it becomes easily part of the same formula.

46 A search in the *PN* for the combination of the honorary titles discussed in Section I with the official title of pagarch reveals an intriguing tendency toward asyndetic connection until the 620s CE, while from the 640s, the connection with *kai* appears to have become standard. This tendency is especially pronounced in the description of the parties in contracts from the Fayum, and may not apply to other types of document that may occasionally use an extended reference

trast, the short form of reference primarily strives for unambiguity and is in most cases limited to one epithet and *either* a current office *or* an honorary title, depending on which is the most distinguished.[47] This means that the short form will not, for instance, be expected to display the title of pagarch if the same man was entitled to the dignity of *patricius*. The short form can be further restricted to a personal name plus *either* epithet *or* a current office *or* a dignity (again preferring the most distinctive of these) or even to the personal name only, the latter usually when an aristocrat himself sent notes to subordinates.[48] Polite addresses such as "lord" (*kyrios*) or "master" (*despotēs*) are complementary and can be used with the extended form and the short form as preferred, but they may as well be absent; the tendency to use them is more pronounced among authors who rank below or similar to the person who is addressed or referred to.[49] Two other components typically used to identify individuals are the patronymic—and sometimes, matronymic—and an indication of origin (that is, the fiscal *origo*), but these were, in general, not used when the person held the rank of *lamprotatos* or higher.[50]

In addressing or referring to someone, the use of either the extended or the short form generally depended on the type of document and the author's relationship to the other person.[51] In general, documents of legal value such as contracts employ the

to an aristocrat—for instance, in the docket addresses of letters such as *P.Louvre* III 236 (later VII; no *kai*) or the reference to honorary and official titles in tax receipts such as *SPP* III^2 58 (VII; with *kai*). But Arsinoite documents that use an extended form of reference and are not contracts are too scant to compare the pre-622 and the post-641 evidence in a meaningful manner regarding the presence of this *kai*. In the sixth-century Antaiopolite nome, this *kai* finds use in contracts (e.g., in *PSI* IV 283.5), which suggests that the Arsinoite pattern (if it is indeed one) was not valid everywhere. The participles *geouchōn* and *prōteuōn*, which are absent from post-conquest documents, are always asyndetically linked to preceding titles and always listed in last position. Judging from the online image, there is no room for either κ̣α̣ί̣ or (κ̣α̣ί̣) in the docket of the Herakleopolite letter *CPR* XXII 4.31 (mid-VII).

47 This is relevant for the purposes of dating, and is often overlooked. See, e.g., Banaji 2007, 139 n. 37 for the argument that documents that address Menas Stratelates only as *stratēlatēs* but not as *stratēlatēs* and pagarch "stem from a period in his career when he had not yet progressed to the pagarchy." Such reasoning ignores the significance of the documentary difference between extended and short form of reference. Menas could well have been pagarch also in those cases where he is referred to as *stratēlatēs* only in, for instance, an account or a business letter.

48 E.g., *P.Cair.Masp.* I 67060, authored by Menas Scriniarius and addressed to village headmen.

49 See Tost 2015, 248–249 on "Höflichkeitsbekundungen" and their distinctiveness in regard to rank epithets and official or honorary titles. For an interpretation of these addresses as a system of politeness, see Papathomas 2007, especially 504–506 on *kyrios* and *despotēs*.

50 There are exceptions, as for instance in *P.Lond.* V 1714, in which the origin is noted because it is different from the current area of activity; similar: *P.Ross.Georg.* III 32.2–3 (Arsinoe; 504).

51 The practice is neatly illustrated by the archive of Dioskoros, which yields an astounding variety within the papers of one single individual. The draft(s) of an imperial rescript, *P.Cair.Masp.* I 67024–25 (Aphrodite; c. 551), for instance, introduces, from the perspective of a court authority, the pagarch Ioulianos with the short form (new ed. Fournet 2018, A 31: Ἰουλιανὸν παγάρχην τῆς Ἀνταιοπολιτῶν; cf. *SB* VI 9102, which has the anonymous form), whereas Dioskoros's petition

extended form when someone is introduced, while subsequent mentions of the same individual stick to the short form.[52] Tax receipts are an exception: because the legal value concerns primarily, if not only, the mentioned party of the taxpayer, the issuing party may sometimes stick with the short form.[53] The short form is prevalent in documentation that served an internal use: accounts, lists, and registers or letters between officials or between people close to each other. Writers of internal official and private documents may under certain conditions still have wanted to apply the extended form in order to demonstrate respect and humility. Subordinate officials and estate administrators, for instance, strongly tended to use the extended form when addressing their masters. Finally, some writers employed an even more rudimentary type of reference, which is limited to the mention of the office only and therefore could be termed an "anonymous form." When used with lower-ranking individuals this presumably means in most cases that the personal name of the incumbent was not known; but in case of aristocrats such as the pagarchs this is at least notable and may be due to a somewhat bureaucratic perception of the pagarchy or to particular circumstances not apparent from the documents.[54]

On the other hand, the fact that someone is addressed as pagarch in a papyrus does not entail that this position is relevant to the content of the document: in the notarial contract *CPR* XIV 10, for instance, Apion Stratelates, even though he is addressed as

---

P.Cair.Masp. I 67002 against the pagarch Menas Scriniarius employs the extended form when Menas is introduced even though it is not a contract. Since Menas was of considerably lower rank than Ioulianos, this seems to highlight the primary importance of identifiability in contexts where the type of document did not necessitate the use of the extended form: Dioskoros was obviously aware of the differentiated use of extended and short references.

52 Cf. *CPR* XXIV, pp. 178–179 on this observation in the case of the pagarch Menas Stratelates. More recently, Sven Tost has conducted a study of a comparable issue for the *riparii*; see Tost 2012.

53 The taxpayer is the only one who would use these documents in case of a conflict, and identifying the formally issuing party (e.g., the pagarchs) by name and rank was not important to the taxpayer.

54 In *P.Cair.Masp.* I 67003, petitioners request the *dux et Augustalis* to give an order τῷ παγάρχῃ τῆς Ἀνταίο(υ) καὶ τῷ τοποτηρητῇ ταυτῆς (l. 25) to help them. The mention of the full official titles "pagarch of Antaiopolis" and "*topotērētēs* of the same (city)" suggests that the references are to the institutions and, therefore, to "whoever is in charge," possibly a reference to a new pagarch yet unknown to the locals. Comparably, many tax receipts mention the responsible pagarchs in anonymous fashion even in cases in which they were obviously known, as proven by the fact that the anonymous form occurs in the singular as well as in the plural. The reason for this seems to be a bureaucratic perception comparable to the one that is present in *P.Cair.Masp.* I 67003: these documents were only nominally issued by the pagarch and it is most likely that the actual incumbent never saw the majority of those receipts for single payments, which suggests that the writer simply referred to the responsible institution. Finally, also *SB* VI 9102 refers to the pagarch by office only, even though the nominally issuing imperial chancery must have known the incumbent's name from the petitioners; apparently, it is the institution that mattered here, or the chancery wanted to provide the incumbent (most likely Ioulianos) with the possibility to save face.

pagarch in this text, probably did not lease out his dye-house in this capacity; instead, he figures as pagarch because the address in this type of document demands the extended form.

III. Career Patterns in the Thebaid

Thanks to the documentary wealth of the papyrus archives from Aphrodite we know of more Byzantine pagarchs from the province of the Thebaid than from anywhere else, though some of them remain anonymous.[55] The papers of Dioskoros—a village official, notary, and intellectual—and his peers show how people on the ground perceived and were confronted with state power through the fiscal authority exercised by the pagarchs. The contrast with the province of Arcadia is striking: the evidence from the Thebaid shows a significantly more balanced distribution of higher- versus lower-ranking pagarchs, and it deals almost exclusively with the pagarchs' official business. The Thebaid thus supposedly reflects the day-to-day reality of the pagarchy to a greater extent than the papers from the Apiones archive or those from the Fayum do.

1. The Upper Tier

Ioulianos, Patrikia, Ioannes & Serenos, Kometes & Euthymios, Phoibammon(?)

Ioulianos is certainly the most illustrious player in our evidence for the pagarchs of Antaiopolis, owing on the one hand to his exalted position, and on the other to his frequent resurfacing over a vast time period. He bears the epithets *megaloprepestatos* and *endoxotatos* and the titles of *illoustrios*, *apo archontōn* (former, or honorary, *praeses*?), and *apo eparchōn* (former, or honorary, prefect?), and there is no evident development of his titulature in the documents we have. Ioulianos's base in the Aphrodite region was an estate (*ousia*) that contributed to the village tax.[56] According to Constantin Zuckerman, this *ousia* comprised approximately 60 percent of Aphrodite's taxable area and should be identified as the obscure *endoxos oikos* of Aphrodite.[57] But this certainly overstates the case, and the figures cited by Zuckerman for Ioulianos's *ousia* are, if

---

55 In this section, documentation is kept to a minimum to preserve the flow of the argument. For full documentation, the reader is directed to Table 4 (pp. 165–167) and the prosopographical notes pertaining to the individual pagarchs in the Catalog.

56 *P.Cair.Masp.* I 67060; Ioulianos's lands are also at issue in *PSI* IV 283. The first document relates to Ioulianos 1 in Ruffini 2011; the second to Ioulianos 2. As I discuss in the Catalog, s.v., these are probably one and the same person.

57 Zuckerman 2004a, 221, on the basis of *P.Aphrod.Reg.* and *P.Ross.Georg.* V 62, the latter misidentified as *P.Ross.Georg.* III 62; Palme 2007b, 335 apparently agrees. The *endoxos oikos* of Aphrodite is discussed in Chapter Six, Section I.

anything, more likely to reflect the fiscal share that he was responsible for[58]—some of which perhaps as pagarch. This means that Ioulianos's lands were more modest than Zuckerman assumes and rather comparable to that of Count Ammonios, Aphrodite's patron, an equally—if not better—suited candidate to have been in control of the *endoxos oikos* of Aphrodite.[59]

In any case, Ioulianos was certainly personally involved in the pagarchy, which he had held since some point in or not long before 547 CE.[60] For it was presumably in that year that Ioulianos got accused by the Aphroditan community of overstepping his authority by violating Aphrodite's *autopragia*, a case that the villagers pursued as far as the imperial court in Constantinople.[61] It has been speculated that the death of Aphrodite's patron Ammonios created a power vacuum that motivated Ioulianos to crack down on the village.[62] The numerous petitions and most imperial rescripts from that episode are, however, drafts by the accusing party, and all are rather vague about the exact occasions. In fact, Ioulianos does not appear to have taken much damage from this episode, and he continued to act as pagarch through at least 559/560 CE.[63]

It is remarkable that a man with such strong local standing and interests as Ioulianos was not a local and not even from the same province. This is revealed by three drafts of the same petition concerning his alleged misdeeds, in two of which Ioulianos goes by the nickname "the Arsinoite."[64] How this relates to his strong Antaiopolite presence is

58 See Bagnall 2008, 188–189 and Ruffini 2018a, 91–92, who highlight this possibility, but there should be little doubt about this.

59 Zuckerman's calculations imply that Ioulianos's *ousia* would not be appearing in the *kōmētika* calculations of *P.Aphrod.Reg.*; Zuckerman may have based this idea on the conception that the classification of a parcel as either *astika* or *kōmētika* depended on the status of its owners; see Chapter Two, Section III 1 for a discussion of this argument. *P.Cair.Masp.* I 67060, however, in which Ioulianos's *ousia* is explicitly mentioned as contributing to the *kōmētika* account, suggests the opposite. I would argue that Ioulianos is not expected to appear in the Aphrodite Register because he was presumably rather young by 526/527 CE, and perhaps still resided in Arsinoe (see below).

60 Personal involvement: *PSI* IV 283 (though based on the restoration of a lacuna in l. 9; see Chapter Two, n. 79); *P.Lond.* V 1660, where Ioulianos, unlike Patrikia, is addressed without a representative; *P.Lond.* V 1674, making the final decisions about tax rates, despite acting at that time apparently through a representative, the *procurator* Christodotos (cf. *SB* XVI 12370). The accusations by the Aphroditans likewise appear to indicate that he was involved in person. Start of the pagarchy: *P.Cair.Masp.* III 67283 (547 CE) implies that Ioulianos's pagarchy already started in a (lost) previous indiction, but that it cannot have been far from the composition of the text. A text relating to some fiscal authority with no explicit link to the pagarchy (but possibly connected to it) is *P.Cair.Masp.* III 67285, in which Ioulianos appears together with a certain Enoch; this text is signed by the *hypodektēs* Ioannes, who is attested from 537 to 551.

61 For a possibly earlier date of *P.Cair.Masp.* III 67283, see Chapter Four, n. 19.

62 Zuckerman 2004a, 222.

63 *SB* XVI 12370. He might have even been promoted to the rank of *endoxotatos stratēlatēs*, if he is identical with Ruffini's (2011) Ioulianos 4.

64 *P.Cair.Masp.* I 67024–25 (new ed. Fournet 2018) A 31: Ἰουλιανὸν παγάρχην τῆς Ἀνταιοπολιτῶν; A'

not clear. The titles *apo archontōn* and *apo eparchōn* indicate that Ioulianos may have served as *praeses* or as prefect (that is, praetorian prefect of the East?), but both titles may also have been of honorary or titular nature. Provided they were not, Ioulianos may have been granted landed estates at Antaiopolis as a reward for his service, which made him a candidate for the pagarchy.[65] We do not know how long Ioulianos stayed in office. He is no longer pagarch in *P.Lond.* V 1674 (c. 570), but it is unclear whether he was still alive at that point;[66] whether he pursued his career following his pagarchy is uncertain.[67] In any case, Ioulianos seems like an exemplary powerful outsider who took on the pagarchy after having retired from imperial service.

The remaining high-ranking pagarchs of Antaiopolis known by name are more elusive. We know that the *endoxotatē* **Patrikia** was not only "responsible for the pagarchy,"[68] but was indeed herself addressed as pagarch, once alongside Ioulianos, but once apparently even as the head of a collegium.[69] That the pagarch Menas Scriniarius is described as her *dioikētēs* possibly points to his function in her estate administration.[70] In any case, there should be no doubt that Patrikia acceded to the pagarchy through her possession of landholdings, or rather, the economic potential arising from it.

Ioannes's pagarchy is mainly known from the collection of Antaiopolite tax receipts in which he is addressed either as *megaloprepestatos* and *endoxotatos* pagarch, or as *endoxotatos* (or *megaloprepestatos*) "pagarch of the two-thirds share of Antaiopolis,"

55–56: Ἰουλιανὸν τὸν ἐπίκλην Ἀρσενοΐτην | καὶ παγάρχην τῆς Ἀνταιοπολ(ιτῶν), and B 29: Ἰουλιανόν, τὸν ἐπίκλην Ἀρσενοΐτην, παγάρχην | τῆς Ἀνταιοπολιτῶν.

65 See Banaji 2007, 101–170, pointedly, e.g., at 128, for the portrait of an aristocracy that achieved dominant local standings due to earlier imperial service. On imperial grants to favorites, see Johnson & West 1949, 22–23 and Banaji 2000, 96. See, e.g., Justinian's *Pragmatic Sanction* from August 13, 554, in which the emperor confirmed that he has bestowed parts of a large estate in Italy on the former praetorian prefect Liberios; see *Prag.Sanct.* 1 and, on Liberios's career, O'Donnell 1981.

66 Because Dioskoros at other times shows himself very meticulous about whether someone was in office or not at a given point of a narration, Bell's restitution of the pagarchy in ll. 37–38: Ἰουλιανο(ῦ) τοῦ [ἀπ]ὸ ἐπάρχων̣ | κ̣α̣ὶ̣ [παγάρχου? seems unlikely. Banaji 2007, 162 n. 168 suspects [ἀπ]ὸ ἐπάρχων̣ κ̣α̣ὶ̣ [ἀρχόντων, which is somewhat odd because of the accumulated titles of honor; cf. the Catalog, n. 214. Presumably, the titulature was already complete in the short form and the sentence continued after κ̣α̣ί̣. For the possibility that Ioulianos might have been dead at that point, see the Catalog, n. 222.

67 The observation that Ioulianos "got away with it" would be even more pronounced if he was identical to the *paneuphēmos stratēlatēs* who represents the *dux* in *P.Cair.Masp.* I 67008, which would suggest a promotion and relocation to Antinoopolis in the 560s.

68 This or similar wording is usually employed to refer to the formalities of *munera patrimonii*, especially when women, who were supposedly not able to exercise the function in person, are referred to (see, e.g., the evidence on the *logisteia* in relation to the Apion household referred to on pp. 174 and 176 above.).

69 *P.Lond.* V 1660.5–7 and *Vat.Aphrod.* 16A.2: [– – – ο]ἱ ἐνδοξότατοι πάγαρχοι Πατρ[ικία καί – – –]. On this passage and Patrikia's pagarchy, see the Catalog, n. 251 and Chapter Four, n. 73.

70 On Menas's position, see Chapter Four, Section III.

in two instances of which the title of *comes* is added.[71] There is no apparent pattern in the use of these epithets or titles that would suggest a career sequence: the different titulatures occur for the same indictions and the variation is therefore likely due to the writers' customs. Some potential prosopographical matches could make Ioannes's background comparable to that of Ioulianos (or Menas Scriniarius, in the other direction), but they are rather speculative and therefore discussed in the Catalog. Ioannes was certainly pagarch with **Serenos** from at least 570/571, yet it is unknown for how long they remained in office. Serenos, for his part, is addressed as *illoustrios* only,[72] as *endoxotatos illoustrios*, as *illoustrios* and pagarch, as *endoxotatos* pagarch, as *endoxotatos illoustrios* and pagarch, and as *endoxotatos illoustrios* and "pagarch of the one-third share (of Antaiopolis)." It seems likely that he is identical with the *peribleptos comes* and *illoustrios megaloprepestatos* Serenos, a *logiōtatos scholastikos* and *endoxotatos illoustrios* who was active in the Hermopolite nome,[73] which, like in Ioulianos's case, adds a "supralocal" element. Possible, albeit uncertain, prosopographical matches may point to an integration into the provincial administrative apparatus.

Not much can be said about **Kometes** and **Euthymios,** apart from their being *endoxotatoi* pagarchs jointly with Ioulianos in 559/560. Also elusive is **Phoibammon**, who appears, in only one text, as "head (*epikeimenos*) of the pagarchy," though his lineage appears to point to someone integrated into the provincial aristocracy.

2. *The Lower Tier*

Menas Scriniarius, Kollouthos Cancellarius, Kollouthos Exceptor, Dorotheos, Athanasios, Kallinikos(?), Theodoros, (at least) four anonymous pagarchs, Makarios(?)

The Dioskoros archive features, in addition, a type of pagarch strikingly different from the *endoxotatoi* mentioned above, and the most famous—or rather, notorious—of them is no doubt **Menas Scriniarius**. A *lamprotatos scriniarius*, Menas was on the one hand a local *geouchōn* from Antaiopolis and on the other a career official who rose to provincial ranks in the ducal bureau of the Thebaid in Antinoopolis. In a contract from 553 CE, he is addressed as pagarch alongside Ioulianos.[74] Around the same time, Menas is referred to as Ioulianos's co-pagarch in a document in which he acts as a proxy of, or stand-in for, the *endoxotatē* Patrikia as "her *dioikētēs*."[75] Probably as early as that

71 The reference to Ioannes as *illoustrios* in *P.Cair.Masp.* III 67325 fol. VIII verso 24 is to be rejected; see n. 198 below.

72 *P.Cair.Masp.* III 67325 fol. III recto 7, but even here the pagarchy is implied by the preceding phrase, which refers to the "one-third share."

73 *P.Cair.Masp.* I 67002 col. II 2–4.

74 *P.Lond.* V 1661.5–6 (Aphrodite; July 24, 553): Φλ(αουίῳ) Ἰουλιανῷ τῷ μεγαλοπρεπεστάτῳ ἀπὸ ἀρχόν̣τ̣ω̣ν̣ καὶ Μηνᾷ λαμπροτάτῳ | σκρ̣ινιαρίῳ καὶ παγάρχαις τῆ̣ς Ἀνταιοπολιτῶ̣ν̣; cf. n. 9 above.

75 *P.Lond.* V 1660.5–8 (Antaiopolites; c. 553): τῶν μ]ε[γ]α̣λ̣οπρ̣επεσ̣τάτων κοινῶν | δεσποτῶν παγάρ-

period we see Menas personally involved in the pagarchy, caring for the proper delivery of tax payments and for the proper registration of land.[76] He then took on the pagarchy again in 566 CE with the inception of the indiction year, and it is this tenure during which Dioskoros's petitions famously paint Menas as a ruthless marauder.[77] As in the case of Ioulianos, however, it is notable that Menas's alleged misconduct apparently did little to reduce his standing: by the time of *P.Lond.* V 1677 (c. 568–570 CE) Menas was still pagarch, and in *P.Lond.* V 1714 (March 14, 570 CE), he is still a man of respected standing and authority.[78] Even more so, Menas is not only called a *lamprotatos scriniarius* in this text—this time attached to the ducal office of the Thebaid[79]—but he additionally bears the more elevated epithet *peribleptos*. It therefore appears that Menas actually even *rose* in status after the events Dioskoros describes so painstakingly in drastic terms. Menas's son Theodoros followed the family pattern of working for the ducal office and became *exceptor* there,[80] but it is unclear whether Menas was the first to pave the way for his son.

How are we to explain Menas's career, especially considering that he is described as *scriniarius* and pagarch at the same time and that he furthermore was a *dioikētēs* of the *endoxotatē* Patrikia? The title of *dioikētēs* is usually taken to indicate that Menas served in Patrikia's estate administration, and in this capacity performed the duties of the pagarchy for Patrikia.[81] Two hypotheses suggest themselves here: The first has Menas as

χων Ἰουλιανο(ῦ) τοῦ μεγαλοπρεστάτου (read μεγαλοπρεπεστάτου) ἀπὸ ἀ̣ρ̣χ̣[όν]τ̣[ων] | καὶ τῆς ἐνδοξοτάτης Πατρικίας δ(ιὰ) τοῦ λαμπρο(τάτου) κυρίου Μηνᾶ αὐτῆς διοικητοῦ καὶ | παγάρχ(ου). See Chapter Four, Section III on the topic of "stand-ins" in this case.

76 Delivery of tax payments: *P.Cair.Masp.* I 67060. Registration of land: *SB* XX 14241. It seems more likely that these and some other letters date to Menas's pagarchy in the 550s instead of that in the 560s. On this issue, see the Catalog, s.v.

77 See *P.Cair.Masp.* I 67002 col. I 10–11: ἀπὸ προοιμίων τῆς ἔναγχος διαδραμο(ύ)σης πεντεκαιδεκάτης ἐπινεμήσεως, ἀφ' ἧς ἀντελάβετο τῆς παγαρχίας | Ἀνταίο(υ). The text does not state that this was Menas's first pagarchy, but only refers to an incipient mandate.

78 It is difficult to tell whether Menas was still pagarch at the time of *P.Lond.* V 1714. On the one hand, the document is from Antinoopolis and therefore one would not expect the Antaiopolite pagarchy to be mentioned here; the dossier of Ioannes and Serenos, moreover, does not reveal whether they were in office already in the third indiction (furthermore, it may still be possible that Menas acted as their representative). On the other hand, if Menas was at that time *scriniarius* in the ducal bureau, he cannot be expected to have run the Antaiopolite pagarchy in person, which he surely does at the least during the events of *P.Cair.Masp.* I 67002, which took place in 566 CE.

79 This does not preclude that Menas was previously involved in provincial administration, given his profession as *scriniarius*. The new rank epithet makes a promotion more likely, however. It is not without irony, but probably also part of an aristocratic pattern that Menas got promoted to a post in the bureau of the *dux* after the villagers of Aphrodite had petitioned an earlier *dux* to help them out against Menas. See Chapter Six, Section V.

80 On the *exceptores* in provincial offices, see Teitler 1985, 73–81.

81 It is possible, however, that Menas was pagarch in his own right *in addition* to his functioning as a stand-in for Patrikia; see Chapter Four, Section III.

a *scriniarius* by profession and a *dioikētēs* on Patrikia's estates. In this capacity—and since he was a trained bureaucrat—he assumed the pagarchy for Patrikia in the early 550s. He then filled this post again in his late-560s pagarchy until becoming a *scriniarius* in the ducal bureau at some point between 568 and early 570. The second possibility is that Menas was already *scriniarius* of the ducal bureau when he took on the Antaiopolite pagarchy for Patrikia; in this sense, his position as *dioikētēs* would either have been a legal construction or refer to an older meaning of *dioikeō* for someone acting as a replacement.[82]

So either Menas came from Patrikia's estate administration and later rose to provincial honors by serving as "her" pagarch, or he was a genuine part of the provincial administration and assumed the pagarchy for a nome in which he controlled land, just like Ioulianos, though probably on a smaller scale. Chronological considerations appear to support the latter interpretation: Menas's son Theodoros would presumably be granted access to the provincial bureau because of his father's career, and Menas therefore probably should be assumed to have been ducal *scriniarius* for some time before 570 CE. Previous considerations would, however, favor the first possibility, for it seems clear that Menas as pagarch resided in Antaiopolis, not in Antinoopolis where the ducal bureau was situated.[83] It may thus be that Menas was indeed promoted to the post of ducal *scriniarius* two or three years after becoming pagarch in 566 CE.[84] What both interpretations have in common, however, is that Menas's way to the pagarchy in Antaiopolis appears to have been linked to his capacities and position as *scriniarius*.

The pagarch **Kollouthos Cancellarius** was a type of mobile career bureaucrat quite comparable to Menas. A *lamprotatos* only, Kollouthos held the position of *cancellarius* in the ducal office of the Thebaid in Antinoopolis.[85] He was a *comes* and pagarch, an Antinoopolite city councilor, and part of a family that produced several influential men at the provincial level:[86] two of his brothers were among the high-ranking staff in the ducal bureau of the Thebaid (at least) under the *dux* Athanasios, and Dioskoros praises Kollouthos and his father Apa Dios in a way highly suggestive of municipal and/or provincial officeholding.[87] Although his precise origin cannot be determined,[88] this suggests that Kollouthos's "home base" was Antinoopolis. At the same time, he

82 See Chapter Four, Section III.

83 *P.Cair.Masp.* I 67002 col. II 1–7, where prisoners are transferred from Antinoopolis to Antaiopolis and Menas explicitly receives them only when they have arrived in the latter city.

84 Menas is *lamprotatos* and *peribleptos* in *P.Lond.* V 1714, but earlier only *lamprotatos*, which would suggest a promotion coming with the office of ducal *scriniarius*, i.e., that he became part of the ducal bureau only after his tenure as pagarch.

85 Potentially, he was also *exceptor* and *scriniarius* during his career; see the Catalog, s.v., for the relevant prosopographical matches.

86 *P.Aphrod.Lit.* IV 14.

87 See Ruffini 2011, s.vv. Kallinikos 17, Dorotheos 12, and Apa Dios 1. For details of Dioskoros's praise of Kollouthos, see the Catalog, s.v.

88 Fournet 1999, 327 suspects that he originated from the Thebaid.

held strong ties to the village of Aphrodite that were presumably grounded in landed estates.[89] Dioskoros's papyri seem to suggest that Kollouthos's pagarchy was that of Antaiopolis, but this is never made explicit: he is said to "come to us" (to the village of Aphrodite, that is), and Dioskoros refers to Kollouthos's "unjust predecessors," by which he may imply the pagarchy, given the villagers' conflict with the pagarch Menas.[90] Given other instances in which Dioskoros may be found to stretch the truth a little, we may grant him a certain amount of literary freedom also in this case.[91] In another papyrus, an Aphroditan woman refers to Kollouthos as "my master," and cites his order to free her from prison.[92] It is unknown for how long he held the pagarchy, or whether he was acting in this capacity on behalf of some higher-ranking aristocrat. It is also unclear whether Kollouthos Cancellarius is identical with the Antinoopolite pagarch **Kollouthos Exceptor**: the personal name is very common, but with the official positions of *cancellarius* and *exceptor*, we are in quite similar territory, although nothing more is known about the latter man. In conclusion, there is indeed the real possibility that Kollouthos Cancellarius—whether identical with Kollouthos Exceptor or not—was not pagarch of Antaiopolis.[93]

In Hermopolis, the *lamprotatos comes* and pagarch **Dorotheos** belongs to the same stratum and, although the prosopographical matches here are not beyond doubt, he can be seen actively engaged in the performance of the pagarchy.[94] The late pagarch **Athanasios** lacks any epithet or title but is instead referred to as "former pagarch," which may indicate a comparatively low rank, but the text offers no clue about his career.[95] Apparently, his heirs had assumed certain "shares," but are these linked to the pagarchy? The pagarch **Kallinikos**[96] equally bears no epithet alongside his title of pagarch, but the relevant papyrus is damaged here and may have originally contained some allusion to a rank. Kallinikos cannot be located based on the document in which he appears, but some probable prosopographical matches suggest that he was a *lamprotatos comes* in Hermopolis who was actively performing his pagarchy. The Hermopolite pagarch **Theodoros**, referenced as "lord" (*kyrios*) only, may fit in this group, although

89 There are possible identifications with homonymous bureaucrats who held estates in Antaiopolis, Antinoopolis, and Lykopolis, but these are uncertain, as the personal name is common; see the Catalog, s.v.

90 *P.Aphrod.Lit.* IV 14.

91 See especially Chapter Six, Sections II and III.

92 *P.Cair.Masp.* I 67005.19.

93 From Table 4 (pp. 165–167) it would appear that he cannot have had much time as pagarch of Antaiopolis. However, we do not know for certain in what capacity Kollouthos was sent to Aphrodite—it may be possible to think of him as a stand-in or as *topotērētēs* (cf. *P.Cair.Masp.* I 67003.26).

94 See *BGU* XII 2196 (VI), a tax receipt issued to a village *boēthos* for aggregated tax payments, which Dorotheos signs in person; see Chapter Two, n. 116. Cf. *BGU* XIX 2772 (V–VI), where possibly the same Dorotheos issues an order to *eirēnarchai*.

95 *SPP* III 436 (VI–VII).

96 Listed in the Catalog in the category "Unknown Province."

the fragmentary text that mentions him yields little information on his standing; he at least seems to personally take care of an issue involving tax payments at the level of an individual village.[97]

The **anonymous** *lamprotatoi* pagarchs from *P.Cair.Masp.* I 67068—their number is not stated—may have been pagarchs in Antinoopolis, Antaiopolis, or Hermopolis. In the latter two cases, their presence in Antinoopolis, presumably for accounting or general reporting to the provincial authorities, would mark their personal involvement. But even if they were pagarchs of Antinoopolis, their active performance of the pagarchy is still suggested by the fact that Dioskoros is said to be about to meet up with them in some matter.[98] No epithets or titles are extant in case of the anonymous pagarchs in both *P.Lond.* V 1865 (Hermopolis)[99] and *O.Sarga* 107 (Apollonopolis Heptakomias or Antaiopolis; but perhaps from the early Islamic period); one admittedly vague reasoning may be that this lack is to be attributed to a rather low rank. The same could be argued for **Makarios**, if he actually was a pagarch,[100] but again, this argument is, on its own, far from compelling.

IV. Career Patterns in Arcadia

The division between the upper and the lower tiers is more refined in Arcadia.[101] Here, we see certain individuals holding the pagarchy—and authority over "pagarched" villages—who clearly exceeded even the exalted rank of the *endoxotatos* Antaiopolite pagarch Ioulianos, oftentimes through their proximity to the imperial center. I therefore distinguish the Arcadian upper tier further into an *imperial elite* and a *regional elite*, although we shall see that the boundaries between these groups were permeable, too. The *megaloprepestatoi* pagarchs Ioulianos from Oxyrhynchos and Theodorakios from Arsinoe are omitted here because they fit into a later pattern.[102]

97 *P.Sorb.Copt.* 30 (VI–early VII).

98 *P.Cair.Masp.* I 67068.9–10: ὑ̣μῶν κατε̣ρχο̣μένων | ἐπὶ τὴν Ἀντινοέων πρὸς τοὺς λα̣μπρ̣[οτάτου]ς ἡ̣μῶν δεσ[πό]τας παγάρχους; the addressee is Dioskoros.

99 New ed. Gascou & Gonis 2022, no. 5.

100 *P.Cair.Masp.* I 67055 col. II 9–10: ὑπὲρ μερίδ(ος) τοῦ̣ [– – –] | Μακαρίου παγάρχ(ου?) κ̣[– – –]. See the discussion in the Catalog, s.v.

101 As in the preceding section, documentation is kept to a minimum to preserve the flow of the argument. For full documentation, the reader is directed to Table 5 (pp. 169–171) and the prosopographical notes pertaining to the individual pagarchs in the Catalog.

102 Ioulianos: *PSI* I 52 (647 CE; see Chapter Three, Section VI for a discussion of the date); Theodorakios: *W.Chr.* 8 (639/640).

1. Imperial and Regional Elites in the Oxyrhynchite
(Strategios II, Apion II, Apion III, Anastasia,) Ptolemaios & Ioustos

The Oxyrhynchite evidence tells us only little about the Byzantine pagarchy proper, but most documents concern the "pagarched" villages (*kōmai pagarchoumenai*) discussed in Chapter Three. The evidence is dominated by the archive of the Flavii Apiones, a family of extraordinary status and responsibilities in Middle Egypt and elsewhere. Due to the abundant material, the family history of the Apiones has been illuminated like few others in the late Roman Empire.[103] Consequently, and because the chronology and prosopography of the Apiones is the subject of ongoing debate due to the continuous publication of new material, I shall not go into much detail here but will instead limit the survey to the points that are important for the argument. Despite the changing paradigm that in recent decades has laid emphasis on the cooperative side of late antique aristocrats, some historical accounts still feature the Apiones as prime examples of insubordinate late antique magnates who infiltrated the provinces and assumed control of local power sources at the expense of the state.[104]

The Apiones so far have furnished three instances of magnates in control of *kōmai pagarchoumenai* in the Oxyrhynchite: Strategios II, Apion II, and Apion III. **Strategios II** comes into the light of history in 489 CE as *lamprotatos* curial and landowner in Oxyrhynchos.[105] At that time, he acted through an intermediary named Theodoros, probably owing to his minority. Theodoros identifies as *hypokatastatos* (or *hypokatastatēs*), which he also does in an instance from 493 in which a "pagarched" village under Strategios appears for the first time, with Strategios being a *lamprotatos* and *aidēsimos politeuomenos* and *geouchōn*.[106] In a third instance, however, Theodoros identifies as *hypokatastatos* and *diadochos*, the latter title being linked by Strategios's appearance as a *riparius* of Oxyrhynchos.[107] Strategios had become "independent" by 497, at which point he bore the epithets *megaloprepestatos* and *endoxotatos* and the title of *comes devotissimorum domesticorum* and is attested as having held the *riparia*, probably that of Herakleopolis.[108] In 492 or 507 he was *comes sacrarum largitionum* for the Egyptian diocese, before being appointed Augustalian prefect of Egypt between 518 and 524, around which time he appears to have become entitled to be *endoxotatos* and *hyper-*

103 For the relevant literature, see the Introduction, n. 47.
104 On this discussion, see Chapter One, Section I.
105 *P.Flor.* III 325.
106 *P.Oxy.* LXXXII 5337.
107 *P.Oxy.* LXVII 4614 (date lost); for the relation of the *diadochos* position to a liturgy, cf. Chapter Four, Section III.
108 Much of the following account of the Apiones' careers follows Hickey 2012, 8–18 (see also Mazza 2013) but pays special attention both to their appearances in relation to "pagarched" villages and to the "Menas formula," neither of which is a subject of Hickey's survey. Especially the recent *P.Oxy.* LXXXII and LXXXIV have added important new material unavailable to Hickey at the time.

phyestatos stratēlatēs and honorary consul (*apo hypatōn*).[109] Strategios obtained the title of *patricius* at some point between 528 and 530, and a little later, probably shortly after 532, he became *comes sacrarum largitionum* of the East. He died probably within the first two months of 542.

Entrusted by Justinian with multiple important missions,[110] Strategios was one of the top elites of the late Roman Empire, part of the imperial circle, and largely absent from Egypt since the 530s. This seems to be supported by the use of the so-called Menas formula, which refers to an apparently institutionalized representation in every legal document involving Strategios from 523 onward:[111]

> To Flavius Strategios, the *endoxotatos* and *hyperphyestatos stratēlatēs*, *eukleestatos patricius*, (and) *prōteuōn* in Herakleopolis as well as in this renowned city of Oxyrhynchos, through Menas, *oiketēs*, who also puts the formal question and supplies for his own master, the same *paneuphēmos* man, the conduct (of) and responsibility (for the transaction).[112]

The prevalence of the formula suggests that Strategios was no longer based in Oxyrhynchos after 523, supposedly because of his holding important offices in Alexandria.[113] The formula should, however, rather be termed "*oiketēs* formula," since it also occurs with *oiketai* other than Menas, notably in a case involving Strategios in 493.[114]

109 In *P.Oxy.* LXIII 4396 (February 18, 542), Strategios is addressed as *paneuphēmos*, *hyperphyestatos*, and *eukleestatos* in the same document. *P.Oxy.* LXX 4785.6–9 (October 19, 530), quoted below, even adds *endoxotatos* to this accumulation of rank epithets.

110 Begass 2018, 348–349.

111 *P.Oxy.* LXXXII, p. 165; the earliest instance, though fragmentary, is *P.Oxy.* XVI 1984 (October 28, 523). Its meaning is discussed by Ruffini 2008a, 51 n. 52 and Sarris 2006, 161 and n. 44. The latter argues that this formula may have been a fiction in the sense that there was not really an *oiketēs* called Menas, given that the Menas formula is attested with the Apiones for close to a century. The parallel evidence for *oiketai* other than Menas and for large landowners other than the Apiones, however, (see n. 114 below) probably suggests that we are indeed dealing with a real *oiketēs*, or most likely, multiple real *oiketai* named Menas. On the meaning of *oiketēs* ("slave," "servant") in late antique Egypt, cf. Berkes 2017a, 89 n. 15, but in the present context, it may also denote a socially or administratively subordinate rank in a more general sense, rather than being the title of a managerial or administrative post.

112 *P.Oxy.* LXX 4785.6–9 (October 19, 530): διὰ Μηνᾶ οἰκέτου τοῦ καὶ | υπερωτοντος (read ἐπερωτῶντος) καὶ προσπορίζοντος τῷ ἰδίῳ δεσπότῃ | τῷ αὐτῷ πανευφήμῳ ἀνδρεὶ (read ἀνδρὶ) τὴν ἀγωγὴν καὶ | ἐνοχήν.

113 Does the formula provide an indication that Strategios assumed the title of *comes largitionum* of the Egyptian diocese only in 522 and that he was appointed Augustalian prefect a little later, with 524 being the *terminus ante quem* here? On these potential dates, see Hickey 2012, 12 and nn. 72 and 73.

114 For some *oiketai* other than Menas who appear as intermediaries of the Apiones in the Oxyrhynchite, see *P.Oxy.* LXIII 4390.4–5 (469 CE; to Flavia Isis, daughter and heiress of Strategios I) and *P.Oxy.* LXXXII 5337.5–6 (493; to Strategios II), perhaps also *P.Oxy.* LXXXII 5332.4–6 (480; perhaps to Apion I, but the name is lost). Notable texts from other nomes are *CPR* XXIV 25.7–9 (Herakleopolis; 598), where a *meizoteros* is the intermediary of a Strategios (perhaps Strategios

This means that both of Strategios's attestations as *geouchōn* of a "pagarched" village fall into a period during which he was either a minor or absent, but this does not seem to be significant for his formal authority over these villages.[115]

Strategios's son **Apion II** reaped the fruits of his father's apogee, illustrating the family's continuing close ties to the emperor by being granted the extraordinary title of *consul ordinarius* as early as 539, at which point he was a mere ten to twenty-one years of age. He is attested in the rank of *paneuphēmos* by 550, as *patricius* by 565, and, though only in posthumous texts, as *protopatricius*, an exclusive title reserved for the leading authority in the senate, certainly implying proximity to the capital. There is no evidence that Apion ever held any office in Egypt or elsewhere; he was known to be dead on November 5, 578.[116] The *oiketēs* formula is attested for Apion throughout his life, which appears to confirm the impression that he was usually not dwelling in Egypt. He turns up as *geouchōn* with responsibility for "pagarched" villages in the 550s, 560s, and 570s.[117]

Apion II's adopted son **Apion III** became head of an Oxyrhynchite estate before March 27, 593, but his activities are not as well documented as those of his predecessors.[118] He regularly bears the epithets *paneuphēmos* and *hyperphyestatos* as well as the titles of *consularis* (*apo hypatōn*) and, after 604/605, of *patricius*. He died around the end of 619; since this date is close to the Sasanian invasion of Egypt it has been suggested that Apion's death may be linked to this event. There is, however, no evidence that he dwelled in Egypt at that time, but quite the contrary: as in the case of Apion II, the legal documents addressed to Apion III deploy the *oiketēs* formula throughout

Paneuphemos, who is discussed below), and *P.Stras.* IV 229.4–6 (Panopolites; 502), where a *singularis* of the *dux* and his intermediary, a "slave" (*pais*), occur (the latter potentially rather being a "servant"). The term "*oiketēs* formula" is also employed by Nikolaos Gonis in *P.Oxy.* LXXXII, p. 165. One may speculate whether the Aurelius Menas, son of Theodoros, who signs in the name of illiterates in four documents from the Apiones archive (see *P.Oxy.* LXXXIII, p. 113) may be identical to this Menas, because one generation earlier, the *oiketēs* formula shows a certain Theodoros in the place of Menas (see, e.g., *P.Oxy.* LXXXII 5337).

115 *P.Oxy.* LXXXII 5337 (June 10, 493) and *P.Oxy.* LXX 4785 (October 19, 530); see Chapter Three, Section III, where this argument is discussed.

116 See now *P.Oxy.* LXXXIII 5380.

117 Cf. Table 3 (p. 127).

118 *P.Oxy.* LXXXIII 5392 (see the discussion by Nikolaos Gonis in the introduction) now shows that Apion III and his brother Georgios were legally "children and heirs" of Apion II. Technically, though, they were two generations younger, as their mother Praiiekte (Lat. Praeiecta) was either the daughter (or daughter-in-law and adopted daughter) of Apion II; on Praiiekte, see also the Catalog, s.v. Strategios Paneuphemos (Arsinoe).

his life.[119] His estate is attested as an economic and administrative actor even after his death, as late as 626 CE.[120]

The *endoxotatē* and *megaloprepestatē illoustria* **Anastasia** certainly played in a lower league than the Apiones, although she as well may with good reason be considered a part of the top aristocracy.[121] Her father was the *endoxotatos illoustrios* Menas, son of Eudaimon, who was in some way linked to the Apion estate.[122] In her papers, she is regularly represented by one of her *dioikētai* and in one instance a village is described as being "pagarched" by her.[123]

Only Ptolemaios and Ioustos can with some confidence be said to have been entrusted with the pagarchy of Oxyrhynchos, although both are not explicitly mentioned as pagarchs. Not much is known about **Ptolemaios** apart from his being *endoxotatos* and that his heirs paid for the pagarchy in a list of public contributions, implying that Ptolemaios was already deceased at that time.[124] The same document also features the *endoxotatos* **Ioustos**, who was, however, alive and paid the same amount for the pagarchy as Ptolemaios's heirs. This man, known to have been a *comes*, was probably Anastasia's uncle.[125] Ioustos also maintained some obscure business or administrative relationship with the Apion estate,[126] although he was in control of an *oikos* of his own.[127] Ptolemaios and Ioustos, though of very elevated standing, certainly did not play in the same socioeconomic league as the Apiones either.

---

119 Apion III is sometimes suspected to be the Apion who is *dux et Augustalis* of the Thebaid in *P.Oxy.* I 130, but this text is undated; for the identification, see Hickey 2012, 16 n. 96 with references. Apion's *hyperphyestatos* son Strategios at the end of this text would in this case be Strategios IV.

120 The administrative structure of the Apion estate proper (that is, without the *kōmai pagarchoumenai*; see Chapter Three, Section IV) appears to be still in place in *P.Oxy.* LXVIII 4704 (August 29–September 27, 626). For its administrative function at this time, see *P.Oxy.* LVIII 3959 (January 12, 620). This deed of surety is addressed to the late Apion III and it involves a village that is, notably, *not* described as *pagarchoumenē*; this may simply be due to the fact that the original formula, styled on a person, would have been odd in this case and was therefore simply suppressed; see Chapter Three, n. 149.

121 Banaji 2007, 150 suggests a promotion from *megaloprepestatē* to *endoxotatē*, but one must exercise caution when using these two epithets as the only arguments for an advancement in rank; see Section I above.

122 See the Catalog, s.v. The Apiones and Anastasia (Oxyrhynchos).

123 *P.Oxy.* XLIV 3204 (January 2, 588).

124 *P.Oxy.* XVI 2040; discussed in detail in Chapter Three, Section II.

125 See Gonis 2002a, 95–96.

126 *P.Oxy.* XVIII 2195.98 and 102 (c. 562/563?), where he receives payments for waterwheels, which is to be accounted for one of the Apiones' *pronoētai*.

127 *P.Oxy.* LVIII 3938 (March 7, 601; posthumous).

2. *Imperial and Regional Elites in the Fayum*

Strategios Paneuphemos, Apion Stratelates, Christophoros & Strategios Stratelates, Kyrillos, Menas Stratelates

The internal division within the upper tier that is notable in Oxyrhynchos can be observed in the Fayum as well, and the Arsinoite equivalent of the Oxyrhynchite Apiones is certainly **Strategios Paneuphemos**.[128] He enters the scene already in possession of the highest honors the empire had to offer, regularly bearing the epithets *paneuphēmos*, *hyperphyestatos*, and (though considerably less often) *eukleestatos*, the highest distinctions imaginable, with no immediately apparent pattern in usage.[129] The documents up to 602/603 CE address him as *hypatos*, while from at least 604 onward he is addressed as *patricius*, which by itself suggests proximity to the imperial circles. He is known to have been in control of an *oikos* in the Arsinoite nome,[130] and is generally thought to have owned *oikoi* also in the Herakleopolite and the Oxyrhynchite nomes.[131] Recently, some papyri have surfaced that indicate that Strategios Paneuphemos may have been the son of the *patricia* Sophia, a well-known landed magnate in the Arsinoite nome.[132] Like

128 On Strategios and his archive, see van Loon 2017, 128–129 with further references; *P.Eirene* IV, pp. 207–208; and *P.Messeri*, pp. 252–253. The nickname "Paneuphemos" came into use in scholarly literature to distinguish him from Strategios IV, the son of Apion III. In some older studies, he is to the same end called Pseudo-Strategios III, because Strategios IV was at that time (i.e., before the Strategios now known as Strategios I surfaced) known as Strategios III.

129 But cf. Chapter Four, n. 42.

130 *CPR* XXIV 26.4 (602/603 CE); *SPP* VIII 1072.2 (c. 610 CE); *SPP* X 1 (posthumous), a γ]νῶ(σις) συνηθειῶ(ν) διδομ(ένων) εἰς τὸν οἶκο(ν) τοῦ ἐν ἁγί(οις) | Στρατηγίου (ll. 1–2). Another postmortem reference is *CPR* XXIV 33.6 (653 CE), restored virtually in its entirety and *exempli gratia*.

131 **Herakleopolites:** *P.Erl.* 73.9–12 (604 CE), where a Belisarios, *trapezitēs* ("banker") of the *endoxos oikos* of a *paneuphēmos patricius* Strategios is mentioned, who also appears (without the *oikos*) in *P.Vars.* 31.1 (609), *SPP* III^2 66.3 (early VII), and *CPR* XXIV 29.1 (c. 616; Belisarios was dead at that time), thus maybe extending the evidence for the Herakleopolite *oikos* a little further. **Oxyrhynchites:** *P.Oxy.* LVIII 3935 (591); three other texts have him as *geouchōn* (always καὶ ἐνταῦθα) in Oxyrhynchos without explicitly mentioning his *oikos*: *P.Oxy.* LVIII 3936.6–9 (598); *SB* XXII 15487.9–13 (598); *P.Oxy.* XVI 1991.7–10 (601). See now also *P.Oxy.* LXXXIII 5398.2–5 (598) for a *mikra ousia* of Strategios at Oxyrhynchos and in general Nikolaos Gonis's short review of Strategios's Oxyrhynchite dossier in *P.Oxy.* LXXXIII, p. 192. Some recent research has become more cautious in identifying these Strategioi as the same person; see *P.Eirene* IV, pp. 207–208 and *P.Messeri*, pp. 252–253. Yet, the extraordinarily high rank of these men gives pause and suggests that these Strategioi are indeed the same person. The problem is getting more complex because of the intricate genealogy of the Apiones, to whom Strategios in some way seems to have been related.

132 These texts will be published in a forthcoming article by Fritz Mitthof, whom I owe thanks for providing me with an earlier version of the manuscript. Further research will show whether this hypothesis will stand, but it is indeed possible that the Arsinoite elites were more closely related than has been assumed. Sophia, whom Mitthof suggests to be the mother of Strategios Paneuphemos, might have also been the mother of the *endoxotatos stratēlatēs* Theodosios, who,

the Apiones, and along with other Arsinoite magnates, Strategios appears to have been responsible for fiscal shares.[133] Unlike the Apiones, however, Strategios bore the title of pagarch, and he does so continuously from 600 to 614 or 615 CE in all documents where it would be expected, which suggests that his pagarchy throughout this period was continuous, and potentially even longer.[134]

Likewise in contrast to the Apiones, Strategios appears to have conducted business in the Fayum on his own,[135] and appears to have been—or was supposed to be—the locally present champion of imperial power. In 617 CE, he was involved, apparently on imperial request, in the reconciliation between the Alexandrian and Antiochean churches at Alexandria, which makes him one of the few individuals known from the papyri who made it to nonpapyrological sources.[136] The date of this meeting falls to a period after February 616, when Menas Stratelates is first attested as pagarch of the Fayum. The clear separation of the documents into texts that attest Strategios as pagarch before that date, and those that attest Menas Stratelates as pagarch afterward, probably means that Menas was Strategios's successor, further attesting to Strategios's personal care for the pagarchy. He is commonly known to have been alive until at least 619,[137] which makes one speculate whether his death was linked to the Persian invasion. Because, however, the pagarch Kyrillos was alive as late as 618, *SPP* VIII 1228, in which Strategios and Kyrillos's heirs surface, must date to 623/624, thus attesting Strategios Paneuphemos even later, alive under the Persian occupation.[138] This point is of great interest since it would

---

like his mother, held a fiscal share in the Fayum; see Gonis 2008, 204–205. The pagarch Kyrillos (see below) also appears in some elusive connection to Strategios's *oikos* (*SPP* VIII 1072, though maybe not as pagarch). Cf. *SPP* X 249, in which these three men all appear jointly, sharing (along with the heirs of a certain Eustochios) an amount to be paid. I am indebted to Sophie Kovarik for discussing these possible links with me, based on her knowledge of unpublished papyri.

133 See *SPP* X 249 and its discussion in Chapter Three, Section VII.

134 On the chronology, see Table 5 (pp. 169–171).

135 This impression cannot be only an illusion due to different notarial practice in the Arsinoite documents, as Mazza 2011, 276–277 hypothesizes (though not specifically in regard to Strategios). In Strategios's case it is even explicit since he is said to have gone *from Arsinoe* to Alexandria in order to mediate in a church council in 617 CE (see below). The *oiketēs* formula is attested for him only once, namely in *CPR* XXIV 25.7–9 (Herakleopolis; 598), provided that this Strategios is indeed Strategios Paneuphemos; this makes sense if he resided in the Fayum. See now also *P.Oxy.* LXXXIII 5399.1–2 (Oxyrhynchos; September 28–October 27, 612), showing that Strategios Paneuphemos was (at that moment) present in the Arsinoite nome.

136 On the event and our main source (Michael the Syrian), see van Loon 2017, 128–129 and Allen 2013, 197–198, with particular attention to the date at 197 n. 44. Strategios's participation suggests that he was himself a miaphysite, in contrast to the imperial Chalcedonian orthodoxy (which also the Oxyrhynchite Apiones adhered to).

137 P.Vindob. G 50349, which is currently being prepared for publication by Sophie Kovarik; see van Loon 2017, 129 n. 10.

138 *SPP* VIII 1228.7: [– – –] Φλ(άουιος) Στρατήγιος (καὶ) οἱ κληρ(ονόμοι) Κ\υ/ρίλλ[ου – – –]. The text mentions an eleventh indiction in l. 3; Kyrillos is alive in *BGU* III 725 (July 21, 618); see van Loon 2017, 129–130.

attest a *patricius*, that is, a person of presumably close proximity to the emperor, as a man of continued position and authority under the Persian invaders.[139] Is this the reason Strategios is only called "Flavius Strategios" in this document and does not bear any of his usual epithets or titles of imperial rank? Also the *patricius* title seems to have been suppressed from his titulature from this period onward, certainly for the obvious close connection to the emperor that this title implied.[140] However, Strategios's estates were visibly not confiscated after the Byzantine reconquest of 629.[141]

The aforementioned **Kyrillos** was a pagarch from a lower, though still rather exalted, aristocratic level than Strategios Paneuphemos, which in the Arsinoite included the pagarchs Apion Stratelates, Christophoros & Strategios Stratelates, Kyrillos, and Menas Stratelates. All of these were *endoxotatoi stratēlatai* at one point in their career.[142] Like Strategios Paneuphemos, three of them can be found to have been granted promotions during their tenures as pagarchs, assuming these tenures were continuous: **Apion Stratelates** started out as *endoxotatos stratēlatēs* but between 556 and 577 appears to have been promoted to *paneuphēmos apo hypatōn*.[143] **Christophoros** and **Strategios Stratelates** also began as *endoxotatoi stratēlatai* but are later seen as *eukleestatoi hypatoi*, still jointly addressed as pagarchs. This permeability between "imperial" and "regional" elites encapsulates that what I call the *upper tier* is a rather coherent stratum when compared to the *lower tier*, which will be further discussed later.

The only pagarch from among these *endoxotatoi stratēlatai* about whom we can gather more detailed information is **Menas Stratelates**.[144] He was a landowner[145] and pagarch at least from 615/616 to 622/623. The documents, in so far as their state of preservation allows for such statements, are mostly linked to private business, includ-

139 Even though the exact content of *SPP* VIII 1228 is obscure, it certainly relates to fiscal matters. It seems to be a tax receipt, but coeval Arsinoite parallels are virtually nonexistent for this type of document. It seems unlikely that *SPP* VIII 1228 (623/624 CE) can be linked to a pagarchy that Strategios and the "heirs of Kyrillos" held at that time. Rather, this document appears to be relating to the fiscal shares of the Arsinoite; it would be unprecedented to see a collective anonymous reference to heirs for only one part of a pagarchic collective when the other part is referred to by name. The Antaiopolite pattern suggests that either all pagarchs were addressed anonymously and collectively, or each is explicitly named; see Chapter Two, Section III 3.

140 Strategios (if this is really Strategios Paneuphemos; see the Catalog, s.v.) is referred to without his *patricius* title in a (posthumous) document from 653 CE, in the early Islamic period (*CPR* XXIV 33), which suggests that he no longer held this title in his latest stages of life, and *SPP* VIII 1228 possibly indicated that he already lost his patriciate (or that writers tend to suppress it) under the Persian regime. But cf. Morelli 2010, 153–154 on the use of the title of *patricius* by Arab elites.

141 An estate, managed by an *antigeouchos*, still bears Strategios's name in *CPR* XXIV 33.5–6 (see the previous note). The estate is mentioned in a lacuna, but should more likely be restored as *ousia* or *oikos* without an epithet; for a discussion, see Chapter Three, n. 243.

142 Strategios Paneuphemos was probably a "hidden" *stratēlatēs*; see the Catalog, s.v.

143 See Table 5 (pp. 169–171).

144 Van Loon 2017, 128 with further references.

145 *SPP* III^2 153 (629 or 644 CE) and *SPP* III 344 (643 or 658 CE; posthumous reference). Both texts refer to an *ousia*, not an *oikos*.

ing some cases that may relate to official activity. In one instance, Menas issues an order that seems to concern a gift for a special day or a festival; the same text contains an obscure reference to a "lamp lighter" (*phanaptēs*) and a (military) *excubitor*.[146] Another text deals with a grain payment to "Theodoros, *hypodektēs* of the *ousia* of Menas, the *endoxotatos stratēlatēs*," which was possibly related to the grain tax.[147] A third document mentions an agent of Menas to whom the collection of apparently official fiscal dues—payments for a stone building and grain contributions—was entrusted.[148] This agent works in connection with a *hypodektēs* and asks Menas to provide *bucellarii* so that he would be able to collect the due amounts.[149]

It is notable that Menas, as one the highest-ranking local elites, is attested in office under Roman *and* the Persian rule. Does this mean that he consciously gambled on cooperating with the invaders? There has been some speculation that Menas may have been subsequently punished for this collaboration after the Byzantine reconquest of 629 CE.[150] But if this were the case, it would be remarkable to find Menas's *ousia* prevailing under his name, including his title of *stratēlatēs*, until even after the Islamic conquest, which makes a loss of status during the Byzantine reconquest somewhat unlikely.[151] We may therefore assume that Menas's conduct was not considered unusual or extraordinary, or was at least deemed excusable.[152] Menas provided administrative

---

146 *SPP* VIII 1048.3 (620 or 635 CE): ἐν τῇ τῶν σίτων ἑορτῖ and l. 2: (καὶ) τοῦ φανάπτ\ου/ (καὶ) τοῦ ἐξσκο[υβίτορος (read ἐξκουβίτορος).

147 *SPP* III² 153.1–2 (629 or 644 CE).

148 *P.Münch.* III 130 (Arsinoites; first half of VII). The payment for the building that is behind l. 4: ἀ]ν̣οικοδομηθ( ) appears to be extraordinary due to the building's previous destruction (ll. 6–8; see *BL* IX 173 and the editor's commentary), while the grain payments are linked to a *katabolē* (ll. 19–20), one of the three regular tax installments. The sender's title is a clearly readable χ*ʃ* on the verso, which the editor expands to χ(ειριστοῦ).

149 *Hypodektēs*: l. 21. *Bucellarii*: l. 11. Cf. the mentions of a *hypodektēs* and a *bucellarius* of Menas's *ousia* in *SPP* III² 153 and *SPP* III 344, respectively, on which see n. 151 below. In addition, ἀπαιτέω (ll. 12, 17, and 32) is obvious official fiscal terminology. Menas is mentioned as deceased in *SPP* III 344, which suggests that we are dealing with the responsibilities for the fiscal shares here; yet, it is unclear how long Menas had been dead by the time that papyrus was written, so perhaps these are still pagarchic responsibilities.

150 *CPR* XXIV, p. 180. On the connected hypothesis on the same page, "daß [on this occasion] für die wieder getrennten Pagarchien Arsinoites und Theodosiupolites neue Pagarchen ernannt wurden," see the Introduction, n. 50.

151 See, again, *SPP* III 344.1–2 (October 8, 643 or October 7, 658): βουκελλάριος οὐσίας τοῦ ἐν ἁγίοις Μηνᾶ γενωμένου (read γενομένου) στ̣ρ[ατηλάτου ταύτης] | τῆς Ἀρσινοιτῶν πόλεως. See also *SPP* III² 153.1–2 (April 11, 629 or 644): [ὑ]π̣οδέκτ(ης) οὐσί(ας) Μηνᾶ τοῦ [ἐν]δ̣ο̣ξ̣(ο)τ̣(άτου) | στρ̣[ατ]η-λ̣ά̣του̣. Menas is reported dead in the former but apparently alive in the latter text. The expression "*stratelates* of the/this city" in the former is a rare particularity of the Islamic period; see n. 32 above. On these texts and their chronology, see also the discussion in the Catalog, s.v. Menas Stratelates (Arsinoe).

152 Compare, for instance, the case of Manṣūr b. Sarjūn, grandfather of John of Damascus, who in 635 CE supposedly opened the city gates of Damascus to the Arab invaders; see Griffith 2016, 29–30.

continuity to the invaders, which the (new) Byzantine authorities may have considered to be a different quality than actively sabotaging Byzantine defensive operations.

3. The Lower Tier

Antiochos & Theon, Theodoros (Oxyrhynchos), Theodoros (Arsinoe)(?)

On the lower level, evidence from Arcadia is scarce. The pagarchs **Antiochos** and **Theon** were most likely *lamprotatoi* or, at most, *peribleptoi*, and although we cannot pin down the precise nome for which they were responsible, their responsibility fell within the province of Arcadia.[153] The relevant text shows both pagarchs in close exchange with the praesidial bureau of Arcadia, where they are said to have submitted a fiscal report (*anaphora*) to the author of the text, which he then passed on. Furthermore, the pagarchs were to provide donkeys for a transport.

The Oxyrhynchite pagarch **Theodoros** is a *megaloprepestatos* and this epithet makes it indeed hard to decide whether he actually is to be added to the group of lower-tier pagarchs or whether he might be a "hidden" *endoxotatos*.[154] The idea that he is the same man as the homonymous *meizoteros* from the Apion estate is based on the combination of the title of *comes* with the personal name, which is common, and should be rejected.[155] The address using only the epithet *megaloprepestatos* is shared by some of the pagarchs known from around the end of the Roman reign in Egypt.[156] In the only extant text, Theodoros, through a *phylax*, sends for a horse from one of the Apiones' *chartoularioi*, but it is unclear whether this relates to official business. On the one hand, the *chartoularios* appears to be assuming Theodoros's familiarity with internal matters of the Apion estate; on the other hand, he appears to shield the estate administration against potential reproaches from Theodoros, and there is a certain distance in the tone. In short, it remains possible that Theodoros assumed the pagarchy for his masters, the Apiones, who would then have held the pagarchy next to their responsibility for fiscal shares[157]—but the evidence is not particularly suggestive of this possibility and I opt for rejecting it.

---

153 *P.Mich.* XI 624 (Arcadia; mid-V–early VI). The early date makes a comparison of the epithets difficult, as the aristocratic hierarchy I described in Section I was built from the sixth- and early seventh-century evidence.

154 *P.Oxy.* XVI 1858 (Oxyrhynchos; early VII). On the epithet *megaloprepestatos* and its occasional use as sole epithet for individuals who were from the rank of *endoxotatos*, see Section I above.

155 See the Catalog, s.v.

156 Notably, this concerns the Oxyrhynchite pagarch Ioulianos (*PSI* I 52) and the Arsinoite pagarch Theodorakios (*W.Chr.* 8.)

157 Cf., again, *P.Oxy.* XVI 2040 where it is made explicit that Ptolemaios and Ioustos (or their heirs) held fiscal shares *and* responsibility for the pagarchy; cf. also the discussion on Strategios Paneuphemos above.

The dating of the Arsinoite pagarch **Theodoros** to the Byzantine period is based on an uncertain attribution of the relevant document to the archive of the *oikonomos* Ioustos.[158] The reference to him as "my pagarch" might indicate a lower standing, but is too vague to take this as a given.

V. Patterns of the Pagarchy

All known pagarchs have one thing in common: they were notables drawn from those ranks that had originally marked membership in the senate. It is the spectrum, however, that is striking here: while some pagarchs apparently did not exceed the rank of *lamprotatos*, many others did, and indeed all "senatorial" epithets can be found among the pagarchs, reaching as far as *paneuphēmos* and *hyperphyestatos*. It follows that a certain status was not by itself a prerequisite for holding the pagarchy, but it is more difficult to determine whether the reverse was true. It seems that in the sixth century, holding the pagarchy did not entitle the incumbent to a particular epithet, but a problem is that we cannot trace any *lamprotatos* pagarch back to the time before he assumed the pagarchy. Since the 630s, pagarchs appear to have been entitled to the epithet *megaloprepestatos* or were recruited from among holders of this rank or higher. Pagarchs generally bore the name predicate of Flavius, which was restricted to higher civic and imperial officials and dignitaries or to the military, whereas the *praepositi pagorum* had regularly been Aurelii. The survey in the preceding sections suggests, however, that two groups can be distinguished: a group of "upper-tier" pagarchs who came into this position while already in possession of significant political and socioeconomic power, and another group of "lower-tier" pagarchs who took up the pagarchy after having held decidedly lower administrative posts.

1. Imperial and Regional Elites

Within the first group of upper-tier pagarchs one can further distinguish two subgroups: a "supraregional" imperial elite whose horizon reached as far as Constantinople through close ties to the imperial administration or even to the imperial family,[159] and a regional elite who lacked visible links to the imperial level or to other dioceses or provinces. The Oxyrhynchite Apiones and Strategios Paneuphemos in Arsinoe certainly number among examples of the "imperial elite," exalted through the epithets *hyperphyestatos*, *paneuphēmos*, and *eukleestatos*, but more decisively through the title

158 Kovarik 2007, 153.

159 The term *supralocal elites* is employed by Slootjes 2011 (in the context of the imperial period) in order to describe elites who were usually active beyond what Slootjes considers their local power-base: e.g., Roman senators or equestrians with landholdings in a distant province.

of *patricius*. The Oxyrhynchite Apiones were, for the most part, absentee landowners active in Eastern and Constantinopolitan politics who would, however, still have borne responsibility at the local level through their authority over villages that were being "pagarched" by their *oikos*, whereas Strategios Paneuphemos, while maintaining close ties to the emperor, was clearly present in the Fayum acting as Heraclius's—and, presumably, Phocas's—local right-hand man and being personally involved in the pagarchy, probably in addition to his own fiscal shares.

Further down the social hierarchy, both the Thebaid and Arcadia furnish more numerous examples of regional elites with the standing of *endoxotatos*, but the line between imperial and regional elites was permeable, as is obvious in the cases of some pagarchs on their way to the imperial level. In the Fayum, Apion Stratelates went from *endoxotatos stratēlatēs* to *paneuphēmos apo hypatōn* and Christophoros and Strategios Stratelates rose from *endoxotatoi stratēlatai* to *eukleestatoi hypatoi*.[160] In Antaiopolis, Ioulianos's title of *apo eparchōn* may hint at an earlier career at the prefectural level, that is, the level immediately subaltern to the imperial sphere, although this title may be dismissed as a simple honor that does not necessarily imply that Ioulianos ever was actually prefect.[161] Ioulianos's exalted standing would, however, be a convincing explanation for why he held the Antaiopolite pagarchy for more than a decade, in which he rivals imperial elites like Strategios Paneuphemos.

Regarding the issue of imperial versus regional horizon, there is not much evidence about how the achievement of imperial titles changed the ways of any of these up-and-coming imperial elites. The case of Menas Stratelates brings an interesting nuance to this issue, for he continued to hold the pagarchy under the Persians but received no apparent blowback to his standing after the Byzantine reconquest. This may suggest that Menas was more focused on his regional standing, which would by itself seem natural for an aristocrat of local means without any immediate links to the imperial level. But it may also be that this is significant not so much for Menas's attitude as it is for how the pagarchy was perceived. The apparently easy transition to a new regime and the absence of a Byzantine reaction to such conduct may, then, emphasize the *local* significance of the pagarchy and its deep integration into the local administrative network. It may have simply not occurred to Menas that he should have refrained from continuing

160 Note that in all three cases, their later epithets (*paneuphēmos* and *eukleestatos*, respectively) are the same as in the case of the *patricii*, but the three did not, so far as we can see, achieve this last breakthrough to the title of *patricius*. They were thus, formally, on the same level as Apion III and Strategios Paneuphemos before each of these two was granted, under Phocas, the patriciate. See also the *endoxotatoi* heirs of a *hyperphyestatos patricius* in *SB* XVIII 13952, suggesting that it was due to their heritage that at least some *endoxotatoi* had a favorable starting position for a run to the level of imperial elites; *patricius* is restored, but convincingly so, by Gonis 2008, 203.

161 The term *apo eparchōn* can be interpreted in different ways, and perhaps it links Ioulianos to the provincial, rather than the prefectural level; see the Catalog, s.v. Note additionally the possibility that Ioulianos may be identical with the Ioulianos in *P.Cair.Masp.* I 67008, a *paneuphēmos stratēlatēs*, which would imply a promotion.

to act as pagarch, and "passive continuation" was apparently nothing for which the Byzantine central administration later would reprimand him.[162]

Next to Menas, there are other pagarchs who remained in office after regime changes, such as Theodorakios, who did so after the Islamic conquest.[163] We do not have unambiguous evidence for how an imperial aristocrat like Strategios Paneuphemos would have acted in the face of a looming foreign invasion, but we have seen above that there is indeed good reason to believe that Strategios in fact not only survived the Persian conquest, but even stayed in Egypt in a position of fiscal responsibility, presumably for the fiscal shares of his *oikos*.[164] We may recall that even before the Persian conquest Strategios Paneuphemos had lived to see two regime changes: from Maurice to Phocas and from Phocas to Heraclius, the second of which had led to bloody clashes even in Egypt itself.[165] Neither of these incidents did anything to damage Strategios's standing; in fact, Phocas even made him a *patricius* shortly after his accession.[166] In Constantinople, surviving a regime change was a more delicate matter for favorites of the overthrown regime.[167] An apparent paradox results: on the one hand there is the drive of these men to the imperial level, on the other the peaceful transition of the pagarchy and other local power positions from one regime to another. Can we style Strategios Paneuphemos as representative of an elite that was courted by the emperors in the interest of maintaining a firm grip in the province but that fell short of providing loyalty once their local power base was at stake? In this picture, elite politics emerges as a dry calculation and weighing of economic profits—for both sides. Notable promotions, certainly not without imperial consent, occurred at times when these elites were holding the pagarchy,[168] suggesting that they were useful enough in the eyes of the central government and that their officeholding at least served to foster their standing. Perhaps their personal loyalty was not the primary factor that made Menas and Strategios important to the regime; instead, they first and foremost had to "function," and the transition between different powers may therefore have been part of the game. These apparently seamless and quiet transitions of pagarchs to new regimes may not be

162 See Section IV 2 above.

163 Cf. *W.Chr.* 8 (639/640) and *CPR* XXIV 32 (May 4, 651).

164 Cf. also *P.Prag.* I 64 (May 28, 636). The *dux* here is Theodosios, perhaps the son of the *patricia* Sophia. If he can be identified as the brother of Strategios Paneuphemos (see n. 132 above), this would suggest that Strategios's family had not fallen out of imperial favor.

165 On the chronology of the transition from Phocas to Heraclius and its traces in Egypt, see Palme 2015, 224–225.

166 The earliest instance of this is *P.Erl.* 73 from March 29, 604. Cf. Christophoros and Strategios Stratelates; their advancement to the rank of *eukleestatoi hypatoi* may be related to the accession of Emperor Mauricius (August 13, 582); cf. Table 5 (pp. 169–171).

167 See Begass 2018, 421–422 for the consequences of regime change in Constantinople.

168 At least Apion Stratelates, Christophoros and Strategios Stratelates, and Strategios Paneuphemos were promoted that way.

representative, but they may attest to an institution well integrated into—and essential to the functioning of—the administrative machinery of the Egyptian provinces.

2. *Career Bureaucrats on the Lower Tier*

Typification for the lower-tier pagarchs is riskier than for the upper tier because much of the evidence we have for this type of pagarch concerns Menas Scriniarius and Kollouthos Cancellarius. Both are exemplary Thebaid officials in that they were mobile: they went from the surrounding cities to Antinoopolis in order to pursue a career in the provincial administration or from the capital to the cities in order to claim central positions there.[169] Many bureaucrats from Antinoopolis are known to have owned landholdings in the Antinoopolite, Hermopolite, or Antaiopolite nomes,[170] which can at least be said for Menas.[171] In addition, Menas and Kollouthos both had professional experience that probably made them the perfect choice for filling this post, all of which further suggests that the story of Menas being pagarch *because* he was Patrikia's *dioikētēs* may not be so simple, and that it may have been the other way around—that the bureaucrat Menas offered himself to Patrikia to perform the Antaiopolite pagarchy and only to this end became her *dioikētēs*.[172] The reasons for which Kollouthos would have assumed the pagarchy of Antaiopolis are, however, not quite clear—if his acting in Antaiopolis was not based on some other capacity anyway.[173] The links of the lower-tier pagarchs Menas, Kollouthos Cancellarius, Kollouthos Exceptor, and, probably, of Kallinikos may thus illustrate the close links the pagarchy had to the spheres of provincial government at least since *Edict* 13. These links are underscored by what Dioskoros has to say about the families of the pagarchs Kollouthos and Phoibammon,

---

169 Rarely do we have information in one document as explicit as in *P.Cair.Masp.* III 67309 (Antinoopolis; February 25–March 26, 569), where the *boēthos logistēriou* Ioannes describes himself as originating from Lykopolis, but dwelling in Antinoopolis. See also, for instance, *P.Coll.Youtie* II 92 (= *P.Cair.Masp.* I 67023) for Flavius Helladios, like Menas Scriniarius a *lamprotatos scriniarius* at Antinoopolis, but originating from Panopolis.

170 See Keenan 2001, 66–68 and 70.

171 *P.Lond.* V 1714.

172 An interpretation that would make him even more the "power-seeking element" described by Banaji 2007, 163.

173 Was he the anonymous pagarch and *topotērētēs* whom *P.Cair.Masp.* I 67003.25 mentions? The text has τῷ παγάρχῃ τῆς Ἀνταίο(υ) καὶ τῷ τοποτηρητῇ ταυτῆς, but these may well be the same person, provided that a specific person is referred to here at all. Cf. *P.Cair.Masp.* I 67002 col. III 19: ἔγραψεν (!) γὰρ αὐτῷ ὁ γραμματεὺς καὶ ὁ διακονητής; the link between these two passages was established by Gelzer 1913b, 361 n. 1. For a man who was both pagarch and *topotērētēs*, one can possibly refer to the pagarch Christophoros from the earliest years of the Islamic period, who might have been *topotērētēs* in *SB* VIII 9754 (Herakleopolis; June 4, 646). On the *topotērētēs* of the city, see Jesenko 2016, 1807–1809.

both of whom were closely linked to or can be considered part of the administrative elite of the province.

There are but two papyri that show lower-tier pagarchs in Arcadia. Antiochos and Theon are noted to have handed a fiscal report (*anaphora*) to the provincial administration, which is also the most plausible reason for the anonymous pagarchs of *P.Cair. Masp.* I 67068 to be present in Antinoopolis. And in the second case, the Oxyrhynchite pagarch Theodoros, it is not even clear if this man was in fact a lower-tier pagarch. He may have held a managing position on the Apion estate and in this function assumed the pagarchy for his *geouchōn*,[174] but the only text to attest him is not particularly suggestive of this possibility. The comparatively small share that the pagarchy held among the *syntelestai* in Oxyrhynchos[175] may also make it plausible in this case that Theodoros held the pagarchy in his own right.

Like the upper-tier elites, the lower-tier bureaucrats illustrate the rigid administrative integration of the pagarchy, mostly through their close ties to the ducal bureau, and—more overtly than the upper-tier elites—they reveal their character as a *Funktionselite*, as an aristocracy of service. The example of Menas suggests that the pagarchy may have been part of the path to higher honors for these bureaucrats, but these opportunities were counterpoised by a higher risk. A responsibility with such immense financial implications certainly posed an existential threat for lower-ranking landowners,[176] which may account for some of Menas's tenacity in the Aphrodite affair.[177] That both Menas and Kollouthos Cancellarius—if the latter actually was pagarch of *Antaiopolis*—are likely to have seen rather limited tenures in comparison to the upper-tier pagarchs may reflect that their career was more unstable or volatile than those of elites of higher standing, or that the office was, after all, still a strain to them, as they were less capable of handling and diverting profit and loss.

3. *Local, but Mobile, Elites*

The career bureaucrats from the lower tier bring yet another issue into this discussion: the mobility displayed by the pagarchs Menas Scriniarius and Kollouthos Cancellarius.

174 Admittedly, Theodoros ranks notably higher than Menas, but *if* he was a part of the Apion estate, then his superior was most likely the *antigeouchos* Biktor, an *endoxotatos illoustrios*, who in turn answered to the head of the *endoxos oikos*, the *hyperphyestatos* and *paneuphēmos patricius* Apion III. The hierarchical distance of Theodoros from Apion may, in this case, therefore safely be equated with how the *endoxotatē* Patrikia would relate to her *dioikētēs* Menas Scriniarius. This is, however, hypothetical, since, as stated above, the evidence hardly suggests that the *meizoteros* Theodoros is identical to the pagarch of that name.

175 See Chapter Three, Section II.

176 Naturally, a lower rank need not be indicative of a smaller fortune, but by and large this equation may be assumed to be valid.

177 This episode is discussed in Chapter Six, Section III.

As outlined at the beginning of this chapter, it is commonly assumed that pagarchs in the Byzantine period originated from the areas they became responsible for, and thus would have formed a "local elite." There is, however, almost no positive evidence regarding the origins of individual pagarchs. Normally, legal documents refer to an individual's origin via *apo* ("from") plus toponym in the genitive but, as we have seen, this formula virtually never occurs in reference to pagarchs or other aristocrats, because these men were distinguished enough without the additional identifier of their origin. Naturally, in the case of large landowners with imperial ties and estates extending into more than one nome, it would certainly have been odd to address them as "hailing from Oxyrhynchos" or the like.[178] A subtle reference to the pagarchs' mobility may be found in *Edict* 13 (539 CE). In one passage that lists all institutions and sections of the population that were subject to the *dux et Augustalis* of the Thebaid, the edict differentiates between permanent residents, temporary residents, and pagarchs and other officials.[179]

One of the rare literary sources for the pagarchy, the Coptic *Life of Aaron*, more clearly challenges the assumption that "mobile" pagarchs were an innovation of the Islamic period.[180] This text, which compellingly can be shown to have been composed before the Islamic conquest, most probably in the late sixth century, features a passage in which the pagarchy is used as a literary device in order to explain an actor's interregional mobility. In the quote below, Aaron recalls a conversation with Makedonios—who would later become the first bishop of Philai—in which he tells Aaron how he came to the region of Philai in the first place:

> For he said to me, "While I was still a magistrate, and had started to obtain wealth, I went south, because I was pagarch over these cities."[181]

What would the audience have assumed to be the reason for Makedonios's taking up the pagarchy in the deep south: recently acquired or granted estates? But Makedonios appears to have had no former ties to this region. Or did he receive a direct appointment

178 We may recall that also the Apiones, whose fiscal share was dominant in Oxyrhynchos, were originally from Herakleopolis and rose to power through the administration of imperial estates.

179 Iust. *ed.* 13.25; see Chapter Two, Section I, especially n. 27. A more straightforward interpretation would hold that the pagarchs are mentioned because of the significance of their business to the imperial cause.

180 On this text, see the in-depth analysis in Dijkstra 2008. A new edition has since been published in Dijkstra & van der Vliet 2020. The *Life*'s depiction of historical events is discussed in Wipszycka 2021, especially on pp. 107–110.

181 *Life of Aaron* 29 (Dijkstra & van der Vliet 2020, p. 78 ll. 27–28; see also the commentary and cf. Dijkstra 2008, 255 and Dijkstra 2007, 193–194): ⲁϥϫⲟⲟⲥ ⲅⲁⲣ ⲛ̣[ⲁï ϫⲉ ⲉⲧ]ⲓ̣ ⲉⲓⲟ ⲛⲁⲣⲭⲱⲛ ⲉⲁⲓϫⲓ ⲁⲣⲭⲏ ⲛⲧⲙ[ⲛⲧⲡ]ⲗⲟⲩⲥⲓⲟⲥ, ⲁⲓⲉⲓ ⲉⲣⲏⲥ ⲉⲓⲡⲁⲅⲁⲣⲭⲏ ⲉ[ϫ]ⲛ̄ ⲛⲉⲓⲡⲟⲗⲓⲥ. For an analysis of the pagarchy in this context and the question of whether this passage was aimed at a Byzantine audience still, see Stern 2020, 41–43.

maybe *bound* to a granted estate?[182] Whatever the imagined reason, it is significant for our discussion that the text assumes that its contemporary audience would accept the idea of a pagarch taking up his position in a region that he had no connection to. This point becomes even more significant when we consider the explicit reference to the pagarchy in a story set in the late fourth century and the beginning of the fifth. First, Coptic literary texts only rarely specify particular offices, usually sticking to the general term *archōn*, which in Coptic serves to denote any official of some significance. And second, given that the pagarchy was, in reality, still a curial office in the narrated period, with authority over individual *pagi*, its appearance in the story qualifies as an anachronism. The pagarchy is thus unlikely to have played a role in the "historical reality" behind this episode and consequently must have been deliberately chosen for its capacity to explain Makedonios's move to Philai. A pagarch's taking up an appointment in a remote region was therefore most likely not an extraordinary event.

Mobile officials were nothing new to Byzantine Egypt, but in case of the pagarchs, scholars have generally stressed precisely the local character of the pagarchy, so that a pagarch taking up appointments somewhere other than at one's primary residence, such as the literary Makedonios, seem to run counter to this conception. Turning to practice, however, there are few obvious candidates for pagarchs who did not originate from the *civitas* in which they were appointed pagarch. One reason for this is that the pagarchs' elevated standing conceals the statement of origin from the documents.[183] The most explicit outsider is Ioulianos, who in one document is referred to as "the Arsinoite."[184] How this relates to his presence at Antaiopolis remains a mystery, however. Ioulianos may have relocated to the Thebaid either due to an appointment as *praeses* or after he had served as praetorian prefect of the East, provided that these titles reflect offices he actually discharged, and not titular ones. Aristocratic landholding in the Roman Empire, moreover, was always political.[185] Ioulianos's Antaiopolite *ousia*, then, may have been some sort of imperial reward for his service as prefect, considerable enough to make him eligible to assume the pagarchy.[186] This case would be well in line

182 We have seen that there are basic indications that this might have been the case in the Antaiopolite nome for the pagarch Ioulianos (*PSI* IV 283) and the situation described in *SB* XX 15016; see Chapter Two, Section II 2.

183 That entails that nearly every pagarch may potentially have been from another region than the one that he was appointed to, but it seems safer to take as starting point the assumption that a pagarch was based in the *civitas* to which he was appointed.

184 See n. 64 above.

185 Cf. Begass 2016 for the links between aristocratic landowning and imperial policy in the Eastern Empire of the fifth and sixth centuries.

186 Admittedly, the idea that imperial favorites were provided with land in a region where they were about to take up office can only draw on ambiguous evidence. The *dux et Augustalis* and *patricius* Athanasios, for instance, controlled an *oikos* in the Antinoopolite nome, that is, in the immediate hinterland of the provincial capital where he served as governor. Note that Athanasios was perhaps the son of the mentioned Ioulianos, "the Arsinoite," as is suggested by an unpublished papyrus that Ruffini (2011, s.v. Athanasios 4) refers to.

with Banaji's model of a bureaucratic elite claiming economically powerful local positions due to completed imperial service and also with what the *Life of Aaron* presents as an apparently common model for a pagarch's career. The example of Ioulianos furthermore points to the role that chance plays for our knowledge. Out of a significant number of texts that have survived to tell us about the doings and dealings of this man, only one tells us of his origin. We may assume, therefore, that there were more outsider pagarchs whose nonlocal origins have simply not found their way into the documents they left us.

A different type of mobility occurred among the lower-tier pagarchs, exemplified by Menas Scriniarius, Kollouthos Cancellarius, and likely others without us knowing. They were part of the provincial administrative staff, whose mobility in the course of a bureaucratic career has already been highlighted in the previous section. This pattern is also visible in Oxyrhynchos, the capital of Arcadia,[187] and thus Antiochos and Theon or the Oxyrhynchite Theodoros would be suitable candidates for such careers, although their origins remain elusive.

It is more difficult to assess the mobility of pagarchs who may have taken up appointment in multiple *civitates*.[188] In Serenos's case, the relevant identification with a Hermopolite landowner is likely, but there is nothing to suggest he was also a pagarch in Hermopolis. In Kollouthos's case, by contrast, it is somewhat plausible that he was indeed pagarch in Antaiopolis as well as in Antinoopolis (presumably not at the same time); but this is hardly certain, and his activity around Aphrodite might have been related to another capacity. There is no pre-Islamic evidence yet that a pagarch was responsible for two nomes, so alternative interpretations seem to be the safer choice.[189] The early Islamic period yields some examples of pagarchs in multiple nomes, though to date, these cannot be evidenced to have been in office in two nomes at the same time.[190]

187 Keenan 2001, 72–73.

188 The *Life of Aaron* mentions "these cities" (ⲛⲉⲓⲡⲟⲗⲓⲥ) that Makedonios says he will be administering as pagarch, but this remark may in the literary context be dismissed as referring to "towns" in the sense of larger settlements, rather than to *civitates* in the legal sense. The question of the legal status of the "cities" in this region, around the First Cataract, is discussed by Dijkstra & Worp 2006. On the topic of multiple "cities" in a single nome, see also Chapter Six, n. 11.

189 The case of the pagarchs of Arsinoe and Theodosiopolis should not count here because this phenomenon is accounted for by the particular history of the Theodosiopolite nome, on which see the Introduction, n. 50.

190 See, for instance, Nājid b. Muslim, who was pagarch of Herakleopolis at least from 728 to late 729 and is generally thought to have been appointed pagarch of Arsinoe afterward, at some point between 729 and 743; see n. 4 above. On the phenomenon of "double pagarchies" in the early Islamic period, see the Catalog, s.v. Anonymous pagarch (Unknown province: Apollonopolis Heptakomias or Antaiopolis).

4. Clusters of Evidence

Comparing the various regions and their attested pagarchs, one primarily notes the striking similarities of the pagarchs' basic career patterns across the two compared regions, which I captured in the upper/lower-tier model. Three differences stand out, however, as regards namely the ratio between upper-tier and lower-tier pagarchs, the distribution of imperial elites, and the prevalence of the title of *stratēlatēs*.

By and large, evidence from the Thebaid shows a more or less equal proportion of pagarchs from the upper tier and those from the lower tier, whereas the upper tier is significantly more prominent in Arcadia, with only two documents attesting lower-tier pagarchs at all, one of whom is even a *megaloprepestatos*. A hypothesis may be that the lower-ranking pagarchs were only performing the pagarchy as stand-ins for ultimately responsible "nominal pagarchs" from the upper tier, in which case the distribution of our evidence would be able to explain the different pattern of occurrence. The evidence from the Fayum, as well as that from Oxyrhynchos, consists, for the most part, of papers from the large estates of high-ranking aristocrats who in some cases happened to be pagarch. By contrast, the overwhelming majority of documents from the Thebaid comes from the archives of Dioskoros and Phoibammon, in which pagarchs are mentioned when Dioskoros (and his family) had to deal with them, mostly at the village level or little above. From this perspective, the evidence from the Thebaid presumably would exhibit a more regular picture of the pagarchs' day-to-day job, which is to say that it features more prominently "active" pagarchs with whom people would actually come into contact. These would, then, be absent from the Fayum evidence because we do not have comparable material from the village level from this region.

But this hypothesis has significant shortcomings. Although Menas Scriniarius and the Oxyrhynchite pagarch Theodoros may have been pagarchs by the delegation of higher aristocrats, there are valid arguments to the contrary in both cases, as presented in Section III of Chapter Four. More decisive, however, seem to be the signatures on the Antaiopolite tax receipts.[191] Here, upper-tier pagarchs such as Ioulianos and Patrikia, who is mostly suspected to have been Menas's "superior" or "nominal" pagarch, are the overall responsible authorities in whose names the writers of these receipts sign, and the petitions against Ioulianos show that these upper-tier pagarchs were also perceived as the ones responsible. Receipts from Hermopolis and Antinoopolis, however, show the lower-tier pagarchs Dorotheos, Kallinikos, and Kollouthos Exceptor in this exact position as overall responsible authorities, which speaks against the notion that they were generally stand-ins.[192] The median aristocratic level may therefore indeed have been higher in the Fayum and in Oxyrhynchos than in Antaiopolis and Antinoopolis.

---

191 See Chapter Two, Section III 3.

192 Moreover, *P.Cair.Masp.* I 67002 col. II 11–12 implies that also Menas Scriniarius in the Antaiopolite had the authority to issue tax receipts in his own authority.

Linked to this issue is the question of why there are no imperial elites attested as holding the pagarchy in the Thebaid. Arcadia shows a handful of pagarchs bearing imperial epithets, some already from the point at which they appear in our documentation, others later after a promotion. In the Thebaid, by contrast, no known pagarch bears any epithet higher than *endoxotatos* or titles such as *patricius*, *hypatos*, or even *stratēlatēs*. Did men like the *dux et Augustalis* Athanasios, a *patricius* after all, assume the pagarchy somewhere, and is it only by chance that we lack any evidence of this?[193] We must not forget, however, that the time span from which we have evidence for pagarchs is considerably shorter in Antaiopolis than in Arsinoe, simply limiting the chance to observe a pagarch from the imperial level in the Thebaid. Furthermore, figures such as the Oxyrhynchite Apiones or Strategios Paneuphemos were so exceptional that there would not have been too many of them throughout the late Roman world of their time anyway. But even in this light, it is still notable that *all* upper-tier elites from the Fayum ranked higher than even the highest-ranking pagarchs known from the Thebaid. The aforementioned different character of the evidence may be a factor here, but the pattern is so striking that this is hardly a sufficient explanation. Again, this may be accounted for by a generally lower-ranking nome aristocracy in the Thebaid than in the Fayum and in Oxyrhynchos, so that the pagarchy was not, as one may think, of higher value in the Fayum, but likely simply adapted to the distribution of elites present in each region.[194]

The third point to consider here is the overwhelming number of *stratēlatai* among the Arsinoite pagarchs.[195] The title of *stratēlatēs* is attested for all known pagarchs from that region apart from Strategios Paneuphemos, but his *stratēlasia* might have been suppressed from his titulature once he became *hypatos*, at some point before the papyri start to attest him.[196] Outside the Fayum, no pagarch is known to have been *stratēlatēs*, although in general *stratēlatai* from other regions are well known: for instance, the *dux et Augustalis* Athanasios in Antinoopolis and Strategios II in Oxyrhynchos.[197] Several men from the ranks of the *endoxotatoi* pagarchs can with certainty be excluded from

193 Athanasios is known to have controlled an *endoxos oikos* at Antinoopolis (*P.Cair.Masp.* II 67166.6–7 from 568 CE), but he is unlikely to be the pagarch of that name in *SPP* III 436; see the Catalog, s.v. Athanasios (Hermopolis).

194 In Chapter Two, Section II 2, I compared Ioulianos's role in the administrative network of Antaiopolis to the role that Strategios Paneuphemos played in the Fayum; their hierarchical difference may in this view be indicative of a general divide in terms of status between Arsinoe and Antaiopolis.

195 See also Kovarik 2023b, 111: "a title typically borne by Arsinoite pagarchs."

196 For a discussion, see the Catalog, s.v.

197 While Strategios II had authority over "pagarched" villages, other landlords with that authority such as Apion II and III are uncertain cases. They are comparable to Strategios Paneuphemos in that they already ranked higher than *stratēlatēs* at the time of their first appearance. Both of them, however, keep at least their patriciate and consulate together in their titulature, while Strategios Paneuphemos is known to have suppressed his consulate once he attained the patriciate. This would appear to suggest that Apion II and III had indeed not been *stratēlatai* before,

having held the *stratēlasia*, since they are attested only with lower-ranking titles: this concerns Ioulianos, Ioannes, and Serenos in Antaiopolis, as well as Ioustos in Oxyrhynchos.[198] The pattern of suppressing the *stratēlasia* in case of higher honors is not consistent,[199] but a comparison with the title of *illoustrios* may be illuminating. This title was borne by pagarchs in Antaiopolis (Ioulianos and Serenos) and possibly in Arsinoe (Strategios Stratelates[200]), as well as by Anastasia, landlady over a "pagarched" village in the Oxyrhynchite nome. Strategios Stratelates may have been an *illoustrios* at an early stage of his career, but in the document in which he holds the pagarchy, he is a *stratēlatēs* and the *illoustrios* title would then have been suppressed from his titulature. This observation may in turn also account for the seemingly complete absence of the *illoustrios* title among the Arsinoite pagarchs: they were all *stratēlatai*, so if one of them had ever been *illoustrios*, this title was suppressed once he became *stratēlatēs*, which is a pattern that can also be observed elsewhere.[201] We can cautiously infer that there was a hierarchy, perhaps even a sort of *cursus*, of the honorary titles *illoustrios*, *stratēlatēs*, *hypatos*, and *patricius*, and that the Fayum featured a higher degree of "aristocratic density" than the Thebaid that cannot be dismissed by referring to the accident of preservation. There is no obvious answer to the question of what drives this difference, apart from the point that the Arcadian *civitates* were closer to Alexandria and the rest of the empire and may for this reason have seen a concentration of higher-ranking elites. Notably, in the early Islamic period, when we can follow the careers of more pagarchs over the course of some time, being pagarch of the Fayum appears to have been more prestigious than being pagarch of any other region,[202] and perhaps this is a late reflection of the apparently higher status of Arsinoite aristocrats in general during the sixth and early seventh centuries.

---

but perhaps their secretaries and notaries simply did not consider the *stratēlasia* worth keeping when compared to the higher-ranking patriciate and the consulate.

198 The documents frequently refer to Ioulianos and Serenos as *illoustrioi*; Ioannes and Ioustos are sometimes given the title of *comes*. If these aristocrats had been entitled to the titles of *stratēlatēs*, *hypatos*, or *patricius*, any of these would have been preferred over *illoustrios* or *comes* in a short reference. The reference to Ioannes as an *illoustrios* is to be deleted; *P.Cair.Masp.* III 67325 fol. VIII verso 24: Φλ[(αούιος)] Ἰωάννης [ἰλ]λ̣(ούστριος) (καὶ?) [πάγ]α̣ρ̣χ(ος) in fact reads: Φλ(αούιος) Ἰωάννης ἐ̣ν̣δ̣ο̣ξ̣(ο̣τ̣α̣τ̣ο̣ς̣) π̣άγαρχ(ος); see Stern forthcoming (a), s.v. Christodoros 1 *notarius*.

199 *Stratēlasia* suppressed: Apion Stratelates, Christophoros, and Strategios Stratelates (the title disappears from their long-form titulature when they rise to become *hypatoi*). *Stratēlasia* kept: Strategios II (who regularly kept his *stratēlasia* next to the honorary consulate and the patriciate, which does not appear to have depended on the writer of the document).

200 If this Strategios is identical with the homonymous *endoxotatos illoustrios* of *BGU* II 364; see the discussion in the Catalog, s.v.

201 See *P.Oxy.* LXXXII, p. 143 for a comparable pattern in the case of *politeuomenoi*, and pp. 123–125 above on the inclusion or exclusion of titles in a document based on the hierarchy of titles.

202 See Garel & Vanthieghem 2022, 87–88 (although we still lack comparative material from Lower Egypt). Arsinoe appears to have become the capital of Arcadia in the early Islamic period.

Finally, different clusters of evidence are certainly responsible to a degree for the contrast of Byzantine "local magnate" pagarchs versus Islamic "bureaucrat" pagarchs in the scholarly literature. Much of the Islamic documentation for the pagarchs is composed from the contents of larger archives: the archive of the pagarch Appa Kyros and his sons Christophoros and Theodorakios, who were also pagarchs, from the 640s; the archive of Senouthios, subordinate administrator to the pagarch Athanasios, from around the same period; the archive of the pagarch Papas from the second half of the seventh century; and finally, and perhaps most prominently, that of the pagarch and *dioikētēs* Basileios from the early eighth century.[203] These are all administrative archives and contain scores of letters that these pagarchs received from, or wrote to, various administrative levels as well as documents with the purpose of internal accounting. We do not have a comparable dossier for the Byzantine period;[204] and our picture of the pagarchy would probably be a different one if we had, for instance, the official inbox of Ioulianos or Menas Scriniarius. Still—to stick with these two Antaiopolite examples—we do have similar types of documents of these two pagarchs, though they are few in number: at least some of these documents must have gone, so to speak, over Ioulianos's and Menas's desks at some point—but we only have them when they reached the hand of, or were copied by, Dioskoros and his family.

VI. Summary

An analysis of the pagarchs' career patterns reveals that they were in fact far from being a coherent "local magnate" elite. Although it is difficult to schematize an *absolute* hierarchy of late antique elites and to attribute them to distinct classes, they can still be allocated within a consistent *relative* hierarchy according to the epithets and titles they bear. Transferring this model onto the Byzantine pagarchs highlights an intriguing diversity in their career patterns. The basic conditions for this hypothesis are shown in Figure 3,[205] which is not intended to be an abstract model that implies that *every* pagarch (never mind other aristocrats), whatever region they might come from, must be placed within the ranges shown here, but rather serves to illustrate what the evidence

203 There are other pagarchs known from multiple texts, such as Ioannes and Theodorakios in the Fayum of the earliest years after the conquest, but these are less frequent than those cited above. The majority of the documents from the archive of Flavius Atias (see n. 4 above), however, relate to a period when he, after having become pagarch, had risen to the position of *dux* of Arcadia (and of the Thebaid).

204 This lack is too prominent to explain it exclusively with the "accident of preservation." Morelli 2010, 147–148, n. 25, in a well-balanced discussion, suggests different archiving practices to be at work here; see also the Introduction, nn. 86 and 33.

205 The epithet *paneuphēmos* in Figure 3 stands for all three epithets of the highest rank: *eukleestatos*, *hyperphyestatos*, and *paneuphēmos*; see Table 6 (p. 196).

has left us, as fragmentary as it is and with sources collated from different contexts and decades.[206]

Arcadia		**Thebaid**
Governor: *lamprotatos–megaloprepestatos* *praeses*		Governor: *endoxotatos–paneuphēmos* *dux et Augustalis*
Arsinoe	***Oxyrhynchos***	***Antinoopolis, Hermopolis, Antaiopolis***
Pagarchs: *endoxotatos–paneuphēmos* (including a *patricius*)	Pagarchs: *megaloprepestatos–endoxotatos* (small overall share)	Pagarchs: *lamprotatos–endoxotatos* (including many lower-ranking "career bureaucrats")

Figure 3: Range of ranks of governors and pagarchs in the provinces of Arcadia and the Thebaid, c. 500–622 CE.

In the Fayum, we regularly witness pagarchs from the ranks of at least *endoxotatos stratēlatēs* taking up the pagarchy, some of whom even received promotions during their tenure and rose to the wider imperial circles, undoubtedly forming the political leadership in the *civitas* of Arsinoe. In Oxyrhynchos, the only pagarchs we see were not the biggest actors in terms of rank amid a group of aristocratic peers, many of whom would exceed these pagarchs in rank and can be clearly found to have wielded fiscal authority themselves. The Thebaid, finally, features pagarchs from the rank of *lamprotatos* in numbers that we do not find in Arcadia, and the idea that all these were only stand-ins for superiors is untenable. While the upper-tier pagarchs leave few traces of their careers before the pagarchy, some *lamprotatoi* conform to a pattern of career bureaucrats to whom the pagarchy was part of their official *cursus*. It is, furthermore, clear that the pagarchs were not necessarily a strictly local elite, and that the number of outsiders may be larger than we are aware of. There were few explicit outsiders among the pagarchs, but we need to recall that our evidence is expected to reveal the origin of aristocrats only in exceptional cases.

The various career patterns for the pagarchs suggest a higher aristocratic density in Arcadia than in the Thebaid. The character of the pagarchy was not inherently different in these provinces, but the office adapted to local elite composition. In Oxyrhynchos, large parts of the fiscal administration of the country villages were dealt with by

206 While most of the evidence from the Thebaid comes from the mid to late sixth century, the Arsinoite papyri largely date from the late sixth and early seventh centuries up to the early 620s. The Oxyrhynchite evidence spans both periods and ends abruptly in the late 620s, just before the Arsinoite evidence becomes more abundant again from the late 630s onward and into the early Islamic period.

the "private" resources of extensive *oikoi*, whereas the pagarchy proper was comparatively small. In the Fayum, where "large estates" seem to have been smaller, the fiscal authority of the *oikoi* was supposedly not as extensive, and the pagarchy was accordingly responsible for a higher share, which may explain that the pagarchy here was sometimes even entrusted to imperial elites. For the Thebaid, speculations about the fiscal value of the local pagarchies are much riskier due to insufficient evidence.

This situation entails that the pagarchs were often not the socially or economically dominant actors in the countryside, and that the resources that the government attributed to the staffing of the pagarchy were also a means to make up for the infrastructural disadvantage some pagarchs would have held vis-à-vis the nome elite and the estate administration under these elites' individual fiscal jurisdictions. This disadvantage may have not been much of an issue for the central government in the case of Oxyrhynchos, where exalted imperial players like the Apiones invested their resources for public purposes through their dominant *oikoi*. This family, part of the imperial entourage, served as the empire's link to the local level, and it may therefore have been less important for the central government to keep a close eye on the local pagarchs. The infrastructural disadvantage was a more serious issue for the low-ranking *lamprotatoi*. In their cases, however, we see the tendency for these men to be linked via office, and some even through family relations, to the provincial offices and the higher-ranking governors. In Arsinoe, finally, where the *oikos* infrastructures apparently did not guarantee as comprehensive a coverage of the fiscal landscape as in Oxyrhynchos, it was of paramount importance to provide the pagarchs with additional resources, and to bring the officeholders closer to the imperial circles.

We have thus seen three ways in which the central government may have exerted its fiscal authority in the countryside of the *civitates*: (1) through the *duces* and their official (and private) networks, mostly in case of lower-ranking bureaucrat pagarchs, (2) through the active courting of locally grounded imperial elites who held either *oikoi*, the pagarchy, or both, or (3) through the deliberate dislocation, backed by granted estates, of merited honorees or retired imperial servants, who then would take on the local pagarchy or the responsibility for a fiscal share. The pagarchy thus emerges as a rather flexible instrument, depending on the composition of the local elite: either guaranteeing a balance vis-à-vis the local nobility or providing (soon-to-be) imperial favorites with the necessary infrastructure to exercise comprehensive authority within the nome.

Chapter Six
Taxes and Social Conflict in Sixth-Century Aphrodite

Following the more comprehensive approach to the pagarchs' careers pursued in the previous chapter, this final discussion places the pagarchy in the context of the conflicts that arose inside one close environment: the Antaiopolite village of Aphrodite in the mid-sixth century. This village has yielded an enormous amount of papyri, the largest sixth-century papyrus archive, and it is the only place where we find sufficient evidence on individual events linked to the pagarchs' activity to contextualize their actions over a certain period of time in a sort of microhistory. Some notable events of Aphroditan history feature in scholarly literature mostly as the "misdeeds" and "abuses," or similar, of two pagarchs: Ioulianos in the late 540s and Menas in the mid-560s CE. Information about these events survives in some rescripts but primarily in petitions and rescript drafts meticulously composed by the poet and notary Dioskoros.[1] What were these confrontations about, where did they lead, and what do they reveal about the balance of power in the countryside on the periphery of the late Roman Empire? Based on the analysis of the pagarchy that has been advanced in the previous chapters, the present chapter reviews these cases to examine their conditions, events, and consequences for the construction of public authority in the countryside. It is thus a testing ground for some results of the previous chapters, using the village of Aphrodite and its surroundings as an enclosed historical laboratory. The chapter starts by looking at Aphrodite and its administrative privilege of *autopragia* as a limit to the pagarchs' authority, about which these conflicts seem to have first evolved.

I. The Limits of Authority

As has been established in the previous chapters, the pagarchs' authority was confronted with certain limits, among them the "self-collecting" estates in the rural parts of the nome. Another limit was the "autopract village." Settlements of that type are thought to have been a regular part of the countryside of Byzantine Egypt,[2] yet the only case known to us is the ancient *kōmē Aphroditēs*, Aphrodite for short (or, in the Islamic period, Aphrodito), today the village of Kom Ishqaw in the heart of Egypt, on the left bank

1 On the issue that many of the "rescripts" in these matters are actually drafts that were (pre)-composed by Dioskoros and his entourage, see Fournet 2015, 259–261 and Zuckerman 2004b, especially pp. 82–83 and 88–90. These rescript drafts thus show Dioskoros's requests rather than the genuine outcome of the villagers' appeal to the imperial court, and will be read accordingly throughout this chapter.

2 See, e.g., Palme 1989, 98; Berkes 2017a, 8; and Ruffini 2018a, 23.

https://doi.org/10.1515/9783111493183-007

of the Nile.[3] The privilege of *autopragia* enabled the villagers of Aphrodite to maintain their own fiscal account (*dēmosios logos*) that entitled them to pay their provincial and imperial taxes directly to the provincial bureau, independently from municipal officials or the pagarch.[4] In this way, the village was able to avoid surcharges by the pagarchs' officials for handling its taxes, such as for commuting the small individual contributions into gold, or for transporting the grain designated for the *embolē*. As part of the Antaiopolite nome, however, the village was not entirely exempt from the authority of the city of Antaiopolis.[5] Scholars have described how Aphrodite's privilege repeatedly came under attack by the local pagarchs, who resided in the nome capital Antaiopolis, about fifteen kilometers or nine miles to the northeast, across the river, and in the immediate range of the pagarchs' orders.[6] In this narrative, the pagarchs of Antaiopolis constantly tried to drag the village into their purview and the "indomitable Gauls" of Aphrodite pulled out all the stops to fight them off.[7] Rather than a conflict between different administrative levels, this is seen mostly as a struggle between smallholders and magnates who abused their official powers for their personal enrichment. In this conception, Aphrodite figures as the last bastion of free villagers in late antique Egypt, encircled by the remainder of a country that had fallen prey to the mounting dominance of a landed aristocracy.[8] In this chapter, I argue for a modification of this view, by more closely embedding these episodes in the context of administrative practice.

In late antiquity, Aphrodite was part of the province of the Thebaid in the south of Egypt, and it was situated about 140 kilometers or 86 miles to the southeast of the provincial capital Antinoopolis. The village thus qualifies as being on the periphery of

3 Berkes 2017a, 13–16 has convincingly rejected the suggestion in the editor's introduction to *BGU* XII 2168, followed by Poethke 1984, that the expression περὶ πρακτορίαν κώμης refers to autopract villages. See also Chapter Three, n. 183 on potential autopract villages in the Oxyrhynchite nome as speculated about by Giovanni Ruffini.

4 The fiscal procedures of the autopract Aphrodite and its official apparatus have been meticulously analyzed by Zuckerman 2004a, 115–142. For the imperial context of the institution of *autopragia*, see Chapter One, Section I.

5 On these links, see Zuckerman 2004a, 138–142: "Malgré son autopragie, le village d'Aphroditô fait partie de la circonscription cadastrale centrée sur et gérée à partir de la cité d'Antaeopolis" (quote on p. 141). The pagarchs Ioulianos and Menas Scriniarius apparently had authority over Aphrodite's liturgies as early as 553 CE (*P.Lond.* V 1661). The autopract village also had to pay to the pagarchs its *kōmētika* and *astika* contributions (*P.Cair.Masp.* I 67060); in this case, *autopragia* entailed collection within the village before the aggregated amount was sent from the village's *own* officials, not from the pagarchs' *hypodektai* and *boēthoi*, to the pagarch's "bureau" at Antaiopolis; see Chapter Two, Section II 3.

6 This statement assumes that Antaiopolis is to be located at the modern town of Qaw el-Kebir.

7 "Indomptables Gaulois": Zuckerman 2004a, 222, in an allusion to the adventures of Asterix the Gaul.

8 The most influential uses of these episodes for drafting the narrative of notoriously repressive large landowners have probably been Gelzer 1909, 92–96; Bell 1917, 99–100 (cf. Bell 1944, 33–35); and Hardy 1931, 137–138. The historiographical context is discussed in Keenan 1993 and Palme 2013a, especially 129–132.

the Roman Empire. The archives of Dioskoros, Phoibammon, and Kollouthos have left us with an unparalleled wealth of evidence from this site for large parts of the sixth century, and if a late antique microhistory were to be written, Aphrodite would have to be its primary theater.[9] Because of this potential for historical analysis, Aphrodite finds frequent mention as the Byzantine-Egyptian village par excellence.

This, however, it was certainly not.[10] The "village" of Aphrodite had probably once been a *polis*—yet without ever being the center of a nome—before being reduced to the status of a *kōmē*.[11] Still, it counted perhaps about seven thousand inhabitants, an unusually large number for a *kōmē*, and was subject to various administrative arrangements that might be conclusively linked to a former city status, as can be the extent of its administrative infrastructure.[12] For instance, Aphrodite had its own *riparii*, liturgical security officials normally found only at *civitas* level.[13] It also had its own *hypodektēs*, who is in one instance explicitly linked to the practice of paying taxes directly to the provincial bureau without having to deal with Antaiopolite officials.[14] This is what the Aphroditans repeatedly refer to as the "autopract mode" (*autoprakton schēma*) of paying their taxes.[15] In most of these cases, they consider

9 Cf. Ruffini 2018a.

10 See also Berkes 2017a, 11–12, particularly his arguments against the overly optimistic view of Ruffini 2008a, 249, who suggested that Aphrodite "probably looks like what we might see in an Oxyrhynchite village."

11 The question is far from settled. The new texts of *O.Trim.* I bring another nuance to this problem, as they seem to feature multiple actual *poleis* within the same nome. Therefore, two different questions arise here: whether Aphrodite ever legally was a *polis* and whether it ever was the center of its own nome. For the relevant sources and their discussion, see Marthot 2013, I 15–30 (a condensed, but less nuanced, rendering of parts of these findings from her unpublished doctoral dissertation can be found in Ruffini 2018a, 10–11) and Marthot 2012, 487–489.

12 On the size of the town, see Zuckerman 2004a, 223; his estimate is considered "modest" by Ruffini 2008a, 247, but is supported by Bransbourg 2016, 332. Aphrodite might have even been more populous than Antaiopolis, the capital of its nome; see Keenan 2007, 232 n. 30

13 Tost 2012, 777 and Gascou 1985, 38 (= 2008, 160–161), linking special arrangements such as Aphrodite's *riparia* and *autopragia* to the village's large size and former *civitas* status. Cf. Palme 2004.

14 *P.Hamb.* III 230.7–11 (mid-VI), especially 7–8: κατα̣[βο]λ̣[ὴ]ν̣ πέ̣μ̣πο̣ντε̣ς̣ | διὰ ἰδίου ὑποδέκτου εἰς τὴν τάξιν καὶ μηδὲν ἐν τῇ Ἀντα[ιο]πολιτῶ̣ν καταβάλλοντες; for the date, see Fournet & Gascou 2002, 34 and Zuckerman 2004a, 138. Illustrative tax receipts for this mode of payment are *P.Cair.Masp.* I 67033, 67034, 67035, and 67039. On Aphrodite's *hypodektēs*, see Chapter Two, n. 129.

15 *P.Cair.Masp.* I 67002 col. III 8: ἐκ προνομίου ἐχόντων κατὰ τὸ αὐτόπρακτον σχῆμα; *P.Cair.Masp.* I 67024–25 (new ed. Fournet 2018) A 33–35: καὶ ταῦτα μηδέ|ποτε τελεσάντων ὑπὸ παγαρχίαν αὐτῶν ἀλλὰ κατὰ τὸ τῶν | αὐτοπράκτων σχῆμα δι' ἑαυ\τῶν/ τοὺς δημοσίους φόρους ἐπὶ ⟦το(ὺ)ς̣⟧ | τὴν ἐπιχώριον τάξιν κατατιθέντων; *P.Cair.Masp.* I 67032.94–95: τὸ προνόμιον τοῦ ἀυτοπράκτου σχήματο̣ς̣ | τῆς ὑμετέρας ὑπαρχθῆναι κώμης. Cf. *P.Cair.Masp.* I 67019 verso 2–6: [τ]ελο̣[ῦσα] δ̣ὲ ἀ̣εὶ ὑπὸ τὴν ἐ[πι]χ̣ώριον σεμνὴν | π̣ο̣λ̣ι̣[τι]κὴν τάξιν, αὐτόπρακτο̣ς οὖσα̣ καὶ αὐτοτελὴ\ς/ τῶν εὐσεβ̣ῶ̣ν̣ καὶ δημοσίων ⟦ὑ̣μῶν⟧ | ε[ἰ]σ̣φόρων, μηδέποτε κ̣λη[ρω]θ̣ε̣ῖ̣[σ]α̣ ὑπ[ὸ π]α̣γα̣ρχικὴν ἐξουσίαν ἀπὸ γονέων | α̣ὐ̣τῶ̣ν καὶ προγόνων, ἐχόντω̣[ν] τὸ προνόμιο̣ν̣ αὐτ̣[ῶ]ν ἀπὸ θείο̣[υ] τύπου | τοῦ τῆς θείας λήξεως Λέ̣[ον]τ̣ο̣ς. The privilege here is in the mode of payment, not the collection as such; see pp. 33–34 above. On the meaning of *politikē taxis*, see Chapter Two, n. 27.

this form of organization a privilege (*pronomion*) that had been granted to them a long time ago.[16]

It is problematic, however, that the legislation on *autopragia* (which does not discuss Egypt) remains exclusively tied to individual landowners (*possessores*), not villages.[17] This observation underlies Miroslava Mirković's hypothesis that the *autopragia* of Aphrodite was valid only for the large landholders (*megaloi ktētores*) of the village.[18] She notes that *autopragia* was designed for those able to pay in advance, and argues that the "smallholders" (*leptoktētores*), as the Aphroditans name themselves on one occasion, would hardly have been in a position to do so. The latter expression is obviously rhetorical and aims at painting the picture of "humble" villagers in a petition before a higher authority. The main idea seems practicable: some of the better-situated landowners would organize the day-to-day business of the *autopragia*, including specific institutions linked to this arrangement such as the village's *hypodektēs*. In his petitions, Dioskoros seems quite clear about attributing *autopragia* either to the village or to "us" in order to evoke the image of an all-unified village society. Yet this rhetorical figure would hide the fact that only parts of that society were in a position to profit from the arrangement—and this makes an intriguing backdrop for the frictions between Dioskoros's faction and other villagers that we see play out in the papyri discussed in this chapter.[19] A relic of this privileged circle of village landowners may be found in the signature of the *boēthos* Makarios in the Antaiopolite tax receipts: Makarios issues multiple receipts in the name of the pagarchs but issues one "as authorized representative (*ex epitropēs,* that is, *per procuram*) of the *koinon* of landowners (*ktētores*)."[20] This

16 It appears that *pronomion* is not a synonym for *autopragia*—the entire city of Antaiopolis also enjoyed a *pronomion* in regard to its *dēmosia*, though we do not know what this privilege might have involved; see *P.Cair.Masp.* I 67009 verso 10, *P.Lond.* V 1678.8, and Rouillard 1928, 97 n. 5. The moment when Aphrodite was granted its privilege (under Emperor Leo I, who reigned 457–474) is given by *P.Cair.Masp.* I 67019 verso 5–6 (for the quote, see the previous note).

17 For the sources, see Chapter One, n. 34.

18 Mirković 2008 and 1996. By contrast, Gascou (1985, 38–44 = 2008, 161–167) used this paradox to argue that there is no evidence of *autopragia* of *oikoi* in Egypt, or at least that when we see the Apiones pay enormous sums in taxes and transport tax grain to Alexandria, this is not *autopragia* but an obligation toward the state.

19 Ruffini 2018a, 51–52 and 59.

20 See *P.Cair.Masp.* III 67325 fol. VII verso 20–21: δι' ἐμοῦ Μ̣ακαρίου | ἐξ ἐπιτροπῆς τῶν κο̣ι̣νῶν τῶν κτητ(όρων) | σεσημ(είωμαι); the document is from the "post-autopract" era. The form τῶν κο̣ι̣νῶν looks odd, but since Makarios's hand does not seem to belong to a particularly consistent or well-trained writer, this must probably be read as τοῦ κοινοῦ. A *koinon* of *ktētores* is not attested elsewhere, however. Cf. *P.Cair.Masp.* III 67286.1–3 (542 CE; new ed. Fournet 2020b, no. 6a): ὑ̣π̣ὲ̣ρ̣ κώμ(ης) Ἀφροδίτης δ(ιὰ) τῶν πρωτοκομητ̣ῶ̣ν̣ (read πρωτοκωμητῶν) τ̣ῆ̣ς̣ [αὐτῆς κώμης] | δ(ιὰ) Βίκτ̣ο̣ρ̣ο̣ς̣ π̣ρ̣ε̣σ̣β̣υ̣τ̣έ̣ρ̣[ου κ(αὶ) Ἀπολλῶτος κ(αὶ) Σενουθίου (ὑπέρ) τε αὐτῶν κτήσεως] κ̣α̣ὶ̣ δ̣ι̣αφόρ(ων) κτητόρο(ν) (read κτητόρων) | τῆς αὐτῆς κώμ(ης). Alternatively, one may read the expression τῶν κο̣ι̣νῶν τῶν κτητ(όρων) in a less technical fashion as "the joint landowners," for which other texts may provide analogies; cf. *P.Lond.* V 1660.5–6: τῶν μ]ε[γ]α̣λ̣οπρεπεσ̣τάτων κοινῶν | δεσποτῶν παγάρχων and *SB* XX 14241.12–13: τῷ κοινῷ δεσπό(τη) τῷ κυρίῳ | Μ̣ηνᾷ.

was the way of handling matters in practice; it does not, to my mind, speak against the idea that Aphrodite's privileges and rather elaborate administrative infrastructure, such as having its own *riparius*, resulted from its former legal status and the size of its population. In other words, the *autopragia* may have constituted some sort of privilege or concession granted to the "village" in acknowledgment of its former position as a *civitas*.[21] The administrative history of Aphrodite as our only known case of village *autopragia*, as well as the treatment of *autopragia* in the laws, suggest that this privilege was only rarely granted, and consequently, we have little reason to assume that a host of tacitly autopract villages pervaded the Egyptian countryside.[22]

Over Aphrodite looms the shadow of Ammonios, a *megaloprepestatos* and *endoxotatos comes sacri consistorii*[23]—widely known as "Count Ammonios" in scholarly literature—who is habitually perceived as a sort of patron to Aphrodite during the second quarter of the sixth century. He was a large landowner in and around the village whose estate accounts have come down to us because Dioskoros's father Apollos was employed as his *dioikētēs*, although his landholdings may not have held a dominant position.[24] The capacity in which he acted is nowhere made explicit,[25] but Ammonios handled tax payments for Aphrodite, had an influence on the composition of fiscal registers, and was responsible for the appointment of the village's *prōtokōmētai*.[26] He was a

21 See n. 13 above.

22 If Aphrodite owed its *autopragia* to its former city status, then comparable cases of switching legal statuses of settlements (see Dagron 1979, 32) may lead to more candidates. On other suggestions by scholars for identifying autopract villages in Egypt, see n. 3 above.

23 Ruffini 2011, s.v. Ammonios 1; see also Ruffini 2008a, 173–177.

24 The identification of Dioskoros's father Apollos with the homonymous *dioikētēs* seems convincing, while the Apollos who was Ammonios's *hypodektēs* was a different person; see Gascou & Fournet 2002, 28; Zuckerman 2004a, 48 and 51 and n. 56; and Vanderheyden 2015, no. 35. For the discussion of the extent of Ammonios's lands, see Zuckerman 2004a, 220 and 2004b, 77 ("modest" estate) versus Ruffini 2008a, 174–176 (and 173: "the closest thing to a Flavius Apion among Aphrodito's protagonists") and Ruffini 2018a, 80–81 ("exceptional" estate); on p. 77, however, Ruffini also argues that Ammonios only held modest lands, ending the chapter with the curious statement that "[t]here are no large estates" at Aphrodite (p. 93).

25 But cf. the reading πατρ̣ωνικίων in *P.Cair.Masp.* I 67029.5 (see Amelotti & Migliardi Zingale 1985, no. 9) in relation to Ammonios's potential successor Theodosios.

26 Tax payments: P.Cair. SR 3733 (2), on which see Fournet 2001, 481–482. Ammonios is probably too high-ranking (and perhaps too young?) to be identical with the homonymous *chrysōnēs*, the provincial fiscal official to receive Aphrodite's gold taxes (for the sources, see Ruffini 2011, s.v. Ammonios 3). Fiscal registers: *P.Cair.Masp.* II 67200. *Prōtokōmētai*: *P.Cair.Masp.* III 67323, on which see Ruffini 2008a, 153. This text perhaps alludes to a position as *praeses*, but Ammonios is nowhere referred to as such (*pace* Sarris 2006, 100, *P.Ross.Georg.* III 37 does not contain any indication that Ammonios had been a *dux*), and furthermore, Dioskoros's father is noted as having had troubles with previous governors (*archontes*, i.e., usually, the *praesides*) in *P.Cair.Masp.* I 67024–25 (new ed. Fournet 2018) A 5–7 and B 5–7; at the time of that petition, a notion of "previous governors" would have included a former *praeses* Ammonios and given him a negative aura, which seems unlikely (though not impossible).

force to be reckoned with not only at Antaiopolis but also in the Hermopolite nome.[27] Ammonios disappears, and probably died, after 545 CE, and it is unlikely to be a coincidence that this is when Aphrodite's struggle with the pagarch Ioulianos began.[28] Ammonios's role as a sort of patron to the village can help explain the workings of its *autopragia*, since an autopract village is nowhere else attested. Namely, it may be possible to link Ammonios's position to the otherwise dubious presence of an "*endoxos oikos* of the village Aphrodite," which occurs in one, and only one, papyrus.[29] Under the supervision of Ammonios, it would not have been any more difficult for provincial authorities to deal with the autopract Aphrodite than with any other aristocrat magnates who were vested with fiscal responsibility over village land through their *oikoi*; such a supervision by Ammonios may thus have been perceived in a similar manner.[30] No other *oikos* "of" a village is attested, and it is tempting to link this singular institution to the equally singular phenomenon of the autopract village. Although Ammonios usually bears higher-ranking identifiers than the *lamprotatos geouchos* in the relevant text, there is no more likely candidate.[31] The alternative candidate, the pagarch Ioulianos,[32] also bore considerably higher rank epithets and honorary titles and, as far as we know, he directed only an *ousia*, not an *oikos*, and this *ousia* was clearly not superior to Aphrodite's village headmen.[33] All this is not to say that Aphrodite's *autopragia* was simply an *autopragia* of the large landlord Ammonios, or that Aphrodite was structurally the

27 In Hermopolis, Ammonios was responsible for the *riparia* (*P.Flor.* III 304), supposedly through his "shares"; see the pattern established by Tost 2012, especially 778–779, regarding *riparii* "of" large landlords. At Aphrodite, apparently provincial administration had its say over the nomination of its *riparii*; see *P.Cair.Masp.* III 67281. For another aristocrat with links to both Antaiopolis and Hermopolis, cf. the pagarch Serenos.

28 *P.Ross.Georg.* III 37 (October 28–November 26, 545) is the last text to have Ammonios alive. He had passed by the time of *P.Hamb.* I 68 (549/550 or 564/565).

29 *SB* III 6704 (January 23, 538); one party of this contract identifies as κοινότης τῶν ἀγρευτῶν τῶν καὶ διαφερόντων τῷ ἐνδόξῳ οἴκῳ | τῆς αὐτῆς κώμης Ἀφροδίτης (ll. 4–5). Other texts seem to imply the presence of this *oikos*; see Zuckerman 2004a, 221 with references.

30 The model proposed in Chapter Three would, *cum grano salis*, also be able to explain how Ammonios and his *oikos* could have attained such a position even though his own property (his *ousia*) may not have been a dominant extension in the village. The fiscal shares in the Oxyrhynchite were, however, clearly linked to civic administration.

31 *SB* III 6704.10; for the identification, see Ruffini 2011, s.v. Ammonios 1 (h).

32 For this identification, see Zuckerman 2004a, 220–221 and Sarris 2006, 101. *Pace* Sarris (ibid.) and Palme 2008b, 205, Ioulianos is not attested as *lamprotatos*; the passage cited in this context (*P.Cair.Masp.* III 67283 col. I 2) is restored *exempli gratia* and should contain an honorary or official title, if it refers to Ioulianos at all; see Chapter Four, nn. 15 and 19. For an argument in favor of Ioulianos being in control of the *endoxos oikos* at Aphrodite, see the Catalog, n. 226.

33 See *P.Cair.Masp.* I 67060.2–3 (addressed to Dioskoros and Apollos as *prōtokōmētai*): ἡ οὐσία τοῦ ἐνδ[οξ(οτάτου) ἀπὸ] ἐπάρχων Ἰουλιανοῦ, | συντελοῦσα εἰς τὸ κωμητικόν. The use of *synteleō* no doubt implies that the role of the *ousia* was equivalent to that of the village's *syntelestai*.

same as a *kōmē pagarchoumenē*; it simply illustrates that there is more at issue here than we currently know.[34]

After Ammonios had left this world, or at least Aphrodite, the ominous figure of the *megaloprepestatos* Theodosios arrived on the scene.[35] He is said to have collected taxes from the village for the eleventh indiction (547/548 CE), without, however, entering these payments into the provincial accounts. Again, it is not clear in what capacity Theodosios acted, but he is important enough to be referred to by a rank epithet only, without an official title, in a rescript from the *curator domus divinae*.[36] In a draft for a rescript, Dioskoros expects Theodosios to be around for the longer term even after his alleged misconduct, so apparently Theodosios did not simply run off with the money;[37] the same draft also does not object to Theodosios's collecting the taxes, but simply argues that they should be properly entered into the accounts. Earlier, I proposed that this Theodosios may be the same as the high-ranking *procurator* in an Aphroditan rent receipt.[38] Based on the evidence available so far, this identification remains uncertain, but if it holds, it may link Theodosios to Christodotos, the *peribleptos comes* and *procurator* discussed earlier in the same context of the pagarch Ioulianos's influence at Aphrodite. These men may have acted as administrators of Ammonios's now-defunct *endoxos oikos*,[39] potentially as managers of the imperial household (*domus divina*) at Aphrodite.[40] The village had obtained imperial patronage, probably in 540/541, after

34 Considering the fact that Ioulianos's pagarchy is first attested after the death of Ammonios, one may even suspect that Ioulianos may have been given control of Aphrodite's *endoxos oikos* after Ammonios's death; this is of course highly speculative, but for a potential parallel case, see Ioulianos potentially taking over (parts of) the *ousia* of the *megaloprepestatos* Kyros based on his pagarchy, as discussed in Chapter Two, Section II 2.

35 Ruffini 2011, s.v. Theodosios 16, and Zuckerman 2004b, 75–77. Zuckerman (77) suggests, on the grounds of a "schema onomastique banal," that Theodosios was the son of Count Ammonios (who was himself the son of one Theodosios). *Pace* Sarris 2006, 101, Theodosios is not attested as a landowner at Aphrodite in *P.Cair.Masp.* I 67107; the text refers to this Theodosios as the father of Ammonios (*BL* IX 43; see also n. 40 below) and it is Ammonios's, not Theodosios's, measure that is at issue here and well known.

36 *SB* VI 9102.9 and 25 (c. September 548).

37 *P.Cair.Masp.* I 67024–25 (new ed. Fournet 2018) A 20–22, which orders the *dux* to act in this matter μὴ χρόνους ἐκ χρόνων αὐτὸν ἤτοι τὴν | κατ' αὐτὸν κώμην τῶν ἐποφειλομένων αὐτοῖς ἀπο|στερεῖσθαι, "lest he (i.e., Theodosios) time and time again divest him (i.e., Dioskoros) or his village of the things that belong to them."

38 See Chapter Four, Section III.

39 Can this hypothesis explain that in *SB* XVI 12370, a receipt for *adespotos* land, Christodotos appears as intermediate instance *between* the pagarchs and their *boēthos*? A perhaps equally probable hypothesis is that Christodotos was *procurator* of Ioulianos's pagarchy; see Chapter Four, Section III.

40 Ammonios was a large landowner in the area before Aphrodite apparently gained imperial patronage in 540/541 (see the next note), but I do not see this as a counterargument. Zuckerman's (2004b, 75–77) alternative hypothesis that Theodosios, as Ammonios's son (see n. 35 above), exercised patronage over Aphrodite seems less convincing; see Azzarello 2012, 24–25 and 84–87

Dioskoros's father Apollos had traveled to Constantinople following persistent conflicts with the provincial authorities.[41] Later, at the time of the Menas affair, we see that the *paneuphēmos patricius* Athanasios, who also became *dux et Augustalis* of the Thebaid, was responsible for the lands of the *domus divina* in the entire Thebaid.[42] In this capacity, Athanasios would have certainly been superior to Theodosios's or Christodotos's successors. Athanasios maintained a residence, and a *dioikētēs* attached to it, at Aphrodite, presumably in his capacity as imperial overseer.[43] The significance of the imperial house in this matter may also account for the fact that one of the rescripts the villagers obtained from Constantinople was authored by the *curator domus divinae*, the superior administrator of all estates of one particular member of the imperial family.[44] We are at the level of high politics here.

II. Taxes, Village Factions, and the Outside World

Whatever exact position Ammonios had, his disappearance marked the start of a new phase in Aphrodite's struggle with the authorities, the first part of which had brought the village under imperial patronage in 540/541 CE. The first petition in this matter, *P.Cair.Masp.* III 67283, must date to immediately after Ammonios's disappearance, for there is not the slightest allusion to him even though he had been the highest-ranking protector of Dioskoros's family.[45] The petition addresses the empress Theodora through the *dux*, and finds strong words for the deeds committed by Ioulianos:

---

and Fournet 2018, 596–597. In addition, one may note that Zuckerman argues that the *curator domus divinae* of *SB* VI 9102 would not have addressed the *dux Thebaidis* if he had any "pouvoir hierarchique" over Theodosios, that is, if the latter was a member of the administrative branch of the imperial household. But I see no reason why the *curator* should not have addressed the *dux* as the highest fiscal authority in the province, particularly since the orders involved dealing with the pagarch and were largely about compensation for the actions of the staff of the *dux*. We should, generally, not refrain from assuming frequently overlapping hierarchies in late antique Egypt.

41 Fournet 2015, 255 and Zuckerman 2004b, 81. On these conflicts, see also *P.Cair.Masp.* I 67024–25 (new ed. Fournet 2018) A 5–7: ἐπειδὴ δὲ | παρὰ τῶν κατὰ καιρὸν ἀρχόντων οὐ τὰς τυχούσας ἀδικίας | ὑπέμεινον, τῷ θείῳ \ἡμῶν/ οἴκῳ σφᾶς αὐτοὺς ἐπιδοῦναι and, on this text, Azzarello 2012, 94–95. What we do not know is whether these conflicts were the *main* reason for Apollos's journey to the capital.

42 Morelli 2008a, 233–237; Azzarello 2012, 101–102.

43 *P.Cair.Masp.* I 67002 col. II 26–col. III 2 (May–July 567 CE).

44 *SB* VI 9102 (c. September 548).

45 On the date of this text, see Chapter Four, n. 19. The traditional date (inferred from *SB* XVIII 13297) is "before November 10, 547," so it is possible that this text preceded the Theodosios affair. If Fournet's dating for *P.Cair.Masp.* III 67283 (i.e., 540–545 CE) holds, then Ioulianos's conduct (or that of another pagarch, since Ioulianos is restored) referred to in the papyrus may in fact be related to Aphrodite's troubles with the provincial officials that started around 540, as discussed in Section I above.

> But the said man attacked our properties and has not shrunk from plundering them more than the lands ravaged by barbarians, on the pretext of taxes. And his entourage, as already said, has plundered all properties around the village in an indescribably evil manner, even the fields of this (village) [– – –] so that we are suffering and no longer capable of paying our customary contributions to the public dues or to live a modest life in possession of our animals and equipment. Instead, in the fields they have left us nothing to feed on and in the village absolutely none of the furnishings of a decent life for us. God knows all that has been done against the law, and the murders that have occurred as part of this plague, which has struck and brought shrieking, and all the inexpressible punishments and crimes that surrounded us then, and for which a papyrus roll has no room unless it narrates with no break.[46]

It is hardly news that documentary papyri are not "objective" sources, but this seems especially evident in the case of petitions, for there was nothing that the petitioners, or Dioskoros supposedly writing on their behalf, were less interested in than in a factual rendering of what happened. The character of petitions such as *P.Cair.Masp.* III 67283 has been described as oscillating "between document and literature,"[47] and the extent of violence described in the petition, for instance, should not be taken at face value, although it is unlikely that it was entirely the product of Dioskoros's imagination.[48] Topoi such as the helpless village community opposing a dominant outside actor occur regularly in such documents and suggest further caution when dealing with narratives of that kind.[49] In reality, Ioulianos may have technically been an outsider, but his landed property made up a considerable part of the village.[50] Obviously, we do not have access to Ioulianos's version of the story, yet we can still place the accusations against him in a larger context.

In 547/548, after the death of Dioskoros's father Apollos, who had been one of Aphrodite's *prōtokōmētai*, a certain *megaloprepestatos* Theodosios, mentioned in the previous section, collected taxes from the village, apparently without attributing it to the corresponding accounts. The Aphroditans thus still owed taxes to the province,

46 *P.Cair.Masp.* III 67283 col. I 5–11. Some parts of the text are lost and restored by the editor partially *exempli gratia*, partially on the basis of Dioskoros's other petitions. There can be little doubt, however, about the argument made and the tone in which it is advanced. The translation given above is adapted from Rowlandson 1998, 45–46 and includes restored text that Rowlandson, mostly, does not translate. On "papyrus roll" (*chartēs*), see Chapter Two, n. 117.

47 See the Introduction, n. 60. The quote is adapted from the title of Fournet 2004.

48 As Bell (1944, 34) writes in regard to the later Menas affair: "[W]e may not have Mênas's version of the story, but [...] we may feel confident that grave abuses occurred." The pagarchs' use of violence in these episodes is also discussed in Section V below.

49 See Bagnall 1989, 211–212 and Bryen 2013, 96–100. For Ioulianos's (and Menas's) connections within the village, however, see Ruffini 2008a, 191–195.

50 In *P.Cair.Masp.* I 67060, Ioulianos's *ousia* is cited as the exemplary *mega(lo)s ktētōr* before others by the pagarch Menas (note that this is based on my interpretation, discussed in the Catalog, s.v., that the *apo eparchōn* Ioulianos is the same person as the homonymous pagarch). On Zuckerman's (2004a, 221–222) suggestion that Ioulianos may have owned about 60 percent of the village's taxable land, however, see Chapter Five, Section III 1.

and Ioulianos paid the village a visit to collect them, apparently not restricting himself to harsh language.[51] Dioskoros composed a petition against both Theodosios and Ioulianos, and in 548 CE went as far as Constantinople to submit it to the imperial court. What this petition says about Ioulianos's conduct bears a similar quality to what had been described in *P.Cair.Masp.* III 67283:

> Without hesitation or mercy he ruined the inhabitants, so that they pledged large parts of their cattle and longed for their untimely death. And thereupon our said estates were torn down to the detriment of the public treasury.[52]

Ioulianos's fiscal role in the village appears to have been larger than Dioskoros is willing to admit. The main point of the petitions and rescript drafts in the Ioulianos affair is the village's *autopragia*, its being part of the *domus divina*, and its resulting fiscal independence from the city of Antaiopolis and Ioulianos in particular.[53] Comparing a rescript draft with an actual rescript in the matter suggests, however, that Dioskoros was trying to hide the fact that Ioulianos's intervention had been instigated by the provincial office.[54] In the rescript draft, Dioskoros frames the intervention by Ioulianos as if it were unrelated to this case: the pagarch is mentioned only in the second part of the document, while in the first part "the men of the provincial office" are the ones to collect the tax a second time.[55] A rescript that was actually obtained in this matter from the imperial chancery gives the presumably more trustworthy reasoning for the pagarch's intervention: here it is Ioulianos who comes to the village to collect the tax a second time because it had not been forwarded to the provincial office.[56] The double role of the pagarchs—as representatives of the city, but also as the link to the provincial administration—is on full display here, and presumably contributed much to the dispute about the extent of the pagarch's authority. The rescript does not question this

51 For narratives of this episode and the documents connected to it, see Zuckerman 2004b, especially 75–77, 82–83, and 88–90; van Minnen 2003, 118–119; Palme 2008b, 205–208; Fournet 2015, 259–261; cf. Stern 2023, 283–284.

52 *P.Cair.Masp.* I 67019 verso 19–22 (548/549 CE): [ἀό]κν̣ως καὶ [ἀ]φ\ε/ιδῶς ἀνα̣τ̣ρέπει τοὺς ἐνοικοῦντας | \ὥ̣στε/ μ̣ακ̣ρ[ᾶς] τῆς ἑαυτῶ̣ν ζωῆς ὑποκεῖσθαι καὶ ἐπικα̣λ̣ε̣ῖν ἐπὶ [τ]ὸ[ν] \πρὸ καιροῦ τὸν/ | θάνατον, καὶ τὰ εἰρημ[ένα ἡ]μ[ῶ]ν κτήματα ἐκ τούτο(υ) ἀ̣π̣ε̣τράπησαν πρὸς λ\ύ/μην | τ̣ο[ῦ] δ̣η[μο]σίου λόγο(υ).

53 *P.Cair.Masp.* III 67283 col. I 2–4; *P.Cair.Masp.* I 67019 verso 1–6; *P.Cair.Masp.* I 67024–25 (new ed. Fournet 2018) A 30–35.

54 The ultimate responsibility of the provincial *officium* was noted early by Geraci 1979, especially 197–199, an article that is (too) often left out of this discussion. See also Gelzer 1913a, 189. On the imperial perspective on such events, cf. Jones 1964, 405.

55 *P.Cair.Masp.* I 67024–25 (new ed. Fournet 2018) A 11–13 (c. 548 or 551): ὥστε τοὺς τῆς ἐπιχωρίου τάξεω\ς/ | πά̣λιν ἐκ δευτέρου τοὺς ἱ̣κέτας τὰς ἐπικείμενας αὐτοῖ\ς/ | συντελείας εἰσπρᾶξαι.

56 *SB* VI 9102.8–15 (c. September 548): φήσαντες | Θεοδόσιον τὸν μεγαλοπρεπέστατον | τοὺς ὑπὲρ τῆς ἑνδεκάτης ἐπινεμ(ήσεως) | δημοσίους ἀποπληρωθέντα φόρο[υς] | μηδὲν ὑπὲρ αὐτῶν ἐπὶ τὸ δημόσιον | καταθεῖναι, τὸν δὲ πάγαρχον | εἰσπράττειν αὐτοὺς τὰ εὐσεβῆ | τελέσματα.

visit to the autopract village, but demands that either Theodosios talk to Ioulianos, or that he properly account for what he has collected.[57]

Two other texts imply Ioulianos's fiscal role at Aphrodite, possibly that of a pagarch, as early as 551 CE, and this role does not seem irregular.[58] Additionally, Dioskoros maintained a professional relationship to Ioulianos even after the incidents of the late 540s, which can be taken to balance the picture of Ioulianos as manifestly evil. Dioskoros and his cousin-in-law Phoibammon paid their taxes (for the shares they had inherited from Dioskoros's father Apollos) to Ioulianos's collectors, mostly for family holdings at Phthla, which was not autopract.[59] But as one of the village headmen of Aphrodite, Dioskoros also acted at least twice as Ioulianos's intermediary in the pagarch's legal undertakings: one is a deed of surety for a church reader, possibly in the context of a crime, the second an acknowledgment of debt to the pagarchs from two minor tax collectors for what might have been an advance payment of the tax.[60] Phoibammon is even attested as a lessee of Ioulianos's property.[61]

In yet another rescript draft, Dioskoros himself adds a possibly revealing detail to the whole affair; here, Ioulianos is accused of having seized Apollos's property because

---

57 *SB* VI 9102.25–29.

58 *P.Ross.Georg.* V 62; *P.Cair.Masp.* III 67285. In both texts, Aphrodite's *hypodektēs* Ioannes occurs, whose *floruit* Zuckerman 2004a, 40–51 dates to 537–551. In the latter text, Ioannes collects seventeen *keratia* "for the account of remainders of the *endoxotatos apo eparchōn* Ioulianos and Enoch" (see also the following note). This Enoch was presumably not on the same hierarchical level as Ioulianos. The editor speculates that Enoch might be identical with the homonymous Antaiopolite *expelleutēs* from *P.Cair.Masp.* I 67105 (September 28–October 27, 532), but the chronological distance seems considerable. More plausible, but still dubious, is the hypothesis that Enoch may have been identical with one *lamprotatos* and *pseudotyrannos* Enoch from *P.Stras.* IV 279.7 (VI): παρὰ τῶν ποιμένων τοῦ λαμπροτάτ[ου κ]αὶ ψευδοτυρ[άν]νου ἐṇωχ[± 10]. He may thus have been another pagarch or a stand-in for Ioulianos. Note especially the link to shepherds so well known from the Antaiopolite pagarchs (on which see Section IV below)! At the end of l. 1 of *P.Cair.Masp.* III 67285 verso, something like καὶ ἑτοίμως ἔχω ταῦτα λογίζεσθαι (cf. *PSI* VIII 937.5) should be expected. The beginning of l. 3: προκ is most likely ọ̔ προκ(είμενος); there is no visible abbreviation marker on the photo, but the writer's hand is not well trained and may have simply missed it.

59 *P.Gen.* IV 193; *SB* XX 15015; *SB* XX 15013; *SB* XVI 12370 (the latter concerning Aphrodite). Presumably, Dioskoros was also the unnamed intermediary payer in *P.Cair.Masp.* I 67046; on the pattern, see Stern forthcoming (b). It is unclear how *P.Cair.Masp.* III 67285 relates to Ioulianos's pagarchy. Ioulianos appears here in the tax title together with a certain Enoch (ll. 2–3: εἰς λόγον λοιπάδ(ων) τοῦ ἐνδọξ(οτάτου) ạ̓π̣ὸ ἐπάρχ(ων) | Ἰο(υ)λιανο(ῦ) κạὶ Ἐνώχ), but the document is signed by Aphrodite's *hypodektēs* Ioannes.

60 Deed of surety: *P.Cair.Masp.* I 67094. Acknowledgment of debt: *P.Lond.* V 1661; see also Ruffini 2008a, 193–194. The pagarchs would probably not have been personally involved in routine procedures such as these, which were handled at the village level. But they probably would have wanted to know about loans given to *boēthoi* in their names, as documented in *P.Lond.* V 1661, although one may have little doubt that the risk of such loans would have been borne by Dioskoros and his colleague.

61 *PSI* IV 283 (December 20, 550).

of Apollos's debts.[62] This adds to the information that a faction within the village had turned against Apollos's heirs, among them Dioskoros, because of the repeated tax demand.[63] That Ioulianos, consciously or unconsciously, may have assisted a competing village faction puts the problems that Dioskoros's kin had with Ioulianos in a different light.[64] The situation would not have been helped by the dramatic increase in the gold taxes on arable land, which (compared to 536 CE) had risen probably by about 50 percent by 551 and by about 100 percent by the mid-560s.[65] In this climate, the frictions within Aphrodite became clearer than ever before, and Dioskoros had recurring clashes with a dominant faction around the *prōtokōmētai* Herakleios and Ioannes. The village's own responsibility for tax collection, the *autopragia*, can in fact be seen as an institution that only one part of the village (elite) actually profited from, sowing the seeds for internal discord.[66] People such as Dioskoros's archrivals Herakleios and Ioannes may have jumped at the opportunity to boost their standing with the help of the pagarch.[67] The petitions of course strive to present to the authorities a picture of social cohesion among a "silent majority," but the conflicts in the Aphroditan society known from the sixth-century papyri suggest a deep internal rift about how to deal with the Antaiopolite officials.[68] These frictions came to a new height when the *megaloprepestatos* Theodosios took the village's taxes, and an unspecified number of Aphroditan landowners turned to Dioskoros and his relatives for compensation, apparently seizing part of their estates. Dioskoros's decision to write with the villagers' voice must thus also be seen as a strategy to cover up that community's internal conflicts—by evoking the impression of a village community that stood united against individual malicious

62 *P.Cair.Masp.* I 67026.7–10 (the Dioskoros in this text is Apollos's nephew, not his son, the poet and notary); Zuckerman 2004b, 77; van Minnen 2003, 122.

63 *P.Cair.Masp.* I 67024–25 (new ed. Fournet 2018) A 24–30 and B 23–28 (not part of the passage redacted in A') and Zuckerman 2004b, 77 and 88–89; cf. Amelotti & Migliardi Zingale 1985, no. 10. Note especially that in version A, Dioskoros provides the reason for the Aphroditan landowners to proceed against Apollos as ἀφορμὴ τῆς τοῦ εἰρημέ(νου) δημοσίου δευτέρας εἰσπράξεως (l. 27), but that this part has been crossed out in A and no longer features in B, the latest version of the text, which may be suggestive of Dioskoros's intention to avoid inadvertently providing a plausible explanation for the "raids."

64 On "Dioskoros's faction," see Ruffini 2008b and Ruffini 2018a, 60–74, which offer compelling analyses of Aphrodite's internal conflicts.

65 Bransbourg 2016, 342–345, Table 14; see also Zuckerman 2004a, 213–219. This increase, as established by Bransbourg from Antaiopolite *and* Oxyrhynchite sources, seems particularly noteworthy since it occurs in the aftermath of the Justinianic plague, which hit Egypt for the first time in 541 CE. For some intriguing speculations about the possible reasons for this situation, see Bransbourg 2016, 399–400, to which I would add the, equally speculative, hypothesis that the imperial government may have taxed less-affected regions more to offset losses elsewhere.

66 See n. 19 above. The "village's"—in fact, Dioskoros's faction's—fierce defense of its *autopragia* would hide that Dioskoros and his kin were among the profiteers of that arrangement, and others in the village therefore may have been looking to undermine that institution.

67 Ruffini 2008b; Zuckerman 2004b, 77, 88–89.

68 Stern 2023, 289 with references.

perpetrators. Conflicts and rivalries with the shepherds of the neighboring village of Phthla, discussed in the following section, also point to more animosity on the ground than Dioskoros is willing to admit.

All in all, it is unlikely that Ioulianos's access to the village was irregular; rather, it seems to have been related to a village in tax arrears. Still, Dioskoros accuses the pagarch of considerable violence. How the authorities responded will be discussed at the end of this chapter, but first we turn to the Menas affair.

III. The Reluctant, or Incapable, Taxpayer

In 567 CE, some fifteen years after the Ioulianos episode, Dioskoros, in the voice of his fellow Aphroditans,[69] filed the petition *P.Cair.Masp.* I 67002 against the pagarch Menas Scriniarius, addressing the latter's direct superior, the *dux et Augustalis* Athanasios.[70] This document strikes a quite similar tone to *P.Cair.Masp.* III 67283 against Ioulianos, but takes the pagarchs' malevolence to another level. In multiple columns, Dioskoros describes at length how Menas and his armed auxiliaries violently entered the village. Not only did they seize land, harvest, cattle, and money and arrest villagers, they also allegedly left a trail of destruction in the fields and set houses ablaze.[71] Some of the most vivid passages may illustrate the extent of the accusations. First, Menas had some villagers persecuted and arrested while they were abroad:

> We inform our good lord that during the past tenure of the *endoxotatos referendarius* Kyros the aforementioned *lamprotatos* Menas wrote a letter to the *peribleptos comes* and *illoustrios megaloprepestatos* Serenos, the most eloquent *scholastikos*, at the time when we attended the traditional cattle market at Thynis, because we habitually go there every year to do business with the livestock for our alimentation and that of our children. But there we were ambushed by the *dioikētai* of the *endoxotatos illoustrios* Serenos and thrown into the local jail, whence we were taken to the prison of Antinoopolis and then to the prison of Antaiopolis. Later, we were handed over to the aforementioned pagarch Menas, who subjected us to manifold abuses and tortures, kept us in custody for a period of six months, and demanded 117 *nomismata* as fines from us in addition to what we had paid when we were being tortured in Thynis and in the prison of Antinoopolis.[72]

Then, under Kyros's successor Athanasios, Menas also had Dioskoros persecuted. Finally, Menas advanced violently toward the village:

69 Keenan 2008b, 178–179; Stern 2023, 274 n. 8.
70 Some background to this document is discussed in Stern 2023 in a different context. Where needed, I retrace relevant arguments from that article, the manuscript of which was basically completed by 2018.
71 See Stern 2023, 271–272 for an introduction to this document with references to earlier scholarship and the main narrative outline.
72 *P.Cair.Masp.* I 67002 col. II 1–7.

> And he came with a force of robbers, *paganoi*, and soldiers, and made the village his prey, laying it waste worse than barbarians could have done and burning certain distinguished houses of the old great proprietors of the village, and he took seven hundred *nomismata* under the name of public taxes without giving receipts for them and credited us with none of the sum.[73]

These and similar descriptions of the pagarch's violence and the villagers' suffering made a lasting impression on modern scholars.[74]

Again, we are well-advised to read Dioskoros's accusations carefully in order to reveal what is actually at issue here. The petition's vivid language and detail prompt us, for instance, to look twice at the poet-notary's own role in the storyline he creates. In the voice of his fellow Aphroditans addressing the *dux*, Dioskoros describes his stay in Antinoopolis, in essence, as exile that he had to resort to because of aggressive interventions by the pagarch:

> We inform your *paneuphēmos* authority that since the beginning of the recently elapsed fifteenth indiction, when he (i.e., Menas) took over the pagarchy of Antaiopolis, he has been reaping the profit of the arouras of our common brother, the wretched servant of your renowned philanthropy, Dioskoros, a man utterly in need, who has young children scarcely knowing as yet their right hand from their left, who need heavy expenses for their maintenance. And the said pitiless man (i.e., Menas) scrupled not to bestow on the *boēthos* of the village of Phthla and on its shepherds—free of rent and taxes, to appropriate to themselves—his (i.e., Dioskoros's) arouras, which they enjoy without rent and taxes, leaving to him, to his utter destruction, the tax quota on them, assigned to his charge. (…) And without a legal redress he remains to date abroad with his children, beseeching that he may obtain your good judgment of the case, master.[75]

This image is daunting and does not appear to leave any doubt about Menas's actions being the essential reason for the move to Antinoopolis. Dioskoros implies that his return only depends on Menas's being brought back in line—a reasoning by and large echoed in modern accounts of that episode.[76] It is no surprise, however, that having to take refuge is a common topos in petitions, notably in the context of "fiscal oppression."[77] Nor is it surprising to find well-educated administrators moving from the countryside to the administrative centers. Dioskoros is certainly not the only example of those,[78] although the best-documented one. Indeed, the provincial capital

73 *P.Cair.Masp.* I 67002 col. II 23–26 (translation adapted from Bell 1944, 34).

74 For more examples, see Stern 2023, 272 with references. The influence that Dioskoros's "emotional strategies" had on modern scholars' perception of his narratives and, thus, of late antiquity in general is discussed in Palme 2021, 338.

75 *P.Cair.Masp.* I 67002 col. I 9–15 and 18–19 (translation adapted from Bell 1944, 33).

76 For a discussion, see Stern 2023, 278, especially n. 27.

77 Fournet 1999, 321 n. 438; Ziche 2006, 128–132.

78 See Gagos & van Minnen 1994, 21 and Keenan 2001, 71–72 for a comparable interpretation. Similar patterns are presented in Keenan 2001, 66–68 and 70 for Antinoopolis and 72–73 for Oxyrhynchos, the capital of Arcadia.

Antinoopolis was not the worst place for him to end up, as we soon find him as notary attached to the circles of provincial administration.[79] It is revealing that Dioskoros emphatically describes firsthand the arrival of the celebratory images on the occasion of Justin II's inauguration.[80] Justin's accession took place on November 14, 565, but according to Dioskoros's own words in the petition, Menas did not become pagarch until April 26, 566, and only then started to supposedly harass Dioskoros.[81] Even if we grant some time for the news of a new emperor to make it to the Thebaid, and some more for the imperial images to follow,[82] this seems an implausible timeline, given that in this storyline the new pagarch Menas would still need at least some time to "sufficiently" pursue Dioskoros to make him leave Aphrodite. Consequently, Dioskoros was probably no longer dwelling in his native village when Menas assumed the pagarchy.[83] Indeed the petition never mentions that Dioskoros was still at Aphrodite or had to endure any personal persecution when it describes the start of Menas's tenure; only Dioskoros's lands are ever mentioned as the target of any concrete actions.[84]

Another chain of events therefore seems more likely: Menas went after Dioskoros's land in and around Aphrodite precisely because the poet-notary no longer dwelled in the village. Otherwise, it would also be difficult to understand why, if Dioskoros really was "persecuted," he left his wife and some of his children behind. Neither does Dioskoros's return to Aphrodite coincide with the end of Menas's pagarchy.[85] What is

79 On Dioskoros's connections to the ducal *officium*, see Palme 2008b, 211 and cf. MacCoull 1986. We know that Dioskoros was with his son Petros, who then became the apprentice of a local intellectual; see Fournet 2008b, 28.

80 *P.Aphrod.Lit.* IV 17 and the editor's commentary on pp. 567–568; see also MacCoull 1988, 72–75. Dioskoros can thus be expected to have been in the city for some time. Dioskoros apparently dwelled at Aphrodite as late as November 7, 565 (*P.Lond.* V 1686). See Chapter Two, n. 113, for a potential echo of this event in Antaiopolis, although I think an alternative interpretation is more likely. On the ceremony of the *adventus* of imperial portraits, see Humphries 2019, 39–40 and Pfeilschifter 2014, 140 n. 57 with further references.

81 Stern 2023, 278 n. 30. See also Chapter Four, n. 15 on the start of Menas's pagarchy.

82 Fournet 1999, 330–331 (cf. 321) places the arrival of these images at the very end of 565 or the beginning of 566 CE. This roughly coincides, he argues, with the commencement of Athanasios's tenure as *dux* and Dioskoros's move to Antinoopolis.

83 If, however, Dioskoros's firsthand view of the arrival of the images was merely a poetic fiction and he still dwelled in his native village at the time the effigies arrived, this would serve as an argument that he embellished Menas's pursuits. The tone of *P.Aphrod.Lit.* IV 17 is entirely in line with the other encomia and we would have to conclude that Dioskoros "applied" for a position in the ducal administration already from Aphrodite.

84 *P.Cair.Masp.* I 67002 col. I 9–19. And while Dioskoros says that he "remains to date abroad with his children," he never actually makes the reasoning that he went there because of Menas's actions; see l. 18–19: καὶ ἀνεκδίκητος ὑπάρχει | ὁ ἄθλιο[ς] ἕως νῦν ἐπὶ ξένης σὺν τέκνοις, αἰτῶν \ὧν καὶ/ ἐκδικίας ἀγαθῆς ὑμῶν τυχεῖν, δέσπο(τα). While Dioskoros is not saying anything untrue, he is certainly insinuating.

85 Menas was probably no longer pagarch in March 570, while Dioskoros dwelled in Antinoopolis until at least November 570; see Stern 2023, 279 and n. 31.

more, this episode alludes to Menas seizing Dioskoros's land in the neighboring village of Phthla and giving it to Kyros, the *boēthos* of that village, whom Dioskoros accuses of cultivating his land without paying rents or taxes.[86] Yet, in one of his poems, Dioskoros quite explicitly states that Kyros and his shepherd entourage came onto Dioskoros's grounds only during harvest season, likely to confiscate the grain.[87] Dioskoros's problems with the shepherds at Phthla moreover reportedly date back as far as the twelfth and thirteenth indictions—three years before Menas took office with the start of the fifteenth—and are, again, motivated by the collection of taxes.[88]

At other times, in striking contrast to the picture of Menas in *P.Cair.Masp.* I 67002, where he is presented as rather diabolical, Menas appears to have maintained a much more pragmatic, perhaps even friendly, relationship with Dioskoros and his kin. Unfortunately, all these documents are undated. In two letters, Menas is linked to orders that certain men must not disturb Dioskoros's lands or farmers, and in another one, he appears to settle some land registration issue, again in favor of Dioskoros's kin.[89] A letter from Menas himself to a *prōtokōmētēs* may document his involvement in a procedure surrounding a legal issue, but the papyrus is very fragmentary and the content largely obscure.[90] Other letters from or about Menas show him in a professional relationship with Aphrodite's *prōtokōmētai*, including Dioskoros, just as we have seen for the pagarch Ioulianos. The contexts of these documents are not always clear, since they

86 *P.Cair.Masp.* I 67002 col. I 13–19; on this man, see Ruffini 2011, s.v. Kuros 26 (Kyros is not *Augustalis*, however, but the son of a certain Augustalia; see Vanderheyden 2015, 154). The same events are alluded to in *P.Lond.* V 1677.13–16.

87 *P.Aphrod.Lit.* IV 11.72–78; for the exact timing, cf. Fournet 1999, 323. I therefore suspect that similar sounding accusations in another case (e.g., *P.Cair.Masp.* I 67021 verso 1–4) may also be explained in this manner, if one were to defend the pagarch here.

88 As shown by the Coptic letter Vanderheyden 2015, no. 15 (new ed. of MacCoull 1993, no. 11). On the role of the shepherds in tax collection, see Section IV below.

89 See *P.Lond.* V 1683.1–2: [– – – ο]ụṣ σọὺς ἐδέξατο ὁ λαμπρότατος κύριος Μηνᾶς. Πάραυτα οὖν | [πρὸς ἡμᾶς κατά?]λαβε ἵνα ἀπαλλάξαι τὸ πρᾶγμα σο(υ) and *P.Lond.* V 1682.2–5: μέλλων (...) | ἀπελθεῖν εἰς Μọυṿκρῆκιν μετὰ το(ῦ) λαμπρ(οτάτου) κυρίου Μηνᾶ καὶ ἐπέτρεψα | τῷ ποιμένι κατὰ τύχην εὑρεθέντι ἐγγὺς μου μὴ ὀχλῆσαι τοῖς γεωργοῖς | σου. Both texts refer to a meeting in the Antaiopolite village of Mounkrechis and probably relate to the same chain of events. They appear to be from Menas's first pagarchy in the 550s, for when Menas became pagarch in 566 CE, Dioskoros was probably no longer village headman, as he was in Antinoopolis; for the chronology of Dioskoros's move to Antinoopolis, see above. The address on the verso of *P.Lond.* V 1682 is heavily abraded, but from the photo it looks like the line was considerably longer than the text provided by the edition. Furthermore, [† τῷ δεσ]π̣ό̣τ̣(η) μ̣ου seems a doubtful restoration to me, since the writer refers to Dioskoros as *adelphotēs* in the main text, meaning he is unlikely to have addressed him as *despotēs* in the address; probably the writer was another *prōtokōmētēs*. The other text that shows Menas bailing Dioskoros out is *SB* XX 14241, in which Menas again takes actions to ensure that certain men will no longer harass Dioskoros (ll. 11–15). Cf. *P.Oxy.* XVI 1831 (Oxyrhynchites; late V–early VI), where a village headman invokes the authority of the pagarch(s?) as a threat to persuade his opponent to concede.

90 *P.Cair.Masp.* I 67083.

were written for those "in the know" and therefore do not provide much context, but they seem to concern issues of tax collection.[91]

These instances show a more favorable side of the Antaiopolite pagarchy and, moreover, that like Ioulianos, Menas was not constantly perceived as Aphrodite's bad guy. That this changed—even if only from the perspective of one of the village's factions—was probably not due to repeated attempts at personal enrichment on Menas's part, but to Aphrodite's repeated failure to fulfill its fiscal obligations. An undated letter, probably dating back to Menas's first pagarchy in the 550s, suggests that the pagarchs had reason to be nervous about the Aphroditans' ability to effectuate their payments in time. In this short note, Menas sends a fierce warning to the village headmen, Dioskoros and a certain Apollos, to hand over due taxes by the next day:[92]

> The *diakonētēs* most beloved of God has reported to me nothing at all from your village, and see that the large landowners of the city, for example, the estate (*ousia*) of the *endoxotatos apo eparchōn* Ioulianos, which contributes (*syntelousa*) to the *kōmētikon*, has (*sic*!) already paid its full quota, and see, it gave me no anxiety in this regard. (I have written) in order that you know that if you do not bring me by tomorrow the quota of the *astikon* and the *kōmētikon* in full, you will not be delighted about your behavior. Be aware, I have written to warn you! And come with Apollos, for I need to talk to you (singular!).[93]

While this letter does thus not immediately relate to the events of *P.Cair.Masp.* I 67002, it suggests that the Aphroditans had a recurring problem with their tax payments.

It has recently been suggested that Aphrodite had lost its *autopragia* before the end of the 550s due to its fiscal problems that had become evident early in the Ioulianos episode, and there is indeed a lot to this hypothesis.[94] At the least, the extent of *autopragia*

91 *P.Cair.Masp.* I 67060 (the *prōtokōmētai* are to hand over the taxes and meet Menas); *P.Cair. Masp.* I 67061 (the *prōtokōmētai* are to meet Menas immediately); *P.Lond.* V 1684; and *PSI* VIII 939 (Menas has to deal with issues concerning the *embolē*).

92 *P.Cair.Masp.* I 67060. This text is probably still from the autopract era. Taxes for local expenses such as the *kōmētika* and *astika* would supposedly not have been affected by the *autopragia*, i.e., the payment to the provincial office. For the date, see Fournet & Gascou 2002, 35 n. 43 and Stern 2023, 280 n. 38, but cf. *P.Lond.* V 1677, which relates to Menas's second pagarchy and in which also an Apollos (Ruffini 2011, s.v. Apollos 154) is *prōtokōmētēs*. Menas's second pagarchy started when Dioskoros was already in Antinoopolis. Would Dioskoros still be addressed in his capacity as *prōtokōmētēs*? Presumably not, and moreover, the document tells Dioskoros to send Apollos to him, who was presumably not in Antinoopolis (cf. nn. 82, 85, and 89 above). On this Apollos, see Ruffini 2011, s.v. Apollos 129.

93 *P.Cair.Masp.* I 67060 (translation adapted from Sarris 2006, 110); especially ll. 4–6 (see *BL* XII 45): ἵνα ṭ[ὲ] (read δὲ) μ̣ά̣θηṭε̣ ὅτι εἰ μὴ δι̣[ὰ τ]ῆς α̣ὔ̣ριον ἐξενέγκητέ μοι | τὸ μέτρον τοῦ τε ἀστικο(ῦ) καὶ κωμητικο(ῦ) ἐπλήρους, ο[ὐ]κ [ἔχετε] ε̣[ὐ]χαριστῆσαι̣ τῷ | πράγματι, ἰδοὺ οὖν, γέγραφα διαμαρτυρο̣(ύ)μενος ὑ̣μ̣[ῖν. The letter *P.Cair.Masp.* I 67061 may be placed in the same context.

94 Admittedly, in the Antaiopolite tax receipts from the 560s and 570s (see Stern forthcoming (b)), receipts for the *embolē* of Aphrodite are never signed in the pagarch's name but only by Aphroditan village officials, whereas two receipts for the *embolē* signed by Matoi, *boēthos* of Phthla,

vis-à-vis the pagarch's authority was significantly limited. Whereas the petitions against Ioulianos put the *autopragia* prominently in the foreground, little of that argument appears to be left in the documents from the 560s.[95] In *P.Cair.Masp.* I 67002 (567 CE) the *autopragia* of old is a distant memory, and the villagers complain that the pagarch Menas did not properly balance their account with what he took from them, nor did they obtain proper receipts.[96] Menas seized animals and "plundered" the pagarchy under the "pretext" of taxes.[97] But then it is acknowledged that the pagarch regularly collects the tax payments, and the villagers are insistent on the point that they (or their ancestors) had always paid on time.[98] Despite modern claims to the contrary, Menas—unlike Ioulianos—is never actually accused of trying to bring Aphrodite under his pagarchy. And it is certainly revealing in this regard that in the 540s the Aphroditans claim that Ioulianos "tries, against all custom, to forcefully drag us into (!) the pagarchy of Antaiopolis," implying that their village is not part of it; in 567, however, Menas's "plundering the pagarchy" and its goods clearly includes Aphrodite—that is, the Aphroditans perceive their village as part of the pagarchy.[99] Unlike the situation during the autopract era, here

---

are indeed signed in the name of the pagarchs. But as argued in Chapter Two, Section III 2, these receipts relate to different stages of the collection procedure: the payment is registered with the *boēthoi* (viz., for *kōmētika*; see *P.Gen.* IV 193.1–2: *embolē* "for the *kōmētika*") or with the *hypodektai* (viz., for *astika*, although there is no testimony for an *embolē* payment "for the *astika*"), whereas the *loading* is confirmed by Aphrodite's village officials. It is conceivable that Phthla also processed its tax grain through the ships belonging to elites from the nearby larger "village" of Aphrodite.

95 Geraci 1979, 201–202; Stern 2015, 127–129.

96 *Autopragia* of old: *P.Cair.Masp.* I 67002 col. III 5–9; see also the preceding section. Accounting: *P.Cair.Masp.* I 67002 col. II 13 and 24–25. See also Mirković 1996, 357 and Zuckerman 2004a, 213. By contrast, the petition's remark that "there have been until now eight pagarchs of Antaiopolis without us having ever been in arrears with the imperial taxes (*basilikoi phoroi*) or the *embolē*" (*P.Cair.Masp.* I 67002 col. II 18–19; for *basilikoi phoroi* as taxes, see *P.Lond.* V 1676.50–51) is ambiguous; see Chapter One, nn. 135 and 136. It may refer, as Zuckerman argues, to the pagarchs in office since the abolition of the *autopragia*, but this would suggest a rather swift turnover among the pagarchs. The comment may, alternatively, refer to the pagarch's authority in the event of arrears (Geraci 1979, 203–205), so that Dioskoros essentially wants to convey that "for as long as there have been pagarchs of Antaiopolis, we have never been in conflict with them over the payment of arrears for the imperial taxes or the *embolē*." This, however, would imply rather long tenures for the—in this case—four pagarchs before Ioulianos (and for Ioulianos himself; see Chapter Four, Section II) and that they were all sole pagarchs. Cf. Chapter Four, Section IV: tax increases in the 540s and 550s could have required additional pagarchs to cover the risk, and the evidence suggests that at least Ioulianos had no colleagues until 552/553 CE.

97 *P.Cair.Masp.* I 67002 col. II 17 and 25; col. III 12–14; *P.Cair.Masp.* I 67021 verso 9; *P.Lond.* V 1677.34–36.

98 *P.Cair.Masp.* I 67002 col. I 16–17; col. II 17 and 22; *P.Cair.Masp.* I 67021 verso 13–14.

99 Cf. *P.Cair.Masp.* III 67283 col. I 2: βούλεται παρὰ τὸ] ἔ̣θ̣ος ἡμᾶς ἑλκ[έσ]θαι εἰς π̣α̣γαρχίαν τῆ[ς Ἀνταιο(υ)]π̣ο̣λ̣ιτῶν ἧς κεκράτηκε̣ν κτλ. and *P.Cair.Masp.* I 67024–25 (new ed. Fournet 2018) A 31–32: τὴν κατ' αὐτοὺς | κώμην ὑπὸ τὴν οἰκείαν παγαρχίαν ποιήσασθαι (Ioulianos) with *P.Cair. Masp.* I 67002 col. III 20: οὐκ' ἐπαύσατο μανιῶν διόλο(υ) διαρπάξαι καὶ ἀθετῆσαί φησιν τὴν

it is Menas who collects the tax (*dēmosion*), which is tellingly not even worth an additional accusation.[100] In another petition relating to this matter, the villagers complain about "the yoke of the pagarchy" under which they now pay their taxes, and report that the *dux* had ordered the pagarch to collect only "the net taxes," so to drop at least the unbearable surcharges, the "punishing *diagrapha*."[101]

Figures are a more difficult matter. According to *P.Cair.Masp.* I 67002, Menas had 200 *nomismata* collected on top of the regular *dēmosion*, probably as exactly that surcharge, as pagarch, so he was considered responsible for the regular tax collection.[102] But

παγαρχίαν, ἣν ἐξεπọ́ρθησεν ἀποτεθεικὼς τὰ τα(ύ)της χρήματα εἰς τὰ Ἄπα Σενουθί̣[ο(υ)] (Menas). An implicit territorial meaning of παγαρχία is apparent here, but an abstract notion of the pagarch's authority would also be a fitting explanation. The ambiguity is probably intended, since the text also seeks to highlight Ioulianos's malevolence and thus is obviously playing with the manifold shades of κρατέω in the relative clause, including "etwas in seine Gewalt nehmen, sich bemächtigen" versus "besitzen, innehaben" (see *WB*, s.v.).

100 *P.Cair.Masp.* I 67002 col. II 22; *P.Cair.Masp.* I 67021 verso 13–14.

101 *P.Lond.* V 1674 (c. 570?). "Yoke of the pagarchy" (of course a play on the word *zygon*, which can be translated as "yoke," but in fiscal contexts usually means simply "measure"): εἰλ]κύσθημεν εὐγενῶ̣ς κ̣[αὶ] | ἐλευθερικῶς τὸν βίον κατ[αγ]ọ́μεṿ[ον ....] τῆς παγαρχίας ζυγὸν παṛ[ὰ?] | τῶν ἀποφθαλμιωσαμένωṿ τῆ[ς? – – –]....[πε?]π̣ραγμẹ́ṿọụ τ̣ε τ̣ῶ̣[ν] | παγάρχων τῶν ἡμᾶς α̣.[– – –]... ἄγειν εἰς δουλẹί̣α̣ṿ (ll. 15–18). "Net taxes": κατελέησεν ἡμᾶς τότε \προσέταξεν/ μηδὲν ἀπαιτῆ\σ̣[αι]/ | εἰ μὴ αὐτὰ μόνα τὰ ξηρὰ δημόσια (ll. 96–97). Unbearable surcharges, "punishing *diagrapha*": καθ' ἑκάστην ἐπινοουμένοι εἴς τε | διαγραφῶν ζημίας ẹụχ.[..] κ[αὶ?] ἀ̣π̣[αιτήσεις? πα]ρὰ τὸ ἔθος (ll. 22–23). This text also informs the debate about tax increases and additional surcharges on the land taxes (Zuckerman 2004a, 120 and 214–217; Bransbourg 2016, 342–345), and the responsibility of the pagarchs for collecting them (ll. 96–97; see Zuckerman 2004a, 214).

102 *P.Cair.Masp.* I 67002 col. II 22–23; Zuckerman 2004a, 213. The petition is explicit here that these exactions, by "the aforementioned pagarch," took place "under the former *endoxotatos referendarius*," i.e., the former *dux* Kyros; see also *P.Lond.* V 1677.16 and the commentary and cf. Zuckerman 2004a, 213 n. 254. This passage therefore poses a problem for Fournet's (1999, 330–331) hypothesis that Athanasios would have taken office at the end of 565 or the beginning of 566 CE, since Menas only took up the pagarchy with the beginning of the fifteenth indiction (*P.Cair.Masp.* I 67002 col. I 10–11), i.e., on April 26/May 1, 566 (for more doubts about this chronology, see n. 115 below and cf. Morelli 2008a, 235 n. 40). To argue that Athanasios was governor "for the second year," and not "for the second time," Fournet points out that in *P.Oxy.* XVI 1920 (563 CE) Athanasios is not referred to as *dux*; but the title of *dux* would not be expected to appear in the documentary context of that papyrus, which does not require an "extended reference" (see Chapter Five, Section II). Athanasios was a *patricius*, which is a far more exclusive title that would be considered sufficient in a short reference. There is a possible explanation of the resulting chronological dilemma, but it is very conjectural: The first aspect of that explanation concerns the supposed synchronism of Athanasios's installation as *dux et Augustalis* with the arrival of the images of the new emperor Justin II (accession on November 14, 565). Athanasios may have just been designated, and received Dioskoros's praise as such, or the news of a new emperor (let alone the arrival of his images) simply took longer to reach the Thebaid than Fournet assumes. I find the latter option realistic; cf. above for my discussion of the start of Dioskoros's stay in Antinoopolis, with references in n. 80 to discussions of the timeline of an "imaginary" imperial *adventus*. The second aspect concerns the collection of the two

the petition, as quoted at the beginning of this section, states that Menas had also taken 117 *nomismata* from the villagers as "fines" (*zēmiōmata*)—probably for arrears from the preceding year that made him go after the villagers in the first place. This amount was paid during their internment in Antaiopolis, whereas an undefined amount had been paid during the earlier detention in Thynis and Antinoopolis, and perhaps both amounts are included in the 200 *nomismata*. After collecting these 200 *nomismata*, Menas supposedly returned with armed forces to the village still in the same fiscal year 566/567, and extracted a further 700 *nomismata* from the villagers, again "under the name of public taxes," but we have little way of knowing whether this constituted Aphrodite's entire gold tax rate for the fifteenth indiction.[103] In any case, Gilles Bransbourg in his study on taxation rates in late antique Egypt has convincingly argued that Aphrodite was not alone in facing tax hikes, but that the whole of Egypt was probably subject to the imperial government's mounting thirst for cash, or rather, gold.[104] The appearance of two and even three pagarchs after the sole pagarchy of Ioulianos at the beginning of the 550s may even reflect the need for higher sureties from affluent aristocrats who could guarantee the flow of gold through commutation. Aphrodite's loss of its *autopragia* may therefore have been, at least in part, due to its insufficient capacity to arrange payments in gold.[105] There is additional evidence that this period saw an

hundred *nomismata* by Menas that supposedly happened under the former governor (*P.Cair. Masp.* I 67002 col. II 22–23). We may assume that these exactions took place immediately after the start of Menas's tenure on April 26/May 1, 566. Athanasios might have taken office with the beginning of a new indiction, i.e., on the same date that Menas assumed the pagarchy. Perhaps, for some reason, it took the new *dux* longer than usual to reach Antinoopolis (see *P.Ant.* II 96 for an official who was "late to work"), so that Menas's collection of the two hundred *nomismata* happened, de facto, still under Kyros. Athanasios's formal tenure might, however, still have been counted starting with the inception of the indiction year. This would result in May–July 567 (the date of *P.Cair.Masp.* I 67002; see col. I 10) being part of Athanasios's "second year," while still leaving a—however small—time window for Menas in May 566 to extract the two hundred *nomismata* under Kyros.

103 *P.Cair.Masp.* I 67002 col. II 22–25 (also quoted at the beginning of this section). Banaji 2007, 27 and 230 adds all these amounts and assumes that the resulting total of 1,017 *nomismata* constitutes Aphrodite's tax payments for a single year. Other scholars apparently count the unspecified amount as part of the 117 *nomismata* and the 200 *nomismata* as part of the 700. Keenan 2008, 176 cautions against the use of this figure (817 *nomismata* plus surcharge of 200 *nomismata*) as the total of Aphrodite's gold tax payments for one year—against Zuckerman 2004a, 213–214, who reads this amount as part of the *dēmosion* mentioned in l. 13. Cf. Bransbourg 2016, 332–333, who operates with Zuckerman's figures (and assigns these payments—erroneously, I believe—to the first instead of the preceding fifteenth indiction) and argues that the 117 *nomismata* were "levied as advances"; however, the text of the petition does not say this. The timeline of events and the wording suggest that the 117 *nomismata* are linked to an earlier demand.

104 Bransbourg 2016; the main conclusions about this increase are assembled in Table 14 on p. 345. Zuckerman 2004a, 120 argues that the increases documented in *P.Lond.* V 1674 were due to the village's recent subjection to the pagarchy.

105 Cf. *P.Lond.Herm.*, which has been conclusively interpreted to show that the Hermopolite village of Temseu Skordon in the early sixth century effectuated most of its payments in copper coinage.

increasing financial burden on imperial subjects throughout the empire.[106] But the entire point of the privilege of *autopragia* was that the privileged payer would be able to provide a stable and secure flow of income for the state, and the privilege was therefore likely to be in peril when this condition could no longer be met.[107]

The petition *P.Cair.Masp.* I 67002, addressed to the *dux et Augustalis* Athanasios, also manifests an intriguing chronological issue in one of the excerpts quoted above that further supports the impression of the Aphroditans' serious and chronic financial struggles. Under the previous governor Kyros, thirteen villagers had attended a cattle market in the village of Thynis in the Hermopolite nome.[108] Menas—in this part of the petition identified simply by his epithet *lamprotatos*, but without the title of pagarch—is said to have written a letter to a certain Serenos, who had the villagers ambushed and thrown into a local jail before transferring them to the prison of Antinoopolis, the nearby provincial capital.[109] From Antinoopolis, the villagers issued a petition to the then-governor Kyros before they were transferred into custody—apparently, of Menas's predecessor—at Antaiopolis, and only "later" were handed over to Menas, whom the petition at that point refers to as "the pagarch."[110] Since a meticulous study

---

The use of "*n nomismata* minus *n keratia*" (the editors use the equivalent form "*n solidi* minus *n siliquae*") in that context appears to show that this formula refers to actual gold payments and not, as the editor of *P.Aphrod.Reg.* argued, to a lower standard of the *nomisma* (= *solidus*) at that time; on this point see Kruse 2015, 204–207. The ubiquity of this phrase throughout *P.Aphrod. Reg.* would then indicate that the Aphroditans collected most of their taxes in copper but paid most of them in gold and got back their "change" in copper coinage. It must have been at this intermediate point that the capacity of the village leaders to convert these amounts was crucial, and this capacity supposedly played a significant role in the conflicts that played out at Aphrodite—namely when only some of the village elite were able to profit from it and when the village was not able to meet the demands.

106 In 566 CE, Justin II considered it worthwhile to remit all tax arrears that were still extant from 552/553 to 559/560. But the main beneficiaries of such measures were the richer landowners, and Justin's decision to repay all public debt may have in fact led to the peak in gold tax rates during the period of 565–568. See Iust. *nov.* 148.1 and Bransbourg 2016, 388–389; cf. Haldon 2005, 54.

107 Geraci 1979, 204; cf. *C.Th.* XI 1.34 (429 CE; see Chapter One, n. 34), which concerns similar arrangements and their potential revocation for Africa, probably due to the particular distribution of civic administrative control in that region.

108 On the identification of Θηνις (*P.Cair.Masp.* I 67002 col. II 2 and 6) with Thynis (*TM* Geo ID 2923), see Keenan 2008 and Gascou 1996, 341 (= 2008, 408). A fragmentary contract with people from Thynis that may belong to the Dioskoros archive is MacCoull 1993, no. 19. Earlier scholarship (e.g., Rémondon 1961, 78) identified Θηνις with This (Girga; *TM* Geo ID 2400), about fourty-five miles south of Aphrodite, but the transport of the prisoners from this place past Antaiopolis to Antinoopolis in the north and then back south to Antaiopolis would make less sense.

109 *P.Cair.Masp.* I 67002 col. II 1–5. On the possibility of identifying this Serenos with the homonymous Antaiopolite pagarch, see the Catalog, s.v.

110 The petition proceeds in a chronological loop here that invites explanation. After describing the imprisonment in Antinoopolis for the first time (col. II 5), the petition proceeds to mention the transfer to Antaiopolis and that "later" (ὕστερον) the villagers were "handed over to the said pag-

by Federico Morelli has suggested that Dioskoros, in drafting *P.Cair.Masp.* I 67002, was highly attentive to the status and offices that an individual held at a given time in the narrated events,[111] there is good reason to believe that the pagarchy is purposely absent in the parts of the story that deal with Thynis and Antinoopolis. This would entail that the petition to Kyros (which the petitioners issued from Antinoopolis) was sent before Menas took office, and that Menas was taking care of business ahead of his tenure.[112] He wrote a letter to his fellow Serenos requesting that notorious tax debtors be arrested so he would be able to receive them in Antaiopolis right at the beginning of his tenure.[113] This chain of events fits perfectly with James Keenan's identification of the cattle market that the villagers attended as the "festival of Thynis." This festival was held in late March,[114] that is, about one month before Menas took on the pag-

---

arch Menas." But then (col. II 7–11) the narrative jumps back to the scene at Antinoopolis and Hermopolis—Serenos, his agents, and the villagers' cattle reappear—and describes the petition to Kyros before the transfer to Antaiopolis is mentioned a second time. On the pagarchs' use of prisons, see Stern 2016. On prisons in late antique Egypt, see also Chapter Three, n. 127.

111 Morelli 2008a, regarding the *dux* Athanasios, who was also *curator domus divinae*, and in *P.Cair. Masp.* I 67002 appears in both capacities in different parts of the text. For instance, when talking about Athanasios during the episode of their initial incarceration in Antinoopolis, the petition does not refer to Athanasios as *dux* (Morelli 2008a, 234–235).

112 I only briefly alluded to this chronological discrepancy in Stern 2023, 281 n. 39, an article that was based on a paper presented in 2016. In the meantime it has come to my attention that also in 2016 Federico Morelli—in a footnote to the edition of *P.Gascou* 48 (p. 312 n. 46)—likewise entertained the possibility that these arrests occured before the start of Menas's tenure as pagarch. Morelli rejects this hypothesis based on the assumption that *P.Cair.Masp.* I 67002 says that Menas started the "persecutions" as pagarch. But the start of his pagarchy is mentioned only in relation to the alleged seizure of Dioskoros's land (col. I 9–13). The story of the villagers at Thynis is told in a new part of the petition (col. II 1, introduced by δεόμεθα δὲ ὑμῶν περὶ το(ύ)[το(υ)] καὶ παρακαλοῦμεν, διδάσκοντες τὸν ἀγαθὸν ἡμῶν δεσπότην ὡς κτλ.), enabling a break in the chronological narrative. Again (see n. 84 above), Dioskoros is technically not stating anything untrue, but apparently made considerable compositional efforts to evoke a connection. Thus I think my point that Menas is mentioned as pagarch only from the time when the villagers are received in the prison of Antaiopolis, at least several weeks after the arrest at Thynis, is valid, and it poses an additional challenge to the established tenure of Athanasios as *dux* starting in late 565 or early 566. On this problem, see also n. 102 above.

113 See Gascou 2004, 99 n. 26 (= 2008, 446 n. 26) for an in-passing interpretation of this episode as a crackdown on tax fugitives. Ruffini 2008a, 158 n. 74 deems this interpretation "curious," but why else would Menas have the villagers arrested abroad? Their "habitual" attendance at the "festival of Thynis" (see below) may have served the villagers as a pretext for getting away, and fear that they might soon be out of reach may explain why Menas chose to act before the start of his tenure. Notably, this crackdown involved authorities at Antaiopolis—including Menas's predecessor, if my interpretation of ὕστερον is correct (see n. 110 above)—as well as at Antinoopolis and perhaps even at Thynis in the Hermopolite nome. The scale of this operation supports the idea that Menas was not on a personal mission here.

114 Keenan 2008b, 177 speculates upon the connection of the date of the festival to the date Menas assumed tenure as pagarch, but does not comment on the potential implication that the arrests happened before the beginning of Menas's pagarchy.

archy in late April or May 1, 566—which is a plausible time span for the villagers to be imprisoned, brought to Antinoopolis, and afterward to Antaiopolis, where Menas, now pagarch of Antaiopolis, received them at the start of his tenure.[115] Otherwise, the pagarchs' responsibility for tax fugitives is virtually absent from the Byzantine documents,[116] although it is frequently attested in the early Islamic period, notably in the archives of Senouthios, Papas, and Basileios. The reason for this is certainly again the different character of the surviving evidence after the Arab conquest, which has left us considerably more documents from the pagarchs' *officia*.

Again, considerable doubts arise about the notion that in this episode the pagarch transgressed his authority by entering an autopract village. Still, the discourse that these petitions create implies an extraordinary amount of violence. I now turn to look at the men behind this use of coercive force: the pagarchy's armed staff and collaborating institutions.

IV. The Means of Authority

The Ioulianos and Menas affairs put the pagarchs' extensive coercive powers into the spotlight, which calls for some structural comments. Since no normative arrangements on these issues survive, we have to evaluate the evidence on the basis of "contextually legitimized powers": who considered what action to be legitimate in a given context? Consequently, by "power," "competence," or "responsibility" I mean actions that are not generally objected to, but at most questioned under specific circumstances.

That fiscal officials such as the pagarchs wielded the power to confiscate property seems natural due to their inherent link to fiscal liability and restitution. This authority is ubiquitous in the documents of the Ioulianos and Menas affairs, and it is nowhere contested as such.[117] Rather, the petitioners contest the underlying justification: that they had been in arrears which the pagarch was supposed to collect. In the 540s and early 550s, the villagers complain about Ioulianos's trespassing on private property: Ioulianos supposedly took livestock and equipment which is characterized as looting and seizure of property, under the pretext of collecting taxes.[118] One text deals specifically

115 If Fournet is correct in putting the beginning of Athanasios's tenure as *dux et Augustalis* to late 565 or early 566 CE, then the detentions (under the governorship of Kyros) would have taken place even longer before the start of Menas's tenure as pagarch, but see n. 102 above: Menas was apparently collecting regular taxes from the villagers of Aphrodite as pagarch (i.e., after April 26/ May 1, 566) still under the *dux* Kyros, which results in a chronological dilemma, and may suggest a different chronology for Athanasios's tenure as *dux*.

116 This responsibility is probably reflected in some of the deeds of surety, although the offense is not expressly stated in these documents; see Stern 2015, 123–125.

117 Stern 2015, 127–129.

118 Plundering and seizure: *P.Cair.Masp.* I 67019 verso 17–22; *P.Cair.Masp.* III 67283 col. I 5–8; *P.Cair.Masp.* I 67024–25 (new ed. Fournet 2018) A 35–37. "Pretext" of taxes: *P.Cair.Masp.* III

with the seizure of Apollos's property, apparently due to debts that Ioulianos attempted to recover after Apollos's death.[119] Some confiscations of animals in this context may relate to requisitions for specific purposes rather than actual confiscations, as suggested by a papyrus from Oxyrhynchos in which a pagarch demands a horse from an estate administrator.[120]

The pagarchs also had tax debtors arrested, and Menas is said to have arranged collective as well as individual detentions.[121] In one case Dioskoros's son might have been taken as a hostage because he was the nephew of the *prōtokōmētēs* whom Menas held responsible for the arrears; but Dioskoros complained that his son was not responsible for the arrears of his brother-in-law, therefore this was apparently considered an illegitimate means of coercion.[122] There is remarkably little explicit evidence of detentions in the Ioulianos episode, given that Dioskoros describes them so vividly for the Menas affair, yet I hesitate to see this as a significant difference.[123] Ioulianos is, however, attested as the recipient of a deed of surety for a church reader (*anagnōstēs*) from Aphrodite.[124] We have little way of knowing why this man was put under bond, but Ioulianos is represented by two village headmen of Aphrodite, one of them being Dioskoros, which suggests that Ioulianos was nominally involved in his official capacity.[125]

Modern historiography has not been kind to the pagarchs and their role in late antique society, and this view results, for the most part, from the dramatic depictions that Dioskoros presented in his petitions. Yet we have seen how Dioskoros not only maintained a working relationship with Ioulianos, but also had help from Menas in his struggles with the local shepherds. Moreover, Menas was repeatedly involved in legal

---

67283 col. I 3–6; *P.Cair.Masp.* I 67024–25 (new ed. Fournet 2018) A 27 (see Geraci 1979, 198–199), notably erased here and absent from B, the latest version of that text. The alleged "seizure" of Dioskoros's property at Phthla by the *boēthos* Kyros, however, was probably a confiscation of the harvest; see n. 87 above.

119 *P.Cair.Masp.* I 67026, especially 9–10; Zuckerman 2004b, 77; van Minnen 2003, 122. This Ioulianos is referred to as *endoxotatos* only, but see the Catalog, s.v., on identifying these Ioulianoi as the same person.

120 *P.Oxy.* XVI 1858 (VI–early VII). Cf. *P.Mich.* XI 624 (mid-V–early VI), in which two pagarchs have the responsibility for the disposition of donkeys for a transport of hay, but these appear to have been their own donkeys.

121 *P.Cair.Masp.* I 67002 col. II 4 (by the *endoxotatos illoustrios* Serenos, following a request by Menas); col. II 14; col. III 4–5; *P.Cair.Masp.* I 67021.16–17. On the topic, see Stern 2015, 129–132.

122 *P.Lond.* V 1677.22–34 and 37–38. The *prōtokōmētēs* is Ruffini's (2011) Apollos 154.

123 Papyri that may allude to detentions during the Ioulianos episode include *P.Cair.Masp.* I 67019 verso 19, *P.Cair.Masp.* I 67024–25 (new ed. Fournet 2018) A 36, and *P.Cair.Masp.* III 67283 col. I 3–5, which bear strong similarities with parts of the documents of the Menas affair, though they never become as explicit. Cf. Stern 2015, 130.

124 *P.Cair.Masp.* I 67094 (April 1–25, 552 or March 27–31, 553).

125 The surety relates to the reader's presence and to his good behavior, but not to particular duties; we may be dealing with a crime suspect here. Note the high number of guarantors (four) and the comparatively high penalty (six *nomismata*).

matters of individuals.[126] The question to what degree the pagarchs were involved in the legal system is not easy to answer as we have no evidence that any pagarch adjudicated individual cases. The "early" pagarchs, or *praepositi pagorum*, appear to have been involved in this branch of authority[127] and in the early Islamic period, adjudication by the pagarchs is a recurring topic in our sources.[128] As subordinates of the *duces et Augustales*, however, the Byzantine pagarchs were *ex officio* involved in assisting the judicial apparatus and in local contexts, their decisions conceivably represented "the law" for large parts of the local population. In one instructive case, Menas assists a shepherd in what seems to be an investigation; he orders the *prōtokōmētai* to hand over some men whom this shepherd had listed. If this is not done, Menas (or, the shepherd?) threatens legal action.[129] The pagarchs were also entrusted by higher authorities with executing decisions. One group of monks petitioned the *dux et Augustalis* to give an order to the pagarch and the local *topotērētēs*, so that one Iezekiel would stop contesting the monks' claim to a particular piece of land.[130]

Other documents multiply the cases of "benevolent" pagarchs, and again some of these instances come from the Dioskoros archive. Pagarchs were approached via petitions, although we have little direct evidence of this or of any decisions.[131] One petition by an imprisoned widow to the *dux et Augustalis* implies an earlier petition she had sent to the pagarch, since the woman mentions the pagarch's order to have her released.[132] This order, however, was apparently ignored, for reasons unknown to us;

---

126 *SB* XX 14241, where Menas is involved in a legal dispute over the registration of a land plot. Likewise, *P.Lond.* V 1683 alludes to a legal dispute and implies that Menas had the authority to influence its outcome. Another legal dispute might be mentioned in *P.Cair.Masp.* I 67083, but the letter is too fragmentary to say much more.

127 For the delegated judicial authority of the *praepositi pagorum*, or "early" pagarchs, see Lewis 1948, especially 54–57, and Chapter One, and here especially Section III on *P.Oxy.* XVI 1831, in which the writer perhaps refers to the pagarch(s) in the context of litigation, but the precise meaning of that passage remains unclear.

128 See Tillier 2013, 20–25 with further references.

129 *P.Cair.Masp.* III 67322. The mention of a *pragma* is probably part of the warning about an official inquiry and the offer of an out-of-court settlement (cf. *P.Oxy.* XVI 1831). The text illustrates that farmers would file petitions to the pagarch, who in turn would rely on the shepherds of Phthla to maintain public order in his area; Makarios is certainly the same man who turns up in *SB* XX 14241. The author of *P.Cair.Masp.* III 67322, a certain Ioannes, is not the pagarch of that name; see the Catalog, s.v. Ioannes (Antaiopolis).

130 *P.Cair.Masp.* I 67003.24–25 (Antinoopolis?; c. 567): ὅθεν παρακαλοῦμεν τὸ ὕψος ὑμῶν (…) εἰ παρασταίη προστάξαι τῷ παγάρχῃ τῆς Ἀνταίο(υ) καὶ τῷ τοποτηρητῇ ταυτῆς ἀφ' ἡμῶν αὐτὸν ἀποτρέψαι, δέσπο(τα) ὑ̣π̣(ερ)φ̣υ̣ε̣σ̣τ̣α̣(τε); on this text, see Stern 2015, 122 and 132–133. It remains unclear whether the pagarch here was Menas, Kollouthos Cancellarius, or an as-yet unknown pagarch, who may have been a colleague of Menas or Kollouthos. It is also not certain whether two officials are being addressed here, or only one; see Chapter Five, n. 173.

131 In addition to the sources mentioned below, see n. 129 above on *P.Cair.Masp.* III 67322.

132 *P.Cair.Masp.* I 67005.19 (Antinoopolis?; c. 568): ἐκέλευσεν ὁ δεσπ(ότης) μου ὁ λαμπρ(ότατος) κύριος Κόλλουθος ὁ καγκελλάριος κ(αὶ) παγάρχης ἀπολυθῆναί με.

hence the widow's follow-up petition to the *dux*. The writer of a fragmentary Coptic letter urges the addressee to meet the pagarch when he arrives in town, apparently to settle the writer's problem with village authorities regarding the proper processing of his tax payments.[133]

Even a literary example can lighten the pagarchs' "dark side." The Coptic *History of the Church* accuses Emperor Marcian (r. 450–457) of trying to gain popularity by denying the *boēthoi* entry to the villages for the purpose of tax collection; instead, he orders that the pagarchs collect the taxes themselves.[134] This note places the pagarchs on a very local level, yet—given the pagarchs' bad reputation in parts of the scholarly discourse—it is remarkable that the conception of the pagarch as the more benevolent or at least neutral authority found its way into the Coptic literary tradition.

The men who executed the pagarchs' authority in the countryside find mention as well, and render themselves susceptible to accusations from Dioskoros, who at times refers to them vaguely as the pagarch's entourage, or "those who followed him."[135] Four texts from the Menas affair provide more detail and divide the pagarch's "auxiliaries" (*boētheiai*) into different groups: (1) "robbers," *paganoi*, and soldiers; (2) soldiers and *paganoi*; (3) "robbers," *paganoi* or soldiers (restoration), shepherds, and other villagers; and, finally, (4) the *paganoi* appear on their own, now themselves linked to the "robber" topos.[136] First, the latter use of the term suggests that the term "robbers" should probably be discounted as rhetoric. The second group are the soldiers, who appear here to be not brigands but regular troops, as they are on another occasion specified as "soldiers of (the detachments of) the Scythians and Macedonians" under a *vicarius*, who assists Menas in collecting the taxes from the villagers, apparently without being subordinate to the pagarch.[137] A pagarch's cooperation with the military was probably

133 *P.Sorb.Copt.* 30 (Hermopolites; VI–early VII). The fragmentary text does not reveal, however, where the addressee is supposed to meet the pagarch (in the city? in the village?) or whether the pagarch's visit was to address this issue, or part of regular "tours" around the countryside.

134 See Chapter One, n. 139 and Chapter Two, n. 182.

135 Ioulianos: *P.Cair.Masp.* I 67026.7–8: τ̣ο̣ὺ̣ς̣ Ἰουλιανῷ τῷ ἐνδοξ(οτάτῳ) | προσ̣ή̣κ̣[ον]τ̣α̣ς̣; *P.Cair. Masp.* III 67283 col. I 6 has οἱ αὐτῷ ἑπόμενοι, but entirely restored. Menas: *P.Cair.Masp.* I 67002 col. III 2: οἱ | συνεπόμενοι αὐτῷ εἰς βοήθειαν; *P.Cair.Masp.* I 67021 verso 11–12: παρὰ τ̣ῆ̣ς̣ | ἑπομένη̣ς̣ τῷ εἰ[ρη]μ(ένῳ) κυρ(ίῳ) Μηνᾷ β[ο]η̣θ̣(είας).

136 (1) *P.Cair.Masp.* I 67002 col. II 23: μετὰ πολλῆς λῃστρικῆς τε καὶ παγανικῆς καὶ [στ]ρ̣α̣τι[ωτ]ικῆς βοηθεί[ας]; (2) *P.Cair.Masp.* I 67021 verso 8–9: μετὰ στρατιωτ(ικῆς) καὶ | π̣[αγανι?]κ̣ῆ̣ς̣ β̣οηθ(είας); (3) *P.Lond.* V 1677.27–28: παρά τε τῶν λῃστῶν καὶ | [τῶν παγανῶν/στρατιωτῶν (see the commentary) καὶ τῶν σὺ]ν τούτοις ποιμένων καὶ τῶν ἀπὸ τῆς κώμης ὅλων οἰκητόρων; (4) *P.Lond.* V 1674.77–79: μετὰ τῶν λῃστρικῶν ἐφόδων καὶ ἀπὸ προόδων | πολλῶν ὡς εἴρηται παγανῶν τῶν καὶ τὴν κώμην ἡμῶν ἐπι|πηδησάντων.

137 *P.Cair.Masp.* I 67002 col. II 11–12; see Stern 2015, 135–136. Mitthof 2008, 256–257 speculates whether these men may have been subordinate to the pagarch, but as we have established together, the quoted *P.Flor.* III 295 + *P.Lond.* V 1678 is a *testimonium delendum* for the pagarch; see the Catalog, s.v. Thomas (Antaiopolis). Zuckerman 2004a, 153–159 highlights the role of the military in collecting local taxes; cf. Chapter 11 of Iust. *ed.* 13 and Gelzer 1913b, 355–356. On brigand sol-

a situational arrangement in cases of continuous and significant resistance on the part of the taxpayers; a factor in this cooperation may have been that the pagarchs and the *vicarii* of such units occasionally found themselves on comparable social strata.[138] Another factor was geopolitical: the unit was stationed in the area during these years as a precaution against hostile incursions by the Blemmyes. In this context, Menas's confiscations have occasionally been interpreted as foresighted acts to ensure safekeeping of grain reserves and valuable mobile property.[139] The third group in the list, the shepherds who followed Menas, were not simply herdsmen, but also regular field guards (*agrophylakes*) at Aphrodite and presumably in the neighboring village of Phthla.[140] The village *boēthos* of Phthla, Kyros, commanded local shepherds to assist him in confiscating Dioskoros's harvest, and it would appear that the *boēthos*, as the local arm of the pagarch, directed such local security forces under the pagarchs' auspices.[141] The shepherds living on the margins of the village community and the *boēthoi* were both outsiders of some sort—and deployed by the biggest outside actors in the picture, the pagarchs.[142] One Oxyrhynchite text from the time of the "early" pagarchy also shows a *boēthos* in some obscure connection to the pagarch and the field guards of a village, apparently within a chain of hierarchy.[143]

Who, in contrast to these three groups, were the *paganoi*?[144] One may be tempted to read the term as "civilian," in contrast to the soldiers,[145] but it should give us pause that

---

diers in Antaiopolis at that time, see Mitthof 2008, 252–253. Note also the close connection in which soldiers and pagarchs are mentioned as subordinates of the provincial governor in Iust. *ed.* 13.12.

138 Liebeschuetz 1974, 166; Mitthof 2008, 254–255.

139 See Rémondon 1961, 77–78 (where Menas appears as a "bon administrateur") and 86. See also Dioskoros's frequent comparisons of Menas's acts to barbarian devastations. On these incursions, see Palme 2007c, 257 n. 57 and Dijkstra 2004, 153. Another rather favorable interpretation of Menas's transferring goods "of the pagarchy" to a monastery in these times is provided by Ruffini 2018a, 127.

140 *P.Cair.Masp.* I 67002 col. I 14; col. III 4 and 13; *P.Lond.* V 1677.14 and 28. On the κοινὸν τῶν ποιμένων and its regular involvement in matters of public security, see *P.Cair.Masp.* I 67001 (December 28, 514), Keenan 1985a, and Maurer & Tost 2016, 1837 n. 24. On the role of the shepherds in the Menas affair, see Ruffini 2008a, 184–187, 194–195, and 218–226. Notably, it is the "evil" pagarch Menas who in *P.Lond.* V 1682 shields Dioskoros against one of these neighboring field guard–shepherds (Ruffini 2008a, 222; the text number is misspelled in n. 92), though this text more likely relates to Menas's first pagarchy in the 550s.

141 On the role of these shepherds in tax collection, see also Vanderheyden 2015, no. 15.

142 On the places of residence of the *boēthoi*, see Chapter Two, n. 184.

143 *P.Oxy.* XVI 1831, especially l. 12: οὐδὲ βοηθὸς ἡμῶ̣ν̣ ε̣μεσ̣..η η..[...]τ̣ε ὁ̣ π̣ά̣γαρχος. Since the writer is a village headman, "our *boēthos*" probably relates to a village *boēthos*, who is here in some way linked to a pagarch, most likely again in his role as intermediary or the pagarch's local representative.

144 On the various meanings of παγανός/παγανικός, see Guilland 1967, I 154–155 and *CPR* XXIII, pp. 204–205.

145 *CPR* XXIII, p. 204 n. 25; Fournet 2018, 613.

in the fourth group above the *paganoi* appear on their own, without any contrasting term. Some two decades earlier, Ioulianos apparently does not draw on support from the military, but Dioskoros's first draft of an imperial rescript in this matter nonetheless orders the provincial governor to take care that "whoever of your administration and of the *paganoi*" unduly confronted the villagers be held accountable.[146] Given that this draft refers to the men of the provincial *officium* and the pagarch advancing toward the village as though these were two distinct episodes,[147] it is conceivable that *paganos* in this context referred to the pagarch's civil security personnel, and it is certainly no coincidence that the *paganoi*, not the soldiers or the shepherds, occur on *all* occasions where the pagarch's "auxiliaries" are specified. The *paganoi* might thus have been understood as the pagarch's security forces, although this was probably not a technical term. In other contexts, *paganos* may indeed refer to the countryside—that is, the area usually administered by the pagarchs—in contrast to what pertains to the urban center of the *civitas*.[148]

In the same rescript draft from the Ioulianos episode that involves *paganoi* and has come down to us in three different versions, Dioskoros appears to change the tone over time. In the later drafts, he no longer talks about *paganoi* but refers to *idiōtai*, "private individuals."[149] This may allude to Dioskoros's opponents in the village community who went after him in the first place, even before the pagarch became involved. It does not necessarily mean that the term *paganoi* in the first version was intended to refer to these opponents and comprises the same group of people as *idiōtai*. This is not simply an exchange of words from one draft to another, but the grammar is slightly different, and in the same sentence Dioskoros rather subtly redirects his accusations from the ducal staff (in the first draft) to those involved "who depend" on the *dux*'s office.[150]

146 *P.Cair.Masp.* I 67024–25 (new ed. Fournet 2018) A 46: τῆς \τε/ σῆς τάξεως καὶ παγανῷ̣ν̣.

147 See Section II above.

148 See *CPR* XXII 1.7 (Hermopolis; April 3, 644; from the early Islamic period) for the use of παγανός for an inhabitant of the countryside in contrast to a city dweller. Cf. also *P.Cair.Masp.* III 67281.5 (Antinoopolis; 538–540 CE): τὴν ἐξ ἔθους δημοσίαν βοήθειαν and *P.Cair.Masp.* III 67282.5 (Antinoopolis?; VI): ἐν τ[ο]ῖς τόποις πολιτικὴν βοήθειαν. The former designates the detachments of police forces under the *riparius*, the main police official of the *civitas* (although here it refers to the *riparius* of Aphrodite; see, however, Tost 2012 on their institutional equality); see Zuckerman 2004a, 133–136. The second expression also refers to police forces, probably those of the province; on the meaning of *politikos* in this context, see Chapter Two, n. 27.

149 *P.Cair.Masp.* I 67024–25 (new ed. Fournet 2018) A 46 (first draft): τοὺς ἄλλους ἢ σὴ ἐνδοξ(ότης) ὅσοι \τῆς \τε/ σῆς τάξεως καὶ παγανῷ̣ν̣/; A' 68–69 (second draft): τοὺς ἄλλ̣ο̣υ̣ς̣ | ὅσοι ὑπὸ τὴν τῆς σῆς ἐνδοξ(ότητος) τυγχάνοντες τάξιν, ἔν τε ἰδιώταις τελοῦσιν; B 43–44 (third draft): τοὺς ἄλλους ὅσοι ὑπό τε τὴν τῆς σῆς *vacat* | τάξιν τελοῦσιν, ἔν τε ἰδιώταις.

150 See n. 149 above, using Fournet's translation "qui dépendent de ton bureau"; see Fournet 2018, 622–623 for an alternative interpretation of the development of this passage. An alternative, and more literal, translation of τελοῦσιν would be "those who *pay* (under the authority of the *officium* of the *dux*)." Together with the use of the word *idiōtai* this may be a way of refraining from accusing officials in an actual rescript.

An analogous development might have shifted blame from the pagarch's local staff to unnamed individuals in the village.

We have no evidence from the Antaiopolite nome about what kind of personnel were counted among these *paganoi*, but we can draw on evidence from Arsinoe, where in one instance two *eirēnarchai* and three *phylakes* commit themselves to the pagarch Strategios Paneuphemos.[151] The *eirēnarchai* were village liturgists and the subordinate *phylakes* may have been minor liturgists or guards hired by the pagarch or the *eirēnarchai* to support their duties.[152] In one case, the pagarch Kyrillos draws on an *eirēnarchēs* to have someone arrested.[153] In Oxyrhynchos, a pagarch makes use of a *phylax* to send a letter,[154] and landlords with authority over "pagarched" villages are also attested as directing security officials, namely *phylakes* and *prōtophylakes*,[155] but it is unclear how this authority fits into the chain of hierarchy of the entire *civitas*. Given the high rank achieved by the Apiones, the most famous of these magnates with extended fiscal shares in villages, we may suspect that their authority in matters of public security was, at least in practive, directly subordinate to the provincial governor, rather than to the pagarch or to the *riparius*, but there is no evidence for this hypothesis. Did the pagarch supervise the coercive authority of the *geouchountes*? Did the *riparius*? Did dominant magnates such as the Apiones?

In any case, *riparii* are notably absent from the evidence for the pagarchy. While there is one document to suggest that the *riparius* was answerable to the pagarch's orders in the early Islamic period,[156] their relationship in the Byzantine age remains obscure.[157]

V. The Politics of Authority

What was the stance of the provincial and imperial authorities toward the Ioulianos and Menas affairs? And did the pagarchs have reason to be worried? Dioskoros is quick to imply that the pagarch Menas—by his alleged disruption of the villagers' ability to pay their taxes—was undermining an essential foundation of the imperial state. The

151 *P.Bodl.* I 53, on which see Stern 2015, 127 and 133–134; Sänger 2005, 195 and n. 153; and Torallas Tovar 2000, 120–121.

152 On the *phylakes* as minor liturgists, see Sänger 2005, 164 and Maurer & Tost 2016, 1838 n. 29.

153 *P.Lond.* V 1786, where Kyrillos is not addressed as pagarch (but cf. Chapter Five, n. 24), but the text is an internal administrative letter, not a contract, and the reference to Kyrillos therefore follows the "short form." Cf. *BGU* XXI 2892, a deed of surety to Kyrillos by an *eirēnarchēs*, among others.

154 *P.Oxy.* XVI 1858.

155 *P.Oxy.* LXX 4802; *P.Oxy.* I 139; *P.Oxy.* LXVI 4536. See Stern 2015, 125–126 and 134 n. 78 for a discussion of these documents.

156 *P.Ross.Georg.* III 23 (Arsinoites; end of VII).

157 But cf. the *riparii* "of" the *oikoi* in Oxyrhynchos and Herakleopolis; see Chapter Two, n. 144.

petition *P.Cair.Masp.* I 67002, in a passage quoted above, explains how thirteen men from Aphrodite were imprisoned by the *endoxotatos illoustrios* Serenos in the Hermopolite village of Thynis and then transferred to the provincial capital of Antinoopolis. Here, the prisoners succeeded in getting the governor Kyros to intervene in their case and order that they be released from prison, "yet we were not released."[158] The passage does not reveal the actual addressee of Kyros's order, possibly intentionally, as if to imply that it was Menas who had been ignoring the governor's order to release them. An alternative interpretation might hold that Kyros had ordered that the Antinoopolite authorities (or the *endoxotatos illoustrios* Serenos) release the prisoners from the jail in Antinoopolis to have them transferred to Antaiopolis—that is, into the hands of the pagarch whose jurisdiction they belong to—which is exactly what happened.[159]

In the same petition, Dioskoros refers to an episode in which "the scribe and deacon wrote to him in the matter lest he come up to the village untimely and disarray the grain tax."[160] Why did Menas not back off when the villagers approached him with a more or less direct threat to appeal to higher authorities? A general point to consider is that Dioskoros wrote these petitions to well-educated addressees who would know about rhetorical conventions, topoi, and literary motifs in these kinds of documents. Dioskoros must have been aware of that, and his accounts of Ioulianos's and Menas's conduct are therefore unlikely to have been, or even meant to be, taken at face value.[161] Justinian's *Edict* 13 (539 CE) states that a pagarch who disrupts the tax collection procedures was to be removed from office, with his estates made subject to seizure.[162] Both *P.Cair.Masp.* III 67283 and *P.Cair.Masp.* I 67002 address the *dux et Augustalis*, who was not himself entitled to dismiss the pagarch, but it was through him that relevant information would reach the praetorian prefect and the emperor.[163] Ioulianos's and Menas's allegedly deadly misconduct would appear to provide an appropriate context for applying these regulations, yet all petitions in both affairs stick to the demand that

158 *P.Cair.Masp.* I 67002 col. II 10–11.

159 Cf. Stern 2023, 281.

160 *P.Cair.Masp.* I 67002 col. III 19: ἔγραψεν γὰρ αὐτῷ ὁ γραμματεὺς καὶ ὁ διακονητὴς τούτου χάριν, \το(ῦ)/ μὴ ἀνελθεῖν τὴν κώμην ἀκαίρως καὶ διαστρέψαι τὴν ἐμβολήν. Again, by referring to the grain tax the villagers allude to the potential interest that provincial authorities would have in events of this kind. Whether the deacon was issuing the notice himself or simply forwarding an appended message (perhaps issued by village elites) is another matter that is not as evident as Dioskoros makes it seem. This is not the only time a deacon is attested as exchanging information between the village and the pagarch; see *P.Cair.Masp.* I 67060.1.

161 In addition to the instances discussed earlier, see Ruffini 2018a, 37–38 for a discussion of the accusation that Menas's men had nuns and virgins raped during these incidents, and also n. 139 above and Ruffini 2018a, 167.

162 See Chapter Four, Section I on the regulations of *Edict* 13 regarding a pagarch's removal from office.

163 The main text of *P.Cair.Masp.* III 67283 addresses the empress Theodora, but the *dux* is implied as an intermediary in col. I 15: διὰ χειρὸ]ς̣ τῆς | εὐσεβεσ[τάτ]ης ἡμῶν̣ δ[εσπο]ίνης (i.e., Theodora) καὶ τῆς ὑμ̣ετέρας ε[ὐ]κ̣λ̣[εί]α̣ς (i.e., the *dux*).

justice be done and that the petitioners not be bothered further so that they can pay their taxes.[164] These petitions do contain explicit demands for punishment, but they restrict these to the pagarchs' auxiliaries, whom the petitioners hope "to be thoroughly destroyed."[165]

This restriction is significant in order to understand what Dioskoros and his fellow villagers could have hoped to achieve, as it is also apparent in Dioskoros's and the government's dealing with the Theodosios and Ioulianos episode. The documents pertaining to Dioskoros's visits to Constantinople in 548/549 and 551 CE support two main impressions: First, Dioskoros—while showering Ioulianos with accusations—did not argue for punishment of the pagarch and explicitly targeted minor personnel for punishment and perhaps compensation requests.[166] Second, the government did not regard Ioulianos entering the village in this case as a point to take issue with and would soften the demands of the petitioners in the resulting rescript.[167] Later documents confirm these two observations: neither did Ioulianos lose any aristocratic standing, nor was he deprived of the pagarchy. Instead, he is seen in what is at least a functioning working relationship with Dioskoros and others in the years immediately following the episode, and in 560, Ioulianos is still (or, again?) attested in the position of pagarch.[168] What does change is that from 553/554 the pagarchy appears to have been held by two or three pagarchs; but rather than a rebuke to Ioulianos, this was more likely due to the increasing fiscal value of the Antaiopolite pagarchy, which, like all of Egypt and the empire, saw a dramatic rise in gold tax demands.[169]

By contrast, Menas indeed seems to have been in office only for a couple of years, perhaps as short as two indictions, after which Ioannes and Serenos may have taken over.[170] How this move is to be interpreted depends on whether Menas was pagarch in his own right or for a higher aristocrat, and whether, and under what circumstances, he

---

164 *P.Cair.Masp.* III 67283 col. I 13–15; *P.Cair.Masp.* I 67019 verso 24–28; *P.Cair.Masp.* I 67002 col. III 22–25, 42–45, and 55–57. The relevant passages are lost or fragmentary in *P.Cair.Masp.* I 67021, *P.Lond.* V 1674, and *P.Lond.* V 1677.

165 *P.Cair.Masp.* I 67002 col. III 22–23: προστάξαι τὸν μὲν εἰρημέ(νον) πάγαρχον ἀποπαύ[εσ]θαι ἡμῶν θυμολεοντ[ο]φθόρον: ἔπειτα δὲ καὶ τοὺς ἀλιτηρίο(υ)ς πλείω βαρβάρων κακούργο(υ)ς καὶ ἀ̣ρ̣χιλ̣ηστὰς μηλονόμους | ἀ̣ν̣αιρεθῆναι σὺν ῥίζαις. See Stern 2023, 283 with further context. A similar wording may hide behind *P.Cair.Masp.* III 67283 col. I 16–17, but the text has been heavily restored by the editor.

166 Whereas the petitions in the Ioulianos episode do not explicitly demand restitutions, the specific amounts mentioned in *P.Cair.Masp.* I 67002 col. II 6, 10, 13, and 23 from the Menas affair may allude to restitutions; cf. Stern 2023, 282 and n. 48.

167 Discussed in Stern 2023, 284–285 with references, notably to Zuckerman 2004b and Geraci 1979. By contrast, Fournet 2015, 260–261 is somewhat more optimistic regarding what was actually transferred from the drafts into the rescript proper, as is Palme 2008b, 208.

168 See Table 4 (pp. 165–167).

169 This hypothesis about the number of pagarchs at Antaiopolis is developed in Chapter Four, Section IV.

170 See Table 4 (pp. 165–167). A short tenure alone would be insufficient to suggest that Menas was

was the sole pagarch of Antaiopolis at that time. What seems certain at least is that the Menas affair did not trigger his dismissal as stipulated by *Edict* 13, including the handover of property.[171] Furthermore, one document from after these incidents attributes to Menas the rank epithets of both *lamprotatos* and *peribleptos*, instead of the simple *lamprotatos* epithet he bears in earlier texts.[172] The document that tells us this is a contract involving Menas's son that was, ironically, or again revealingly, drawn up by Dioskoros during his alleged "exile" in Antinoopolis after Menas's pursuits. Again, their relationship cannot have been so bad after all. But what did this entail for Menas's career? Was he promoted, and therefore stepped down from the pagarchy of Antaiopolis? Or was he promoted to get him off the scene, without, however, making him subject to punishment? As in the case of Ioulianos, the consequences of the conflict for Menas were probably rather modest, to say the least.

The question remains as to why both Ioulianos and Menas got away with it. When we bear in mind the close connections that some of these aristocrats from the nome and provincial levels had to each other—sometimes through family ties even—we might assume they harbored a certain hesitation to act against their peers.[173] But it should give us pause that actual consequences are all but absent from the rescript drafts *P.Cair. Masp.* I 67024–25 (in the case of Ioulianos) as well as from the petition *P.Cair.Masp.* I 67002 (in the case of Menas)—that is, from documents that contain Dioskoros's demands. Dioskoros obviously did not go as far as requesting to have Ioulianos or Menas removed from the pagarchy, which suggests that structural political considerations were also at play: either Dioskoros thought that the pagarchs' actions were in essence covered by their authority, or he figured that the government would not take issue with them. Even if Dioskoros's accusations may have been exaggerated, there is little doubt that at least Menas's incursions at Aphrodite involved a great deal of violence, and the villagers were indeed seeking material compensation, so the violence may have been perceived as going too far to simply endure it.[174] What contributed to aggressive interventions was the existential risk in which fiscal administrators at this level found themselves. Given the villagers' repeated shortfall in their tax payments, confiscation

removed from the pagarchy due to the events described by *P.Cair.Masp.* I 67002, since there is no apparent pattern in the length of the pagarchs' tenure.

171 See Stern 2023, 286.

172 *P.Lond.* V 1714.12–15 (Antinoopolis; March 14, 570): Φλαυΐῳ Θεοδώρῳ υἱῷ τοῦ λαμπροτάτου καὶ περιβλέπτου κυρίου | Μηνᾶ σκρινιαρίου τῆς κατὰ Θηβαΐδα λαμπρᾶς δουκικῆς τάξεως | τῷ λαμπροτάτῳ ἐξκέπτορι τῆς αὐτῆς τάξεως ὁρμωμένῳ | ἀπὸ τῆς Ἀνταιοπολιτῶν ἐφ' ἧς καὶ γεουχοῦντι. Menas bore the title of *scriniarius* during his pagarchy but it is hard to tell whether this referred to a continuous assignment to the ducal office, or to a marker of profession, referring to an earlier duty.

173 Ruffini 2008a, 193; Palme 2008b, 214–215; Fournet 1999, 327–329.

174 On this and the following thought, see Stern 2023, 287; Palme 2008b, 217; Ziche 2006, 132; Geraci 1979, 205.

of their property was less greedy than mere self-preserving, and violence may have only been Menas's last resort.[175]

The next question is whether the state cared all that much or even relied on such interventions as a sort of officially condoned means to ensure tax revenues, even though it may have "contradicted government policy."[176] We must not forget the other side of the "oppressive official" narrative: that local communities and individuals alike, at least some of them, could and would refuse to pay tax rates that the state considered appropriate; in other cases, they simply exerted violence themselves against local collectors, thereby disrupting the imperial collection scheme at its root.[177] For the state, maintaining fiscal authority in the countryside meant not least the capacity to deal with taxpayers' attempts to cheat the system, and in general keep a watchful eye over any other potential disruptions. As pagarchs, Ioulianos and Menas were crucial to the imperial enterprise and their conduct seems to have been tolerated; Menas even received a promotion, albeit possibly only to get him off the scene. Both episodes occured in a particularly challenging fiscal environment. In the 540s and 550s demands for taxes, especially for contributions in gold, were continuously increasing, and at one point may have been too much for the village leaders to handle on their own.[178] And the extraordinarily high tax demands of the mid-560s were probably a reaction to the financial turmoil of Justin II's early reign.[179] No administration interested in the long-term stability of its tax income could have endorsed the major devastations described by the petition *P.Cair.Masp.* I 67002, but as we have seen, the situation on the ground was probably different from Dioskoros's vivid description. As "Good Officials of Byzantine Egypt,"[180] the pagarchs had to be rigid enough, but not too rigid, so that the government deemed their ends acceptable, and the taxpayers their means at least endurable. Thus the pagarchs served as mediators between the empire and its subjects, whose needs would sometimes apparently be regarded as a nuisance to the central government.[181] We can imagine that this was always a delicate balance, but especially so

175 The overall loss of most ancient documentation entails that we are missing a potentially large number of documents—let alone verbal exchanges—between Menas, his staff, and the villagers that are likely to have preceded these interventions; cf., for instance, *P.Cair.Masp.* I 67060.

176 On this sort of violence and how people, to a degree, expected and accepted it (in many cases because they had little choice), see Bagnall 1989, 209 and 212–213 (quote); Bell 2013, 270–272; and Ziche 2006. See also Bryen 2013, 66–68 for some theoretical reflections and cf. Wickham 2005, 66–67 and 145.

177 For examples, see Sessa 2018, 148 and Droß-Krüpe 2023.

178 It remains to be seen how far this mounting burden on Egypt resulted from its relative stability after the Justinianic plague had hit other regions more critically. On the potential impact of the plague, see Zuckerman 2004a, 217 and Bransbourg 2016, especially 322, 343–344, and 388.

179 Zuckerman 2004a, 215–217; Banaji 2007, 59–60; Bransbourg 2016, again especially 322, 343–344, and 388.

180 On the concept of the Good Official in Ptolemaic Egypt, see Crawford 1978. Cf. Haldon 2005, 46–51.

181 See the passing remark by the *curator domus divinae*—who authored the actual rescript *SB* VI

when the financial situation of the empire was strained to a point rarely seen, such as when Ioulianos and Menas were in charge. In this environment, what they did might have been what, fundamentally, was expected of them.

VI. Summary

The village of Aphrodite is so valuable for our understanding of the pagarchy because it allows us to evaluate the pagarchs' purview within a comparatively close environment. Legally a village, Aphrodite was subject to a special form of administration, *inter alia* to organize its *autopragia*, a privilege granted (or renewed) under Emperor Leo I. Under the autopract regime, the village paid provincial and imperial taxes, most prominently the *embolē*, directly to the provincial office without the pagarchs as intermediaries. Local taxes, after they had been collected and aggregated for the village, were nonetheless handed over to the pagarch, who was also supervising several liturgists active at Aphrodite in the early 550s. While this suggests that the pagarchs had a closer link to the village than often acknowledged, the situation may not have been as straightforward as that. Rather, the relationship between the pagarchs and the autopract village appears to have evolved over time. This evolution is most plausibly to be explained by continuous difficulties that the village officials faced in matters of tax collection, which apparently date back as far as the late 530s, when the first conflicts with provincial officials are documented. It is around this time that Count Ammonios's presence in Aphroditan activities becomes more pronounced, although he may have already assumed this role earlier. The strong presence of the imperial *oikos* at Aphrodite further begs the question of how the involvement of the imperial household relates to the *autopragia* and to the authority wielded by Ammonios, himself a *comes sacri consistorii*. Ammonios's "patronage" for Aphrodite may perhaps in some aspects be conceived in terms comparable to that of large landowners' authority over villages that we see in Oxyrhynchos, although at different levels and less formalized, in order to ease the government's dealings with the village's "smallholders" and make village *autopragia* work in practice.

Aphrodite's fiscal strains became more palpable in the late 540s, when Dioskoros was directly involved with village administration. The *megaloprepestatos* Theodosios, possibly linked to the imperial household and a successor of Ammonios as "supervisor" of Aphrodite's fiscal business, collected what may from his perspective have been arrears, but what the Aphroditans considered their regular tax payments for the indiction of 547/548. Apparently as an intermediary for the provincial office, the pagarch Ioulianos advanced to the village to collect the missing taxes, which the Aphroditans argued they had already paid to Theodosios. Ioulianos used force to extract the taxes, but, like Theodosios, remained in his post, with the imperial chancery calling only for

9102—according to which the villagers of Aphrodite, in addressing the imperial court, had made themselves "bothersome" (l. 8; Ruffini 2008a, 157 n. 63).

his subordinates to be brought into line for any potential overly violent extractions. The frequent conflicts resulted in the abolition, suspension, or at least limitation of Aphrodite's *autopragia*. In 566/567, the pagarch Menas collected the regular taxes, and appears to have been on constant alert regarding the village's notorious payment behavior, or payment capacity, even before his term of office actually started. Dealing with the large landholders in the nome was probably not much of a hazard for a pagarch since these men and women were usually his peers with similar interests; confronting a headless—or multiheaded—(former?) autopract village that owed taxes may have been expected to soon turn nasty. In his responsibility for tax fugitives, Menas had absent debtors arrested even ahead of his tenure and executed public fiscal authority in the village through obviously violent means of coercion, drawing on local army detachments, the field guard–shepherds, and his own liturgical security personnel. Despite Dioskoros's fierce accusations before the *dux*, however, Menas moved from his pagarchy to a new position in the ducal office at Antinoopolis, elevated to the rank of *peribleptos*. Ioulianos and Menas were effective tools of the late Roman fiscal regime in the countryside, and they were acknowledged as such.

In his microhistory of sixth-century Aphrodite, Giovanni Ruffini argues that ordinary village life should be placed at the lower end of the scale when it comes to state involvement.[182] The perspective taken in this chapter suggests higher stakes. Ruffini is certainly right to argue that what happens at the ground level in the village of Aphrodite cannot be understood exclusively from the perspective of the central government, but the claim that the state was absent from Aphrodite goes too far to the other extreme. The state was a fact of life at Aphrodite, and it was tangible especially for Dioskoros and his fellows from the village elite who, as representatives of their village community, faced its demands and regulations most immediately. Granted, one may conceive of Ioulianos as a rich landowner, and of Menas as an aristocratic parvenu, but seeing them entirely in terms of their socioeconomic position means ignoring the fact that their authoritative positions were vested in them by the government. More importantly, unlike for Dioskoros and his fellows for whom Aphrodite was the center or at least the bedrock of their ambitions, for Ioulianos and Menas, the village was always just a *part* of their careers. As pagarchs, Ioulianos and Menas were integrated into a web of expectations from their peers in the *civitas* of Antaiopolis and from superior authorities at Antinoopolis and Constantinople, which may in part explain why the conflicts with the village of Aphrodite apparently did little to damage their standing.

182 Ruffini 2018a, 25–26, 207, and 213.

Conclusion

Rulers rose and fell, taxes went on forever.[1]

I. Findings

The vast majority of the late Roman Empire's subjects dwelled in the innumerable villages, estates, and scattered hamlets of its rural regions, which through their labor, taxes, and commodities sustained the political and economic centers and the state apparatus all the way up to the capital. But although fundamental to the empire's prosperity, the provincial countryside was far removed from the imperial center in terms of both distance and administrative layers. These regions are only rarely covered by our traditional literary sources, whose authors were usually not interested in the ordinary and everyday. By contrast, the papyrological evidence from Egypt gives us a precious opportunity to see how local communities responded to the demands from above and how empire looked on the ground.

To understand how the late Roman Empire built and sustained its authority in these remote spaces, the present study has investigated the fiscal administration of the Egyptian provinces. Fiscal concerns were a major motivation of day-to-day state business in the provinces, and Egypt, with its exceptional wealth of documentary material from the local level, provides us with more substantial evidence on this topic than any other region. In the last two decades, important scholarly works on several institutions have refined our understanding of the late antique Egyptian countryside, notably including an intense debate over the validity of the model of fiscal participation. This debate and its consequences for our perception of late antique aristocratic aspiration and the role of the state has to some degree obscured the pagarchs' role in the administrative network. That role has therefore been the focus of the present book, which has analyzed the pagarchs' doings and dealings at different levels, from the ground level to the cities and up to the level of the province, along with the repercussions at the imperial level, and has applied the heuristic concept of state *infrastructural power* to evaluate how the pagarchs and related actors contributed to the creation of public authority in the late antique Egyptian countryside.

The pagarchs first surface in documents from the fourth and fifth centuries, when *pagarchos* and *pagarchēs* emerged as synonymous Greek renderings for the well-known *praepositus pagi*. Chosen from among the city councilors, this "early" pagarch presided over one of about ten to fifteen *pagi* per city territory, or nome, and seems to have been responsible for virtually everything that happened in his district. The office was implemented in Egypt in 307/308 CE as one of the final steps toward the country's

1 MacMullen 1976, 197.

https://doi.org/10.1515/9783111493183-008

municipalization, which formally applied the Roman administrative principle of civic self-government to the Egyptian nome capitals. In the course of the fifth century a regime of notables increasingly replaced civic officials as the main administrative body in the *civitas*, and aristocratic landholders began to assume much of the scattered fiscal authority of the "early" pagarchies. The pagarchy—the office of the pagarch—adapted to these developments, and the pagarchs' status increased. The villages whose administration could not be effectively organized by an *oikos* administration were united and placed under the authority of one single incumbent or of collegial pagarchs, who were now distinguished aristocrats.

These newly empowered pagarchs operated at two tiers. At the level of the city—alongside the *dēmosion logistērion*, the central accounting office of the *civitas*—they aggregated taxes that their various agents collected from the villages. The pagarchs also administered civic land in the countryside. Not being a municipal office, the pagarchy was funded from revenues that the cities directed to "external" purposes, such as provincial expenses. Its incumbents were not answerable to the city councils but directly to the provincial governors, and apparently reported their accounts to the provincial offices on a regular basis. In addition to supervising accountants such as *trakteutai* and *logographoi*, the pagarchs had a number of collectors at their disposal. These included most notably the *hypodektai*, liturgists from the city level, and the *boēthoi*, who contracted with the pagarchs for individual villages. The division of responsibilities between these officials still respected the now somewhat anachronistic separation between the land categories of *astika* and *kōmētika* in the rural parts of a city's territory.

But the pagarchy was only *one* fiscal actor in the countryside—and sometimes far from the most important one. An analysis of the evidence for *kōmai pagarchoumenai* in the Oxyrhynchite nome revealed that these "pagarched" villages represented a fiscal entity separate from the pagarchy proper. Instead, the authority of *geouchountes* over these villages is most plausibly to be identified with the administrative responsibilities that some *oikoi* and their magnates had assumed over the course of the fifth century, which in this context were found to have been more wide-ranging than previously assumed. Unlike the pagarchs, these magnates were not vested with an official apparatus and instead deployed their own estate administration to arrange the collection of taxes from land they did not own. This elaborate estate management both covered the collection of rents and taxes from estate plots and provided the upper-level administrative tier for these villages. The lower tier in the village parcels not owned by the magnate seems still, however, to have been formed by the village officials and the *boēthoi*, who in other villages were subordinate to the pagarchs. Although this model has been established mainly from Apion evidence, there are indications that similar arrangements existed outside the Oxyrhynchite nome.

This comparison with the "private" *oikos* administration revealed a more pronounced "official" character of the pagarchy, which prompted a reassessment of the widespread idea that the office took the form of a *munus patrimonii*. The formal framework did indeed include liturgical elements such as collegial responsibility, divided shares of the office, and the inclusion of women among the eligible candidates, but evidence of a potential formal delegation to liturgical stand-ins is ambiguous. Pagarchs could only be dismissed by the emperor, recalling other "semi-imperial" officers such as the *defensores civitatum*. But whereas the latter were chosen biannually from among a pool of eligible candidates from the city nobility, we have no evidence that the pagarchy alternated between the leading families of the cities at regular intervals. Quite the contrary, some pagarchs served tenures of a decade or more. Despite such long tenures and the link to personal wealth, the office does not seem to have been a permanent burden on on the largest landholders of the nome.

The pagarchs were not an internally coherent elite, but came from a wide range of aristocratic backgrounds. Local elite composition differed throughout the Egyptian provinces and nomes, and the pagarchy adapted to this composition. But there is also evidence that the pagarchy itself had an influence on the balance of authority in the countryside, at times even through outsiders. In Oxyrhynchos, the lion's share of rural administration was managed through *oikoi*, the most dominant of which was run by imperial confidants—the Apiones family—while the pagarchy played a comparatively minor role. In the Arsinoite, where the shares of the *oikoi* compared with the pagarchy appear not to have been as large, the office was generally held by the leading players, some of whom rose to imperial honors during their tenure. In the Thebaid, pagarchs from lower aristocratic ranks appear to have been more numerous, and many can be linked to the (semi)professional staff of the provincial administration. In these cases, the reach of the state depended on its control of the *duces et Augustales*, the direct superiors of the pagarchs.

A case study of the village of Aphrodite suggested that the pagarchs were closer to the reach and interests of the central government than often assumed. Aphrodite enjoyed wide-ranging, but not complete, fiscal autonomy from its *civitas* Antaiopolis, but the obligations that this privilege entailed repeatedly brought village leaders into conflict with the local pagarchs and other authorities. Our main source on these conflicts, the poet, notary, and village headman Dioskoros, naturally takes every effort to create the impression of a unified, harmonious village community threatened by disruptive outsiders and malicious individuals—for instance, in his account of the confrontation with the mysterious *megaloprepestatos* Theodosios, who allegedly embezzled the villagers' taxes. But internal discord appears to have added quickly to the heat of the conflict, or was perhaps at the heart of the problem. The mounting fiscal pressure of Justinian's reign mixed with, or may have even caused, internal frictions among the village elite, as Dioskoros's side got into violent quarrels with a competing faction. The pagarchs Ioulianos and Menas were drawn into this conflict. No doubt mindful of Aphrodite's recent unstable fiscal history, they took increasingly drastic steps to ensure the extraction of the village's overdue taxes. These interventions were certainly violent, but were, equally certainly, embellished by Dioskoros in his petitions. Apparently, the central government not only approved of the pagarchs' interventions in principle, but regardless of propaganda also had little, if any, objection to the means they resorted to. Even outside these episodes, the pagarchs' use of liturgical guards underscores their role in maintaining public security and securing the steady flow of revenue. They were also approached by people regarding legal matters and were thought to be able to influence the outcomes.

II. Prospects

The results of this study have implications for our understanding of the extent and the mechanisms of late Roman administration in the countryside of late antique Egypt. These implications span three levels: (1) the local world of the *civitates* and below; (2) the world beyond the cities: province, diocese, and empire; and (3) the transitional perspective: from the Roman administration to the decade of Persian occupation (619–629 CE) and reestablished Byzantine control (629–639), and finally to the Arab reign.

1. Fiscal Authority in the Countryside

This book has laid out in detail the business of the pagarchy at the local level, considering aspects ranging from collection on the ground to aggregation and accounting at the top. Apart from providing a refined understanding of individual procedures and related documents, its findings also situate the pagarchs within an intricate web of fiscal authority exercised by various actors in the rural hinterlands of the Roman cities.

Two points are particularly noteworthy. The first concerns the relationship between pagarchy and *civitas*. Although curial authority and capacity were much reduced during the fifth century, fiscal procedures still revolved around institutions originally grounded in the curial system.[2] The *dēmosion logistērion* remained the center of fiscal organization in the *civitas*, and its staff did not simply turn into another instrument serving the pagarchy. Furthermore, even the pagarchs' own staff followed an ancient practice of arranging different procedures for land plots taxed as *astika* and land plots taxed as *kōmētika*, and the curial class filled the ranks of some of the pagarchs' subordinate collectors and accountants. But although they operated at the city level, the pagarchs of the sixth century were no longer the municipal officers of old, the *praepositi pagorum*. Instead, they were now directly subordinate to the provincial governor, as

2 The continuous influence of institutions of curial origin on what has sometimes been called a "postcurial" order in the late Roman Empire was notably highlighted by Laniado 2002.

the distinction between municipal and state offices had in general become somewhat artificial.[3]

The second significant observation is the division of authority between the pagarchs and the heads of institutional *oikoi*—large estates with extended administrative responsibilities for territories not owned by them. The model proposed in this study disentangles the two institutions, establishes a clearly defined relationship between them, and supports Jean Gascou's model of fiscal participation from an administrative standpoint by removing a major uncertainty. It also serves to support and refine Todd Hickey's and Gilles Bransbourg's seminal analyses of the internal workings of the Apion estate. But the revisions to the model of fiscal participation suggested here also have implications beyond the Oxyrhynchite, and may serve as an additional argument for the hypothesis that the model of fiscal participation is, in essence, valid for Egypt as a whole. The evidence that has so far been adduced in favor of this hypothesis has not found universal acclaim; separating the pagarchy and the "pagarched" villages in the Byzantine period offers a compelling explanation for why the term *pagarchia* was "territorialized" in the early Islamic age and became synonymous with the entire administrative circumscription of the nome/*civitas*. This phenomenon can be seen for the first time in the first decades of Arab rule and probably resulted from the permanent incorporation of "pagarched" villages into the pagarchies around the middle of the seventh century. Since that development can be detected in all parts of Egypt from which we have sufficient evidence, we may indirectly infer that it was common practive for large estates throughout the country to exercise fiscal authority over villages, although the extent of that authority was probably greater in Oxyrhynchos than in other regions.

A number of aspects remain unclear pending the discovery of further sources. For one, we have little idea of exactly how and on what basis the city notables—the large landowners, the bishops, and imperial dignitaries—partitioned and negotiated authority among themselves. Under their regime, the allocation of the responsibilities traditionally assumed by the city councilors seems to have become more informal.[4] Certain responsibilities and offices were apparently handed to certain magnates on the basis of elaborately calculated shares, but the pagarchy clearly did not rotate between families at short, regular intervals. The precise mechanism by which the notables, or the government, had pagarchs appointed is yet to be discovered.

3 See Eich 2015, 130 for a more general perspective and Bowman 1986, 81–83 for an Egyptian one.

4 Directives from above may, however, have been more prevalent than appearances suggest, as the example of the contributions for the heating of public baths indicates. *P.Oxy.* XVI 2040 (c. 566/567 CE) is a schedule that shows how these contributions were shared among the leading landowners of Oxyrhynchos, that is, in the province of Arcadia, but Iust. *ed.* 13.14 (539 CE) reveals that at least in the two eparchies of Aegyptus it was a central official, the *vindex* of Alexandria, who was tasked with drawing up schedules of this kind; the part of the edict concerning Arcadia is lost.

It is relevant in this context that it is unclear whether the magnates' authority over *kōmai pagarchoumenai* was, at the city level, equal to that of the pagarchs.[5] Justinian's *Edict* 13 would appear to suggest that it was not,[6] but this question cannot be answered solely through an administrative-bureaucratic lens. Late antique administration, for all its formalism, was much more fluid and flexible than the sophisticated and abstract bureaucracy of modern states. Among the notables in each city and province, the balance of authority was certainly situational and built from negotiations, rumors, and local politics that elude us. If we ask who had the last word in local policy decisions, it would seem difficult to argue for anyone other than the Apiones in the city of Oxyrhynchos, or Strategios Paneuphemos in the city of Arsinoe. Strategios held the pagarchy; the Apiones, as far as the evidence goes, did not. Yet it is unclear how any potential dispute between an Oxyrhynchite pagarch and the Apion estate management would have been resolved.[7] Or whether the Antaiopolite pagarch Menas, a *lamprotatos scriniarius*, would have dared to speak out in the event that he disagreed with his pagarchic colleague, the *endoxotatos apo eparchōn* Ioulianos.

A different question is whether absentee magnates like the Apiones, who resided in Constantinople, had much interest to intervene in negotiations among the Oxyrhynchite nobles as long as their *oikos* provided themselves, and the state, with a consistent and reliable income, particularly since Todd Hickey has convincingly argued in favor of the essentially autarkic nature of the Apion estate at Oxyrhynchos.[8] Christoph Begass points to extensive estates in the hands of the senatorial elite of the Eastern Empire. However, it is not clear whether these were the senators' actual source of wealth, because the evidence does not allow us to adequately quantify the production of these estates against the fiscal commitments of their senatorial owners.[9]

Ultimately, it is unclear whether the fiscal responsibility over villages was *imposed* on the *geouchountes* or whether these magnates exercised this authority voluntarily. Hard evidence is absent, though I find myself tending toward the latter interpretation.[10] In the beginning, the unified pagarchy may have been a way to facilitate tax collection

5 On different ways of interpreting the position of, for instance, the *ousia* of the ex-*eparchos* Ioulianos in this regard, see Chapter Three, n. 27.

6 The edict does not differentiate between landowners who wielded fiscal authority over villages and those that did not, which is not surprising insofar as these magnates did not have a particular official title as seen in Chapter Three, Section III. However, because the relevant provisions of the edict concerning the provinces of Arcadia and Augustamnica are lost, it is unclear whether this lack of differentiation in the passages concerning Aegyptus and the Thebaid is significant. If it is, it may be a vague indication that in most nomes the fiscal shares of the *oikoi* might not have been as extensive as in Oxyrhynchos.

7 One may recall *P.Oxy.* XVI 1858 (early VII), in which the pagarch Theodoros, through a guard (*phylax*), demands horses from the *endoxos oikos*, prompting excuses from the responsible estate manager.

8 Hickey 2012.

9 Begass 2016 and 2018, 434–456.

10 Here, I side with Hickey (2012, 159), who argued that "though 'willing participation' need not

from those villages that could not be effectively covered by infrastructure provided by the large estates, and thus only represented an internal shift of resources among the city's elite. But to see the pagarchs simply as managers of what was left over after the villages had been allocated to *oikoi* possibly overestimates the importance of the phenomenon of public administration through *oikoi* in *civitates* other than Oxyrhynchos. In many if not most nomes, in environments where aristocratic *oikoi* were less prominent, the pagarchy was probably the dominant fiscal authority in the countryside, not least because of the official resources that backed it.

Some scholars have recently argued that the late antique countryside saw the rise of an increasingly empowered peasantry.[11] It would be conceivable, then, to understand the regime of notables and the elevation of the pagarchy to the city level in part as a way to push back against this development, but one does not see much clear evidence for this kind of peasants in the rural areas of late antique Egypt.[12] Perhaps this is not to be expected for a stratified peasantry like the Egyptian.[13] This topic, and in particular the bargaining power that taxpayers had vis-à-vis the government, merits a more detailed examination through the lens of fiscal sociology.[14]

2. *The Reach of Empire*

Considering how the pagarchs were integrated at the level of the *civitates* leads us to the imperial government and its relationship to these local functionaries—even though parts of this venture are speculative for the time being, due to the localized nature of the clusters of evidence. In the fourth century the pagarchs, as *praepositi pagorum*, started out as an emblem of civic self-government, but this "self"-government proved to be a double-edged sword. Despite the introduction of city councils to the Egyptian nome capitals by Septimius Severus in 200 CE, central nome officials, notably the *stratēgoi*, remained the de facto nodes of public authority. The reforms of the early fourth century—involving the demotion of the *stratēgoi*—did not do much to elevate the cities' autonomy, as the new positions of authority, despite being held by curials,

have the good of the state as a motive, I do think that it is a mistake to discount the role of euergetism." See also Tuck 2011, 288 and Mazza 2011, 278–279.

11 See Dossey 2010 on North Africa, and Grey 2011 and Weisweiler 2017 for an imperial perspective; cf. Stern 2023, 289–290.

12 Grey 2011 includes papyrological evidence, although he uses it largely anecdotally.

13 The village of Aphrodite would appear to be a case study for this kind of "emboldened" peasantry, but the historical and documentary situation is more complex than that. These villagers' confidence must be seen in the context of their fiscally privileged status, as they enjoyed the right of *autopragia*, and Dioskoros's "filtering" voice taken into account; see especially Chapter Six, nn. 66 and 69. These different groups are manifestations of the different socioeconomic strata within the peasantry that Banaji 2007, 192–196 points to.

14 Cf. Kiser & Levi 2015, 561–566.

were bound closer to the provincial level as "semi-imperial officials." Against this backdrop, the administrative and sociopolitical observations made in the preceding chapters raise the question of whether the pagarchs were part of a continuous effort by the central government to obtain more direct access to the resources in the provinces and the countryside.

On the ground, the pagarchs dealt with civic matters in the rural parts of the city territories. But although they worked in collaboration with civic institutions, they were not subordinate to any of them. Rather, the pagarchs formed part of the new regime of notables in the cities, but at the same time acted as the local arm of provincial administration. This places them in the larger context of the administrative reforms enacted by Justinian and his praetorian prefect John the Cappadocian during the 530s, an inherent feature of which was the closer link between local power positions and the upper administrative levels.[15] These reforms were intended, among other things, to make the governors less reliant on networks of local patronage, as suggested also by Justinian's *Edict* 13 (539 CE), quoted right at the start of the present book.[16] This proclamation also effectively did away with the intermediary administrative layer of the Egyptian diocese, while the installation of higher-ranking provincial governors, the *duces et Augustales*, streamlined the chain of hierarchy from the prefecture to most parts of the Egyptian countryside: the pagarchs were to take orders from the provincial level, but their tenure was always subject to praetorian and imperial approval.

Edict 13 should also be seen as a document of imperial propaganda. In terms of legitimacy, Justinian found himself in an unfavorable position from the start, which his early legislation reflects in its attempt to cultivate the emperor's patronage for his subjects.[17] The complaint about the pagarchs and other local authorities, especially those involved in tax collection, forms a topos that was essential to this program but also part of a propagandistic tradition among late Roman emperors.[18] In a region that had housed about 10 percent of the entire population of the (united) empire in the second century CE, Egypt would have been one of the important places to spread this message.[19]

---

15 See Jones 1964, 279–285; Haldon 2005, 48–55; and Palme 2013a, 103–105. It is difficult to gauge the exact degree to which John was behind many imperial decisions until his fall in 541 CE. On the larger context of the "centralisation" and "efficiency" of late antique administration, cf. the classic account by Jones 1964, 401–410.

16 See Iust. *ed.* 13.4, which increased the remuneration of the staff of the ducal *officium* to three times its previous amount. Chapter 10 suggests that a significant factor obstructing the collection of taxes in Egypt was the frequent granting of tax exemptions by provincial administrators.

17 See Bell 2013, 275–317 on the context of Justinian's vulnerability and for a reading of much of his legislation as a response to this situation. Sarris 2006, 2–4 briefly refers to this aspect in regard to *Edict* 13, but then prefers to interpret the latter in terms of conflict between the emperor and the provincial aristocracy. Cf. Pfeilschifter 2014 for the view that imperial activity was largely directed at the elites and the masses in Constantinople.

18 On the context, see most recently Weisweiler 2017.

19 For estimates, see Bagnall 2009a, 19.

Justinian's position in particular was precarious. In 532 CE, five years into his reign, the emperor went through a dramatic baptism of fire when the bloody Nika riots set parts of Constantinople ablaze. Justinian ultimately prevailed by resorting to extensive violence, but his relationship to the senatorial elite remained strained.[20] Reaching out to potential new allies, Justinian followed the path his predecessors had laid out for him, and which his successors likewise adhered to, by granting offices and honors to select confidants. Historians have long seen such phenomena in terms of an intense struggle for power between the "despotic" late Roman emperors and their senatorial aristocrats. In this conception, the rise of a new imperial bureaucracy and the integration of private resources for the purpose of public administration took the form of an aristocratic takeover of state institutions. In recent decades, however, important studies have further explored the meritocratic and nonhereditary nature of the late Roman aristocracy, and its implications for the aristocrats' relationship to the emperor. In an environment in which increasing numbers of ambitious men (and women) competed for titles and privileges, the emperor established himself as the central source of social power for an aristocracy of service.[21] Christoph Begass recently published a monumental study on the constitution of the senatorial elite under the Leonid dynasty that promises to become an authoritative source for this view. Begass points out that at the dawn of the sixth century a clear distinction was established between the senatorial class as such and a more exclusive circle that claimed and exercised actual political leadership in the capital by means of imperial office. This division created an increasing number of aristocrats who were formally of senatorial rank, but in practice far removed from the imperial center, though they were at times rewarded with imperial titles and privileges for local service in the *civitates*.[22]

The findings of this book contribute to our understanding of these matters by providing examples of how the relationship between the empire and "local imperial" elites was institutionalized at the local level.[23] Conceiving of "pagarched" villages as distinct from the pagarchy opens up a more nuanced view of the balance of social power in the countryside, as it can explain the regionally varied career patterns that we see the

20 On the circumstances surrounding Justinian's relationship to the senatorial elites in the capital, see Sarris 2006, 14–17, including an intriguing analysis of the participation of Egyptian elites in the Nika revolt. The argument of Meier 2003 that Justinian staged the incident has not found much support, and indeed seems less likely. The vast literature on this episode is accessible through Ayaita 2016, who essentially follows the traditional narrative.

21 For recent analyses, see Begass 2018, 41 and 415–456, especially 419, with references to the most important studies. This topic is explored in the Egyptian context by Banaji 2007, 101–133, although one has to take into account the influence that the old curial networks still had on the composition of the "new" nome elite even in the sixth century.

22 Begass 2018, *passim*; especially 480–485; cf. Haldon 2005, 39–40. Begass only hints at the existence of this second group, since his study focuses on the mechanisms among the political elite of the senatorial class. He assigns an important role in this system to the title of *patricius*, which served to acknowledge imperial servants of outstanding merit.

23 Cf. Haldon 2005, 53–54.

pagarchs follow. The basic conditions for this hypothesis were outlined in Figure 3,[24] to which we can refer back at this point. The first thing to note here is the strong standing of the Thebaid *duces et Augustales*, and the best-known representative is the *endoxotatos stratēlatēs*, *consularis* and *hyperphyestatos patricius*, *dux et Augustalis Thebaidis* Athanasios.[25] His standing was certainly exceptional when compared with other aristocrats of late antique Egypt, but most of the *duces* we know of in the Thebaid of the sixth and early seventh centuries came close to it.[26] The installation of such men as *duces* of the Thebaid would presumably have provided an acceptable degree of central control over the local pagarchs, who by virtue of the public resources entrusted to them controlled the fiscal landscape of the nomes. But not every provincial governor was a *hyperphyestatos patricius* or an *endoxotatos stratēlatēs*. The governor of Arcadia was "only" a *praeses* with the rank of *lamprotatos, peribleptos,* or *megaloprepestatos*,[27] and thus found himself confronted with a number of much higher-ranking regional and imperial elites.[28] It is here, at least in Arsinoe and Oxyrhynchos, that the central government instead ap-

24 See p. 229 above.

25 *P.Cair.Masp.* I 67002, *praefatio*. On Athanasios, see Ruffini 2011, s.v. Athanasios 4; Fournet 1999, 330–332; and Kaiser forthcoming.

26 See, for instance, Fournet 1999, 332–336 on the *duces* Ioannes (Ruffini 2001, s.v. Ioannes 227) and Kallinikos (Ruffini 2011, s.v. Kallinikos 17). Concerning Ioannes, cf. also the potential identification of Ioannes with the *hyperphyestatos patricius* of *P.Ant.* II 110.5 from sixth-century Antinoopolis, and see now *P.Christodote,* p. 9 for more evidence. Concerning Kallinikos, Ruffini (2011, s.v. Kallinikos 17) dismisses the identification of the second *dux* in *P.Cair.Masp.* I 67005—a *hyperphyestatos comes domesticorum*—with Kallinikos, but it is still endorsed by Jean-Luc Fournet in *P.Bagnall*, pp. 98 n. 9 and 99 n. 13 (referring to Fournet 1999, 332–336). Other *duces* of the Thebaid rank comparably high, as the following list illustrates. *Paneuphēmoi and hyperphyestatoi duces*: *P.Münch.* I 2.4–7 (Elephantine; 578) and *P.Oxy.* I 130.1–3 (Oxyrhynchos, but concerning the *dux* of the Thebaid; 548/549). *Paneuphēmoi duces*: *SB* VI 9616 verso 15–16 (Antinoopolis; 550–558?) and *P.Laur.* III 110.13–19 (Hermopolis; 600 or 615). *Endoxotatoi duces*: *P.Cair.Masp.* I 67031.1 (Antinoopolis; c. 543–545); *P.Cair.Masp.* I 67002 col. II 10 (Antinoopolis; 567), which is a reference to the *dux* Kyros, not to the *dux* Athanasios who is the addressee of the petition; and *P.Lond.* V 1675.8 (Antinoopolis; 567/568). The latter papyrus is the lower part of *P.Lond.* V 1674 and the reference might thus be to the *dux* Ioannes, who actually ranked higher than *endoxotatos* (see Fournet 2008c, 330). It has to be borne in mind that *endoxotatos* could be used for men of higher standing in short references (cf. *SB* VI 9616 verso 15–16 and 18, where *endoxotatos* is used for a *paneuphēmos dux*), so we might ask whether the *endoxotatoi duces* listed in this note were perhaps closer to Athanasios in terms of social hierarchy than the use of *endoxotatos* alone would seem to suggest.

27 An *endoxotatos archōn* occurs in *SB* IV 7436.4 (end of VI) from Thebes, that is, in the Thebaid, but this is exceptional, and can perhaps be explained by some other title or function not mentioned in this reference.

28 Cf. *P.Oxy.* XVI 1829, in which a *megaloprepestatos praeses* has to approve official records of a pagarchy submitted by one or two individuals who are *endoxotatos*, *hyperphyestatos*, and *paneuphēmos*. On this text, see the Catalog, s.v. Anonymous pagarch (Arcadia). Federico Morelli (2008a) believes there are indications that the *dux et Augustalis* Athanasios, mentioned above, also held some authority in or over Arcadia, but Palme 2021, 329 n. 50 notes that it is unclear whether

pears to have resorted to a less hierarchical, or at least less bureaucratic, approach to the local level. In Arsinoe, which had a higher "density" of aristocrats than the Thebaid, the government seems to have courted the individual pagarchs,[29] who, again through public administrative infrastructure, exercised fiscal authority vis-à-vis their peers of comparably high ranks. In Oxyrhynchos, a family of imperial acquaintances, the Apiones, controlled the largest individual share of the fiscal landscape. It is, finally, notable that this system, if accepted as such, transcended the reigns of individual emperors.

If we accept this reconstruction, it is unclear which factor should be given primacy: did the central government court individuals or families that already held important positions at the local level, or did it promote and perhaps even delegate its protégés *in order to claim* these positions? This question cannot yet be answered conclusively, although the cases of explicit outsiders in positions of local fiscal authority do make the question ever more intriguing.[30]

3. Toward Transition

The findings of this study also have implications for questions about change and continuity at the turn from Byzantine to early Islamic Egypt. Four developments in the early seventh century may illuminate a major shift in the position of the pagarchy to the form that scholars usually associate with early Islamic Egypt.[31] These observations are largely, though not exclusively, confined to Arcadia. (1) In Oxyrhynchos, we see that the administration of villages through *oikoi* was probably abolished or restricted around the middle of the seventh century; shortly after, the term *pagarchia* became synonymous throughout Egypt with the entire nome, likely reflecting this development.[32] (2) By 636 CE at the latest, Arcadia was no longer governed by a simple *praeses*, but by its own *dux et Augustalis*. This man was a *eukleestatos stratēlatēs*; likewise, virtually all known *duces* from the 620s until the end of the seventh century were *eukleestatoi*.[33]

Arcadia at that point formally fell under the purview of the *dux et Augustalis* of the Thebaid or whether this authority was based on some other Arcadian responsibility of Athanasios.

29 It is even possible that many of the highest Arsinoite elites, and the pagarchs, were in fact related by family (Sophie Kovarik, personal communication), comparable to large parts of the elite of the Thebaid as depicted in the poems of Dioskoros (see Fournet 1999, 328–329 and Mazza 1995, 204–205). Such a "local official tradition" would have made it even easier for the central government to patronize the right men (and women) in the right positions.

30 See also Haldon 2004, especially 232–233 with comparable examples from an imperial context.

31 On the point that several phenomena formerly interpreted as Arab innovations have since been revealed to be developments from the periods of the Persian occupation (619–629 CE) or after the Byzantine reconquest (629–639), see Morelli 2013, 173 and Morelli 2010, 147–148, n. 25.

32 See Chapter Three, Section VI and the Introduction, n. 99.

33 *P.Prag.* I 64 (May 28, 636). Exceptions are a *paneuphēmos* and *eukleestatos patricius* and *dux* in *SB* XXVIII 17144.2–3 (Hermopolis; 641/642) and a *paneuphēmos dux* in *P.Apoll.* 9.2 (Apollonopolis Ano; 660/661 or 675/676). No *dux* is actually attested from the period of the Persian occupation.

(3) The pagarchs of the Fayum changed their title from "pagarch of (the cities of) Arsinoe and Theodosiopolis" to "pagarch of this city of Arsinoe" at some point between 623 and 639 CE.[34] Finally, (4) the first attested pagarch to bear this shorter title was apparently of lower status than all his known predecessors: a "simple" *megaloprepestatos* who did not bear the title of *stratēlatēs*, which had previously been a distinctive feature of the pagarchs of the Fayum.[35] *Megaloprepestatos* appears to have become the proper epithet pertaining to a pagarch from the 630s until c. 700; when pagarchs of that period ranked higher (*endoxotatos*), they generally did so because of other titles, such as Theodorakios and Ioannes, *endoxotatoi stratēlatai,* in Arsinoe and Athanasios, *endoxotatos illoustrios*, in Hermopolis.[36]

At the moment it cannot be determined whether the change in titulature of the Fayum pagarchs was merely a nomenclatorial formality or a result of the abolition of the Theodosiopolite nome,[37] but the other three observations are striking when set in relation to one another, as captured in Figure 4.

The resulting picture approaches the former Thebaid pattern and includes pagarchs without exalted standing—that is, without the epithets *eukleestatos, hyperphyestatos,* or *paneuphēmos*—under higher-ranking *duces*. Did Arcadia become more like the Thebaid? And was this development connected to the more or less contemporaneous abolition, or reduction in scale, of the system of *oikos* administration over villages? That does seem plausible, though evidence to prove such a connection will be hard to come by, and it would certainly only have been a part of interlinked developments.

If this hypothesis is accepted, what might have prompted this reorganization? Did the Persians or the post-629 Byzantine administration in Egypt implement a general policy of no longer conferring local authority for tenures as long as those previously enjoyed by some pagarchs and *geouchountes*? Menas Stratelates and, probably, Strategios Paneuphemos remained in their positions under the Persian regime,[38] but it is unlikely

34 See the Introduction, n. 50 and Chapter Five, n. 32.

35 Theodorakios in *W.Chr.* 8, although he is later attested as *endoxotatos stratēlatēs* and pagarch. Cf. the Oxyrhynchite pagarch Ioulianos of *PSI* I 52, also a simple *megaloprepestatos* without any title of honor, though in Oxyrhynchos we do not have much to compare this Ioulianos with (perhaps *P.Oxy.* XVI 2040, in which Ptolemaios and Ioustos are *endoxotatos*, provided that they personally were the pagarchs). Both *W.Chr.* 8 and *PSI* I 52 are legal documents that would be expected to use the extended form of reference when addressing a pagarch, that is, to mention honorary titles. Cf., in the early seventh century, Theodoros, *megaloprepestatos* pagarch of Oxyrhynchos.

36 Papas, a *megaloprepestatos* pagarch and the protagonist of the homonymous archive of the second half of the seventh century, is in a number of letters addressed only as *peribleptos*. Petterios (*SB* XVI 12481 from 668 CE) and Zacharias (*P.Ross.Georg.* III 52 from 674 CE), both of Arsinoe, are *endoxotatoi* pagarchs, apparently without further titles; this perhaps reflects a development of the later seventh century. *SB* I 4659 has been revised and does not refer to Menas; see the Catalog, n. 70.

37 See the discussion in Stern forthcoming (c).

38 Their staying in power (Menas as pagarch; Strategios probably not as pagarch, but as *geouchōn* with extended fiscal shares) suggests that there was no extensive bloodshed, if any, among the

Arcadia (before 623 CE)		**Thebaid** (before 623 CE)	**Arcadia / Thebaid** (623–c. 700 CE)
Governor: *lamprotatos–megaloprepestatos praeses*		Governor: *endoxotatos–paneuphēmos dux et Augustalis*	Governor: *eukleestatos dux* (*et Augustalis*)
Arsinoe	***Oxyrhynchos***	***Antinoopolis, Hermopolis, Antaiopolis***	***Arsinoe, Herakleopolis, Oxyrhynchos/ Hermopolis, (Antaiopolis,) Apollonopolis Ano***
Pagarchs: *endoxotatos–paneuphēmos* (including a *patricius*)	Pagarchs: *megaloprepestatos–endoxotatos* (small overall share)	Pagarchs: *lamprotatos–endoxotatos* (including many lower-ranking "career bureaucrats")	Pagarchs: *megaloprepestatos–endoxotatos*

Figure 4: Expanded version of Figure 3 (see p. 229 above), including the period after 622 CE, which is only a *terminus post quem* for the establishment of the new pattern.

that this alone would have been the reason for the Roman government to change the system after the reconquest, since—as we have seen—there is no evidence of condemnation of either of these men.[39] An alternative explanation is that the local administrative system changed because its economic foundation had eroded.[40] The Persian conquest possibly undermined the economic potential of the *oikoi* to a degree that over the medium term rendered them incapable of performing their administrative role for the adjoined villages. But if we accept Hickey's explanation that the economic mechanisms of the Apion estate at Oxyrhynchos were essentially autarkic in nature, then at least this *oikos* would not have been seriously affected by a breakaway of interregional economic networks after the Persian conquest.[41] Might violence be (part of) the explanation? Did the invaders significantly damage the infrastructure of the aristocratic estates? Even if we approach with skepticism the literary accounts of widespread devastation and bloodshed in the Roman East during the Persian conquest, the papyrological record

Roman aristocrats after the Persian conquest. In the case of the more or less synchronous demise of Apion III, it is unclear whether he was even in Egypt at that time.

39 I have noted before that Strategios Paneuphemos is no longer referred to as *patricius* in his later mentions, but this is perhaps to be explained by the early Islamic administration's hesitation to employ titles that once suggested proximity to the Roman emperor. Cf. Chapter Five, n. 140.

40 On economic disruption in the wake of the Persian conquests, see Booth 2022, 247–248.

41 Hickey 2012, discussed in the Introduction, Section III. See also Bransbourg 2016, 372, who suggests the Apiones may have had an "aversion" to exposing their grain economy to interregional markets; this is in line with Hickey's findings about the Apiones' wine economy. Recently published documents from the Apiones archive also support this point; see *P.Oxy.* LXXXIV 5465 and 5472 and *P.Oxy.* LXXXIV, p. 156. On the economic capacities of the Apion estate under Persian occupation, see also Chapter Three, n. 206.

reveals traces of Persian violence in Egypt, but the extent and dating of this violence are disputed.[42]

All three explanations have their appeal, but must remain hypothetical for now. Certainly, multiple factors were at play here, since it also seems plausible that the installation of a *dux et Augustalis*, that is, of a governor with military authority, was called for on military grounds after the experience of the Persian conquest. That Menas's and Strategios's reputations did not suffer any obvious damage from the major political changes suggests, in addition, that the pagarchy was strongly embedded in a well-running local administrative machinery.[43]

III. Final Remarks

The Introduction of this book highlighted the limitations of the papyrological evidence when it comes to generalizable claims about late antique Egypt. The "clusters of evidence" allow us to make assertions that are valid for specific dates, areas, and contexts, but in no case do they reveal the complete picture. For instance, not much is known about the administrative workings of the many *civitates* in the Thebaid and Arcadia beyond Antaiopolis, Antinoopolis, Hermopolis, Oxyrhynchos, Herakleopolis, and Arsinoe—and almost none at all when it comes to the cities of Aegyptus and Augustamnica. Since our view depends to a great extent on the two largest papyrus archives of the late antique period, any newfound papyrus from these under-documented regions could shift the grounds of debate. Comparisons with other parts of the empire face the major challenge that the available sources are fundamentally different in character from the Egyptian papyri. Going beyond merely anecdotal assertions requires a more in-depth approach than is possible here.

That said, I believe that the model developed here presents a tenable conception of central actors in the countryside of late antique Egypt, especially because it integrates various clusters of papyrological evidence from different decades and from a wide range of localities. Not only does it reconcile regional variations and establish a plausible overall picture, it also draws a continuous line from the pagarchs of the fourth century, who were minor curial officials, to the homonymous nome chiefs of the early Islamic period four centuries later. The model presented here makes it less likely that any of these clusters of evidence was a pure anomaly within Egypt; although socioeconomic realities

42 Cf. Foss 2003, 164–170 and Booth 2022, 238–239. See also the fragmentary *P.Münch.* III 130, in which the pagarch Menas Stratelates is involved in the reconstruction of a building that appears to have been destroyed by "them"; see Chapter Five, n. 148.

43 So perhaps the pagarchy (see also p. 219 above on Byzantine regime change) is here following the same pattern as lower-ranking offices, where we also find many indications of careers continuing and even advancing after the conquest; see Booth 2022, 244. At those lower levels, personal continuity is generally less surprising. On the continuities of late Roman administrative structures under Persian occupation, see also Sänger 2011.

varied from Antaiopolis to Oxyrhynchos, and from Oxyrhynchos to the Fayum, the *institutional framework* of fiscal administration at this level appears to have been essentially similar. The preceding chapters have, however, also laid out possible alternative interpretations of detail. If this book in any way helps inspire further research, it will have succeeded in its aims.

Throughout its existence, the pagarchy and its powers were used, challenged, and negotiated by all sides—the state, the elite, and the common people—ultimately keeping an important balance that allowed it to prevail for more than four centuries and to outlive the empire for longer than many other institutions of Roman administration. While the institution continued to change and adapt and thus lived on,[44] the titles *pagarchos* and *pagarchēs* disappeared under the Abbasid dynasty (from 750 CE) as Greek gradually fell out of favor as the administrative language of Egypt.[45] A ninth- or tenth-century manuscript from the White Monastery preserves a probably centuries-old form of a litany in which a prayer for the pagarch still occurs, but the misspelling of this pagarch's title and the Coptic translation of his Greek epithet suggest that the writers were no longer familiar with the meaning of this term, its essence.[46] *Stat rosa pristina nomine …*

I hope that this book, proceeding from an administrative perspective on local power networks, has demonstrated how studying "the state" and its apparatus at the local level uncovers a complex interplay of some of the administrative, economic, and sociopolitical factors that contributed to the construction of authority in the late antique countryside. The Roman Empire's approach to most of its provinces was for a long time defined by decentralized governance by largely autonomous metropolitan elites. Late antiquity marked a divergence from that principle insofar as it saw an increasingly professionalized state apparatus and rising numbers of imperial officeholders. The administration of the empire was still far from becoming a bureaucracy in the modern sense of the term, but in the late antique Egyptian hinterland we witness the govern-

44 A later alternative title was ἐπικείμενος (τῆς) παγαρχίας ("headman of the pagarchy"), which probably mirrored the Arabic title of the pagarch, *ṣāḥib al-kūra*; see Garosi 2022, 234; Sijpesteijn 2013, 120; and Gonis 2004, 190. The equivalence of the titles *epikeimenos pagarchias* and *pagarchos/pagarchēs* is made likely by the example of Yaḥyā b. Hilāl, who is attested with both titles; see Garel & Vanthieghem 2022, 89. In some papyri, Yaḥyā is titled "*epikeimenos* of the pagarchy of the Arsinoite nome"—see, e.g., *SPP* VIII 1333.3 from after 751 CE: ἐπικ]ειμ(ένου) π(αγαρ)χ(ίας) Ἀρ[σινοίτου—but in *P.Christ.Musl.* 16.4 (758 CE), he appears as ⲡⲁⲧⲁⲣⲭ(ⲟⲥ) (read ⲡⲁⲅⲁⲣⲭⲟⲥ).

45 Late instances include *SPP* X 65.1 (780 CE) in Greek and *CPR* XII 8.17 (VIII–IX) in Coptic. A Coptic graffito from Gebel el-Teir in Kharga Oasis is translated in Winlock 1941, 49 (cf. Bagnall & Tallet 2015, 176) as "In the year of Diocletian 500+, I, Severus, the son of the Pagarch of Hibis," suggesting the mention of a pagarch between 784 and 883 CE. The text, however, does not refer to a ⲡⲁⲅⲁⲣⲭⲟⲥ but to ⲡ̣ⲗⲁϣⲁⲛⲉ ⲛϩⲏⲃ, "the *lashane* of Hibis."

46 On this manuscript and its two parallels, see the introduction to the Catalog. The spelling ⲡⲁⲧⲁⲣⲭ- is of the kind that we repeatedly encounter in other later manuscripts of sources that refer to pagarchs, e.g., the *Codex Theodosianus* and Justinian's *Edict* 13, and also in later Coptic documentary papyri, for instance, in *P.Christ.Musl.* 16.4 (see n. 44 above).

ment actively seeking to shape and refine its instruments in order to extend the reach of the state. Balancing tendencies for increasingly informal ways of exercising authority, the elevation of the pagarchy in the fifth century can probably be taken as an attempt at centralization in the rural areas at a time when the institutional role of the aristocratic large estates started to take hold. For various and not always intended reasons, this development would—at least structurally—come to fruition around the time of the Arab conquest or in the decade prior. Ultimately, from the perspective of the late Roman emperors, the pagarchy and the delegated authority of aristocrats over villages via their *oikoi* established a balance of power in the Egyptian countryside that enabled government in a peripheral region of a “postcurial” world.

Catalog
Prosopographical Notes

The following catalog lists the pagarchs we know from the period from c. 500 CE up to the Islamic conquest in 639–642. The individual entries discuss potential prosopographical identifications, social status, and other points of interest, such as the allocation of a pagarch to a certain *civitas*. This catalog thus aims to make the arguments of the main chapters easier to follow—by preventing them from getting bogged down in excessive detail—while at the same time ensuring transparency, especially considering that new evidence could modify the arguments presented here.

The Catalog goes through the attested pagarchs by province and nome from north to south; within a nome, the entries follow alphabetical order, as the chronologies are sometimes inconclusive, with anonymous pagarchs listed at the end. "Anonymous" in this catalog means that either the papyrus does not provide this pagarch's personal name or the name is lost. Names in parentheses refer to individuals whom scholars frequently identify as pagarchs but who in my opinion were not actually pagarchs.[1] A "(?)" can mean two things: (1) this person does not actually bear the title of pagarch in any document but is instead linked to a *pagarchia* or (2) the reading of the title or its attribution to the person is uncertain.[2] This leads to the following ordering:

1 With the exception of "Alexandros," who is a ghost pagarch, these individuals may have been pagarchs, but this cannot be inferred from the evidence currently available.

2 Some of these "pagarchs" followed by "(?)" nonetheless appear as pagarchs in the main chapters—for instance, in the discussions of Chapter Five, Sections III and IV. The individual entries in the Catalog discuss the degree of certainty of the identifications. In variation of (1), I count *P.Oxy.* XVI 1829.2–3 as certain, i.e., without "(?)," because the pagarchy in that text is expressly the pagarchy "of" an individual: οἱ τύποι τῆς | π̣αγαρχίας τοῦ τῆς ἐνδόξου μνήμης ὑμῶν πατρός.

https://doi.org/10.1515/9783111493183-009

Within each entry, I refer to the pagarch concerned by using the initial letter of the personal name only (for instance, Menas Scriniarius = M.), so that namesakes can be easily distinguished at first glance; this is in order to avoid confusion about which documents certainly refer to the pagarch and which only relate to potential homonymous matches. Possible but uncertain identifications discussed in this catalog are only occasionally mentioned in the main chapters. Most of the Thebaid pagarchs figure in Giovanni Ruffini's prosopography of Byzantine Aphrodite and are always listed with their relevant entries below; references to the *PLRE* for pagarchs can be accessed through Roberta Mazza's catalog.[3]

The basis of this catalog is formed by papyri that contain words based on the stem παγαρχ- and have been dated to before the Islamic conquest of Egypt.[4] In general, I include documents dated "VI–VII,"[5] but not those dated "mid-VII" or later, "VII" or later,[6] or "after 639/640/641/642" (vel sim.). There are exceptions to these principles,

3 Ruffini 2011 and Mazza 1995, 226–242. The latter includes some pagarchs whose tenures are probably dating from the early Islamic period. I will only in exceptional cases mention where I differ from Ruffini's or Mazza's identifications. For the sake of concordance with these works, I retain and explain obsolete entries.

4 The texts that mention a pagarchy and not the pagarch's title will, of course, play a role in this prosopography if it is possible to link the pagarchy to an individual, such as in the case of Ptolemaios and Ioustos in the Oxyrhynchite nome.

5 Still, *P.Lond.* V 1753 and *SPP* XX 273 may be from the early Islamic period and will always be marked as uncertain here as well as in the main chapters. *PSI* I 52, discussed in Chapter Three, Section VI, most likely dates from the early Islamic period but is included here since it has thus far usually been considered within the scope of scholarly discussions about the Byzantine pagarchs.

6 Therefore, the two pagarchs called Sabinos are absent. The first is the author of *SPP* VIII 1187, which is of unknown origin (perhaps from Arsinoe) and was dated to the sixth century in the *editio princeps*, but has later been assigned to the seventh (*CPR* X, pp. 155–156). The second appears in *SPP* III^2 94, which was assigned to the seventh century and possibly comes from Arsinoe or Herakleopolis; cf., however, the editor's arguments against an Arsinoite provenance in the commentary. It is possible, of course, that these two pagarchs are the same person. However, *P.Ant.* II 96 and 97 (both Antinoopolis; VII) are included for discussion, since the Phoibammon

but they are marked as such and discussed where relevant. Also excluded here are texts that refer to "early" pagarchs of the fourth and fifth centuries, as these texts are discussed separately in Chapter One.[7]

Virtually all relevant Greek documentary papyri from the Byzantine era containing παγαρχ-, including the most recent publications, have now been entered into the *PN*. In addition, *P.Prag.* III 219 should be restored to refer to a pagarch.[8] The texts of *P.Aphrod.Lit.* IV 13 and 14 have not been entered into the *PN* due to their literary character. A host of notarial documents from the Arsinoite nome that mention pagarchs are currently being edited by Sophie Kovarik, four of which I refer to in this study: Louvre E 6573, P.Berol. 3387, P.Vindob. G 24302, and *CPR* XIX 14 + P.Vindob. G 21029 + P.Vindob. G 25638.[9] No Coptic document attesting Byzantine pagarchs has been entered into the *PN* to date; Coptic papyri that certainly refer to Byzantine pagarchs are *P.Sorb. Copt.* 30, MacCoull 1993, nos. 6 and 11 (the latter has been re-edited as Vanderheyden 2015, no. 15), and Vanderheyden 2015, nos. 11 and 13. A less likely instance is *O.Sarga* 107.

All individuals identified that way can then be subjected to prosopographical analysis, resulting in additions to the Catalog that are discussed in the individual entries below. Not included are various men and women whom some scholars have identified as pagarchs by virtue of their being *illoustrios* or *illoustria*. This title is often taken as a de facto synonym for *pagarchos/pagarchēs* or it is said to refer "typically" or "almost exclusively" (vel sim.) to pagarchs.[10] The first assumption goes back to a claim by Jean Gascou that he has since retracted,[11] the second is, to a certain degree, valid for the Islamic era of the seventh century and the first part of the eighth. In the Byzantine period, the title of *illoustrios* can be shown to fit well into a hierarchy of honors; some

mentioned in these documents may be the same as the Phoibammon mentioned in *P.Aphrod. Lit.* 13; but because this is very uncertain and both *P.Ant.* II 96 and 97 may well be from the early Islamic age, neither appears as evidence for Byzantine pagarchs in the main chapters of this book.

7 *P.Mich.* XI 624 (mid-V–early VI) is a borderline case, but has been included here as it probably shows "later" pagarchs. *P.Oxy.* LXXXII 5337 (June 10, 493) is included because it forms part of the evidence on *kōmai pagarchoumenai*, discussed in Chapter Three.

8 *P.Prag.* III 219.1 (mid to late VI–early VII): read παγάρχῳ τ]ῆ[ς] Ἀρσινοιτῶν καὶ Θεοδοσιουπολιτῶν. The combination of Arsinoe and Theodosiopolis occurs exclusively with the pagarchs' official title, and l. 4: παρὰ τῆς ὑμετέρας ὑπερφυείας suggests that only one pagarch is addressed. This was de facto already suggested by Sophie Kovarik in her unpublished doctoral dissertation; the data in Kovarik 2014, xxiii (in Chapter 3) lists the pagarch as addressee (although only with Arsinoe, which is certainly unintentional).

9 See pp. 168–169 for references. I am grateful to Sophie Kovarik for allowing me to use these documents as discussed in her unpublished dissertation on the late antique notaries; see Kovarik 2014.

10 See, for instance, *P.Heid.Kopt.*, p. 100 and Hickey 2012, 108 and n. 69; cf. Berkes & Mihálykó 2019, 298.

11 Original passage: Gascou 1972a, 69. Revised version: Gascou 2008, 49. Despite this deletion, the revised article retains traces of the argument, such as when Oxyrhynchite "pagarchs" are listed; cf. Gascou 1972a, 70–71 n. 3 and Gascou 2008, 49–50 n. 33.

pagarchs bore the title, most did not.[12] The hypothesis that the *illoustrios* title serves to identify a pagarch is therefore not adopted in the present catalog.

With the exception of the abovementioned *P.Aphrod.Lit.* IV 13 and 14, literary, "semi-literary," and normative sources that mention pagarchs or the pagarchy have not been included in the Catalog, since they do not refer to specific pagarchs (Iust. *ed.* 13; Coptic *History of the Church*) or the pagarch referred to is fictional (*Life of Aaron*).[13] Probably also to that first group belongs a litany that contains a prayer "for the *endoxotatos* and God-loving, the *illoustrios* and pagarch, and with all his children and with those who are with him."[14] The text of this part of the litany is preserved in three late bilingual manuscripts from the White Monastery in the Thebaid.[15] It must have grown and changed over time, and we are probably dealing with a generic prayer for whoever was in charge and not one that was intended only for one specific pagarch at a certain time. Specific orthographic slips in the various manuscripts indicate that their writers no longer had a clear idea of parts of that passage,[16] and such texts go back to compositions from perhaps centuries earlier, as the conserved prayers for the emperor and his

12 See Chapter Five, Section I. Immediately after the conquest, the pagarchs Athanasios in Hermopolis (who appears in the Senouthios archive) and Theodorakios in Arsinoe bear the titulature of *endoxotatos illoustrios* and pagarch, but before the conquest Theodorakios is addressed simply as *megaloprepestatos* pagarch in a receipt in contract form, which we would expect to give the full-fledged titulature of rank epithet, office, *and* title of honor if there is one.

13 In Berkes & Mihálykó 2019, the authors republish a papyrus that they interpret as "an acclamation performed by the citizens of Arsinoe in honor of their pagarch" from the seventh century, but from the period of Byzantine control over Egypt (p. 302). The text does not mention the title of pagarch but instead refers to an *illoustrios* (perhaps an *endoxotatos illoustrios*; see the commentary on ll. 1–2). While it seems perfectly plausible that this person may have been a Byzantine pagarch (since *illoustrios* is the higher title and would be preferred in a short reference), a problem for this hypothesis is that the papyrus comes from an Arsinoite context and virtually all known pagarchs of Byzantine Arsinoe were at least *stratēlatai*. The only exception is Theodorakios, who in *W.Chr.* 8 from 639/640 CE is addressed as *megaloprepestatos* pagarch (see the previous note), but after the Islamic conquest is referred to as *endoxotatos illoustrios*. It is, therefore, not unlikely that Berkes and Mihálykó's pagarch is actually from the early Islamic period; the reference to the Roman emperor does not speak against this (on late prayers to the emperor, cf. n. 17 below). According to the hypothesis presented in the Conclusion of this book, the period from 623 to 639 CE might have witnessed a general reduction in the ranks of the Arsinoite pagarchs, so the acclamation may also have been written during this period. I find, however, the authors' alternative suggestion more plausible, namely that the *illoustrios* may have been a military officer, which would fit the Roman and military contexts of the acclamation; see, again, the commentary on ll. 1–2 of the papyrus.

14 P.Vindob. K 9743 verso 7–11 (written on parchment): ὑπὲρ τοῦ ἐνδοξοτάτου καὶ τοῦ φιλοχρίστου | τοῦ δὲ ἰελλουτρίου (read ἰλλουστρίου) καὶ παγάρχου καὶ | μετὰ πὰντων τῶν δέκνων (read τέκνων) αὐ|τοῦ καὶ μετὰ πάντων συμπαρον|τῶν αὐτῷ.

15 P.Vindob. K 9743 (= *SPP* XV 251); MS Insinger 29; Borgia Copto 109/101. The texts and earlier editions and literature are accessible through Henner 2000, 146, 147–150, and 161–182. Only P.Vindob. K 9743 has been assigned with some confidence to the ninth or perhaps tenth century.

16 See Henner 2000, 165 (notes on ll. 8 and 14) and 200.

court illustrate.[17] Notably, all three Coptic versions of this part of the prayer do not render the Greek rank epithet *endoxotatos* in its Graeco-Coptic form (ⲉⲛⲇⲟⲝⲟⲧⲁⲧⲟⲥ), but translate it with an Egyptian word.[18] The combination of the rank epithet *endoxotatos* and the title of *illoustrios* for this "standard pagarch" suggests a date between the mid-seventh and early eighth century for the original composition.[19] This fits the position of one pagarch as the single central authority at the city level that is manifest in the composition of the text: the prayers for the pagarch are placed between prayers for the imperial court and the army on one side and prayers "for this city and the entire city and the countryside and the village (...)" on the other.[20]

Arcadia I: Arsinoe

For a long time it has been assumed that the Apiones and Strategioi in the Fayum are the same as the individuals that we see as absentee landlords in Oxyrhynchos, the "Apiones" in the strict sense, as it were. Doubts have been raised about these identifications, however, and today scholars are more cautious.[21] From the evidence currently available, it appears safer to assume that Apion Stratelates, Strategios Stratelates, and Strategios Paneuphemos, if at all related to the Oxyrhynchite Apiones, form an Arsinoite branch of this family.[22] Many new insights will emerge from Sophie Kovarik's forthcoming editions of a host of new documents concerning the Fayum aristocracy.

17 On (partially adapted) prayers for the "emperor(s)" under non-Roman rule, see Treu 1974, 53–54 and n. 27 as well as Henner 2000, 175–178.

18 See the synoptic table in Henner 2000, 171: ⲉⲧⲃⲉ ⲡⲉⲧϩⲁⲉⲟⲟⲩ. The term ⲉⲛⲇⲟⲝⲟⲧⲁⲧⲟⲥ is still used in the eighth century, for instance in *P.Lond.* IV 1497.3 (708/709 CE).

19 This interpretation assumes that the combination of the titles of *illoustrios* and pagarch became frequent in the Thebaid at about the same time as in Arsinoe. A sixth-century example of an *endoxotatos illoustrios* who was pagarch in the Thebaid is Serenos, but at that time this was by no means close to a standard titulature that could serve to explain its use in the litany.

20 P.Vindob. K 9743 verso 17–18: ὑ̣π̣ὲ̣ρ τῆς π̣όλεως ταύτης καὶ πάσης πόλε|[ως κα]ὶ χώρας καὶ κώμης κτλ.

21 On this discussion, see Nikolaos Gonis in *P.Oxy.* LXX, p. 93. For instance, Mazza 1995, 234–237 argues that Apion Stratelates and Apion II are one and the same man.

22 Scores of papyri from the fifth to seventh centuries mention individuals called Apion and Strategios, and many of these men bear high ranks. Therefore, the prosopographical matches should be handled with care, especially when they transgress nome borders—one needs only to look at the numerous Apiones and Strategioi in Oxyrhynchos and Herakleopolis. It is therefore advisable not to identify any Apion or Strategios with a contemporary namesake until there are multiple matching titles or contexts.

Apion Stratelates

A. is addressed as *endoxotatos stratēlatēs* in *BGU* I 305 and as *paneuphēmos apo hypatōn* (of consular rank/honorary consul) in *CPR* XIV 10; in both papyri he is pagarch of Arsinoe. A. was once thought to be identical with Apion II, *consul ordinarius* of 539 CE, but more recent scholarship has put this into doubt especially due to A.'s titulature.[23] A.'s titles are very different in both aforementioned papyri; an explanation would be that by the time of *CPR* XIV 10, A. had advanced from *endoxotatos stratēlatēs* to *paneuphēmos apo hypatōn*.[24] His earliest attestation is possibly *P.Erl.* 120 (unknown; 546–547?), where two *endoxotatoi prostatai*, Menas and Apion, are somehow involved in fiscal business, apparently the transport of tax grain, under the new *dux et Augustalis*.[25]

A. is thought to have been deceased by December 20, 578, since the pagarchs then were Christophoros and Strategios Stratelates (see s.v.).[26] This hypothesis, though possible, rests on two assumptions: that the pagarchy was held for life and that the three could not have been in office together. There is evidence against both assumptions,[27] although it is still possible that Apion died during his tenure.

A tempting match would be another *endoxotatos stratēlatēs* Apion, who had interests in Oxyrhynchos and is known from *P.Oxy.* LXX 4786 (July 27, 551). This Apion had some relation to a certain Christophoros (l. 8) and it would be a curious, though not improbable, coincidence if this man was not the aforementioned Christophoros who later held the pagarchy jointly with Strategios Stratelates. This text is also remarkable for its lack of the *oiketēs* formula that is a regular feature of the Apionic contracts from that period in the Oxyrhynchite, which further suggests different branches of the Apiones or two independent families, of which the Arsinoite branch also had interests

23 See Nikolaos Gonis in *P.Oxy.* LXX, p. 93 and Mazza 2013. If A. were identical with Apion II, his titulature would be expected to contain a reference to his having held the ordinary (not honorary, as A.) consulate. The name Apion was very common in Egypt.

24 *P.Oxy.* LXX, p. 93; add the observation that the link of the epithet *hyperphyestatos* to the title of *apo hypatōn* mentioned in this commentary is possibly present earlier in the case of Apion I in 489 CE; see *P.Flor.* III 325 (with *BL* VII 53) and Hickey 2012, 11.

25 *P.Erl.* 120.7–8: τοὺς ἐνδοξ[οτά]τους πρ̣ο̣σ̣τ̣ά̣τας | Μηνᾶν καὶ Ἀπίωνα. On the identification with A., see Gonis 2002a, 96 and Gonis 2005, 93 n. 35. The Menas in this text is possibly the same Menas who fathered the Oxyrhynchite *geouchousa* Flavia Anastasia (Gonis 2002a, 96) and who may be the brother of a Dorotheos (*PSI* VIII 953.70; cf. *PSI* VIII 956.20) who is possibly the Hermopolite pagarch (see s.v.), but the names Menas and Dorotheos are too common to encourage these identifications. On the use of *prostatēs* as a polite reference comparable to *kyrios* or *despotēs*, see s.v. Theodoros (Oxyrhynchos) below.

26 *CPR* XIV 11. It should be noted that this would fit the fact that Apion II died (or his death became known) between March 25, 578 and January 19, 579 (Hickey 2012, 16), but in light of the arguments against both Apiones' identification, I consider this a coincidence.

27 See Chapter Four, Section II.

in Oxyrhynchos (see also s.v. Strategios Paneuphemos above).[28] No evidence has yet been found to support the hypothesis that the Oxyrhynchite Apiones would have had interests in the Fayum.[29] The property A. rents out in *BGU* I 305 is located in the same neighborhood (*amphodon*) in which Christophoros and Strategios lease out property in *CPR* XIV 11, which may indicate another vague connection between the three men. The Apion from *P.Oxy.* LXX 4786 may also be a good match for the *endoxotatos stratēlatēs* Apion who owned an Oxyrhynchite *ousia* in *P.Oxy.* LXXXIII 5375 (June 18, 557).

Other matches are less certain: A. may be the *stratēlatēs* of *BGU* II 364 (Arsinoe; 553), who is the brother of an *illoustrios* Strategios; both are sons of a *peribleptos* Theodoros.[30] The late Apion of *CPR* XXIV 25 (Herakleopolis; 598) is not a valid match, since he is referred to here "in *euklees* memory,"[31] and thus is undoubtedly no other than Apion II.

Christophoros & Strategios Stratelates

Ch. and S. appear collectively as *endoxotatoi stratēlatai* and pagarchs of Arsinoe in *CPR* XIV 11 (578 CE), where they lease out a workshop. Both were presumably heading their family estate, given that they are addressed in a private context, and were joint pagarchs because of this. In the unpublished papyrus Louvre E 6573 (586/587 CE), they resurface as pagarchs, having been promoted to *eukleestatoi hypatoi*.[32] At least S. appears in another unpublished text from 588 CE (P.Berol. 3387), again as *eukleestatos hypatos*, but the pagarchy is restored in this document.[33]

There are several possible identifications of varying degrees of plausibility. Ch. may have been somehow linked to Apion Stratelates, if the latter is the same Apion who figures in *P.Oxy.* LXX 4786 (551 CE).[34] Note that the property Ch. and S. rent out in *CPR* XIV 11 is in the same neighborhood where Apion Stratelates rents out property in *BGU* I 305. Less certain seems the identification of S. with the *endoxotatos illoustrios* Strategios of *BGU* II 364 (553 CE), who occurs together with a *stratēlatēs* whose name is

28 On the *oiketēs* formula, see pp. 209–211 and 213 n. 135.

29 *P.Oxy.* LXX, p. 93.

30 *P.Oxy.* LXX, p. 93.

31 *CPR* XXIV 25.6: τοῦ ἐν εὐ]κλεεῖ [τ]ῇ μνήμῃ Ἀπίωνος.

32 On Louvre E 6573 and P.Berol. 3387, see Chapter Four, nn. 35 and 36. Because of this late appearance as *eukleestatos hypatos*, Strategios Stratelates cannot be the late *endoxotatos* Strategios whose wife and daughters are *prōteuousai* of Arsinoe in *CPR* X 127 (584 CE). This man's wife Theophania is addressed as *stratēlatissa*, which probably means that the late Strategios was a *stratēlatēs*. Theophania for her part is linked in some way to the *patricia* Sophia (see Gonis 2008, 203–204), possibly the mother of Strategios Paneuphemos (see s.v. below).

33 See Table 5 (pp. 169–171).

34 See also s.v. Apion Stratelates above.

lost in a lacuna. Because of the pairing with this Strategios, the anonymous *stratēlatēs* has been suggested to be either Ch. (who appears alongside S. in *CPR* XIV 11) or Apion Stratelates (who probably appears alongside Ch. in *P.Oxy.* LXX 4786, who in turn appears alongside S.).[35] As for the space on the papyrus, both restorations seem possible. Both *endoxotatoi* in *BGU* II 364 are sons of a Theodoros who was probably *periblep-tos*,[36] and they are *geouchountes*, which would fit Ch.'s and S.'s joint holding of the pagarchy, though in this case they were not pagarchs at the time of this document. Furthermore, due to the different patronymic, identifying the Strategios of *BGU* II 364 with S. would make it clear that this line was distinct from the Apiones and Strategioi in the Oxyrhynchite nome. Neither identification, however, is beyond doubt.

Kyrillos

A *megaloprepestatos*[37] and *endoxotatos stratēlatēs*, K. appears as pagarch in one recently published and in one unpublished deed of surety from the last years of the sixth century: *BGU* XXI 2892 (October 5, 595) and P.Vindob. G 24302 (after 591/592).[38] In *SB* XXX 17412 (October 5, 596),[39] a *compromissum* between K. and a certain Apollos, apparently an employee of K.'s *ousia*,[40] K.—while being an *endoxotatos stratēlatēs*—is clearly not pagarch and the argument from silence gains substance from the type of document, which one would expect to contain an extended form of address and thus K.'s full titulature. On the other hand, it is notable that the text contains one of the few attestations of the term λογοποιία, which also occurs in *P.Lond.* V 1660.20 (Antaiopolites; c. 553), a text concerning the collection of taxes from a village under the pagarchy.[41] Is λογοποιία here connected to K.'s past pagarchy? In that case, the dispute

35 See the discussion about the relationship of these men by Nikolaos Gonis in *P.Oxy.* LXX, p. 95.

36 See *P.Oxy.* LXX, p. 95; ἐνδόξου μνήμης appears to be too short for the lacuna. Cf. *P.Cair.Masp.* II 67151.285–286 (Antinoopolis; November 15, 570): τῷ λαμ[π]ρ(οτάτῳ) κ[υ]ρ[ί]ῳ | Χριστοφόρῳ υἱῷ Θεοδώρου; this text is adduced by Mazza 1995, 240. The latter match is possible in terms of chronology, but a career advancement from *lamprotatos* to *eukleestatos hypatos* seems spectacular.

37 *P.Lond.* V 1786.2–4. This text is said to be from c. 610 CE, but since Kyrillos's pagarchy is now dated to the early 590s, it should probably be dated then, since the context very likely shows him as pagarch. See Table 5 (pp. 169–171).

38 For P.Vindob. G 24302, see *BGU* XXI, p. 92.

39 *SB* XXX 17412 (= Gagos 2008). Of course, with the new P.Vindob. G 24302, the editor's note that Kyrillos was not pagarch is no longer tenable, though certainly true for the moment in which *SB* XXX 17412 was written.

40 It is notable that Apollos's position is absent in the demarking of the parties in ll. 6–8, which probably means that he no longer held this position at the time the text was written. In ll. 14–16, however, the document clearly alludes to Apollos's (former) attribution to Kyrillos's *ousia*, possibly as *dioikētēs* (l. 14: ἐδιοίκησεν; Gagos 2008, 60). Apollos's epithet *thaumasiōtatos* would certainly fit the *dioikētēs* of an *endoxotatos*.

41 See Chapter Two, Section II 3.

may have been about the accuracy of the accounts that K., or rather his subordinate, left his successor in the pagarchy and for which the subordinate was held responsible.[42]

Although K.'s archive has long been known to scholars, it only recently became certain that he was a pagarch. The documents in which he appears are too fragmentary to tell much about the context but seem to concern mostly private business.[43] Apart from having an *ousia*, workers, and managers at his disposal, Kyrillos organized transports via the Nile to Alexandria, which probably indicates a *munus* of transporting the tax grain.[44] Official business is certainly behind *SPP* VIII 1114, addressed(?) to a *megaloprepestatos osprigitēs*, an official responsible for the collection and transport of tax grain,[45] and possibly behind *SPP* VIII 1115, by the means of which K. is ordering a payment to a *zygostatēs*, with a *logographos* involved.[46]

P.Lond. V 1786 also certainly relates to official issues. The text is a letter from a certain Alos, who humbly styles himself as "your servant" vis-à-vis "my master, the *megaloprepestatos* and *endoxotatos stratēlatēs* Kyrillos."[47] Only the second part of Alos's title is preserved, but he was apparently an official entitled to order detentions, certainly an *eirēnarchēs* or a *kōmarchēs*.[48] The content is difficult to reconstruct owing to the rather idiosyncratic Greek displayed in the text. It seems that Alos had received an order from

---

42 The formula λογοποιείαν (read λογοποιίαν) θέσθαι in the London text suggests that Gagos's (2008, 66) hypothesis is correct according to which λογοθεσία, a term used in the labor contracts to προνοῆται ἤτοι ὑποδέκται (see pp. 129–130 above) from Oxyrhynchos must be equivalent.

43 On his archive, see *TM* Arch ID 389 and *CPR* X, p. 155 n. 4; both, however, are incomplete. The earliest certain testimony is *SB* XXX 17412 from 596 CE (see above). In addition to the documents mentioned in Table 5 (pp. 169–171 above), the following texts (all from the Arsinoite nome and VII, if not stated otherwise) are believed to be part of this dossier: *BGU* III 725.10 (Arsinoe; 618); *P.Lond.* V 1786 (c. 592–596); *SB* I 4907 (name and title restored); *SB* I 4908; *SB* XIV 12195 (608); *SPP* VIII 1072 (610); *SPP* VIII 1105 (name and title restored); *SPP* VIII 1113 (name only); *SPP* VIII 1114; 1115; 1116; 1117 (title restored); *SPP* VIII 1118 (name only; possibly *stratēlatēs* in a lacuna); *SPP* VIII 1119 (title restored); *SPP* VIII 1121 recto (name restored but rejected by Gonis 2008, 208 n. 31); *SPP* VIII 1123 (name restored); *SPP* VIII 1189 (c. 613/614?); *SPP* VIII 1228 (name only, but see the discussion below); *SPP* VIII 1247 (name only, but K.'s *ousia* is mentioned); *SPP* X 249.10 (c. 620; on the identification, see Gonis 2008, 208 n. 31). See also *SPP* XX 133 for a [– – – † Κύ]ριλλ̣[ος – – –] in a very fragmentary receipt (VI–VII). Three other texts (Arsinoites; V–VI) give only the name and are possibly too early for K. as *stratēlatēs* but perhaps relate to a time before he obtained this title, or to an ancestor: *SPP* VIII 1069; 1070; 1071.

44 *SB* I 4907; *SPP* VIII 1105.

45 On the *osprigitēs*, see *SPP* III^2 pt. I, p. 118 and pt. V, pp. 38–39.

46 According to the edited text (there is no online image) the lacuna in l. 2: [παράσχες . . . . . .] (καὶ) Μηνᾷ ζυγ[οστάτῃ provides space only for a short personal name, not another office designation, so possibly we are dealing with ζυγ[οστάταις, but perhaps παράσχες (vel sim.) was still part of l. 1. On the *logographos*, see Chapter Two, Section II 3.

47 *P.Lond.* V 1786.2–5: † τῷ δεσπότῃ μο(υ) τῷ μεγαλω|πρεπεστάτῳ (read μεγαλοπρεπεστάτῳ) καὶ ἐνδοξωτάτῳ (read ἐνδοξοτάτῳ) | στρδηλατ̣ο (read στρατηλάτῃ) Κυρίλλῳ | παρὰ τ̣οῦ εσο(ῦ) (read σοῦ) δ̣ούλου Ἀλῶτ[ος.

48 The continuation of the formula that refers to the sender in *P.Lond.* V 1786.5–6 reads, according to the editor: Ἀλῶτ[ος ἀ̣π̣ὸ̣] | χορ̣(ίου) Καμ̣ίνων. Gonis 2008, 208 n. 31, however, has convincingly

K. to summon the—unnamed—son of a certain Apa Nakios, but later discovered he had detained the wrong guy, for which Alos is now apologizing to K.[49] These events apparently concerned the payment of taxes,[50] and K. therefore most probably received this letter in his capacity as pagarch, to which the involvement of a village *eirēnarchēs* or a *kōmarchēs* lends further support.[51] In this sort of internal correspondence, a reference to K.'s pagarchy would not be expected; instead, the writer sticks to the more exclusive title of *stratēlatēs*. Moreover, Alos is an official of the village of Kaminoi, which is known to have been under the authority of the pagarch at least in 639/640 CE, that is, immediately before the Islamic conquest.[52] Jean Gascou dated *P.Lond.* V 1786 to c. 610 CE, certainly based on the attribution to K.'s dossier, whereas Nikolaos Gonis more broadly assigned the text to the early seventh century for palaeographical reasons.[53] Since it is now known that K. was pagarch in the last decade of the sixth century (c. 592–596 CE, assuming he was sole pagarch), *P.Lond.* V 1786 may be assigned to this period with some confidence. The name of the subject's father, Apa Nakios, is extremely rare, and given that Alos does not name the person under surety but only identifies him through his father, this Apa Nakios must have been easy to identify.[54] This makes it highly probable that this Apa Nakios is the same man who appears in *SB* XXVIII 16873 (late 592 CE), a loan agreement with, presumably, Strategios Paneuphemos.[55] In this document, Strategios is not yet pagarch, which makes it even more probable that *P.Lond.* V 1786 dates to the early 590s, when Kyrillos was pagarch instead.

More mysterious is *SPP* VIII 1228, which appears to contain two receipts (for taxes?) from an eleventh and a twelfth indiction, issued by "Flavius Strategios and the heirs of Kyrillos."[56] Our knowledge of tax receipts from the Fayum at that time is, literally, very fragmentary and there is no evidence of tax receipts written in the name of pagarchs. Still, both Strategios Paneuphemos and K. are known to have been pagarchs, and both appear collectively at the end of the two tax receipts. We might thus speculate whether we are dealing with receipts issued by the pagarchy, which Strategios and the heirs of K.,

argued that the beginning of l. 6 has χοụ instead of χοṛ, and that therefore εἰρηνάρ]|χοụ Καṃίνων or κωμάρ]|χοụ Καṃίνων is to be read.

49 *P.Lond.* V 1786; cf. the editor's reconstruction and the one suggested in *BL* VI 65.

50 Cf. *P.Lond.* V 1786.15–21, especially 19–20.

51 See Chapter Five, n. 24 and *BGU* XXI 2892 (October 7, 595), a deed of surety to Kyrillos as pagarch by an *eirēnarchēs*.

52 *W.Chr.* 8. See also *SPP* III^2 23 (VI?), a receipt issued by a *hypodektēs* of the village of Kaminoi; on *hypodektai* under the pagarch's authority, see Chapter Two, Section III 1.

53 On both dates, cf. Gonis 2008, 208 n. 31. The *editio princeps* assigns the text to the fifth century, and indeed some features of this hand seem to be curiously early.

54 The rarity of the name makes it somewhat likely that also *P.Lond.* III 1032 originates from the Arsinoite nome if the date (VI–VII) holds. Due to the repercussions of the cyber incident at the British Library, the online image is currently inaccessible to check the palaeography.

55 See Chapter Four, n. 40.

56 *SPP* VIII 1228.4: [– – – Στρατήγ]ιος (καὶ) οị κληρ(ονόμοι) Κụρ[ίλλου – – –] and l. 7: [– – –] Φλ(άουιος) Στρατήγιος (καὶ) οἱ κληρ(ονόμοι) Κ\υ/ρίλλ[ου – – –].

following the latter's death, may have held collectively. However, the parallel evidence suggests that "the heirs of Kyrillos" would probably not feature as such collectively in place of one pagarch.[57] Therefore, the responsibility for fiscal shares is likely to be at issue in these receipts. Some connection between K. and Strategios Paneuphemos is apparent from *SPP* VIII 1072,[58] but since only a minor part of the document is preserved it remains unclear whether K. himself held any position within the *oikos* of Strategios or whether he issued the document—probably some sort of receipt—to a representative of Strategios's *oikos*.[59] *SPP* X 249 is another instance of some connection of K. to Strategios Paneuphemos.[60] K. was probably alive until 618 CE, so the eleventh and twelfth indictions of *SPP* VIII 1228 would be 622/623 and 623/624 CE, respectively.[61] In 622/623, however, Menas Stratelates is attested as pagarch, which fits the above suggestion that *SPP* VIII 1228 relates to the responsibility for fiscal shares.

A Kyrillos, *endoxotatos comes*, figures in *SPP* XX 140 (Arsinoe; 533) as the father of a Flavius Eustochios, possibly the *stratēlatēs* of the same name.[62] Though this Kyrillos is too early to be K., he may be an ancestor. If these two identifications hold, though both are speculative, it would again yield close connections among the Fayum elite.[63]

Menas Stratelates

M. is first attested in the recently published P.Vindob. G 26585 (ed. van Loon 2017) from February 20, 616, with the elevated titles of *endoxotatos stratelatēs* and pagarch of Arsinoe and Theodosiopolis.[64] Since his personal name is common throughout late antique Egypt, there have been doubts about whether some documents concerning several *stratēlatai* and *endoxotatoi stratēlatai* named Menas from the early seventh-century Fayum all relate to the same individual. Yet, Bernhard Palme has convincingly

57 See Chapter Five, n. 139.

58 *SPP* VIII 1072.1–2: Φλ(άουιος) Κύριλλος σ[ὺ]ν θ(εῷ) στρατηλ̣[άτης – – –] | ἐνδόξου οἴκ(ου) Στρατηγίου [– – –].

59 Cf. Gonis 2008, 208 n. 33, correctly dismissing a suggestion by Banaji 2007, 139 n. 36 that Kyrillos was a *stratēlatēs* of (!) Strategios's *oikos*. Sophie Kovarik makes me aware of the possibility that Kyrillos and Strategios were related by family.

60 See Gonis 2008, 207–208. Cf. pp. 150–153 above on whether this text illustrates fiscal shares held by the *stratēlatēs* Theodosios, Strategios Paneuphemos, K., and the heirs of Eustochios.

61 Hoogendijk 1998, 27 n. 10 (*BL* XI 262); cf. Worp 1984, 115–116 and Diethart 1980, 361 n. 406 (the latter referring to *BGU* III 725, the latest text to have K. alive); I owe these references to Guus van Loon. By contrast, Palme 1997a, 122 n. 77 suggests that this may be a different Kyrillos and places this papyrus in an earlier indiction cycle. *SPP* VIII 1072, however, shows K.'s connections to Strategios Paneuphemos and the name "Kyrillos" is not very common in our evidence.

62 See Gonis 2008, 208.

63 In this case, *CPR* XIX 18.3 (Arsinoites; V–VI): ὑ(πὲρ) κτ(ήματος) Κυρίλλου λαμπρο(τάτου) may also refer to an ancestor of this line.

64 The evidence published earlier is collected in *CPR* XXIV, pp. 180–181.

argued that the epithets involved are so elevated that we are likely dealing with the same person.[65]

The pagarch Menas from *SPP* III 303 is generally thought to be M.; Bernhard Palme places the document's sixth indiction to 617/618 CE, arguing that M. would have been called *stratēlatēs* in the short form if he was one.[66] Because *CPR* XIX 32 from 622 CE was the earliest testimony for M. available to Palme, he consequently suggested that M. was given the epithet *stratēlatēs* only after *SPP* III 303. The new P.Vindob. G 26585 has changed that picture insofar as it shows M. as *endoxotatos stratēlatēs* as early as 616 CE; it has therefore become possible again, as implied by the editor Guus van Loon, to date *SPP* III 303 to 632 CE. The occurrence of simply "pagarch" in *SPP* III 303, at a time when Menas had higher-ranking titles, is unusual for the Byzantine period, but the hierarchy of such titles was occasionally less strictly adhered to in third-person references in nonlegal documents such as this one. In view of the Arsinoite pagarchs currently known, an identification with M. still seems the most plausible option.

It is unclear for how long M. exactly held the pagarchy. In any case it is remarkable that a man of such an exalted standing remained pagarch of Arsinoe and Theodosiopolis even during the Persian occupation. He is attested in this position in *CPR* XXIV 30 from April 27, 622 and *CPR* XIX 32 from December 29, 622.[67] In 639/640 CE, however, Theodorakios is pagarch in the Fayum;[68] consequently, M. must have stepped down from or lost the pagarchy in the time span 623–639/640 CE.[69] *SB* I 4659.5–6 (Arsinoe; 668), often taken as evidence of the late M. and his supposed daughter Marous, has been convincingly reread by Sophie Kovarik, who rejects the reference to M.[70]

M. was dead by the time of *SPP* III 344, a text from either 643 or 658 CE, that is, after the Islamic conquest.[71] Technically, 628 CE would be possible,[72] but the expression

65 *CPR* XXIV, p. 178.

66 As for instance in *SPP* VIII 1048.1 (620 or 635 CE), an internal order from Μηνᾶς σὺν θ(εῷ) στρατηλ(άτης).

67 *SB* XXIV 16287 has been assigned to the Persian occupation and attributed to M. in Palme 1997b. This seems likely, if largely because we do not know other Arsinoite pagarchs from 619 to 629 CE. In any case, this text does not add anything to our understanding of M.'s role.

68 *W.Chr.* 8.

69 *BGU* II 694, attesting a pagarch Theodoros, may be part of the archive of the *oikonomos* Ioustos. If it is, the text should probably date to 628 CE and thus may indicate that Menas was no longer in office—assuming he was sole pagarch; see s.v. Theodoros (Arsinoe) below.

70 Kovarik 2014, 229 n. 68, confirming Palme's doubts about the 668-date in combination with the presence of M. (*CPR* XXIV, p. 181 n. 12). See also Kovarik 2022, 61–62.

71 *SPP* III 344.1–2: οὐσίας τοῦ ἐν ἁγίοις Μηνᾶ γενωμένου (read γενομένου) στ̣ρ̣[ατηλάτου] | τῆς Ἀρσινοιτωνπόλεως (*sic*). The papyrus is dated only by indiction. The parallels at this time suggest the reconstruction στ̣ρ̣[ατηλάτου ταύτης (!)] | τῆς Ἀρσινοιτῶν πόλεως; see Chapter Five, n. 32.

72 The dates 643 or 658 CE originally were based either on the idea that *SPP* III 303 (where M. appears as pagarch in a sixth indiction) must be from 632 CE (*CPR* X, p. 156 n. 8) or on the notion that M. was the father of Flavia Marous of *SB* I 4659 (*CPR* XXIV, p. 180 n. 11) and therefore must have been alive in the 630s. The first argument has lost its force because Menas is now attested as

"*stratēlatēs* of (!) the/this city of Arsinoe" appears peculiar to the early Islamic period; usually, the dignitaries of the Byzantine period were simply referred to as *stratēlatēs*, without any further definition.[73] Moreover, M. was apparently still alive at the time *SPP* III² 153 was written, and since this text is likely to be from either 629 or 644,[74] *SPP* III 344 is unlikely to date from 628.

Some other texts may relate to M. or have been cited as part of his dossier, but cannot be firmly linked to him. *P.Rain.Unterricht* 111 (VII) is a writing exercise and probably relates to M. (l. 54) but does not yield any further information. The Menas in *SPP* III² 58.2 (VII) is referred to as *makarios*, meaning he is deceased and unlikely to be the *endoxotatos stratēlatēs* of l. 1. In *SB* I 1449 (Byzantine), a *stratiōtēs* or *stratēlatēs* Menas authorizes an inscription for the renovation of a church.[75] Yet another Flavius Menas appears in *SPP* III 400 (VII), which is said to be of Arsinoite or Herakleopolite origin and may thus relate either to M. or to the later Herakleopolite pagarch Menas from the late seventh century—or, of course, to someone completely different. There is no reason to identify the "former *stratēlatēs*" of *SPP* III² 72bis.3 with M., as the editor did, because the text probably dates from the latter half of the seventh century.[76]

Strategios Paneuphemos

S. enters the scene possessed of the highest honors the empire has to offer, regularly bearing the epithets *paneuphēmos* and *hyperphyestatos*, the highest distinctions within the highest senatorial class.[77] In one instance, he is addressed as *eukleestatos*.[78] The documents up to 602/603 CE address him as *hypatos*, with *CPR* XXIV 26 (c. June 602–June 603) being the last instance. *SPP* VIII 1158.1 (Arsinoites; December 12, 602; *non vidi*) supposedly has Στρατήγιος σὺν θ(εῷ) ἀπὸ ὑπάτων Φ[– – –], but since the papyri attest a number of high-ranking Strategioi in this period, the identification with

pagarch earlier than 617 and because it assumes that Menas would always be referred to as pagarch if he was one; but *SPP* III 344 uses a short form of reference (see Chapter Five, Section II), in which the higher-ranking *stratēlasia* is preferred. The second argument no longer holds due to Kovarik's correction (see n. 70 above).

73 See Chapter Five, n. 32.

74 If *SPP* III² 153 were placed one indiction cycle earlier, this would result in the date of April 11, 614, while Strategios Paneuphemos was pagarch of the Fayum at least until October 5, 614 (*P.Eirene* IV 40), and as yet it seems that he and Menas were not in office at the same time.

75 For a discussion of these two possible expansions of the abbreviation, see *CPR* XXIV, p. 181.

76 Kovarik 2014, 664–665 n. 239.

77 On the variations in his titulature, see *CPR* XXIV, p. 154 (cf. Palme 1997a, 102). The documents from the dossier of Strategios Paneuphemos are listed in van Loon 2017, 129 n. 8; *P.Eirene* IV 40, p. 207 n. 9; and *P.Oxy.* LXXXIII, p. 192. Essential literature is also listed in *P.Messeri* 44, p. 252 n. 1.

78 *CPR* XXIV 27.8–10 (Arsinoe; 610); but see l. 17: παρὰ τῆς [ὑ]μετέρας ὑπε[ρ]φυίας (read ὑπερφυείας), alluding again to the epithet *hyperphyestatos*.

S. is not certain, given that he is nowhere else called *apo hypatōn*, but rather *hypatos*. Perhaps by December 12, 602, S. was no longer *hypatos* and *CPR* XXIV 26 may thus be dated earlier in that indiction year.[79] On September 16, 605, S. is attested with the title *patricius* for the first time.[80] Possibly earlier mentions of the patriciate occur in the following texts (all from the Arsinoite nome with no date):

- *SPP* X 114.2–3: The patriciate is certain; but there is no personal name.
- *SB* I 4781: S. is pagarch here. The lacuna in l. 1, however, might have contained the title of *hypatos* instead of *patricius*; this does not help to date the text.
- *SB* I 5253: The patriciate is restored but certain; S. is pagarch.

It has been argued that S. never held the title of *stratēlatēs*.[81] The fact that all other pagarchs in the Fayum are known to have been *stratēlatēs*, however, gives pause. S. is easily the most distinguished persona from that region, which is a compelling explanation for the missing title: when S. appears in our evidence, he bears the title *hypatos*, which would be preferred over the less distinguished *stratēlatēs*, a pattern for which the titulatures of the pagarchs Apion Stratelates, Christophoros, and Strategios Stratelates furnish precedents. Whereas the comparably high-ranking Oxyrhynchite Apiones keep all their honorary titles in their long-form titulature, S. drops the allusion to his consulship once he is *patricius*, and it would, analogously, be possible for him to have been *stratēlatēs* before he was granted the *hypateia*.

S.'s personal name makes him a natural candidate to be included in the stemma of the Oxyrhynchite Apiones. The hypothesis that he was the husband of Praiiekte, the daughter (or daughter-in-law and adopted daughter) of Apion II,[82] has been rendered obsolete by two unpublished texts.[83] Some unpublished papyri provide indications that S. might have been the son of the *patricia* Sophia.[84] But S. might also have been the son or adopted son of Apion II.[85] Further evidence will show whether any of these hypotheses stand. It used to be common among scholars to identify S. with some Strategioi in Oxyrhychos and Herakleopolis who were of similar status.[86] Given the coupling of the

79 A *paneuphēmos patricius* Strategios appears in *P.Erl.* 73 (Herakleopolis; March 29, 604), that is, with a higher honor; on the evidence for S. beyond the Arsinoite, see below.

80 *P.Bodl.* I 53.

81 For instance, Bernhard Palme (1997a, 125) argues that the anonymous *endoxotatos stratēlatēs* of *SB* I 4721 cannot be S. because S. has never been *stratēlates*.

82 On the status of Praiiekte (Lat. Praeiecta), see Nikolaos Gonis in *P.Oxy.* LXXXIII, p. 173.

83 P.Vindob. G 13381 + 22003 (Herakleopolis; 607) has Praiiekte married to a Strategios, but this man must have been dead by the time of that text; see Hickey 2012, 16 and, for provenance and date of the unpublished papyrus, Kovarik 2014, 682 n. 280 and https://data.onb.ac.at/rec/RZ00007746. An unpublished papyrus from Oxford suggests an even earlier time of death of this Strategios (595/596 CE as *terminus ante quem*); see Bernhard Palme's comments in *P.Eirene* IV, p. 207.

84 These texts will be published by Fritz Mitthof, whom I owe thanks for providing me with an earlier version of the manuscript.

85 *P.Oxy.* LXXXIII, pp. 173–174.

86 These identifications have in recent years been approached more cautiously (see *P.Eirene* IV, pp.

personal name with such a rare rank epithet and title, S. may, for instance, be identical with the *paneuphēmos patricius* of that name in *P.Erl.* 73 (Herakleopolis; March 29, 604), who was in control of an *endoxos oikos* in the Herakleopolite nome. In any case, a recent publication has now demonstrated close links between S., described as a resident of the Fayum, and the Oxyrhynchite estate of Apion III in Oxyrhynchos.[87]

The first document with a fixed date that attests S.'s pagarchy is *SB* XXIV 16288 from June 2, 600, though *CPR* XXIV 24 may date from some years prior.[88] Subsequently, the Arsinoite evidence consistently addresses him as pagarch *when appropriate*[89] until and including *P.Eirene* IV 40 (October 5, 614–April 25 or 30, 615).[90] The later documents all concern third-person references linked to S.'s employees, and thus generally feature only the most distinct attribute. Until recently, S. was generally thought to have died in office, which reinforced the hypothesis about a lifelong tenure for pagarchs. The recently published P.Vindob. G 26585 may suggest that S. was still alive on February 20, 616, when Menas Stratelates is first attested as pagarch of Arsinoe and Theodosiopolis.[91] But since the reference in this new text is only to S.'s *antigeouchos*, a reference to the pagarchy is not expected here. Therefore, the passage does technically not prove that S. was no longer pagarch; he could have held the pagarchy jointly with Menas. The distribution of the evidence between S. and Menas as pagarchs, however, appears to make this an unlikely hypothesis, since their attestations do not overlap, although new papyri may change this picture at any time. The *patricius* in *SPP* X 249.9 (c. 620?) is most likely to be S.[92] and probably shows him in his responsibility for fiscal shares apart from the pagarchy. I believe that the same is true for *SPP* VIII 1228, and

207–208 and *P.Messeri*, pp. 252–253). For a contrast, see Nikolaos Gonis in *P.Oxy.* LXXXIII 5398 and 5399 with discussion. The parallel titulatures and the extraordinarily high ranks involved speak in favor of identifying (many of) these *paneuphēmoi* Strategioi with S., but perhaps more evidence will change the picture.

87 *P.Oxy.* LXXXIII 5399 (612 CE) and the introduction on pp. 107–108. On S.'s Oxyrhynchite dossier, see also *P.Oxy.* LXXXIII, p. 192.

88 Based on the recently identified fragment P.Vindob. G 21202, *CPR* XXIV 24 has been dated to before 600 CE; see *P.Eirene* IV, p. 206 n. 5. Cf. Chapter Four, n. 42.

89 When the title of pagarch is omitted during this period, it is in all cases due to the use of a short form that employs only the most distinctive title (see Chapter Five, Section II)—either due to the type of document or because the attestation is a third-person reference: *SPP* VIII 1158 (602 CE), which is fragmentary, appears to be an internal order for payment, using the honorary title *apo hypatōn*; *CPR* XXIV 26.3–5 (602/603) and *P.Erl.* 73.9–12 (604) refer to S.'s *oikos*; *SPP* X 114.2–3 (after 602/603) employs the short form to mark the ownership of an *epoikion*; and *SB* XXIV 15899.6–7 (608) and *SPP* XX 209.7–9 (610) refer to S.'s employees.

90 On the date, see Chapter Four, n. 43.

91 Van Loon 2017. Sophie Kovarik makes me aware of the unpublished P.Vindob. G 50349, which may attest that S. was alive as late as May 11, 619 (cf. van Loon 2017, 129 n. 10).

92 Gonis 2008, 208. See Chapter Three, Section VII.

that in this document we witness S. bearing fiscal responsibility under the Persian regime, since Kyrillos, whose heirs appear in this document, was still alive in 618.[93]

Finally, there are some texts whose connection to S. is uncertain. Bernhard Palme included *P.Oxy.* XVI 1829 here, but has since retracted this identification.[94] Guus van Loon has pointed to a small dossier of texts relating to a *comes* Georgios, *antigeouchos* of S., which sheds further light on the structure of S.'s Arsinoite estates.[95] Comparable here is a posthumous appearance in *CPR* XXIV 33.6 (653 CE), which refers to an *antigeouchos* [τοῦ ἐνδόξου οἴκου ? τοῦ τῆς πανευφ(ήμου) μνήμης Στρατ?]ηγίου γενομένου παγάρχ(ου). Eta seems certain and I consider the restoration of S.'s name as the only likely possibility with this ending, but the ***endoxos*** *oikos* is doubtful.[96] Under Byzantine administration, we would expect S. to be referred to as "former *patricius*" in short, using his most distinctive title, rather than "former pagarch." Conceivably after the Islamic conquest the writer hesitated to invoke a title that suggested proximity to the Roman emperor.[97] The editor of *SB* XXIV 16222 suggested that the *patricius* mentioned therein is S., but Federico Morelli has argued convincingly that Athanasios, the *dux et Augustalis* of the Thebaid, is the likelier match.[98]

Strategios Stratelates

See s.v. Christophoros & Strategios Stratelates.

Theodorakios

Th. appears for the first time as pagarch in the receipt *W.Chr.* 8, which dates from 639/640 CE and concerns requisitions for military purposes. This text is mostly taken to illustrate Byzantine preparations against the Arab incursion, whereas Federico Morelli suggested that this text may also date from the time when the patriarch Kyros, as de facto authority in Egypt, had recognized Arab rule.[99]

Th.'s dossier has been assembled and discussed in *CPR* XXIV, pp. 197–199. The editor based some of his chronology on the assumption that the use of the epithets *mega-*

---

93 On this text, see s.v. Kyrillos above.

94 See s.v. Anonymous pagarch (Arcadia) below.

95 Van Loon 2017, 139–140.

96 The editor explicitly noted that τοῦ ἐνδόξου οἴκου was supplied *exempli gratia*. For a discussion, see Chapter Three, n. 243.

97 Cf. Chapter Five, n. 140.

98 Edition: Hoogendijk 1998; for the identification with Athanasios, see Morelli 2008b.

99 Morelli 2010, 155 n. 65. On Kyros and his relationship to the invaders, see also Gascou 1983, 98–99 (= 2008, 100–101).

loprepestatos and *endoxotatos* in different texts reflects a hierarchical development.[100] In two texts from 643 and 644 CE, Th. is an *endoxotatos stratēlatēs* and pagarch[101] and in *W.Chr.* 8, Th. is addressed as *megaloprepestatos* pagarch only. Based on this supposed development, the editor of *CPR* XXIV dates *SB* I 4856, cautiously, to before 643 because Th. appears only as *megaloprepestatos* pagarch in this papyrus.[102] Then, however, he discusses *CPR* VII 51 (629 or 644 CE) and opts for dating it to 629, arguing convincingly that in this document Th. is referred to by a patronymic and not yet addressed as pagarch (or *stratēlatēs*). But the text addresses Th. as *endoxotatos*, so if it is earlier than the *megaloprepestatos* references, the idea of a hierarchical development of these two epithets cannot stand.[103] In Section I of Chapter Five, I discussed other instances that make the argument of a hierarchical progression from *megaloprepestatos* to *endoxotatos* in such contexts doubtful. It is therefore possible that Th. was an *endoxotatos stratēlatēs* also in 639/640, but was not addressed as such in *W.Chr.* 8.[104] The mentioned *CPR* VII 51 also reveals that Th. was the son of an *ellogimōtatos scholastikos,* but there is no other glimpse into his life before he became pagarch.

In *CPR* XXIV 32 from May 4, 651, Th. is apparently still pagarch. Since it is possible that the tenure of an early Islamic Arsinoite pagarch named Ioannes is to be dated 645 to 651,[105] one may ask whether Ioannes and Th. were joint pagarchs, perhaps based on a

---

100 *CPR* XXIV, p. 197 n. 3.

101 *P.Ross.Georg.* III 50 (July 21, 643) and *BGU* I 320 (February 9, 644).

102 On this text, see the corrections in Jördens 1992, 288. It is not beyond doubt that *megaloprepestatos* refers to the Theodorakios of this text.

103 It is, of course, also possible that the Theodorakios of *CPR* VII 51 is not the pagarch, but the personal name does not appear to be very common, and it would be remarkable to find two men of the same name from the rank of *endoxotatos* in the same nome at around the same time and without any obvious distinction.

104 Cf. Chapter Five, n. 24 on the case of Kyrillos in *P.Lond.* V 1786. In Th.'s time, this probably illustrates that *megaloprepestatos* was the (minimum) epithet pertaining to a pagarch (see Chapter Five, Section I). Or, if *W.Chr.* 8 was indeed written under Arab authority (see n. 99 above), perhaps Theodorakios did not use his "Byzantine" title in the first months of Islamic rule.

105 On this discussion, cf. Bernhard Palme in *CPR* XXIV, pp. 197–200 (who cautiously argues that Ioannes was pagarch 660–666 CE, rather than 645–651) on the one hand and Morelli 2013, 169 and Kovarik 2014, xxviii–xxix (Chapter 3) on the other. This Ioannes is perhaps the pagarch and *dux* of *CPR* XXIV 33 (though the editor deemed this identification unlikely; see *CPR* XXIV, pp. 199–200 and 205). With Sophie Kovarik's and my suggestion concerning that man's titulature (see the Introduction, n. 93), the remaining space for the personal name is quite limited. This encourages the reconstruction of ll. 4–5 as [Φλ(αουίῳ) Ἰωάννῃ τῷ εὐκλεεστάτῳ δουκὶ ταύτης τῆς Ἀρκάδω]ṿ ἐπαρχίας καὶ παγάρχ(ῳ) ταύτη[ς τῆς | Ἀρσινοϊτῶν πόλεως κτλ., although one may object that εὐκλεεστάτῳ might have been abbreviated, which would leave space for a longer name. Ioannes is, however, a virtually inevitable restoration for *P.Berl.Monte* 15.1–2 (Arsinoites; mid-VII): [± 25] .ρ . . | [± 10 ταύ]ṭ[ης τῆ]ς̣ [Ἀ]ρσι[νο]ịṭῶν πόλε(ως). The editor de facto makes this connection herself. In the commentary, she suggests the reconstruction [N.N. τῷ ἐνδοξοτάτῳ ἰλλουστ]ρί̣[ῳ | καὶ παγάρχῳ ταύ]ṭ[ης τῆ]ς̣ [Ἀ]ρσι[νο]ịṭῶν πόλε(ως) and notes that the only known Arsinoite *illoustrioi* from these years who were also pagarchs are Ioannes and Theodorakios—but she does not deem either of them a sufficiently certain restoration. Ioannes's name and tit-

system comparable to the *skelē* (subdistricts), which at least in the Herakleopolite of the 640s saw two or three pagarchs in office at the same time.[106] However, Sophie Kovarik questions the date of *CPR* XXIV 32 based on a new reading,[107] which would render the hypothesis of Ioannes and Th.'s joint pagarchy unnecessary, as Th.'s pagarchy could in this case have ended after the indiction of 643/644 CE (*BGU* I 320). Kovarik's earlier date for *CPR* XXIV 32 is underscored by the argument that Th. would probably not have been addressed as *illoustrios* when earlier papyri attest him bearing the higher-ranking title of *stratēlatēs*.[108]

Th. is not identical with the pagarch of the same name who was active in the Herakleopolite nome soon after the Islamic conquest, as their different filiation makes clear.[109]

Theodoros

Th. is referred to as "my pagarch"[110] by a church *notarius* in *BGU* II 694, in which he has received some wine from the addressed church *oikonomos* for a festivity. It is unclear in what role he appears here. The text is *possibly* to be connected to the dossier of the *oikonomos* Ioustos,[111] which spans from 621 to 635 CE; in this case, Choiak 30 of

ulature, however, fit the space perfectly, counting twenty-seven characters in the first lacuna, including one for the abbreviation of the Flaviate: [Φλ(αουίῳ̣) Ιωάννῃ τῷ̣ ἐνδοξοτάτῳ̣ ἰλλουσ]τ̣ρ̣ίῳ̣ | [καὶ παγάρχῳ̣ ταύ]τ̣[ης τῆ]ς̣ [Ἀ]ρσιν̣[ο]ι̣τ̣ῶν πόλε(ως). As Theodorakios's name is even longer and the writer does not abbreviate any of the extant titles and rank epithets, this restoration becomes close to certain.

106 On the *skelē*, see Chapter Four, Section Four, especially n. 92. The *skelē* existed also in Hermopolis, where, however, one pagarch was responsible for the entire nome; Oxyrhynchos probably also knew such subdistricts, but we cannot say what effect they had on the administration by the pagarch.

107 Kovarik 2014, 95 n. 91.

108 See Chapter Five, Section I on the hierarchy of these titles. But perhaps the early Islamic period saw changes in the use of these titles that I missed; cf. the discussion of *W.Chr.* 8 above. If the argument is accepted, then the reference to Ioannes as *endoxotatos stratēlatēs* and pagarch in *BGU* III 737 (November 3, 648 or 663) is doubtful, since the *stratēlasia* is entirely restored here and nowhere else attested for the Arsinoite Ioannes. Moreover, Ioannes is later (in *CPR* XIV 1 from July 8, 651 or 666) attested as *endoxotatos illoustrios* (i.e., with a lower-ranking title) and pagarch; the name is mostly restored but fits the length of the short lacuna at the beginning of l. 6. Consequently, *BGU* III 737.4–5 should be restored as: Φλ(αουίῳ̣) Ἰωάννῃ τῷ̣ ἐνδοξοτάτῳ̣ [ἰλλουστρίῳ καὶ παγάρχῳ̣ ταύτης] | τῆς Ἀρσινοιτῶν πόλε(ως).

109 *CPR* XXIV, p. 199, referring to *CPR* VII 51, which probably names Th.'s father. That an Appa Kyros was father to the Herakleopolite Theodorakios is made explicit in the Arabic part of the bilingual document *P.Vind.EarlyIslamic* 4, the Greek part of which is *SB* VI 9576.

110 *BGU* II 694.3: Θεοδώρῳ̣ παγάρ(χῳ̣) ἐμήν (read ἐμῷ̣). The form πάγαρχος is indeed the more common one but the use of ἐμήν for ἐμῷ̣ may be explained by an adaptation to the "pseudo-feminine" singular παγάρχην (including a confusion of case), so perhaps one should read παγάρ(χη). The abbreviation παγαρ(χ-) is not uncommon.

111 Kovarik 2007, 153 n. 4.

the second indiction would translate to December 27, 628.[112] Assuming that Menas Stratelates was sole pagarch of the Fayum, Th.'s presence in *BGU* II 694 may then indicate that Menas's pagarchy ended even before the Byzantine reconquest.

Anonymous pagarchs

Several anonymous pagarchs can be found in the Arsinoite papyri of the sixth century. Three of the texts can be dated to a year and are therefore included in Table 5 in Section II of Chapter Four, where possible matches are also discussed.[113] Other anonymous pagarchs are only roughly dated to centuries and any speculation about their identity would be futile.[114]

Arcadia II: Oxyrhynchos

(The Apiones and Anastasia: magnates of kōmai pagarchoumenai*)*

Three of the four aristocrats known to have borne responsibility for "pagarched" villages—Strategios II, Apion II, and Apion III—are part of the magnate family of the Apiones.[115] Scholarly literature on the prosopography of the Apiones is legion and the main lines are captured in Section IV of Chapter Five.[116] For clarification, I note that I separate the Oxyrhynchite Apiones from the Arsinoite aristocrats Apion Stratelates, Strategios Stratelates, and Strategios Paneuphemos, who might still somehow be related to the Oxyrhynchite Apiones.[117]

The only non-Apionic instance of a *kōmē pagarchoumenē* occurs in *P.Oxy.* XLIV 3204 (January 2, 588 CE), in which the village name is lost. The document is addressed to Flavia Anastasia, whose links to the Apiones are still not very clear.[118] She is usually an *endoxotatē illoustria,* but is very likely to be the Anastasia who in two or three papyri appears as *megaloprepestatē.*[119] In *P.Oxy.* XLIV 3204, where Anastasia is addressed as *en-*

112 628 CE was a leap year. On the date, see also *CPR* X, p. 155 and n. 25.
113 *SB* I 4721; *SB* XVIII 13952; *CPR* XIX 14 + P.Vindob. G 21029 + P.Vindob. G 25638. See pp. 169–171 above.
114 *P.Prag.* III 219 (see the introduction to this catalog for the restoration of the pagarchy here); *SB* I 5256; *SPP* III 392.
115 The *geouchōn* from *P.Oxy.* LXX 4802, whose name is lost, is most likely Apion III.
116 For references, see the Introduction, n. 47.
117 See the introduction to the Arsinoe section above and the discussion therein about Strategios Paneuphemos's possessions in the Oxyrhynchite nome.
118 On Anastasia and her archive, see *P.Oxy.* LXIX, p. 210 and the literature assembled in Papathomas & Vergados 2021, 132–133.
119 *P.Oxy.* XVI 2020 (580s CE) and *SB* VI 9368 (577/578 or 592/593 CE), perhaps also in P.Col. inv.

doxotatē illoustria, she is also referred to as *hyperphyeia*.[120] Her father was the *endoxotatos illoustrios* Menas, son of Eudaimon, who stood in some obscure relation to the Apiones.[121] The *endoxotatos* Ioustos is a good candidate to have been her uncle,[122] which probably puts her *floruit* to the 580s and 590s; see s.v. Ptolemaios and Ioustos below. This situation fits the fact that Anastasia is absent from *P.Oxy.* XVI 2040 (566/567 CE) but does appear in *P.Oxy.* XVI 2020 (580s).[123] In this context, Anastasia's connection to the village of Ieme is noteworthy. Ieme appears in the earlier list *P.Oxy.* XVI 2040 as the only village contributor but is missing from the later *P.Oxy.* XVI 2020, where Anastasia appears. Was the village "independent" or did it possess some special status, but was later "pagarched" by Anastasia? Ieme is the only village that is known in connection to Anastasia and is thus the only available candidate for a *kōmē pagarchoumenē* of/by her *oikos*.[124] Nikolaos Gonis tentatively suggests some connections that may link Anastasia's family and a significant portion of the Oxyrhynchite nobility to Antaiopolite nobles.[125]

Ioulianos

I. appears in *PSI* I 52, probably to be dated to September 18, 647 CE.[126] Although his tenure as pagarch thus probably dates to the period after the Arab conquest of Egypt, I. is listed here because he has often been discussed as a Byzantine pagarch, based on earlier datings of *PSI* I 52 to 602 and 617. There are no compelling identifications to suggest. I. could be identical with the "lord Ioulianos" who is accused of having taken

---

523.4 (ed. Papathomas & Vergados 2021) from May 16, 571, where the name is restored but likely, based on the circumstances of the find and the filiation, if this is not a sister of Anastasia's. The distribution of the other documents does not suggest that the differing epithets manifest a "career advancement" from *megaloprepestatē* to *endoxotatē*; on this issue in general, see Chapter Five, Section I. Notably, in P.Col. inv. 523, the *megaloprepestatē* addressee (i.e., probably Anastasia) is later referred to as *endoxotēs* (l. 21) in contrast to a *megaloprepeia* (l. 22).

120 *P.Oxy.* XLIV 3204.4 and 18.

121 *PSI* VIII 956.20 and *P.Erl.* 120.7–8, where possibly Menas and Apion II occur as joint *prostatai*. On Eudaimon, see Gonis 2002a, 93–97. Cf. the discussion about *PSI* VIII 955 + *SB* XX 15181, s.v. Anonymous pagarch (Oxyrhynchos) below.

122 Gonis 2002a, 95–96.

123 On the dates, see Chapter Three, Section II.

124 *P.Oxy.* LXIX 4757.14 (undated) features Ieme (as Εἰέμη); the passage that could have contained the *pagarchoumenē* formula is lost. In *P.Oxy.* XLIV 3204 (January 2, 588), probably written by the same man, Ieme can perhaps be restored in ll. 11–12: ἀπὸ | [κώμης Εἰέμη πα]γαρχουμένης. In *P.Oxy.* LXIX 4756.9 (March 10, 590), where a short village name (not *pagarchoumenē*) is lost, it does not seem possible to restore ἀπὸ κώμης Εἰέμ]η because the traces after the lacuna do not fit eta.

125 Gonis 2002a, 95–97; he concedes that this must remain speculation.

126 For the date, see Chapter Three, Section VI.

something unjustly in *P.Oxy.* XVI 1865 (VI).[127] A more likely candidate for this "lord Ioulianos," however, is the *stratēlatēs* of the same name (*P.Oxy.* LV 3805 col. VI 73: after 566 CE), since *P.Oxy.* XVI 1865 probably refers to military requisitions.[128]

Ioustos (?)

See s.v. Ptolemaios (?) & Ioustos (?).

Ptolemaios (?) & Ioustos (?)

P. and I., both *endoxotatoi*, appear in connection with the pagarchy in *P.Oxy.* XVI 2040 (566/567? CE), a list of contributions, and in a comparable context without the pagarchy in *P.Oxy.* XVI 2020 (580s CE). I. is probably the *endoxotatos comes* Ioustos, son of Eudaimon, who appears in several papyri and may have been the uncle of Anastasia, granddaughter of a Eudaimon.[129] P. was apparently dead by the time of both *P.Oxy.* XVI 2040 and 2020, while I. was apparently alive at the time of the former but dead at the time of the latter. *P.Oxy.* XVI 2020 would thus have to be assigned to the period after 576/577 CE, the date of *P.Oxy.* XVIII 2195, in which I. is alive,[130] which would match Anastasia's *floruit* in the 580s and 590s, given the alternation of generations.

Theodoros

Th. appears in *P.Oxy.* XVI 1858, where a *chartoularios* hails him as "my master and in every respect *megaloprepestatos*, worthy of every honor and praise, D.V., *prostatēs* Theodoros, *comes* and pagarch."[131] The editor proposed that Th. is identical with the *comes* and *meizoteros* who is addressed and referred to in several letters from the archive of Biktor, the *antigeouchos*.[132] This collection is considered a subarchive of the Apiones archive

127 Gascou 1972a, 70–71 n. 3 (= 2008, 49–50 n. 33).

128 See *P.Oxy.* XVI 1865.10–11, which is hardly a metaphorical passage. This does not mean that the *stratēlasia* was a military office, though; it was the honorary title by which Ioulianos was identified in this context.

129 Gonis 2002a, 93–97 and Gonis 2019a, 353–355. See above, s.v. The Apiones and Anastasia.

130 Gonis 2002a, 95–96.

131 *P.Oxy.* XVI 1858.7: δεσπό(τῃ) ἐμ\ῷ/ τὰ πά(ντα) μ(ε)γ(αλοπρεπεστάτῳ) πά(σης) τιμ(ῆς) (καὶ) πρ(οσ)κ(υνήσεως) ἀξίῳ γνη(σίῳ) με(τὰ) θ(εὸν) προστά(τῃ) Θεοδώρῳ κόμε(τι) (καὶ?) παγάρχ(ῳ).

132 Theodoros *meizoteros*: *P.Oxy.* XVI 1849; 1850; 1851; 1852. Theodoros *comes* and *meizoteros*: *P.Oxy.* XVI 1857. On this subarchive, see *P.Oxy.* XVI, pp. 27–28, where the editor takes all these Theodoroi to be one and the same person.

and the connection puts Th. to the early seventh century.[133] But in a papyrus that was published after *P.Oxy.* XVI 1858, a *lamprotatos meizoteros* Theodoros appears alongside a *comes* and *meizoteros* Theodoros, which illustrates the difficulty of identifying men with such a common name.[134] The title of *comes* is also not distinctive enough as to immediately suggests that the two individuals named Theodoros are the same person.

Again, we can get a little further by looking at the documentary context of the titles in question: on the one hand we find a *megaloprepestatos prostatēs*, *comes*, and pagarch (= Th.); on the other, a *comes* and *meizoteros* (assuming that there were not multiple *meizoteroi* named Theodoros). A link between the two men other than the name and the title of *comes* is only apparent from the openings of *P.Oxy.* XVI 1857 and 1858, which address Theodoros *meizoteros* and Th., respectively. Both letters refer to their Theodoros as "your *prostatikē megaloprepeia*,"[135] which may appear to suggest that the *meizoteros* Theodoros was also *prostatēs* and *megaloprepestatos* even though he is only termed *lamprotatos* in the address. This is, however, more easily explained by the fact that both papyri are written in the same hand, which is that of the *chartoularios* Menas. In this light, the formula "your *prostatikē megaloprepeia*" from l. 1 in each papyrus seems to be a signature phrase of Menas's that probably should be understood in a general sense: "your protecting magnificence" or similar.[136] Therefore, Menas may have been deliberately attempting to distinguish Theodoros, the *meizoteros*, from Th., the pagarch, by employing distinctive epithets in the dockets of both documents; after the context was clarified, there was was less need for a distinction in the main text. The comparison also shows that *prostatēs* in *P.Oxy.* XVI 1858 takes the same place in the address as *adelphos* ("brother," "fellow colleague") in *P.Oxy.* XVI 1857, which suggests that *prostatēs* does not designate an actual position here, but functions as a relational term, as a polite way of addressing a higher-ranking authority.[137]

133 Gonis 2015b; Mazza 2001, 38. Cf. *P.Oxy.* LVIII 3954.8–11 (February 12, 611), which provides the explicit link between the *dioikētēs* Georgios, one of the main correspondants in the Biktor archive, and the estates of Apion III.

134 *P.Oxy.* LVI 3871. The *lamprotatos meizoteros* may be identical with the Theodoros who figures in *P.Oxy.* XVI 1861.9 and *P.Oxy.* XXVII 2480.3, 13, and 16; this man is a *meizoteros* but lacks any other distinctive title or epithet and is active in the Kynopolite. The *tribunus* Theodoros from l. 29 in the same document, however, may well be another person, as Lajos Berkes (2017a, 58 n. 180) has argued contra Todd Hickey. There are other Theodoroi in ll. 99 and 129, which illustrates the frequency of this personal name and strengthens Berkes's (2017a, 99 n. 93) point that the name is too common to allow the *prostatēs* (see below) to be identified with the *meizoteros*.

135 *P.Oxy.* XVI 1857.1: τῇ ὑμετέρᾳ προστατικῇ μεγαλοπρεπείᾳ; *P.Oxy.* XVI 1858.1: τῆς ὑμετέρας προστατικῆς μεγαλοπρεπείας.

136 This translation is used by the editor.

137 This was put forward in a different context by Morelli 2008b, 151 (see n. 39 for a reference to *P.Oxy.* XVI 1858). Compare two of the letters from Biktor the *antigeouchos* to Theodoros the *meizoteros* that, at this position, refer to him as "your worthy brotherliness" (*P.Oxy.* XVI 1849.1: ἡ ὑμετέρα γνησία ἀδελφότης) and "your worthy *lamprotēs*" (*P.Oxy.* XVI 1852.1: τῆς ὑμετέρας γνησίας λαμπρότητος) instead of "your *prostatikē megaloprepeia*" (*P.Oxy.* XVI 1857 and 1858).

Still, since none of the texts in this dossier has a fixed date, one cannot exclude the possibility that the *comes* and *meizoteros* Theodoros was promoted and thenceforth entitled to the epithet *megaloprepestatos* once he assumed the pagarchy.[138] A *megaloprepestatos* lord Theodoros, *princeps*, appears in *P.Oxy.* VIII 1108 (late VI–VII), but again, the name is too common to encourage this identification. The Theodoros addressed in *SB* XXIV 16312 (Oxyrhynchos; October 12, 549?), however, is an *endoxotatos comes domesticorum* and former *dux et Augustalis*, and thus, with all due respect to Th.'s ambitions, probably too high-ranking to be our pagarch.

(Anonymous pagarch)

The edited text of *PSI* VIII 955 + *SB* XX 15181, part of the Apiones archive, refers to an unnamed *endoxotatos illoustrios* as pagarch. No Apion is ever referred to as *illoustrios* in our evidence, so this man would then probably be a non-Apionic pagarch;[139] Todd Hickey speculates whether this man may have been the *endoxotatos illoustrios* Menas, the father of Anastasia.[140] Yet, the restoration of *PSI* VIII 955.39 as μετ]ᾰ̣ τοῦ ἐνδοξ(οτάτου) ἰλλουστρ(ίου) παγ̣[άρχου? raises doubts.[141] The document is an account and does not give us any reason to assume that an extended reference would have been used, as discussed in Section II of Chapter Five; we rather expect the writer to use only the most distinctive title of honor or office, which in this case is the title *illoustrios*. The editor suggests the alternative that this is the beginning of a personal name, Παγ̣[-, which I find more convincing, and judging from other parts of this papyrus, γ could also be τ̣. There is thus no compelling reason to identify this man as pagarch (although he might have been one).

138 The link of the epithet *megaloprepestatos*, which is more than a rank epithet in the strict sense, to the title of pagarch seems to have developed in the early seventh century; see the Conclusion, Section II 3.

139 Or this man is a high-ranking employee of the Apion estate, filling the post for his master, but cf. Chapter Four, Section III, for my discussion of Menas Scriniarius and the Oxyrhynchite pagarch Theodoros, the two pagarchs that are most often cited in the context of the "stand-in hypothesis."

140 See s.v. The Apiones and Anastasia (Oxyrhynchos) above and Hickey 2012, 107–108.

141 For the restoration of μετ]ά̣, see Hickey 2012, 107 n. 68, which I deem far from certain. Because of the ascender at the left end of the fragment—which also makes the reading [Μην]ᾶ̣ impossible—this should then actually be μ]ε̣[τ]ά̣, and the space for the supposed tau seems almost impossibly narrow. See, however, *PSI* VIII 953.51, also an account from the Apion estate: μετὰ τοῦ αὐτ(οῦ) ἐνδόξ(ου) ἰλλου(στρίου) Α̣[. . . . . .]; the epithet here and earlier in this line should of course be ἐνδοξ(οτάτου). *Pace* Hickey 2012, 108 n. 69, this man should not be identified as pagarch based on the title of *illoustrios* alone; on this point, see pp. 285–286 above.

Arcadia III: Unknown Nome

Antiochos & Theon

A. and Th. are mentioned in *P.Mich.* XI 624 (mid-V–early VI),[142] an internal administrative letter of Oxyrhynchite provenance.[143] Because they appear in proximity to Herakleopolis in this text, it has been assumed that they were pagarchs of that city.[144] But the situation is more complex than that. The sender of *P.Mich.* XI 624 was most likely a member of the *officium* of the *praeses* (see the commentary) or more specifically, as ll. 9–10 suggest, a member of the *scrinium* of the *ab actis*, a subsection of the praesidial *officium*.[145] The sender addresses an *exceptor* Kyrillos about several apparently unconnected topics. He dwells in a different city from Kyrillos (l. 7) and shows himself to be familiar with details of the locality he is sending the letter to. Among the several matters discussed in the letter is the following: "And inform my lords (and) fellow colleagues Antiochos and Theon, the pagarchs, that I have submitted without delay their report (*anaphora*) while my lord, the *ab actis*, was not in Herakleopolis but in Arsinoe."[146] A little later, A. and Th. are mentioned again: "Be good and have all the hay transported while you are still in the city, and remind the said men, that is, Antiochos and Theon, to provide their donkeys for its transportation as he (!) announced."[147]

In order to harmonize the many issues and institutions alluded to in this letter—which belong to either the writer's or the sender's city—there are two options: Either the writer was in Oxyrhynchos, which is generally seen as the capital of Arcadia, while

142 The editor assigns this text to the early sixth century, identifying "a highly practiced sixth-century cursive," whereas Gascou 2023, 306 n. 223 argues instead that this hand dates from the middle or the second half of the fifth century, "notamment d'après la forme du κ." I do not consider the latter argument compelling enough to make this text evidence for an "early pagarch" (or for a "later pagarch" before 493 CE, although this would not invalidate the reconstruction put forward in Chapter One, Section IV). The pagarchs clearly belong to the city level here.

143 The papyrus belongs to one of the "Nahman lots" that come from Oxyrhynchos; see the entry of *P.Mich.* XI 624 in the University of Michigan's digital collection (https://quod.lib.umich.edu/a/apis/x-2133/4013v.tif).

144 Gascou 1972a, 44 (= 2008, 62), in a passage in which he appears to assume that all of ll. 8–13 relates to Herakleopolis. Mazza 1995, 188 and 240 accepts the allocation of A. and Th. to Herakleopolis.

145 The writer is apparently dealing with A. and Th.'s report (*anaphora*) and several others (see ll. 16 and 28) *because* the *ab actis* was absent. On the *scrinium* of the *ab actis*, see *CPR* XXIII, pp. 197–198.

146 *P.Mich.* XI 624.8–11: καὶ μετάδος τοῖς κυρίοις μου ἀδελφοῖς Ἀντιόχῳ καὶ | Θ̣έωνι τοῖς παγάρχοις ὡς παραυτὰ μηδὲν μελλήσας ὑπέβαλα τὴν ἀναφορὰν | αὐτῶν, τοῦ κυρ(ίου) μου τοῦ ἀβάκτης μὴ ὄντος ἐπὶ τῆς Ἡρακλεοπολιτῶν ἀλλ' ἐπὶ | τῆς Ἀρσιν̣οειτῶν.

147 *P.Mich.* XI 624.13–15: καταξίωσον δὲ ἔτι ἐπὶ τῆς πόλεως τυγχάνοντος ποιῆσαι ὅλον | τὸν χόρτο̣ν κοβαλευθῆναι, ὑπομνήσας τοὺς αὐτούς, τουτέστιν Ἀντίοχον καὶ Θέωνα, | τὰ κτήνη αὐτῶν παρασχῖν (read παρασχεῖν) πρὸς μετ[α]φορὰν τούτων καθὼς καὶ ἐπηγγίλατο (read ἐπηγγείλατο). The singular at the end may indicate that Antiochos was the head of the collegium; see Chapter Four, n. 118.

Kyrillos was in Herakleopolis, or the writer was in Herakleopolis and Kyrillos, the *exceptor*, in Oxyrhynchos. The first option would be an argument, albeit not a decisive one (see below), for the conclusion that A. and Th. were pagarchs of Herakleopolis; the second would suggest they were pagarchs of Oxyrhynchos. For a start, ll. 9–11 suggest that the presence of the *ab actis* in Herakleopolis was expected because of either a permanent or a temporary residence.[148] This would appear to speak in favor of option no. 2: the writer of *P.Mich.* XI 624 was dwelling in Herakleopolis, whereas Kyrillos was located in Oxyrhynchos, presumably as it was the place of residence of the *praeses Arcadiae*.[149]

However, at the beginning of the letter, the writer says to Kyrillos, "If you are feeling better, come to us; for my lord, the *praeses*, is looking hard for everyone." Later, the writer refers to a particular moment "when all the *officiales* were sent up."[150] "Up" in such contexts in Egypt usually means upstream, that is, up the Nile, suggesting "all the *officiales*" went south to Oxyrhynchos.[151] Finally, the writer reports: "and (although/because/when I was) *anakeimenos*, I gave the reports (*anaphorai*) to my lord, the *praeses*."[152] Again, there are two possible scenarios: (1) A considerable number or all members of the *officium* of the *praeses* resided—permanently or, for unknown reasons, temporarily—in Herakleopolis before they relocated (back?) to Oxyrhynchos. On this occasion, the writer took the various *anaphorai* with him to Oxyrhynchos, while Kyrillos had to stay behind due to an illness. In Oxyrhynchos, the writer handed the *anaphorai* to the *praeses* and then wrote to Kyrillos, asking him to settle some matters in or around Herakleopolis while Kyrillos was "still" (l. 13: *eti*) in the city.[153] In this case, we would have to translate *anakeimenos* along the lines of "when I had the chance to" or "as I was (very) motivated to do so," that is, once he had arrived in Oxyrhynchos

148 See n. 145 above. See also *CPR* XXIII 32 (July 20, 450), issued by a *pater civitatis* of Herakleopolis, which the *scrinium* of the *ab actis* received in the harbor of Neilopolis, only about fifteen miles from Herakleopolis (see ll. 2 and 14–16).

149 This fits the Oxyrhynchite provenance of the papyrus; see n. 143 above. To reconcile an Oxyrhynchite provenance with the abovementioned option no. 1, we may assume that Kyrillos, having received the letter in Herakleopolis, brought the letter with him to Oxyrhynchos when he finally rejoined his colleagues (see below).

150 *P.Mich.* XI 624.7–8: καὶ ἐὰ̣ν̣ ῥᾷ̣ον ἔχῃς ἐνκατά̣λ̣αβε ἡμᾶς· πάνυ γὰρ ἐπιζητῖ (read ἐπιζητεῖ) πά̣ντα̣ς | ὁ κύρ̣ιός μ̣ο̣υ ὁ ἄρχων and ll. 26–27: πάντων δὲ τῶν ὀφφ(ικιαλίων) | ἀναπεμφθέντων. In the first passage, ἐὰ̣ν̣ ῥᾷ̣ον is damaged but certain.

151 Cf. ἀναπέμπω versus καταπέμπω. The former, alternatively, may also be translated as "to send back."

152 *P.Mich.* XI 624.27–28: καὶ ἀνακίμενο̣ς (read ἀνακείμενος) | τὰς ἀναφορὰς παρεσχόμην τῷ κυρίῳ̣ μου τῷ ἄρχοντι.

153 In this scenario, because the submission of the pagarchs' report clearly took place in Herakleopolis in any case, we would need to assume that the writer simply had no time to inform A. and Th. of the submission of their report before he left the city.

again.[154] If however, *anakeimenos* here means "although (I was) laid up ill,"[155] then the writer would still have been in Herakleopolis when he wrote the letter—along with the *praeses* (whose presence the writer implies in ll. 7–8)—and thus writing to Kyrillos about Oxyrhynchite matters. This would suggest option 2, although in that case it is unclear why the *praseses* would still be around Herakleopolis when all the *officiales* had already gone "up" to Oxyrhynchos.[156]

In conclusion, while it seems possible that A. and Th.'s place of residence was Herakleopolis, the largely unexplained context of the letter does not allow us to rule out Oxyrhynchos.[157] It is also conceivable that A. and Th. were only temporarily in Herakleopolis or Oxyrhynchos, whether because they stayed around for a while after handing in their reports or because they had to deal with other business that they had with the provincial administration. I therefore allocate A. and Th. only generally to the province of Arcadia.

A. and Th. do not bear rank epithets in *P.Mich.* XI 624 but the way they are referred to ("brothers," i.e., "fellow colleagues," and "lords") suggests that both had about the same rank as the writer, at most *lamprotatos* or *peribleptos.*[158] As for their business in this letter, it is theoretically possible that the "report" of the pagarchs concerned the construction works mentioned later or fiscal contributions for these works. The docu-

---

154 Cf. *LSJ* and *WB*, s.v. ἀνάκειμαι, where these meanings are not directly attested but fall within a plausible semantic range.

155 This is the, albeit tentative, interpretation of the editor, but this elliptic or euphemistic use does not really seem to be attested; cf., for instance, the explicit rendering ἐνόσησα καὶ ἔτι ἀνάκειμαι in *P.Neph.* 1.11 (Alexandria; c. 350–370).

156 Cf. Gonis 2022, 112 (on Arcadia): "The capital of the province in the fifth and sixth centuries was a curious share between Heracleopolis and Oxyrhynchus." It seems that the contents of *P.Mich.* XI 624 can indeed be best explained by assuming that, at the time of the papyrus, Herakleopolis and Oxyrhynchos shared the function(s) of the provincial capital, either by periodically relocating or by (temporarily?) dividing provincial staff between the two cities.

157 In addition, Herakleopolite documents only make up a very small portion of the attestations for the names Antiochos and Theon for the fifth and sixth centuries. Theon (*TM* Nam ID 5538): 159 attestations (including Arsinoites/Fayum: 44; Herakleopolites: 5; Oxyrhynchites: 55). Antiochos (*TM* Nam ID 2087): 15 attestations (including Arsinoites/Fayum: none; Herakleopolites: 1; Oxyrhynchites: 4). "Herakleopolites" here includes *TM*'s "Herakleopolites" and "Herakleopolis"; the same goes for the Oxyrhynchite nome. Some of these attestations concern the same individuals, but what is relevant here is the probability of finding the name among the surviving evidence. The distribution is only partially accounted for by the general distribution of papyrological texts between the Herakleopolite and Oxyrhynchite nomes for the fifth and sixth centuries, which, according to *PN* data (strict search), is in the ratio of about 1 : 3.5.

158 The address as *kyrios* (Lat. *dominus*) was originally reserved for the highest aristocratic class but from 400 CE onward it also appears with members of lower classes (Koch 1903, 82–83). It is therefore not decisive in our case; cf. the Antaiopolite pagarch Menas, who is regularly addressed as *kyrios* and *lamprotatos*. The *praeses Arcadiae* himself would likely be of *megaloprepestatos* rank in the sixth century. If *P.Mich.* XI 624 is from the fifth century, then the spectrum of ranks of the people involved would in general be lower, but there is no comparative material for the rank epithets of "later pagarchs" before the mid-sixth century.

ment deals, however, with a number of apparently unrelated matters and judging from parallels, *anaphora* more likely relates to a routine report about tax payments or the transport of grain for the *embolē*.[159]

There are two possible matches, if A. and Th. are compared with Menas Scriniarius and the Oxyrhynchite Theodoros, who might have been pagarchs by virtue of being employed by a large estate:[160] in one account from the Apion estate, an Antiochos *epikeimenos* occurs,[161] and Th. may have been a *comes* and *dioikētēs* of the Apion estate or an Oxyrhynchite *politeuomenos* and *pater civitatis*.[162] Neither of these identifications can build on more than the personal name and the plausible scenario, and the sources they rely on are possibly too late.

It might be pure coincidence that *P.Mich.* XI 624 features three men named Theon (= Th.), Timagenes, and Eudaimon in official positions, but this potential coincidence is too curious to not mention it here. A Theon, a Timagenes, and an Eudaimon were responsible for fiscal shares in the Oxyrhynchite nome and, probably, were heads of the first "private" late antique institutional *oikoi* in the fifth century.[163] While Theon is a relatively common name even in the fifth and sixth centuries, Timagenes and Eudaimon are less common, and many of the attestations in fact concern the same individuals and show a strong tendency toward the Oxyrhynchite nome.[164] We would then, potentially, have part of their earlier careers attested in *P.Mich.* XI 624, in which case the papyrus should be assigned to the early fifth century.[165] In addition, an Antiochos and a Theon appear together in *PSI Congr.* XVII 29, from the fifth century. Here, one

159 See *nFWB*, s.v. ἀναφορά and the references in § 3, especially *CPR* XXIII, p. 198, where the role of the *ab actis* in relation to *anaphorai* is discussed. Thus, the writer's link to the staff of the *ab actis* in *P.Mich.* XI 624 and the other *anaphorai* mentioned in this papyrus (see n. 145 above) support this interpretation of A. and Th.'s *anaphora*.

160 Although I have argued in Chapter Four, Section III that this is a less likely scenario for either of them.

161 *P.Oxy.* LV 3805.118 (late VI): δ(ιὰ) Ἀντιόχου ἐπικ(ειμένου); cf. the estate account *P.Oxy.* XVIII 2195.55 (576/577?): καὶ ἀπὸ δικαίο(υ) Ἀντιόχο(υ) and l. 132: δι(ὰ) Ἀντιόχο(υ) χορτοπαραλήμπτ(ου). The honorific of the *scholastikos* Antiochos of *PSI* VIII 891.12 (V–VI), presumably part of the praesidial staff, fits the pattern, but there is no other argument for an identification; see also the *embolatōr* Antiochos in *P.Oxy.* XVI 1999.1–2 (VI–VII).

162 *P.Oxy.* XVI 1908.11 (VI–VII): δ(ιὰ) [τ]οῦ κόμ(ετος) Θέωνος διοικ(ητοῦ) and *SB* XX 14987.2–3 (IV–VI?): Θέωνι πολιτευομένῳ | πατρὶ πόλεως.

163 See Gonis 2009, 91–92 and Chapter One, Section I. The rather well-known Eudaimon is attested way later than Theon and Timagenes and we would have to assume this was his homonymous ancestor; cf. Gonis 2002a, 93–97. But it may also be the other way around.

164 Theon (*TM* Nam ID 5538): 159 attestations (55 of which are from the Oxyrhynchite nome). Timagenes (*TM* Nam ID 6247): 27 (Oxyrhynchites: 24). Eudaimon (*TM* Nam ID 3074): 45 (Oxyrhynchites: 22). Many of these attestations concern the same individuals. Cf. n. 157 above.

165 On the dating, cf. n. 142 above. As A. and Th. appear to be accountable to the *praeses* and not to the city level, they are certainly "later" pagarchs. Therefore, an early date of *P.Mich.* XI 624 would require reconsideration of the dates and contexts of some of the fifth-century documents discussed in Chapter One, Section III.

Flavius Horion, son of Theon, *nauarchos* of Oxyrhynchos, is mentioned close to an *onoma* of, perhaps, one Antiochos; but the text is fragmentary and the connection therefore obscure.[166] While intriguing, these links are not compelling enough to assign *P.Mich.* XI 624 to the early fifth century, at least not on current evidence.

Theon

See s.v. Antiochos & Theon.

Anonymous pagarch

In *P.Oxy.* XVI 1829, two undated letters or rather drafts of letters are preserved that share roughly the same content but have different addressees.[167] Following the death of a high-ranking aristocrat,[168] the writer addresses, in the first letter, the late man's son or daughter (whose sister is, as l. 19 shows, the writer's *despoina*) and, in the second letter, the late man's child-in-law,[169] concerning the records of the late man's pagarchy.[170]

The address on the verso "to Flavius Strategios, *endoxotatos* and *hyperphyestatos* and *hyperphyestatos* (*sic*!) and *paneuphēmos*" is in any case not complete (the rank epithets are not accompanied by any title) and stands amid some illegible lines of tachygraphy. Alternatively, two Strategioi were being addressed, one of them *endoxotatos* and *hyperphyestatos*, the other *hyperphyestatos* and *paneuphēmos*. But this scenario depends too much on a complicated interpretation of the suspiciously unusual "address" on the verso.

All in all, the names and high ranks vaguely point to the environment of the Apiones and the family of Strategios Paneuphemos, but as yet this cannot be made further plausible, and we may be confronted with a different Strategios here. Therefore, it is

166 *PSI Congr.* XVII 29.5–7 (August 31, 432): Φλάουιος Ὡρίων Θέωνος | ναύαρχος τῆς αὐτῆς Ὀξυ̣ρ̣[υγ]χ̣ι̣[τῶ]ν̣ π̣[όλ]ε̣[ως]. κ̣[..]φ̣[..]α̣[.]ε̣[– – –] | ἀπὸ̣ ὀνόματος Ἀντ̣ι̣[οχ- – – –].

167 For details on this text and much of what follows, see Palme 1998, but cf. Palme's short review of the issue in *P.Eirene* IV, p. 207 and *P.Messeri*, p. 253 and n. 6, taking into account the evidence that has been published since.

168 *P.Oxy.* XVI 1829. 2–3: οἱ τύποι τῆς | π̣αγαρχίας τοῦ τῆς ἐνδόξου μνήμης ὑμῶν πατρός, "the acts/minutes of the pagarchy of your father of *endoxos* memory"; cf. ll. 12–13: τῶν τύπων τοῦ τῆς ἐνδόξου | [μν]ήμης ὑμῶ[ν] πενθεροῦ.

169 The term πενθερός may also refer more generally to someone related by marriage, such as a brother-in-law (see *LSJ*, s.v.), although this meaning does not seem to be attested or obvious in the papyri. The use of "your *exousia*" (ll. 4, 10, and 24) a term that invokes official authority, appears to suggest that both addressees are male. Cf., however, the case of Patrikia as pagarch of Antaiopolis. See *BL* XIII 154 (Joëlle Beaucamp) for the view that this document is addressed to a married couple.

170 Cf. Chapter Two, Section II 3 and n. 118.

unclear to which pagarchy the document refers: The letter is clearly a draft that was never sent in this form. The writer was obviously a representative or envoy of the late pagarch's family in the provincial capital, where the *praeses Arcadiae* approved the records of this man's pagarchy. It is thus uncertain whether the letter concerns the Oxyrhynchite, Arsinoite, Herakleopolite, or yet another Arcadian pagarchy.

Thebaid I: Antinoopolis

Kollouthos Exceptor

K., an "*exceptor* and pagarch of Antinoopolis," appears in *P.Leid.Inst.* 72 and his possible Antaiopolite connections are discussed below, s. v. Kollouthos Cancellarius (Thebaid: Unknown nome). An independent match may be the Kollouthos *exceptor* from BL Pap. 1069a (ed. Gonis 2021, no. 2), who asks a *paneuphēmos comes* to release one of his employees from prison. Two possible restorations concern a Kollouthos *exceptor* who is among the staff of the *officium* of the *dux*, but they are restored partially with the potential connection of K. to Aphrodite (and thus to Kollouthos Cancellarius) in mind.[171]

An *exceptor* named Kollouthos appears in *P.Sorb.* II 69 (618/619 or 633/634?) and the context of one of his appearances there (col. 91 A.3) suggests that he is, like K., based in Antinoopolis.[172] In *P.Laur.* II 26 (609/610?), finally, from nearby Hermopolis, a Kollouthos *exceptor* acts as a witness. If one of these two Kollouthoi is K., then K. cannot be identical with Kollouthos Cancellarius, simply for the chronological distance.

Phoibammon (?)

Ph. (Ruffini's Phoibammon 151A) appears in the poem *P.Aphrod.Lit.* IV 13 (Antinoopolis; end of 565–early 566/567), praised by Dioskoros as "headman (*epikeimenos*) of

171 Fournet 2008d, 290–293 (cf. Fournet 1993, 234 n. 42) restores *P.Stras.* I 47.7–8 (Antinoopolis; 566) as: Φλ(άουιος) Κολλοῦθος | [ἐξκέπτωρ τῆς δουκικῆς ? τ]ά̣ξεως (cf. Ruffini's Kollouthos 47). Fournet 1993, 234 n. 42 wonders whether this man may also figure in *P.Flor.* III 294 (Aphrodite; VI), where ll. 1–3 read: τοῦ παναρε̣ ̣ τον ̣ ̣ ̣ ̣ ̣ ̣ ̣ ̣ [– – –] | προγεγραμμένος Κολλοῦθος ο[– – –] | τῆς αὐτῆς δουκικῆς τάξεως δ̣[– – –] (Ruffini's Kollouthos 9). The link to the ducal *officium* makes it tempting to identify this Kollouthos with K., especially because the lacuna behind his name is of unknown length and could have easily contained ὁ [λαμπρότατος ἐξκέπτωρ] or the like. The preceding προγεγραμμένος probably indicates, however, that this Kollouthos has been presented in this text beforehand; if so, the reference to the ducal bureau may not be part of Kollouthos's titulature. In both cases, Fournet qualifies his hypothesis by pointing to the frequency of the personal name, which represents a problem for any identification.

172 Gonis 2021, 99.

the pagarchy." The editor Jean-Luc Fournet suggests that this particular form may mean that Ph. was exercising the pagarchy ad interim.[173] But it also may be accounted for by Dioskoros's literary intentions, given that the title is part of an acrostic.[174] The poem goes on to describe Ph. as part of the lineage of a certain Kometas (Ruffini's Kometas 2; perhaps the pagarch Kometes?) and Eustochios, and makes Ph. a relative of the *patricius* Athanasios. Apart from this, the text yields no concrete information on Ph.'s doings and dealings. His lineage as presented in the text suggests that he had at least a considerable potential to rise higher than simply *lamprotatos*, but his name is too common for conclusive identifications. On the potential match with the Phoibammon from *P.Ant.* II 96 and 97, see s.v. Phoibammon (Thebaid: Unknown Nome) below.

Anonymous pagarchs

In *P.Ant.* II 96, an internal administrative letter found in Antinoopolis,[175] the unknown writer urges the unknown addressee to demand, probably from a land measurer (*geōmetrēs*), "the *nomisma* that he is accustomed to give to the pagarchs."[176] The apparently repeated payments and the fact that no specific locality is provided seem to suggest a local context and that these are pagarchs of Antinoopolis, even though pagarchs from other cities visited the provincial capital on an apparently regular basis. It is elusive whether this is a collegium of pagarchs or whether the plural is due to the repeated payments that may have spanned multiple tenures.[177] The text was originally assigned to the sixth century, but has been reassigned recently to the seventh, in both cases for palaeographical reasons.[178] Because of this latter dating, *P.Ant.* II 96 is not used as evidence for Byzantine pagarchs in the main chapters. It is possible, however, that the *lamprotatos cancellarius* Phoibammon who appears here can be assigned to the earlier part of this century; see the discussion s.v. Phoibammon (Thebaid: Unknown Nome) below.

173 Fournet 1999, 554.

174 It is notable that the title ἐπικείμενος τῆς παγαρχίας later appears to replace the formal title of pagarch from the beginning of the eighth century, apparently as a derivation from an Arabic expression; see the Conclusion, n. 44.

175 On the provenance, see the preface to *P.Ant.* II.

176 *P.Ant.* II 96.4–5: καὶ [ἀ]ξιώσατε ἀπαιτῆσαι αὐτὸ[ν] τ̣ὸ̣ | νόμισμα ὅπερ ε̣[ἴω]θεν διδόν[α]ι τ[οῖ]ς παγάρχοις.

177 See Mazza 1995, 187.

178 Benaissa 2009, 59 n. 7, who reports the result of an inspection of the original by Nikolaos Gonis.

Thebaid II: Hermopolis

Athanasios

A. bears a name that was a favorite among the late antique aristocracy throughout Egypt, and is identified without epithets, only as pagarch, in *SPP* III 436 (Hermopolis; VI–VII).[179] He may be identical with the *endoxotatos illoustrios* and pagarch Athanasios known from the papers of one of his subordinates, Senouthios, in the Hermopolite nome. In fact, the identification as pagarch without any epithets, exclusively by official title and personal name, seems to be more common in documents from the Islamic period, although the Byzantine pagarchs Ioulianos and Menas Stratelates, both *endoxotatos*, are occasionally referred to that way.[180] The mention of a certain Christodotos in our text may give pause, since all three other extant attestations of this name in the papyri most probably pertain to the same individual, a Flavius Christodotos who was *lamprotatos comes* or *peribleptos comes* and *procurator* in the second half of the sixth century in Antaiopolis and was dead by 570 CE.[181] If the Christodotos from *SPP* III 436 is identical to the *procurator*, then this text must date to before 570. Identifications across nome borders should, however, always be dealt with cautiously. A.'s appearance in this papyrus is presumably due to his "share" of the pagarchy that his heirs assume, but this is uncertain.[182] It is hardly an option to identify A. as the *dux et Augustalis* Athanasios from the Dioskoros archive—an *endoxotatos stratēlatēs*, *apo hypatōn*, and *hyperphyestatos patricius*—for that man would not have been referred to simply as pagarch in this "short form" in a text like *SPP* III 436, but rather as *patricius*.

Dorotheos

A *lamprotatos comes* and pagarch in the tax receipt *BGU* XII 2196 (VI),[183] D. may be identical with the *lamprotatos* Dorotheos from *BGU* XVII 2705 who requests a *notarius* to send two large jugs to a former *actuarius*,[184] although this Dorotheos is only referred to as *lamprotatos*. Another parallel might be *BGU* XIX 2772, in which a Dorotheos issues an order to *eirēnarchai* to summon a prison guard. Though this document

---

179 The date and provenance of this text rest on a remark without context by Johannes Diethart; see *CPR* X, p. 153.

180 Ioulianos: *SB* VI 9102 (anonymously); Menas Stratelates: *SPP* III 303.

181 On this man, see s.v. Ioulianos (Antaiopolis) below and Chapter Four, Section III.

182 *SPP* III 436.2: τῶν κλ(ηρονόμων) Ἀθ⟨α⟩νασίου παγάρχου. It is notable that Athanasios is neither "former pagarch" nor "of … memory."

183 *BGU* XII 2196.1: τῷ . [– – – τ]ᾳ̣τ(ῳ), which should be restored as τῷ θ̣[αυμασι]ῳ̣τ(άτῳ). The trace after the lacuna fits omega much better than alpha; the theta starting rather low has its parallels in Δωροθέου (l. 1) and Ἀθύρ (l. 3); see *P.Lond.* V 1753.1 (VII) for the parallel structure of this receipt.

184 *BL* XII 27.

does not preserve any indication of office or rank, it is probably the capacity to give orders to the *eirēnarchai* that is distinctive here, although we cannot achieve certainty about this.[185] That the two latter Dorotheoi are not called pagarch does not mean that they cannot be D., since they are the higher-ranking senders of these texts and the addressees would know who they were, even with no title given. Possibly, D.'s heirs occur in *SB* XVIII 13756 recto 31 and *P.Sorb.* II 69 col. X 15.[186] With the name "Dorotheos" being so widespread, it must remain uncertain whether any of these men is D.

Also worthy of note is *SB* XXIV 16140, which has one Dorotheos sign a receipt to a *chrysōnēs* (an eparchy official):[187] In both this text and in *BGU* XII 2196, the handwriting of the signature differs markedly from that of the main text. But if we assume this means that these two Dorotheoi indeed signed these receipts personally, then they are most likely not identical: The Dorotheos of *SB* XXIV 16140 shows a pronounced fluency in his cursive signature, which is more than one can say for D. Finally, D. should not be identified with Ruffini's Dorotheos 12, *magister* of the *dux et Augustalis* without further evidence. Although this man is occasionally also referred to as *lamprotatos*, he is clearly of higher status.

Ioannes

A "D.V., *praeses* and pagarch of Hermopolis,"[188] I. is attested in *P.Lond.* V 1753, a receipt for village taxes that I. issued to a *boēthos* via a *trakteutēs*. On palaeographical grounds, the papyrus was assigned to the sixth or seventh century in the *editio princeps*, and the editor Harold I. Bell posited that it "probably dates from before the Arab conquest." Recently, it has been argued that the handwriting is consistent with a seventh-century date, possibly from after the Arab conquest.[189]

The terminology suggests that the document is still from the Byzantine period. I translated the Greek term *archōn* as *praeses* because it clearly designates a specific official position in our text; in the early Islamic period, the word *archōn* does not appear to be used for specific positions, but is used for higher-ranking authorities in general.[190] Similarly, a *trakteutēs* has yet to appear in documents from the early Islamic age. On the other hand, the combination of the positions of *praeses* and pagarch would seem unusual for the Byzantine period. Such a high-ranking office combined with the pagar-

185 See *P.Bodl.* I 53 and Chapter Six, Section IV; cf. *P.Lond.* V 1786 and the discussion s.v. Kyrillos (Arsinoe) above.
186 *P.Sorb.* II 69, p. 212 (note on col. X 15; see *BL* X 24); cf. *BL* XII 27.
187 On the *chrysōnēs*, see Chapter Six, n. 26.
188 *P.Lond.* V 1753.1: † Φλ(αύιος) Ἰωάννης σὺν Θε(ῷ) ἀρχοντος (read ἄρχων) καὶ πάγαρχ(ος) Ἑρμοπο̣λ(ίτου).
189 Nikolaos Gonis (personal communication) and Berkes 2017a, 236.
190 See Gesa Schenke's remarks in *P.Gascou*, p. 410.

chy is attested, however, for the pagarch of Arsinoe and *dux Arcadiae* in *CPR* XXIV 33 from 653 CE.[191] I therefore leave the question open in the main chapters.

Some matches have been proposed:[192] *SB* VI 9144 (VII–VIII) is the only one of these that features a Ioannes who was a pagarch; an identification with the Ioannes of *SB* XVIII 13170 (VII) would assume a promotion from *singularis* to pagarch and *praeses*; *BKU* III 420 (undated but probably also later than the Arab conquest). While all are possible, none of them seems compelling to me, as the personal name is very common. The common name also renders uncertain the association with the Antaiopolite pagarch Ioannes or with a *megaloprepestatos* Ioannes, the father of Demetrios, *megaloprepestatos comes* and *politeuomenos* of Hermopolis.[193]

Theodoros

A "lord (*kyrios*) Theodore, pagarch" is mentioned in the recently published Coptic letter *P.Sorb.Copt.* 30 (Hermopolites; VI–early VII). The letter survives only in fragmentary state and the context is therefore obscure. The letter writer urges the addressee to meet the pagarch to speak to him apparently about problems the writer has with some village authorities about the proper prodecures regarding taxes paid by him, possibly as a representative of a monastery. The pagarch is said to "come" apparently to the place of the addressee, yet it is neither clear where the addressee finds himself (the village? the monastery? the city?) nor whether this visit was part of regular tours of this pagarch to the countryside or was motivated precisely to take care of the matter himself. In any case, Th. was personally involved as a pagarch. There is no indication that he was the same person as the other known pagarchs of that name. It is also not convincing to identify Th. with namesakes in the same region and period that are referenced as *kyrios* or bear a rank epithet that might fit a pagarch.[194]

---

191 It is possible that this man, whose name is lost, is the Arsinoite pagarch Ioannes from the early Islamic period, on whom see s.v. Theodorakios (Arsinoites) above. This Ioannes is unlikely to be identical with I.

192 Sijpesteijn 1981, 361; Kruit 1994, 72; Cromwell 2017, 189 n. 130. For the date of *SB* VI 9144, see *BL* XII 194.

193 This identification was deemed possible by Banaji 2007, 167; cf. Giacometti 2019, 361 on the issue.

194 The most intriguing candidate for a match might be Flavius Theodoros from *P.Lond.* V 1714 (570 CE), a *lamprotatos exceptor* of the provincial office in Antinoopolis and very likely the son of the Antaiopolite pagarch Menas (see s.v. Menas Scriniarius below), but there is no evidence of any links this man had to the Hermopolite nome, although in general the close connection of the Antinoopolite and Hermopolite administrations and elites are clear enough.

Anonymous pagarch

A pagarch from Hermopolis appears in the former *descriptum P.Lond.* V 1865, now edited in Gascou & Gonis 2022, no. 5, and dated to the sixth or seventh century. The document is a text receipt or certificate of payment for the *embolē* and was issued by a *trakteutēs* in the pagarch's name. Apparently, the writer did not attribute any rank epithets or honorary titles to the pagarch, whose personal name is in a lacuna.

Thebaid III: Antaiopolis

(Alexandros)

This man, thought to appear in *PSI* IV 283.5–6 (December 20, 550), is in fact the pagarch Ioulianos.[195]

Euthymios

See s.v. Kometes & Euthymios.

Ioannes

Ruffini's Ioannes 197, but the reference to Ioannes as *illoustrios* pagarch is to be deleted.[196] A *megaloprepestatos* and *endoxotatos comes*, I. was "pagarch of the two-thirds share of Antaiopolis" at least in the early 570s.[197] It may seem tempting to assume that I. is identical with the Ioannes (Ruffini's Ioannes 45) of *P.Cair.Masp.* III 67322 (Aphrodite; VI). The way this man handled public security and deployed Aphrodite's *agrophylakes*-shepherds recalls a lot of the business of the pagarch Menas Scriniarius. In this interpretation of *P.Cair.Masp.* III 67322, I. had taken over an order from his predecessor, the "*lamprotatos* lord Menas" to the *prōtokōmētēs* and was now urging compliance.[198] The tone between the two parties is, however, rather familiar. Moreover, a person of I.'s standing is perhaps unlikely to have had much to fear from the anger of the *lamprotatos* Menas to which the papyrus alludes. Finally, Dioskoros had been abroad in Antinoopolis for some years when I. was pagarch in 570, and is thus unlikely to be still addressed as *prōtokōmētēs* here if the Ioannes of this text really was the pag-

195 Lemaire 2010, 398.
196 See Chapter Five, n. 198.
197 For the sources, see Table 4 (pp. 165–167).
198 *P.Cair.Masp.* III 67322.3–5.

arch. Therefore, the Ioannes of *P.Cair.Masp.* III 67322 is more likely to be someone of lower rank than the pagarch Menas, perhaps a *prōtokōmētēs*,[199] and the papyrus should probably be assigned to Menas's first pagarchy. Comparably, the way the Ioannes who authored *SB* XX 14119 makes use of polite attributes to address a *prōtokōmētēs* makes me refrain from identifying this man with I., who, in addition, bears a very common name.[200] I. has also been suspected to be identical with the *megaloprepestatos comes* Ioannes who is asked to investigate the affairs of the monastery of Stratonikis in *P.Fouad* 87 (Aphrodite; VI),[201] and the matching rank makes this a more likely match than in the case of *P.Cair.Masp.* III 67322, in which the description of the relationship to Menas points to a lower status of the writer than *megaloprepestatos comes*.[202]

I.'s earlier career may be reflected in *P.Köln* V 240 (Antaiopolites; VI), in which a *lamprotatos politeuomenos* Ioannes (Ruffini's Ioannes 9; cf. Ioannes 129) is apparently responsible for tax collection. The close appearance of a *hypodektēs* (l. 9) and a *trakteutēs* (l. 13) is reminiscent of the milieu of *P.Cair.Masp.* I 67057 col. II 24–36, which lists expenses for the pagarchy. A pagarch would, however, certainly not have been referred to as *politeuomenos*, even if he was one, because the pagarchy was the more exclusive of these two titles. Another match may be the Ioannes of *P.Berl.Zill.* 6.7 (Antinoopolis; 527–565), a *lamprotatos* and *aidēsimos scriniarius* of the ducal bureau of the Thebaid originating from Hermopolis, which would make his career strikingly parallel to Menas Scriniarius, but this is highly speculative. The personal name is too common and the move from a *lamprotatos* or *lamprotatos* and *aidēsimos* to a *megaloprepestatos* and *endoxotatos* seems a big step up, though not insurmountable. I.'s titles would match perfectly Ruffini's Ioannes 124, the *megaloprepestatos* and *endoxotatos comes* of *P.Cair. Masp.* I 67104 (Aphrodite; 530). Yet, the revised timeline of the Antaiopolite pagarchs established in my analysis of the Antaiopolite tax receipts and the resulting chronological distance render this identification unlikely, though not impossible.[203] Further matches, including some former or later *duces* of the Thebaid, would be intriguing but must remain speculative, as the name is among the most common of late antique Egypt.[204]

199 Ruffini's Ioannes 20, 188, 193, and 194 are conceivable matches. Also the (uncertain) reading of the verso τ̣[ῷ] . . . . ἀ̣δ̣[ελ]φ̣[(ῷ)] Δ̣ι̣ο̣σ̣κ̣ό̣ρ̣ῳ̣, relating to Dioskoros as a "brother" or "colleague," fits the interpretation that the Ioannes of *P.Cair.Masp.* III 67322 is not the pagarch. The Apollos in this letter (Ruffini's Apollos 2A) was certainly one of the *prōtokōmētai* of this name, Apollos 128 and 129 being the likeliest candidates. It is not surprising to have a *prōtokōmētēs* issuing orders to a colleague, nor are there two separate areas of influence at stake: in *P.Lond.* V 1681, the *prōtokōmētēs* Apollos 2 also receives a complaint about a newly installed *prōtokōmētēs* whose impeachment is requested.

200 Ruffini 2011, s.v. Ioannes 54; cf. Mazza 1995, 229.

201 Gascou 1976, 177 n. 1; Banaji 2007, 162 n. 164.

202 See n. 199 above.

203 See Table 4 (pp. 165–167). Cf. Banaji 2007, 162.

204 See the various "Johns" in Banaji 2007, 254. However, I. cannot be identical with Ruffini's Ioannes 201. This was put in doubt by Ruffini himself; for a definite rejection, see the new edition

Ioulianos

In Ruffini's prosopography of Byzantine Aphrodite, the Ioulianos whom I describe in this study is treated as two different individuals: an "ex-prefect" (*apo eparchōn*), Ruffini's Ioulianos 1, and a pagarch and former *praeses* (*apo archontōn*), Ruffini's Ioulianos 2.[205] I think that these two have to be identified as one and the same person.[206] Ioulianos 2 is referred to in various ways: as pagarch, as *endoxotatos* pagarch, as *endoxotatos illoustrios* and pagarch, as *megaloprepestatos* pagarch, as *megaloprepestatos illoustrios* and pagarch, and as *megaloprepestatos* pagarch and *apo archontōn*, that is, former *praeses*.[207] Ruffini, apparently taking the pagarchy as the decisive element, takes all these to be identical and to this adds attestations in which a Ioulianos is mentioned by name only or even by epithet only.[208] Given that the attestations for Ioulianos 2 overlap in the early 550s,[209] and since the personal name is not common, such a combination of high-ranking epithets presumably means that there was only one Antaiopolite pagarch Ioulianos in this period.[210] It is notable that the titles *illoustrios* and *apo archontōn* are never men-

---

of *SB* XIV 12116 in Keenan 2015, whose new readings eliminate this Ioannes from the list of potential matches.

205 Ruffini 2011, s.vv. In Ruffini 2008a, 168 n. 55, the author expressly distinguishes these two Ioulianoi.

206 Comparably, Mazza 1995, 228–229, whose argument is the "rather homogenous" titulature: "La titolatura […] mi pare piuttosto omogenea."

207 **Pagarch:** *P.Cair.Masp.* I 67024–25 (new ed. Fournet 2018) A 30–32; *SB* VI 9102 (the anonymous pagarch is certainly Ioulianos). ***Endoxotatos* pagarch:** *P.Cair.Masp.* I 67046; *SB* XVI 12370. ***Endoxotatos illoustrios* and pagarch:** *P.Gen.* IV 193; *PSI* IV 283; *SB* XX 15013.4–7, missed in Ruffini's prosopography under (j); *SB* XX 15015. ***Megaloprepestatos* pagarch:** *P.Cair.Masp.* I 67094. ***Megaloprepestatos illoustrios* and pagarch:** *SB* XX 15013.1–3. ***Megaloprepestatos* pagarch and *apo archontōn*:** *P.Lond.* V 1660 (Ruffini's prosopography under (m) misses the title *apo archontōn*); *P.Lond.* V 1661. In the lacuna of *P.Cair.Masp.* III 67283 col. I 2, λαμπρ(ότατος) is highly unlikely, and I.'s titulature should be restored differently here; see Chapter Four, n. 15.

208 Name only: *P.Cair.Masp.* III 67354; *P.Cair.Masp.* I 67019 verso. Epithet only: *P.Cair.Masp.* III 67283 (on the restoration of the epithet in this case, see the previous note); *P.Cair.Masp.* I 67026. The pagarchy occurs in all these texts apart from the latter.

209 Admittedly, only *P.Lond.* V 1661 and *P.Cair.Masp.* I 67094 have fixed dates, but the indiction dates for the tax receipts issued by Ioulianos are a good fit for the time of these contracts; see Table 4 (pp. 165–167).

210 Ioulianos's epithets, prima facie, appear to undergo a chronological development: Ioulianos is *endoxotatos* in all documents until the first indiction of 552/553 CE, and *megaloprepestatos* in every document afterward before he resurfaces some years later as *endoxotatos* in 559/560 CE (*SB* XVI 12370; the text is less likely to be one indiction cycle older, as Ioulianos appears to have been sole pagarch initially). Given this seeming pattern, it would appear plausible to "divide" Ruffini's Ioulianos 2 and to distinguish a Ioulianos, *megaloprepestatos apo archontōn*, from another Ioulianos, *endoxotatos*, both of whom were pagarch and *illoustrios*, and to identify the latter with Ruffini's Ioulianos 1, i.e., Ioulianos *endoxotatos apo eparchōn*. This reconstruction is especially tempting because of *P.Lond.* V 1661 (Aphrodite; 553), where Ioulianos is "only" *megaloprepestatos*, while the *endoxotatē* Patrikia is mentioned right after him. Yet, *SB* XX 15013 (Antaiopolites;

tioned in unison; only one at a time (or neither) is employed, which may indicate that the *illoustrios* title related to Ioulianos's former official position.[211]

By contrast, Ioulianos 1 is a roughly contemporary *endoxotatos apo eparchōn* (former prefect) for whom Ruffini adduces *only* instances that give the title *apo eparchōn*. This Ioulianos 1 is known to have owned an *ousia* that contributed to the village taxes in the vicinity of Aphrodite[212] and was apparently in some way involved in tax collection in the Antaiopolite nome.[213] The editor of *P.Lond.* V 1674 restored the title of pagarch to him, but this is not very likely.[214] Ioulianos 1 may have been pagarch or had some fiscal responsibility for Aphrodite as early as the 540s, perhaps for lands granted to him after his tenure as prefect.[215] A potential identification with Julian the Egyptian, a poet who somehow was involved in the Nika revolt of 532 and may have been identical with a Ioulianos who was praetorian prefect (*eparchos*) of the East in 530/531, must remain speculative.[216]

But why should Ioulianos 2, as in Ruffini's prosopography, be easily identifiable by virtue of his personal name alone, or by virtue of his being *endoxotatos*, if a namesake of about the same status was active in the area? The name is not common in the Aphrodite papyri: apart from Ioulianos 1 and 2 there are only two other attestations. We are

---

552/553), written during this first indiction, contradicts this apparent pattern. The papyrus contains two tax receipts: one for the second installment (*katabolē*) of the tax, and another one for the third, and whereas Ioulianos *megaloprepestatos* issues the former, Ioulianos *endoxotatos* issues the latter, thus contradicting a transfer of the pagarchy from a Ioulianos *endoxotatos* to a Ioulianos *megaloprepestatos*. On this overlapping use of *megaloprepestatos* and *endoxotatos*, see Chapter Five, Section I.

211 *P.Lond.* V 1660.6 and *P.Lond.* V 1661.5, which address Ioulianos as *apo archontōn*, do not address him as *illoustrios*. See Chapter Five, Section I on this hypothesis regarding the use of *illoustrios* in the sixth century.

212 *P.Cair.Masp.* I 67060 (mid-550s).

213 *P.Cair.Masp.* III 67285 (537–551 CE, according to Zuckerman 2004a, 40–51), signed by Ioannes, *hypodektēs* of Aphrodite, records a payment εἰς λόγον λοιπάδ(ων) τοῦ ἐνδο̣ξ(οτάτου) ἀ̣π̣ὸ ἐπάρχ(ων) | Ἰο(υ)λιανο(ῦ) κ̣α̣ὶ Ἐνώχ (ll. 2–3), "on the account of remainders of the *endoxotatos apo eparchōn* Ioulianos and Enoch." In *P.Lond.* V 1674.37 (568–570), Ioulianos is referred to in the context of fixing a particular tax rate for Aphroditan soil at some point before the document was drafted.

214 *P.Lond.* V 1674.37–38: Ἰουλιανο(ῦ) τοῦ [ἀπ]ὸ ἐπάρχων̣ | κ̣α̣ὶ [παγάρχου?. Apparently, Bell took Ioulianos 1 and 2 to be identical, but even though I support this identification, the context of the petition and the *fasti* of the Antaiopolite pagarchs (see Table 4 on pp. 165–167) suggest that I. was no longer pagarch by that point. The restoration [ἀπ]ὸ ἐπάρχων̣ κ̣α̣ὶ [ἀρχόντων (Banaji 2007, 162 n. 168) seems even less likely. On the restoration of that last lacuna, see Chapter Five, n. 66.

215 The collegiality with Enoch in *P.Cair.Masp.* III 67285 seems to suggest the pagarchy here. But the post of *chrysōnēs* seems possible as well; cf. Ammonios and Biktor in *P.Cair.Masp.* I 67037, 67041, and III 67344.

216 See Sarris 2006, 15–16 with references, assuming that Ioulianos/Julian, the *praefectus praetorio per Orientem* of 530/531 (*PLRE* III, s.v. Iulianus 4) is the same man as Julian the Egyptian (*PLRE* III, s.v. Iulianus 11). But the concerns given by the *PLRE* against this identification—especially about the different titulature and the use of the nickname "the Egyptian"—seem valid; in that case, Julian the Egyptian had not been *eparchos*. On the Nika revolt, see the Conclusion, n. 20.

thus asked to believe that there were two men of this name active in this area who were of about the same rank—a rank that usually only a handful of people in the nome, if not the province, would have been entitled to—and who are not subject to any obvious consistent distinction in the documents. For instance, *P.Cair.Masp.* I 67026 (Aphrodite?; c. 551) is a petition, which per se aims to unmistakably identify the culprit. And here, we see a Ioulianos—and according to Ruffini, this is Ioulianos 2—referred to by a simple *endoxotatos*, which would be odd if there were two Ioulianoi of this rank in the area.[217] Moreover, both titles, *apo eparchōn* and *apo archontōn*, are quite rare in the sixth century, and it would not be too much of a stretch to suppose that they were somehow related; perhaps *apo eparchōn* here refers to a former high official on the level of the eparchy (if the title was not honorary),[218] one of the Egyptian provinces, and may in this regard be comparably able to denote a former *praeses*, as is likely attested in one case.[219] More decisively, both Ioulianos 1 and Ioulianos 2 enjoyed professional links to the *peribleptos comes* and *procurator* Christodotos in a fiscal context,[220] all of which makes Ioulianos, the *apo eparchōn*, likely to be identical with the *illoustrios* and pagarch Ioulianos, the *apo archontōn*. In one document, I. bears the epithet "the Arsinoite,"[221] which may point to his origin or a former office. While the edited text of *P.Lond.* V 1674.36–38 suggests that I. was alive until at least 570 CE, a tempting restoration has him dead by this point.[222]

The recently edited *BGU* XXI 2887 (Hermopolites; VI–VII) may now reflect I.'s earlier career as *praeses* but may also be from the time of I.'s pagarchy.[223] The editor's

217 All the more so if Ioulianos, the *apo eparchōn*, was really the dominant player described by Zuckerman 2004a, 221–222 on the basis of *P.Ross.Georg.* V 62 (Aphrodite; VI; accidentally cited by Zuckerman as *P.Ross.Georg.* III 62). See Chapter Three, n. 221 on this text.

218 On the two titles and the concept of "honorary" officeholders, see the nuanced but ultimately skeptical discussion in Gonis 2021, 94–95.

219 See, e.g., *P.Sijp.* 35 (p. 225) from sixth- or early seventh-century Arcadia, governed by a *praeses*; see also Benaissa 2022, 168. However, *apo archontōn* may also be a general use of *archōn* in the sense of a higher official dignitary. For Greek instances of *archōn* referring generically to offices of significance such as that of governor, see *P.Erl.* 120.9–10 (unknown origin; 546–547?): τοῦ ἐνδο-[ξ]οτάτου κ[αὶ] πανευφήμου Ἡφαίστου ἀντιλαβοτος (read ἀντιλαβόντος) | τῶν ἀρχῶν, referring to the *dux et Augustalis* Hephaistos, on whom see Gonis 2005, 93–94.

220 Cf. *P.Lond.* V 1674.36–38: κατὰ πεισμονὴν Χριστοδότ̣ο̣[υ] | τοῦ ἀπογενομέ(νου) π̣ρ̣οκ̣[ουράτορος ± 14]ης Ἰουλιανο(ῦ) τοῦ [ἀπ]ὸ ἐπάρχων̣ | κ̣α̣ί̣ [– – –] (on the lacunae, see n. 222 below and Chapter Five, n. 66) and *SB* XVI 12370.2–3: οἱ ἐνδοξ(ότατοι) π[ά]γαρχοι Ἰ̣ουλια̣ν̣ὸ̣ς καὶ Κομήτης καὶ Ε̣[ὐ]-θύμ̣[ιος] | διὰ τοῦ περυβλέπτου (read περιβλέπτου) κ̣όμ̣ιτο̣ς̣ Χριστοδότο\υ/ προκ[ο]υρ(άτορος). This man is Ruffini's Christodotos 1; the link to Ruffini's Christodoros (*sic*) 11 is weak, as Keenan 2015 highlights, and is rendered impossible by my new dates for the dossier of the pagarchs Ioannes and Serenos, on which see Table 4 (pp. 165–167).

221 *P.Cair.Masp.* I 67024–25 (new ed. Fournet 2018) A 31, A' 55–56, and B 29.

222 In *P.Lond.* V 1674.36–37: κατὰ πεισμονὴν Χριστοδότ̣ο̣[υ] | τοῦ ἀπογενομέ(νου) π̣ρ̣οκ̣[ουράτορος ± 14]ης Ἰουλιανοῦ τοῦ [ἀπ]ὸ ἐπάρχων̣, it is possible to restore π̣ρ̣οκ̣[ουράτορ(ος) τοῦ τῆς ἐνδόξ(ου) μ̣νήμ]ης before the personal name, with υ of τοῦ in superscript.

223 The editor notes that *BGU* XXI 2887 must come from the *officium* of the *praeses*, but despite the

argument that the absence of an official title means that the Ioulianos of this text did not hold any office at that time—and therefore should probably not be identified with I.—does not seem valid. In internal administrative letters, subordinate officials would, among themselves, usually stick to the "short form" of referring to a superior, for which a title of honor as high as *endoxotatos illoustrios* is adequate.[224]

Another Flavius Ioulianos, an *endoxotatos* and *paneuphēmos stratēlatēs*, is the intermediary of the *dux* Athanasios, and probably his father.[225] If this man is identical to I., this would suggest a promotion and a move to Antinoopolis during the 560s, but this is speculative.[226]

If Zuckerman's reasoning for dating *P.Cair.Masp.* I 67030 and *P.Cair.Masp.* III 67321 to 546 and 548/549 CE, respectively, is accepted,[227] I. was probably not the *megaloprepestatos comes* and *praeses* of the Thebaid Flavius Theodoros Menas Ioulianos Iakkobos who appears in these documents, as I. was pagarch of Antaiopolis by 547 at the latest. The alternative dates 531 and 533/534, suggested by Gascou,[228] would fit better, assuming I. was born around 500 CE, although it is notable that I.'s title of *illoustrios* does not appear before 550 (*PSI* IV 283) and a promotion would fit the pattern of aristocratic promotion from *comes* to *illoustrios*.[229] Ruffini hypothesizes that the Kyros whose former land I. rents out in *PSI* IV 283 was I.'s father,[230] but this seems unlikely since I. was, as mentioned, an "Arsinoite," and the relationship between father and son/heir would be expected to be made explicit in such a context. This text therefore probably refers to some other arrangement.[231]

editor's discussion, the Ioulianos of this text need not be addressed in his capacity as landowner (see below), but may have been involved as an official. The fact that the *singularis* in this text "went up (the Nile) to bring" (l. 2: ἀνελθόντι παρενεγκεῖν) Ioulianos's *procurator* may indicate that this is a *procurator* of I.'s *ousia* at Antaiopolis (i.e., south of Antinoopolis, the provincial capital); for this *ousia*, see *P.Cair.Masp.* I 67060. It is not clear from the text whether Ioulianos was himself at Antaiopolis when the letter was written, or not.

224 On "short" and "extended" forms of referring to aristocrats, see Chapter Five, Section II.

225 Ruffini's Ioulianos 4. On the intermediary of Athanasios, see *P.Cair.Masp.* I 67008; on his father, see the introduction to Ruffini's Athanasios 4, though Ruffini does not suggest a link to his Ioulianos 4, but only to Ioulianos 1 and 2. Cf. Ioulianos 3A.

226 This would shed a different light on the question of who controlled the *endoxos oikos* of Aphrodite, on which see pp. 236–237 above. There has been speculation about a link between the status of *endoxoi oikoi* held by certain families (notably, the Apiones) and these families' involvement with the *domus divina*. If Ioulianos (= here, hypothetically, Ruffini's Ioulianos 1, 2, *and* 4) was the father of Athanasios, the latter being *curator* of the imperial grounds at Aphrodite, this would be suggestive of such a model, and make I. perhaps a better candidate to exercise control over Aphrodite's *endoxos oikos*.

227 Banaji 2007, 162 n. 167. See *BL* XI 52 and *BL* XIII 52 on both dates and cf. Fournet 2008c, 314 and 325.

228 *BL* XI 42.

229 See Table 6 (p. 196).

230 Ruffini 2011, s.v. Kuros 16, referring to a new reading by Florence Lemaire.

231 A hypothesis to explain this arrangement is discussed on pp. 73–74 above.

Kometes & Euthymios

Ruffini's Kometes 3 and Euthymios 1. K. and E. are joint pagarchs together with Ioulianos in 559/560 CE, as attested in *SB* XVI 12370. They appear to have acted through the *procurator* Christodotos, whose appearance alongside Ioulianos in *P.Lond.* V 1674 suggests that Ioulianos served as the head or "performing" pagarch of this collegium.[232] Whereas E. is unknown from anywhere else, K. may have been the *comes* Kometes registered as landholder in the Aphrodite Cadaster, *SB* XX 14669.3 (Aphrodite; early 524?), although in this case he must have been fairly old by the time of *SB* XVI 12370 (559/560).[233] Is this the Kometas (*sic*) of Dioskoros's poems, who fits so well into the family links of the Thebaid elite of the sixth century, including the *dux* Athanasios and the pagarch Phoibammon?[234] K. and E. both have rare personal names, befitting the elite habitus of the period.

It is possible that K. is identical to the Oxyrhynchite Kometes who appears to have been in a promising position to be eligible for the pagarchy in that nome.[235] This link, if connected to a possible but not very probable identification of the pagarch Ioannes (see above), would yield an even closer network of Byzantine Egyptian provincial elites but must remain speculative.

Makarios (?)

Ruffini's Makarios 55. On the recto of *P.Cair.Masp.* I 67055, a very fragmentary papyrus, one encounters, possibly, a pagarch with the common personal name Makarios.[236] The poem on the verso probably dates to c. 567 CE and assuming that it was written after the recto,[237] it offers a *terminus ante quem* for the beginning of M.'s tenure. But even so, the list on the recto, which mentions a ninth indiction, may have been much older at the point when the papyrus was put to new use to draft a poem on the verso; the pattern of other reused documents from the Dioskoros archive suggests that M. may have been in office several decades earlier.[238] The same text also features a *prōtokōmētēs* Herakleios (col. II 16) whose tenure can with some certainty be dated to

232 On divisions of authority between joint pagarchs, see Chapter Four, Section IV.

233 Ruffini's Kometes 1.

234 Ruffini's Kometas 2, though Ruffini does not link him to K.

235 *P.Oxy.* XVI 2040 (c. 567/577 CE).

236 *P.Cair.Masp.* I 67055 col. II 9–10: ὑπὲρ μερίδ(ος) τοῦ̣ [– – –] | Μακαρίου παγάρχ(ου?) κ̣[– – –].

237 Judging from the online images, it appears that the sheet was cut based on the layout of—that is, to fit—the text of the verso, which would make the text on the verso the younger document.

238 Cf. *P.Cair.Masp.* III 67325 (first phase starting from 559/560 CE) and *P.Aphrod.Reg.* (from 525/526 CE), both of which were reused for a series of receipts starting in 569/570; in the case of *P.Aphrod.Reg.*, these were edited as *P.Flor.* III 298 and *P.Stras.* VII 699. See Stern forthcoming (b) on the use and reuse of these documents and Chapter Four, n. 17 on the dates.

the lifetime of Count Ammonios,[239] which leads to the plausible assumption that M. was pagarch in the 530s or 540s, in which case the ninth indiction would conform to 530/531 or 545/546 CE.[240] But this is not certain, nor is anything else known about M., which is why his name is accompanied by a question mark in Chapters Four and Five.

Menas Scriniarius

Ruffini's Menas 13. M.'s links to the pagarchy come from two different contexts, the first of which is apparent in two London papyri: in *P.Lond.* V 1661 (July 24, 553), he and Ioulianos jointly serve as Antaiopolite pagarchs, and this is also attested in *P.Lond.* V 1660, which must therefore be dated to a year from Ioulianos's pagarchy around 553 CE, but probably not earlier.[241] M. then appears a second time as pagarch from 566 CE onward, but with a clear marker that this constituted a new mandate.[242] M. is attested with a variety of titles and epithets, and their accumulation in various documents makes it highly likely that they refer to the same man. Although the name is among the most common in late antique Egypt, I am also convinced that this is the same person as Ruffini's Menas 66.[243] The epithets given to Menas 66 are not only strikingly parallel those given to M.; his son is also explicitly said to be *geouchōn* at Antaiopolis.[244] This Menas appears only as a patronymic reference, and one would not expect this reference to reveal his origin or his being *geouchōn* somewhere, but we may deduce it from his son's titulature. It is therefore safe to assume that Menas 66 was also from, and/or was *geouchōn* in, Antaiopolis, strengthening the likelihood of the match with Menas 13.

A number of undated documents can be safely attributed to Menas 13, even though he appears without the title of pagarch. All of them appear to touch on business that M. is known to have been involved with and it is often uncertain to which of M.'s tenures they belong: *P.Cair.Masp.* I 67060; *P.Lond.* V 1682, 1683, and 1684 (probably the first tenure); *P.Aphrod.Lit.* IV 11 (certainly the second). I find it at least as likely that the "lord" Menas who is mentioned in *SB* XX 14241 alongside a *boēthos* and *lampro-*

239 See *P.Cair.Masp.* II 67200. In Ruffini 2011, the Herakleios of this text is Herakleios 2, and Ruffini is cautious to identify this man with the homonymous *prōtokōmētēs*, Herakleios 35 (see also Herakleios 34), but discusses the possibility.

240 *P.Cair.Masp.* III 67319, in which the *prōtokōmētēs* Herakleios also occurs, should, for different reasons, be assigned to 552/553 rather than 567/568 CE; cf. n. 246 below.

241 Earlier, Ioulianos appears to have been sole pagarch.

242 It does not follow from *P.Cair.Masp.* I 67002 col. I 10–11: ἀπὸ προοιμίων τῆς ἔναγχος διαδραμο(ύ)σης πεντεκαιδεκάτης ἐπινεμήσεως, ἀφ' ἧς ἀντελάβετο τῆς παγαρχίας | Ἀνταίο(υ) that this was Menas's first pagarchy.

243 Harold I. Bell, the editor of *P.Lond.* V 1714, argued that it is "hardly doubtful" that the Menas in this text is the pagarch. Ruffini appears to be more cautious about this but still calls the match "likely."

244 *P.Lond.* V 1714.

tatoi trakteutai (Menas 60; not considered to be a possible match by Ruffini) is also M., given the clear association of these officials with the pagarchy.[245] The events here, concerning the *topos* (P)Karkarou, probably relate to 552/553 because the text features "the son of Tachymia;" this can only be the Biktor, son of Tachymia, who damaged this exact *topos* in *P.Cair.Masp.* III 67319.20.[246] In the cases of Ruffini's Menas 5, 11, and Anonymous 111, the contexts are not as clear, but still suggestive. In *PSI* VIII 939 (Menas 5), a *lamprotatos* "lord" Menas has to come to the harbor to take care of the grain shipping and storage,[247] which seems to concern a similar matter as in *P.Lond.* V 1684. In *P.Cair.Masp.* I 67083 (Menas 11), the allusion to someone's *pragma* ("matter" or "legal proceedings") and the address to a *prōtokōmētēs* (a village headman) are suggestive, while in *P.Cair.Masp.* I 67061 (Anonymous 111), it is the urgency and the demanding tone of the letter, addressed to all (!) village headmen of Aphrodite. *P.Cair. Masp.* I 67061 probably relates to similar events as *P.Cair.Masp.* I 67060, as the editor thought. The *descriptum P.Cair.Masp.* II 67185 recto contains six effaced lines with the end of a letter, including a reference to a "lord" Menas that is, however, too general to attribute this text to M.

Banaji's suggestion that Menas, the [*peribleptos*] *comes* and *procurator* of *P.Cair. Masp.* I 67104 (Ruffini's Menas 28) from August 19, 530, is M. is implausible not only because Banaji's proposed link to Patrikia is impossible,[248] but also because the titles do not match: "Menas" is too common a name in late antique Egypt, we have no evidence of M. being a *comes* or of his being *peribleptos* before 570.[249] Moreover, it is not compelling to equate a *procurator* with a *dioikētēs*, although both positions may relate to the same environment.

245 See Chapter Two, Section III 2 and II 3, respectively.

246 Tachymia (the name is rare and probably always refers to the same individual in the sixth-century papyri from Aphrodite) must be distinctive enough a person that *her* name is used instead of a patronymic (which is frequently the case with this Biktor) and overall it would be too much of a coincidence if there were two Biktors, sons of two different women both named Tachymia and connected to the same *topos*. The events of *SB* XX 14241 therefore must relate to the events described in *P.Cair.Masp.* III 67319 recto; in the latter, the first indiction is the "present" one (l. 20: παρούσης). This text should be dated to 552/553 and not to the next cycle; see Fournet 2008c, 324 and add the even earlier occurrences of this Biktor in Ruffini 2011, s.v. Biktor 44, from as early as 517 (fixed date)! The ὑπό (the *topos* "under" him) in *SB* XX 14241.14 thus relates to the time when Biktor had seized the *topos* of Pkarkarou, before he was ordered to leave. The text was written after the events (the Kollouthos here is said to have been (!) *diadotēs*), i.e., after 552/553 CE when the *topos* was returned, making it more likely that M. was serving in a responsible position during these years, and was not merely a formal partner to Ioulianos; see also *P.Cair.Masp.* I 67060.

247 Ἀποθήκη (l. 3) here is probably a *horreum*, a grain storage; cf. Brandes 2002, 293–294.

248 See s.v. Patrikia (Antaiopolis) below.

249 We may recall that M. was still alive and active in the ducal bureau of the Thebaid on March 14, 570 (*P.Lond.* V 1714).

Patrikia

Ruffini's Patrikia 1. The *endoxotatē* P. is known to have held the pagarchy collegially with Ioulianos sometime around 553 CE, as shown in *P.Lond.* V 1660, where she acts with Menas Scriniarius as her representative.[250] A restoration of the tax receipt *P.Vat.Aphrod.* 16A now shows her also as part of a collegium of pagarchs, probably as its head; the text was possibly written by the *hypodektēs* Petros who is attested in *P.Cair.Masp.* I 67046, under the pagarch Ioulianos.[251] Otherwise, P. is only known from one of Dioskoros's poems from 567 CE, but neither her father Kallinos nor her husband Paulos, whom she married in that year, can be further identified.[252] Notably, P. married Paulos about fifteen years after she is attested as pagarch, which had Ruffini speculate that either she held the pagarchy at an extremely young age, that she married late, or that this was her second marriage,[253] of which the latter seems the safest choice. There is evidence that may show her to originate from Aphrodite.[254] Banaji identifies P. as the addressee of *P.Cair.Masp.* I 67104 (Aphrodite; 530) and thus as the daughter of the *megaloprepestatos* and *endoxotatos comes* Ioannes (Ruffini's Ioannes 123). To do so, however, Banaji needs to reject Fournet's identification of P. with the Patrikia of Dioskoros's poem, in which he is certainly mistaken.[255] There is no strong connection to the *paneuphēmos* Patrikia in *PSI* III 238 (unknown origin; VI–VII), as has been proposed;[256] this may have been a title rather than a personal name: "the *paneuphēmos patricia*."

Serenos

Ruffini's Serenos 9 (b) and (c). As Ioannes's co-pagarch (at least) in the early 570s, S. is an *endoxotatos illoustrios* and appears as formal issuer of a number of tax receipts concerning Aphrodite and the Antaiopolite nome. Since the name is not common in

250 On the circumstances of her pagarchy and her deputy Menas, see Chapter Four, Section III.

251 *P.Vat.Aphrod.* 16A.2 must without a doubt be read as [– – – ο]ἱ ἐνδοξότατοι πάγαρχοι Πατρ[ικία καί – – –]; see Stern forthcoming (a), s.v. Anonymous *hypodektēs* 2. Cf. Fournet 2016, 133, especially n. 110 (where he restored Patrikia tentatively), and see, for instance, *SB* XVI 12370 for the position of καί. The signatory Anonymous *hypodektēs* 2 is possibly to be identified with Petros *hypodektēs*, the signatory of *P.Cair.Masp.* I 67046 from 550/551 CE.

252 *P.Aphrod.Lit.* IV 35.

253 Ruffini 2018a, 162.

254 Ruffini 2018a, 161–162, citing an obscure pun in one of Dioskoros's poems.

255 See Banaji 2007, 162 and 254. Banaji further suggests that this Ioannes is the homonymous Antaiopolite pagarch, which would entail that P. probably was responsible for the pagarchy ad interim because of her late father. This Ioannes is, however, unlikely to be the Antaiopolite pagarch, based on my timeline for this pagarch's tenure; see Table 4 (pp. 165–167). On Banaji's implausible suggestion that Menas, the [*peribleptos*] *comes* and *procurator* of *P.Cair.Masp.* I 67104 (Ruffini's Menas 28), was Menas Scriniarius, the pagarch of 553 CE, see s.v.

256 Fournet 1999, 634–637.

our evidence from Aphrodite, it is tempting to identify him with the only other Flavius Serenos from this period, attested in *P.Ross.Georg.* V 37 (Aphrodite; mid-VI), Ruffini's Serenos 9 (a), but there is nothing, save the Flaviate and the personal name, to support this identification.[257]

In the case of *P.Cair.Masp.* I 67002 (Antinoopolis; 567), the accumulation of distinguished titles strongly suggests that this Serenos is S.[258] He is introduced as the "*peribleptos comes* and *illoustrios megaloprepestatos* Serenos, the *logiōtatos scholastikos*" (col. II 2), and thus clearly bears the exemplary epithets for a provincial bureaucrat.[259] Later in the document, he is once referred to as *endoxotatos illoustrios* (col. II 4) and on a later occasion simply as *illoustrios* (col. II 8). This Serenos helped the soon-to-be pagarch Menas Scriniarius detain thirteen villagers of Aphrodite and seize their cattle while they were visiting an annual cattle market in the Hermopolite nome.[260] According to the petition, the villagers were arrested by Serenos's *dioikētai*; later, the text mentions a *meizoteros* as well as a "private" jail, which supposedly means that this Serenos had estates in the area. One wonders in what capacity this Serenos was acting; if he had held any office at the time he had the Aphroditans detained, he would have probably relied on soldiers or minor security personnel such as *eirēnarchai*.

The same man almost certainly also appears in *P.Rain.Cent.* 80 (VI), a letter found in Hermopolis, as "my master, the *megaloprepestatos* and *peribleptos comes* Serenos."[261] He is asked to relieve some villagers of their duties before they regularly end, but it remains unclear whether these duties concern estate work or public liturgies; in any case, it shows that this Serenos was present in the Hermopolite area. The name has been read only recently and the titulature is so high-ranking and so close to the one presented for the Serenos in *P.Cair.Masp.* I 67002 that these papyri must refer to the same person. If that man was identical with S. it would explain the connection to, and his interests at, Aphrodite, which motivated the pagarch Menas to write to him and urge him to become engaged in the matter, as narrated by *P.Cair.Masp.* I 67002. Also, a new dating of the dossier of the pagarchs Ioannes and S. to the early 570s instead of the late 550s puts S. chronologically in close proximity to *P.Cair.Masp.* I 67002, so I think the match of S. with the Serenoi of both *P.Cair.Masp.* I 67002 and *P.Rain.Cent.* 80 is very

257 The editors of *P.Ross.Georg.* V 37 speculate whether references to his being *illoustrios* or pagarch may have been lost in the lacuna in l. 14. Gascou 1972a, 61 n. 4 (= 2008, 44 n. 6) accepts the identification.

258 Ruffini's Serenos 10. Banaji 2007, 161 assumes without discussion that Serenos 10 and S. are the same man. Mazza 1995, 231 does not consider *P.Cair.Masp.* 67002 in this context.

259 Cf. Fournet 1999, 688.

260 On the identification of the nome, see Keenan 2008b, 177. On the episode and its chronology, see pp. 251–253 above.

261 *P.Rain.Cent.* 80 verso (with the new reading by Gonis 2021, 95): τῷ δεσπότῃ μ\ου/ τῷ μεγαλοπρ(επεστάτῳ) καὶ ... περιβλ(έπτῳ) κόμ(ετι) Σ̣ε̣ρ̣ήνῳ; the traces after καί may represent either an elusive siglum or two or three erased letters.

likely.[262] The latter papyrus is then probably to be dated to before 566 CE, as S. is still addressed as (*megaloprepestatos* and *peribleptos*) *comes,* rather than as (*megaloprepestatos* and *endoxotatos*) *illoustrios*.[263]

This Serenos—so, in my view, S.—may also be identical with the Serenos of *P.Ant.* III 206.14 (Antinoopolis; mid to late VI, following *BL* XII 6),[264] who was an *illoustrios* and figures in a list of official payments from high-ranking men, probably (provincial?) officials or major landowners.[265] If this man is identical with S., then S. may—like Kollouthos, Menas, and, possibly, Ioulianos and Kallinikos—belong to the circles of the provincial administration of the Thebaid.

(Thomas)

The text of the *editio princeps* of *P.Flor.* III 295.11 identifies Th. as pagarch, but this man was in fact a *cancellarius*.[266]

Anonymous pagarchs

There are a number of anonymous pagarchs in the Antaiopolite tax receipts who can be identified with known pagarchs through coeval receipts and who are captured in Table 4 (pp. 165–167). Six further papyri feature anonymous pagarchs:

- The pagarch of *SB* VI 9102 is certainly Ioulianos.

262 See Table 4 (pp. 165–167). Gonis (2021, 95) asserts that no *comes* Serenos had been attested from Hermopolis before and does not identify this Serenos with S. This is probably due to the misleading entry in *PLRE* III, s.v. Serenus 3, in which the Serenos of *P.Cair.Masp.* I 67002 is connected to Antinoopolis—where the petition was written—instead of Hermopolis. But this Serenos had *dioikētai* acting in the Hermopolite village of Thynis, as presented above, and he was a *comes* (in fact, Gonis thinks that he is "probably the same" as S.). Therefore, all three Serenoi—the one in *P.Cair.Masp.* I 67002, the one in *P.Rain.Cent.* 80, and S.—are most likely the same person.

263 *P.Cair.Masp.* I 67002 was written in May–July 567, but S. is mentioned in a story dating to March or April 566; on this chronology, see n. 260 above. On the hierarchy of titles, see Table 6 (p. 196).

264 This Serenos does not figure in Ruffini's prosopography because *P.Ant.* III 206 does not deal with Aphrodite. Gascou 1972a, 61 n. 4 (= 2008, 44 n. 6) identifies him with S. More cautious ("forse") is Mazza 1995, 231.

265 One of them is the *patricius* Athanasios, i.e., the *dux et Augustalis* of *P.Cair.Masp.* I 67002, and the amount attributed to Serenos (by an *entagion* from a certain *katholikos* Theodoros) is just about a tenth of Athanasios's share. It is unclear what precisely this account is about, but the presence of an *exceptor*, a *trakteutēs*—new readings by Nikolaos Gonis (2024, 146–147) eliminate the "*prakteutai*" in both *P.Ant.* III 206 and *SPP* VIII 1270—and the references to Hermopolis (l. 16) and the Hermopolite village Skordon (l. 3) in a text found at Antinoopolis (see the preface to *P.Ant.* II) suggest that some official inter-city or provincial matter seems at stake here.

266 Based on a reading by Jean-Luc Fournet; see Stern 2015, 144.

- *P.Cair.Masp.* I 67003: Menas or Kollouthos Cancellarius would seem most likely, but also an unknown pagarch (who perhaps was also a *topotērētēs*) is possible.
- MacCoull 1993, no. 6: This Coptic letter was written in Antinoopolis and is addressed to Dioskoros and his wife Sophia by one of their sons.[267] We know that Dioskoros's son Petros stayed with him, at least for some time, in Antinoopolis during his "exile," but the tax receipts from the "receipt codices" of Dioskoros's family show Petros back in his native village Aphrodite in the early 570s.[268] Perhaps when this letter was written, Dioskoros had returned to Aphrodite, but Petros still remained in the provincial capital.[269] This would entail that "the pagarch" referred to in this letter was not Menas, who was probably no longer in office then, but Kollouthos, Ioannes, or Serenos (provided that an *Antaiopolite* pagarch is indeed mentioned here). In an alternative scenario, Petros may have gone to Antinoopolis before Dioskoros, or one of Dioskoros's two other sons may also have dwelled there for some time. Both these latter hypotheses would date the text earlier, to when Menas (or a predecessor) was still in office, but this is far from certain.
- MacCoull 1993, no. 11 = Vanderheyden 2015, no. 15: This pagarch cannot be Menas, because Menas was not yet in office. What is more, the pagarch title added a specification that is lost in a lacuna,[270] which I believe to indicate that this is not the pagarch of Antaiopolis as this would have been clear from the context. Similar letters speak only of "the pagarch" when the *local* pagarch is meant.
- Vanderheyden 2015, no. 11: Since this text in all likelihood relates to the Menas affair, the pagarch mentioned here is probably Menas.
- Vanderheyden 2015, no. 13: This text may also relate to the Menas affair. Although this is less certain than in Vanderheyden's no. 11, Menas still seems the most convenient identification.

Thebaid IV: Unknown Nome

Kollouthos Cancellarius (Antaiopolis or Antinoopolis)

Ruffini's Kollouthos 36. It seems likely that the attestations collected by Ruffini do indeed refer to the same person. At a time when Dioskoros dwelled in Antinoopolis, *P.Aphrod.Lit.* IV 14 has him glorifying K., who is *comes* and pagarch, a city councilor,

267 See Fournet 2008b, 27–28 for a refined reading of the address.

268 See Chapter Two, n. 3 and Stern forthcoming (b) for a discussion of the timeline.

269 The tax receipt that was most probably received by Petros at Aphrodite, *P.Flor.* III 298.72–73, dates from December 7, 572; he must have returned at least by then. Dioskoros dwelled in Antinoopolis until at least November 15, 570 (*P.Cair.Masp.* II 67151), possiby as late as October 573 (cf. *P.Cair.Masp.* I 67096). The reading of *P.Flor.* III 298.72–73 cannot be checked, however, as the fragment appears to be lost.

270 Vanderheyden 2015, no. 15.1: ⲡⲡⲁⲅ̣ⲁⲣ̣ⲭⲟⲥ̣ ⲛ̣̄ . [± 10] ("the pagarch of …").

and part of an important family that held key offices in the Thebaid capital.[271] Like his father, K. is addressed as "leader of cities," having "saved" Antinoopolis.[272] While this appears to suggest that K. was pagarch in Antinoopolis, there are strong indications that he was also active around Aphrodite. In fact, K.'s relationship to the village is the central issue of this poem: he is "eagle of the whole land of Aphrodites Kome" (l. 25), has "*come to us* to take pity on the whole land of Aphrodites Kome, suffering from lamentable troubles at the hands of unjust predecessors" (ll. 35–36; my emphasis), and finally is said to have "helped all the cities of the Thebaid" (l. 41).[273] The degree of metonymy and exaggeration is difficult to gauge but it is clear enough that K. had been to Aphrodite to take care of some issues, though this is not to say that he went because Dioskoros asked him to. The explicit reference to "predecessors," then, should probably be understood to mean that K. succeeded Menas Scriniarius, the main target of much of Dioskoros's written output at that time, in the post of pagarch, but again it is difficult to gauge how literally we can take this poetic wording. In *P.Cair.Masp.* I 67005 (Antinoopolis; 567 or 568), an Aphroditan widow states that "my master, the *lamprotatos* lord Kollouthos, the *cancellarius* and pagarch" ordered to release her from prison,[274] which has been taken to suggest that he may have been pagarch of Antaiopolis.[275] Although Kollouthos is a common name, the interlinked Aphroditan and Antinoopolite contexts make the conclusion that the Kollouthos of *P.Cair.Masp.* I 67005 is K. probable. Still, it remains uncertain whether K. was pagarch *for Antaiopolis* or whether his activity there was based on some other capacity. The widow refers to him as "my master," but this can also be understood as a general term of respect.

Some potential matches may underscore the ties that K. had to the village of Aphrodite, but the common personal name and the lack of more distinguished epithets make this far from certain. An undated *scriniarius* and *lamprotatos* "lord" Kollouthos (Ruffini's Kollouthos 8) is a landowner in the Antinoopolite and Lykopolite nomes.[276] Maspero identified this man with K., who is also a *lamprotatos* "lord," and a *cancellarius* (K. in *P.Cair.Masp.* I 67005) operates in roughly the same environment as a *scriniarius*. But instead of being K., Ruffini's Kollouthos 8 may well have been identical with

271 *P.Aphrod.Lit.* IV 28 (Aphrodite?; 542/543 or 547/550?) is a comparable document, and the Kollouthos in this text certainly K., based on his description as γλυκύφορμος (l. 1; cf. *P.Aphrod.Lit.* IV 14.25; see the editor's commentary), though this text yields no valuable information on his career.

272 K.'s father, Apa Dios, is additionally hailed as πτολίουχος, a "protector of cities" (l. 8). In this paragraph, I mainly follow the translations of MacCoull 1988, 100–102 and 96–98.

273 In the first two cases, Dioskoros employs poetic aliases for the village. In translating προηγητήρων (Fournet: l. 36; MacCoull: l. 12), I adopt Fournet's "prédécesseurs" over MacCoull's "administrators." In *P.Lond.* V, p. 147, Bell also assumed that Kollouthos succeeded Menas.

274 *P.Cair.Masp.* I 67005.19: ἐκέλευσεν ὁ δεσπ(ότης) μου ὁ λαμπρ(ότατος) κύριος Κόλλουθος ὁ καγκελλάριος κ(αὶ) παγάρχης ἀπολυθῆναί με. On *cancellarii*, see Benaissa 2009, 59–61.

275 As suggested by Gelzer 1913b, 361 and Liebeschuetz 1974, 164 n. 10.

276 *P.Cair.Masp.* I 67099 (Aphrodite/Antinoopolis?; VI) and *P.Cair.Masp.* III 67313 (Antinoopolis; VI). The professional title *scriniarius* figures only in the latter text, but the family links in both documents suggest that they relate to the same man.

the *scriniarius* Kollouthos who appears as landholder in two other papyri (Ruffini's Kollouthos 27).[277] This man was the son of a certain Ammonios—there is no reason to assume that this was Count Ammonios—and the differing filiation undercuts the hypothesis that this man was K. The title of *comes* that *P.Aphrod.Lit.* IV 14 attests[278] is lacking in all other instances cited here, but this is not necessarily significant, given that *comes* in this period was no longer the distinctive attribute it once had been, and may not have been consistently used.

The question of whether K. was pagarch of Antaiopolis or Antinoopolis becomes more complex because of *P.Leid.Inst.* 72 (Antinoopolis; VI), which attests a Kollouthos who is "*exceptor* and pagarch of Antinoopolis" (= Kollouthos Exceptor). Equating an *exceptor* with a *cancellarius* would be tempting but not unproblematic, not least as Kollouthos is a common name; yet this identification is suggestive because of K.'s links to Antinoopolis, and because of the fact that Dioskoros in the poem *P.Cair.Masp.* I 67004 is praising simply a *lamprotatos* Kollouthos, which implies unambiguity. But *P.Leid.Inst.* 72 cannot be dated and several possible matches with other *exceptores* called Kollouthos are not conclusive.[279] Therefore, we may either be dealing with one pagarch Kollouthos who acted in this capacity in both Antaiopolis and Antinoopolis—which I find unlikely, because we have yet to encounter Byzantine pagarchs responsible for two nomes—or there was one Kollouthos from Antinoopolis who became pagarch in Antaiopolis (= K.) and another one who was pagarch of Antinoopolis at some other point in the sixth or early seventh century (= Kollouthos Exceptor). A third possibility is that K., whether identical with Kollouthos Exceptor or not, was pagarch of Antinoopolis and came to Aphrodite by virtue of some other capacity that eludes us or by virtue of his personal authority. The jury is still out on this one,[280] but separating these two men may be the safer working hypothesis. Ultimately, I would tend to prefer the third interpretation, because I would expect Dioskoros—who was the writer of the petition *P.Cair.Masp.* I 67005—to be more specific, at least in his petitions, about attributing K.'s pagarchy to Antaiopolis if that were the case.

K. might also have been the same man as the *lamprotatos* Kollouthos who is praised by Dioskoros in *P.Cair.Masp.* I 67004 for help against a culprit whose name is lost.[281] On the question whether K. is the same individual as the Kollouthos of *P.Ant.* III 206, see the Kollouthos of the following entry.

---

277 *P.Cair.Masp.* III 67327.37–49 (Aphrodite; 539) and *P.Lond.* V 1702 (Aphrodite; 542/543). See also Keenan 1985b, 148–150.

278 See Fournet 1993, 234 n. 42.

279 See s.v. Kollouthos Exceptor (Antinoopolis) above.

280 Fournet 1993, 234 n. 42 urges caution about K.'s relationship to Kollouthos Exceptor; Mazza 1995, 204–205 and 232–233 suggests that K. and Kollouthos Exceptor are the same man.

281 Ruffini's Kollouthos 53. On the interpretation of this text, see Dijkstra 2004 and 2008, 4 and n. 15.

Kollouthos (?) (Lykopolis?)

The “lord” K. of *P.Ant.* III 206 (Antinoopolis; mid to late VI; see *BL* XII 6) is connected to a payment in kind “for the pagarch(y?) of Lykopolis, of the 4th indiction,” based on an *entagion* by a *katholikos*. This is based on new readings by Nikolaos Gonis, although he expresses caution about the reading of Lykopolis.[282] “Pagarchy” may in this context refer to the fiscal responsibilities of the office—in a way comparable to cases such as *P.Oxy.* XVI 2040—perhaps because Lykopolis did not have a pagarch at the time, or because Lykopolis (or its pagarchy) in some way contributed to expenses that formed the basis of this list. Consequently, K. might be the same as the pagarchs Kollouthos Exceptor (Antinoopolis) or/and Kollouthos Cancellarius (see the previous entry), both of whom were at some point active in Antinoopolis. In addition, Lykopolis was situated between Antinoopolis and Hermopolis to the north and Antaiopolis to the south. Therefore, Kollouthos Cancellarius—who was at some point (in whatever capacity; see the preceding entry) active around Aphrodite—was potentially capable of assuming this sort of extra responsibility, and a reference to a “lord” (*kyrios*) fits his standing. The fourth indiction mentioned in *P.Ant.* III 206 may correspond to 555/556, 570/571, or 585/586 CE and if the *illoustrios* Serenos of this text is the same as the Antaiopolite pagarch (see s.v. above), who held this pagarchy during a fourth indiction, then *P.Ant.* III 206 should not be dated to the pagarch Serenos’s tenure at Antaiopolis.[283] But K. could also be the *trakteutēs* of l. 7.[284]

Phoibammon (?) (Antinoopolis?)

Ph., a *lamprotatos cancellarius*, appears in *P.Ant.* II 97 and is probably the same as the *lamprotatos cancellarius* Phoibammon of *P.Ant.* II 96. In the former document, Ph. potentially appears as “managing (*dioikōn*) the pagarchy.”[285] Both papyri were found in Antinoopolis and were assigned by their editors to the sixth century, but have been redated recently to the seventh century by Nikolaos Gonis, in both cases for palaeo-

282 *P.Ant.* III 206.11: (ὑπὲρ) τοῦ κυρ(ίου) Κολλούθου (ὑπὲρ) παγαρχ( ) Λὐ̣κ(ων) δ ἰνδ(ικτίονος); see Gonis 2024, 142–143. Because of the parallels for this expression, I deem (ὑπὲρ) παγαρχ(ίας) more likely than (ὑπὲρ) παγάρχ(ου). The *editio princeps* had πατρ\χ/ λόκ(ου) (read πατρ(ι)κ(ίου) λόγου) instead of παγαρχ( ) Λὐ̣κ(ων).

283 Jean-Luc Fournet places Serenos’s fourth indiction as pagarch in 555/556, whereas I assign it to 570/571, and Sofie Remijsen to 585/586; see Chapter Four, Section II for references on the dates of the tenure of Ioannes and Serenos.

284 Not “*prakteutēs*”; see above n. 265.

285 *P.Ant.* II 97.5–6: Φοιβάμμωνος τοῦ λαμπρ(οτάτου) καγκελλαρί̣[ου – – –] | παγαρχίας διοικοῦντος. On διοικέω in the sense of being someone’s deputy, see Chapter Four, Section III. On a *cancellarius* as pagarch, see s.v. Kollouthos Cancellarius (Thebaid: Unknown nome) above.

graphical reasons.[286] Jean-Luc Fournet, based on the sixth-century dating, points to a potential match with the Antinoopolite Phoibammon whom Dioskoros describes as "*epikeimenos* of the pagarchy."[287] But the new dates of *P.Ant.* II 96 and 97 cast doubt on this identification.[288] Moreover, in view of the document's severely fragmentary condition, Fournet concedes that it is not certain whether the pagarchy in *P.Ant.* II 97.6 is actually part of Ph.'s description in the preceding line. In the case that it is, the use of *dioikōn* seems ambiguous in this text. In Ph.'s case, it would probably signal that Ph., as *cancellarius*, was in charge of the pagarchy only due to extraordinary circumstances. The writer of this text, however, probably refers to "the pagarchy managed (*dioikoumenē*) by me."[289] The precise context of that passage is unclear due to the fragmentary state of the papyrus, but it may seem a bit of a stretch to assume the appearance of two extraordinary administrations of, apparently, different pagarchies, in the same document. Because Antinoopolis was the provincial capital of the Thebaid, pagarchs appearing here need not be the local pagarchs; but in *P.Ant.* II 96, Ph.'s position as *cancellarius* and his appearance in an apparently local context may be vague indications that his responsibility was indeed the pagarchy of Antinoopolis. Due to the uncertain dating of both *P.Ant.* II 96 and 97, Ph. does not figure as Byzantine pagarch in the text of the main chapters.

Theo[... (?)

The writer of *P.Ant.* II 97, probably the Flavius Theo[... in l. 13, mentions "the pagarchy managed (*dioikoumenē*) by me," then, after a lacuna, refers to "places" (*topoi*) and "land plots" (*ktēmata*) that are perhaps "pagarchic," immediately followed by another lacuna.[290] On the combination of *dioikoumenē* with the pagarchy, see the preceding entry on Phoibammon. Th. goes on to mention, among other things, an amount of thirty-six *nomismata*, a delivery, "wrongdoers," and an account linked to the unknown addressee.[291] Nonetheless, due to the fragmentary preservation of the papyrus, the context of this probably administrative letter is nebulous. Jairus Banaji (2007, 163 n. 177) implicitly suggests that the *endoxotatos* Theodosios from *P.Flor.* III 377 (Ptol-

---

286 On the provenance, see the preface to *P.Ant.* II. On the dates, see Benaissa 2009, 59 n. 7.

287 Fournet 1999, 554; see s.v. Phoibammon (Antinoopolis) above.

288 For the possibility that both men are the same and that *P.Ant.* II 96 and 97 may date from the early seventh century, see Benaissa 2009, 59 n. 7.

289 *P.Ant.* II 97.2: τῆς διοικουμένης παρ' ἐμοῦ παγαρχ[ίας – – –]. On the writer of this text, see the following entry, s.v. Theo[...

290 *P.Ant.* II 97.2–3: τὰ ὑπὲρ συστάσεως τῆς διοικουμένης παρ' ἐμοῦ παγαρχ[ίας – – –] | τόπων τε καὶ κτημάτων διακειμένων παγαρχικῶ[ν – – –]. The term *systasis* in the beginning is ambiguous without further context and most likely relates to Th.'s own appointment or to an allocation of taxes; see *WB*, s.v. σύστασις.

291 *P.Ant.* II 97.7a, 9, 10, and 11.

emais Hermeiou; VI) might be the same man, but because *P.Ant.* II 97 has now been assigned to the seventh century, this seems doubtful. Since Th. writes to a Flavius in the provincial capital, his responsibility was probably not related to the Antinoopolite pagarchy but that of another nome. Due to the uncertain dating, Th. does not figure as Byzantine pagarch in the main chapters.

Anonymous pagarch (Apollonopolis Heptakomias or Antaiopolis)

In the Coptic letter *O.Sarga* 107, four suckling pigs are to be given to "the pagarch's bride."[292] The text is usually dated between the sixth and eighth centuries, in accordance with the range of the finds from Wadi Sarga (*TM* Geo ID 237), but Hans Förster, in his dictionary of Greek words in Coptic documentary texts, assigned it to the sixth or seventh century without further comment.[293] Wadi Sarga is situated in immediate proximity to Apollonopolis Heptakomias Mikra (modern Kom Isfaht; ⲥⲃⲉϩⲧ in Coptic; *TM* Geo ID 268),[294] a city suspected to have been under the administrative purview of the nearby city of Antaiopolis. This phenomenon is indeed prominent in documents from the early Islamic period,[295] but the situation is unclear for the Byzantine age.

Apollonopolis Heptakomias is listed between Hypsele and Antaiopolis in both Hierocles's *Synecdemus* and George of Cyprus's *Descriptio orbis Romani*.[296] Moreover, the nome frequently appears under Byzantine administration. Admittedly, a legally proper *civitas* administered by another city during the Byzantine period would find a parallel in Theodosiopolis in the Fayum, which was administered by the neighboring city of Arsinoe.[297] We do, however, find Apollonopolite officials during the Byzantine period, among them a *dioikētēs*,[298] a *trakteutēs*,[299] and an *ekdikos*,[300] which marks a contrast to the Theodosiopolite nome. It might well be that the taxes of the Apollonopolitan countryside were under the purview of the pagarch of nearby Antaiopolis in the Byzantine period, too, but the texts cannot be taken as evidence for or against this hypothesis. Lines 3–4 of the probably Byzantine ostracon *SB* XX 14550 (Aphrodite;

292 *O.Sarga* 107.7–8: ⲧϣⲉⲗⲉⲉⲧ ⲙⲡⲡⲁⲕⲁⲣⲭ̣ⲟⲥ (read ⲙⲡⲡⲁⲅⲁⲣⲭⲟⲥ).
293 Förster 2002, s.v. πάγαρχος: ⲡⲁⲕⲁⲣⲭⲟⲥ.
294 This Apollonopolis is not to be confused with its more southern namesakes Apollonopolis Ano (modern Edfu; *TM* Geo ID 269) and (another) Apollonopolis Mikra (modern Qus; *TM* Geo ID 270).
295 For instance, in *P.Lond.* IV 1347.4–5 (January 10, 710): χωρί\ου/ Μουναχθη' παγαρχίας Ἀνταίο(υ) καὶ | Ἀπόλλωνος.
296 Hierocl. *Synecd.* 731.3 (c. 527–535 CE); Georg.Cypr. 767 (c. 603–606 CE).
297 On Theodosiopolis and its administration by the city of Arsinoe, see the Introduction, n. 50.
298 P.Drexel (ed. Benaissa 2008, no. 1), ll. 1–2. On this post, see Chapter Four, Section III.
299 P.Drexel (ed. Benaissa 2008, no. 1), l. 2. On this post, see Chapter Two, Section II 3.
300 *SB* XX 14550; O.Cair. SR 18953/4 (ed. Aish 2013, no. 2). On this post, see Chapter One, n. 105.

VI–VII) read τοῖς | β ἐκδ(ίκοις) Ἀνταίου καὶ Ἀπόλλωνος̣, which certainly refers to one *ekdikos* in either city and does not necessarily indicate two *ekdikoi* of an administratively united territory. Similarly, the reference to a *lamprotatos dioikētēs* of Apollonopolis in P.Drexel (late VI–early VII) is, to my mind, not sufficient to argue that this man was the local representative of the pagarch of Antaiopolis.[301] Notably, Antaiopolis, which had its own pagarch, also had a *dioikētēs* in the sixth century (*P.Köln* V 240.5).[302]

Therefore, the question of whether *O.Sarga* 107 shows a pagarch of Apollonopolis Heptakomias or of Antaiopolis must remain open (assuming it is from the Byzantine period). There is also no indication of whether this pagarch belonged to the "upper" or "lower" tier according to my categorization in Chapter Five. The reference to his office instead of a rank epithet plus honorary title vaguely suggests he might have been a lower-tier pagarch, but this is far from certain.

Anonymous pagarchs

In *P.Cair.Masp.* I 67068, two (or more) pagarchs referred to as "our *lamprotatoi* masters"[303] are present in Antinoopolis, but it is not clear whether this is a permanent residence or an occasional stay. They may be pagarchs of Antinoopolis, as Gelzer proposed,[304] but they may also have been there in order to consult or report to the provincial administration.[305] The letter was written by a certain Phoibammon, who refers to Hermopolis as "my city," and was sent to Dioskoros, who may still have been resident of Aphrodite at that time, given that the sender alludes to Dioskoros's recent presence in the village of Euphrosynon. Therefore, Hermopolis and Antaiopolis would be alternatives for these pagarchs' administrative allocation.

MacCoull 1993, no. 11 = Vanderheyden 2015, no. 15 refers to another anonymous pagarch. The document is from the Antaiopolite nome, but the pagarch is unlikely to have been the pagarch of Antaiopolis; see above, s.v. Anonymous pagarchs (Antaiopolis).

301 For this hypothesis, see Benaissa 2008, 186–187 and 191–192.
302 On various official positions referred to as *dioikētēs* in the Byzantine period, see Chapter Four, n. 58.
303 *P.Cair.Masp.* I 67068.10 (VI): τοὺς λαμπρ̣[οτάτου]ς ἡμῶν δεσ[πό]τας παγάρχους.
304 Gelzer 1913b, 361.
305 Cf. Mazza 1995, 187–188. For a comparable situation, see *P.Mich.* XI 624.

Unknown Province

Ammonios (?) (Hermopolis?)

One of the Vienna papyri with the provenance "angeblich Hermopolites," *SPP* VIII 1028 (VI), has two small isolated lines, apparently the beginning of an order by a certain *politeuomenos* Ammonios.[306] This man seems to be a pagarch or responsible for a pagarchy, and orders that something be paid or given to an *advocatus fisci*. There is no particular reason to identify this Ammonios with Count Ammonios, discussed in Section I of Chapter Six. The context is obscure as more text would be necessary to complete the document in a meaningful way. The online image suggests that surface damage may be responsible for the lack of text in the parts surrounding the extant passage.

Kallinikos (Hermopolis?)

K. is referred to in *P.Münch.* III 152 without any status designation.[307] This is somewhat surprising, as the numerous Antaiopolite tax receipts usually add rank epithets to the pagarch's titles if they are identified by name;[308] therefore, one may suspect either a comparatively low rank such as *lamprotatos* or that the title of pagarch was modified afterward where the text is illegible.[309]

There are several possible matches that may point to K.'s being from the same milieu of provincial bureaucrats as Menas Scriniarius and Kollouthos Cancellarius; all of these potential matches are from Hermopolis: in *SB* XX 14169 (VI), a *comes* Kallinikos issues a receipt to a man who is *thaumasiōtatos.* The latter's function in relation to the village of Telbonthis mentioned in the document is lost, but given that the receipt concerns the *dēmosia* of the village, this man may have been the *boēthos* of Telbonthis.[310] This Kallinikos is represented by a *scriniarius* and an *exceptor*, which probably means that he was a high-ranking official in the provincial administration,[311] rather than a pagarch, at least at the time the receipt was written.

---

306 *SPP* VIII 1028.1–2 (see *BL* I 417 and Laniado 2002, 94): παγαρχ( ) Ἀμμωνίου πολ(ιτευομένου) [– – –] | παράσχου Πα̣̃ φισκοσυνηγόρ(ω̣) [– – –].

307 *P.Münch.* III 152.3–4: Φλ(άουιος) Καλλίνικος πάγαρχος ..... |............. σεσημείωμαι. The title of pagarch might have been followed by the name of the city or that of a subordinate official "through" (διά) whom Kallinikos acted, but the traces are faint and difficult to make sense of.

308 But cf., from Antinoopolis, *P.Leid.Inst.* 72.5 (VI): Φλ(άουιος) Κολλοῦθος ἐξκ(έπτωρ) (καὶ) πάγαρχ(ος) Ἀντι(νόου).

309 Cf. Ioannes's and Serenos's being referred to as "pagarch of the two-thirds/one-third share of Antaiopolis," for instance, in *P.Cair.Masp.* III 67325 fol. III verso 5–9 and 9–12.

310 *Thaumasiōtatos* is a common epithet for village *boēthoi*; see *P.Lond.* V 1753 and *BGU* XII 2196, in the latter of which this epithet can be read with ease (for the correction, see n. 183 above).

311 Cf. *P.Lond.* III 1035, a similar receipt issued by a *magister* to the *thaumasiōtatos boēthos* of the

A more likely match is the *lamprotatos* Kallinikos from *SB* XIV 11353 (VI): he writes to an *archiphrouros* (who apparently acts as a debt collector) that he has received the *dēmosia* of the village of Tanemois through a certain Oros. This Kallinikos may in turn be identical with a number of Kallinikoi who appear in similar contexts in matters pertaining to the collection of taxes,[312] and whom Nikolaos Gonis assigns to the early sixth century.[313]

There might be a number of other options. One of the preceding Kallinikoi or K. himself would be a good match for the *comes* Kallinikos from BL Pap. 1325 (ed. Gonis 2021, no. 1), who is about to go to an estate and "bring the men." The letter stems from a Hermopolite/Antinoite context but is not from Antinoopolis (see l. 7).

Jairus Banaji points to the possibility of identifying K. with the *comes* Kallinikos in *P.Ant.* III 189 (Antinoopolis; VI–VII), a list of wanted persons from villages in the northern Hermopolite nome.[314] But there is no institutional link to the pagarchy here apart from the fact that the phrasing "his villages" points to some sort of official responsibility.[315]

Another possible match for K. is the *lamprotatos* Kallinikos, son of Achilleus, from *P.Sorb.* II 69.83.C3 (618/619 or 633/634), which would only be possible if K. is not identical with one of the *lamprotatoi* Kallinikoi mentioned in the *SB* and *SPP* texts above.[316] The homonymous *dux et Augustalis* of the Thebaid from the late 560s may be yet an-

village of Sinape (l. 1). The fact that a *magister* issues a receipt here possibly links the document to the provincial bureau. See also the discussions of the careers of the pagarchs Menas Scriniarius and Kollouthos Exceptor in Chapter Five, Section III 2 (and s.vv. above).

312 ***SB* XVI 12699** (501/516 CE): the *ekdikos* of Hermopolis acknowledges that a *lamprotatos* Kallinikos has paid for the "cleaning" (*anakatharsis*) of the city. ***SPP* III 369** (IV–V): a Flavius Kallinikos appears in a fragmentary papyrus of obscure context, but the references to a *kephalē*, *apochē*, and the *logisteia* (cf. Gonis 2000b) strongly suggest that it is about taxes. ***SPP* VIII 989** (V–VI): a *lamprotatos* Kallinikos orders the *boēthos* of Tanemois (the same village as in *SB* XIV 11353 mentioned above) to remunerate some guards (*phrouroi*). ***SPP* VIII 1049** (VI): a fragmentary text of obscure content sent by a Kallinikos, but the document mentions again the village Tanemois; the position of the indiction before (!) the amount of money may suggest a fiscal context. ***SPP* VIII 1050** (VI): a *lamprotatos* Kallinikos sends an order of payment for a soldier (*scutarius*) to the *boēthos*, again, of Tanemois. A new reading (Gonis 2019a, 353) adds ***SPP* VIII 1173** (V–VI) to this group: once again, a *lamprotatos* Kallinikos sends an order of payment possibly to the *boēthos* of Tanemois. The village name in l. 2 is certain, and restoring the beginning of that line as either [– – – βοηθ]ῳ̣ or [– – – βοηθ](ῳ̣) poses no difficulty, but must remain tentative, of course. The admittedly small trace of ink after the lacuna may be the right end of omega or part of an abbreviation marker.

313 Gonis 2019a, 353.

314 Banaji 2007, 165, but cf. his Appendix 4, with reservations.

315 The fact that the text was found in Antinoopolis may be a vague indication that there is some authority at the provincial level at work here. Cf. Gonis 1998, whose suggestion would imply that it is Kallinikos himself who is to look for these men on his estate.

316 Cf. Gonis 2019a, 353.

other option[317] and would bring the pagarch K. again into a web of career bureaucrat circles using the pagarchy on their way to the top, but this must remain speculation.

Menas (?) (Hermopolis?)

According to Fournet & Bénazeth 2020, 153–154 (no. 24), M. appears as *eparchos*[318] (prefect or *praeses*) or pagarch in a monogram (deciphered as Μηνᾶ ἐπάρχου or Μηνᾶ παγάρχου) on a silver spoon (V–VII) that was found in Tuna el-Gebel, the necropolis of Hermopolis. There is no way of telling how it got there or whether M. was its last owner, so even if M. was a pagarch, it would not be certain that he was the pagarch of Hermopolis. The editors note that the readings of both name and title are uncertain, which is why this potential pagarch does not figure elsewhere in this book.

Neilammon (Arsinoe?)

In *SPP* VIII 1061, one of the Viennese papyri "supposedly" from the Arsinoite nome,[319] the *pronoētēs* of an *ousia* is ordered to send a considerable amount of hay to the pagarch N. This amount consists of sixty *gomoi* ("loads"), more than one metric ton in total,[320] but there is no way to tell on account of what this amount was paid or sent. If it was for a public contribution, this would be evidence of an *ousia* that paid its dues to the pagarch.[321] But we may also imagine that the pagarch was helped by a peer to cover contributions that the pagarch had not yet been able to collect for various reasons. N. does not bear any other titles, though an epithet or rather a reference to "Flavius" may be hidden at the end of l. 2, where faint traces can be seen on the online image.[322] A possible, but speculative, match may be Flavius Neilammonas in *P.Prag.* I 34 A 5 (Arsinoe; VI), who was probably a *geouchōn*.[323]

317 Gonis 2021, 91.

318 On this title, cf. p. 320 and nn. 218 and 219 above.

319 See *CPR* X, pp. 155–156 n. 26, which refers to a note by Wessely ("angeblich Arsinoites").

320 The exact weight of a *gomos* is not really clear and probably varied locally and in different contexts. In *SB* VIII 9920 (Arsinoites; VI), one *gomos* of hay translates to 19.6 kilograms, apparently for different transport animals; see Reekmans 1962, 28–31. By contrast, in the first-century archive of Nikanor, concerning caravans in the Eastern Desert, one *gomos* of grain, not hay, seems to translate to c. 186 kilograms and apparently concerns camel transports (see Bülow-Jacobsen 2013, 564) but as we have no indication that *SPP* VIII 1061 concerns a desert transport, this is probably less likely. The vast majority of *gomoi* amounts mentioned in the papyri are much lower than sixty, most of them in the single digits.

321 On *ousiai* paying taxes to the pagarch, see Chapter Three, Section VII.

322 *SPP* VIII 1061.1–3: † Γεροντίῳ προνοοιτ(ῇ) (read προνοητῇ) οὐσί(ας) | Σιττᾶ Ἀσαὰρ παράσχ(ου) *traces* | Νειλάμμ(ωνι) παγάρχ(ῃ), κτλ.

323 For this reading of l. 5, see *BL* IX 213.

The sender and estate owner in *SPP* VIII 1061 goes by the exceptionally rare name of Sitta,[324] son of Asaar. There are about a dozen attestations of a Sitta(s) or Tzitta(s) in the *PN* and only one of a man called Asar (*sic*).[325] While *SPP* VIII 1061 has been assigned to the sixth century, it is curious that Sitta is identified by his patronymic and without titles or epithets, as this man owns an *ousia* and is having a significant amount of hay transported and thus was probably an aristocrat or official. Can this be explained by the fact that Sitta signed the document himself? Or is this text from the early Islamic period, which preferred the use of the patronymic in some contexts where titles were used in Byzantine documentary practice? One fairly well-known Sitta(s) or Tzitta(s) is the *megaloprepestatos comes* and *meizoteros* (estate administrator) of Flavius Strategios Paneuphemos in *BGU* II 368.8–10 (Arsinoe; June 25, 615), who also appears in this role in *SPP* X 138 col. I 4 from the beginning of the seventh century (see *BL* XI 264). We encounter another Tzittas in *SPP* VIII 1111, a *lamprotatos dioikētēs* and *chrys(o)hypodektēs* who is in service of the *stratēlatēs* Theodosios. The *meizoteros* and the *dioikētēs* are certainly the same man, given Tzitta's rare personal name, his role as estate administrator, the close links between Flavius Strategios Paneuphemos and the *stratēlatēs* Theodosios, and Nikolaos Gonis's arguments for dating *SPP* VIII 1111 to 618 or 603, rather than to 633.[326] This earlier date for *SPP* VIII 1111 allows for the assumption that this Tzittas experienced a smooth career transition from *lamprotatos* (without an honorary title) to *megaloprepestatos comes*. It also adds to the impression of a family business run by Theodosios and Strategios, who may have been brothers,[327] that Tzittas worked for, although he may have worked first for Theodosios and then for Strategios.

This connection, then, makes one wonder whether the Gerontios who was *lamprotatos chartoularios* of Theodosios's *ousia*[328] might be identical with the *pronoētēs* Gerontios who is addressed by Sitta (= Tzittas?) and asked to make a payment of hay to the pagarch N. in *SPP* VIII 1061. However, *pronoētai* were usually of lower rank than *lamprotatos*. Therefore, while not impossible, both matches—between the two Gerontioi and between Sitta and the *comes* Tzittas—fail to convince (despite the rarity of the name), at least based on the evidence so far available. Consequently, not much can be said about the pagarch N. that is certain.

324 On this name, see Palme 1997a, 110 n. 33.

325 *P.Lond.* IV 1556.7; there is no online image.

326 Estate administrator: In *SPP* X 138 col. I 4, Tzittas's function is lost in a lacuna, but since three of the four surrounding entries are for *dioikētai* (col. I 14 and col. II 8 and 12), it is possible that Tzittas was also referred to as *dioikētēs* in this document. On the connection between Strategios and Theodosios, see Chapter Three, Section VII. On the date, see Gonis 2008, 206–207 contra Palme 1997a, 112 n. 40. Palme distinguishes the *meizoteros* and the *dioikētēs*, partially because of the 633 date of *SPP* VIII 1111.

327 See Chapter Five n. 132 and the references there.

328 *P.Lond.* I 113.6C.3–6 (Arsinoe; 620 or 635?).

Sources and Bibliography

All online resources were last checked on May 30, 2024.

Ancient Sources

All abbreviated sources not listed below are papyrological editions, including editions of ostraca and tablets, and are cited according to the *Checklist of Editions* (https://papyri.info/docs/checklist). Texts from *P.Aphrod.Lit.* are conventionally cited not according to the number of the volume, but the internal numbering of parts I–IV. Three of the papyrological abbreviations used in this book, *O.Sabil, P.Aphrod.Let.Copt.* I, and *P.Vind.EarlyIslamic*, are not (yet) part of the *Checklist* and defined below. Non-italicized citations of papyri or ostraca (starting with P., O., or Pap.; cf. the Index of Sources) refer to inventory numbers and are provided with the relevant publications in the main chapters.

AE
L'Année Epigraphique, 1889–

Basil. *epist.*
J. Henderson (ed.) and R. J. Deferrari (trans.), *Basil: Letters*, vol. I: *1–58*, Cambridge 1926;
Y. Courtonne (ed. & trans.), *Saint Basile: Lettres*, vol. I, Paris 1957.

CIG
Corpus Inscriptionum Graecarum, 5 vols., 1828–1877.

CIIP
Corpus Inscriptionum Iudaeae/Palaestinae, 5 vols., 2011–

CIL
Corpus Inscriptionum Latinarum, 17 vols., 1863–

C.J.
B. W. Frier et al. (eds. & trans.), *The Codex of Justinian: A New Annotated Translation with Parallel Latin and Greek Text*, 3 vols., Cambridge 2016.

C.Th.
Th. Mommsen (ed.), *Theodosiani libri XVI cum constitutionibus Sirmondianis,* Berlin 1905;
C. Pharr (trans.), *Theodosian Code and Novels and the Sirmondian Constitutions,* Princeton 1952.

Dion.Hal. *ant.*
C. Jacoby (ed.), *Dionysii Halicarnasei antiquitatum Romanarum quae supersunt*, 4 vols., Leipzig 1885–1905;
E. Cary (trans.), *The Roman Antiquities of Dionysius of Halicarnassus*, 7 vols., London 1948.

Georg.Cypr.
E. Honigmann (ed.), *Le Synecdèmos* [sic] *d'Hiéroclès et l'opuscule géographique de Georges de Chypre*, Brussels 1939.

Hdt.
N. G. Wilson (ed.), *Herodoti Historiae*, 2 vols., Oxford 2015;
A. L. Purvis (trans.), *The Landmark Herodotus: The Histories*, New York 2007.

Hierocl. *Synecd.*
E. Honigmann (ed.), *Le Synecdèmos* [sic] *d'Hiéroclès et l'opuscule géographique de Georges de Chypre*, Brussels 1939.

https://doi.org/10.1515/9783111493183-010

History of the Church
D. W. Johnson, "Further fragments of a Coptic History of the Church: Cambridge OR. 1699 R," *Enchoria: Zeitschrift für Demotistik und Koptologie* 6 (1976) 7–17.
ICG
C. Breytenbach and Ch. Zimmermann (eds.), *Inscriptiones Christianae Graecae (ICG): Eine Datenbank frühchristlicher Inschriften*: https://icg.uni-kiel.de
Isid.Pel. *epist.*
J. P. Migne (ed.), *Patrologia Graeca,* vol. LXXVIII: *Isidorus Pelusiota*, Paris 1912 (= 1860).
Iust. *ed.*
R. Schöll and W. Kroll (eds.), *Corpus iuris civilis,* vol. III: *Novellae*, Berlin 1912;
C. E. Zachariae von Lingenthal (ed.), *Imp. Iustiniani pp. a. Novellae quae vocantur sive Constitutiones quae extra codicem supersunt, ordine chronologico Digestae*, Leipzig 1891;
D. J. D. Miller and P. Sarris (trans.), *The Novels of Justinian: A Complete Annotated English Translation*, 2 vols., Cambridge 2018.
Iust. *inst.*
J. A. C. Thomas (ed. & trans.), *The Institutes of Justinian*, Oxford 1975.
Iust. *nov.*
R. Schöll and W. Kroll (eds.), *Corpus iuris civilis,* vol. III: *Novellae*, Berlin 1912;
D. J. D. Miller and P. Sarris (trans.), *The Novels of Justinian: A Complete Annotated English Translation*, 2 vols., Cambridge 2018.
Life of Aaron
J. H. F. Dijkstra and J. van der Vliet (eds. & trans.), *The Coptic Life of Aaron: Critical Edition, Translation and Commentary*, Leiden 2020.
Lydus *mag.*
A. C. Bandy (ed. & trans.), *Ioannes Lydus: On Powers or The Magistracies of the Roman State,* Philadelphia 1983.
O.Sabil
D. Mahmoud Masoud, R. Ast, and R. S. Bagnall, "Two archives of ostraka from Ain es-Sabil," *BASP* 58 (2021) 87–134.
P.Aphrod.Let.Copt. I
L. Vanderheyden, *Correspondre en copte dans l'Égypte du VI*[e] *siècle: Les lettres coptes des archives familiales d'Aphrodité*, forthcoming.
Prag.Sanct.
R. Schöll and W. Kroll (eds.), *Corpus iuris civilis,* vol. III: *Novellae*, Berlin 1912;
D. J. D. Miller and P. Sarris (trans.), *The Novels of Justinian: A Complete Annotated English Translation*, 2 vols., Cambridge 2018.
Proc. *bell.*
J. Haury and G. Wirth (eds.), *Procopii Caesariensis opera omnia*, 4 vols., Leipzig 1962–1964;
H. B. Dewing and A. Kaldellis (trans.), *Prokopios: The Wars of Justinian,* Indianapolis 2014.
P.Vind.EarlyIslamic
L. Demiri and C. E. Römer, *Texts from the Early Islamic Period of Egypt: Muslims and Christians at Their First Encounter*, Vienna 2009.

Instrumenta and Online Databases Abbreviated in This Study

BL
Berichtigungsliste der griechischen Papyrusurkunden aus Ägypten, 13 vols., 1922–

*CSBE*²
R. S. Bagnall and K. A. Worp, *Chronological Systems of Byzantine Egypt*, 2nd ed., Leiden 2004.

LSJ
H. G. Liddell, R. Scott, and H. S. Jones, *A Greek-English Lexicon*, 9th ed., Oxford 1996 (= 1940).

nFWB
Mehrsprachiges Online-Wörterbuch zum Fachwortschatz der Verwaltungssprache des griechisch-römisch-byzantinischen Ägypten:
https://www.organapapyrologica.net/content/dictionary_start.xed

PLRE
A. H. M. Jones, J. R. Martindale, and J. Morris, *The Prosopography of the Later Roman Empire*, 3 vols., Cambridge 1971–1992.

PN
The Papyrological Navigator: https://papyri.info/search

SB
Sammelbuch griechischer Urkunden aus Ägypten, 30 vols., 1915–

TM
Trismegistos: https://www.trismegistos.org

TM Arch
Trismegistos Archives: https://www.trismegistos.org/arch/

TM Geo
Trismegistos Places: https://www.trismegistos.org/geo/

TM Nam
Trismegistos People (Names): https://www.trismegistos.org/ref/

WB
Wörterbuch der griechischen Papyrusurkunden, mit Einschluss der griechischen Inschriften, Aufschriften, Ostraka, Mumienschilder usw. aus Ägypten, 4 vols., 3 suppl., 1925–

Journals and Encyclopedias Abbreviated in the Bibliography

AnPap
Analecta Papyrologica, 1989–
APF
Archiv für Papyrusforschung und verwandte Gebiete, 1901–
BASP
The Bulletin of the American Society of Papyrologists, 1963–
BCPS
Bulletin of the Center of Papyrological Studies, 1985–
BIFAO
Bulletin de l'Institut Français d'Archéologie Orientale du Caire, 1901–
CdÉ
Chronique d'Égypte: Bulletin périodique de la Fondation Égyptologique Reine Élisabeth, 1925–
CE
A. S. Atiya (ed.), *The Coptic Encyclopedia*, 8 vols., New York 1991.
EAH
R. S. Bagnall, K. Brodersen, C. B. Champion, A. Erskine, and S. R. Huebner (eds.), *The Encyclopedia of Ancient History*, 13 vols., 2013.
GRBS
Greek, Roman, and Byzantine Studies, 1958–
JHS
The Journal of Hellenic Studies, 1880–
JJP
The Journal of Juristic Papyrology, 1946–
JLA
Journal of Late Antiquity, 2008–
JRS
The Journal of Roman Studies, 1911–
ODLA
O. Nicholson (ed.), *The Oxford Dictionary of Late Antiquity*, 2 vols., Oxford 2018.
RÉG
Revue des Études Grecques, 1888–
Tyche
Tyche: Beiträge zur Alten Geschichte, Papyrologie und Epigraphik, 1986–
ZPE
Zeitschrift für Papyrologie und Epigraphik, 1967–

Bibliography

Contributions in papyrological volumes are generally cited according to the *Checklist of Editions*; see the Ancient Sources above. Selected scholarly works appear under their papyrological abbreviations when their editions are quoted or referred to, but are otherwise generally cited as monographs to acknowledge their extensive introductions (cf. Keenan 2009, 187); this applies to Fournet 1999 (*P.Aphrod.Lit.*), Gagos & van Minnen 1994 (*P.Aphrod.Mich.*), and Zuckerman 2004a (*P.Aphrod.Reg.*). The numerous articles collected in Gascou 2008 are cited in the form of their original publication for the sake of clarity, but since these articles were (sometimes critically) revised in Gascou 2008, a reference to the latter has been added in each case. As I learned immediately before this book went to press, Vanderheyden 2015 will be published in revised form as *P.Aphrod.Let.Copt.* I (see the Ancient Sources above); while the text of the original dissertation has been significantly revised, the numbers of the edited documents remain identical.

Actes 1978
(no eds. given) *Actes du XV*e *Congrès International de Papyrologie, Brussels, 29 August–3 September 1977*, Brussels 1978.

Aish 2013
S. D. A. Aish "Two orders of olive-oil delivery," *BCPS* 30 (2013) 23–28.

Allen 2013
P. Allen, "Religious conflict between Antioch and Alexandria c. 565–630 CE," in: W. Mayer and B. Neil (eds.), *Religious Conflict from Early Christianity to the Rise of Islam*, Berlin 2013, 187–199.

Alston 2002
R. Alston, *The City in Roman and Byzantine Egypt*, London 2002.

Amelotti & Migliardi Zingale 1985
M. Amelotti and L. Migliardi Zingale, *Le costituzioni giustinianee nei pariri e nelle epigrafi*, 2nd ed., Milan 1985.

Ando 2017a
C. Ando, "Introduction: States and state power in Antiquity," in: Ando & Richardson 2017, 1–16.

Ando 2017b
C. Ando, "The ambitions of government: Territoriality and infrastructural power in ancient Rome," in: Ando & Richardson 2017, 115–148.

Ando & Richardson 2017
C. Ando and S. Richardson (eds.), *Ancient States and Infrastructural Power*, Philadelphia 2017.

Appl 2012
M. Appl, "*Anazetesis* und *parastasis* anhand der Dokumentation zu den Nyktostrategen," in: Schubert 2012, 49–54.

Atti 1966
(no eds. given) *Atti dell'XI Congresso Internazionale di Papirologia, Milano, 2–8 settembre 1965*, Milan 1966.

Ayaita 2016
J. J. Ayaita, *Justinian und das Volk im Nikaaufstand*, doctoral dissertation, Heidelberg 2016.

Azzarello 1998
G. Azzarello, "Einbruchsanzeige an einen *procurator*," *Tyche* 13 (1998) 20–27.

Azzarello 2006
G. Azzarello, "*P.Oxy.* XVI 2039 e la nascita della *domus gloriosa* degli Apioni," *ZPE* 155 (2006) 207–228.

Azzarello 2012
G. Azzarello, *Il dossier della* domus divina *in Egitto*, Berlin 2012.
Azzarello 2013
G. Azzarello, "'Distretti' nell'Oxyrhynchites del VII sec.? *P.Mert.* II 98 rivisitato," *APF* 59/2 (2013) 401–405.
Azzarello 2015
G. Azzarello, "Auf der Suche nach verborgenen Quellen: Zur Rekonstruktion des Dossiers der Apionenfamilie," in: R. Lafer and K. Strobel (eds.), *Antike Lebenswelten: Althistorische und papyrologische Studien*, Berlin 2015, 353–359.
Azzarello 2019
G. Azzarello, Review of McConnell 2017, *BASP* 56 (2019) 342–349.
Azzarello forthcoming
G. Azzarello (ed.), *Power and Wealth in Late Antique Egypt: The Apiones and Other Aristocratic Houses*, Berlin, forthcoming.

Bagnall 1989
R. S. Bagnall, "Official and private violence in Roman Egypt," *BASP* 26 (1989) 201–216.
Bagnall 1992
R. S. Bagnall, "Landholding in late Roman Egypt: The distribution of wealth," *JRS* 82 (1992) 128–149.
Bagnall 1993
R. S. Bagnall, *Egypt in Late Antiquity*, Princeton 1993.
Bagnall 1995
R. S. Bagnall, "Women, law, and social realities in late antiquity: A review article," *BASP* 32 (1995) 65–86.
Bagnall 2003
R. S. Bagnall, "Periodizing when you don't have to: The concept of Late Antiquity in Egypt," in: B. Sirks (ed.), *Gab es eine Spätantike? Vier Vorträge, gehalten auf der Tagung des Graduiertenkollegs für Antike und Europäische Rechtsgeschichte am 21. Juni 2002*, Frankfurt am Main 2003, 39–47.
Bagnall 2007
R. S. Bagnall (ed.), *Egypt in the Byzantine World 300–700*, Cambridge 2007.
Bagnall 2008
R. S. Bagnall, "Village landholding at Aphrodito in comparative perspective," in: Fournet 2008a, 181–190.
Bagnall 2009a
R. S. Bagnall, *Early Christian Books in Egypt*, Princeton 2009.
Bagnall 2009b
R. S. Bagnall (Hg.), *The Oxford Handbook of Papyrology*, Oxford 2009.
Bagnall 2009c
R. S. Bagnall, "Practical help: Chronology, geography, measures, currency, names, prosopography, and technical vocabulary," in: Bagnall 2009b, 179–196.
Bagnall 2011
R. S. Bagnall, *Everyday Writing in the Graeco-Roman East*, Berkeley 2011.
Bagnall 2020
R. S. Bagnall, *Reading Papyri, Writing Ancient History*, 2nd ed., New York 2020.
Bagnall 2021
R. S. Bagnall (ed.), *Roman Egypt: A History*, Cambridge 2021.

Bagnall & Tallet 2015
R. S. Bagnall and G. Tallet, "Ostraca from Hibis in the Metropolitan Museum of Art and the archaeology of the city of Hibis," *ZPE* 196 (2015) 175–198.
Bagnall & Worp 1980
R. S. Bagnall and K. A. Worp, "Papyrus documentation in Egypt from Constantine to Justinian," in: R. Pintaudi (ed.), *Miscellanea Papyrologica*, Florence 1980, 13–23.
Bagnall & Worp 1985
R. S. Bagnall and K. A. Worp, "Two nominations of goldsmiths to collect taxes," *ZPE* 59 (1985) 67–70.
Banaji 1999
J. Banaji, "Agrarian history and the labour organisation of Byzantine large estates," in: A. K. Bowman and E. Rogan (eds.), *Agriculture in Egypt from Pharaonic to Modern Times*, Oxford 1999, 193–216.
Banaji 2000
J. Banaji, "State and aristocracy in the economic evolution of the late empire," in: E. Lo Cascio and D. W. Rathbone (eds.), *Production and Public Powers in Classical Antiquity*, Cambridge 2000, 92–99.
Banaji 2007
J. Banaji, *Agrarian Change in Late Antiquity: Gold, Labour, and Aristocratic Dominance*, 2nd ed., Oxford 2007.
Bang 2015
P. F. Bang, "Tributary empires and the New Fiscal Sociology: Some comparative reflections," in: Monson & Scheidel 2015, 537–556.
Beaucamp 1990
J. Beaucamp, *Le statut de la femme à Byzance (4e–7e siècle)*, vol. I: *Le droit impérial*, Paris 1990.
Beaucamp 1992
J. Beaucamp, *Le statut de la femme à Byzance (4e–7e siècle)*, vol. II: *Les pratiques sociales*, Paris 1992.
Beck et al. 2008a
H. Beck, P. Scholz, and U. Walter (eds.), *Die Macht der Wenigen: Aristokratische Herrschaftspraxis, Kommunikation und "edler" Lebensstil in Antike und Früher Neuzeit*, München 2008.
Beck et al. 2008b
H. Beck, P. Scholz, and U. Walter, "Einführung: Begriffe, Fragen und Konzepte," in: Beck et al. 2008a, 1–13.
Begass 2012
Ch. Begass, "Bemerkungen zum spätantiken Rangtitel ὑπερφυέστατος in den Papyri," *ZPE* 180 (2012) 279–286.
Begass 2016
Ch. Begass, "Property and power of the senatorial aristocracy of the Eastern Roman Empire in the fifth and sixth centuries," *JLA* 9/2 (2016) 462–482.
Begass 2018
Ch. Begass, *Die Senatsaristokratie des oströmischen Reiches, ca. 457–518: Prosopographische und sozialgeschichtliche Untersuchungen*, München 2018.
Bell 1908
H. I. Bell, "The Aphrodito papyri," *JHS* 28 (1908) 97–120.
Bell 1917
H. I. Bell, "The Byzantine servile state," *The Journal of Egyptian Archaeology* 4 (1917) 86–106.

Bell 1944
H. I. Bell, "An Egyptian village in the age of Justinian," *JHS* 64 (1944) 21–36.
Bell 1948
H. I. Bell, *Egypt from Alexander to the Arab Conquest: A Study in the Diffusion and Decay of Hellenism*, Oxford 1948.
Bell 2013
P. Bell, *Social Conflict in the Age of Justinian: Its Nature, Management, and Mediation*, Oxford 2013.
Benaissa 2007
A. Benaissa, "An estate overseer's work contract and the meaning of *exotikoi topoi*," *BASP* 44 (2007) 75–86.
Benaissa 2008
A. Benaissa, "Two bishops named Senuthes: Prosopography and new texts," *ZPE* 166 (2008) 179–194.
Benaissa 2009
A. Benaissa, "Receipt for a gratuity to a *cancellarius*," *APF* 55/1 (2009) 56–62.
Benaissa 2010
A. Benaissa, "Korr. Tyche 643," *Tyche* 25 (2010) 208.
Benaissa 2012
A. Benaissa, "Miscellanea toponomastica," *ZPE* 183 (2012) 191–196.
Benaissa 2015
A. Benaissa, "Korr. Tyche 767," *Tyche* 30 (2015) 211–212.
Benaissa 2020
A. Benaissa, "*P.Oxy.* LXXVII 5123 and the economic relations between the Apion estate and its *coloni adscripticii*," *JJP* 50 (2020) 49–66.
Benaissa 2021
A. Benaissa, *Rural Settlements of the Oxyrhynchite Nome: A Papyrological Survey*, 3rd ed., 2021, Trismegistos Online Publications IV: https://www.trismegistos.org/top/
Benaissa 2022
A. Benaissa, "Late antique papyri from Hermopolis in the British Library III," *ZPE* 223 (2022) 161–182.
Berkes 2014
L. Berkes, "Eine oxyrhynchitische Enthaftungsbürgschaft aus dem 7. Jh.," *JJP* 44 (2014) 71–81.
Berkes 2015
L. Berkes, "An estate prison in Byzantine Egypt: *PSI* VII 824 reconsidered," *ZPE* 193 (2015) 241–243.
Berkes 2016
L. Berkes, Review of Mikhail 2014, *The Journal of Ecclesiastical History* 67 (2016) 390–392.
Berkes 2017a
L. Berkes, *Dorfverwaltung und Dorfgemeinschaft in Ägypten von Diokletian zu den Abbasiden*, Wiesbaden 2017.
Berkes 2017b
L. Berkes, "Korr. Tyche 834," *Tyche* 32 (2017) 252.
Berkes & Haug 2016
L. Berkes and B. Haug, "Villages, requisitions, and tax districts: Two Greek lists from the eighth-century Fayyūm," *BASP* 53 (2016) 189–222.
Berkes & Mihálykó 2019
L. Berkes and Á. Mihálykó, "A Greek acclamation in praise of an *illustris* from seventh-century Egypt: P.Berol.inv. 5603 reconsidered," *GRBS* 59 (2019) 295–310.

Bianchini 1984
M. Bianchini, "L'imperatore Costantino e una certa Agrippina: Riflessioni su *C.Th.* 8.15.1," in: V. Giuffre (ed.), Sodalitas: *Scritti in onore di Antonio Guarino*, 9 vols., Napoli 1984, 1191–1206.
Bjornlie 2007
M. S. Bjornlie, Review of Sarris 2006, *Bryn Mawr Classical Review* 2007.06.04: https://bmcr.brynmawr.edu/2007/2007-06-04.html
Bogaert 1997
R. Bogaert, "La banque en Égypte byzantine," *ZPE* 116 (1997) 85–140.
Bonney 1999
R. Bonney, "Introduction: The rise of the fiscal state in Europe, c. 1200–1815," in: R. Bonney (ed.), *The Rise of the Fiscal State in Europe, c. 1200–1815,* Oxford 1999, 1–17.
Booth 2022
Ph. Booth, "Egypt under the Sasanians (619–29): 'Stability, continuity, and tolerance'?," in: Ph. Booth and M. Whitby (eds.), *Mélanges James Howard-Johnston*, Paris 2022, 233–258.
Börm 2010
H. Börm, "Herrscher und Eliten in der Spätantike," in: H. Börm and J. Wiesehöfer (eds.), Commutatio et contentio*: Studies in the Late Roman, Sasanian, and Early Islamic Near East*, Düsseldorf 2010, 159–198.
Bowman 1971
A. K. Bowman, *The Town Councils of Roman Egypt*, Toronto 1971.
Bowman 1986
A. K. Bowman, *Egypt after the Pharaohs*, Berkeley 1986.
Bowman 2008
A. K. Bowman, "Oxyrhynchos in the early fourth century: 'Municipalization' and prosperity," *BASP* 45 (2008) 31–40.
Brandes 2002
W. Brandes, *Finanzverwaltung in Krisenzeiten: Untersuchungen zur byzantinischen Administration im 6.–9. Jahrhundert*, Frankfurt am Main 2002.
Bransbourg 2015
G. Bransbourg, "The later Roman Empire," in: Monson & Scheidel 2015, 258–281.
Bransbourg 2016
G. Bransbourg, "Capital in the sixth century: The dynamics of tax and estate in Roman Egypt," *JLA* 9/2 (2016) 305–414.
Breytenbach & Zimmermann 2018
C. Breytenbach and Ch. Zimmermann, *Early Christianity in Lycaonia and Adjacent Areas: From Paul to Amphilochius of Iconium*, Leiden 2018.
Brown 1991
R. Brown, "The value of 'narrativity' in the appraisal of historical documents: Foundation for a theory of archival hermeneutics," *Archivaria* 32 (1991) 152–156.
Bryen 2013
A. Z. Bryen, *Violence in Roman Egypt: A Study in Legal Interpretation*, Philadelphia 2013.
Bülow-Jacobsen 2013
A. Bülow-Jacobsen, "Communication, travel, and transportation in Egypt's Eastern Desert during Roman times (1st to 3rd century AD)," in: F. Förster and H. Riemer (eds.), *Desert Road Archaeology in Ancient Egypt and Beyond*, Cologne 2013, 557–574.

Carrié 1981
J.-M. Carrié, "L'Égypte au IVe siècle: Fiscalité, économie, société," in: R. S. Bagnall, G. M. Browne, A. E. Hanson, and L. Koenen (eds.), *Proceedings of the Sixteenth International Congress of Papyrology, New York, 24–31 July 1980*, Chico 1981, 431–446.
Carrié 1999
J.-M. Carrié, "Économie et société de l'Égypte romano-byzantine (IVe–VIIe siècle): À propos de quelques publications récentes," *Antiquité Tardive* 7 (1999) 331–352.
Cassia 2009
M. Cassia, "Πάγοι e κῶμαι nell'Helenoponto: La lettera basiliana a Candidiano," in: M. Cassia (ed.), *La piaga e la cura: Poveri e ammalati, medici e monaci nell'Anatolia rurale tardoantica*, Rome 2009, 75–97.
Clackson 2010
S. J. Clackson, "Coptic or Greek? Bilinguism in the Papyri," in: A. Papaconstantinou (ed.), *The Multilingual Experience in Egypt from the Ptolemies to the Abbasids*, Burlington 2010, 73–104.
Clarysse & Vandorpe 1997
W. Clarysse and K. Vandorpe, "Viticulture and wine consumption in the Arsinoite nome (*P.Köln* V 221)," *Ancient Society* 28 (1997) 67–73.
Connor et al. 2024
A. J. Connor, J. H. F. Dijkstra, and F. A. J. Hoogendijk (eds.), *Unending Variety: Papyrological Texts and Studies in Honour of Peter van Minnen*, Leiden 2024.
Cooper 2007
K. Cooper, "Closely watched households: Visibility, exposure and private power in the Roman *domus*," *Past & Present* 197/1 (2007) 3–33.
Corcoran 1996
S. Corcoran, *The Empire of the Tetrarchs: Imperial Pronouncements and Government A.D. 284–326*, Oxford 1996.
Crawford 1978
D. J. Crawford, "The Good Official of Ptolemaic Egypt," in: H. Maehler and V. M. Strocka (eds.), *Das ptolemäische Ägypten: Akten des internationalen Symposions 27.–29. September 1976 in Berlin*, Mainz 1978, 195–202.
Cromwell 2017
J. A. Cromwell, *Recording Village Life: A Coptic Scribe in Early Islamic Egypt*, Ann Arbor 2017.

Dagron 1979
G. Dagron, "Entre village et cité: La bourgade rurale des IVe–VIIe siècles en Orient," Κοινωνία 3 (1979) 29–52.
Danielewicz 2022
J. Danielewicz, "ΙΝΔΙΚΤΙΩΝ in editions of papyri and inscriptions: A philologist's comment on the spelling and declension of the term," *JJP* 52 (2022) 209–215.
Davis 1987
N. Z. Davis, *Fiction in the Archives: Pardon Tales and Their Tellers in Sixteenth-Century France*, Stanford 1987.
Delmaire 1988
R. Delmaire, "Le personnel de l'administration financière en Égypte sous le Bas-Empire Romain (IV–VI siècles)," *Cahier de Recherches de l'Institut de Papyrologie et d'Égyptologie de Lille* 10 (1988) 113–138.
Derda 2006
T. Derda, *Ἀρσινοίτης νομός: Administration of the Fayum under Roman Rule*, Warsaw 2006.

Derda et al. 2016
T. Derda, A. Łajtar, and J. Urbanik (eds.), *Proceedings of the 27th International Congress of Papyrology, Warsaw, 29 July–3 August 2013*, 3 vols., Warsaw 2016.
Diethart 1980
J. M. Diethart, *Prosopographia Arsinoitica I: s. VI–VIII*, Vienna 1980.
Diethart & Worp 1986
J. M. Diethart and K. A. Worp, *Notarsunterschriften im byzantinischen Ägypten*, 2 vols., Vienna 1986.
Dijkstra 2004
J. H. F. Dijkstra, "A cult of Isis at Philae after Justinian? Reconsidering *P.Cair.Masp.* I 67004," *ZPE* 146 (2004) 137–154.
Dijkstra 2007
J. H. F. Dijkstra, "'Une foule immense de moines': The Coptic *Life of Aaron* and the early bishops of Philae," in: Palme 2007a, 191–197.
Dijkstra 2008
J. H. F. Dijkstra, *Philae and the End of Ancient Egyptian Religion: A Regional Study of Religious Transformation 298–642 CE*, Leuven 2008.
Dijkstra & van der Vliet 2020
J. H. F. Dijkstra and J. van der Vliet, *The Coptic Life of Aaron: Critical Edition, Translation and Commentary*, Leiden 2020.
Dijkstra & Worp 2006
J. H. F. Dijkstra and K. A. Worp, "The administrative position of Omboi and Syene in late antiquity," *ZPE* 155 (2006) 183–187.
Di Segni 2011
L. Di Segni, "Epigraphic finds reveal new chapters in the history of the Church of the Holy Sepulchre in the 6th century," in: K. Galor and G. Avni (eds.), *Unearthing Jerusalem: 150 Years of Archaeological Research in the Holy City*, Winona Lake 2011, 351–360.
Dossey 2010
L. Dossey, *Peasant and Empire in Christian North Africa*, Berkeley 2010.
Drake 2006
H. A. Drake (ed.), *Violence in Late Antiquity: Perceptions and Practices*, Aldershot 2006.
Drecoll 1997
C. Drecoll, *Die Liturgien im römischen Kaiserreich des 3. und 4. Jh. n. Chr.: Untersuchung über Zugang, Inhalt und wirtschaftliche Bedeutung der öffentlichen Zwangsdienste in Ägypten und anderen Provinzen*, Stuttgart 1997.
Droß-Krüpe 2023
K. Droß-Krüpe, "Not paying taxes in Roman Egypt," in: K. Schönhärl, G. Hürlimann, and D. Rohde (eds.), *Histories of Tax Evasion, Avoidance and Resistance*, New York 2023, 71–83.
Durliat 1990
J. Durliat, *Les finances publiques de Dioclétien aux Carolingiens (284–889)*, Sigmaringen 1990.

Eich 2015
P. Eich, "The common denominator: Late Roman imperial bureaucracy from a comparative perspective," in: W. Scheidel (ed.), *State Power in Ancient China and Rome*, Oxford 2015, 90–149.
Eller 2022
A. Eller, *Nomes et toparchies en Égypte gréco-romaine: Réalités administratives et géographie religieuse d'Éléphantine à Memphis*, Cairo 2022.

Feissel 2003
D. Feissel, "Bulletin épigraphique 580," *RÉG* 116 (2003) 668.
Feissel & Gascou 2004
D. Feissel and J. Gascou (eds.), *La pétition à Byzance*, Paris 2004.
Fikhman 1974
I. F. Fikhman, "Kurienland in Oxyrhynchos?" in: W. Müller (ed.), *Festschrift zum 150-jährigen Bestehen des Berliner Ägyptischen Museums*, Berlin 1974, 343–346, now in: Jördens 2006, 106–109.
Fikhman 1976
И. Ф. Фихман, *Оксиринх: город папирусов*, Moscow 1976.
Fikhman 1978
I. F. Fikhman, "Les 'patrocinia' dans les papyrus d'Oxyrhynchus," in: *Actes* 1978, 186–194; now in: Jördens 2006, 152–160.
Fisher & van Wees 2015
N. Fisher and H. van Wees, "The trouble with 'aristocracy,'" in: N. Fisher and H. van Wees (eds.), *"Aristocracy" in Antiquity: Redefining Greek and Roman Elites*, Swansea 2015, 1–57.
Förster 2002
H. Förster, *Wörterbuch der griechischen Wörter in den koptischen dokumentarischen Texten*, Berlin 2002.
Foss 2003
C. Foss, "The Persians in the Roman near East (602–630 AD)," *Journal of the Royal Asiatic Society* 13/2 (2003) 149–170.
Fournet 1992
J.-L. Fournet, "Appendice sur le nom d'Ἀφροδίτης κώμη," *RÉG* 105 (1992) 235–236.
Fournet 1993
J.-L. Fournet, "À propos de *SB* XIV 11856 ou Quand la poésie rencontre le document," *BIFAO* 93 (1993) 223–235.
Fournet 1999
J.-L. Fournet, *Hellénisme dans l'Égypte du VIe siècle: La bibliothèque et l'œuvre de Dioscore d'Aphrodité*, 2 vols., Cairo 1999.
Fournet 2000
J.-L. Fournet, "Le système des intermédiaires dans les reçus fiscaux byzantins et ses implications chronologiques sur le dossier de Dioscore d'Aphrodité," *APF* 46/2 (2000) 233–247.
Fournet 2001
J.-L. Fournet, "Du nouveau dans les archives de Dioscore d'Aphrodité," in: I. Andorlini, G. Bastianini, M. Manfredi, and G. Menci (eds.), *Atti del XXII Congresso Internazionale di Papirologia, Firenze, 23–29 agosto 1998*, Florence 2001, 475–485.
Fournet 2004
J.-L. Fournet, "Entre document et littérature: La pétition dans l'Antiquité tardive," in: Feissel & Gascou 2004, 61–74.
Fournet 2008a
J.-L. Fournet (ed.), *Les archives de Dioscore d'Aphrodité cent ans après leur découverte: Histoire et culture dans l'Égypte byzantine, Actes du colloque de Strasbourg, 8–10 décembre 2005*, Paris 2008.
Fournet 2008b
J.-L. Fournet, "Archive ou archives de Dioscore? Les dernières années des 'archives de Dioscore,'" in: Fournet 2008a, 17–30.
Fournet 2008c
J.-L. Fournet, "Liste des papyrus édités de l'Aphrodité byzantine," in: Fournet 2008a, 307–343.

Fournet 2008d
J.-L. Fournet, "Les papyrus des archives de Dioscore à Strasbourg," in: Fournet 2008a, 285–306.
Fournet 2009
J.-L. Fournet, "The multilingual environment of late antique Egypt: Greek, Latin, Coptic, and Persian documentation," in: Bagnall 2009b, 418–451.
Fournet 2015
J.-L. Fournet, "Des villageois en quête de lettres officielles: Le cas des pétitionnaires d'Aphrodité (Égypte, VIe s. ap. J.-C.)," in: Procházka et al. 2015, 255–266.
Fournet 2016
J.-L. Fournet, "Sur les premiers documents juridiques coptes (2): Les archives de Phoibammôn et de Kollouthos," in: A. Boud'hors and C. Louis (eds.), *Études coptes XIV: Seizième journée d'études, Genève, 19–21 juin 2013*, Paris 2016, 115–141.
Fournet 2018
J.-L. Fournet, "Les Égyptiens à la capitale ou Quand la papyrologie s'invite à Constantinople: Édition comparée des *P.Cair.Masp.* I 67024–67025," in: C. Morrisson and J.-P. Sodini (eds.), *Constantinople réelle et imaginaire: Autour de l'œuvre de Gilbert Dagron*, Paris 2018, 595–633.
Fournet 2020a
J.-L. Fournet, *The Rise of Coptic: Egyptian versus Greek in Late Antiquity*, Princeton 2020, 109–147.
Fournet 2020b
J.-L. Fournet, "Trois nouveaux reçus d'annone civile transportée par le monastère de la Métanoia (Égypte, VIe siècle)," *JJP* 50 (2020) 109–147.
Fournet 2024
J.-L. Fournet, "Une nouvelle paire de brouillons d'un rescrit impérial," in: Connor et al. 2024, 137–149.
Fournet & Bénazeth 2020
J.-L. Fournet & D. Bénazeth, "Quand les cuillers se mettent à parler," in: A. Boud'hors, E. Garel, C. Louis, and N. Vanthieghem (eds.), *Études coptes XVI: Dix-huitième journée d'études, Bruxelles, 22–24 juin 2017*, Paris 2020, 129–159.
Fournet & Gascou 2002
J.-L. Fournet and J. Gascou, "Moines pachômiens et batellerie," *Études alexandrines* 8 (2002) 23–45.
Fournet & Papaconstantinou 2016
J.-L. Fournet and A. Papaconstantinou (eds.), *Mélanges Jean Gascou: Textes et études papyrologiques*, Paris 2016.

Gad 2016
U. A. Gad, "Who was who in the aristocracy of Byzantine Oxyrhynchos," in: Derda et al. 2016, 1787–1799.
Gagos 2008
T. Gagos, "*Compromissum*," *BASP* 45 (2008) 59–67.
Garel & Vanthieghem 2022
E. Garel and N. Vanthieghem, "Nouveaux textes sur les pagarques du Fayoum au VIIIe siècle," in: L. Berkes (ed.), *Christians and Muslims in Early Islamic Egypt*, Ann Arbor 2022, 87–125.
Garosi 2022
E. Garosi, *Projecting a New Empire: Formats, Social Meaning, and Mediality of Imperial Arabic in the Umayyad and Early Abbasid Periods*, Berlin 2022.

Gascou 1972a
J. Gascou, "La détention collégiale de l'autorité pagarchique dans l'Égypte byzantine," *Byzantion* 42 (1972) 60–72; rev. ed. "La pagarchie collégiale en Égypte byzantine," in: Gascou 2008, 43–50.
Gascou 1972b
J. Gascou, "Notes critiques sur quelques papyrus des Ve et VIe siècles," *CdÉ* 47/93–94 (1972) 243–253.
Gascou 1976
J. Gascou, "P.Fouad 87: Les monastères pachômiens et l'état byzantin," *BIFAO* 76 (1976) 157–185.
Gascou 1983
J. Gascou, "De Byzance à l'Islam: Les impôts en Égypte après la conquête arabe," *Jesho* 26 (1983) 97–109; rev. ed. in: Gascou 2008, 99–112.
Gascou 1985
J. Gascou, "Les grands domaines, la cité et l'état en Égypte byzantine: Recherches d'histoire agraire, fiscale et administrative," *Travaux et Mémoires* 9 (1985) 1–90; rev. ed. in: Gascou 2008, 125–213.
Gascou 1986
J. Gascou, "Comptabilités fiscales hermopolites du début du VIIe siècle," *Tyche* 1 (1986) 97–117; rev. ed. in: Gascou 2008, 223–245.
Gascou 1987
J. Gascou, "Le Cadastre d'Aphroditô (*SB* XX 14669)," *Travaux et Mémoires* 10 (1987) 103–158; rev. ed. in: Gascou 2008, 247–305.
Gascou 1992
J. Gascou, Review of Palme 1989, *Jahrbuch der Österreichischen Byzantinistik* 42 (1992) 352–354.
Gascou 1996
J. Gascou, Review of Bagnall 1993, *Topoi* 6 (1996) 333–349; rev. ed. in: Gascou 2008, 401–415.
Gascou 2004
J. Gascou, "Les pétitions privées," in: Feissel & Gascou 2004, 93–103; rev. ed. in: Gascou 2008, 441–451.
Gascou 2008
J. Gascou (ed.), *Fiscalité et société en Égypte byzantine*, Paris 2008.
Gascou 2009
J. Gascou, "The papyrology of the Near East," in: Bagnall 2009b, 473–494.
Gascou 2014
J. Gascou, "Deux mandats d'amener byzantins (P.Sorb. inv. 2743 r° et v°)," *CdÉ* 89/177 (2014) 131–141.
Gascou 2023
J. Gascou, "Στιππίον κογχισθέν (*P.Yale* IV 186) et le commerce linier dans l'Égypte tardive, II: Aspects de l'économie linière à l'époque tardive," *CdÉ* 98/195–196 (2023) 252–312.
Gascou & Gonis 2022
J. Gascou and N. Gonis, "Six receipts from the *demosion logisterion* of Hermopolis," *APF* 68/1 (2022) 146–162.
Gelzer 1909
M. Gelzer, *Studien zur byzantinischen Verwaltung Ägyptens*, Leipzig 1909.
Gelzer 1913a
M. Gelzer, "Zum αὐτόπρακτον σχῆμα der P. Aphrodito Cairo," *APF* 5 (1913) 188–189.

Gelzer 1913b
M. Gelzer, "Altes und Neues aus der byzantinisch-ägyptischen Verwaltungsmisere, vornehmlich im Zeitalter Justinians," *APF* 5 (1913) 346–377.
Geraci 1979
G. Geraci, "Per una storia dell'amministrazione fiscale nell'Egitto del VI sc. d. C.: Dioskoros e l'autopragia di Aphrodito," in: *Actes* 1978, 195–205.
Giacometti 2019
D. Giacometti, "Reuniting the dossier of Flavius Demetrios, an aristocrat and landowner in late antique Hermopolite [*sic*]," *APF* 65/2 (2019) 357–363.
Giardina 1989
A. Giardina, "Egitto bizantino o tardoantico? Problemi della terminologia e della periodizzazione," in: L. Criscuolo and G. Geraci (eds.), *Egitto e storia antica dall'ellenismo all'età araba: Bilancio di un confronto*, Bologna 1989, 89–103.
Gonis 1998
N. Gonis, "Korr. Tyche 252," *Tyche* 13 (1998) 260.
Gonis 2000a
N. Gonis, "A *symmachos* on mission and his paymaster: *P.Herm.* 80 enlarged," *ZPE* 132 (2000) 181–183.
Gonis 2000b
N. Gonis, "Korr. Tyche 368: The acting *logistes* Hermogenes again?," *Tyche* 15 (2000) 200.
Gonis 2002a
N. Gonis, "Studies on the aristocracy of late antique Oxyrhynchos," *Tyche* 17 (2002) 85–97.
Gonis 2002b
N. Gonis, "*P.Oxy.* XVI 1979 *desc.*: Deed of surety," *JJP* 32 (2002) 29–34.
Gonis 2004
N. Gonis, "Another look at some officials in early 'Abbāsid Egypt," *ZPE* 149 (2004) 189–195.
Gonis 2005
N. Gonis, "Prosopographica," *APF* 51/1 (2005) 87–94.
Gonis 2007a
N. Gonis, "Recent news from Flavius Magistor & sons," *JJP* 37 (2007) 125–133.
Gonis 2007b
N. Gonis, "Notes on miscellaneous documents III," *ZPE* 159 (2007) 267–272.
Gonis 2008
N. Gonis, "Notes on the aristocracy of Byzantine Fayum," *ZPE* 166 (2008) 203–210.
Gonis 2009
N. Gonis, "Prosopographica II," *APF* 55/1 (2009) 90–95.
Gonis 2015a
N. Gonis, "Seventeen Beinecke papyri," *APF* 61/2 (2015) 323–351.
Gonis 2015b
N. Gonis, "Korr. Tyche 793," *Tyche* 30 (2015) 225.
Gonis 2016
N. Gonis, "Payments to *bucellarii* in seventh-century Oxyrhynchus," in: Fournet & Papaconstantinou 2016, 175–192.
Gonis 2019a
N. Gonis, "Prosopographica III," *APF* 65/2 (2019) 348–356.
Gonis 2019b
N. Gonis, "Notes on personal names and abbreviations in late Arsinoite and Heracleopolite documents," *CdÉ* 94/187 (2019) 188–205.

Gonis 2021
N. Gonis, "Prosopographica IV," *APF* 67/1 (2021) 90–101.
Gonis 2022
N. Gonis, "A view of Arcadia in the seventh century," *Tyche* 37 (2022) 109–112.
Gonis 2024
N. Gonis, "Abbreviations in late documents resolved III," *APF* 70/1 (2024) 141–149.
Grey 2011
C. Grey, *Constructing Communities in the Late Roman Countryside*, Cambridge 2011.
Griffith 2016
S. H. Griffith, "The Manṣūr family and Saint John of Damascus: Christians and Muslims in Umayyad times," in: A. Borrut and F. M. Donner (eds.), *Christians and Others in the Ummayyad State*, Chicago 2016, 29–51.
Grohmann 1964
A. Grohmann, "Der Beamtenstab der arabischen Finanzverwaltung in Ägypten in früharabischer Zeit," in: H. Braunert (ed.), *Studien zur Papyrologie und antiken Wirtschaftsgeschichte*, Bonn 1964, 120–134.
Grubbs 2002
J. E. Grubbs, *Women and the Law in the Roman Empire: A Sourcebook on Marriage, Divorce, and Widowhood*, London 2002.
Guilland 1967
R. Guilland, *Recherches sur les institutions byzantines*, 2 vols., Berlin 1967.

Haarer 2022
F. K. Haarer, *Justinian: Empire and Society in the Sixth Century*, Edinburgh 2022.
Habermann 1998
W. Habermann, "Zur chronologischen Verteilung der papyrologischen Zeugnisse," *ZPE* 122 (1998) 144–160.
Haensch 2013
R. Haensch, "Die Statthalterarchive der Spätantike," in: M. Faraguna (ed.), *Archives and Archival Documents in Ancient Societies*, Trieste 2013, 333–349.
Hagedorn 2005
D. Hagedorn, "Bemerkungen zu Urkunden," *ZPE* 151 (2005) 127–132.
Haldon 2004
J. F. Haldon, "The fate of the late Roman senatorial elite: Extinction or transformation," in: J. Haldon and L. I. Conrad (eds.), *The Byzantine and Early Islamic Near East VI: Elites Old and New in the Byzantine and Early Islamic Near East*, Princeton 2004, 179–234.
Haldon 2005
J. F. Haldon, "Economy and administration: How did the empire work?" in: Maas 2005, 28–59.
Hall & Schroeder 2006
J. A. Hall and R. Schroeder (eds.), *An Anatomy of Power: The Social Theory of Michael Mann*, Cambridge 2006.
Hardy 1931
E. R. Hardy, *The Large Estates of Byzantine Egypt*, New York 1931.
Harrauer & Pintaudi 2012
H. Harrauer and R. Pintaudi, "Due ordini di pagamento in denaro dall''Archivio' degli Apioni (?) (PL III/721; PL III/449)," *AnPap* 23–24 (2011–2012) 137–142.
Harries 2001
J. D. Harries, "Resolving disputes: The frontiers of law in late antiquity," in: R. W. Mathisen (ed.), *Law, Society, and Authority in Late Antiquity*, Oxford 2001, 68–82.

Henner 2000
J. Henner, *Fragmenta Liturgica Coptica: Editionen und Kommentar liturgischer Texte der Koptischen Kirche des ersten Jahrtausends*, Tübingen 2000.
Heinen 1991
H. Heinen, "Taxation in Roman Egypt," *CE* VII, 2002–2007.
Heisler 1984
R. J. Heisler, "Coptic documents from the Michigan collection," *ZPE* 57 (1984) 125–129.
Hickey 1998
T. M. Hickey, "Notes on some Cairo papyri from Byzantine Oxyrhynchus," *ZPE* 123 (1998) 161–164.
Hickey 2007
T. M. Hickey, "Aristocratic landholding and the economy of Byzantine Egypt," in: Bagnall 2007, 288–308.
Hickey 2008
T. M. Hickey, "An inconvenient truth? *P.Oxy.* 18.2196 verso, the Apion estate, and *fiscalité* in the late antique Oxyrhynchite," *BASP* 45 (2008) 87–100.
Hickey 2012
T. M. Hickey, *Wine, Wealth, and the State in Late Antique Egypt: The House of Apion at Oxyrhynchus*, Ann Arbor 2012.
Hoogendijk 1998
F. A. J. Hoogendijk, "Der Scribo behindert die Flotte des Patricius: Ein Brief aus dem Dossier des Flavius Strategius Paneuphemos (= Pseudo-Strategius III)," in: A. M. F. W. Verhoogt and S. P. Vleeming (eds.), *The Two Faces of Graeco-Roman Egypt: Greek and Demotic and Greek-Demotic Texts and Studies*, Leiden 1998, 21–35.
Hornickel 1930
O. Hornickel, *Ehren- und Rangprädikate in den Papyrusurkunden: Ein Beitrag zum römischen und byzantinischen Titelwesen*, doctoral dissertation, Gießen 1930.
Huebner 2019
S. R. Huebner, *Papyri and the Social World of the New Testament*, Cambridge 2019.
Humphries 2019
M. Humphries, *Cities and the Meanings of Late Antiquity*, Leiden 2019.

Jesenko 2016
A. Jesenko, "Die *topoteretai* im spätantiken und früharabischen Ägypten," in: Derda et al. 2016, 1801–1823.
Johnson 1976
D. W. Johnson, "Further fragments of a Coptic *History of the Church*: Cambridge OR. 1699 R," *Enchoria*: *Zeitschrift für Demotistik und Koptologie* 6 (1976) 7–17.
Johnson & West 1949
A. C. Johnson and L. C. West, *Byzantine Egypt: Economic Studies*, Princeton 1949.
Jones 1964
A. H. M. Jones, *The Later Roman Empire 284–602: A Social, Economic, and Administrative Survey*, 3 vols., Oxford 1964.
Jördens 1992
A. Jördens, "Nachlese in Pariser Papyri," *ZPE* 90 (1992) 285–288.
Jördens 2001
A. Jördens, "Papyri und private Archive: Ein Diskussionsbeitrag zur papyrologischen Terminologie," in: E. Cantarella and G. Thür (eds.), *Symposion 1997: Vorträge zur griechischen und hellenistischen Rechtsgeschichte, Altafiumara, 8.–14. September 1997*, Cologne 2001, 253–268.

Jördens 2006
A. Jördens (ed.), *Wirtschaft und Gesellschaft im spätantiken Ägypten: Kleine Schriften Itzak F. Fikhman*, Stuttgart 2006.
Jördens 2009
A. Jördens, *Statthalterliche Verwaltung in der römischen Kaiserzeit: Studien zum* praefectus Aegypti, Stuttgart 2009.

Kaiser forthcoming
A. M. Kaiser, "Flavius Athanasius, *dux et Augustalis Thebaidis*: A case study on landholding and power in late antique Egypt," in: S. Procházka and S. Tost (eds.), *Land and Power in the Ancient and Post-Ancient World: Proceedings of the 3rd International Conference of the NFN "Imperium and Officium,"* Vienna, forthcoming.
Kaldellis 2015
A. Kaldellis, *The Byzantine Republic: People and Power in New Rome*, Cambridge 2015.
Karayannopoulos 1958
J. Karayannopoulos, *Das Finanzwesen des frühbyzantinischen Staates*, München 1958.
Keenan 1973
J. G. Keenan, "The names Flavius and Aurelius as status designations in later Roman Egypt," pt. I, *ZPE* 11 (1973) 33–63.
Keenan 1974
J. G. Keenan, "The names Flavius and Aurelius as status designations in later Roman Egypt," pt. II, *ZPE* 13 (1974) 283–304.
Keenan 1983
J. G. Keenan, "An afterthought on the names Flavius and Aurelius," *ZPE* 53 (1983) 245–250.
Keenan 1985a
J. G. Keenan, "Village shepherds and social tension in Byzantine Egypt," *Yale Classical Studies* 28 (1985) 245–259.
Keenan 1985b
J. G. Keenan, "Notes on absentee landlordism at Aphrodito," *BASP* 22 (1985) 137–169.
Keenan 1991
J. G. Keenan, "The 'New Papyrology' and ancient social history," *Ancient History Bulletin* 5 (1991) 159–169.
Keenan 1993
J. G. Keenan, "Papyrology and Byzantine historiography," *BASP* 30 (1993) 137–144.
Keenan 2001
J. G. Keenan, "'Die Binnenwanderung' in Byzantine Egypt," *GRBS* 42 (2001) 57–82.
Keenan 2007
J. G. Keenan, "Byzantine Egyptian villages," in: Bagnall 2007, 226–243.
Keenan 2008a
J. G. Keenan, Review of Zuckerman 2004a, *BASP* 42 (2005) 285–297.
Keenan 2008b
J. G. Keenan, "Tormented Voices: *P.Cair.Masp.* I 67002," in: Fournet 2008a, 171–180.
Keenan 2009
J. G. Keenan, "Egypt's 'special place,' " in: E. P. Cueva, S. N. Byrne, and F. Benda (eds.), *Jesuit Education and the Classics*, Newcastle 2009, 177–192.
Keenan 2012
J. G. Keenan, "Receipt for *embole* from Aphrodito," *BASP* 49 (2012) 147–150.
Keenan 2015
J. G. Keenan, "Payment order for cavalry fodder: *SB* XIV 12116," *ZPE* 193 (2015) 244–248.

Kelly 2004
Ch. Kelly, *Ruling the Later Roman Empire*, Cambridge 2004.
Kiser & Levi 2015
E. Kiser and M. Levi, "Interpreting the comparative history of fiscal regimes," in: Monson & Scheidel 2015, 557–571.
Koch 1903
P. Koch, *Die byzantinischen Beamtentitel von 400 bis 700*, doctoral dissertation, Jena 1903.
Kovarik 2007
S. Kovarik, "Von Zitronen, Melonen und Pfirsichen: Zum Obst- und Gartenbau im spätantiken Ägypten," *APF* 53/2 (2007) 152–181.
Kovarik 2014
S. Kovarik, *Das spätantike Notariat: Kanzleipraxis des 4.–8. Jh. n. u. Z. am Beispiel Arsinoites (Mittelägypten)*, doctoral dissertation, Vienna 2014.
Kovarik 2022
S. Kovarik, "Domänenland in Damenhand," in: B. Palme (ed.), *Halbmond über dem Nil: Wie aus dem byzantinischen das arabische Ägypten wurde*, Vienna 2022, 55–64.
Kovarik 2023a
S. Kovarik, "A generous salter and a noble landlady: Two new contracts from late antique Arsinoe in the British Library," *BASP* 60 (2023) 185–212.
Kovarik 2023b
S. Kovarik, "The evolution of the notarial signature in late antique Egypt: A diachronic comparison of the Middle Egyptian evidence (province of Arcadia: Arsinoite, Heracleopolite, Oxyrhynchite)," in: A. Ghignoli, M. Boccuzzi, A. Monte, and N. Sietis (eds.), *Segni, sogni, materie e scrittura dall'Egitto tardoantico all'Europa carolingia*, Rome 2023, 71–118.
Kovelman 1991
A. B. Kovelman, "From *logos* to myth: Egyptian petitions of the 5th–7th centuries," *BASP* 28 (1991) 135–152.
Kramer 2011
J. Kramer, *Von der Papyrologie zur Romanistik*, Berlin 2011.
Krause 1996
J.-U. Krause, *Gefängnisse im Römischen Reich*, Stuttgart 1996.
Krause & Witschel 2006
J.-U. Krause and C. Witschel (eds.), *Die Stadt in der Spätantike: Niedergang oder Wandel? Akten des internationalen Kolloquiums in München am 30. und 31. Mai 2003*, Stuttgart 2006.
Krüger 1989
J. Krüger, "Die Badeanlagen von Oxyrhynchos: Eine historisch-terminologische Untersuchung," *Tyche* 4 (1989) 109–118.
Kruit 1994
N. Kruit, "Three Byzantine sales for future delivery: *SB* XVI 12401 + 12402, *SB* VI 9051, *P.Lond.* III 997," *Tyche* 9 (1994) 67–88.
Kruse 2002
Th. Kruse, *Der Königliche Schreiber und die Gauverwaltung: Untersuchungen zur Verwaltungsgeschichte Ägyptens in der Zeit von Augustus bis Philippus Arabs (30 v. Chr.–245 n. Chr.)*, 2 vols., Munich 2002.
Kruse 2015
Th. Kruse, "Urkundenreferat 2011 (1. Teil)," *APF* 61/1 (2015) 203–234.
Kruse 2016
Th. Kruse, "Die Kompetenzen des administrativen Hilfspersonals der enchorischen Beamten in der römischen Kaiserzeit," in: Derda et al. 2016, 1761–1771.

Lallemand 1964
J. Lallemand, *L'administration civile de l'Égypte de l'avènement de Dioclétien à la création du diocèse 284–382: Contribution à l'étude des rapports entre l'Égypte et l'Empire à la fin du III*[e] *et au IV*[e] *siècle*, Brussels 1964.
Laniado 2002
A. Laniado, *Recherches sur les notables municipaux dans l'Empire protobyzantin*, Paris 2002.
Legendre 2016
M. Legendre, "Neither Byzantine nor Islamic? The duke of the Thebaid and the formation of the Umayyad state," *Historical Research* 89/243 (2016) 3–18.
Lemaire 2010
F. Lemaire, "*Antimisthosis* in the Dioscorus archive," in: T. Gagos and A. Hyatt (eds.), *Proceedings of the 25*[th] *International Congress of Papyrology: Ann Arbor, July 29–August 4, 2007*, Ann Arbor 2010, 397–408.
Lewis 1948
N. Lewis, "Two petitions for recovery (P.Col. inv. nos 61 and 62; 318 A.D.)," *JJP* 2 (1948) 51–66.
Lewis 1990
N. Lewis, "*Notationes legentis*: Women in public offices," *BASP* 27 (1990) 38–40.
Lewis 1992
N. Lewis, "*Notationes legentis*," *BASP* 29/3–4 (1992) 127–133.
Lewis 1997
N. Lewis, *The Compulsory Public Services of Roman Egypt*, 2nd ed., Florence 1997.
Liebeschuetz 1973
J. H. W. G. Liebeschuetz, "The origin of the office of the pagarch," *Byzantinische Zeitschrift* 66 (1973) 38–46, reprinted in: Liebeschuetz 1990, no. XVII.
Liebeschuetz 1974
J. H. W. G. Liebeschuetz, "The pagarch: City and imperial administration in Byzantine Egypt," *JJP* 18 (1974) 163–168, reprinted in: Liebeschuetz 1990, no. XVIII.
Liebeschuetz 1990
J. H. G. W. [*sic*] Liebeschuetz (ed.), *From Diocletian to the Arab Conquest: Change in the Late Roman Empire*, Aldershot 1990.
Liebeschuetz 1996
J. H. W. G. Liebeschuetz, "Civic finance in the Byzantine period: The laws and Egypt," *Byzantinische Zeitschrift* 89 (1996) 389–408.
Liebeschuetz 2000
J. H. W. G. Liebeschuetz, "Administration and politics in the cities of the fifth to the mid seventh century: 425–640," in: A. Cameron, B. Ward-Perkins, and M. Whitby (eds.), *The Cambridge Ancient History*, vol. XIV: *Late Antiquity: Empire and Successors A.D. 425–600*, Cambridge 2000, 207–237.
Liebeschuetz 2001
J. H. W. G. Liebeschuetz, *Decline and Fall of the Roman City*, Oxford 2001.
López 2013
A. G. López, *Shenouthe of Atripe and the Uses of Poverty: Rural Patronage, Religious Conflict, and Monasticism in Late Antique Egypt*, Berkeley 2013.

Maas 2005
M. Maas (ed.), *The Cambridge Companion to the Age of Justinian*, Cambridge 2005.
MacCoull 1986
L. S. B. MacCoull, "Dioscorus and the dukes: An aspect of Coptic Hellenism in the sixth century," *Byzantine Studies/Études byzantines* 13 (1986) 30–40.

MacCoull 1988
L. S. B. MacCoull, *Dioscorus of Aphrodito: His Work and His World*, Berkeley 1988.
MacCoull 1993
L. S. B. McCoull, "The Apa Apollos monastery of Pharoou (Aphrodito) and its papyrus archive," *Le Muséon* 106 (1993) 21–63.
MacMullen 1976
R. MacMullen, *Roman Government's Response to Crisis, A.D. 235–337*, New Haven 1976.
Magie 1905
D. Magie, *De Romanorum iuris publici sacrique vocabulis sollemnibus in Graecum sermonem conversis*, Leipzig 1905.
Mann 1986a
M. Mann, *The Sources of Social Power*, vol. I: *A History of Power from the Beginning to A.D. 1760*, Cambridge 1986; rev. ed. 2012.
Mann 1986b
M. Mann, "The autonomous power of the state," in: J. A. Hall (ed.), *States in History*, Oxford 1986, 109–136, first: *Archives européenes de sociologie* 25 (1984) 185–213.
Mann 2008
M. Mann, "Infrastructural power revisited," *Studies in Comparative International Development* 43/3–4 (2008) 355–365.
Manning 2003
J. G. Manning, *Land and Power in Ptolemaic Egypt: The Structure of Land Tenure*, Cambridge 2003.
Maresch 1994
K. Maresch, *Nomisma und Nomismatia: Beiträge zur Geldgeschichte Ägyptens im 6. Jahrhundert n. Chr.*, Opladen 1994.
Maresch 2007
K. Maresch, "Vom Gau zur Civitas: Verwaltungsreformen in Ägypten zur Zeit der Ersten Tetrarchie im Spiegel der Papyri," in: R. Haensch and J. Heinrichs (eds.), *Herrschen und Verwalten: Der Alltag der römischen Administration in der Hohen Kaiserzeit*, Cologne 2007, 427–437.
Marthot 2012
I. Marthot, "Homonyms causing confusion in toponymy: Examples from Aphrodito and the Antaiopolite nome," in: Schubert 2012, 487–490.
Marthot 2013
I. Marthot, *Un village égyptien et sa campagne: Étude de la microtoponymie du territoire d'Aphroditê (VIe–VIIIe s.)*, 3 vols., doctoral dissertation, Paris 2013.
Martin 1994
A. Martin, "Archives privées et cachettes documentaires," in: A. Bülow-Jacobsen (ed.), *Proceedings of the 20th International Congress of Papyrologists, Copenhagen, 23–29 August 1992*, Copenhagen 1994, 569–577.
Maspero 1911
J. Maspero, Review of Gelzer 1909, *Journal des savants* 9 (1911) 180–184.
Maurer & Tost 2016
K. Maurer and S. Tost, "Polizeiliche Erzwingungs- und Verwaltungsstäbe im spätantiken Ägypten," in: Derda et al. 2016, 1825–1841.
Mayerson 2007
Ph. Mayerson, "The case for 8,000,000 *modii* in Justinian's Edict 13.8," *BASP* 44 (2007) 167–174.

Mazza 1995
R. Mazza, "Ricerche sul pagarca nell'Egitto tardoantico e bizantino," *Aegyptus* 75 (1995) 169–242.
Mazza 2001
R. Mazza, *L'archivio degli Apioni: Terra, lavoro e proprietà senatoria nell'Egitto tardoantico*, Bari 2001.
Mazza 2008
R. Mazza, Review of Sarris 2006, *Journal of Agrarian Change* 8/1 (2008) 150–156.
Mazza 2011
R. Mazza, "Households as communities? *Oikoi* and *poleis* in Byzantine Egypt," in: Van Nijf & Alston 2011, 263–286.
Mazza 2013
R. Mazza, "Apiones," in: *EAH* II, 524–526.
Mazza 2018
R. Mazza, "*Pagus* and pagarch," in: *ODLA*, 1122.
McConnell 2016
R. E. McConnell, "More land, more production, or more taxes? Growth and the Apion estate," *BASP* 53 (2016) 355–366.
McConnell 2017
R. E. McConnell, *Getting Rich in Late Antique Egypt*, Ann Arbor 2017.
McGing 2002
B. C. McGing, "Illegal salt in the Lycopolite nome," *APF* 48/1 (2002) 42–66.
Meier 2003
M. Meier, "Die Inszenierung einer Katastrophe: Justinian und der Nika-Aufstand," *ZPE* 142 (2003) 273–300.
Métivier 2005
S. Métivier, *La Cappadoce (IV*[e]*–VI*[e] *siècle): Une histoire provinciale de l'Empire romain d'Orient*, Paris 2005.
Mikhail 2014
M. S. A. Mikhail, *From Byzantine to Islamic Egypt: Religion, Identity and Politics After the Arab Conquest*, London 2014.
Millar 1981
F. Millar, "The world of the *Golden Ass*," *JRS* 71 (1981) 63–75.
Mirković 1996
M. Mirković, "*Autopragia* and the village Aphrodito," *Zeitschrift der Savigny-Stiftung für Rechtsgeschichte: Romanistische Abteilung* 113 (1996) 346–357.
Mirković 2008
M. Mirković, "Les *ktêtores*, les *syntelestai* et l'impôt," in: Fournet 2008a, 191–202.
Mitchell 1988
S. Mitchell, "Maximinus and the Christians in A.D. 312: A new Latin inscription," *JRS* 78 (1988) 105–124.
Mitchell 1993
S. Mitchell, *Anatolia: Land, Men, and Gods in Asia Minor*, 2 vols., Oxford 1993.
Mitthof 1999a
F. Mitthof, Review of *P.Sorb.* II 69, *Gnomon* 71/2 (1999) 134–139.
Mitthof 1999b
F. Mitthof, "Zur Pagusordnung des Herakleopolites," *Tyche* 14 (1999) 211–218.

Mitthof 2001
F. Mitthof, Annona militaris*: Die Heeresversorgung im spätantiken Ägypten: Ein Beitrag zur Verwaltungs- und Heeresgeschichte des Römischen Reiches im 3. bis 6. Jh. n. Chr.*, 2 vols., Florence 2001.

Mitthof 2008
F. Mitthof, "Das Dioskoros-Archiv und die militärischen Reformen Justinians in der Thebais," in: Fournet 2008a, 248–259.

Monson & Scheidel 2015
A. Monson and W. Scheidel (eds.), *Fiscal Regimes and the Political Economy of Premodern States*, Cambridge 2015.

Morelli 2008a
F. Morelli, "Zwischen Poesie und Geschichte: Die 'flagornerie' des Dioskoros und der dreifache Dux Athanasios," in: Fournet 2008a, 223–245.

Morelli 2008b
F. Morelli, "*SB* XXIV 16222: Due patrizi e un Liciniano," *Tyche* 23 (2008) 139–157.

Morelli 2010
F. Morelli, "'Amr e Martina: La reggenza di un'imperatrice o l'amministrazione araba d'egitto," *ZPE* 173 (2010) 136–157.

Morelli 2013
F. Morelli, "Egitto arabo, papiri e papirologia greci," *JJP* 43 (2013) 163–186.

Morelli 2024
F. Morelli, "Atias ritrovato, Atias perduto: un conto del periodo arabo senza 'Aṭiyya ibn Ǧuʿaid (*CPR* VIII 72)," in: Connor et al. 2024, 172–178.

Nielsen 1997
B. E. Nielsen, "Early fourth century tax bases in the Oxyrhynchite nome," in: B. Kramer, W. Luppe, H. Maehler, and G. Poethke (eds.), *Akten des 21. Internationalen Papyrologenkongresses, Berlin, 13.–19.8.1995*, Leipzig 1997, 756–764.

O'Callaghan 1963
J. O'Gallaghan, *Cartas Cristianas griegas del siglo V*, Barcelona 1963.

O'Donnell 1981
J. J. O'Donnell, "Liberius the patrician," *Traditio* 37 (1981) 31–72.

Oertel 1917
F. Oertel, *Die Liturgie: Studien zur ptolemäischen und kaiserlichen Verwaltung Ägyptens*, Leipzig 1917.

Orlandi 2007
T. Orlandi, "The Coptic *Ecclesiastical History*: A survey," in: J. E. Goehring and J. A. Timbie (eds.), *The World of Early Christianity: Language, Literature, and Social Context: Essays in Honor of David W. Johnson*, Washington, DC, 2007, 3–24.

Palme 1989
B. Palme, *Das Amt des ἀπαιτητής in Ägypten*, Vienna 1989.

Palme 1997a
B. Palme, "Die *domus gloriosa* des Flavius Strategius Paneuphemos," *Chiron* 27 (1997) 95–125.

Palme 1997b
B. Palme, "Die Invokation von *SB* I 4805," *ZPE* 117 (1997) 171–174.

Palme 1998
B. Palme, "Flavius Strategius Paneuphemos und die Apionen," *Zeitschrift der Savigny-Stiftung für Rechtsgeschichte: Romanistische Abteilung* 115 (1998) 289–322.
Palme 1999
B. Palme, "Die *officia* der Statthalter in der Spätantike," *Antiquité Tardive* 7 (1999) 85–133.
Palme 2004
B. Palme, "Die *riparii* des Dorfes Aphrodite: Claudius bzw. Flavius Apollos, Aurelius Apollos und Flavius Victor," in: H. Heftner and K. Tomaschitz (eds.), Ad fontes! *Festschrift für Gerhard Dobesch zum 65. Geburtstag*, Wien 2004, 841–854.
Palme 2007a
B. Palme (ed.), *Akten des 23. Internationalen Papyrologenkongresses in Wien, 22.–28. Juli 2001*, Vienna 2007.
Palme 2007b
B. Palme, "Bauernsterben und Fiskalverwaltung im byzantinischen Aphrodite," *CdÉ* 82/163–164 (2007) 330–336.
Palme 2007c
B. Palme, "The imperial presence: Government and army," in: Bagnall 2007, 245–270.
Palme 2008a
B. Palme, "Law and courts in late antique Egypt," in: B. Sirks (ed.), *Aspects of Law in Late Antiquity*, Oxford 2008, 55–76.
Palme 2008b
B. Palme, "Dioskoros und die staatlichen Autoritäten," in: Fournet 2008a, 203–222.
Palme 2013a
B. Palme, "Staat und Gesellschaft des spätantiken Ägypten im Spiegel der Papyri," *JJP* 43 (2013) 95–133.
Palme 2013b
B. Palme, "Administration, late antique Egypt," *EAH* I, 82–85.
Palme 2013c
B. Palme, "Arcadia, Egypt," *EAH* II, 622–624.
Palme 2015
B. Palme, "Byzantinisches Ägypten: Der Beitrag der Papyri zur Geschichte des frühbyzantinischen Reiches," in: Ch. Gastgeber and F. Daim (eds.), *Byzantium as Bridge Between West and East: Proceedings of the International Conference, Vienna, 3rd–5th May 2012*, Vienna 2015, 217–240.
Palme 2016
B. Palme, "Neue Texte zum Dossier des Flavius Flavianus und Flavius Ptolemaeus," in: Fournet & Papaconstantinou 2016, 339–350.
Palme 2021
B. Palme, "Emotional strategies in petitions of Dioskoros of Aphrodito," in: A. Chaniotis (ed.), *Unveiling Emotions III: Arousal, Display, and Performance of Emotions in the Greek World*, Stuttgart 2021, 321–342.
Palme forthcoming
B. Palme, *Form und Funktion der byzantinischen Gestellungsbürgschaften*, forthcoming.
Papaconstantinou 2015
A. Papaconstantinou, "The rhetoric of power and the voice of reason: Tensions between central and local in the correspondence of Qurra ibn Sharīk," in: Procházka et al. 2015, 267–281.
Papathomas 2007
A. Papathomas, "Höflichkeit und Servilität in den griechischen Papyrusbriefen der ausgehenden Antike," in: Palme 2007a, 497–512.

Papathomas & Vergados 2021
A. Papathomas and A. Vergados, "An Oxyrhynchan deed of surety for a registered sailor from the dossier of Flavia Anastasia," *Tyche* 36 (2021) 131–137.
Parker 2001
B. J. Parker, *The Mechanics of Empire: The Northern Frontier of Assyria as a Case Study in Imperial Dynamics*, Helsinki 2001.
Pedone 2020
M. Pedone, Apud acta: *Studi sul processo romano alla luce della documentazione papirologica (IV–VI sec. d. C.)*, Turin 2020.
Pfeilschifter 2014
R. Pfeilschifter, "Drinnen und draußen: Die Herrschaft des Kaisers über Konstantinopel und das Reich," in: M. Meier and S. Patzold (eds.), *Chlodwigs Welt: Organisation von Herrschaft um 500*, Stuttgart 2014, 111–142.
Pieler 1990
P. E. Pieler, "Erwägungen zur Novelle Justin [*sic*] II. über die 'Wahl' der Provinzstatthalter (Nov. Just. 149)," in: E. Forsten (ed.), Novella Constitutio*: Studies in Honour of Nicolas van der Wal*, Groningen 1990, 177–193.
Poethke 1984
G. Poethke, "*Metrocomiae* und Autopragie in Ägypten," in: P. Nagel (ed.), *Graeco-Coptica*, Halle 1984, 37–44.
Procházka et al. 2015
S. Procházka, L. Reinfandt, and S. Tost (eds.), *Official Epistolography and the Language(s) of Power: Proceedings of the First International Conference of the Research Network "Imperium & Officium. Comparative Studies in Bureaucracy and Officialdom," Vienna, 10–12 November 2010*, Vienna 2015.

Ramsay 1888
W. M. Ramsay, "Laodiceia Combusta and Sinethandos," *Mitteilungen des Deutschen Archäologischen Instituts: Athenische Abteilung* 13 (1888) 233–272.
Ramsay 1918
W. M. Ramsay, "The utilisation of old epigraphic copies," *JHS* 38 (1918) 124–192.
Rathbone 2008
D. Rathbone, "Villages and patronage in fourth-century Egypt: The case of *P.Ross.Georg.* 3.8," *BASP* 45 (2008) 189–207.
Rebenich 2008
S. Rebenich, "*Pars melior humani generis*: Aristokratie(n) in der Spätantike," in: Beck et al. 2008a, 153–175.
Reekmans 1962
T. Reekmans, *A Sixth Century Account of Hay (P.Iand. inv. 653)*, Brussels 1962.
Reiter 2003
F. Reiter, "Datierungen nach dem Postkonsulat des Basilius in Papyrusdokumenten," *ZPE* 145 (2003) 231–245.
Reiter 2013
F. Reiter, "Liturgy, Greco-Roman Egypt," *EAH* VIII, 4117–4119.
Remijsen 2024
S. Remijsen, "The archive after Dioscorus: The dates of the receipts in *P.Cair.Masp.* III 67325 and *P.Flor.* III 298 + *P.Stras.* VII 699," in: Connor et al. 2024, 198–206.

Rémondon 1961
R. Rémondon, "Soldats de Byzance d'après un papyrus trouvé à Edfou," *Recherches de Papyrologie* 1 (1961) 41–93.
Rémondon 1965
R. Rémondon, "*P.Hamb.* 56 et *P.Lond.* 1419: Notes sur les finances d'Aphrodito du VIe siècle au VIIIe," *CdÉ* 40/80 (1965) 401–430.
Rémondon 1966
R. Rémondon, "L'Égypte au 5e siècle de notre ère: Les sources papyrologiques et leurs problèmes," in: *Atti* 1966, 135–148.
Rémondon 1974a
R. Rémondon, "Les contradictions de la societé égyptienne à l'époque byzantine," *JJP* 18 (1974) 17–32.
Rémondon 1974b
R. Rémondon, "[Situation présente de la papyrologie byzantine]," in: E. Kießling and H.-A. Rupprecht (eds.), *Akten des XIII. Internationalen Papyrologenkongresses, Marburg, 2. bis 6. August 1971*, München 1974, 367–372.
Rendsburg 2017
G. A. Rendsburg, "The etymology of χάρτης 'papyrus roll,' " *Scripta Classica Israelica* 36 (2017) 149–169.
Rey-Coquais 2002
J.-P. Rey-Coquais, "Inscriptions de l'hippodrome de Tyr," *Journal of Roman Archaeology* 15 (2002) 325–335.
Rouillard 1928
G. Rouillard, *L'administration civile de l'Égypte byzantine*, 2nd ed., Paris 1928.
Rowlandson 1998
J. Rowlandson, *Women and Society in Greek and Roman Egypt: A Sourcebook*, Cambridge 1998.
Ruffini 2008a
G. R. Ruffini, *Social Networks in Byzantine Egypt*, Cambridge 2008.
Ruffini 2008b
G. R. Ruffini, "Factions and social distance in sixth-century Aphrodito," in: Fournet 2008a, 157–170.
Ruffini 2009
G. R. Ruffini, Review of Sarris 2006, *Topoi* 16/2 (2009) 627–640.
Ruffini 2011
G. R. Ruffini, *A Prosopography of Byzantine Aphrodito*, Durham 2011.
Ruffini 2018a
G. R. Ruffini, *Life in an Egyptian Village in Late Antiquity: Aphrodito before and after the Islamic Conquest*, Cambridge 2018.
Ruffini 2018b
G. R. Ruffini, Review of McConnell 2017, *Topoi* 22/2 (2018) 741–746.

Sänger 2005
P. A. Sänger, "Die Eirenarchen im römischen und byzantinischen Ägypten," *Tyche* 20 (2005) 143–204.
Sänger 2011
P. A. Sänger, "The administration of Sasanian Egypt: New masters and Byzantine continuity," *GRBS* 51 (2011) 653–665.

Sarris 2004
P. Sarris, "Rehabilitating the Great Estate: Aristocratic property and economic growth in the late antique East," in: W. Browden, L. Lavan, and C. Machado (eds.), *Recent Research in the Late Antique Countryside*, Leiden 2004, 55–71.
Sarris 2006
P. Sarris, *Economy and Society in the Age of Justinian*, Cambridge 2006.
Sarris 2022
P. Sarris, "Egypt in the age of Justinian: Connector or disconnector?," in: J. Bruning, J. H. M. de Jong, and P. M. Sijpesteijn (eds.), *Egypt and the Eastern Mediterranean World: From Constantinople to Baghdad, 500–1000 CE*, Cambridge 2022, 19–45.
Scharf 1994
R. Scharf, Comites *und* comitiva primi ordinis, Mainz 1994.
Scheidel 2013
W. Scheidel, "Studying the state," in: P. F. Bang and W. Scheidel (eds.), *The Oxford Handbook of the State in the Ancient Near East and Mediterranean*, Oxford 2013, 5–57.
Schmelz 2002
G. Schmelz, *Kirchliche Amtsträger im spätantiken Ägypten nach den Aussagen der griechischen und koptischen Papyri und Ostraka*, München 2002.
Schmidt-Hofner 2008
S. Schmidt-Hofner, *Reagieren und Gestalten: Der Regierungsstil des spätrömischen Kaisers am Beispiel der Gesetzgebung Valentinians I.*, München 2008.
Schubert 2012
P. Schubert (ed.), *Actes du 26e Congrès international de papyrologie, Genève, 16–21 août 2010*, Geneva 2012.
Scott 1998
J. C. Scott, *Seeing Like a State: How Certain Schemes to Improve the Human Condition Have Failed*, Yale 1998.
Sessa 2018
K. Sessa, *Daily Life in Late Antiquity*, Cambridge 2018.
Sheridan Moss 2009
J. Sheridan Moss, "Two Michigan papyri," *BASP* 46 (2009) 37–57.
Shue 1988
V. Shue, *The Reach of the State: Sketches of the Chinese Body Politic*, Stanford 1988.
Sijpesteijn 1981
P. J. Sijpesteijn, "Some corrections to Greek elements from *BKU* III," *CdÉ* 56/112 (1981) 360–361.
Sijpesteijn 2013
P. M. Sijpesteijn, *Shaping a Muslim State: The World of a Mid-Eighth-Century Egyptian Official*, Oxford 2013.
Slootjes 2011
D. Slootjes, "Local elites and power in the Roman world: Modern theories and models," *Journal of Interdisciplinary History* 42/2 (2011) 235–249.
Stern 2015
M. Stern, "Der Pagarch und die Organisation des öffentlichen Sicherheitswesens im byzantinischen Ägypten," *Tyche* 30 (2015) 119–144.
Stern 2016
M. Stern, "Welche Gefängnisse kontrolliert der Pagarch?," in: Derda et al. 2016, 1843–1870.

Stern 2020
M. Stern, “Local magnates, but mobile: Elite dynamics in Byzantine provinces,” in: S. R. Huebner et al. (eds.), *Living the End of Antiquity: Individual Histories from Byzantine to Islamic Egypt, Proceedings of an International Conference, Basel, May 18–20, 2017*, Berlin 2020, 33–48.

Stern 2023
M. Stern, “Disputing public authority in the late Roman countryside: *P.Cair.Masp.* I 67002 revisited,” in: S. Waebens, K. Vandorpe, and N. Vaneerdewegh (eds.), *Seeking Justice in and out of Court: Dispute Resolution in Greco-Roman and Late Antique Egypt*, Leuven 2023, 271–290.

Stern 2024
M. Stern, “Παγάρχης oder πάγαρχος? Zum Gebrauch stammgleicher Synonyme in dokumentarischen Texten und einer hypothetischen ‘Notarschule’ im Dorf Aphrodito,” in: S. Killen, S. Scheuble-Reiter, and S. Schmidt (eds.), Caput studiorum*: Festschrift für Rudolf Haensch zu seinem 65. Geburtstag*, Wiesbaden 2024, 283–296.

Stern forthcoming (a)
M. Stern, “The writers of the Antaiopolite tax receipts,” forthcoming.

Stern forthcoming (b)
M. Stern, “Public accounting and private recordkeeping in the Dioskoros archive,” forthcoming.

Stern forthcoming (c)
M. Stern, “The city solution: Theodosiopolis and the system of joint administration in the late antique Fayyum,” forthcoming.

Stolk 2022
J. V. Stolk, “ΙΝΔΙΚΤΙΩΝ in editions of papyri: A sociolinguist’s comment on the spelling and declension of the term,” *JJP* 52 (2022) 217–222.

Syrkou 2021
A. Syrkou, *Horrorscope: The Gallery of Tortures in Late Antiquity*, Pisa 2021.

Tedesco 2013
P. Tedesco, “Note sulla genesi e l’evoluzione dell’autopragia demaniale nei secoli IV–VI,” in: G. Barone, A. Esposito, and C. Frova (eds.), *Ricerca come incontro: Archeologi, paleografi et storici per Paolo Delogu*, Rome 2013, 3–17.

Teitler 1985
H. C. Teitler, Notarii *and* Exceptores*: An Inquiry into Role and Significance of Shorthand Writers in the Imperial and Ecclesiastical Bureaucracy of the Roman Empire (from the Early Principate to c. 450 A.D.)*, Amsterdam 1985.

Tillier 2013
M. Tillier, “Du pagarque au cadi: ruptures et continuités dans l’administration judiciaire de la Haute-Égypte (Ier–IIIe/VIIe–IXe siècle),” *Médiévales* 64 (2013) 19–36.

Thomas 1959
J. D. Thomas, “The office of *exactor* in Egypt,” *CdÉ* 34/67 (1959) 124–140.

Torallas Tovar 2000
S. Torallas Tovar, “The police in Byzantine Egypt: Hierarchy in the papyri from the fourth to the seventh centuries,” in: A. McDonald and Ch. Riggs (eds.), *Current Research in Egyptology*, Oxford 2000, 115–123.

Tost 2012
S. Tost, “Die Unterscheidung zwischen öffentlicher und privatgeschäftlicher Sphäre am Beispiel des Amts der *riparii*,” in: Schubert 2012, 773–780.

Tost 2015
S. Tost, "Diktion und Funktionalität verwaltungsinterner Korrespondenz von Amtsträgern des Sicherheitswesens im spätantiken Ägypten," in: Procházka et al. 2015, 237–254.
Treu 1974
K. Treu, "Liturgische Traditionen in Ägypten (zu *P.Oxy.* 2782)," in: P. Nagel (ed.), *Studia Coptica*, Berlin 1974, 43–66.
Tuck 2011
J. Tuck, "The *oikoi* and civic government in Egypt in the fifth and sixth centuries," in: Van Nijf & Alston 2011, 287–305.
Turner 1968
E. G. Turner, *Greek Papyri: An Introduction*, Oxford 1968.

Valk 2021
J. Valk, "A state of extraction: Navigating taxation in ancient polities," in: Valk & Soto Marín 2021, 1–35.
Valk & Soto Marín 2021
J. Valk and I. Soto Marín (eds.), *Ancient Taxation: The Mechanics of Extraction in Comparative Perspective*, New York 2021.
Van Bremen 1996
R. van Bremen, *The Limits of Participation: Women and Civic Life in the Greek East*, Amsterdam 1996.
Van der Vliet 2013
J. van der Vliet, "Coptic documentary papyri after the Arab conquest," *JJP* 43 (2013) 187–208.
Vanderheyden 2015
L. Vanderheyden, *Les lettres coptes des archives de Dioscore d'Aphroditê (VIe siècle; Égypte)*, 3 vols., doctoral dissertation, Paris 2015.
Vandorpe 2009
K. Vandorpe, "Archives and dossiers," in: Bagnall 2009b, 216–255.
Van Haelst 1966
J. van Haelst, "De nouvelles archives: Anastasia, propriétaire à Oxyrhynchus," in: *Atti* 1966, 586–590.
Van Loon 2017
G. A. J. C. van Loon, "An orchard lease from the reign of Heraclius," *BASP* 54 (2017) 127–142.
Van Minnen 2003
P. van Minnen, "Dioscorus and the law," in: A. A. MacDonald, M. W. Twomey, and G. Reinink (eds.), *Learned Antiquity: Scholarship and Society in the Near East, the Greco-Roman World and the Early Medieval West*, Leuven 2003, 115–133.
Van Minnen 2006
P. van Minnen, "The changing world of the cities of later Roman Egypt," in: Krause & Witschel 2006, 153–179.
Van Minnen 2007
P. van Minnen, "The other cities in later Roman Egypt," in: Bagnall 2007, 207–225.
Van Minnen 2019
P. van Minnen, Review of McConnell 2017, *JLA* 12/1 (2019) 260–262.
Van Nijf & Alston 2011
O. M. van Nijf and R. Alston (eds.), *Political Culture in the Greek City after the Classical Age*, Leuven 2011.

Venticinque 2014
Ph. F. Venticinque, "Social capital and economic strategies on late Roman estates in Oxyrhynchus," *Historia: Zeitschrift für Alte Geschichte* 63 (2014) 463–486.
Verbeeck 1991
B. Verbeeck, Pagarch: *CE* VI, 1871a–1872a.

Weisweiler 2017
J. Weisweiler, "Populist despotism and infrastructural power in the later Roman Empire," in: Ando & Richardson 2017, 149–178.
Wickham 2005
Ch. Wickham, *Framing the Early Middle Ages: Europe and the Mediterranean 400–800*, Oxford 2005.
Wilcken 1892
U. Wilcken, "Bemerkungen zur ägyptischen Strategie in der Kaiserzeit," *Hermes* 27 (1892) 287–300.
Wilcken 1912
U. Wilcken, *Grundzüge und Chrestomathie der Papyruskunde: Historischer Teil, Erste Hälfte: Grundzüge*, Leipzig 1912.
Wilcken 1913
U. Wilcken, "Referate," *APF* 5 (1913) 198–300.
Winlock 1941
H. E. Winlock, *The Temple of Hibis in El-Khārgeh Oasis, Part I: The Excavations*, New York 1941.
Winterling 2014
A. Winterling, "'Staat' in der griechisch-römischen Antike?," in: Ch. Lundgreen (ed.), *Staatlichkeit in Rom? Diskurse und Praxis (in) der römischen Republik*, Stuttgart 2014, 249–256.
Wipszycka 1971
E. Wipszycka, "Les reçus d'impôts et le bureau des comptes des pagarchies aux VI–VII siècles," *JJP* 16–17 (1971) 104–116.
Wipszycka 1972
E. Wipszycka, *Les ressources et les activités économiques des églises en Égypte du IV*[e] *au VIII*[e] *siècle*, Bruxelles 1972.
Wipszycka 2021
E. Wipszycka, "What can the lives of saints tell us about history: The case of the Coptic *Life of Aaron*," *JJP* 51 (2021) 105–117.
Worp 1984
K. A. Worp, "Flavius Strategius: Some notes," *ZPE* 56 (1984) 113–166.
Worp 2005
K. A. Worp, "Chronological notes on Byzantine documents," *ZPE* 151 (2005) 153–158.

Ziche 2006
H. Ziche, "Making late Roman taxpayers pay: Imperial government strategies and practice," in: Drake 2006, 125–134.
Zuckerman 2004a
C. Zuckermann, *Du village à l'Empire: Autour du registre fiscal d'Aphroditô 525/526*, Paris 2004.
Zuckerman 2004b
C. Zuckerman, "Les deux Dioscore d'Aphroditè ou Les limites de la pétition," in: Feissel & Gascou 2004, 75–92.

Indexes

Due to the frequent occurrence of various sources, places, and terms, the page numbers in all indexes provided here include the corresponding footnotes.

Index of Ancient Sources

Bold page numbers indicate suggested readings, dates, or provenances.

Citations by conventional abbreviations

For expansions of the conventional abbreviations, see the Ancient Sources in Sources and Bibliography.

Inscriptions

Legal sources

https://doi.org/10.1515/9783111493183-011

Literary sources

Papyri, ostraca, and tablets

Citations by inventory numbers

Unpublished and recently edited documents without a conventional abbreviation. For the editions, see the Bibliography.

Papyri and ostraca

Other manuscripts

Citations by edition number in books or articles

Index of Persons

Pagarchs

Only pagarchs whose names are known have been included; anonymous pagarchs can be more conveniently found by consulting their respective source texts. In this index, "early seventh century" refers to the period up until the Islamic conquest (639–642 CE); the criteria for categorizing pagarchs into three groups are explained in the introduction to the Catalog. Corresponding Catalog entries are highlighted in bold. This index also includes uncertain cases as discussed in the Catalog.

Fourth and fifth centuries

Sixth and early seventh centuries

Early Islamic Egypt

Emperors and empresses

Other notable dramatis personae

An asterisk indicates that this aristocrat or their *oikos* is attested as holding authority over *kōmai pagarchoumenai*; bold page numbers refer to the corresponding entries in the Catalog.

Index of Places

A forward slash (/) indicates place name variants also commonly found in scholarly literature. Villages and smaller settlements are listed with their respective nomes in parentheses. Page numbers in parentheses indicate that the place appears solely in parentheses as the provenance of a source text.

Places in Egypt

Places outside Egypt

Index of Transliterated Terms

Where relevant, some entries are distinguished by grammatical gender or number, or are listed exclusively in the plural form (e.g., in the case of certain taxes). In selected cases, specialized English equivalents for transliterated terms have been provided for convenience. Entries sharing an obvious connection to adjacent entries have not been cross-referenced (e.g., *peribleptos* and *peribleptos oikos*). Some nontechnical terms, transliterated solely to indicate the origin of an English translation, have not been included.

Bei Fragen zur Produktsicherheit wenden Sie sich bitte an:
If you have any questions regarding product safety, please contact:

Walter de Gruyter
Genthiner Straße 13
10785 Berlin
productsafety@degruyterbrill.com